The Making of the
African Diaspora

The Making of the African Diaspora in the Americas 1441–1900

Vincent Bakpetu Thompson

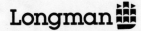
Longman

Longman Group UK Limited,
Longman House, Burnt Mill, Harlow,
Essex CM20 2JE, England
and Associated Companies throughout the world

Published in the United States of America
by Longman Inc., New York

© Vincent Bakpetu Thompson 1987

First published 1987

Set in 11/12 Bembo

Produced by Longman Group (FE) Ltd
Printed in Hong Kong

ISBN 0-582-64238-8

This book is dedicated to my mother who strove for my education and to the memories of my late maternal grandmother who taught me the English alphabet and the kindest parent anyone could have had, to my late father who bore most of the burden of my early education and my late maternal grandfather whose enlightenment and generosity provided immense inspiration during my adolescent period, and whose home was a safe sanctuary.

Library of Congress Cataloging-in-Publication Data

Thompson, Vincent Bakpetu.
  The making of the African diaspora in the Americas, 1441–1900.

  Bibliography: p.
  Includes index.
  1. Slavery–America–History. I. Title.

HT1048.T48 1986   306′.362′091812   86–15332

ISBN 0-582-64238-8

British Library Cataloguing in Publication Data

Thompson, Vincent Bakpetu
  The making of the African diaspora in the
  Americas, 1441–1900.
  1. Slavery–America–History
  2. Blacks–America–History
  I. Title
  306′.362′097   HT1048

ISBN 0-582-64238-8

Contents

Maps

Acknowledgements

In writing this book I have profited from the searching criticisms of
friends, notably Professors Edward Reynolds and Godfrey Uzoigwe.
Their advice has been most valuable. The former read all of Part Two and
also supplied other sources of information, and together with his wife,
Dr Kay Reynolds, gave me hospitality during a visit to their home in San
Diego, California. Professor Uzoigwe read the entire work and was
incisive in his criticisms and suggestions. I am indebted to Joseph
Murumbi (former Vice-President of Kenya) and his wife, Sheila, whose
hospitality during the years of my sojourn in Kenya cannot be fully
repaid. Their Africana Library, regrettably now the possession of the
State, provided me with very useful material. Dr Terry Ryan and
Professor Peter Marshall commented on the chapter dealing with 'wealth
and power' and compelled me to rethink the entire subject. My friend,
Mr Andrew Townley, who read most of the earlier chapters, has always
been a friendly critic and his insights have been helpful. Others gave me
encouragement and hospitality during research trips to the Americas.
They include Professor and Mrs J. B. Webster in Halifax, Nova Scotia,
my brother, Professor Emmanuel Thompson of Illinois University, and
his wife too. Professor J. H. Franklin, an early pioneer, now Emeritus of
the University of Chicago, not only proved hospitable but presented me
with two of his books. Both he and Mrs Franklin were most gracious.
Professor St Clair Drake at Stanford University, California, now
Emeritus, further enlightened my understanding with his lively·
discussions, hospitality, and the present of a very useful book. Professor
Drake is a less well-known authority on the diaspora. My thanks also go
to Basil Davidson for past encouragement and to Professor George
Shepperson of Edinburgh University for reading and reporting on the
manuscript. Apart from Davidson, he is the one well-known diaspora
expert on this side of the Atlantic.

Miss Valerie Coburn in New York was helpful and accompanied me on
my visits to Harlem and the Arthur Schomburg Collections in New York
City. I also received encouragement and lavish hospitality in
San Francisco, California, at the home of my close friends, Mr and Mrs
K. Babb. Professor Nathan Shapirra of the Department of Fine Art and
Design at the University of California at Los Angeles helped me in my
travels through the city and proved a most gracious friend. The
unsurpassed hospitality of Dr and Mrs J. T. Willis in their Bethesda,

ACKNOWLEDGEMENTS

Maryland, home gave me time for reflection on the chapters I had written.

I wish also to express my thanks to the archivists and librarians of the following institutions: Dalhousie University, Halifax, Nova Scotia; the Library of Congress in Washington, D.C.; the University of Chicago; the Arthur Schomburg Collections in New York; the University of California at San Diego; the University of the West Indies at St Augustine (Trinidad), Cave Hill (Barbados), and Mona (Jamaica); the Free Public Reference Library in Barbados; the University of Guyana Library; the British Library including the Newspaper Library in Colindale (particular thanks to Mrs Theresa Mowah, Miss Merle Chandler, Messrs Roy Juggessur and Harry Budhram); the Public Record Office, London; the Institute for Historical Research, London; the Society for the Propagation of the Gospel, London; King's College (London University) Library, London; the University of Brasilia, Brazil; the University of Nairobi, Kenya; and last but not least, Streatham Vale Public Library. My indebtedness to archivists and librarians in all these institutions as well as others not mentioned, and to my guides in Haiti, Puerto Rico and Surinam, is immense and cannot be easily repaid except by a comprehensive acknowledgement. I am also grateful for valuable and dedicated typing help provided by Miss Virginia Bareto, Miss Sally Gimber, Mrs Rosemary Osborne, Mrs Alice Gaant and Mrs Ann O'Connor.

These acknowledgements cannot be complete without expressing thanks to my students of the course 'Africa and the Black Diaspora' between 1971 and 1975 at the University of Nairobi, Kenya, who raised numerous and interesting questions, and stimulated me to persist in the effort, arming me with the strength to complete the task I had undertaken. The work which has emerged is completely different from the lectures they heard, though some of its outlines are discernible. I hope that the appearance of the book will deepen their understanding and stimulate some of them to further research. It is also hoped that it may serve as an introductory text for students approaching the African diaspora for the first time.

Professor B. A. Ogot, former Head of the History Department at the University of Nairobi, deserves my thanks for inviting me to teach the course.

All these people and many more provided a climate in which I could work and furnished me with every help and kindness when I most needed it. However, my thanks must also be given to my publishers, who have turned a cumbersome manuscript into a book, and I mention especially Julian Rea and Peter Warwick. It only remains to say that the exigencies of teaching for a number of years inhibited the early completion of this work. It is offered here with all the humility that the author can muster.

Vincent Bakpetu Thompson

Gold is most excellent. Gold is treasure, and he who possesses it does all he wishes to in this world, and succeeds in helping souls into paradise.

Christopher Columbus while on his Fourth Voyage,
in a letter to Ferdinand and Isabella, July 7, 1503

Is it not enough that we are torn from our country and friends, to toil for your luxury and lust of gain? Must every tender feeling be likewise sacrificed to your avarice? . . . Why are the parents to lose their children, brothers their sisters, or husbands their wives? Surely this is a new refinement in cruelty, which while it has no advantage to atone for it, thus aggravates distress and adds fresh horrors even to the wretchedness of slavery.

Olaudah Equiano (Gustavus Vassa), *The Interesting Narrative of the Life of Olaudah Equiano or Gustavus Vassa, The African, written by himself*, 1789

Introduction

This study is designed to meet the needs of those who wish to know more about the African diaspora into the Americas during the centuries of the slave trade and slavery between the fifteenth and nineteenth centuries.

The term 'diaspora' is used here synonymously with dispersion, deriving inspiration from the Jewish concept of diaspora enshrined in the Book of Deuteronomy: 'The Lord shall cause thee to be smitten before thine enemies: thou shalt go out one way against them, and flee seven ways before them; and shalt be removed into all the kingdoms of the earth' (Deuteronomy 28: 25). The term comes from the Septuagint translations of the Book of Deuteronomy concerning the Jews, but, as Professor George Shepperson has observed, while it might not be said that the African peoples have been dispersed into all the kingdoms and countries of the world, 'they have certainly migrated to a very large number of them'. Moreover, the forces which drove them abroad, slavery and imperialism, are not dissimilar to those which dispersed the Jews.[1] Here the discussion centres on the dispersion of Africans through four centuries in the slave trade, and on the evolution of Africans in those New World societies known collectively as the Americas – North and South America and the Caribbean.

From the middle of the fifteenth century, and persistently from the mid-sixteenth, Africans were exported from their homeland to the Americas to develop and sustain a plantation system of agriculture and to work the mines of South America in a new and unfamiliar environment. This forced migration through the slave trade continued until well nigh the end of the nineteenth century, although officially it was terminated by the middle of the century. The smuggling of slaves that persisted was in the main carried on by interlopers, by ships flying 'flags of convenience',[2] and by nations which refused to accede to an international covenant on the ending of the trade in slaves. Smuggling continued well after the formal abolition of the trade, a step initiated by Britain in 1807 and followed by the United States in 1808, but which proved difficult to follow for other nations until diplomatic activity backed by some display of force compelled the defaulters to abandon the trade. But, in spite of the acts of abolition, nationals of countries like France,

1

Portugal, Spain, Brazil, Cuba and even the United States, continued to participate in the slave trade. The overall implications of these gigantic migrations of the African peoples to the New World form too large a subject to be undertaken in one book. Since there are numerous aspects to the study of the African diaspora, an all-embracing study would involve a lifetime of study and research. What, however, is attempted here is partly an interpretative exercise of the Euro-African connection and partly a synthesis of the activities surrounding the slave trade, the major factor in the African dispersion through four centuries. A second intention arises from the preoccupation of scholars with comparative studies of slavery in the Americas. Such studies have resulted from the assertion that there were fundamental differences between slave zones in the Americas, especially in the handling and treatment of slaves and their consequences. Accordingly, an effort is made here to observe the zones of African dispersion as an entity from which one can generalise the situation, taking account of local variations of degree rather than kind. But, above all, this work is also intended as a corrective exercise to the distortions which have encumbered the subject of the European enslavement of Africans. Hitherto, Eurocentric writers have sought to salve their consciences by employing rationalisations to obscure the issues involved and the long-term implications of this sordid episode in human experience. An additional reason for the work is to impose some semblance of pattern on the study with the aim of encouraging more enterprising and more ardent research, concerned with upholding decent human values and preoccupied with the future destiny of man, to unravel as much of the truth as is attainable, and to undertake in-depth studies which time and space have precluded me from doing.

The work, therefore, seeks to examine from the point of view of the African diaspora to the Americas how the slave trade contributed to the establishment in the New World of new communities of Africans, as well as communities of people of mixed descent, and how the experiences of the time conditioned their consciousness towards the mother continent of Africa as well as the societies in which they dwelt. For with that perception began a number of conflicting tendencies conditioned both by environmental factors and by an insight into the meaning of their degradation in the Americas. This gave rise to a kind of pan-African tradition manifested in several ways — by an attempt to recreate the mother continent in the imagination; by the persistence of African return and redemption movements; by emphasising a separate identity *vis-à-vis* the Euro-American world which dominated every aspect of their lives; by religious expression and a desire to become missionaries to Africa, by returning to the continent both on an individual and group basis (the most notable and creditable of these endeavours being those of Afro-Brazilians following the emancipation of slaves in Brazil); by the creation of intellectual movements from the second half of the nineteenth century which had as their objective the rehabilitation of Africa in every sense of that word; and by historical and cultural researches and efforts to demonstrate that African civilisation was the one from which other civilisations, especially the Euro-Christian ones, have derived their inspiration. These endeavours among descendants of Africa in the diaspora were to result in the foundation of the American Negro Academy in 1895, the Negro Society for Historical Research in 1916, the Association for the Study of Negro Life and History, founded by Professor Carter G. Woodson in 1916, and the Negro History Week (another of Woodson's achievements). These were the forerunners and pioneers of the African Studies programmes, which Eurocentric scholars have sometimes appropriated in the post-Second World War period without giving due credit to their original founders.

A milestone in this endeavour was the publication in 1883 of the Afro-American lawyer and historian, George Washington Williams, whom W. E. B. DuBois rightly named the 'father of African Studies in America'. His monumental work published in 1883, based on solid research and scholarship, was entitled *The History of the African Race in America*, and it remains a clear indication of that pioneering spirit which animated others to follow in his footsteps and to perfect the work which he so conscientiously undertook. Even a cursory glance at the publication cannot fail to impress on one where George Washington Williams felt the roots of Afro-Americans in the New World lay. He saw it posited in Africa and in his book he laid the foundations of his history on the evolution of African civilisation prior to African peoples being beached in the Americas. In spite of its pitfalls, judged even by modern standards the work shows the endeavours of a genuine seeker after truth, painstaking, persistent, an African and Africanist, as well as a real and warm human being. No part of his writing reveals rancour. The book derives from work clinically undertaken to guide mankind's footsteps to a less dishonourable future. It was in the same tradition that a later Afro-American scholar, William Ferris, produced in 1912 his publication, *The African Abroad*.

Not all aspects of the African diaspora are given equal emphasis in this work. The story of settlements in Latin America is given less weight and is treated only in so far as it relates to the handling of Africans in the slave theatres and reflects similar patterns to other slave societies. Detailed studies of individual territories persist, but instinctively one does not feel that they will illuminate more than what is already known about the factors which conditioned the stimulation of an African consciousness outside Africa in the

Americas. They could, of course, shed light on the apparent failure of that consciousness to materialise fully in some places, as a recent study indicates.[3] The African consciousness is a large subject which could form the subject of several works, but need not detain us here. Accordingly, the focus of this work is on those aspects of the dispersion (with correctives here and there) which contributed to the growth of a pan-African tradition and, at the same time, a tradition too of ambivalence towards Africa, the former linking Africa and the Africans of the diaspora, and the latter separating them. This ambivalence has bequeathed a tradition of acceptance and rejection of Africa simultaneously. The tradition of acceptance has tended to link the African diaspora in a common destiny with that of Africa in an endeavour to transcend the problems posed by the Euro-American domination of their lives, while the tradition of rejection, first encouraged by conditioning under servitude and extended beyond it, focuses on why the endeavour to transcend that domination has had such a career of ambivalence. This ambivalence is hardly understandable without a knowledge of the factors which played on the slaves' sensibilities during the centuries of their enslavement in the Americas; such an understanding gives gravity to the present study.

The present work is broadly conceived in four parts. The first takes account of the factors behind the diaspora and here consideration is given to the European pursuit of wealth and power which impinged on Africa and the Americas with differing results and which had long-term implications for Africa in terms of the slave trade. It was also felt that the slave trade background to the dispersion would illuminate the mental attitudes of Africans who were dragged by circumstances into slavery. Since there is very little that is extant for most of the period, material has been assembled, however imperfect it might be, from the journals and writings of captains of slave ships, surgeons of slave-trading vessels, and officials, in order to gain some impression of African attitudes to enslavement before their arrival in the Americas. Knowledge of such attitudes helps to illuminate the response of Africans to their enslavement in the New World theatres of slavery. In particular, resistance at the point of embarkation helps to focus attention on the refusal by slaves to accept their status throughout the centuries in which the institution persisted in the Americas.

The second part of the book deals with the strategy adopted by the slavocracy to make Africans adaptable and amenable to slavery and to sustain the system. This strategy enables us to understand some of the factors in the tenacity of slavery in the Americas. While economic gain was central to the operations of both the slave trade and slavery, it was the techniques of handling slaves which introduced both the severities and subtleties of slave societies and which kept the institution of slavery in existence for such a protracted period. Consequently, consideration is given to certain aspects of strategy such as the development of a plantation hierarchy, the principle of 'divide and rule', the treatment of slaves, and the denial to slaves of the right to education and the right to practise religion (both Christian and African religions in fact flourished from the entrenched principle of divide and rule). The efforts made by Africans to defeat these stipulations of both law and custom are seen as 'a conflict between darkness and light'.

The third part naturally flows from the second in that it examines some aspects of slave strategy, the ways and means which slaves devised and adopted for defeating the system. Thus, African techniques of resistance, both passive and active, are examined and are reinforced by a special study of the French colony of St Domingue, which became the independent state of Haiti in 1804. The international dimensions of the Haitian struggle led to the achievement of a kind of independence which has remained to plague the country even to the present day. The succeeding chapter discusses aspects of anti-slavery involving the fight for abolition of the trade and the emancipation of slaves in the various slave theatres. It is needless to stress that the intensity was greater in some countries than in others. The special place of descendants of Africa in the abolitionist movements is highlighted, but since the entire anti-slavery endeavour was essentially multi-racial and international in scope the efforts of others are examined too. Yet the place of blacks is specially emphasised because previous literature on the subject, with a few exceptions, had tended to deflate this aspect of the contribution of Africans of the diaspora to the achievement of freedom.

Finally, in an epilogue, some of the preceding strands are drawn together and particular attention is drawn to the character and preoccupations of leadership.

In summarising the layout of chapters it can be seen that the work in all essentials divides between the earlier period of the slave trade and slavery, with all its implications, through anti-slavery seen within the framework of a broader internationalism with the rehabilitation of the role of the descendants of Africa in that particular crusade. The second part relates to the emergence and problems of early and later leadership and how it laid the foundations for later leadership as well as a tradition of struggle, which still finds echoes in contemporary black movements, whether in the Americas or in Africa. It is in the latter section that the crosscurrents of ideas, thoughts and actions, both within and without the African communities, created the apparent divergencies in objectives and goals, both limited and long term, as well as the divergent strategies for realising them. Thus, motivations and behavioural patterns are examined against the background of constraints imposed by the system of slavery – geographic, political, legal, religious, economic and administrative.

There are a number of ways in which the study can be regarded. First, as a contribution to an understanding of the plight and experiences of descendants of Africa in the Americas. Secondly, as a general contribution to the growing literature on the African slave experience beginning in Africa and terminating in the Americas, where the actions of the slavocracy and slaves and freemen and freewomen contributed to the societies which emerged in the post-emancipation era. Thirdly, as a historical contribution which highlights certain aspects of transformation in the lives, values and perceptions of Africans nurtured in a different environment under conditions of draconian restrictiveness previously unknown to most of them. It is hoped that the study will be of interest to historians of Africa, the Americas and Europe as well. There is an additional contribution in that the study indicates certain areas in which further research would be valuable. Above all, the entire focus and emphasis of the work involves an attempt to evolve a new way of looking at the African slave experience as is evident in the links between European mercantilism, the transfer of Africans, the strategy evolved to make the slave system durable, and the attempts by Africans of the diaspora to contribute to their own liberation. Such considerations emphasise the need for further reappraisals of these and other aspects of the African diaspora.

The study relies heavily on English-language sources for this study, both primary and secondary. Fortunately this is not too much of a handicap since many important works have been translated into English, and many of the authors whose work this writer has used have themselves undertaken extensive research in archival materials written in such languages as Spanish, Portuguese, Dutch and French. A number of translations of important documents have also been kindly undertaken by colleagues on my behalf.

Throughout, the use of statistics has been limited and a detailed quantitative analysis of slavery and the slave system eschewed. This approach has been undertaken elsewhere and would have added little to the arguments presented here. In fact one should be wary of the methods employed by statistician-historians, who in some cases have sought to dispel certain myths only through the creation of new ones. The authors of *Time on the Cross*, for example, have argued that the notion that 'the typical slave was poorly fed' is 'without foundation in fact', yet evidence abounds in contemporary accounts by slaves themselves that under-nourishment was commonplace in many slave theatres.

One has tried to break new ground by writing a broad interpretative book that examines four centuries of history and encompasses North and South America as well as the Caribbean. Few modern writers have attempted such a wide sweep, and in this effort one has been able to draw upon the researches of historians who have had more limited canvases to paint. Works that have been especially useful include Professor J. H. Franklin's monumental study *From Slavery to Freedom*, which is mostly concerned with the North American experience. Jamaican history has been well served by Edward Brathwaite's *The Development of Creole Society in Jamaica, 1770–1820* (1971) and Orlando Patterson's *The Sociology of Slavery* (1967), both of which clearly demonstrate the functions of divisive techniques in sustaining slave societies and the implications of this in the post-emancipation era, though neither writer has tackled in depth all the factors that contributed to the durability of the slave system. Both Philip Curtin's *Two Jamaicas* (1955) and Fernando Henriques' *Jamaica: land of wood and water* (1957) illustrate the importance of colour divisions during the slavery era, a topic dealt with in some detail in the present study. Pierre de Vaissière's *St Domingue* (1909) and C. L. R. James's *Black Jacobins* (1963, first published 1938) contain important material on the same theme, namely by calling our attention to the conflicts in Haiti generated as a result of the creation of a hierarchy of colour, though neither book deals with the international dimension to the revolution in the depth covered here. Numerous other publications of value have also been consulted and these are listed in the bibliography. Throughout one has also used material from the various slave narratives and autobiographies which hitherto have been largely ignored by scholars.

A final importance of this study may be seen in the fact that it also seeks implicitly to illuminate the contemporary social scene, which has evolved in different ways in different places out of the practices of previous centuries. For example, a proper focus on Haitian history is more likely to be obtained from a clear understanding of the revolution, and this can assist in illuminating the phenomenon described in modern parlance as 'neo-colonialism', for in the struggle for independence and the retention of it, the Haitians have long striven, in the face of abject poverty coexisting with extreme wealth and privilege, to stave off the status of a dependent colony incapable of autocentric development. Parts of the Americas, and more especially the West Indies and the Guyanas, remain basically plantation-type economies dependent on single primary products, with plantation culture being all-pervasive. The mental legacy of slavery lingers on and its overthrow requires, first, knowledge of how it all evolved, and then a systematic onslaught upon it by the inculcation of useful ideas and values and the formulation of policies designed to erode the painful, slavish legacies of centuries of persistent and ingrained callousness in the treatment of the slaves.

It would be presumptuous even to suggest that one has exhausted the subject. This has not been the intention. In the four years between 1971 and 1975 when this writer taught courses at the University of Nairobi on 'Africa and the Black Diaspora' he became even more convinced of the need for a text which synthesised some of the cross-currents of these four centuries in the Africans' experience in the Americas; in short, a text capable of setting the Africans of the diaspora in a continuum from the time of their first transfer from Africa until their descendants attempted to forge some kind of a link with the parent continent. If this aim has been only partially fulfilled in this work, its purpose will have been served.

Notes

1 G. Shepperson, 'The African Abroad or the Africa of the Diaspora', in *Emerging Themes of African History*, T. O. Ranger (ed.), Nairobi, 1968, p. 152.
2 See *The National Anti-Slavery Standard*, No. 24, 18 Nov. 1841, for the controversy which arose between the British and the U.S. governments on the question of the right to search ships suspected to be engaged in the slave trade.
3 Leslie B. Rout, Jr., *The African Experience in Spanish America*, Cambridge, 1976.

1   Slave societies in the Americas

The term 'slave societies' is employed here to refer to those parts of mainland America and the Caribbean islands in which, between the sixteenth and nineteenth centuries, slaves were used to develop and sustain economic life. The Americas contain a large variety of relief and climatic features, ranging from arctic conditions in the north, through temperate regions in North America to the subtropical and tropical areas of Central and South America and the Caribbean islands. Continental America is characterised by a rich variety of topography, some areas being mountainous, others forming plateaux, still others constituting vast lowland plains whose surfaces are broken by extensive river systems, some of which empty into the sea while others drain into lakes forming valuable navigable waterways. On the western side of the American mainland mountain chains extend from the north (the Rockies), through Central America to the south (the Andes), while in the east the landscape is configured by the Appalachian mountains of North America and the Guyana and Brazilian highlands of South America.

The topography and vegetation of the Americas decisively shaped the pattern of European conquest and settlement. The eastern seaboard of the two continents was the region of the earliest and most densely populated settlements, and in North America it was only in the nineteenth century that substantial progress westward was made and large permanent centres in the interior and in the west came into being. Even today, the eastern seaboard of North America remains the most densely inhabited region of the continent. In South America coastal cities such as Santiago in Chile and Buenos Aires in Argentina, both founded in the sixteenth century, remain substantial centres of population.

The age of discovery set the pace for European westward expansion across the Atlantic Ocean, and notable among the early explorers were men from the Iberian peninsula – from Spain and Portugal – and navigators of Genoese origin. Christopher Columbus carries the credit of being the first European voyager in modern times to 'discover' the Americas, in 1492, an expedition made under Spanish auspices. The Spanish were quickly followed to the New World by the Portuguese, by the English, French and Dutch, and later by the Danes, Swedes and Germans.

The factors behind the movement of European peoples across the Atlantic were various and are difficult to define with precision; indeed, it is not easy in describing events of the period to define exactly cause and effect, as two historians have noted:

> In the investigation of significant historical development it is often impossible to follow, with any conviction, the old logic of cause and effect. Events crowd upon circumstances, seemingly unrelated details coincide, individuals, unknown to each other and inspired, it would seem, by motives that are utterly disparate, set to work in the same direction, but in various parts of the world accident plays its part, and then suddenly and almost fortuitously, the pieces fall into place and mankind has changed direction. It was thus with the early exploration and exploitation of the New World: economics, scientific progress, religion, personalities, and what is loosely called 'the spirit of the age', all conspired together to bring about events that made possible the voyages of discovery and settlement; these things, geography, national characteristics, and again accident (it is impossible for historians to ignore the force of accident) gave dominion over what was eventually to prove the greatest empire of them all, to the countries of the North West Atlantic Seaboard, to France, Holland and England.[1]

There was thus a complexity to the human movements which determined and shaped the kinds of settlement that were initially established and later developed across the Atlantic. A combination of mixed motivations impelled and shaped the settlements – among them were featured greed, the quest for riches, political and religious persecution and economic failure at home.

The theatre of European activity in the New World rapidly grew during the sixteenth century. The islands of the Caribbean, which formed the first area of European contact with the Americas, very quickly became staging posts for the exploration and conquest of Central America and the southern landmass. The search by Europeans for new frontiers of adventure and opportunity was a constant feature of life in the Americas during the early centuries of conquest and settlement. So, too, was the turbulence and bloodshed inseparable from European activity. Though they resisted valiantly, the bows and arrows of the indigenous peoples of the Americas were no match for the firearm technology of the invaders. The Arawaks and Caribs of the Caribbean region, and the various Amerindian peoples of North, Central and South America, perished in their hundreds of thousands from military conquest, imported diseases and maltreatment as labourers. In the vanguard of European conquest of the Americas were ambitious and brutal leaders from the Iberian peninsula. Preoccupied with the search for

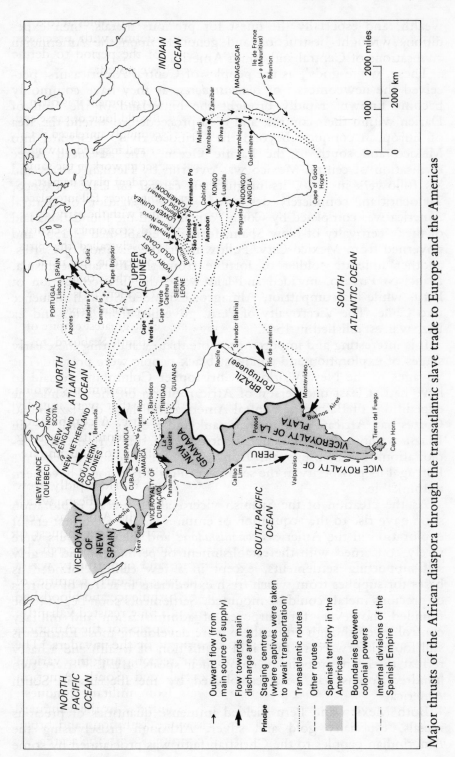

Major thrusts of the African diaspora through the transatlantic slave trade to Europe and the Americas

wealth, and especially the quest for precious metals, their expeditions wrought destruction and genocide upon the Amerindian
civilisations of Central and South America.

These 'white gods', as the peoples of Central America first perceived the newcomers,[2] or *conquistadores*, as they have commonly
become known, rapidly brought the hinterland of the Gulf of
Darien within their control, and then proceeded to extend the area
of European conquest beyond the Orinoco river, westward into
Mexico and south to the Pacific Ocean. The advanced Aztec
civilisation of central Mexico was overrun by Hernán Cortes and
his followers in 1520, its magnificent capital on Lake Texcoco,
Tenochtitlan, completely destroyed. The subjugation of Central
America was completed by Cortes' captains and the foundations laid
of the Viceroyalty of New Spain, formally established in 1535 and
governed from Mexico City. Following in the tradition of Cortes,
another illiterate soldier of fortune from the Iberian peninsula,
Francisco Pizzaro, invaded and laid waste the Inca civilisation of
Peru, while his compatriot, Almagro, expanded Spanish influence
into Chile. The Viceroyalty of Peru, governed from Lima and La
Paz, was established in 1542.

It is interesting and important to note that even during these early
stages of exploration and conquest black people were present. The
voyages to the New World of Christopher Columbus are said to
have had at least one person of African origin on them, while the
expeditions of Balboa in Central America and those of Pizzaro and
Cortes had Africans among their rank and file. As we shall see, in
Brazil without the involuntary introduction of Africans the exploitation of immense wealth from sugar and minerals, which gave
Portugal its prosperity in the seventeenth century, would have been
unthinkable.

As the creation of the Spanish viceroyalties reveal, exploration
soon gave rise to the acquisition of empires. During the first era of
exploration in the Americas *conquistadores* and their followers were
rarely concerned with the establishment of permanent and largely
self-supporting settlements, except in a few centres founded as
bases for supplies from which fresh expeditions in search of sources
of precious metals could be mounted. Settlements soon began to be
founded, however, for purposes of administration and military
control, even though while these were developing most Europeans
still looked forward to the rapid acquisition of wealth and a hasty
retreat to the metropolis to enjoy their spoils. By 1580 over two
hundred towns had been established by the Iberians in South
America.

Both Mexico and Peru yielded immense quantities of precious
metals, especially gold and silver. Although proselytising the
Amerindian peoples to the Christian faith was proclaimed by some

Spaniards to be the foremost aim of their exploration and colonisation of the New World, essentially what was involved was an all-embracing preoccupation with material enrichment and personal aggrandisement. Local peoples were ruthlessly put to work in gold and silver mines, bringing about an untold loss of life. Wherever mines existed the Amerindians fared badly. In areas where mines were absent, as in North America, the survival possibilities of the indigenous peoples were later greatly influenced by their substitution as forced workers by imported African slaves. Both formal and informal resistance to European tyranny was mounted by the Amerindians, and a notable rebellion of a later period was that of the Incas in 1781 which, like all previous challenges to European authority and control in the New World, was suppressed by the Spanish without mercy.

Spanish activity was not confined to Central and South America. In 1519 Ponce de Leon, who a decade earlier had brought Puerto Rico under Spanish control, landed in Florida in North America and the first Spanish settlement in the region was founded in 1528, though most of the pioneering settlers were massacred by local Amerindians. This did not deter Spanish expansion in the continent, however, and Spain's preoccupation with the search for gold and silver led settlers from the Iberian peninsula to extend Spanish exploration beyond Florida into Louisiana, Arkansas and Texas as far as the Rio Grande in the south and westward to the Colorado region.

Following Columbus' first voyage to the Americas Spain had acted quickly to make an international claim to all the territory in the New World. By decree Pope Alexander VI, himself a Spaniard, divided the world outside Europe into two zones, one each side of a line which ran from north to south 100 leagues (640 kilometres) west of the Azores. All lands discovered in the western zone were to belong to Spain and those in the east to Portugal. The Portuguese objected to the arrangement and refused to recognise Spanish claims to the New World unless the line was moved to 370 leagues (2400 kilometres) west of the Azores. Spain relented and the new division was enshrined in the Treaty of Tordesillas in 1494. In this way Brazil, whose coast and hinterland lay to the east of the Tordesillas line, was claimed by Portugal following the expedition in 1500 of Pedro Alvares Cabral, who named the territory 'the land of the true cross', though the Portuguese initially did little to colonise and develop the region.

From the outset no other European nation would accept Spain's claim to rule all the world to the west of the line of the Treaty of Tordesillas. In 1497 a Genoese navigator, Giovanni Caboto (John Cabot) landed in Newfoundland on behalf of the English monarch; in 1524 the king of France sponsored an expedition led by another

Italian, Giovanni de Verrazano, who mapped the North American coastline from Carolina to Nova Scotia; and in 1534 a Frenchman, Jacques Cartier, made the first of several journeys up the St Lawrence river into the North American interior. But for a long time the English and French, together with the Dutch, were less interested in pioneering new discoveries and settlements than in sharing in the spoils of the Spanish empire. The activities of their sailors introduced into the English language a new word, 'filibustering', a term used to describe English piracy against Spanish treasure vessels in Caribbean and American waters. Throughout the sixteenth century repeated attempts were made by French, English and Dutch sailors to break Spain's commercial monopoly. Important French privateer expeditions were led by Jean Ango in 1536–7, François le Clerc in 1554 and Jacques de Sore in 1555; the English sailors, John Hawkins and Francis Drake, led a number of expeditions of piracy and pillage in the New World, Hawkins in 1562, 1564–5 and 1567–9, Drake in 1571–3 and 1585–6, and jointly in 1595–6; and Dutch privateers became active in the Caribbean from the 1570s.

The arrival of the English, French and Dutch marked the beginning of the end of Spain's previously unchallenged commercial supremacy, especially in the Caribbean islands, from where in time Spain was gradually all but eliminated. Between the fifteenth and eighteenth centuries the Spanish nonetheless clung tenaciously to their mainland possessions and to their ostensible monopoly of colonisation, trade and navigation, regimenting commerce in order to stave off (or in practice, restrain) the depredations of pirates and Spain's national enemies. A system of sending two convoys annually from Andalusia across the Atlantic was established, one leaving Seville in May and collecting the treasures of New Spain at Vera Cruz (the Flota), while the other (the Galleons), which departed from Seville in August, sailed to Cartagena in modern Colombia and to Nombre de Dios in modern Panama. This second fleet received the goods of South America, silver shipments from Peru being transported overland to the awaiting vessels across the isthmus from Panama on the Pacific coast. Goods from Buenos Aires on the South Atlantic coast of modern Argentina were initially conveyed by overland routes to Peru, but after 1620 trade was begun from the Rio de la Plata directly to Spain. Nevertheless, all the routes proved very uneconomical and conveyance costs made Spanish goods expensive in Europe. This harsh fact gave rise to much smuggling, which continued unabated into the eighteenth century. The intensity of European rivalry in the Americas ultimately resulted in Spain being expelled from Jamaica by the English and losing Louisiana and Florida to the French. Yet Spain was able to retain much of its empire, especially those colonies on the mainland of South America, until the nineteenth century.

Although Portuguese contact with Brazil began at the turn of the sixteenth century, no attempts were made towards effective occupation until 1531, when an expedition was sent from Lisbon to establish a Brazilian colony. Portugal's neglect of Brazil at this time can be explained by the general preoccupation of Europeans with precious metals and goods of commercial value; no minerals were initially discovered in Brazil, whose only potential export commodities seemed to comprise dyewoods, monkeys and parrots. Moreover, having established themselves on the West African and East African coasts, which they regarded as strategically more important than Brazil, and immersed in their quest for the legendary Christian king, Prester John, who they believed would make a useful ally in their struggles against the Muslims of the Mediterranean region, the Portuguese found no real incentive during the first quarter of the sixteenth century for turning to Brazil. But the arrival of the French in the region to obtain dyewoods soon compelled them to make an effort towards establishing some semblance of control.

The years that followed saw the Portuguese carve out the coastline of Brazil into a number of captaincies, bestowed upon court favourites and those patronised by the Portuguese Crown. Captains were granted extensive powers to establish their fiefs, to govern and trade, and to found urban centres. There was little uniformity of development, for while some captaincies were almost untouched others became important producers of sugar, a crop which the Portuguese had successfully cultivated in their plantations in the Azores and Madeira with the aid of African slave labour. The coastal and sectional method of early Portuguese colonisation left its imprint on the development of modern Brazil, which still consists of thickly populated coastal strips, with difficult communications between them, and behind which lies a vast, sparsely populated interior.

The advent of more intense international rivalry in the New World in the sixteenth century encouraged Portugal to strengthen its hold on Brazil and to impose greater administrative unity on the colony. In the middle of the century a governor for the entire territory was appointed, based in the northern city of Salvador Bahia (Salvador). In 1567, largely in response to increasing French activity in the region, a major southern settlement was founded, St Sebastian (Rio de Janeiro), which became the colony's capital, superseding Salvador. Brasilia has since become the country's capital.

During the period between 1580 and 1640 when the Portuguese crown was held by the Spanish monarch, Portugal was disastrously handicapped in the New World. Whenever Spain acquired national enemies Portugal automatically acquired them too, albeit reluctantly. Dutch hostilities towards Spain were borne, in the main, by the Portuguese throughout their colonies in Africa, Asia and the Americas, and for twenty-four years the Dutch occupied the Brazilian city of Olinda. It was only when the Portuguese eventually succeeded in releasing themselves from Spanish domination that sufficient encouragement was given to the Brazilian settlers to organise against the Dutch and expel them. The Portuguese also successfully regained from the Dutch their West African territory of Angola, though they failed to dislodge the Dutch from their erstwhile Gold Coast possessions. The strategic importance of Angola to the Portuguese was to be found in the fact that they drew their major supply of slaves from this region to sustain the Brazilian sugar industry, and the steady supply of African slaves from Angola to South America averted what would otherwise have been a major commercial crisis. After 1640 the Portuguese were also even more compelled to concentrate their attention on the exploitation of Brazil since they also failed successfully to regain their Asian possessions from the Dutch.

During the last years of the seventeenth century precious metals were discovered in Minas Gerais. The discovery resulted in a gold rush both from metropolitan Portugal and from the northern regions of the colony. Brazil, whose economy had hitherto hinged almost entirely on sugar, suddenly became an important producer of gold and diamonds. The Portuguese crown, like that of Spain, continued to claim one-fifth of mined bullion. Portuguese national energy was unleashed following the separation from Spain, and the mineral discoveries in the New World lured members of various social groups from the metropolis to Brazil. Yet, as it turned out, nothing added more to Portugal's success than the introduction of a large population of African slaves to work the mines and till the soil, slaves whose industry contributed enormously to Portuguese achievements.

Colonial society in the New World was highly stratified – by class, by colour and also by country of origin. A distinction very rapidly emerged between on the one hand *ladinos* or *peninsulares*, Spaniards or Portuguese born in the Iberian peninsula, and on the other hand creoles (*criollos*), who were born of European parents in the American colonies. Discrimination precluded Spanish creoles from holding important administrative posts, and tensions between local whites and *peninsulares* grew more serious as the creoles increased in population. Social distinction on the basis of colour was also of profound importance. The term *castas* was used collectively to signify people of mixed descent, and embraced a complex system of colour classification whose gradations increased as time passed by.[3] Similar divisions developed in Portuguese Brazil and in the English, French and Dutch colonies in the Caribbean.

Already by 1700 Spain had lost ground in the Caribbean, retaining only Cuba, Santo Domingo, Puerto Rico and Trinidad, though its mainland empire in the Americas remained intact. Both England[4] and France[5] had created large Caribbean empires by the close of the seventeenth century, and the Dutch,[6] too, although generally uninterested in settlement, had gained a series of possessions, though by this time Holland had already ceased to be a major power in the area. English interest in the North American mainland developed as a result of the discovery in 1614–16 that Virginia could produce crops of tobacco that sold readily in Europe. Religious persecution in England – above all of the Puritans in the 1630s, but also of royalists at the end of the 1640s – encouraged further emigration across the Atlantic. During the eighteenth century conflicts between the European nations in the Americas continued, and seven major European wars were fought in American waters between 1702 and 1814. British power in the region was consolidated by the acquisition of St Kitts in 1713 and in 1763 of Granada, Dominica, St Vincent and Tobago. At the end of the Seven Years War Britain was also firmly established as the dominant power in North America, France relinquishing its claims to Canada and to land east of the Mississippi river. The tight grip in which Britain held its colonial possessions was loosened, however, between 1775 and 1783 by the War of American Independence and the creation of the United States, whose independent status was recognised by Britain in the Treaty of Versailles of September 1783, and whose constitution came into force in June 1788.

By the end of the eighteenth century Spain still occupied Mexico, Central America, the whole of South America with the exception of Brazil and the Guyanas, Cuba, St Domingo, Puerto Rico and Trinidad. In 1763 it had acquired Louisiana from France and in 1783 regained Florida after losing the territory to Britain twenty years earlier.[7] Moreover, a vigorous reform programme designed to rationalise the administration of the Spanish empire was undertaken during the reign of Charles III (1759–88). The success of Charles's scheme, however, heightened tensions throughout Spain's colonies. Creoles were angered by new taxes, the more efficient collection of old ones, and their continued exclusion from the most lucrative official appointments. The downfall of Spanish colonialism in the New World was ultimately precipitated by the French revolution and the upheavals to the world order that followed the collapse of the *ancien régime* in Europe. The French revolution, like the American revolution before it, provided a precedent for the overthrow of established authority, and the ideas of the Enlightenment began to permeate the colonies. Napoleon's invasion of Spain

17

in 1808 served to underline its weakness. St Domingo had already been ceded to France in 1795. The fourteen years between 1810 and 1824 marked a turbulent period of power struggle in the Spanish American empire which culminated in the achievement of independence for all Spain's former colonies in Central and South America. Puerto Rico and Cuba remained as Spain's only colonial outposts in the New World.

The achievement of Brazilian independence followed a different course from that of Spanish America. When in 1807 Napoleonic armies invaded Portugal the Braganza court fled to Rio de Janeiro, and Brazil enjoyed a *de facto* independence. In 1822 that independence was consolidated when Dom Pedro, the son of the Portuguese monarch – who was left as regent in Rio when his father, Dom João, returned to Lisbon – declared the colony's independence from the metropolis and proclaimed himself Emperor Pedro I. The empire survived in Brazil until as late as 1889 when Pedro II, who had ruled since 1830, was ousted in a bloodless coup and control of the political system fell into the hands of a small elite of planters, professionals and military officers.

The societies that took root in the New World represented a curious mixture of metropolitan patterns of life – in culture, architecture, language and religion – and patterns of life determined by the colonial environment and the economic system that underpinned it. The phenomenon of absenteeism was ingrained at a very early stage. With the notable exceptions of the New England settlements, founded in the seventeenth century, and the later colonies of the North American mainland, and also some of the smaller island societies in the Antilles, such as Antigua and Guadaloupe, absenteeism was an important and persistent feature of most colonial settlements in the New World. It influenced the social structure of plantation colonies so profoundly that the sociologist Orlando Patterson has concluded that colonial Jamaica represented an 'absentee society', a description that could be generally applied to most settlements in the New World from the seventeenth to nineteenth centuries.[8] Absenteeism was especially characteristic of the English Caribbean colonies, and was the subject of numerous despatches between the settler administrations and the British government.[9] At any one time about a third of the plantation owners were likely to be absent, living in enormous wealth in the metropolis while their estates were run by attorneys, overseers or managers on their behalf.

Absenteeism became so entrenched that it even extended to clergymen. A case cited by Governor Maitland of Grenada in 1805 relates to the Rector of the Parish of St George, Grenada, who had been absent from the island for nine months while still earning his 'living'. The clergyman concerned, the Rev. W. Austin, when requested to return to the island from Surinam where he was the proprietor of a sugar estate, suggested instead that he exchange places with another clergyman, the Rev. W. Wicks of Surinam, who would assume his clerical duties in Grenada. The arrangement failed to win the governor's approval.[10] In 1808 Governor Barnes of Dominica reported the case of another clergyman, the Rev. John Audain, who had been absent for nearly twelve months, during which time he had 'openly and notoriously been engaged in commercial mercantile concerns'.[11] In a subsequent despatch in 1811, from Governor Elliot of the Leeward Islands, it was stated:

> The conduct of the Reverend Mr Audain, the only regular
> Clergyman of the Church of England who holds a living in this
> island, has been so notoriously derogatory to His sacred office, that I
> shall immediately suspend him. He has been several years absent
> from Tortola without leaving any Curate to officiate in his place. He
> has not only engaged in Commerce but has actually commanded
> Privateers, and would have perished at St Domingo (and I believe
> deservedly) if Christophe, whom he deceived, could have again got
> him into his possession.[12]

In developing the New World it became clear from an early stage that the successful pursuit of wealth, whether in mining for precious metals or in plantation agriculture, demanded a supply of dependable and cheap labour. The Amerindian peoples of the Americas were unfamiliar with the relentless and rigorous labour demands of the conquerors, perishing in enormous numbers from disease and maltreatment. Some free or indentured workers were obtained from Europe, but the numbers fell far short of the demand. Black slaves were already being utilised in commercial agriculture in southern Spain and Portugal, and it was but a small step to look towards Africa as the reservoir of labour for the development of the Americas.

The societies into which Africans were imported varied much in character, but all were founded upon an economic system based on slave labour, at whose core lay the brutalisation and depersonalisation of the individual. Slavery in the Americas curtailed in large measure the African's right to independent thought and action, to enlightenment and progress. It is impossible to read the lives of former slaves such as Frederick Douglass, Ottabah Cugoano and Olaudah Equiano,[13] and many others, without coming face to face with the inhuman suffering and cruelty of plantation slavery. 'No slave could possibly escape being punished. I care not how attentive they might be, nor how industrious, punished they must be, and punished they certainly were.' This was the assessment of Austin Stewart writing in 1859 of his twenty-two years as a slave in the

United States.[14] Racism and slavery were closely entwined, and as concepts they are sometimes difficult for the historian to satisfactorily disentangle for the period under review. Eric Williams has argued that 'slavery was not born of racism but rather racism was the consequence of slavery';[15] yet there is much evidence which demonstrates that racism was already prevalent in Europe before the sixteenth century and was merely further heightened by the Atlantic slave trade.[16]

It was through slavery and the slave trade that the histories of Africa, the Americas and Europe converged, and it is the cluster of ideas and preoccupations which fathered the experience that forms the subject of the next chapter.

Notes

1 R. B. Nye and J. E. Murpurgo, *A History of the United States*, Vol. 1, *The Birth of the United States*, Harmondsworth, Penguin, 1955, p. 1.

2 See Richard Friedenthal, *The White Gods*, trans. from the German by Charles Hope Lumley, New York and London, 1931.

3 See Appendix 2.

4 England's Caribbean possessions at this time consisted of Antigua, Barbados, Jamaica, Montserrat, Nevis, the Virgin Islands and part of St Kitts.

5 Cayenne, Desirade, Granada, Guadeloupe, Marie Galante, Martinique, St Bartholomew, St Domingue, St Kitts.

6 Aruba, Berbice, Bonaire, Curaçao, Demerara, Essequibo, St Eustasius, Saba.

7 Louisiana was ultimately ceded to the French by Spain in 1800 and subsequently sold to the United States by France in 1803; the United States gained Florida from Spain in 1819.

8 See generally L. J. Ragatz, *Absentee Landlordism in the British Caribbean 1750–1833*, London, 1931.

9 See, for example, Public Records Office, London (PRO), CO 78/51, Petition by the Assembly of Barbados delivered by Mr Walker, Agent for the Island; address to the King; and Earl of Hillsborough to Mr Rous, President of the Council of Barbados, 31 Jan. 1768. Also CO 71/4, Sir William Young to Earl of Hillsborough, 29 July 1772, and William Stuart to Earl of Dartmouth, 10 March 1773.

10 CO 101/42, Governor Maitland to Lord Castlereagh, 3 Nov. 1805.

11 CO 71/43, Governor Barnes to Lord Castlereagh, 8 Dec. 1808.

12 CO 152/97, Governor Elliot to the Earl of Liverpool, 15 May 1811.

13 Frederick Douglass, *Life and Times 1817–1882*, John Lobb (ed.), London, 1882; Ottabah Cugoano, *Thoughts and Sentiments on the Evil . . . Traffic . . . of Slavery*, London, 1787; Olaudah Equiano, *The Interesting Narrative of the Life of Olaudah Equiano or Gustavus Vassa, the African*, 2 vols., London, 1789.

14 Austin Steward, *Twenty-two Years a Slave and Forty Years a Free Man*, Rochester, N.Y., 1859, p. 24. See also W. W. Brown, *Narrative of the Life of William Wells Brown: an American Slave*, London, 1850, p. 16.

15 E. E. Williams, *The Negro in the Caribbean*, Manchester, 1942. See also the

arguments of Moses I. Finlay in L. Foner and E. D. Genovese (eds.), *Slavery in the New World: a Reader in Comparative History*, Englewood Cliffs, N. J., 1969, pp. 256–61 and esp. pp. 260–1.

16 For example see Carl Degler, 'Slavery and the Genesis of American Race Prejudice', *Comparative Studies in Society and History*, I (1959), pp. 49–66; J. Pope Hennessy, *Sins of the Fathers: the Atlantic Slave Traders 1441–1807*, Sphere Books, 1970, pp. 95, 110–13.

2 Wealth and power

Mercantilism

The term 'mercantilism' has been coined to describe the basic principles regulating the economic relations of European states in the sixteenth, seventeenth and eighteenth centuries. The objective of mercantilists was to encourage private trade and industry through state action, and to increase the wealth and power of the state through the prosperity thereby engendered. Economic policy was founded upon certain assumptions scarcely contested at the time: namely, that precious metals constituted wealth; that every effort should be made to accumulate them; and that the gain of one nation must perforce be at the expense of another. The token of success of a mercantilist policy was therefore a healthy inflow of gold and silver, the token of failure the reverse. A favourable balance of trade was to be achieved by tariffs and other measures designed to discourage imports, and bounties and rebates to encourage exports.

The classical expression of the mercantile theory of foreign trade is contained in a pamphlet dating from the seventeenth century:

> No man ever doubted but that Foreign Trade and Commerce is the
> great concern and Interest of every Nation, because the increase and
> Wealth of all States is evermore made upon the Foreigner, for
> whatsoever is gained by one Native from another in one part of this
> kingdom must necessarily be lost in another part, and so the public
> Stock nothing thereby Augmented. But Trade and Commerce
> cannot be maintained or increased without Government, Order, and
> regular Discipline; for in all confused Traffique it must necessarily
> happen that while every single Person pursues his own particular
> Interest the Publique is deserted by All and consequently must fall to
> Ruine.[1]

Implicit in the application of the mercantilist doctrine was the idea of autarky, or national economic self-sufficiency. Monopoly was an important ideal and outside traders were to be excluded from national commerce except on closely regulated terms. Spain's economic relations with its New World possessions, for example, were in theory pre-eminently monopolistic, though it contracted with individuals and nations for the supply of slaves from Africa through the *Asiento* system. Mercantilism was not generally concerned in practice with stimulating industry *per se*, as Eli Heckscher, the outstanding author on the subject, has noted,[2] but rather with directing or promoting it along certain defined channels such as shipping and fishing, industries whose development was closely associated with national defence. The interests of individuals and groups of individuals on the one hand, and the interests of the state on the other, were closely entwined in the formulation of mercantilist ideas. In his assessment of the mercantilist 'mind', Lawrence Harper has deduced from the numerous writings of contemporaries on the subject that 'In so far as seventeenth-century theorists attempted any reconciliation of individual interest and public welfare, it rested on the assumption that there was an ideal balance which, if attained, would secure national prosperity as well as individual advancements'.[3] Mercantilism in these various ways became embedded in the commercial practices of European states and in turn gave rise to 'commercial capitalism' and later 'monopoly capitalism'.[4]

At the root of mercantilist thought lay the twin concepts of wealth and power. The means of achieving these objectives were the various Navigation Acts, the most prominent of which were enacted in England in the seventeenth century. The English Navigation Acts enforced after 1651, with amendments and additions after 1660, had a number of purposes such as the exclusion of foreign vessels from the coastal and colonial trades; the advancement of English seamanship; the encouragement of the building of large ships that were suitable for the Atlantic crossing and for conversion into warships; and the creation of a virtual monopoly in such tropical raw materials as tobacco, sugar, cotton and dyewoods, by enacting that these should be landed only in England from where a large proportion of the goods would be re-exported to other European states. Navigation laws designed to promote national prosperity and the naval power to protect and extend maritime wealth had a long history. Aragon introduced such legislation in the fourteenth century and the Hansa cities and Castile in the fifteenth, while the first Navigation Act in England dates back to 1381 and was designed to arrest the decline in English naval strength.[5] France and Denmark enacted navigation laws in the seventeenth century and Sweden in 1720.

For most of the European maritime nations wealth and defence were crucial factors in the power equation and were inextricably bound. The policy was particularly demonstrated and effectively applied in shipping, and it was in shipping that England, between the seventeenth and eighteenth centuries, achieved ascendancy over its European rivals, becoming a great naval power at a time when the slave trade from Africa had also become of major importance. England proceeded to base its shipping policy on what it considered to be its defence interests and in part too on the attitudes and policies of its European rivals. These preoccupations with the realities of power thus became intertwined with commercial motives.

The Navigation Acts were to play their part in the rise of nations to commercial supremacy and at times provided the pretexts for wars of aggression against rivals, as in the series of Anglo–Dutch wars of the seventeenth century, and this in spite of the fact that very little was achieved in these conflicts in the way of accumulating wealth, except by acts of piracy. In order to encourage shipbuilding numerous concessions were made to shipbuilders which proved advantageous in time of war, but these need not detain us here. However, we are concerned to identify the inter-relationship between mercantilism on the one hand and the Atlantic slave trade on the other, and their link with the plantation economies of the Americas, which, in turn, also generated the demand for labour and gave the slave-trading activities of Europeans in Africa further impetus.

Mercantilism and the slave trade

When a distinguished writer on migration and British capital export, C. K. Hobson, wrote early in this century on the origin of capital, he observed that it could be located in trade.[6] But Hobson, unlike a number of subsequent writers, showed no awareness of the importance of the slave trade in the raising and accumulation of capital. George Frederick Zook, writing in 1910 and employing English and Dutch sources, first demonstrated the inter-connection between the slave trade and the policy of wealth and power.[7] Eric Williams was later to insist that the slave trade played a major part in the accumulation of capital, though the issue is still a matter of historical controversy.[8]

At this point we need to examine how the development of the European settlements in the New World linked Africa with the fortunes of the plantations they were establishing. As has been shown in the previous chapter, the early European settlers in the Americas were the Spanish, soon to be followed by the Portuguese and other Europeans – the English, French, Dutch and the Danes. Initially, the Spanish enslaved the indigenous peoples of the Indies and set them to labour; and it is now generally asserted that this usage of the Amerindians so considerably reduced their number that a plea to the government of metropolitan Spain to allow for the introduction of substitute labour became necessary. This was

24

achieved after a passionate plea on behalf of the Amerindian communities by Bartolomé de las Casas, Bishop of Chiapas in Mexico, and the Jeronomite Fathers.

But the Africans entered the scene early, for some of those who had been taken as slaves from Africa to Europe were later transported to the Indies. As already noted, Africans were present in the fighting ranks of the Spanish *conquistadores* of the New World. The Amerindians had initially been used for work in the mines, but as the settlers also had to survive they had to be employed in cultivation as well. These little settlements were, in time, to grow into larger plantations and some of these were to become important production areas of the major staples – tobacco, rice, sugar, and later, cotton. In time, each of the settlements was to decide its own specialisation, but sugar from early times remained a constant factor throughout the centuries of the slave trade. Other crops such as rice, dyewoods and indigo became important too. But the staples created a demand in Europe, and the demand became a stimulus to further production. As a consequence of the persistence of labour scarcity the settlers in the Americas perfected ways of introducing Africans into their plantations. A notable feature in this development was the growth of trading companies, many of them trading to Africa and the Americas.

Trading companies

Trading companies, which had been known to Europe since the fifteenth and sixteenth centuries, became the means by which the restrictive policies of the mercantilists were put into practice. Most of the companies possessed royal patronage as well as a royal charter;[9] often they also had exclusive privileges conferred on them in their various areas of operation that amounted to a virtual monopoly of trade. Earlier European trading companies, preoccupied with the discovery of passages to the Orient through the north west and the north east in the temperate regions of the world, and concerned to obtain wealth either through the discovery of minerals or through trade, or both, were in time superseded by companies that felt no restraint in challenging the Luso-Hispanic monopoly in areas where the Spanish and Portuguese had established themselves. This challenge began early in the sixteenth century.

Since the areas outside Europe in which the Portuguese and Spanish were operating included Africa, the Orient and the Americas, it was into these theatres that rival European nations, as represented by trading companies and individual adventurers, intruded. Although some commodity trading had attracted

Europeans to the West African and North African coasts, it was the gold trade, the legend of which had existed since the time of the Emperor of Mali's visit to Egypt and the Middle East in the fourteenth century,[10] which aroused European covetousness. The gold trade became a preoccupation of Europeans, who sought to divert it to the Atlantic coast.[11] Initially it was of greater importance than slaves; but, in time, it was superseded by the slave trade. Both the gold trade and the slave trade for a while coexisted; but the growth of one tended to choke the other, and it has been recorded in many accounts that where the gold trade prospered the slave trade was of minimal importance; but, where the slave trade prospered, there was little prospect of finding much gold. As most of the west coast of Africa did not produce gold, and because of the constant labour demands of plantations in the Americas, the slave trade became more important – indeed, the only trade worthy of the name from Africa from the seventeenth century.

Among the companies that became prominent in the African trade were the Dutch West India Company (1621), later superseded in 1674 by a New Dutch West India Company; the French Rouen Company (1633), the French West India Company (1664), the Senegal Company (1672), the New Senegal Company (1681), and later the Guinea Company (1684), renamed at the time of the receipt of the French *Asiento* in 1702 as the Asiento Company; the Prussian Emden African Company (1682); the Swedish African Company (with Dutch patronage, 1647); the English London Adventurers (1618), followed by the Royal Adventurers (1660 and 1663), superseded by the Royal African Company (1672), the Gambian Adventurers, an offshoot of the Royal Adventurers (1669), the South Sea Bubble Company (1713), which had to implement the English *Asiento*, and the Merchant Adventurers of London, free traders (1750); the Havana Monopoly Company, the Caracas Company (1728), and finally the Barcelona or Catalan Company (1755).[12] The London Adventurers had been preceded by the Senegal Adventurers (not an incorporated company), which from 1588 received a charter granting it a monopoly of trade between Senegal and Gambia for ten years. Its activities have remained shrouded in mystery, but in 1618 there emerged a Governor and Company of Adventurers of London trading to Guinea and Benin ('Guinney and Rynney'), by which was meant the entire coast of West Africa. The company survived into the Restoration and was the first incorporated English company in the African trade with a monopoly. But like other companies subsequently, it experienced many of the difficulties that handicapped trading companies of the time: a shortage of capital, interference by interlopers, and harassment by companies of rival nations. It fell to these various trading companies to build fortifications and factories on the west coast of Africa.

The charter company was not a feature of Portuguese trade with Africa, though Portuguese traders and companies did receive royal patronage, the royal family expecting a reasonable return on its ventures. The feature of monopoly was enshrined in the activities of various companies. The Portuguese Brazil Company, for example, established in 1648, was confined in its activities to South America, and its monopoly did not extend to commerce in slaves. It was only in the late seventeenth century that a joint stock organisation emerged in the Portuguese Guinea trade.[13]

Trading companies filled the role which states found too burdensome to undertake; governments not anxious to be burdened directly by the problems that arose from long-distance trading arrangements were content to allow companies to exercise the functions of national envoys or trade consuls. As a result the companies were saddled with heavy financial commitments. As compensation the national company representatives received the rights and privileges to act on behalf of their respective states. Thus, the companies not only erected fortifications for the protection of their trade but acted as agents of their governments to ensure the smooth conduct of trade with foreign nations, and, in this connection, trade with African kings and potentates. It was these privileges which enabled company agents on the spot to make agreements with African kings, thereby giving these agreements the importance of national ones. In short, they conducted diplomatic relations on behalf of their states. It is out of this that trading agents became consuls, and later, ambassadors.

The establishment of colonies

The colonies and settlements established by the European nations in the New World became the outposts of the metropolitan countries and the proving ground for the application of mercantilist ideas. But colonisation came before attempts to apply the regulations of control. Without making a detailed analysis of the factors and motives for European colonisation of other lands in earlier periods, it can be said that the motives involved were basically economic, social and prestigious. A nineteenth-century writer, C. P. Lucas, listed four main reasons for colonisation: love of adventure, desire for wealth, political or social discontent and religion.[14] But a more modern historian in his consideration of early colonial theories listed the following as some of the major reasons: 'spread of the Gospel' (which he discounts as hardly sincere), 'search for

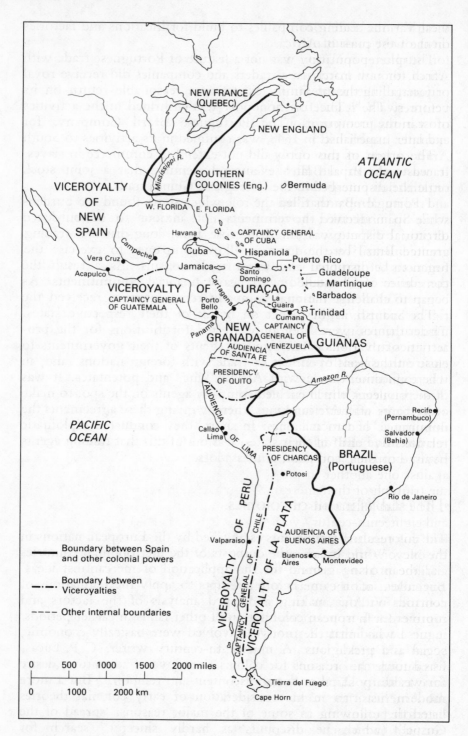

Spanish and Portuguese territories in the Americas in the sixteenth century

wealth' – the search for precious metals being an important ingredient of the pursuit of wealth – 'strategic considerations, an outlet for surplus population inclusive of criminals and undesirables, search for raw materials, markets, for the augmenting of revenue, or forestalling the intentions of rival powers by arriving on the spot before rivals'.[15] The final part of this observation seemed uppermost in the preoccupations of mercantilists as well as those of early and later imperialists.

The origin of this outward expansion in modern times can be traced to the Papal Bull of demarcation of 1492, which sought to settle the dispute between the then rival European powers, Spain and Portugal. By that Bull, Portugal received the eastern world while Spain received the western world, but final settlement of the territorial dispute was only achieved in 1494, when Portugal was granted Brazil by the Treaty of Tordesillas. These arrangements began to be disrupted once the European Reformation had rocked the edifice of Christendom and the rebellious 'Protestant' nations began to challenge the world *status quo*.

The Spanish, as the pioneer European settlers of the Americas in modern times, were later followed by others, who extended their activities to various parts of the New World. The Portuguese were close on the heels of the Spanish after they received Brazil in 1494, where, in time, they established sugar production. The challengers of the pioneers, the Dutch, English, Danes and Catholic French, in order to be effective in their rivalry for territorial and commercial dominance, had to maintain efficient shipping services and navies for offensive and defensive operations against, not only the early rivals, but their competitors as well. In time they were all pitted against one another in the struggle for commercial supremacy and the triumph of their mercantilist preoccupations.

The aim of nations that became embroiled in the seventeenth- and eighteenth-century wars was to achieve commercial supremacy, and this resulted from time to time in the loss or gain of territory by one or other of the contending parties. These rivalries in the Caribbean also asserted themselves in African waters, and the exigencies of the planters' preoccupations imposed additional demands on Africans by the transfer of their people as articles of commerce. In spite of this, it was not the Spanish but the Portuguese who initiated the modern slave trade in Africa; and what began as a trickle later became a flood. As the eastern hemisphere was outside the ordained province of Spain, and since Spain did not have as many ships as Portugal for transporting African labour to the Americas, the carrying role fell upon the Portuguese, who therefore became the first suppliers of slaves to the Spanish Indies.[16] Portugal had begun kidnapping Africans from around Cape Bojar in the 1430s, transporting a small number of slaves to metropolitan

Portugal.[17] Although the focus of their early activity in West Africa was the pursuit of trade in commodities, including gold, the slave trade soon took precedence for the Portuguese above all other considerations.

By the mid-seventeenth century the British, French, Danes and Dutch had established themselves in various parts of the Americas: the English settled on the American mainland in Virginia, Maryland, Rhode Island, Plymouth, Connecticut and Massachusetts (between 1600 and 1650) and in the islands of the Antilles — Bermuda (1609), St Christophers, St Kitts (1623), Barbados (1625), Antigua (1632), Nevis (1628), Montserrat (1632), Barbuda, Anguilla and the British Virgin Islands. The Dutch established themselves on the North American mainland at New Amsterdam and in the West Indies in Curaçao, Saba, St Martin, St Eustatius,[18] and, in the 1630s, in Tobago. The French on the American mainland were installed on the St Lawrence river and in French Acadia (later Nova Scotia, when it fell to the English); in the West Indies their most important settlements were in Guadeloupe (1626), Martinique (1635) and St Domingue (1697). The Danes took over St Thomas (1671). Until 1655 Jamaica remained Spanish but in that year it fell to the English after the failure of Cromwell's 'Western Design'.[19] In time, some of these acquisitions, because of the intense nature of commercial rivalries, changed hands either temporarily or permanently.

As T. S. Floyd has reminded us:

> The capture of Jamaica by England . . . coincided with a fundamental change in the Caribbean economy: sugar was becoming the main crop, and large plantations with Negro slavery were displacing small tobacco farms with white indentured labour. As a result, hundreds of poor whites were pushed off the land; rather than return to England or Holland or France many preferred raiding Spanish towns, especially those where gold and silver might be obtained. These raiders, who operated from several bases in the Caribbean of which Tortuga and Jamaica were among the most important, were called buccaneers.[20]

The ruthless activities of buccaneers proved a thorn in the flesh of nations.

A consequence of the capture of Jamaica by the English was that the island and its coastal areas were swamped by buccaneers, who continued their depredations and harassments on defenceless Spanish frontiers. For twenty years afterwards, buccaneers operating from Jamaica continued to dominate the Caribbean: no Spanish town accessible by water was insulated from their attacks.

Incentives

Professor Sheridan has shown that the plantation colonies, although 'variously described as "treasure islands" or "precious gems in the crown of trade", were in the age of mercantilism widely regarded as valuable adjuncts to European nations'.[21] The wealth of Spain in the Americas, which had aroused the covetousness of other European nations, who kept up their raids on the Spanish Main and the islands in the Caribbean and used pirates on the high seas to plunder Spain, contributed eventually to weakening Spain's hold of the New World. By 1600 its position had been undermined. Yet, the prospects for European colonisation of the western hemisphere grew with the diversion of the focus of trade from the Baltic, the Levant and Europe to long-distance overseas trade. At the same time the new colonies became the receptacles for surplus population from Europe in order to reduce what Sheridan rightly observed as 'social tension at home'.[22]

Thus, from 1621, when the Dutch West India Company began its efforts to wrench away by conquest from the Portuguese the northern part of Brazil, they were engaged in wars of supremacy for the wealth of the Indies and the new lands. Since Portugal was under Spanish domination at the time,[23] Spain became engaged in the defence of Brazil; simultaneously, other powers who were Spain's European rivals occupied themselves by seizing more of Spain's possessions in the Antilles. In the first half of the seventeenth century, therefore, new European powers in the western hemisphere contributed to the dislodging of Spain from its possession of a number of key territories in the New World. In this combination of Europeans for ascendancy over Spain in the west, the newcomers came into conflict, like the Spanish before them, with the indigenous inhabitants. These new arrivals pursued a vigorous and relentless policy of extermination of the indigenous peoples. Its consequences are too well known to be recounted here.

The sugar revolution in the 1640s and the 1650s, following the introduction of sugar cultivation into the English colonies, generated new prosperity and an influx of fresh settlers from Europe.[24] Sugar had been first introduced by the Portuguese into Madeira and later into Brazil. The early settlements therefore led to the movement not only of people but also of crops across the Atlantic; sugar, which came to be one of the greatest staples in the Americas, was the reason why the Dutch became so intent upon the dispossession of the Portuguese of their sugar colony in northern Brazil. The sugar revolution reached the English colonies in the 1640s and 1650s, first in Barbados, and later in other parts of the West Indies, aided by Dutch émigrés from Brazil. The plantation colonies were filled with all types — good, bad, indifferent, ne'er-do-wells and questionable characters. It was into this situation that African slaves were introduced.

In spite of the mercantilists' preoccupations with gaining the lion's share of their colonies' production, they demonstrated ambivalence in their dealings with the colonies. They wanted colonial wealth on the one hand, which they hoped would accrue to the metropolitan country through linking their respective countries with the slave- and gold-producing centres of West Africa, and with the crop-producing plantations of the Americas. Yet, on the other hand, they failed to see the necessity for sending respectable artisans to the plantations. Taking the English colonies as an example, among those sent were vagrants, paupers, undesirables, and all the ne'er-do-wells of England, as well as foreigners, whom they easily persuaded to take up residence on the plantations. As Minchinton observes in his study of the port of Bristol in the eighteenth century, they sent among their contingents both prisoners and former convicts.[25] Arriving in the New World, therefore, were captives taken after Cromwell's Irish, Scottish and Worcester expeditions; prisoners reprieved after being sentenced to death; royalists who exiled themselves from the metropolitan country after the ascendancy of the 'Commonwealth'; soldiers disembarked from Cromwell's 'Western Design'; religious fugitives such as the Huguenots from France; and last but not least slaves forcibly brought from Africa, of whom there was a continuous flow into the colonies even beyond the time of the official abolition of the slave trade in 1807. These deportees and slaves became vital for the survival of the plantations. Thus, as J. A. Williamson observed, the mercantilists filled their empire with very 'dubious elements – good Englishmen, who went with a grievance, bad Englishmen who went to save their necks, foreigners who could have no natural loyalty to England, and the luckless Africans abducted from their homes'.[26] The significance of this is to be found in the fact that these elements played a major part in influencing and moulding the morals, outlook and values of the unfortunate Africans transferred to the colonies; for, in the days when the slave trade was being rationalised and justifications were being advanced for the enslavement of African peoples, one of the claims made was that the Africans were being civilised and that no matter the plight of the Africans in the Americas they were better off there than in their ancestral home in Africa. The plantations were thus the melting pot of various nationalities, attitudes and characters, as well as divergent religious groups, which, in time, blended to mould plantation society, its values and standards. Thus, between 1600 and 1660, the English, Dutch and French, as well as the Danes, had established themselves on the mainland of America and in numerous Caribbean islands, principally in the Greater Antilles.

European cultivators in the New World had hitherto grown tobacco on a large scale. In the early years of cultivation tobacco, like sugar, was a scarce commodity in Europe, but overproduction of tobacco glutted the European market and generated a fall in prices.[27] It was this switch from tobacco to sugar production in the West Indies which ushered in the sugar revolution. Only Virginia and Maryland, of the English colonies, were allowed to continue the production of tobacco. Much of the sugar used in England came initially from Brazil until the English colonies, beginning with Barbados, adopted sugar cultivation. Thereafter sugar became an English industry and came to be more cheaply produced than in Brazil.[28]

Because labour shortage remained a constant feature of the plantations, both sugar and tobacco cultivation led to the demand for an abundant supply of workers. In time cotton cultivation was to be elevated to the status of sugar and tobacco production. Cotton was cultivated in the Leeward Islands and on the mainland of America, though less successfully than sugar in the Caribbean islands; but, after the invention of the cotton gin in North America, it graduated to the dubious dignity of 'King'.

Sugar production, which had outstripped tobacco in the English plantations within a short period of twenty years, accounted for nearly half the value of London's imports from the plantations.[29] After France had acquired the western third of the island of Hispaniola, by the Peace of Ryswick in 1697, she renamed it St Domingue and embarked on making it a plantation colony; and, by the second quarter of the eighteenth century, St Domingue had outstripped its English rivals, notably Jamaica and Barbados, in the production of sugar. In this way,

> between 1720 and 1775 its sugar exports increased in tonnage by nearly fivefold, while in the latter year total exports amounted to about 4 million sterling, one half of which was sugar. Moreover, in 1775 St Domingue exceeded Jamaica by 77 per cent in the number of whites, 72 per cent in free coloureds, 22 per cent in Negro slaves, 18 per cent in sugar exports and 67 per cent in the value of all exports to Europe.[30]

St Domingue's prosperity was at first not fashioned out of sugar but from indigo, of which it was the leading exporter in the early eighteenth century. Coffee cultivation was also introduced by the Jesuits. All these were later outstripped by sugar production. During the early decades of the eighteenth century St Domingue forged ahead of Jamaica, Barbados and Martinique in the production of sugar and possessed more than 200 sugar works, the number increasing annually.[31] Two of Sheridan's tables which appear in Appendix 3 provide an insight into sugar production in the American tropical colonies between 1740 and 1770. They not only reveal a picture of the overall production capacity in the colonies but show that throughout the period from 1741 St Domingue (later Haiti) surpassed all the other producers in sugar production, Jamaica producing only about half the quantity credited to St Domingue.[32]

The cultivation of sugar enhanced the prestige and value of the colonies and helped to establish the social structures of the old colonial system within a generation. It also led to political centralisation. This, at once, began to have a profound effect on the African trade because the cultivation of tobacco, rice, cotton, indigo and, in particular, sugar, increased the demand for African slave labour. Thus, the demand for slaves and the cultivation of sugar and other staples became inextricably bound. African slaves became crucial to the plantations since it was widely believed that their labour requirements could not be satisfied by European indentured servants. The establishment of trading companies to engage in the African slave trade gave the mercantilist theory and practice additional expression. But before considering the rivalries of divergent national interests in African, Caribbean and American waters it is necessary to examine the *Asiento*, which became a vital ingredient of the conduct of the slave trade.

The *Asiento*: illusion and reality

The *Asiento* was a contract and a special privilege conferred on deserving clients by monarchs for the supply of slaves to the Spanish colonies. It was used by the Spanish crown and government as an instrument of foreign policy as soon as its importance was realised.[33] First and foremost it was an instrument for revenue-raising for the Spanish monarchy, but it was also seen by its recipients as a means of enhancing their wealth and economic power. Because of the high premium placed on the *Asiento*, its importance was exaggerated out of all proportion to its promise. Nevertheless, in the period in which it was available from the end of the sixteenth century to the middle of the eighteenth century, it was looked upon as a coveted prize. Individuals, trading companies and governments all sought to acquire it, and their ambitions produced many complications in the relations between states, their respective nationals and trading companies.

The *Asiento* was a contract concluded between the Spanish government on the one hand and a contractor on the other. It farmed out the business of supplying slaves. To the contractor was granted the right to supply slaves to the Spanish Indies. He took up the function of the government to organise the entire business of supplying slaves and maintaining stations in Spain, in Africa and in the Spanish Indies, and was empowered to issue licences to sub-contractors. He was expected to forward licence fees to the Spanish crown. Both contractor and subcontractors could transfer slaves directly from Africa to the Spanish Indies and arrange for their convoy and escort where necessary. As the contracts were generally bestowed on favourites of the Spanish crown and not on rebels, enemies, heretics or religious opponents, the *Asiento* had a mono-poly character to it that was very much in keeping with the principles of the mercantilists.

Three of the maritime rivals of the succeeding centuries, England, France and Holland, all of whom continued through piracy to harass the Spanish in their New World colonies, became convinced that whoever among them acquired exclusively the trade of the Spanish Indies would become master of one of the greatest sources of commercial wealth in the world.[34] Furthermore, their expectations were raised by the likelihood of obtaining markets for the disposal of European manufactures in the Spanish Indies, which they believed would open up new opportunities of employment for their peoples at home. Implicit in these preoccupations was the principle of monopoly in the supply of slaves through the *Asiento*, which it was hoped would bestow on the recipient that exclusive right which has been aptly described as a 'mercantilised version of the legend of Eldorado – a coveted prize, equally elusive, and no less a cause of misunderstanding and war'.[35] But the *Asiento* had a further attraction since it provided gold or bullion, which the Spanish used to pay for slaves. The acquisition and hoarding of bullion was of major importance in the seventeenth and eighteenth centuries, in accordance with the mercantilist creed.

From Appendix 1 (page 406 below) it can be seen that the revived *Asiento* came into operation on 30 January 1595 and that the early recipients were Portuguese citizens, who were at the time Spanish subjects, since the two kingdoms were united. The right was lost following Portugal's successful secession from Spain in 1640. During the period in which the Portuguese citizens lost the *Asiento*, Spain was at first unsure who should receive their favour. Up until the English Restoration of Charles II in 1660, the Spanish government sought to confine the *Asientos* to the subjects of nations friendly to Spain; the government was understandably hesitant to grant con-tracts to enemies of Spain (France), to rebels (Portuguese), to heretics (the English) or to 'rebels and heretics' (the Dutch). Between 1640 and 1662 the *Asiento* was in suspense, which led to a labour shortage in the Spanish colonies and gave rise to clandestine trade on a scale that exceeded the commerce that legitimately passed through the ports of Seville and Cadiz. The trade involved nationals of foreign countries with whom the Spanish government would have openly avowed not to have dealings.

When the *Asiento* was revived from 1662, therefore, it was a fiscal necessity,[36] and was not so much concerned with the welfare of the colonies but rather with the raising of revenue, which Spain hoped would derive from the delivery of slaves, to finance a programme of shipbuilding.[37] The revival was an economic imperative and revealed a preoccupation with both of the pivots on which mercantilism revolved, wealth and power. Nowhere was mercantilist policy more developed than in shipping. A modern historian has argued that for the Spanish government the slave trade was always 'first and foremost a source of revenue, and only secondarily a method of supplying the colonies with labour'.[38]

From this observation it can be seen that those who engaged in the slave trade sought profits. It was not just simply business for business's sake. It is necessary to emphasise this point, especially when arguments have been advanced to suggest that profitability did not come into the slave trade or into slave traders' calculations. There is a tendency today to insist that the *Asientos* and the slave trade were not as profitable as made out and that, if anything, the general picture was one of losses on all sides.[39] But this is immaterial. The *Asientos* were taken up on the expectation of substantial profits, and the difference between the illusion and reality does not diminish their significance. The contracts also have a further importance in that they stipulated the number of slaves to be removed from their parent continent and delivered to the Spanish Indies. It is because the agreements specified the removal of a substantial number of slaves that gives them added significance for the African diaspora.

When Pedro Gomez Reynal received his *Asiento* in January 1595 he was to supply the Spanish colonies with 4250 African slaves annually for a period of nine years. This agreement, which was extended to his successor, Juan Rodrigues Cutino, after Reynal's death in 1600, was intended to fulfil the expectations of the previous agreement. It was assumed that at least 3500 of the slaves would arrive at their destination.[40] Within the terms agreed on by the next recipient, Antonia Roderigues de Rivas, an agreement which lasted until 1662, 29 574 African slaves were shipped.[41] These, of course, were the legal arrangements, but extensive clandestine trading also took place with the Spanish Indies involving the Dutch, who at this time had begun to challenge seriously the Portuguese claims to monopoly on the West African coast. But this clandestine trade was not confined only to the Dutch. English planters and merchants in the newly established English plantations, notably in Barbados, began to buy slaves from the Dutch in return for their products. This was frowned upon by mercantilists in England and was to lead them to devise means of curbing Dutch trade with their colonies.

When Dominco Grillo and Ambrosio Lomelin (Lomoline) received the *Asiento* in 1662 they were obligated for seven years to introduce 3000 African slaves annually into the Spanish Indies at the rate of 100 pesos per pieze de Indias. Lomelin died in 1668 without completing negotiations with subcontractors, but being allowed by the terms of the agreement to negotiate with countries that were at peace with Spain negotiations were opened with the English Company of Royal Adventurers and the Dutch West India Company. At this juncture the English and the Dutch were once again confronting each other in the battle for commercial supremacy. In agreement with Grillo, the English Company were to supply 3500 African slaves annually for delivery in Jamaica and Barbados.[42] It remained an unfulfilled agreement and a factor was that the English monopoly terminated at the end of the second Anglo–Dutch War (1664–7). Although the Grillo *Asiento* ended in 1671, he was still trying to negotiate with the Dutch three years later.

The next recipient of the *Asiento* from the Queen Mother was Antonio Gracia and Don Sebastian de Silica for five years on the payment of 450 000 reals of eight for introducing 4000 piezas (pieces) of African slaves into the Indies. The *Asientistas* were compelled to rely on the Dutch, while Englishmen, through the Royal African Company, continued to hope for a share in the Spanish trade. All sorts of backdoor and clandestine activities took place between the English and the Spanish in Jamaica and Barbados, but it was allegedly 'disproportionate to the noise and passion it aroused'.[43]

The potential benefits seemed great. Furthermore, the Spanish promised to pay a higher price for slaves than the English planters in Jamaica were prepared to pay. Nevertheless, the English Company made considerable gains. From the cargo of the *Robert* (of Bristol) in December 1685, 1113 slaves were sold at Olivero at 23.10s apiece, and 26 at 13.10s apiece.[44] Moreover, the Spanish were prepared to pay in hard cash while the Jamaican planters were not. The English Company was still hoping to profit through these backdoor channels, but the Spanish relied heavily on the Dutch, and Antonio Gracia purchased his cargoes of slaves in the main from Curaçao and drew upon capital advanced by the Amsterdam House of Coymans. But the failure of the Spanish Banking House, which stood surety for him, led to his imprisonment for debt. The Spanish government, which had hoped to prevent the illegal entry of African slaves into the Spanish Indies through Curaçao, found its expectations unfulfilled.

After Gracia's imprisonment the responsibility for his *Asiento* devolved on a body of Seville merchants in 1676 known as the

Council (Consulado) of Commerce of Seville. They too were anxious to prevent the illegal entry of slaves through Curaçao and therefore sold licences to merchants and forbade them to go there. But being inexperienced and unable to gain direct access to the West African slave trade because of the entrenched Dutch and Portuguese presence, they became reconciled to treating with the Dutch West India Company for slaves at Curaçao. The implication was clear: the Spanish had swallowed their pride as far as trading with 'heretics' was concerned.

When the *Asiento* expired in 1682 it was received by Don Nicolas Porcio through the power of attorney conferred on his father by law, a Portuguese businessman of Cadiz named Don Juan Barroso y Pozo. It was approved for five years and in 1685 fell to Balthazar Coymans, who assumed it on behalf of Don Nicolas Porcio. It could be said from this point that the *Asiento* was split between two rival factions, of Nicolas Porcio on the one hand and the Dutch firm of Coymans on the other, and this in turn adversely affected Anglo-Spanish trade. Both factions for a time pursued each other through the courts in Jamaica to the embarrassment of the governor of the island.[45]

As a result of these developments the Royal African Company refrained from making long-term agreements with the Spanish but continued to hope for some kind of prosperity, as the Dutch had done before them. The English therefore took advantage of the visit to England in 1689 of the former Agent of Porcio in Jamaica (St Jago de Castillo) and sought to forge an agreement enabling the Royal African Company to supply 2000 Africans as slaves to Jamaica within twenty months as a price of 80 pieces of eight per 17½ dwt. each.[46] This was seen in some quarters as an attempt to infringe the English Navigation Acts,[47] and at this juncture the English government set the regulations aside in order to achieve a temporary advantage. What prevented the English Company from fulfilling the contract was the outbreak of war.

Castillo on his return to Jamaica in 1690 sued the English Company, who entered a plea of 'restraint of princes', but this also meant the end of the Company's participation in the slave trade to the Spanish Indies. In spite of trade continuing by fits and starts during the War of Spanish Succession (1702–13), the Royal African Company merely played second fiddle and if any profits accrued at all they were to private traders.[48]

The complicated story of the *Asiento* which led to the failure of the Coymans agreement and resulted in a crisis in international relations involving Spain, the Dutch government and the firm of Coymans in Holland (headed by John Coymans who incorporated the brother of the late Balthazar Coymans and by extension the Dutch West India Company and the English) has been told in

Donnan[49] and no attempt is made to retell it in any detail here. After the Dutch and Spanish governments had made representations to each other and held positions which, for a time, remained irreconcilable, in 1692 the Spanish government agreed to establish a committee to arbitrate between the Coymans and Porcio factions.

The singling out of the Coymans *Asiento* in this study is intended to emphasise that there was a greater propensity to losses than is generally imagined in attempting to implement the *Asientos*. It was this particular incident, among others, which has led a modern historian to pronounce the *Asientos* a catalogue of 'broken contracts and frustrated expectations'.[50] While it may be true that the hopes of substantial profits were not often realised and the contracts not often kept, this does not invalidate the point that the numerous *Asientos* were concluded on the expectation of immense gains by the parties to the agreement. As the expectations were high their seekers considered themselves privileged as recipients. That the Coymans *Asiento* did not deter other seekers is seen by the fact that the French became its recipients in 1702, the *Asiento* thereafter to be exercised by the French Senegal Company.[51] This immediately evoked adverse reactions from France's rivals, the English and the Dutch. Thus, while in the War of Spanish Succession 'the English were concerned to keep Louis XIV from the Spanish throne, the Dutch had a subsidiary motive, which was to prevent the French company from retaining the slave *Asiento*'.[52]

At the conclusion of the War of Spanish Succession in 1713 England received the *Asiento*, which was to be exercised by the South Sea Company (1713–20), formed expressly for the purpose. The War of Jenkin's Ear (1739–44) which was occasioned, in the main, by the English failure to deal with the problem of contraband in the Caribbean, later interfered with the English exercise of the *Asiento*. This thirty-year monopoly for supplying the Spanish Indies with 4800 African slaves annually terminated in 1750 when England was again at war with Spain. Nevertheless, England acquired the *Asiento* at a time when it was believed to be the greatest slave trader. Recent research seems to indicate the immense benefits which England derived as the recipient of the 1713 *Asiento*.[53] It has been shown that, in the five years of the War of Jenkin's Ear, England employed about four hundred ships in the contraband trade alone, while Spain hardly employed ten in 'legitimate traffic'; the French ambassador in Madrid claimed that the British made far more profit from the Spanish empire than the Spaniards themselves.[54] Yet, as K. G. Davies reminds us, the *Asiento* 'proved a chimera pursued in the hope of profits, which were generally found to be illusory. Nevertheless, its importance in promoting the quest for slaves and in exciting European interest in West Africa was real enough.'[55] It is immaterial whether the *Asiento* quota contracted for was ever attained; for, where attempts were made to fulfil the agreements, they resulted in the major dispersion of African peoples through the Atlantic slave trade.

But, as has been observed, there were times when, in order to share in the wealth of the Spanish Indies, the Navigation Acts were set aside for temporary advantage. In the period in which the clandestine slave trade continued between the Spanish and the English employing the islands of Barbados and Jamaica, and between the Spanish and the Dutch using Curaçao, the English government at home sent out instructions to the governors of the English West Indian colonies to receive cordially Spanish slave-trading vessels, while barring the vessels of other nations.[56] These instructions, which allowed not only trade with Spain but also in Spanish instead of English ships, breached one of the cardinal principles of mercantilism and evoked hostility among the planters and colonial assemblies.[57] There were numerous protests, and that of the Jamaican Assembly on 26 July 1685 is worthy of note. The members regretted that the governor was conniving in the sale of much-needed slaves to the Spanish, and complained that the practice resulted in a scarcity of labour in the English islands that was damaging to their economy. They then asserted that, had the number of those Africans in their service who had died in the previous six years lived and worked in moderate numbers, the net proceeds from the islands' products would have produced a considerable increase in revenue to the royal exchequer. However, the *Asiento* arrangement meant that the English planters, not possessing the ready cash of the Spanish, found themselves at a disadvantage and consequently the best slaves went to the Spanish Indies at the expense of the English planters, who were compelled to receive the 'refuse', often sickly and unhealthy slaves who died easily. These protests show that the policy of wealth and power, and the interests of the metropolitan country, took precedence over the interests of the colonies. Mercantilism was in confusion.[58]

Although the English planters in the islands were unhappy with the favoured treatment accorded the Spanish in Jamaica and Barbados, and although the Spanish willingness to pay for slaves in hard cash undermined efforts to replenish their plantations with slaves, the English planters nevertheless demonstrated ambivalence. While they deplored the arragement with Spain they still used the same channel for ridding themselves of refractory, truculent and 'undesirable' slaves, thereby shifting their problems on to the shoulders of the Spanish and at the same time receiving cash for their sales. The English planters also showed another ambivalence in their attitude to mercantilist policies. They objected to the monopoly exercised by joint stock companies in the supply of slaves, insisting that the companies could never adequately meet the labour demands of the colonies, but they still expected the metropolis to safeguard their products against the vicissitudes of external competition by guaranteeing them a monopolist position in the English market. In other words, while planters sought free trade in the supply of slaves they did not in turn approve of free trade in the supply of plantation products for the English market.[59] In fact in 1669 the British government eventually conceded the principle of free trade in the supply of labour by abolishing the Royal Africa Company's monopoly; by doing so an important concession was made against one of the strict canons of mercantilist practice. The French (in 1670) and the Dutch (in 1674) quickly followed suit, their respective companies losing their monopolies in the African slave trade. This ushered in a period of interloping activity, which had already for a long time plagued the trading activities of companies engaged in the African trade.

The French government, like the English, found it difficult to impose restrictive policies on planters in their colonies. When the governor sent out by Colbert's new French West India Company (1664) arrived in the Caribbean, planters pressed for the right to purchase slaves and goods from the English islands, claiming that the monopoly company could not adequately supply their needs. The new governors of the French colonies of Martinique and Guadeloupe, however, possessed strict instructions from Colbert not to allow trade with foreigners. The colonists rebelled and were only brought to obedience with difficulty. Fortunately for the French, sugar production in Hispaniola (St Domingue) increased rapidly in the years following the creation of the French West India Company, largely as a result of the efforts of the colony's governor, Bertrand d'Ogeron,[60] who had previously been a sugar planter in Martinique. D'Ogeron had been contemplating residence in Jamaica when, in 1665, he was offered the assignment of governing Tortuga, from where he extended French influence to Hispaniola until the French acquired the western third of the island, which became the French colony of St Domingue. He persuaded unruly French buccaneers to settle down on the island, which soon flourished on slave labour from Africa to become in the eighteenth century the largest sugar producer of the Antilles.

Mercantilism and European rivalries in Africa

It had been gold that first brought Europeans to West Africa, but gold was eventually superseded in importance by the slave trade, which by 1713 had achieved dominance over the former trade. As the commerce in slaves developed, the rivalries engendered by the pursuit of commercial supremacy implicit in European mercantilist thought and action were extended beyond the confines of Europe and the Americas into West African waters. There, from the latter part of the sixteenth century, they became intense, spanning the seventeenth and eighteenth centuries. Apart from the Luso-Hispanic rivalries, which had led to the triumph of Portugal in the Upper Guinea Coast, the Dutch were soon to assail the Portuguese monopoly. Other nations – the French and the English, and even the small competitors, the Swedes, the Danes and the House of Brandenburg (Prussia) – also added to the intense competition and rivalry. Hostilities ensued as Europeans sought spheres of influence and trade depots, erected forts,[61] and adjusted to their newly found clients.

English slave trading on the West African coast dates back at least to the 1560s when John Hawkins made three slave-trading voyages between 1562 and 1567. William Towerston also made three voyages to West Africa. Captain Richard Jobson was another who visited the region. Historians past and modern have reminded us that Englishmen had been appearing on the West African coast for some time, and there is every likelihood that they engaged in the slave trade.[62] Captain Jobson's much quoted statement that 'We are a people who did not deal in any such commodities, neither did we buy or sell one another or any that had our shapes',[63] has not been widely accepted at face value. The late Professor Walter Rodney has maintained that 'This widely quoted statement is as inaccurate as it is pious'.[64] 'This statement of Jobson was made in spite of the fact that Englishmen had been trading in slaves from the sixteenth century with the full sanction and the participation of the English Queen.'[65]

Of the significance of the Guinea trade to the English economy, K. G. Davies has written:

> West Africa, for instance, was the only gold-producing region to which England had either pretensions or access, and the Gold was still widely and properly regarded as a commodity to be esteemed above all others. When, in the mid-seventeenth century, Englishmen began to go to Africa for a different cargo, slaves, the trade took a new significance without losing the old. The potential wealth of the West Indies was universally recognised, and their development was believed to depend upon a sufficient supply of negroes. The African trade was converted into an appendage of Barbados and Jamaica, and partook of the esteem in which the West Indian colonies were held. Sugar transformed the trade, from a desirable if dangerous branch of English commerce, into an essential instrument of imperial expansion.[66]

With these considerations in mind it is no surprise that so much attention was lavished on the African trade by parliaments, governments and pamphleteers, while at the same time the exports of the African Company assumed a significance of their own within the wider framework of expansion of English trade overseas in the seventeenth century. These were the reflections and embodiments of the commercial trends transforming the country into a great trading nation.[67]

Not only did African slaves prove crucial for the sustenance of the plantations but the rival European nations were determined to do their own carrying trade without giving the advantage to their rivals. This view was in keeping with the principles enunciated in the Navigation Acts, an essential factor in mercantilist practice. This set all the maritime powers on a collision course with one another and numerous wars resulted. Thus, thirty years after Jobson's statement, the English were seriously engaged in the act of procuring Africans as slaves for the Americas and so also were their rivals. European and Caribbean rivalries now moved to the Guinea coast, and the consequences were profound. The Luso-Dutch wars set the pattern, so that by the early seventeenth century the Dutch had built a fort on Cape Mount on the Upper Guinea Coast in order to protect their trade in gold with the interior, and soon after they began cultivating sugar there. The king of Cape Mount, advised by his brother, the king of Sierra Leone, and at the prompting of the Portuguese middlemen (Afro-Portuguese) who feared that the Dutch would usurp his powers, destroyed the fort.[68] As the Afro-Portuguese middlemen were the progeny of Portuguese and Africans, the action might have been inspired by the Portuguese with a view to safeguarding their trade monopoly in the area. The Dutch and the Portuguese continued to assail each other from the Upper Guinea Coast to Angola and later to Brazil. Eventually the Portuguese also drove out the Dutch from Pernambuco (Brazil) in 1654.

The wars of supremacy spread to other European powers, and the Dutch, who had been driven out of Brazil, revived their interest in West Africa. Like other rivals, they found the opportunity to erect forts while capturing those of others. They were determined to be the sole suppliers of slaves and African products to their own colonies and, clandestinely, to the Spanish and Portuguese colonies as well. By 1640 the trade had increased by leaps and bounds. By the eighteenth century large numbers were being lost to Africa through the slave wars and the slave trade. International rivalries converted the slave trade into a 'matter of colonial policy' and 'an important affair of state'.[69] The trade in African slaves by Europeans became important in the consideration of European governments owing to the increasing European demand for sugar and the spread of sugar culture, and so the value of slave labour in the colonies of the Americas was enhanced, thus making that supply 'an essential feature of imperial strategy'.[70]

The seventeenth century saw Anglo–Dutch rivalry assume dangerous proportions, and there was an additional factor in the struggle for supremacy between the two. During the seventeenth and eighteenth centuries Amsterdam was England's greatest creditor, for Amsterdam was then the financial centre of the world. It was not until the Napoleonic Wars that London began to outstrip Amsterdam as the world's financial capital.[71] Yet English ascendancy over the Dutch in commerce was the result of a policy pursued over time. An aspect of that ascendancy was the financial triumph of London over Amsterdam as a centre of world trade. The transition had begun by about the middle of the seventeenth century and gained some momentum at the beginning of the eighteenth. The English Navigation Acts played their part in this rise to commercial supremacy since they provided the pretexts for wars of aggression against the Dutch and other rivals, even though the wars themselves rarely led to the accumulation of wealth, except that gained through acts of piracy.

Yet the attitudes of the English manufacturers indicated their approval in the effort to conquer world trade. It was implicit in the formation of trading companies, notably joint stock companies. But the English made a determined bid to extricate themselves from the situation of undue dependence on the products of Holland and they did this by attempting to diversify their sources of supply. This began with articles which had been more cheaply and more competently supplied by the Dutch. Prior to the middle of the seventeenth century they had obtained textiles, mainly Dutch linen (Anabasses) and scarlet cloth, beads, irons, metal goods (including knives and swords) and firearms from the Dutch. These goods were exchanged for gold, ivory, amber, camwood, pepper and other minor articles, and later, slaves on the African coast. When, therefore, England embarked on the diversification of its supply sources it obtained iron goods from Sweden from 1680, amber from the Baltic, beads from Venice and substituted English for Dutch textiles and guns. The latter, which had earlier been obtained from the Dutch, had in 1684 evoked the protest of the English gunsmiths, who were concerned about the consequences of Dutch imports on their trade. But these English gunsmiths soon found a new outlet for their manufactures and within four years from 1701 the English Royal African Company exported to Africa '32 954 muskets, carbines, pistols, snaphances, fowling pieces and fuses to the African coast – enough to equip a fair-sized army'.[72] The products derived by the Company soon became subordinated to the exigencies of the slave trade.

The quest for commercial supremacy ushered in a series of

44

Anglo-Dutch Wars – the first 1652–4, the second 1665–7, and the third 1672–8. The details of these need not concern us since they are recorded elsewhere.[73] However, it is necessary to consider briefly the manner in which they affected Africa, the Caribbean, and the struggles for supremacy induced by the mercantilist pre-occupations of the time.

Although the First Anglo-Dutch War was confined to Europe there was 'tacit understanding between the Dutch and the English to preserve neutrality' in the Caribbean.[74] Yet, in the contest, the English sought commercial supremacy over the Dutch while the Dutch struggled for the maintenance of their supremacy in the commercial sphere, and against the monopoly position which the English sought to impose by excluding Dutch trade from the English colonies. The English brought the conflict to a head by the promulgation of the Navigation Acts of 1650 and 1651, aimed mainly at curtailing Dutch contact with the English colonies of the western hemisphere. At the end of the war both sides were ex-hausted, but the points at issue were not resolved because the Dutch reluctantly acquiesced in their exclusion from the English colonies through their agreement to abide by the English Navigation Laws and the limitations it imposed on commercial opportunities, instead of insisting on free commercial relations, the issue which had drawn them into war with the English in the first place.[75]

Hostilities soon built up and produced a second war. In the meantime the English had passed the 1660 Navigation Acts and the Staple Act of 1663. But hostilities soon loomed large in West African waters and between April 1661 and June 1663 rivalry spilled over into conflict without a formal declaration of war. The Dutch seized six English vessels and Captain Robert Holmes expelled the Dutch from Gorée and other points on the Guinea coast, including Cape Verde, and occupied their factories. Holmes then in 1664 dislodged the Dutch from Cape Coast from which time it became English.[76] These formed the preliminaries to the Second Anglo-Dutch War (1665–7).

The Dutch West India Company, anxious to preserve what remained of its monopoly of the slave trade in West Africa, sent out a squadron under Admiral De Ruyter. De Ruyter appeared in West African waters in January 1655, dislodged the English from Gorée and re-occupied it. Gorée was strategically important as it formed the entrance to the valuable trade in guns and slaves down to the Senegal river. De Ruyter followed up his exploit and expelled the English from various positions on the Gold Coast, except Cape Coast Castle, and captured and confiscated many English-owned slavers under the pretext that their cargoes were obtained from regions where the Dutch had retained exclusive rights after they had been taken from the Portuguese. De Ruyter now crossed the

Atlantic to Barbados and without warning, in April 1665, attempted unsuccessfully to destroy the forts and capture English shipping in the harbour. He then sailed to Martinique, where the French helped him to effect repairs after which he began raiding English settlements in the Leeward Islands. Although he failed to secure a foothold, he nonetheless captured a number of English ships lying in the harbours of Montserrat and Nevis and utterly destroyed the season's export cargoes.[77]

Prior to the declaration of war, the English Company of Royal Adventurers had been able to transport about 3075 African slaves to Barbados within a short span of seven months from August 1663.[78] The events which ensued after the declaration of war form a complicated episode of European rivalries. They were reflected in the African theatre from which the slaves were drawn, and in the West Indies and the American mainland which absorbed them and where the struggles for supremacy were also conducted and inspired by the mercantilist preoccupation of both countries.

The war had the effect of interrupting the steady flow of slaves to the colonies and evoked protests and criticism from English colonists against the existence of a monopoly company in the Guinea trade. The planters in the English and French colonies protested against the mercantilist policies of their respective governments, and the English planters further resented the attempt to share the trade in African slaves with the Spanish colonies. Furthermore, the criticisms and resentments arose from the fact that the English Company had failed in an earlier attempt, in 1663, to secure an *Asiento* for the supply of 3500 Africans to the Spanish colonies.

The Company was eventually ruined by financial difficulties, the details of which need not concern us here. The rivalries were seen both in Africa and in the Caribbean.[79] In this second confrontation the Dutch lost all their colonies, except Curaçao, and most of their shipping and their previous illicit trading with the Spanish colonies, and the conflict led to the reorganisation of a New Dutch West India Company in 1674.

The Anglo-Dutch wars also ushered in a period of Anglo-French wars which resulted in exchanges of territory in the Caribbean. These were to continue into the eighteenth century, and in turn the monopoly companies of the three rival nations were eventually ruined by many factors beyond their control, war being one of them, the challenge of the interlopers being another. In these confrontations between the trading companies and the interlopers, the latter triumphed.

The Third Anglo-Dutch War initially saw the English and the French fighting as allies, while in the Second the French had fought against the English. But even before the conclusion of the third war it had been transformed into a Franco-Dutch war because of

England's withdrawal following the accession of William, Prince of Orange, as King William III of England. As a result the English concluded the Treaty of Westminster in 1674 with the Dutch. The treaty brought on a final divergence between French and English policies and interests in the colonial sphere, and as Newton asserts, thereafter, 'Their rivalry came to be looked upon as one of the fundamental axioms of international politics and it is interesting to note that it immediately coincided with the opening of the active career of William of Orange.'[80]

The conflict eventually ended in 1678 with the French retaining Gorée and other Dutch posts in the Senegal as well as St Louis. But in spite of these losses the departure of the Dutch from West Africa was not immediate. The treaty far from satisfied the Dutch, the chief carriers for the French colonies in the Antilles, because an 'open door' policy for the West Indies was not accepted by the French. The wars of rivalries complicated the activities of the various trading companies on the west coast of Africa. The interlopers, too, proved a nuisance.

Interlopers versus charter companies

The advantage which the interlopers had over the trading companies was that the latter operated with numerous encumbrances and responsibilities while the former freely came and went and took advantage of the forts established by their national trading companies to shelter from adverse circumstances on the coast. These interlopers must not be confused with pirates, of which there were many both in the Caribbean and West Africa. The joint stock companies had difficulty in barring interlopers from their operational spheres. They failed in representations to African potentates to bar interlopers and in attempts to assert control over those potentates. They also introduced a system of granting licences to private shippers, but by fostering the system they conferred legitimacy on private ventures. Licences were issued by the French, Dutch and English alike, and Heckscher has noted of the practice: 'The Joint Stock Companies, besides their activity as economic undertakings for the benefit of their members, also filled the role, whether intentionally or unintentionally of "Regulated Companies" for the benefit of outsiders, and in exceptional cases, even members.'[81] Writing of the Company of Royal Adventurers, Zook had observed that the issuing of licences was common practice; they were issued to those desiring to carry on trade in their own ships and also by officers of the ships of the Company of Royal Adventurers who wished to engage in private ventures. Many licences, he observed, were granted to various individuals during the wars of the 1660s; one of the recipients was Prince Rupert. The issuing of licences was therefore common practice.[82] Right from the beginning of the rivalries on the African coast in the sixteenth century the task of curbing interlopers proved daunting, and in time their numbers increased on the Upper Guinea Coast between 1562 and 1640. With their increase as many as 5000 slaves were exported annually.

The advantages of private shippers over the joint stock companies were numerous. They had no forts to maintain and were not saddled with the financial costs involved in their maintenance, though they used them as shelters from the enemy or from other difficulties in the region. Yet the companies bore the burden of the expenses both for establishing and using them in the slave trade. The immense cost of maintenance was a serious handicap to profitability. Interlopers were freed from these encumbrances. Although the forts gave the illusive impression of protection to their occupants and a feature of some permanence against rival nations, yet, in the day-to-day conduct of trade, and especially the slave trade, their maintenance remained of doubtful value. Moreover, the companies, though not allowed to pass that additional burden of cost to the planters of the Americas by an increase in the price of slaves, were still expected to supply slaves cheaply and at a competitive price in order to ensure that the planters were competitive in sugar production with rival nations. Furthermore, the planters acted as watchdogs and were quick to oppose any attempts at what they considered an 'unfair' increase in slave prices. They sustained campaigns both in the English and French colonies against the monopoly of company slave supply, especially their national companies. Anything approaching an increase in price merely strengthened the case of the opponents of monopoly. But the weight of prejudice by the colonies – notably planters – against the monopoly of companies was both immense and in accordance with the sentiments of the times.

While the companies received royal backing, and while the mercantilist interests were prominent in government, the opposition to monopoly achieved very little. But once the monopoly was removed the interlopers in the slave-trading business found themselves in a fiercely competitive situation which proved disastrous to the companies. Moreover, where the national companies were unwilling to offer weapons for the conduct of the slave wars in Africa, the interlopers felt no such inhibition and did not preoccupy themselves with questions of security and territorial gain as did the companies.[83] Interlopers of rival nations followed this example. Furthermore, rum, which became an exchange commodity for slaves in West Africa in the eighteenth century, is believed to have been introduced by the interlopers, who at the time were searching for a West Indian cargo that would be readily acceptable to West African middlemen.[84] Throughout the confrontations the interlopers proved the bane of the trading companies whose monopoly of the African trade they sought to erode.

While the bulk of the slaves supplied to the Americas in the seventeenth century were drawn from West Africa (and the term is used here to refer to the area extending from the Upper Guinea Coast to Angola), there was an alternative source of supply from which the interlopers drew when the English African Company was unable to satisfy the demands of the planters. That alternative source was Madagascar, which fell within the province of the English East India Company. Between 1675 and 1690 the interlopers drew their supplies from there, and the Royal African Company failed to prevail on the English East India Company to exclude the interlopers from Madagascar. The consequence of the persistence of the interlopers was the triumph of free trade in slaves and this gave the interlopers free rein in the dispersion of Africans to the Americas.

Some implications of the European presence in Africa

The Europeans' quest for commercial supremacy, which had obtained leverage from their mercantilist preoccupations, and had led to their intrusion into the African continent, had divergent effects, most of which were not necessarily healthy. Their activities not only spanned the Guinea coast but extended beyond Angola and the Cape to Moçambique and later to north-eastern Africa in succeeding centuries. The Portuguese were the first to establish forts on the coast to be followed by European rivals. The forts themselves became centres of instability on the African landscape. The frequency with which the forts changed hands, the expulsion by one European group of rival contenders, their intrigues among African potentates to support one or other group against others, their intrigues against Africans, intrigues induced among various African groups in order to set them up against one another, or later African-initiated intrigues in playing one European group against another, all these left Africa, and especially West Africa, from the seventeenth century to the late-nineteenth century, in a state of endless ferment. These were the so-called unending 'intertribal wars' of biased European writers of the period and later. They were far from healthy for the body politic. With some of the coastal kings and potentates well entrenched, with new rulers in the ascendance, it was not expedient for Europeans to attempt conquest at the time, although the Portuguese attempted it both in Upper Guinea and Angola as well as in eastern Africa. Nevertheless, the

49

Europeans periodically found ways of exerting considerable influence on the social scene, and sometimes they stipulated the modes of African behaviour in their commercial dealings with rival Europeans.

Apart from those features peculiar to the era, these intense rivalries pervaded other areas of European intrusion, and the coast of Guinea, in time, manifested its own peculiar feature of this competitiveness. The psychology of the period of intense rivalry has been appropriately summed up in this way: 'Although Africans involved could not know the exact motives and methods of these rival strangers and how they amassed and shared their profits, yet Africans, from their previous long-standing experience of trade, soon came to terms with the new arrivals on the West Coast.'[85]

A notable case of European involvement in African politics occurred on the Gold Coast (modern Ghana) where the Dutch intrigues with the 'Fetu' and the people in the neighbourhood of Komenda achieved the great feat of eliminating Portuguese influence from the Gold Coast in the early seventeenth century.[86] Sometimes, as in Upper Guinea, the Portuguese forbade Africans to trade with rival European nationals. At one point the Portuguese ordered the people of El Mina to destroy a village for having traded with interlopers. Response to such orders often meant the burning down of settlements.[87]

The records are replete with numerous attempts by European companies or individuals trading on the west coast to browbeat Africans into conformity in order to maintain the monopoly of trade and political influence or control which each of them sought.[88] A few examples will suffice. For instance, in Upper Guinea in 1640 the Portuguese tried unsuccessfully to ban the Spanish, but Africans desired Spanish goods which the Portuguese could not supply. The Africans there were conscious of the fact that stagnation would result from barring other competitors, for 'no ship meant no imports, no custom duties, no perquisites'.[89] Attempts to bribe or buy off potentates, in spite of alluring gifts, did not always make African middlemen compliant. Sometimes the use of armed patrols and forts to secure the compliance of Africans or other European rivals proved counter-productive.[90]

From the end of the seventeenth century the Portuguese had begun to lay down conditions of conduct expected of Africans and to impose restrictions on their actions. An example was the directive which they suggested in 1696 as policy for the king of Bissau. It was a seven-point prohibition. It suggested the building of a fort on a chosen site. Christians were to be separated from non-Christians. The king of Bissau was to be a Christian and encourage others to become Christians. It prescribed the non-inheritance of Christian goods by non-Christians. There was to be an embargo on trade with foreigners and ports must be defended against them. Furthermore, Christians committing crimes were to be returned to the captain-major for punishment according to Portuguese law and were not to be harboured by the king. There was even a succession dispute in the same year into which the Portuguese intruded and a clash of interests and sovereignties occurred.[91] But the Portuguese were to learn at great cost to themselves that the erection of forts for the protection of their slave-trading monopoly and for controlling Africans did not even assure them of their pretensions to monopoly of the trade. Interlopers remained (to them as to other European nations and companies) a persistent source of embarrassment, a militating factor in the maintenance of national or company monopolies in the slave trade.

The Portuguese extended their constraints to Angola and to East African waters. Writing in *African Glory* Professor J. C. DeGraft Johnson mentions another feature of Portuguese intrusion into the area of Kongo-Angola in the early slave-trading centuries. He reminds us that Portuguese efforts to use Christianity for imperial or commercial ends were not confined to the Upper Guinea Coast or the Gold Coast alone, but were extended through the Cameroons and further down into the Kongo region. With insights from the writings of a Capuchin missionary, Jerom Merolla de Sorrento, who had visited the Kongo kingdom in 1688, DeGraft Johnson remarks that by the end of the seventeenth century European priests were attempting to command Kongolese counts and dukes, and executing and enslaving Kongolese ancestral priests and indigenous doctors and were advancing pretensions of having power to control the elements. All these, he argues, were aimed at confounding the Kongolese Christians, who had become 'tools and pawns in the hands of unscrupulous European priests, soldiers and merchants'. The position took a turn for the worse when mere parish priests from Europe could dethrone Kongolese kings. These intrigues and interventions, he maintains, in the long term contributed to the destruction of the Kongo kingdom.[92]

DeGraft Johnson's observations may have been too facile about the factors responsible for the destruction of the Old Kongo kingdom, but he certainly describes some of the elements which made for internal dissension and disruption and which had a bearing on its final demise. Excessive slaving was another factor in the disruption, and in this the Portuguese excelled in the region, except for a brief period of Dutch ascendancy. Another factor was the support of the Portuguese for spurious claimants for the various principalities constituting the kingdom. Thus, internal and external factors contributed to its ultimate destruction, but the external factors, involving the Portuguese and the Dutch, induced fissiparous tendencies within the state, generating internecine warfare, instability and lack of purposeful industry, once slaving had become a major Euro-African preoccupation.

The use of Africans from the Kongo region for the production of sugar in São Tomé, and for the cultivation of tobacco and cotton later in Brazil, drew upon African manpower to secure the triangular and polyangular trades, resulting in a large dispersion of Africans. Professor David Birmingham has dealt at length with this development in his consideration of the Mbundu.[93] He has also examined the implications in relation to the Imbangala invasion of Angola and has argued persuasively that slave-trading activities had consequences beyond those regions within the sphere of European operations. They took the form of attacks on the comparatively wealthy states of Ndongo and Kongo, offensives undertaken in order to benefit from the wealth derived from overseas trade. Invasion came from three major quarters: first, the Teke, from the north, with little or no direct effect on the Mbundu; the second was from Jaga, from the east, involving Kongo; the third set of invaders were the Imbangala from the east who invaded Ndongo (i.e. Angola).[94] The Kongo kingdom thus succumbed both to external pressures (mainly Portuguese-inspired and directed) and to internal divisions and strife, as well as centrifugal tendencies, which the external invasion had generated. Portuguese intrusion, therefore, ultimately led to the destruction of the Kongo kingdom.

Yet, in this period of intense rivalries translated from the milieu of Europe, Asia and the Caribbean on to the African scene, some African communities began to take sides in the European quarrels and rivalries, and thus became what Basil Davidson has observed as 'protected clients or agents of one or other of the European fortresses'.[95] The evidence concerning this mode of conduct is ubiquitous.[96]

The implications in the long term were more sinister for African potentates, for they were thus enabled to undermine themselves through their own local rivalries and jealousies and those induced through European activities, the motives of which remained a closed book to them. Later, Europeans found them an easy prey to dispense with singly. There also arose upstart potentates, many of whom were the products of slave-trading activities and had no legitimate basis for their ascendancy in the traditional arrangements. These constituted a new middle class – but a middle class that did the drudgeries for their European benefactors.

This stage was reached on the African social scene, in the main, as a result of the preoccupations of the mercantilist minds in Europe who sought commercial supremacy over others and who equated private fortune with national wealth and power. They wrought havoc on African shores in the pursuit of the twin mercantilist goals of wealth and power, which, in turn, disoriented and disorganised

African societies, while, at the same time, facilitating the dispersion of Africans into the Americas to become the mainstay of the plantations. Davies, referring to the accusations and counter-accusations of Europeans, has said, 'There can be no doubt that both sides were guilty of concealed aggression on a number of occasions.'[97] Friendly agreements in Europe were not always matched by harmony among European rivals in Africa.[98]

These incidents, numerous as they were during the greater part of the seventeenth century, extended in a minimised form into the eighteenth, and while Dutch threats to the English lessened, those of the French became real to both the English and the Dutch. These intermittent threats operated in a cycle of ebb and flow, leading to the loss and gain of territory in Africa as footholds for operations. Thus the French consolidated their hold on Senegal prior to the treaty of Utrecht and also in Gorée, which they had captured from the Dutch in 1677, but they failed in their endeavours to obtain a foothold on the Gold Coast in 1688 owing to staunch Dutch resistance. Nevertheless, they gained a vital foothold in Whydah in 1704 and, as a result, gained entry into one of the greatest slave-trading ports. While the French confined much of their influence to Senegal and Gorée, the Dutch concentrated their efforts on the Gold Coast. Only the English attempted to extend their activities from the Gambia to Whydah and the Niger Delta, in short, throughout the entire length of the Guinea Coast.[99]

Between 1678 and 1687 the French established factories in Sene-gambia and encouraged among Africans a demand for brandy and silver which the English could not supply. The French challenge resulted in an Anglo-French war between 1689 and 1697. At first the French were singularly successful, but in January 1693 the English decisively beat and secured the surrender of the French Governor of Senegal, and the English then completed their campaign by capturing Gorée on 8 February 1693. The French suffered a temporary eclipse in Africa, but inadequate garrisoning by the English of Senegal and Gorée led to their reoccupation by the French. The withdrawal of the English from Senegal and Gambia in 1694 ended, for a while, Anglo-French rivalry in North West Africa. In spite of hostilities to each other in Africa, England and France were able to reach an agreement in Europe to compel African potentates to trade only with their respective companies and to discourage interlopers, but these agreements hardly stemmed the conflicts of the European rivals. The war which followed, that of the Spanish Succession, in which the English strove to exclude the French from the Spanish throne and in which the Dutch were intent on preventing the French from retaining the Spanish *Asiento*, which they acquired in 1702, saw the English acting on behalf of Spain and at the conclusion earning the *Asiento* for themselves. In these confrontations may be seen a combination of political and commercial motives inherent in the mercantilist preoccupations of the European maritime powers in the eighteenth century. The rivalries continued after the eighteenth century and had their adverse effects on Africa.

From 1704 the French began to settle Whydah, and this settlement gave a boost to the slave trade so that in 1711 the English Factor in Whydah was able to report that in the preceding twenty-two months the French had carried away nine thousand slaves.[100] Yet, in spite of the embittered rivalries, in the period of the War of Spanish Succession (1702–13) Whydah had the appearance of a free port open to all-comers in spite of their ambitions to achieve ascendancy over one another. Dutch, French, English and members of minor powers like the Danes, Swedes and Brandenburgers (Prussians) all came, though the activities of the latter were dwarfed by the maritime giants.

One other occurrence on the West African coast in the period of European rivalry needs to be mentioned, for it sheds light on the complexities of relationships engendered by the European presence among Africans inspired by the principles of wealth and power. The Royal African Company inherited one of the legacies of the conflicts from its predecessor, the Company of Royal Adventurers, and in 1686 this became a matter for contention between the Company and the Danes. The story of the conflict is complicated but the main outlines are as follows. The London Adventurers, who had been invited by the king of Fetu to erect a fort at Cabo Corso (Cape Coast), embarked in 1650 on erecting a castle. The English claimed that they had bought the land on which they intended to erect the castle for the princely sum of £64.[101] Shortly afterwards, Henrick Carloff (Carliff), a Dane in the service of the queen of Sweden,[102] obtained permission from the king of Fetu to erect a Swedish castle, notwithstanding the existing agreement with the English. In 1655 the English still insisted that their castle was being built. Here was a case which appeared to the outsider as a case of double dealing, in which each of the contestants expected a clear monopoly to conduct trade. The occurrence also showed the difficulty which European powers had in trying to claim all the trade for themselves and it mirrored the difficulties of the mercantilists. Some African historians have suggested that the action of the king of Fetu was not as illogical as might at first appear and that it should be placed squarely within the African concept that hospitality be given to all visitors and that no-one who indicated a desire to trade should be turned away.[103]

Yet the arrival of the Swedes led to the expulsion of the English from Cape Coast. In 1686 Carloff, who had quarrelled with his former employers and had left their service, reverted to his own people, the Danes, and seized Cape Coast on behalf of the Dutch-financed Swedish Company, which he then transferred to the Danes.[104] Later in that century the Germans – i.e. Prussians or Brandenburgers – came to the coast. This initial struggle for Cape Coast inaugurated a dispute between the English Royal African Company and the Danes in 1686. The story of the Cape Coast confrontations is a classic example of confusion brought about by European rivalries and fierce competition brought to the area. While the Swedes had the castle first after turning out the English, the Danes then acquired it in 1659 by the back door through the action of Carloff, who was formerly in the service of the Dutch-sponsored Swedish African Company.[105] Then the Dutch captured it in 1663, and finally it fell to the English in 1664. Yet, in 1686, it became a matter for adjudication between the English and the Danes. The latter claimed it because of their castle at Frederieksborg, which stood in the neighbourhood of Cape Coast castle.

In the eighteenth century the field was left for the English and the French to struggle for the attainment of political and commercial dominance of the world. These rivalries continued into the first two decades of the nineteenth century, properly belonging to European affairs but spilling over into the colonies in the western hemisphere and into Africa as well. They set the stage for the European colonisation of Africa later in the century, but their roots are to be found in the pursuit of wealth and power, alias mercantilism, the idea which obsessed European minds and European policy-makers in those early days of the slave trade, and which contributed immensely to the transfer of Africans to the Americas. This is the appropriate point to continue our study of the African dispersion across the Atlantic by reconsidering the slave trade. It has been the purpose of this chapter to establish the linkage between the pursuit of wealth and power on the one hand, and the slave trade and the development of the plantations in the Americas on the other. Let us now examine how this pursuit of wealth and power heightened the slave trade, thus contributing to the creation of the African diaspora.

Notes

1 This quotation from a pamphlet published in 1680 is in K. G. Davies, *The Royal African Company*, London, 1957, p. 108.

2 Eli F. Heckscher, *Mercantilism*, 2 vols., trans. M. Shapiro, rev. by E. F. Soderlund, London, 1951.

3 L. A. Harper, *The English Navigation Laws*, New York, 1939, p. 18.

4 W. Rodney, 'European Activity and African Reaction in Angola', *Aspects of Central African History*, T. O. Ranger (ed.), London, 1969, p. 49; also

F. Clairmont, *Economic Liberalism*, New York, 1960, p. 19. It is this point which Eric Williams made explicitly in his study, *Capitalism and Slavery*, Chapel Hill, N. C., 1944. See also V. I. Lenin, *Imperialism*, Petrograd, 1916 (1st edn.), and L. J. Ragatz, *The Fall of the Planter Class in the British Caribbean, 1763–1833*, London and New York, 1928, pp. 3–21, 30–1, 81–107, esp. 93–100.

5 Heckscher, *Mercantilism*, Vol. 2, pp. 37–8.

6 C. K. Hobson, *The Export of Capital*, London, 1st edn., 1914, 2nd edn., 1963, p. xvi. Generally, overseas trade was considered to be the main source of wealth and power. The slave trade was also a source of wealth and power for some.

7 G. F. Zook, *The Company of Royal Adventurers Trading to Africa*, Philadelphia, 1919, pp. 1–8, 12ff, 62–3, 83–6; also Heckscher, *Mercantilism*, Vol. 2, pp. 300, 323–4.

8 William, *Capitalism and Slavery*, pp. 40–1 *et seq.*, and his *From Columbus to Castro*, London, 1970, where he insisted that the slave trade played a major part in the accumulation of capital, though the issue is still a matter of historical controversy. The main critic of this view was the late Professor Roger Anstey; see in particular his 'Capitalism and Slavery: a critique', *Economic History Review*, 2nd series, xxi, 2 (1968), pp. 307–20, and *The Atlantic Slave Trade and British Abolition*, pp. 51–2 and ch. 2.

9 The notable exception initially was Portugal, as the charter company was not a feature of Portuguese trade in Africa, though it came to be eventually.

10 Mansa Musa, Emperor of Mali, made his pilgrimage to Mecca through the desert and through Egypt in 1324–5. His benevolence in the bestowal of gold on the people he met has remained a legend, and at the time caused inflation in Egypt.

11 Among them were Cornelius Hodges and Richard Jobson.

12 This company, although chartered for trade with Santo Domingo, Puerto Rico and other islands outside the sphere of the Havana Company, was disappointing, but it contributed to the further development of Puerto Rico by importing 9450 African slaves into the island between 1766 and 1770 (cf. Richard Sheridan, *The Development of the Plantations to 1750*, London, 1970, p. 69).

13 E. Donnan, *Documents Illustrative of the History of the Slave Trade to America*, Vol. 1, p. 107. Also W. Rodney, *A History of the Upper Guinea Coast*, Oxford, 1970, p. 139. It was through this company that Guzman contracted with Spain for the supply of African slaves to the Indies.

14 C. P. Lucas, *Introduction to a Historical Geography of British Colonies*, Oxford, 1887, pp. 4–14. This author ignored the quest for power.

15 Klaus E. Knorr, *British Colonial Theories, 1570–1850*, London, 1963, pp. 26–62, 1st impression, 1944.

16 Initially Spain and Portugal had carried slaves from West Africa but Spain suffered setbacks after the destruction of its fleet during the Spanish Armada.

17 This aspect of the Euro-African connection is discussed in the next chapter. The implications of the introduction of Africans into Portugal is another aspect of the African diaspora which needs to be fully explored. But in the present state of knowledge the slaves were distributed in Latin Europe mainly in Italy, Portugal and Spain. In time, even the royal family in Portugal had become mulatto. See W. E. B. DuBois, *The World and Africa*, New York, 1947 and 1965, p. 47.

18 These were not plantation colonies but rather trading depots as the Dutch showed a preference for the carrying trade rather than agriculture, and this initially proved profitable to them. But the English and French established cultivation in which crops such as indigo, tobacco, ginger, rice and other staples were grown.

19 Cromwell had really sought to capture Puerto Rico or Hispaniola (Haiti). See T. S. Floyd, *The Anglo-Spanish Struggle for Mosquitia*, Albuquerque, N. M., 1967, pp. 26–8.

20 *Ibid.*, p. 28.

21 Sheridan, *Development of the Plantations*, p. 9.

22 *Ibid.*

23 In 1580 Portugal lost its independence to Spain and so Spain became the mistress of the western and eastern hemispheres. Britain helped Holland to secure independence from Spain but later became engaged in wars of commercial rivalry with Holland. The Dutch captured Pernambuco in Brazil from the Portuguese in 1630 and lost it in 1654. In dislodging the Dutch black soldiers contributed their part – the most celebrated of these leaders was Henriques Dias. Commenting on this loss of Dutch Brazil, C. R. Boxer has written that 'The natural chagrin of the Dutch at their loss of Netherlands Brazil was greatly increased by their realisation that they had been defeated by what was in great part a coloured army', Boxer, *The Portuguese Seaborne Empire 1415–1825*, London, 1969, p. 113, also pp. 119, 131, 262. Some of these coloured soldiers, including Dias, received knighthoods for their outstanding services in fighting the Dutch between 1630 and 1654.

24 The early plantations were at first small and tended by the families settled there; their labour was supplemented by those of white indentured servants brought from Europe. See N. Deerr, *The History of Sugar*, 1949, Vol. 1, p. 160. Bermuda also had convict settlers.

25 W. E. Minchinton, *The Port of Bristol in the Eighteenth Century*, Bristol, 1962, pp. 3–4. Minchinton also reveals that 'Sugar was refined in twenty or more houses in Bristol'. But according to him the prisoners and ex-convicts were a trifle compared to the African slaves which were taken to the colonies. Bristol triumphed over London in the eighteenth century as a slave-trading port, only Liverpool surpassing it.

26 J. A. Williamson, *The British Empire and Commonwealth*, London, 1954, 3rd edn., pp. 97–114. See also Richard Pares, *Merchants and Planters*, Cambridge, 1960, pp. 14–19, and Sheridan, *Development of the Plantations*, p. 58, for a comparable situation in relation to the elements who went to the French plantations.

27 Ralph Davis, 'English Foreign Trade 1660–1700' in W. E. Minchinton (ed.), *The Growth of English Overseas Trade in the Seventeenth and Eighteenth Genturies*, London, 1969, pp. 80–1. Davis indicates that tobacco was a luxury at the end of the sixteenth century; less than a century later it was the solace of all classes.

28 A. P. Poley, *The Imperial Commonwealth*, London, 1921, p. 181. The conventional viewpoint is that it was Dutch émigrés from Brazil after their expulsion by the Portuguese from that country in 1654 who aided the English and the French in the process of sugar cultivation and manufacture, and who supplied the credit until they were eliminated by the mercantilist pursuits of both France and England. Professor C. R. Boxer in *The Portuguese Seaborne Empire*, p. 113, takes a contrary view in which he suggests that improved

57

methods of sugar cultivation and cane-growing were introduced into the British and French West Indies during the Dutch occupation of Pernambuco, probably through the agency of Luso-Brazilian Jews. The origin and development of the sugar industry in the English West Indies, with Barbados in the lead, remains a contentious point. Sir Thomas Dalby (once Agent for the Royal African Company) in 1690 noted that in 1650 a 'Hollander' arriving in Barbados from Brazil had observed that the English knew no other good use for the sugar cane save to make refreshing drinks. He then instructed them in the art of making sugar. But Ligon (an author on the West Indies) observed that the industry had arisen in Barbados prior to 1650, for on his arrival in the island in 1647 he found 'the great work of sugar-making but newly practised by the inhabitants'. 'But as Robert Schomburgk (an early historian of the West Indies) pointed out the Barbados sugar industry was due to the Dutch', see *Barbados Standard*, 13 Sept. 1920, p. 5.

29 Davies, *The Royal African Company*, p. 15, also n.1. Davies' figures, derived from manuscripts in the British Museum (British Library), put the value of London's imports of all commodities from the plantations in 1662–3 at £484 641. 2s. Of this, brown sugar accounted for £175 500 and white sugar for £44 800. The value set on brown sugar, 27s for 100 lb., does not seem excessive.

30 Sheridan, *Development of the Plantations*, p. 48.

31 *Ibid.*, p. 50. This observation was made in 1724, but in 1739 the colony had 'approximately 350 plantations producing upwards of 40,000 tons of sugar directed by the labour of 117,411 Negro slaves'.

32 The figures are extracted from Sheridan, *Development of the Plantations*, pp. 22–3.

33 J. H. Parry and P. Sherlock, *A Short History of the West Indies*, London, 1966, p. 99.

34 A. P. Newton, *The European Nations in the West Indies, 1493–1688*, London, 1933, 2nd edn., 1966, p. 278.

35 Parry and Sherlock, *West Indies*, p. 96. The authors discuss the *Asiento* in ch. 7.

36 L. B. Rout, Jr., *The African Experience in Spanish America*, London, New York and Melbourne, 1976, pp. 43–7; also Donnan, *Documents*, Vol. 1, pp. 105 *et seq.*

37 Donnan, *Documents*, Vol. 1, pp. 105–7; Vol. 2, pp. 326–7.

38 Davies, *The Royal African Company*, p. 327.

39 Anstey in another context was arguing the non-profitability of the slave trade to the 'mother country' and quoted Seymour Drescher's 'A Case of Econocide', to be found in Anstey, *The Atlantic Slave Trade and British Abolition*, p. 52, n. 33. For the further development of this theme, see S. Drescher, *Econocide: British Slavery in the Era of Abolition*, Pittsburg, University of Pittsburgh Press, 1977.

40 'Resumé of the Origin of the Introduction of Slaves into Spanish America', in Donnan, *Documents*, Vol. 1, pp. 342–6, and introduction.

41 *Ibid.*

42 Another account gives the figure of 5000, see Davies, *The Royal African Company*, p. 327. Davies also observes that the *Asiento* was vested in Gracia for a decade.

43 *Ibid.*, p. 330. These backdoor activities continued sporadically until England finally became the recipient of the *Asiento* in 1713 by the Treaty of Utrecht.

44 *Ibid.*

45 *Ibid.*, p. 333.

46 PRO, T, 70/82, folios 61,62,66d.

47 T 70/57, folios 45,45d.

48 Davies, *The Royal African Company*, pp. 334–5.

49 Donnan, *Documents*, Vol. 1, pp. 106–7, also pp. 325–9, 357–9, 362–3, 364–8, 363, 367–9. The story of the Coymans *Asiento* begins in Donnan, *Documents*, Vol. 1, pp. 335–52, and continues on pp. 357–9, 363–71, 373. See also I. A. Wright, *The Coymans Asiento (1685–1689)*, S'Gravenhage, Martinus-Nijhoff, 1921.

50 Donnan, *Documents*, pp. 364–7. We see even from this earlier venture at the commencement of the eighteenth century that commercial capitalism mirrored a tendency to become international.

51 Rout, *African Experience*, pp. 49–53. Parry and Sherlock refer to the company as the French Guinea Company and their date of 1702 is correct; Parry and Sherlock, *West Indies*, p. 99.

52 It was during this war of rivalries between European nations that England acquired the island of St Kitts (St Christopher) which had been a bone of contention between England and France. After its acquisition in 1702, the English retained it. Parry and Sherlock, *West Indies*, p. 99.

53 Sheridan, *Development of the Plantations*, p. 99.

54 *Ibid.*, pp. 67–8.

55 Davies, *The Royal African Company*, p. 14.

56 Donnan, *Documents*, Vol. 1, pp. 351–2, see 'Instructions to Sir Phillip Howard as Governor of Jamaica', 25 Nov. 1685, and 'Address of the Council and Assembly of Jamaica to the King and Queen', 26 July 1689.

57 *Ibid.*, pp. 370–1. The Jamaican Assembly regretted the connivance of the governor in the practice of selling much-needed slaves to the Spanish from the English islands, which made their own labour shortage more acute.

58 There were also other sources of grievance among the planters. See PRO, CO 71/4, Memorial from the Island of Dominica through Ag. Governor to Lord North, First Lords Commissioner of H.M.'s Treasury, and William, Earl of Dartmouth, First Lord of Trade and Plantations and Principal Secretary of State for the Colonies, No. 2, 3 March 1772. Also see CO 239/29, Vol. 1, William Nicolay to Viscount Goderich, No. 39, 2 May 1832, enclosing the petition of the Council of Anguilla pleading for relief of distresses imposed by restrictive legislation.

59 Had the English colonies' monopoly position not been retained in the English market, it would have been seen that their sugar prices could not have withstood the competitive prices of their rivals in the French and Spanish colonies, since it would appear that the English colonies' sugar prices were higher compared to those of their foreign neighbours. It was the pressure of these English colonists which prevented England from maintaining its hold on the colonies of Guadeloupe, Martinique, and Curaçao, which she had captured in the Seven Years' War (1759). Instead, England traded them for Canada, since the products of Canada did not compete with those of the English Caribbean plantations. The retention of the three would have resulted in their glutting the English market with sugar and therefore depressing the prices obtained by the English colonies.

60 Newton, *European Nations in the West Indies*, pp. 237–41.

61 The first fort to be built by the Portuguese was on the island of Arquim in 1448; it was rebuilt and improved in 1461.

62 J. W. Blake, *European Beginnings in West Africa*, pp. 109–14; also Rodney. *Upper Guinea Coast*, pp. 126, 438–40.

63 Richard Jobson, *The Golden Trade*, 1623, reprint, p. 120.

64 Rodney, *Upper Guinea Coast*, p. 126.

65 *Ibid.*

66 Davies, *Royal African Company*, p. 166.

67 *Ibid.*, pp. 166–7.

68 Rodney, *Upper Guinea Coast*, p. 126.

69 B. Davidson, *Black Mother*, London, 1968, p. 76.

70 Davies, *Royal African Company*, pp. 16–17.

71 Hobson, *The Export of Capital*, p. xv.

72 Davies, *Royal African Company*, pp. 173, 177.

73 Newton, *European Nations in the West Indies*, pp. 209, 236–55. Also see Zook, *Company of Royal Adventurers*, pp. 62–3. Zook rightly observed that the Second Anglo-Dutch War was for 'trade privileges on the West African coast', and underlying it was the mercantilist element.

74 Newton, *European Nations in the West Indies*, p. 209.

75 *Ibid.*, pp. 210–11.

76 The capture of New Netherlands by the Duke of York in 1664 (renamed New York) was part of the preliminaries for war.

77 Newton, *European Nations in the West Indies*, pp. 236–7.

78 Zook, *Company of Royal Adventurers*, p. 82; also Davies, *Royal African Company*, pp. 42–3. The Company is recorded as having furnished the plantations in 1667 with 6000 slaves, but Zook (p. 82) casts doubt on this because of the raging Anglo-Dutch war.

79 K. Y. Daaku, *Trade and Politics on the Gold Coast, 1600–1720*, Oxford, 1970, chs. 4–7; A. P. Newton, *European Nations in the West Indies*, chs. 4–19; Zook, Company of Royal Adventurers, pp. 71–96.

80 Details of the Third Anglo-Dutch War are given in Newton, *European Nations in the West Indies*, pp. 296–307. See esp. p. 300, also ch. 19 for causes.

81 Heckscher, *Mercantilism*, Vol. 1, p. 407.

82 Zook, *Company of Royal Adventurers*, pp. 21–2, 69.

83 *Ibid.*, p. 173.

84 Davies, *Royal African Company*, p. 115.

85 Davidson, *Black Mother*, p. 68.

86 *Ibid.*, pp. 67–9. Although K. G. Davies casts doubt on the extent to which European fortifications impressed and influenced Africans (*Royal African Company*, p. 261), he agrees that it drew Europeans into the expensive complexities of African politics (p. 262); see also pp. 278–9. See, too, PRO, T 70/102, pp. 47–50, letter from John Snow to the Royal African Company, 13 July 1705.

87 E. Reynolds, *Trade and Economic Change on the Gold Coast, 1807–1874*, London, 1974, p. 60.

88 Blake, *European Beginnings*, pp. 11, 14, 141, 152–3, 155, 156–7; Daaku, *Trade and Politics*, chs. 3, and 4, esp. pp. 52–63, 75–7, 79 *et seq.*, 82–5, 129–33, 140–1; Rodney, *Upper Guinea Coast*, ch. 5 and pp. 141–51.

89 Rodney, *Upper Guinea Coast*, p. 129, for general argument; pp. 128–30.

90 *Ibid.*, p. 132.

91 *Ibid.*, pp. 145, 151.

92 J. C. DeGraft-Johnson, *African Glory*, London, 1954, p. 143, for the entire account, ch. 14.

93 David Birmingham, *Trade and Conflict in Angola*, Oxford, 1966, pp. 24–6, 27–32, 80, 92–4, 100, 104–10 and ch. 7.

94 *Ibid.*, pp. 64–6.

95 Davidson, *Black Mother*, p. 70.

96 *Ibid.*, pp. 68–70; K. Y. Fynn, *Asante and Its Neighbours, 1700–1807*, London, 1971, pp. 50–4, 63–4, 124–36, 142; Davies, *Royal African Company*, pp. 278–89; Davidson, *Black Mother*, pp. 88–93 and 118–25 *et seq.*; Daaku, *Trade and Politics*, pp. 96–144, also ch. 6; H. A. Wyndham, *The Atlantic and Slavery*, Oxford, 1939, p. 26; A. W. Lawrence, *Trade, Castles and Forts of West Africa*, London, 1963, p. 66.

97 Davies, *Royal African Company*, pp. 267–8, 269. It was observed that a temporary truce was reached between the English and the Dutch at Kommenda by the end of the century without the signing of a formal agreement.

98 *Ibid.*, p. 269. This can also be seen in PRO, T 70/51 folios 17, 39, 44, 108.

99 Davies, *Royal African Company*, p. 270.

100 *Ibid.*, p. 274. Of Whydah it had been observed in 1678 that about 6000–7000 slaves could be obtained there annually (see Wyndham, *The Atlantic and Slavery*, p. 34). Two years later John Mildman indicated that given the appropriate trade goods he could despatch a ship with 500 African slaves at five-weekly intervals (see PRO, T 70/76 folio 18, and Davies, *Royal African Company*, p. 228). These citations testify to Whydah (variously known as Ovidah, Juda, Guydah and Fida) as a large slave market. All the rival slave-trading nations – the Portuguese, French, Dutch and English – operated there in the eighteenth century, and affirmed its importance as a slave market; indeed, slaves were obtained beyond their expectations. The Royal African Company, failing to find enough slaves on the Gold Coast, supplemented its cargoes with slaves from Whydah.

101 Davies, *Royal African Company*, p. 41; Davidson, *Black Mother*, p. 68; Zook, *Company of Royal Adventurers*, p. 7.

102 The Swedish African Company for which Carloff worked was Dutch-sponsored.

103 Daaku, *Trade and Politics*, pp. 59–61; Reynolds, *Trade and Economic Change*, pp. 6–7.

104 Davidson, *Black Mother*, p. 68; Davies, *Royal African Company*, p. 41.

105 The Dutch are said to have backed the company to act as a brake on the monopoly of the Dutch West India Company.

3 The Euro-African connection: myth and reality

It was stated in the preceding chapter that the transatlantic slave trade was the major factor in the African diaspora to the Americas. Because so many routine accounts of the slave trade abound, this chapter is not another conventional history of the slave trade. It is aimed at examining some existing myths relating to the period of African enslavement by Europeans in order to focus more accurately on the European as well as African contributions to this peculiar episode. For the myth is not only ubiquitous, but persistent, that European intrusions merely constituted an extension of a practice which was endemic in African societies from a remote antiquity, and that African reluctance to terminate the trade, when the Europeans did, was indicative of an African refusal to forego the profits which had derived from the activity. In short, the purpose of this chapter is to re-evaluate, briefly, these controversial assertions in the light of the growing body of material and increasing interest in the subject of the transatlantic slave trade. A reappraisal of the often assumed, but often unproven, African contributions to their own enslavement and consequently their own dispersion is long overdue. The endeavour here is merely to scratch the surface of this important but endless debate with a view to stimulating further research. This effort, therefore, is merely the beginning of a reconsideration of many of the distortions which have befuddled the study of the slave trade in Africans to the Americas.

When the book *Black Cargoes*[1] was published in 1963 its authors believed they were telling anew the story of the slave trade, a story which had not been told for upwards of sixty years. They felt that they were breaking new ground, and so they were. But even their enthusiasm has not rescued them from the reassertion of some old myths. That this should have occurred is no reflection on the authors, but serves not only to emphasise the strength of the traditional school, whose interpretations have long dominated the subject, but also to demonstrate how traditional interpretations have fossilised into dogmatic 'truths'. It emphasises the tenacity of some of these distortions. Nevertheless, since *Black Cargoes*, many other attempts have been made to reappraise the Atlantic slave trade from widely divergent angles; some from the demographic point of view,[2] from the purely interpretative angle,[3] or the mere re-examinations of assertions,[4] as a purely economic activity[5] (with attempts at quantifying the activity both in terms of scope and profitability), from a moral and historical angle, from a sociological perspective[6] and from a combination of these. Such reappraisals not only make the study of the slave trade important but compelling.

Myths and assertions

For too long there has been, and still persists, the assertion, as if by way of justification – often emanating from the European and Euro-American quarter – that slavery existed in Africa from 'time immemorial'. This is an error into which even well-intentioned and eminent scholars have fallen. That it still persists can be seen from the vast amount of literature which still asserts it.[7] Professor Walter Rodney focused our attention on the need for a reappraisal of unsubstantiated assertions concerning the existence of slavery in African societies. In spite of Rodney's admonishment, however, the assertion persists. Moreover, attempts have been made to compare the pattern of slavery observed by travellers from the eighteenth to the twentieth centuries in Africa with that which prevailed in the Americas until the end of the nineteenth century. These modern analysts have then proceeded to project their observations backward and have drawn unsupportable conclusions from them. Such exercises have led them to assert that slavery and the slave trade existed in Africa from a remote past. The error of such an approach cannot be over-emphasised.

Walter Rodney noted that chattel slavery did not appear in the early records of Portuguese observers and travellers, many of whom were meticulous chroniclers. He has argued that had chattel slavery existed, and had it been endemic or been known to the societal arrangement, those outside observers, who hardly recorded its existence, would not have been slow to be explicit on the issue.[8]

Furthermore, in the middle of the last century, two descendants of Africa had visited the continent and remarked on what they considered to be 'domestic slavery'.[9] The 'slaves' they saw were an integral part of the African families they were in contact with. They also asserted that cruelty (a feature of Atlantic slavery) was absent from what they had observed. Moreover, the so-called 'domestic slaves' addressed their master as 'father' while he in turn addressed them as 'children'. While observing that the so-called slaves had certain functions, it was not suggested by those authors that what they observed had its origin from a remote antiquity. Since then there have appeared other studies of the slave status in Africa, but they relate to the period after the transatlantic slave trade had come to an end and relate more to the consequences of the slaving centuries of the Euro-African connection than to the assertions so widespread in the works of scholars. The legitimacy of projecting studies of later periods into the past, and for that matter into a remote past, remains a questionable exercise in the absence of hard evidence.

From the English quarter there came early the observation of Mungo Park during his travels in West Africa in the late eighteenth and early nineteenth centuries.[10] This has since been quoted as proof that slavery existed in Africa from very early times. Yet, Park merely conjectured but could not say whether it was recent or was of some antiquity. Moreover, Park could not have had more than a superficial knowledge of the people and places he visited and could not, therefore, be an authority on their past history. His was merely speculation. Yet some writers, as distinguished as Professor Curtin, have employed Park to reinforce their assertions of the old myths of slavery and the slave trade being of antiquity to Africa. Curtin wrote: 'Long before the Atlantic slave trade began, a trade in slaves had existed in West Africa. Part was an export trade to North Africa, but much of the West African slave trade (probably most of it) was internal.'[11]

We are warned again by Professor Rodney that one of the most widely held generalisations about 'indigenous' African society was the assertion that slavery prevailed on the African continent prior to the advent of the European and facilitated the growth of the Atlantic slave trade. He insisted that the assertion was in need of reappraisal.[12] Rodney argued that from a chronological assessment it can be demonstrated that these tenets were not only inapplicable but, on the contrary, it was the transatlantic slave trade which 'spawned a variety of forms of slavery, serfdom and subjection in this particular area'.[13] He observed that the Upper Guinea Coast from the 1460s had a long period of association with the Atlantic slave trade, which spanned four centuries. This he saw as a useful example for evaluating the problem posed by those facile assertions of 'African slavery'. He further stated that this so-called 'African slavery' was observed only in the colonial period to be widespread in this region, till it was suppressed by the metropolitan powers, who had previously engaged in it. He maintained that often what the region sometimes revealed were cases of 'quasi-feudal' exploitation of labour by a ruling elite, who reaped a greater proportion of the harvests, as in the case of the *rounde* or 'slave towns' of Futa Djalon. These so-called 'domestic slaves' were members of their masters' households. 'They could only be sold for serious offences; they had their own plots of land and/or rights to the proportion of the fruits of their labour. They could marry and their children had a right to inheritance, and, if born of one free parent, aften acquired a new status, and such persons could rise to positions of great trust, including that of chief.'[14] In quoting Rattray's work on the Asante, Rodney argued that the usage of the term 'slave' was not fully applicable to Upper Guinea. Rattray, he stated, 'was principally concerned with the slave child (*Odonko ba*), whose privileges were quite different from those of his parents and ancestors'. In Upper Guinea servants born in the household were distinguished from war captives or from those pledged and not redeemed. It was the latter who were vulnerable to sale, being exchanged for goods as well as serving as currency in a number of transactions, such as marriage payments. In the latter part of the nineteenth century, after the transatlantic slave trade had been officially abolished, the colonial administration was plagued with a recurrent problem of how to abolish the internal slave trade which persisted – especially the notable example of those who fell victims to Fula and Mande. Accordingly, a relatively recent examination of the Upper Guinea Coast revealed 'a category of local slavery, as well as agricultural serfdom and personal service'.[15] Rodney emphasised the absence of any reference to African slavery in the sixteenth and seventeenth centuries 'when such evidence could reasonably be construed to mean that the institution preceded the advent of Atlantic slaving'.[16] He argued that there was a loose usage of 'slave' to refer to the common people, but when the slave traders were being accused of injustice to Africans in the practice of New World slavery, it was said that 'Negroes were slaves of absolute kings and the king of Casanga, on the river Casamance, was pointed out as one such absolute king whose subjects were slaves'. In response to such assertions, Rodney observed: 'This is a purely arbitrary use of the word "slave" for propaganda purposes.' He continued the argument by saying that there was only one clear instance where labour services were associated with the limitation of privileges, with reference to Sierra Leone 'at the beginning of the seventeenth century, when if a subject was in danger in one kingdom, he could flee to the protection of another ruler, becoming a "slave" of the latter, either remaining in his service or becoming liable for sale (to the Europeans)'.[17] This, Walter Rodney has insisted, was a time when local custom had already been 'influenced by the presence of slave-buying Europeans, as well as by the arrival of the Manes as an alien ruling element some decades previously, but the essentials of the practice almost certainly preceded these two external factors'.[18] He maintained that John Hawkins' experience on Sherbro Island, when the Sape were used as 'slaves' by the Mane for producing varieties of agricultural crops, showed that no institutionalised slavery or serfdom resulted at that time as the invaders were rapidly integrated and had essentially the same relations with their subjects as previous rulers. With so much antipathy between rulers and subjects, sales of Sape by Mane were explicable in terms of warfare and of class exploitation and, besides, the transatlantic slave trade was in existence before the arrival of the Mane. Rodney, therefore, suggests that 'In so far as the society can be constructed at the moment of contact with the Portuguese, one can discern, at the very most, the presence of a small number of political clients in households of rulers. If they were to constitute the pad for launching the Atlantic slave trade it would never have left the ground.'[19] It would, therefore, be difficult to believe that any observer could have glossed over features such as chattel slaves, agricultural serfs or even household servants, if these were numerous and unprivileged. From several Portuguese accounts details of the structure of Upper Guinea emerge, and they were consistent in emphasising rulers and subjects, fidalgos[20] and plebus.[21] The phenomenon of 'slave', observed by Valentim Fernandes in Senegambia and de Almada on the Wolof in the sixteenth century, was not, he argued, a widespread phenomenon, and that Portuguese chroniclers scrupulously recorded the detail and rarely gave hints of slaves in terms of a commerce to the north. In spite of the failure to identify any slaves during the first phase of the European contact, it was from that region of Upper Guinea that the first slaves were taken and exported – a practice which was taking place in earnest in the sixteenth century. The slaves so obtained were 'victims of inter-tribal feuding', but if any internal slave trading was necessary for the initiation of trans-oceanic slave trading, it was not in the relationship of free versus slave but rather because of the contradiction between nobility and commoners.[22]

The essential point in the Rodney argument is that there is no legitimate basis for projecting into the past the condition of servitude observed in Africa after the Atlantic slave trade had been in operation for more than two centuries in order to assert that slavery and the slave trade had existed in Africa for centuries prior to the coming of the Europeans. What is happening is that more contemporary writers such as G. I. Jones, A. G. Hopkins, P. D. Curtin and many more, are responsible for asserting this old myth of slavery in Africa.[23] The list could be extended. This is another example of how myth can fossilise into an orthodox truth because it has the pronouncement of authority and yet is without any shred of evidence, Curtin stresses it again in the following manner. While observing that there was a difference between Atlantic slavery and slavery in Africa, he wrote, 'Although Africa, Europe and the Middle East all had traditions of slavery going back for millennia, the form of slavery differed so much from one society to another that it can be misleading to talk of slavery as a single institution.'[24] He then proceeded to assert that slavery in West Africa was highly variable from one country to another.[25] From this he deduced that

'Few of the forms of slavery practised in the Ancient Mediterranean or in Africa were very close to the type of slavery that developed in the South Atlantic System'.[26] The point at issue is that one cannot assert that slavery and the slave trade existed in Africa from 'time immemorial' by merely assuming it, or because it has been observed in other societies, and this is not to suggest, as James Pope Hennessy reminds us, that African societies consisted of societies of saints,[27] while others were those of sinners. Furthermore, there has been a tendency to speak of the slave trade and slavery as if they were both the same thing. The assertion about the existence of the slave trade and slavery in Africa prior to the appearance of Europeans in African waters might have been true, yet, as few modern historians have observed 'no self-respecting and honest scholar can fail to be indifferent' to what was essentially a sordid period in the evolution of human beings. Some of the apologists of the slave trade have been quick to speak of the 'Arab slave trade', or what is now currently known as the trans-Saharan slave trade, and the east coast slave trade.

Professor Raymond Mauny has asserted that the number of Africans exported as slaves from the Sudan in the Middle Ages totalled two million,[28] a claim which has been hotly disputed by another scholar, Marian Malowist.[29] Yet, one scholar, Professor Tadeusze Lowicki of the University of Cracow, has already asserted that in a period of one century, the sixteenth, the number taken through Cairo by the trans-Saharan slave trade amounted to between twelve and nineteen million slaves. The figure, according to him, exceeds the number of slaves carried to America during nearly three centuries of the transatlantic slave trade, reckoned at between five and fourteen million slaves.[30] We are nonetheless still in the speculative stages of the exercise. It is an attempt to reverse the hitherto held views by some scholars that the overland slave trade, which appeared in the writings of missionaries travelling in Africa in the nineteenth century, did not amount to much and was not as catastrophic as the Atlantic counterpart.[31] This was how an English historian, E. W. Bovill, writing in 1933, observed the trans-Saharan slave trade:

> Appalled though we may be by the horrors of the trans-Saharan slave traffic, they were not equal, in the opinion of those qualified to draw the comparison, to those of the trade which Europeans carried on between the coast of Guinea and the West Indies. Repulsive though this trade [in eunuchs] seems, we should remember, before condemning the Sudanese for their barbarity, that not only was it common throughout the Mohammedan world, but that it was long practised in Europe. During the Middle Ages large establishments, mostly under the direction of Jews, were maintained in France,

notably at Verdun, for the supply of eunuchs to Muslim Spain. A still more deplorable example was the *Soprani* of the Sistine Chapel, 'the musical glory and moral shame of the papal choir. Although the *Soprani* were not finally abolished till late in the nineteenth century by Pope Leo XIII, the gelding of boys continued to be practised in Italy till even more recent times.[32]

Against this disclosure of Bovill on the trans-Saharan trade is the comparison of another English historian who wrote that, 'the scale of the overseas slave trade so much surpassed anything of its kind before or since as to be quite distinct, in its impact on Africa, both from overland slaving long practised by the Arabs and many negro states, or from the "domestic slavery" of African iron age feudalism. It was much more than the merely peripheral bleeding vitality that was represented by overland slaving. It was quite different in its catastrophic effects, from the subjection of weak peoples to strong peoples that occurred through African warfare and conquest'.[33] He likened the Atlantic slave trade to the Black Death, but admitted that the Black Death, though similarly catastrophic, lasted a few years, while the overseas slave trade 'endured for more than four centuries and that it degraded thought and action, African as well as European, through generations of ingrained contempt for human life'.[34]

But even Bovill, while admitting that the Carthaginians 'were far from being dependent on Africa for slave labour', instead of providing evidence for the assertion which follows, again introduced conjecture more than forty years afterwards when he rewrote his *Caravans of the Old Sahara*, with its new title *The Golden Trade of the Moors*, in an era when apologists for European colonialism[35] were again becoming numerous with the demands of the colonial peoples for the right of self-determination. He says: 'It is unlikely that they hesitated to enslave as many Berbers as they required, nor were so brutal a people likely to have drawn the line at doing the same to their own peasantry. The evidence of negro blood is, however, significant and it seems probable that they imported slaves from the Fezzan. It was a likely source, for the Garamantes cannot have hunted the Troglodyte Ethiopians except to enslave them. The slave trade with the Fezzan may even have been important to the Carthaginians, but there are no grounds for assuming that it was so.'[36] Much of what Bovill says later in his book about the trans-Saharan slave trade relates to the eighteenth century, after the European slave trade had commenced and was in progress in an era in which African greed might have matched European cupidity, and in which it would appear that slave trading was proving a profitable activity. All his other references relate to the nineteenth century, in which it could not be doubted that slavery and the trade were part of the African economic system but which, from mere observation, does not lead us to conclude that slavery was traditional. That the trans-Saharan slave trade was also an episode in the African experience, and that the East African littoral was also the entry point of Arab-Swahili caravans into the interior to forage for slaves, was also true. These latter developments, however, did not begin before the eighteenth century, and whatever must have been delivered on the coast was delivered by some African groups, notably the Yao, Nyamwezi and Kamba, but this does not lead to the conclusion that slavery was endemic to African society from very early times.

Those who had mentioned slaves in early accounts – for example the author of the *Periplus* – did not say that it existed from times past and did not specify the magnitude of any trade in slaves, if any existed. It is modern pseudo-scholarship that reads this into the records. While historians like Reginald Coupland have asserted[37] that the East African slave trade had existed from earliest times, other scholars· disagree and suggest that only since the arrival of Omani Arabs from about the seventeenth century[38] had slaves begun to be exported from the East Africa coast around the Horn. The truth is that the time of origin of the slave trade from East African, or the trans-Saharan trade, as well as their magnitude, remains shrouded in mystery. Most assertions are conjectures unsupported by any hard evidence. That it increased in magnitude in the nineteenth century is attested in the records, as indeed it increased even into the twentieth century.

Some writers have persisted in citing Gustavus Vassa[39] (alias Olaudah Equiano, the Nigerian ex-slave of the eighteenth century) to support assertions that slavery existed for a long time in Africa. Those who use Vassa as evidence ignore two important facts. First, that Vassa did not say that slavery existed in Africa for any length of time. His travelling horizon was limited. He merely indicated that his father, besides many slaves, had a numerous family.[40] The implication of the statement was that slaves were part of the family. One could not generalise for Vassa's society in the light of his mention of slaves in his own family. The slave trade was at its height in the century in which Vassa was captured, the eighteenth century. The second fact is that Vassa was taken away from his society at the tender age of eleven – an age in which young people begin secondary education in the European world. Vassa might have known a number of things about his society, but not enough, as a child, to pontificate on. As a child of that age he thought European ships were propelled by magic. Those who use him to generalise even for the Niger Delta or, more broadly, for Africa, must do so on rather thin evidence. The combination of evidence from Gustavus Vassa and Mungo Park, which some authors have used, does not prove the point of ancient slavery in Africa. The fact that Vassa was sold from one master to another testified to the slave trade in the eighteenth century, after it had already become the chief preoccupation of coastal and hinterland Africans, as well as the European buyers; but this is not testimony to its existence in some remote antiquity.

One point which has yet been unresolved is how to categorise what Europeans considered to be slavery in Africa and whether slavery existed from a remote past. While this writer admits that more research is needed to clarify the issues that are raised by assertions and counter-assertions, from his personal observations of African societies in both East and West Africa, he has not found any evidence for this assertion of the existence of slavery dating from a remote antiquity. It does not even surface in the people's idiom. It has been impossible to locate many words for the term 'slave'. This writer is more inclined to agree with Professor Rodney that the European insistent demand for slaves heightened slave raiding and trading and resulted in various forms of production relationships not only among Africans themselves but between Africans and Europeans. Moreover, from this writer's knowledge of five West African languages he has failed to pinpoint a word which would coincide with the European conception of slave.[41] A recent study has also failed to unearth the existence of slavery from a remote past.[42]

The myth of African sellers

Beneath the myth that Africans sold Africans into slavery is the serious implication that Africans were solely to blame for the slave trade. It was drummed into the ears of this writer in childhood that Britain stopped the slave trade. Often the statement was silent on who began it. Nonetheless, the presentation at the time was to leave one with the impression that Africans themselves started the slave trade, encouraged it, and refused to put an end to it when a benevolent and humanitarian Europe decided that it was time to call a halt. This is what Basil Davidson has referred to in *Old Africa Rediscovered*[43] as the 'great distortion', about which more will be said presently. It has continued to surface in a modified form, both in the writings of people of European and African origin. That it has worked itself effectively into the consciousness of African scholars is evidenced by this citation from no less a person than Professor Adu Boahen, who, in a school textbook, appeared to be rehabilitating the argument that the Africans sold their kith and kin. Boahen wrote, 'African scholars and politicians today must be honest and admit that the enslavement and sale of the Africans from

the seventeenth century onwards were done by Africans themselves, especially the coastal kings and their elders, and that very few
Europeans actually ever marched inland and captured slaves themselves.'[44] One must note the emphasis on 'honesty'. The statement
implies that African scholars and politicians have not been honest
on the question of the enslavement of African man. This again is an
example of that conscious effort, in an attempt to be fair-minded,
to put across what essentially has been the prevailing Eurocentric
viewpoint. So far as the records of writers have shown, the lack of
honesty in discussing the enslavement of African man has been
more profuse from the European quarter. If Africans have complained at all, they have merely called attention to the consequences
of this period of the Euro-African connection. Furthermore, as has
been observed already, it is the Europeans who have attempted to
distort the picture. Then the assertion that it was Africans who,
from the seventeenth century, went inland to enslave their kind,
ignores the fact that the enslavement of Africans was in progress
from just before the mid-fifteenth century and it began with kidnapping, not with sales by Africans. Furthermore, the depredations
of the Portuguese on the Old Kongo kingdom, including Angola,
reveal evidence of the Portuguese actually carrying out wars against
those peoples for the procurement of slaves, and that these intermittent wars provoked by the Portuguese lasted throughout the
slave-trading centuries. Furthermore the kidnapping (popularly
known as 'panyaring') activities of John Hawkins provide the
evidence of European involvement inland.[45] An over-simplistic
statement of the kind quoted above is hardly illuminating, for it
attempts a simplification of what essentially was a complex relationship and, in addition, ignores the warlike alliances between
African notables and European slavers to gratify the needs of
Europe. Boahen's statement is far from being an unconscious
effusion of what was the current myth which had dominated
thinking on the slave trade and slavery for the greater part of the
twentieth century, but it showed how well the lie had gained the
validity of truth. It continues to be repeated by numerous authors,
some of whom have been mentioned in the footnotes of this
chapter. With only two exceptions[46] no author of the slave trade,
apart from Dr Walter Rodney, since the 1950s has been able to
introduce a meaningful corrective to this misleading assertion.[47]

Yet the impression left by the numerous depositions of captains
of slave-trading ships,[48] especially in an era in which they had to
justify their practice, and by later observers, was that the African
was by nature barbaric, bloodthirsty, cannibalistic, prone to human
sacrifices, and, accordingly, it was no surprise that he sold his own
kith and kin. It was they who, 'like the sons of Jacob', sold their
kith and kin[49] to the stranger, bear the blame. Yet the facts of this

encounter, as many authors tell us, are more complex than is at first presented. When the ex-slave from the Gold Coast, Ottobah Cugoano, in the late-eighteenth century produced his *Sentiments on the Evils of Slavery* and indicated that his shame was that his own countrymen of his own complexion had kidnapped and betrayed him, resulting in his exile in slavery,[50] he was showing the extent to which the slave trade had corrupted most of the people whom it had touched like the plague. The infliction on Africa of this vice did not suggest that Africans consisted of saints and no sinners prior to the coming of the Europeans. Without going into the full effects of the slave trade that had been initiated by the Europeans from the fifteenth century, the general picture indicated some very negative features; and, as Davidson observed, it 'stained and ruined much of the fabric of African society while permitting nothing better to replace it. As the slaving wars continued, men grew more callous. African demoralisations matched European cupidity.'[51] And although Davidson reminds us that 'Colonialist Europe may have succeeded, here and there, in fastening on African minds a sense of special guilt for the slaving centuries, the truth is that the guilt was shared all round, and that Africans were not the prime movers in the matter.'[52]

Academic historians of the slave trade seem almost to have ignored one of the major recent contributions to the study of the slave trade.[53] This book, *Sins of the Fathers*, by James Pope Hennessy, whose grandfather was in charge of the West African forts in about 1872, was published in 1967 and again as a paperback in 1970, but it does not even receive mention in the works of Curtin, Hopkins and others of their stamp. Yet not only does Pope Hennessy assemble vital data but he also attempts re-interpretations which are cogent. His revelations on the contemporary attitudes of Europeans and Euro-Americans on the episode merit mention. In trying to unravel who sold whom, he wrote, 'While working on the subject of this book I have often been admonished (and in places as far apart as London and Lagos, as Charleston and Gstaad) to "make it quite clear that it was the Blacks who sold each other". Implicit in this statement of the obvious lies the unspoken question "And so how can you blame us for having bought what the Africans themselves were willing to sell?"'[54] The further implication in all this is the theory that Africans principally had themselves to blame for the slave trade and this viewpoint has many proponents. Hennessy has argued with logic and fact that 'until the Europeans came upon the scene, "slaves" were regarded inside Africa as useful and helpful people whose ownership carried with it specific obligations – to feed, to clothe, to shelter and protect. To kings and noblemen they were also a status symbol, and necessary to the maintenance of rank.' But he argues that 'the phrase "Blacks selling Blacks" has neither pertinence nor meaning, for in those days the concept of African solidarity could not and did not exist'.[55] The crux of the matter is that had there been no buyers there would have been no sellers. He puts the accusation squarely where it lies: 'It was the European traders who assiduously taught Africans to sell other Africans; and moreover taught them to sell slaves, as they taught them to sell gold and ivory for trash.'[56] Hennessy did not fall into the error of asserting that the Africans alone participated; but, like Davidson before him, and Barbot before them, he clearly identified the class of Africans who engaged in this slave trade in an era in which the vast majority of Africans were victims of slave hunting and slave trading. The part played by Africans in their dispersion will be examined presently.

The African refusal to abolish the slave trade

Another point which also calls for a reappraisal is the distortion concerning the African refusal to give up the slave trade even after European abolition of the trade had taken place, largely because of the huge profits which some Africans are said to have amassed through the slave trade. This issue need not long detain us, but it is essential to observe certain points. Although the slave-trading era was inaugurated by piracy with Portuguese kidnapping Africans in the 1440s around Cape Bojador, and was continued by latecomers such as John Hawkins, some European interlopers and some coastal agents of the numerous trading companies in Africa (a practice never completely eliminated from the Euro-African connection), it was generally a 'peaceful partnership'[57] which superseded the earlier but infamous activities of European slave catchers all along the Guinea Coast. With peaceful partnership, the slave-trading business settled down with certain defined rules and regulations for its conduct, the infringement of which could put a temporary halt to the trade. One of the things forbidden to Europeans was kidnapping of Africans. The rules and regulations in the main guided the conduct of trade, even though on both sides of the connection subterfuges were introduced, which tended to bedevil the relations of the two trading groups, the African traders and the European buyers.[58] The question of profitability for African merchants, including mulattos, who gained ascendancy on the entire coast as middlemen of the Euro-African connection, remains dubious. Without considering the question of profitability for the Europeans, and the records speak volumes, and in spite of the claims that there were losses elsewhere, African societies had their manpower exported, which essentially was their capital, and there might have been benefits here and there, but because they came in consumption goods, they were merely acquisitions for display of false affluence. The Rev. H. M. Waddell, a missionary to West Africa in the 1840s, describing some of this display in Old Calabar in the home of King Eyo Honesty, observed, 'Eyo's house was . . . crowded with good furniture of all kinds – tables, sideboards, sofas, chairs, chests of drawers, clocks and all going, barrel organ, chinaware, pictures, chandeliers and mirrors of all shapes and sizes.'[59] Captain Hugh Crow in his *Memoirs* observed Duke Ephraim of Calabar, who was equally powerful and, thinking that the title of duke was higher than that of king, therefore preferred the title. Crow found that the interior of the duke's great house brimmed with articles such as 'numerous clocks, watches, and other articles of mechanism, sofas, tables, pictures, beds, porcelain cabinets of European manufacture; most of which were huddled together in confusion, among numerous fetiches, and in a state of decay, from disuse, carelessness and want of cleaning. Articles of crockery, knives, forks, spoons, plate, etc. appear at the king's table, which is set out with considerable taste and splendour, although here and there a calabash presents its less assuming appearance; and unless the guest be "great men" and strangers much thought of, the fingers are sometimes used, even at the ducal board, as the more convenient purveyors for the mouth.'[60] The picture could be repeated elsewhere among the potentates and prime merchants of the west coast.

We see numerous examples of the acquisitions which African potentates had accumulated through the slave trade and contact with Europeans. Essentially they were goods for display. They might have enhanced the prestige of these potentates in their locality but they did not expand the economy towards growth and development. In the long term they were to prove catastrophic because the coastal Africans had merely been producers of a monoculture in slaves. We get a glimpse of these articles for the display of false affluence. In order to impress the king of Warri, with whom King Pepple of Bonny carried on trade, he sent the king of Warri presents at the time of the betrothal of the king of Warri's daughter to King Pepple of Bonny. The present consisted of 'English, French, Spanish and Portuguese merchandise . . . extracted from his warehouse – gold and silver plate – costly silks and exquisitely fine cloths with embroidered laces, and other articles too numerous to mention'.[61] When the king of Warri eventually brought his daughter for the marriage ceremony an even more dazzling display met the eye. Apart from the firing of a number of gun salutes, the home was highly decorated with fine cloth – the roof, the walls and all around were decorated with superior fine silks and the palace was well adorned. The king of Warri's foot was not even allowed to touch the ground – he walked on the cloth (carpet). In addition, King Pepple gave his guest assortments of drinks consisting of wines and intoxicants, such as brandy puncheons. In addition the king presented all his own subjects, numbering more than a thousand, with pieces of cloth and an exuberant display of shot and shell. Commenting on this, Basil Davidson observed, There in a nutshell lay the truth about 'capital accumulation' during the high days of the Delta trade. Merchants who were also monarchs spent their wealth as traditional rulers must: to glorify their name and reputation and enlarge their power by winning allies from among their peers. The system was stable within its limits; but its limits stopped short of economic growth that could have led to systematic investment. And the slave trade continually fortified those limits by enhancing the power of kings and prime merchants, while siphoning off those pressures of population or political dissent which had pressed elsewhere, to- wards economic expansion.[62] The implication is that the slave trade was more a depressant on economic growth for African potentates, and the picture that emerges for the Niger Delta area could be generalised for all those parts of Africa that became involved in the Atlantic slave trade. But this is not to deny that the enslavement of people had become a way of life. The tenacity of the system that had been installed led a modern Nigerian historian of the Niger Delta, observing the area in the 1880s, to suggest that the whole economy of the Itsekeri and the entire Niger Delta hinged on slavery. According to him 'It was the slaves who manned the war canoes, carried on most of the actual trading, and cultivated their food on such land as was cultivable.'[63] He mistakenly went on to assert that 'Even the British Consuls realised how vital slaves were to the economic system of the coastal peoples'.[64] How vital it was remains a questionable assertion and an arguable thesis; the author conveys the impression that most of the coastal peoples (having been schooled in nothing else as a result of centuries of their Euro- African connection in the slave trade) wished to be assured that they could maintain the institution of slavery.[65] Among the suppliers were Bonny, Opobo, New Calabar and Nembe (Brass). Later the British sought to impose their will on the entire area. It is easy to see how conflict could have arisen from a unilateral rescheduling of commercial activity in the zone.

The point must be made that the European nations who, after they had seen the futility of kidnapping their victims from African waters, agreed to settle for peaceful partnership because it suited them, ignored the fact that the unilateral abrogation of agreements was productive of conflicts. The slave trade had served its purpose for the European nations who, wishing to switch over to commo- dity trading, had not found the same courtesy which they are said to have displayed in settling for peaceful partnership in the early stages of their relations with Euro-African potentates. They did not even make any effort at convincing their erstwhile trading partners with arguments as to why the slave trade was less to be preferred than commodity trading which they were then peddling as 'legitimate' trade. In thus behaving they were ignoring the fact that the slave trade had been legitimate trade because both of the trading partners had sanctioned it. What they later called 'legitimate' trade was a misnomer and should rightly have been identified for what it was – commodity trading. Yet the textbooks are even today replete with the use of the misleading term 'legitimate trade', which should have long been abandoned.

Furthermore, the unilateral abrogation of the trade by Europeans, first by the British and then by the United States followed later by other European nations, and lastly by Brazil very late in the century, was a breach of faith. African potentates and traders understandably reacted against it, and this must, in part, explain their persistence in the slave trade. It was a unilateral decision in which their agreement was not sought, and if anything an attempt was made to browbeat them into conformity. Moreover, their reactions were not unlike those of the slave dealers and their representatives in Parliament[66] who, every time the issue of abolition of the slave trade and emancipation of slaves was mooted, tended to raise the alarm that they would be ruined, the plantations would be ruined and, ultimately, the nation would be ruined. African potentates were no different from those who raised that clamour of ruin. Having been schooled in the art of producing a monoculture in slaves for a period spanning four centuries, it was difficult for habit to change overnight and it was expressed in the reactions of many West African potentates. The tenacity of the slave trade was manifested in the *volte face* made by King Eyo Honesty, writing to some merchants in Liverpool in June 1850 to indicate his willingness and that of King Archibong to resume the slave trade. Hitherto, in December 1842, King Eyo and King Eyamba V had written to Commander Raymond signifying their desire to abandon the slave trade and had called upon the British government to help them with seed cotton and coffee so that the many emancipated people among them could find worthwhile occupations and that trade could flourish.[67] The desire to resume the slave trade in 1850[68] testified to the fact that the habit died hard or that those potentates who wished to resume had not found some alternative role for their subjects and themselves. How far this desire to resume the trade produced the resistance of the Society of Blood Men (the society of freed slaves in Calabar) against their masters, the Egbo, in the following year, which led to Consul Beecroft's intervention, has not been ascertained by this writer. But it would appear surprising if that backward-looking decision of the kings of Calabar did not, in fact, precipitate some fresh crisis with the slaves who then determined to free themselves.

Since Britain was the pioneer, apart from Denmark, in the field of carrying abolition of the slave trade into effect, we ought to examine another example of this attempt at imposition on African traders and potentates. Between 1841 and 1850 Britain signed forty-two treaties with African kings to stop the slave trade. But they went unheeded as other Europeans were not honouring their treaties.[69] When Britain in 1850 sent a commission to King Gezo of Dahomey to terminate the slave trade, he returned the compliment of the queen of England and remarked that the presents she had sent him were acceptable, but as far as the slave trade was concerned he could not see how he and his people could do without it. He begged the queen of England to put a stop to the slave trade everywhere else and allow him to continue it and expressed the hope that the queen would send him some good Tower guns and blunderbusses and plenty of them to enable him to make. war.[70] Another objection to the stopping of the slave trade was mentioned by King Holiday on the Bonny river in July 1807 to Captain Crow, the last English captain legally to take slaves from West Africa. In fact the king could not have expressed his objections to a more ardent supporter of the slave trade than Captain Crow, who in his *Memoirs* denounced the activities of abolitionists such as Wilber-force.[71]

The chiefs of Nembe (Brass)[72] expressed themselves in no uncertain terms in early 1895 when it appeared that the Niger Company was encroaching on their cherished rights to trade and on their domain. Not only did they assert that 'Every river has markets to trade and feed themselves', but that the trade which had just been ended had only just begun and they expressed unhappiness about the stoppage. They continued, 'But the trade with Europeans had begun since our forefathers' time up to date. And as it is snatched away from our hands by the Niger Company, we really felt it keenly. You must please consider and investigate this matter. A person who has been accustomed to eat bread and knows its sweetness from his youth to manhood happens to be offered by another man to eat dust instead of bread. At the very time he hears the word dust he will go mad. Starvation brings a man to insanity. As we before said, if part of the Niger River is not given to us the war with the Niger Company will not stop; if given we shall be glad and thankful'.[73]

But a more telling statement appears later, in June of the same year, from the Nembe (Brass) chiefs. In it they refer to the fact that they obtained their slaves as a rule from the Igbos which cost from £10–£20 per slave. These slaves, they insisted, attained, if they were worthy, the social status of headmen and chiefs. The surfacing of the word 'slave' in these proceedings was a reminder that African potentates and merchants had not fully reconciled themselves to the unilateral abrogation of the slave trade by the British, and later by other Europeans, without according them the courtesy of pronouncing on a trade which, once it ceased to be kidnapping, had been worked out into a state of partnership with rules and regulations guiding its conduct. Unilateral abrogation[74] was a situation of dominance, not a relationship of equals, but African potentates had not perceived that the relationship, which it was assumed was to their advantage, had continued to change adversely against them during the centuries of the Euro-African connection. This fact alone gives credence to the claim that Europe dominated the connection, and not the other way round, on the pretext that the potentates retained their sovereignty and could dictate the terms. It was Europe that set the pace in the connection. While African potentates, kings and merchants could sometimes state the terms on which they could proceed, power was fast slipping out of their hands; first, into the hands of the mulattos – Afro-Portuguese in the main – who became at a certain time the middlemen of the coast with some of them acceding to the position of potentates or advisers to potentates; later, into European hands. These are by no means all the myths regarding this connection, but they are major ones in need of revision.

The enslavement of Africans

Contrary to popular belief, the enslavement of the African in modern times did not begin as a trade, although it quickly became part of a scheme for buying and selling .The year 1441, which is often cited as the commencement of the slave trade, is in fact incorrect as the proper starting date. In that year, it is true, a Portuguese captain, Antão (Antam) Gonçalvez and an associate, Nuno Tristão, in the service of Prince Henry of Portugal, popularly known as 'Henry the Navigator', seized some ten[75] Africans around Cape Bojador. On their return to Portugal the Africans were presented to Prince Henry, who, in turn, sent them to Pope Martin V, and Henry revealed his intention to continue his efforts in this direction.[76] This, in turn, induced the Pope to sanction the endeavour to capture Africans and the conferment on Portugal of sovereignty of any possession discovered by them in Guinea. But what had now been initiated was not *trade* but a scheme for the capture of Africans all along the Guinea Coast, and although some writers now put the official date for the commencement of the slave trade at 1444, this date is only justifiable on the grounds that the slaves kidnapped from the coast of Guinea and the neighbouring islands were taken and sold in European markets. But from the

African source it was not trade, it was just plain seizure, or man-stealing. This practice soon generated a trade in human beings, and, according to an account of Cadamosto, the sellers on the Upper Guinea Coast were said to be Arabs who acted as middlemen in selling Africans among other articles, including gold. But the word 'Arab' may not be taken too literally, for Europeans in those days tended to think of Muslims as Arabs, and Islam had been penetrating the western Sudan since the tenth century A.D. Those who were observed as Arab middlemen might, in fact, have been West African Muslims, who wore the familiar Muslim attire so widespread in Arab lands, the cradle of Islam, and in the Islamic world generally.

Prince Henry the Navigator (whose mother was an English-woman) saw his Guinea exploits as a holy crusade and sought Papal approval to maintain this claim to monopoly. Although in 1443 Pope Eugenius IX had decided to be neutral in the dispute between Portugal and Spain in respect of Guinea, Pope Nicolas V in 1452 had given King Alfonso general power to 'conquer and enslave pagans', but had not conferred on Portugal the right of exclusive control of Guinea. Nevertheless, after the seizure of a Spanish ship in Guinea by Portugal in 1454, John II of Castile protested, and soon after the Pope's authority granting Portugal exclusive monopoly was proclaimed.[77]

From Portuguese sources it was observed that between 1441 and 1448, 927 captives described as 'Moors and Negroes' were carried to Portugal.[78] The Portuguese built their first fort on the island of Arguin in 1448,[79] and rebuilt and refurbished it by 1461, the year of Prince Henry's death. A year before the death of Henry the Navigator it was observed that about 'seven to eight hundred slaves were being carried to Portugal annually'.[80] One of the elements of confusion in the history of the slave trade concerns the numbers involved, often differing in accounts of writers on the subject, but these Portuguese accounts about their activities tell us something of the magnitude of the trade. In speaking of the slave trade beginning as a trickle and becoming a flood, there is justification when, from mere hundreds taken away, figures begin to approximate thousands and tens of thousands. The flood did not come until the mid-fifteenth century. Although the enslavement of Africans began by forcible removal by the Portuguese, there were three stages in this modern Euro-African connection. Kidnapping yielded place to warlike alliances of the kind employed by Hawkins with the kings of 'Castros' and 'Sierra Leone' against the rival kings of Zacina and Zetecama during his third slave-trading voyage to the west coast.[81] Other alliances were used by the Portuguese. But the final stage which eventually prevailed was that of peaceful partnership. Peaceful partnership became the norm in spite of the continuation of occasional kidnapping, which never ceased, but open kidnapping was frowned upon by African potentates and middlemen, who jealously guarded their own role as middlemen.

Clearly, what we have observed so far is that the slave trade began violently, yielding place to a period of warlike alliances between African kings and Europeans, which meant the persistence of violence. Even the peaceful partnership and bargaining which ultimately triumphed was not smooth sailing, for occasionally the old methods re-emerged, and in spite of the prevalence on the west coast of 'respectable' or recognised purchasing groups, representing companies, individuals and royalty, trading activities were sometimes disturbed by pirates and interlopers. Interlopers, as has been observed earlier, were not pirates. Pirates constituted a different breed of operators and they often represented a threat to interlopers and companies alike. There is, for instance, a recorded incident of a confrontation in West African waters between the British government and pirates in the eighteenth century. Twice pirates captured the fort on Bence Island – in 1719 (Davis and Cocklyn) and again in 1720 (Bartholomew Roberts). Even after the capture, according to their own accounts, they found friends in the neighbourhood, these friends being pirates as well. Finally, however, the British government despatched warships against them. Most of the pirates were killed fighting, while many of those captured were executed in 1722 at Cape Coast.[82] Furthermore, around the Sierra Leone river about thirty Englishmen had settled as traders, but part of their lives had been spent in privateering, buccaneering or piracy and they were still reputed to retain the 'love for rioting and humour'. Their relationship with the coastal Africans was regarded as 'friendly' and they had servants among Africans of both sexes, who were reputed to be faithful and obedient to them. Moreover, the women of those parts were prepared to prostitute themselves to whomsoever their European masters wished.[83] But once the system of peaceful partnership was installed, neither seizure by Europeans of Africans nor warlike alliances were any longer legitimate, though both seem to have lasted throughout the slave trade era.

The procurement of weapons, guns and powder enabled the middlemen to organise their own band of retainers effectively and embark on the necessary raids for the capture of slaves. The introduction of these firearms provoked warfare between one African community and another, though we are warned by Walter Rodney not to attach undue emphasis to it. He demonstrates with vital quotations from European sources how it was neither in the interest, nor the intention, of the Europeans to aid the middlemen to become self-sufficient and independently minded, as this might undermine the initiative which the Europeans had made in the conduct of the trade. He reminds us that firearms came late in the slave trade, and when they did come they were often introduced either by interlopers and privateers or by rival European nations (notably the English, Dutch and French) who desired to outflank their European rivals by ingratiating themselves with the local people.[84]

From this we can see the entire relationship that was forged in time between Europeans on the one hand and Africans with mulatto middlemen on the African coast on the other, became more complex. What essentially reigned was confusion, but it proceeded by its own idiosyncrasies and the slave trade advanced. The relationships between the outsiders and insiders were not always harmonious and the records are full of complaints by both sides. Yet it is at this point that we must examine to what extent Africans contributed to their own dispersion. But before we consider this, it is necessary to observe that the Portuguese continued to send slaves to Europe and to some of the plantations they were establishing on islands along the west coast of Africa. Such plantations were to be found in Arguin, St Thomas (São Tomé) and, at a later stage, in Principé. The Portuguese pressed their advantage and reached the Gold Coast in 1481 under Diogo d'Azambuja, the man who, by display of force, by plea and cajolery, persuaded a Gold Coast potentate, Kwame Ansa, to permit the Portuguese to erect a fort, and here was erected on the African mainland the first fort, that of St George at Elmina, the name given to the place by the Portuguese because of their expectations of finding the source of gold. Four years after this the Portuguese king assumed the title of 'Lord of Guinea'.[85] The series of Papal Bulls, which were issued in the years in which the Portuguese claimed monopoly of the Guinea trade, were designed to bolster up this exclusive claim. Attempts to contest it by the French, English and Spanish were abandoned in due deference to the Pope, although they later reversed their policy. But the Papal Bull of 1493, which has already been mentioned, and its augmentation by the Treaty of Tordesillas, clearly apportioned to the rival Portuguese and Spanish their respective spheres.

The Spanish themselves, who began to establish their colonies in the Americas after the discovery of minerals, now needed labour for their mines. They had first used the Amerindians, but had been so severe in their ill-usage that the Amerindians had died like flies. Thus they began to be preoccupied with an alternative source of supply of labour. Soon they turned their attention to Africa. But not until 1513 did the Spanish consider the issue of licences for the importation of Africans into their colonies, the issuing of licences being considered as a source of profit for the Spanish government. Yet, in 1502, the first Africans were taken from Europe and transferred to the island of Hispaniola, and with that began the substantial transfer of men of African origin across the sea to the west. Later the transfer was to be made directly from Africa.

The transfer of people from Africa to metropolitan Portugal, which had begun in the 1440s, contributed to the growth of people of African origin in some of the cities of Latin Europe, notably those of Portugal, Spain and Italy. It has implications for those societies, as has been observed elsewhere.[86] African blood intermingled with that of the Latin people and was to be identified even with royalty. This strain of colour was observed in the Medici family, especially Alessandre Medici, the coloured duke of Florence, whose father was said to be the Pope. It extended to Albania, Austria and Italy. The transfer of Africans to Latin Europe belongs to another aspect of the study of the African diaspora, which has yet to be undertaken *in extenso*. But without wishing to divert attention, the transfer established Lisbon as a slave market and it is no surprise that in the sixteenth century the Pope approved of the slave market in Lisbon, granting the Portuguese the right to enslave 'infidels', and in 1537 about 10 000–12 000 African slaves were brought to the city for transhipment across the Atlantic to the New World.[87]

A book well worth reading concerning the Christian Church's participations in the slave trade is *Christianity, Slavery and Labour* (London, 1931) by Chapman Cohen. Among some of the Popes who approved the slave trade were Popes Martin V, Nicholas V and Innocent VIII, who even accepted a hundred Moors in 1488 from Ferdinand of Spain. Yet the following Popes, Pius II (fifteenth century), Paul III (sixteenth century), Urban VIII (seventeenth century) and Benedict XIV (eighteenth century) protested against the slave trade – but to no avail.[88] Other Christian denominations engaged in enslaving the African but this does not concern us here. What gave rise to the transatlantic transfer and the diversion from Europe of African importation was the establishment of colonies – the Spanish colonies of the Indies and the Portuguese colony of Brazil. The establishment of other colonies in the seventeenth century by other Europeans, and the cultivation of staple crops of sugar, tobacco and cotton, were to give a boost to the slave trade. But initially the slaves were required to augment the rapidly diminishing Amerindians, who had been decimated by mishandling. In the early stages before this appeal was made to the Spanish monarch, slaves continued to be imported to Hispaniola. The glutting of the island with African slaves led to a temporary stoppage. But it must be remembered that the first slaves introduced into the New World were obtained from the European markets of Latin Europe. Not until pleas came from the Indies by religious prelates were they imported directly from Africa. Elizabeth Donnan writes, 'Much has been made of the fact that Las Casas requested that importation [of Africans] be encouraged, but he was but one of several petitioners. The Jeronomite Fathers also were requesting it, the difference being only that Las Casas asked for Spanish or Christian negroes, while Jeronomites recommended that "bozal" negroes (or those direct from Africa) be used.'[89]

Thus, from 1518, the importation was again in progress and Africans were being transferred directly to the New World.[90] The Portuguese, who themselves were vested with the task of conveying the slaves to the Spanish Indies, and cashed in on the earlier contracts or *Asientos*, explored the Guinea coast and beyond the Cape of Good Hope into East African waters. But, in spite of Portuguese claims to the overlordship of Guinea, they had very little contact with the majority of the people, only through intermediaries – often Portuguese priests – who attempted to plant Christianity on the west coast, but who failed dismally. Nevertheless, in extending its activities to the Kongo and Angola, Portugal began to draw labour for its sugar plantations in nearby São Tomé. An anonymous Portuguese pilot visiting the island in 1520 found some planters owning as many as 300 slaves.[91] Portugal continued to be dominant in the Guinea trade until about the end of the sixteenth century. The great traffic in slaves by the Portuguese from the Old Kongo kingdom (including modern Angola) had been noted by a Portuguese, Edward Lopes, in 1578. Furthermore, Master Thomas Turner, an English resident in Brazil on a visit to Angola, also observed that Angola was shipping out about 28 000 slaves annually.[92] This figure might seem an exaggeration, but how can one ascertain the contrary? We have no means even of denying it. But what emerges from this account is that the procurement of slaves resulted from internal upheavals. These upheavals have been given different interpretations and need not concern us here. But European rivals in the late-sixteenth century, and even more so in the seventeenth century, successfully challenged Portuguese claims to monopoly of the Guinea trade. The challengers included the Dutch, English and French.[93] The order of their arrival is not important. What is important is that in the seventeenth century, and from very early in that century, they constituted strong challengers of the Portuguese and were to alter the power balance in the West African Coast area, establishing fortifications in the pursuit of the trade, fortifications which periodically changed hands or became targets for one or other of their European assailants.

When C. L. R. James touched on the history of the slave trade in *Black Jacobins* (1939)[94] some might have thought that he had been highly sensational, especially in citing the evidence of Professor Emile Torday, a Hungarian once in the service of Belgium, who visited the Congo. The lines in *Black Jacobins* read as follows:

The slavers scoured the coast of Guinea. As they devastated an area they moved westward and then south, decade after decade, past the Niger, down the Congo coast, past Loango and Angola, round the Cape of Good Hope, and by 1789, even as far as Mozambique on the eastern side of Africa. Guinea remained their chief hunting ground. . . . They set the simple tribesmen fighting against each other with modern weapons over thousands of square miles. The propagandists of the time claimed that however cruel was the slave traffic, the African slave in America was happier than in his own African civilisation. Ours, too, is an age of propaganda. We excel our ancestors only in system and organisation; they lied as fluently and as brazenly . . . . It was on a peasantry, in many respects superior to the serfs in large areas of Europe, that the slave trade fell. Tribal life was broken up and millions of detribalised Africans were let loose upon each other . . . . Tribes had to supply slaves or be sold as slaves themselves. Violence and ferocity became the necessities for survival, and violence and ferocity survived.[95]

John Barbot, in his *Description of Guinea*, asserts again that those sold by blacks were for the most part prisoners of war,[96] or taken in fights or pursuit, or in the incursions made by some on their enemies' territories. Others were stolen by their own countrymen and there were others who would sell their own children, kindred or neighbours. Those abducted were sold away notwithstanding their protestations that they were not originally slaves. There was one recorded incident in the 1680s when a son sold his father and was returning home with the goods he had received; others captured him, took away his acquisitions, and ordered him to be sold as a slave as well. The kings, Barbot observed, were 'absolute' and faked offences against their subjects in order to sell them. Little children of both sexes (like Vassa, already mentioned) were stolen away from their parents by neighbours, or when found on the road or in the woods or farms. But some of the middlemen purchased some of their slaves from the interior in order to sell on the coast. Such slaves travelled long distances to reach the coastal market and often were ill-treated on the way by flogging, so that at the time of their arrival on the coast many were weak. This, in a nutshell, was the way in which the slave trade proceeded. The complexity of the system has been described by others in numerous pages and it would be superfluous to repeat them here.[97] The attendant cruelty is far from being an exaggeration, and, in fact, the records are more sordid than has been portrayed by C. L. R. James. Kidnapping became a full-time employment.

The African contribution to dispersion

Having considered the development of the slave trade without going into the details of its conduct, we need to consider the question of African participation. We have already quoted authors who have tended to write carelessly of African contributions to their own dispersion through the slave trade. The aim here is to introduce a corrective, since African participation requires some qualification. The points that surface concern those who traded in slaves and the client potentates. The dual role or duplicity of mulattos, who were often by sentiment more European than African, and the intellectual aspect of the African contribution, together with the perversion of African political and social institutions to serve the ends of commerce and the general role of the silent majority, all these points are examined. Until account has been taken of these essential features the role of Africans cannot be properly assessed.

John Barbot, who was an agent of the French Royal African Company in the second half of the seventeenth century, observed that the slave trade was 'the business of kings, rich men and prime merchants'.[98] This statement is crucial to an understanding of the Euro-African connection, and, as Davidson tells us, 'within its "tribal-feudal" context, the slave trade became inseparable from the workings of chiefly rule. Wherever the trade found strong chiefs and kings, it prospered almost from the first; wherever it failed to find them, it caused them to come into being'.[99] Curtin himself has observed that the system functioned where the organised perpetrated depredations on the less organised – the implication is the same.[100] The records are replete with kings and merchants on the Gold Coast who participated in the trade, and they could form the subject of another major study. Among rich merchants various names have been mentioned; among mulattos, John Kabes and Edward Barter stand out, though there were many more. These were the men who welcomed the slave traders from Europe, consulted with them or sent their chief men or Caboceers (from the Portuguese *cabocero*) to discuss the terms of trade; they entertained the slave traders and also laid the rules as to which slaves should be bought first, as well as the preconditions of trade. They received the gifts that were a prerequisite for the opening of trade. They approved the dwelling of Europeans among Africans and sanctioned the allocation of land for building fortifications, factories and barracoons. The granting of land, on which the Europeans erected their settlements, forts and factories, and from which they carried out their activities, by African potentates and kings, constituted part of the African potentate contribution to their own dispersion.

Castles emerged all along the Guinea Coast all the way to Angola. It was, of course, due to the collaboration of the ruling class.[101] Furthermore, they provided protection for the European traders as part of their obligations in cases of misunderstanding with the king's subjects. They also developed the appetite for exotic goods which became, early on, necessary trade goods imported by Europeans for their use and display of false affluence. They were to ask for the necessary weapons for the capture of slaves, and it was they who developed appetites for intoxicants. Though these things might have been imported by Europeans in the first place, we find that African potentates developed a taste for them. It was the potentates and rich merchants who organised their bands of retainers for conducting slave raids into the interior. While the Portuguese in the beginning would have preferred to limit the importation of arms even to the coastal traders, Africans on the coast, by the acquisition of the weapons, also developed a vested interest and did not want any benefits accruing to them from the slave trade to filter through to the interior peoples. These, for instance, became factors in the Asante–Fante conflicts. A point in the rivalry between the Fante potentates and the Asante kings was the desire of the latter to have direct access to the coastal trade with the Europeans.[102] It was by no means the only factor in the contest, but it was a very important one. One of the accusations which the kings of Asante levelled against the Fante middlemen was that they adulterated pure gold[103] by combining it with other base metals and sold it to the Europeans, thus giving the Asante a reputation for dishonesty. A desire for direct trade with the Europeans was expressed many times by the Asante.

But this was not all. It was the kings, who, in a desire to stand high in the Euro-African connection, changed their political system from being democratic in nature to become an instrument for autocratic control.[104] Once they acquired firearms and could disburse patronage their callousness came to match the cupidity of the Europeans. It was they who, in the long run, converted African societies from being societies of rulers and commoners into those of dictators, freemen and slaves. On quite a number of occasions it was ruling potentates or claimants for the kingship or chiefship who called in European assistance to secure them in their positions as kings. Once this was done it meant the acceptance of interference in their internal affairs. The story can be repeated from the Upper Guinea Coast through the Gold Coast and on to the Old Kongo kingdom from Angola and beyond, even on to East Africa. By so doing they weakened their position, and at times were removed by the Europeans and a more amenable African installed as ruler in their place.

The ruling class constituted the chief traders. The typical king, as Walter Rodney argued, was not a dictator but simply *primus inter pares* as far as other nobles were concerned.[105] But the king could not act on his own against his subjects or any of the nobles without support. The coming of the slave trade altered this mode of conduct and both kings and nobles acquired the means of terrorising their subjects. While Europeans treated with Africans through the ruling class, it was not the rulers but the commoners who suffered from the partnership forged between their rulers and the Europeans. Since this partnership was forged between the kings, rich men and prime merchants with European slavers, the relationship by which the ruling class protected itself, while serving the European exploitation of the commoners, is seen as a 'proto-colonial' relationship in which the European accumulated wealth while the African potentates appeared to exercise control in the area.[106]

One cannot discuss the participation of African kings and prime merchants without some reference to alcoholic beverages. Although Walter Rodney has contended that to consider alcohol as having a degenerative effect on the African population in terms of the quantity exported is misleading, and that only after the demise of the slave trade was alcohol brought into Africa in large quantities, one must not, however, ignore the fact that in the slave-trading days the importation of alcohol, even though in small quantities, certainly whetted the appetites of coastal merchants and potentates, and the fact that such alcohol continued to be received as articles of trade from Europeans reveals its desirability as far as they were concerned.[107] The appetite grew on what it fed, and so the importation of larger quantities at the conclusion of the slave trade era would be consistent with that growing appetite for the exotic which the potentates and their forefathers had cultivated in an earlier period. True, the clamour for the ban on liquor was to reverberate throughout West Africa and the world from the mid-nineteenth century. The records are replete with the pleas for a ban, whether it be by Africans or by Aborigines Rights' Protection Societies in Europe or other Temperance Societies in the U.S.A., the West Indies and Europe. In fact one of the revelations made about the American Colonisation Society, which served as a blot on its activities and professions of 'divine providence', was that it had exported a substantial quantity of liquor to Liberia.[108] Depravity there must have been in some quarters,[109] but the subject needs further research, and considering the records of these times it is difficult to see that any useful information to warrant a conclusion would result. But the accounts of slave captains who wined and dined with African kings could be illuminating.

Potentates and kings who resisted

Not all African kings accepted the slave trade, although the vast majority entered into it. There were still some honourable ones. Among them were the Mani-Kongo, Nzinga Mbemba of the Kongo kingdom, baptised by the Portuguese as Dom Affonso I. Close to him was Nzinga Mbande, the queen of the Matamba (in what is modern Angola), baptised by the Portuguese as Donna Anna de Sousa. Then there was Agaja Trudo Adote of Dahomey[110] and also a Wollof king of Cayor. Although these attempts to resist failed, the case of Dom Affonso.I, as the records reveal, is one of the most unfortunate cases of Portuguese double-dealing and insincerity. The alliance which the king of the Kongo had entered into with the Portuguese early in his reign proved illusory. The Portuguese were after gold and slaves and used all sorts of subterfuges to undermine the king. Nzinga Mbemba showed a desire in his letters[111] to his 'brother' the king of Portugal, for know-how, requesting technical aid and medical staff, consisting of physicians, surgeons, apothecaries and also educationists. He also asked that he be given a ship. But the Portuguese were too preoccupied with the slave trade and the greed of gain. Having observed the consequences of the slave trade upon his territory, the king in 1526 made a bold effort to put a stop to the slave trade which had begun in his kingdom thirty years previously, 'almost imperceptibly' as Davidson reminds us. The king attempted to control, then reduce, and finally halt the slave trade. He wrote of the harm which the slave trade was doing to his country. He wrote, 'We cannot reckon how great the damage is, since the above-mentioned merchants daily seize our subjects, sons of the land and sons of our noblemen and vassals and our relatives . . . . Thieves and men of evil conscience take them because they wish to possess the things and wares of this kingdom . . . . They grab them and cause them to be sold: and so great, Sir, is their corruption and licentiousness that our country is being utterly depopulated.'[112] While pleading with the king of Portugal not to countenance such malpractices, he pleaded for no other than priests and teachers, together with some wine and flour for the holy sacrament. He neither wanted merchants nor wares because, as he said, 'It is our will that in these kingdoms [of Kongo] there should not be any trade in slaves nor markets for slaves.'[113]

Observing the whole episode of Portuguese perfidy in its relations with the kingdom of the Kongo, Davidson remarks that the case was typical. Although these attempts to resist failed, yet Dom Affonso's failure to achieve a reversal of Portuguese policy or to evoke a response from the Portuguese king centred on the fact that the slave trade by the Portuguese was a royal monopoly. In desperation the king ultimately called his subjects to take up arms against the Portuguese and defend their land, but that was after the Portuguese intrigues had interfered with the stability of his kingdom. They had induced the Ngola – that is, the vassal ruler of the territory of Ndongo, which the Portuguese mistakenly called Angola from the name of the ruler – to throw off his vassalage. In the confrontation the Portuguese defeated the Kongolese army and the Mani-Kongo was killed (1543). Instability had been induced and was to plague the territory in succeeding centuries[114] till its ultimate collapse. Here was a kingdom in which, as Professor Birmingham has said, the Portuguese had used the 'euphemism of redemption' for the enslavement of Africans.[115]

We now turn to Queen Nzinga Mbande, described as 'the unconquerable'.[116] 'Unconquerable' is an apt expression for this woman with an indomitable spirit, for all through her life in which she resisted Portuguese encroachment on her land and the efforts to undermine her authority by the substitution of a puppet, she employed a combination of diplomacy and war to exclude the Portuguese from Ndongo (i.e. Angola). While she was not success-ful in expelling them she nevertheless ensured that their fortunes were at a low ebb during her lifetime. The Portuguese in their efforts to undermine her used intrigue by supporting rival claimants against her. Only after her death in 1663 at the ripe age of eighty-one years did they become more hopeful of gaining ascendancy over the territory. But in the period of confrontation, rather than succumb to Portuguese domination, she moved her territory inland in an easterly direction, while the other part of the kingdom of Ndongo, which had hived off, remained allied to the Portuguese. She made her kingdom of Matamba so strong that it remained impregnable to Portuguese machinations and so staved off their influence in her kingdom. Her temporary alliance with the Dutch (who were also hunting for slaves) was made with a view to dislodging the Por-tuguese and she manifested a desire to sell to the Dutch some of the prisoners of war whom she had captured in her campaigns. But she aimed ultimately at ridding her country of both the Portuguese and Dutch presence and terminating the slave trade. Thus, the complete abstention from slave trading could not be avoided as it became a necessary adjunct to survival, not for economic reasons but out of sheer necessity to achieve the ultimate objective of re-establishing her sovereignty over Ndongo and reuniting her split kingdom. As Birmingham has aptly stated, the queen 'realised the advantages of the Dutch presence in Luanda and began to use them to her own commercial and political benefit. . . . The Dutch had come to Angola exclusively to obtain slaves. They expected to find an export trade of up to 16 000 slaves per annum. Their negotiations with the African states to obtain slaves were similar to those of their Por-tuguese predecessors. Queen Nzinga was especially anxious to sell them any prisoners of war whom she could capture.... Apart from the raids and skirmishes conducted mainly for commercial purposes, there was a more fundamental war going on in Angola which led to several major campaigns. This was the war between Nzinga and the Dutch on the one side and Ngola Ari (her rival and Portuguese protégé) and the Portuguese on the other.'[117]

The Portuguese, however, became aware that their success in keeping Nzinga at bay had been due to the help they had received from Ngola Ari and that once she ceased to threaten his right to the throne of Ndongo he would throw off his alliance with them and would cease to support their campaigns.[118] Thus, because of internal dissensions often induced by outsiders (Portuguese and Dutch), the entire territory was kept in a state of ferment, and with the wars came slaves which were sold to Europeans, but the slaves which Nzinga would have despatched were prisoners of war, whom she would have categorised as disloyal subjects, rebels or potential dangers to her regime. We see here that there were extenuating circumstances, but the slave trade was too strong and the Portuguese traders were so determined as to brook no opposition or consider a total ban on it. It must also not be forgotten that one of the factors which earlier on won Nzinga Mbande her support was the intense pressure imposed on Mbundu potentates forcibly brought under the domination of the Portuguese forts. This factor drove them into eastern Ndongo to link their forces with those of Queen Nzinga in active opposition to the Portuguese.[119] It enabled her to build up her forces against the Portuguese by sheltering runaway slaves from Luanda. The Portuguese, feeling powerless, unsuccessfully tried diplomacy with the queen; later they resorted to their usual subterfuge of supporting a candidate closer to Nzinga's domain; and so they dug up Ari Kiluanji, a chief of the rock enclosures of Pungu a Ndongo. But she declared war on Ari Kiluanji, which prompted him to seek Portuguese assistance. Although the Portuguese drove out Nzinga from Kwanza Island, the death of Ari Kiluanji led them to impose another Ngola in Ndongo, whom they baptised as Dom Filippe.

The complexities of the confrontations do not concern us here. What is essentially important was that Queen Nzinga's confrontations with the Portuguese in the 1650s imposed severe restraints on the supply of slaves to the Portuguese and, as David Birmingham has observed in his excellent narrative, this inadequacy demonstrated 'that it was almost impossible to conduct the trade satisfactorily without the partnership of one, and preferably more than one, powerful African state'. He points out that one of the main reasons for the sluggishness of business was probably the withdrawal into the interior of Queen Nzinga, who had failed in her ambition to recapture Ndongo and to dominate the entire Mbundu country, while ousting the Portuguese and establishing the Dutch as the major commercial power in Angola. She retreated into Matamba from Dande and remained silent for several years.[120] Her relentless war against the Portuguese from her accession in the 1620s till her death in the 1660s merely demonstrated that the onslaught of outsiders, and slave traders at that, was really determined.

The same experiences which Queen Nzinga had in Mbundu country in modern Angola in the seventeenth century were to be parallelled by another West African king, Agaja Trudo of Dahomey, in the eighteenth century. His efforts to put a stop to the slave trade were frustrated by a combination of factors. Agaja, who had extended the territory of Dahomey by the capture of Whydah, was a unifier of the kingdom, which was to be continued by his successors. Agaja's initial opposition to the slave trade and his warning to the British, telling them of the havoc that the slave trade was doing to his country, in spite of his expedition to capture Adrah (Allada) and other slave-dealing centres on the coast, like Whydah in the 1730s, revealed that the pull of the slave trade was too formidable to ignore.[121] A curious combination of factors led him and Dahomey to succumb to the slave trade, but the most important factor was that of the security of Dahomey, which was a vassal state of the Oyo empire with its humiliating demand for tribute. In order to extricate himself completely from Oyo it became necessary to secure the weapons to maintain that sovereignty against Oyo incursions. But the suppliers of the weapons were European slave traders on the coast, and in the long term Agaja of Dahomey succumbed to the temptations of the slave trade in order to ensure the independence of his kingdom from Oyo rule. It paid off. He then found it necessary to make forages into the interior parts of the Oyo empire to procure slaves for the exchange of weapons. Here was the tragedy of the African rulers. The international combination pressurising Dahomey from the outside left him with no alternative but to militarise the state at the high cost of slave trading.[122]

The last of our resisters among the African potentates was a Bagga chief of Cayor, named Tomba, but unlike the others he eventually succumbed and the Europeans were thus enabled to treat with amenable potentates, who themselves came to assume vested interests in the prosecution of the slave trade.[123]

Intellectual and mystical aspects of the African contribution

There is another aspect to the refusal of African potentates to sanction the quartering of Europeans on African soil with a view to perpetrating depredations on Africans. It is a case in which an attempt at diplomacy failed to produce the desired effect on the insistent European demand for the right of settlement and which, in the long term, proved disastrous to Africans. The case of Kwame Ansa, a Gold Coast king of the fifteenth century, and his encounter with the Portuguese demonstrates another case of Portuguese bad faith once it was poised on its scheme of exploiting Africans. It is essential to record the incident here merely because those who emphasised the role of African kings in the slave trade tend to think of them as unlettered and universally foolish, but the case of Kwame Ansa tells us a different story. After the Portuguese had initiated trade with the Gold Coast in the fifteenth century they sought gold with great enthusiasm. But soon they were also preoccupied with slaves and the capture of slaves. In December 1481 a Portuguese, Captain Diogo d'Azambuja, distinguished as a knight in the royal household, set out for Guinea equipped with timber, hewn stone, lime tiles, bricks, tools, nails, munitions and provisions. He carried with him a hundred craftsmen, including masons, and five hundred soldiers. Elmina at this time consisted of two townships — east of the river Benya was under the rule of the state of Fetu, and west of it was under the control of the Commanis or Kommendas. On arrival at Elmina the captain sought an audience with King Kwame Ansa in order to lay before him Portuguese plans. When the king and his entourage arrived the next morning Diogo d'Azambuja seated himself on an imperial chair on the beach of Elmina after hoisting the Portuguese flag and then mooted the idea for the erection of a fort. Using veiled and direct threats, cajolery and later bribes, he tried to gain his objective. The contact which had begun hitherto as equals between the Portuguese and African potentates was about to be tilted against the African kings. But the letter of Kwame Ansa, who would normally be regarded as an 'unlettered native', speaks volumes.[124] It is fitting to quote it *in extenso*:

> I am not insensible to the high honour which your great master the Chief of Portugal has this day conferred upon me. His friendship I have always endeavoured to merit by the strictness of my dealings with the Portuguese, and by my constant exertions to procure an immediate lading for the vessels. But never until this day did I observe such a difference in the appearance of his subjects; they have hitherto been meanly attired, were easily contented with the commodities they received; and so far from wishing to continue in this country, were never happy until they could complete their lading, and return. Now I remark a strange difference. A great number richly dressed are anxious to be allowed to build houses, and to continue among us. Men of such eminence, conducted by a

commander who from his own account seems to have descended from the God who made day and night, can never bring themselves to endure the hardships of this climate; nor would they here be able to procure any of the luxuries that abound in their own country. The passions that are common to us all men will therefore inevitably bring on disputes; and it is far preferable that both our nations should continue on the same footing they have hitherto done, allowing your ships to come and go as usual; the desire of seeing each other occasionally will preserve peace between us. The Sea and Land being always neighbours are continually at variance, and contending who shall give way; the Sea with great violence attempting to subdue the Land, and the Land with equal obstinacy resolving to oppose the sea.[125]

By the use of all the pressures which he could muster, Diogo d'Azambuja succeeded in obtaining a foothold at Elmina, where the Portuguese built their first fort on the mainland of Africa. He remained as governor of the castle for two-and-a-half years, and at the time of his departure in 1848 a cynic credited him with having left a 'gallows and a pillory at the castle'.[126] What happened was that Portuguese threats had paid dividends and the fast erection of the castle forestalled any machinations of Kwame Ansa. Here was an indirect way in which the Portuguese succeeded in enlisting the support of an African potentate to serve their ends. The possible consequences were reflected in Kwame Ansa's speech, but the long-term implications at the time were not apparent, for he could neither know the motives nor the intentions of the newcomers.

While this potentate might have attempted by the language of diplomacy to forestall the intentions of Europeans who were to plague the coast with slave trading, there were others among Africans, not initially of kingly status, who became the protégés of slave traders and active defenders of the slave trade. Some of these children of coastal Africans were sent overseas for some training and returned to the Gold Coast. Among them were Philip Quaque, Anton Wilhelm Amo and Jacobus Elisa Capitein.[127] Of the three the last was the only advocate of slavery. Some of the Africans had been brought to Europe as protégés of European slave traders who sent them to school and they became educated in France, Holland, Britain and Germany. Philip Quaque became a chaplain on his return to the Gold Coast. William Amo was taken to Europe in 1707 at the age of four and distinguished himself as a scholar in a German university. He wrote a learned treatise on logic, psychology and history. He also became a counsellor of state. But the African who gave comfort to the slave traders and the protagonists of slavery was a young man who at the age of twelve had been sold to a ship's captain who, in turn, sold him to a Dutch merchant in

Holland. He became educated and studied theology at the University of Leyden at the age of twenty, in 1737. He was baptised as Jacobus Elisa Johannes Capitein. He defended his doctoral thesis, in which he argued that slavery was consistent with Christianity, in 1742. The dissertation appeared in several Latin and Dutch editions which apologists of slavery used to uphold the enslavement of Africans. Later that year he assumed his duties as chaplain to Elmina Castle on the Gold Coast; his career was short-lived, however, for he died at the age of thirty on 1 February 1747, having been disregarded by the Europeans at Elmina because of his colour and previous condition of servitude, and by his own people because of his attitude to slavery. These two citations are examples of the intellectual African contribution to their own dispersion. The thesis of Capitein might have helped to cheer European advocates and participants of the slave trade. William Amo, by contrast, identified himself as an African and defended African values, and the writings of two other ex-slaves of West African origin[128] later in the same century, Ottobah Cugoano and Olaudah Equiano, showed that there were other Africans who intellectually loathed the slave trade.[129]

Another aspect of the African contribution which may be linked up with the intellectual aspect relates to the realm of metaphysics or mysticism. It revealed how African trading communities as well as rulers perverted African social institutions in order to accommodate the slave trade. African political and social institutions were bent to accommodate the demand of Europeans for slaves. Hence societies, which hitherto were democratic, soon became oligarchic and later dictatorial. From the moment they accepted the slave trade, rulers perverted the political systems, framing people on the flimsiest of pretexts; some of those who found their way into slave ships bound for the Americas were those categorised as 'criminals' – many were actual offenders but many more were just victims of chicanery. The most telling example is that of the notorious Aro Chukwu Oracle,[130] known to the British as 'Long Juju'. The people of Aro, Umu Chukwu, were regarded as the Children of God (*Les Enfants du Paradis*) by their neighbours and they had evolved a system of oracular consultation in order to propitiate the gods. (One is reminded of Delphi, the religious capital of ancient Greece, and its oracle.) The use of the Aro Oracle to play on people's religious credulity and susceptibilities, and thereby further the slave trade, is another example of that perversion. The system continued, using the tunnel of Bonny to transfer people to the slave ship while pretending to their relatives that God had claimed his victims. The story of the oracle has been told by Professor Dike and needs no recounting here. What is important is that such a structural arrangement devised by Africans to serve a different purpose later, because of the corrupting influence of the slave trade, became perverted to accommodate and promote the slave trade. The oracle continued in existence until it was destroyed by the British in 1900.

The ascendancy of mulatto middlemen

One must not forget again that the Atlantic slave trade threw up the middlemen on the West African coast and although, initially, they consisted of kings and their subordinate princes, later on they included upstarts who had achieved some prestige through trading. In time there was to arise in the seventeenth century, and probably much earlier, a group of Afro-Portuguese or mulatto middlemen. A boost to slave catching in the interior and the slave trade in general was given as a result of the rise of this class of people. They spanned the entire Guinea Coast and became factors to be reckoned with. Walter Rodney, in his excellent book on the history of the Upper Guinea Coast, devotes a whole chapter to the ascendancy of these mulatto middlemen,[131] and it would be pointless to repeat this here. These mulattos were the progeny of one African parent (usually an African woman) and a Portuguese slave trader or factor on the coast. As other Europeans came to the coast this process of hybridisation continued. Out of these there evolved a language for the conduct of the slave trade described as 'Creole-Portuguese'.[132] The Afro-Portuguese fulfilled their functions as middlemen on the coast by acting as pilots on the rivers and serving as commercial advisers to local potentates and rulers, as well as interpreters and sometimes factors and brokers for European traders. Many are the names noted in the records. There were in the Upper Guinea region names as prominent as those of Antonio Duarte from the Casamance, Manuel de Andrade of Farim, and many from Cacheu, including Senhor Lopes, Ambrosio Vaz, Santos de Vidigal Castonho, Manuel de Sousa Mendoca, Senhora Bibiana Vaz,[133] and many more. They were especially prominent in the seventeenth century. In Sierra Leone there were names which have survived into the twentieth century. Among them were Tucker, Rogers and Caulker.[134] Many of them became mulatto chiefs during the second half of the eighteenth century. The Gold Coast also saw a proliferation of mulattos, beginning with a few in the seventeenth century, among whom were Edward Barter and John Kabes. The former was connected with the English African Company and the latter became a broker from whom the British and the Dutch sought services. Kabes was an example of a coastal African who switched allegiances from one European group to another. When he abandoned trading with the Dutch in the 1680s he invited the British to Komenda in 1695, and played off both the English and the Dutch against each other.[135] The mulattos continued to grow in number in West African societies and by the early nineteenth century and into the twentieth century names like James Bannerman, George Kuntu Blankson, Samuel Kantor Brew (described as an 'insolent mulatto' by the English), Samuel Collins Brew, Frank Clealand, Robert Hutchinson, Francis Chapman Grant, John Sarbah, Thomas Hughes, John Smith, and many more, were among the merchant mulatto class which has been identified with the slave trade and which had left its mark on West African society.[136] We are informed that some, like Samuel Brew of Anomabo, Frank Clealand and James Bannerman – both of Accra – were related to traditional authority, either by birth or marriage.[137]

Some of these middlemen by their activities sometimes provoked wars between communities, as happened between the Asante and the Nzima, allegedly provoked by John Konny, another prominent trader and potentate of the Ahanta in the eighteenth century.[138] These mulattos were not just individuals but constituted a powerful group. It was these mulattos who, in the main, ensured that the products of the interior reached the Europeans on the coast; and they also often diverted trade to one or other of their European favourites and even to interlopers when the diversion promised a better return. Among mulatto descendants were names in the nineteenth century such as Curtis, Lightbourne and Wilkinson, based on the Nunez, Konkoure and Pongo. Thus, spanning the centuries from the seventeenth to the nineteenth and into the twentieth, the mulattos continued to be a dominant influence on the coast of West Africa. Although they were of one European parent and one African parent, they suffered from a kind of double-life. They wore European dress, adopted European values and names, and tended to identify with either Europeans or Africans according to circumstances. The Europeans despised them and in some cases referred to them as 'monkeys', and they were not regarded by the early Portuguese or by later-comers as representatives of Portugal or the European world. They were not the true representatives of European values, Europeans did not always trust them, and did not wish to aid them to become capitalists and independent of European influence. Rodney gives us a glimpse of how these Afro-Portuguese middlemen achieved ascendancy in West Africa over African potentates. When with the Europeans they wished to be identified with Europeans; when with Africans they wished to be identified with Africans.[139]

If one is to assess further the contributions of Africans to their own dispersion, an additional qualification emerges, that of the ascendancy of the mulattos. With European women scarce on the west coast, these mulattos formed their associations with African women and their progeny became darker in stock, so that through the passage of time the mulatto stock became darker and darker. By their persistence and dogged determination, as well as skill and diplomacy, they were able to ingratiate themselves with African kings and potentates, using every opening to map out a sphere of influence for themselves till they were powerful enough to dislodge some African potentates,[140] or carve out niches for themselves from which they exercised their influence or defied the potentates. Rodney has ably argued, and as gleaned elsewhere, these mulattos region,[141] but reveals too how through careful and clever manipulation they could not properly be considered as traditional or hereditary rulers – terms still used in reference to African potentates' and prime merchants' participation in the slave trade. For, as Rodney has ably argued, and as gleaned elsewhere, these mulattoes were creatures of the Euro-African trading connection, destined for the role of middlemen, groomed for it sometimes even by being educated abroad in Europe for the purpose of fulfilling this function, and while a few European traders on the coast might have been disenchanted with them or even called them uncomplimentary names, they had been called into existence by the Atlantic trade and had no traditional function in society once deprived of their position.[142] Accordingly, they succeeded in attaining a position of influence in their respective societies from which it was not easy to dislodge them. That they became, as Rodney observed, an 'efficient comprador class of the Upper Guinea Coast in a proto-colonial situation', and while they squeezed Africans to make as many immense personal gains as possible, essentially they served the wider interests of European commercial capitalism.[143] As slave procurers they were able to maintain their link with the interior to ensure a steady supply of slaves. Another factor in their operation (because of their demand for slaves to satisfy the demands of European slave traders) was the provoking of wars in the interior for the procurement of slaves. A notable feature were the *jihads* (the so-called holy wars of Islam) of the western Sudan in the eighteenth century, which Rodney has cogently argued were not motivated primarily by any religious considerations for the conversion of the 'infidel', but rather were pretexts for the capture of slaves on the Upper Guinea Coast and elsewhere in the interior of West Africa.[144] The *jihads*, far from being acts of piety, were acts of depredation by the powerful class and their clients against their victims, the commoners. Elsewhere, untouched by the *jihads*, the wars were, in fact, wars for the capture of slaves and for feeding the insatiable appetites of the European slave traders who, in turn, had to satisfy the greed of the plantation owners in the Americas. The spread of firearms through middlemen and their retainers also provoked incidents which led to the further supply of slaves.

In all this the commoners and the vast majority of the people were the victims and could not be said to have participated. They were the victims on whom the stronger kings, princes and prime merchants let loose their greed for gain, and they suffered in large measure as they constituted the vast numbers who were carried away during the slaving centuries, for them and their descendants to become the Africans of the diaspora. If, therefore, they failed to assert themselves, it was not for want of trying,[145] but because the whole connection was already a conspiracy against them, and it was so overwhelming that they could not even successfully revolt against it. The introduction of firearms, and the use of bands of retainers by the potentates, as well as African collaborators seeking ascendancy over rival claimants,[146] as well as the frequency of surprise attacks at night, consistent with night prowling, hardly gave them any effective means of defending themselves against capture. Once African potentates had accepted what essentially was begun by the prime movers of Europe, once they indicated the willingness to forge the Euro-African partnership, the slave trade was made possible and the dispersion a certainty. Irrespective of his having swallowed Curtin 'hook, line and sinker' in terms of the numbers involved in the slave trade, Professor Hopkins, at least, admits that 'the Atlantic slave trade still remains one of the greatest migrations of all time'.[147] What is missing in this citation is that the migration was forced on the Africans, it was not voluntary. Moreover, contrary to the assertion of one writer on the slave trade (after describing an incident in which Africans around Cape Roxo attacked some Europeans who had attempted to kidnap Africans into slavery), that had Africans acted as a body to reject the trade from the beginning it would have ended just as it had begun,[148] the position was otherwise and was not as easy to overthrow. The observations we have made of the Euro-African connection and the kind of subterfuges grafted on to the system, the intrigues introduced by European interference in African affairs so numerous in the records, and the willingness of some kings and notables to serve as participants, hardly justify such a facile assertion. The slave trade was in progress and with it a massive dispersion of Africans into the western hemisphere.

Notes

1 D. Mannix and M. Cowley, *Black Cargoes*, London, 1963.

2 P. D. Curtin, *The Atlantic Slave Trade: a Census*, Madison, Wis., 1969, is the major work in this field.

3 J. E. Flint, 'Economic change in West Africa', in *History of West Africa*, Vol. 2, J. Ajayi and M. Crowder (eds.), London, 1974. pp. 380–401.

4 J. Pope Hennessy, *Sins of the Fathers*.
5 Fogel and Engerman, *Time on the Cross*, Boston, 1974, and Fogel and Engerman (eds.), *The Re-interpretation of American Economic History*, New York, 1971; A. G. Hopkins, *An Economic History of West Africa*, London, 1973, ch. 3; T. C. Rayan, 'The Economics of Trading in Slaves', Ph.D. thesis, Massachusetts Institute of Technology, 1975.
6 Arnold Sio, 'An Interpretation of Slavery: the slave status in the Americas', in E. D. Genovese and Laura Foner (eds.), *Slavery in the New World: a Reader in Comparative History*, N.J., 1969, pp. 96–112.
7 P. D. Curtin, 'The Atlantic Slave Trade 1600–1800', in *History of West Africa*, Vol. 1, Ajayi and Crowder (eds.), ch. 7, esp. pp. 241–5; Curtin, *The Atlantic slave Trade*, p. 272; B. Quarles, *The Negro in the Making of America*, New York, 1973, p. 21; and R. S. Rattary, *Ashanti Law and Constitution*, London, 1928, p. 33. Both Quarles and Rattary use the expression 'time immemorial'. This of course is mere conjecture as neither of them provides any evidence for their assertions. Much of what they say is conjectural. For instance, Rattary wrote: 'I think slavery possibly existed at a very early date in one or other of the general forms which will be described presently' (p. 32). See also Hopkins, *Economic History*, pp. 82–3; J. D. Fage and R. Oliver, *A Short History of Africa*, Harmondsworth, 1962, pp. 41, 61. No evidence was supplied; rather, these authors assumed the export of slaves to be 'traditional'. See what B. Davidson in *Old Africa Rediscovered*, London, 1968, says. He observed that slaves had existed in the Kongo prior to the arrival of the Europeans and had formed an organic part of the social framework and in it slaves had their clearly defined place, but that after the growth of the Atlantic slave trade the possession of slaves was 'transformed into a savage man-hunt'. Furthermore, Davidson did not say that slavery or the slave trade existed over a wide area of the continent of Africa or formed part of a long-standing tradition.
8 Rodney, *A History of the Upper Guinea Coast, 1545–1800*, Oxford, 1970, pp. 260–1, 263.
9 M. R. Delany, *Report of the Niger Valley Exploring Party 1850–60*, London, 1861, and Robert Campbell, *A Pilgrimage to My Motherland*, London, 1861. Both books are now incorporated into a bound volume entitled *Search for a Place: Black Separatism and Africa*, Ann Arbor, Mich. (paperback), 1971, with an introduction by Howard H. Bell.
10 Mungo Park, *Journal of Travels in the Interior Districts of Africa . . . 1795, 1796, and 1797 . . . 1805*, London, Vol. 1, ch. 22, esp. p. 452.
11 Curtin, 'The Atlantic Slave Trade', in Ajayi and Crowder (eds.), p. 245. Note the conjecture in parenthesis.
12 Rodney, *Upper Guinea Coast*, p. 40.
13 *Ibid.*, p. 260.
14 *Ibid.*, p. 261.
15 *Ibid.*, pp. 261–2.
16 *Ibid.*, p. 262.
17 *Ibid.*, pp. 262–3.
18 *Ibid.*
19 *Ibid.*
20 A Portuguese name for nobles on the west coast of Africa.
21 The term refers to the commoners, see C. R. Boxer, *The Portuguese Seaborne Empire*, pp. 386–91, for an excellent glossary of many terms then in use.

22 *Ibid.*, p. 263.

23 See their works in the bibliography; also n. 7 above.

24 Curtin, 'The Atlantic Slave Trade' in Ajayi and Crowder (eds.), pp. 241–2.

25 *Ibid.*, p. 242.

26 *Ibid.*, p. 243.

27 J. Pope Hennessy, *Sins of the Fathers*, p. 18.

28 Raymond Mauny, *Tableau géographique de l'Ouest Africain au Moyen Age d'après les sources écrites, la tradition et l'archéologie*, IFAN, Dakar, 1961, Mémoires de L'IFAN, No. 61, p. 379.

29 Marian Malowist, 'Le commerce d'or et d'esclaves au Soudan Occidental', in *Africana Bulletin* (Warsaw), iv (1966), pp. 49–72, esp. p. 60.

30 See Alicja Malecka, 'African Studies Symposium in Cracow' in *Africana Bulletin* (Warsaw), vi (1967) pp. 108–13, in which she summarises Tadeusze Lowicki's 'Arab Trade in Negro Slaves up to the End of the XVIth Century: Summary of an Unpublished Paper', esp. pp. 109–11.

31 Davidson, *Old Africa Rediscovered*, p. 120.

32 E. W. Bovill, *Caravans of the Old Sahara*, London, 1933, pp. 257–8. The statement is shortened and slightly modified in his *Golden Trade of the Moors*, Oxford, 2nd edn., 1970, p. 247.

33 Davidson, *Old Africa Rediscovered*, pp. 119–20.

34 *Ibid.*, p. 120. Bovill, who observed that Carthaginian society employed slaves and that archaeological finds from Punic cemeteries revealed numerous skulls of negroid characteristics, testifying to the presence of dark-skinned Africans, says 'to what extent the Carthaginians employed negro slaves is doubtful', *The Golden Trade of the Moors*, p. 21.

35 One such example was M. Perham, *The Colonial Reckoning*, London, 1963.

36 Bovill, *The Golden Trade of the Moors*, p. 22. We see that the citation is based on an assumption rather than fact, but quite easily this conjecture in another context may be quoted as fact and help to reinforce orthodoxy. It is against assertions of this kind that we must guard.

37 Reginald Coupland, *East Africa and Its Invaders*, Oxford, 1938, pp. 17–18.

38 G. S. P. Freeman-Grenville, 'The Coast, 1498–1840', in *History of East Africa*, R. Oliver and G. Matthew (eds.), London, 1963, Vol. I, p. 152.

39 See Olaudah Equiano (Gustavus Vassa), *The Interesting Narrative . . .*, London, 1789, 2 vols.

40 *Ibid.*, Vol. 1, p. 46.

41 In correspondence with Professor G. N. Uzoigwe of the University of Michigan, Ann Arbor, Michigan, Professor Uzoigwe has stated that in his study of Bunyoro Kitara (a former African kingdom in Uganda) he has been unable to identify a word for slave or even the concept within the context of that African kingdom. We must, therefore, be wary in our present state of knowledge to avoid pontificating on so vital a subject. It is, therefore, impolitic to suggest that the scope of the slave trade was already large prior to the European advent on the west coast of Africa. While no evidence exists for this belief there is a greater danger in using the forms of slavery prevalent in the eighteenth to the twentieth centuries heightened by the Atlantic slave trade to infer an African slave past. Mere conjecture is not proof. Also see G. N. Uzoigwe, 'The Slave Trade and African Societies', in *Transactions of the Historical Society of Ghana*, 1973.

42 See contributions, especially that by Nyakatura, in G. N. Uzoigwe (ed.), *Anatomy of an African Kingdom*, New York, 1973.

43 B. Davidson, *Old Africa Rediscovered*, pp. 119–20.

44 A. A. Boahen, *Topics in West African History*, London, 1964, p. 110.

45 Rayner Unwin, *The Defeat of Sir John Hawkins*, London, Allen and Unwin, 1960. Cf. Michael Lewis, *The Hawkins Dynasty: Three Generations of a Tudor Family*, London, pp. 76–80, 88.

46 Pope Hennessy, *Sins of the Fathers*, pp. 182–99, and Davidson, *Old Africa*, n. 43 above and the text cited n. 47 below.

47 Davidson not only castigates Europe for distortion but he cites John Barbot, who revealed that the slave trade on the African side was the 'business of kings, rich men and prime merchants', *Black Mother*, p. 92.

48 These are ubiquitous and so there is no need to mention any one slave captain. A list of their accounts appears in the bibliography.

49 Edmund d'Auvergne, *Human Livestock*, London, Grayson and Grayson, 1933, p. 45.

50 O. Cugoano, *Thoughts and Sentiments on the Evil . . . Traffic of Slavery . . .*, London, 1787, p. 12.

51 Davidson, *Old Africa Rediscovered*, p. 121.

52 *Ibid.*, p. 123.

53 The only exception is Walter Rodney: see *How Britain Underdeveloped Africa*, Dar es Salaam, 1973, pp. 91–2.

54 Pope Hennessy, *Sins of the Fathers*, p. 182. This reference and all hereafter are to the 1970 edition.

55 *Ibid.*, pp. 183–4.

56 *Ibid.*

57 This is an expression of Basil Davidson. Its application has been recognised by writers like J. Pope Hennessy. Peaceful partnership, however, as Rodney has warned, did not mean the activity of hunting slaves inland was peaceful for its victims. See *Upper Guinea Coast*, pp. 252–9.

58 Some examples of conflict situations recounted by Dr Thomas Winterbottom, a physician to Sierra Leone in the eighteenth century, are worthy of note. See his *An Account of Native Africans in the Neighbourhood of Sierra Leone*. London, 1803, Vol. 1, pp. 206ff.

59 H. M. Waddell, *Twenty-nine Years in the West Indies and Central Africa*, London, 1863, 2nd edn., Cass, 1970, pp. 244, 250. According to the report, 'Eyo and his gentlemen did not use their fingers for forks, nor do anything indecorous' (p. 250). On a visit to King Eyamba of Creek Town, the king sat in an armchair inlaid in solid brass under a handsome canopy. Four sofas were wheeled round in front for the company, and a small table placed in the centre for the gift Bible (p. 245).

60 *Memoirs of the late Captain Hugh Crow of Liverpool*, 1st edn., 1830; later edn., London, 1970, p. 273.

61 Davidson, *Black Mother*, p. 240.

62 *Ibid.*, p. 241.

63 Obaro Ikime, *Niger Delta Rivalry*, London, 1969, p. 95.

64 *Ibid.*

65 For 'people' read potentates, House heads, merchant princes and other vested interests; it did not extend to commoners who were the victims of these

depredations. The House system was a complex trading arrangment which developed in the Niger Delta; see K. O. Dike. *Trade and Politics in the Niger Delta*, Oxford, 1956, esp. pp. 34–7.

66 See the statement of Barnave, the French parliamentarian, who observed that 'to relinquish her colonies is therefore to relinquish the naval power of France; in which case the English power will acquire an unrivalled ascendancy in the ocean.' Quoted in E. E. Williams, *From Columbus to Castro: the History of the Caribbean 1492–1969*, London, 1970, p. 241. We see in the quotation a strong objection to abolition of the slave trade. Yet, it was the same Barnave who advised the mulattos not to forget their brother negroes when they acquired their rights of equality with Europeans. It seemed that many of the French actors in the slavery drama at the time the Haitians finally cast off the French yoke always appeared in contradictory roles.

67 Waddell, *Twenty-nine Years*, p. 210, tells of the treaty that had been made with Commander Raymond for abandoning the slave trade. See also his Appendix II, pp. 663–4.

68 *Ibid.*, p. 435, and Appendix IV, p. 667.

69 Private English traders in West Africa were not among the least offenders.

70 Mannix and Cowley, *Black Cargoes*, pp. 227–8.

71 *Memoirs of the Late Captain Hugh Crow of Liverpool*, pp. 158–9, 176–7.

72 The people called themselves 'Nembe' while Europeans referred to them as 'Brass'.

73 *Report of Disturbances in Brass 1895*, Cmd. 7977, Africa No. 3 (1896), chiefs of Brass to C. MacDonald, 14 February 1895. Also see proceedings of the first day, 10 June 1895, evidence of the Brass chiefs. Also in T. L. Hodgkin, *Nigerian Perspectives*, Oxford, 1960, pp. 311–12.

74 In the Gold Coast the mulatto slave traders complained in the early nineteenth century, while continuing the slave trade, that they had not been informed of its abolition. See Norregard, *Danish Settlements in West Africa*, p. 184, quoted in E. Reynolds, *Trade and Economic Change on the Gold Coast*, London and New York, 1974, p. 39.

75 See G. E. Azurara, *Chronicles of the Discovery and Conquest of Guinea*, London, English translation, 1896, Vol. 1, pp. 39–50, esp. 48–50. The capture and abduction of these Africans (Moors) was not attended without the hostility of their brethren. So it cannot be said that Africans accepted the capture of their brethren with equanimity. A reading of Azurara leaves one with no other impression but that the raids on Africans continued but the numbers were still not substantial until it became trade. Some modern historians have tended to put the figure at twelve; an example is to be found in Leslie Rout, Jr., *The African Experience in Spanish America*, p. 7, but this mistaken figure arises from a too rapid reading of Azurara's Chronicles. The initial captives were two – a man and a woman – followed by the capture of ten others indicated as consisting of men, women and boys. The first two were later set ashore, especially as the man spoke Arabic and could play the role of translator. Those two were to proceed to persuade others to come over for bargaining, a stratagem the Portuguese captains hoped would lead to the capture of more Africans, but the plan misfired and the Portuguese, anxious to avoid an ambush, sailed away with the ten captives.

76 Donnan, *Documents Illustrative of the History of the Slave Trade to America*, Vol. 1, pp. 18–41; Azurara, *op. cit.*, Vol. 1, pp. 52–4.

77 Donnan, *Documents*, Vol. 1, p. 5.
78 Quoted from Azurara, *Chronicles of Guinea*, by E. Donnan, *Documents*, Vol. 1, p. 4.
79 See Azurara, Chronicles, Vol. 1, p. 320, n. 75.
80 Donnan, *Documents*, Vol. 1, p. 3. The citation is from G. Azurara's *Chronicles of Guinea*, Vol. II, pp. xxvi–xxvii. See also R. C. Beazley, *Prince Henry the Navigator*, London and New York, 1895, p. 315.
81 Davidson, *Black Mother*, pp. 89–90. Also note the partnership of Dutch and Portuguese dissidents in Angola and Kongo, See Birmingham, *Trade and Conflict in Angola*, pp. 109–22.
82 C. Fyfe, *Sierra Leone Inheritance*, Oxford, 1964, p. 69.
83 *Ibid.* Philip Quaque (Quaco, Kweku), the Gold Coast chaplain at Cape Coast, in a report in 1767 complained of the custom too common among the English on the coast living with African women without marriage, and then discarding them for the flimsiest reasons and taking on others for pleasure. See Attoh Ahuma, *Memoirs of West African Celebrities*, Liverpool, 1905, p. 53.
84 Rodney, *Upper Guinea Coast*, pp. 173–6, 207–8. This reveals that in the second half of the seventeenth century the English Company of the Gambia Adventurers was poised on a policy of not doing anything which would enable the Afro-Portuguese middlemen on the coast to accumulate capital of their own so as to become independent, but the plan was of no avail, for some who grew rich encouraged interlopers, and interlopers were the bane of the trading companies.
85 Beazley, *loc. cit.*
86 W. E. B. DuBois, *The World and Africa*, pp. 46–8. But this was not the beginning of an African presence in the Iberian peninsula. There had been an earlier presence as a result of Moorish domination from the eighth century and the extension of the Almoravid (Al-Murabitun) crusade of medieval times. Its implications in terms of racial admixing are spelled out in Gilberto Freyre, *The Masters and the Slaves*, 4th English edn., New York, 1946, pp. 215–16. J. H. Parry, *The Spanish Seaborne Empire*, pp. 28–37.
87 Bovill, *Caravans of the Old Sahara*, 1933, p. 205. This quotation appeared again in his *Golden Trade of the Moors*, 1958 version, but thereafter it disappears from revised editions. It is interesting to speculate on this omission after more than a generation. It is a pertinent point which needs to be taken into consideration.
88 J. C. DeGraft Johnson, *African Glory*, p. 157. Some popes approved of the slave trade, while others rejected it, but they were powerless against the determination of their wards.
89 Donnan, *Documents*, Vol. 1, p. 15. There is a quotation of the request of the Jeronomites on the same page. See also E. G. Bourne, *Spain in America, 1450–1580*, London and New York, 1904, ch. 8, esp. p. 271.
90 It was in 1517 that Charles V of Spain approved the export of 15 000 slaves to Española (alias Hispaniola or San Domingo) part of which was renamed Haiti, the name known to the indigenous population.
91 Donnan, p. 6.
92 *Ibid.*, p. 7.
93 Donnan suggests that the French, contrary to popular belief, were the first challengers; the records of Rouen show a considerable trade to Brazil in the 1540s, and by 1541 French merchants were reaching Guinea on their way to Brazil, *Documents*, p. 13.

94 C. L. R. James, *Black Jacobins*, London, 1938 and 1963, ch. 1.

95 *Ibid.*

96 Donnan, *Documents*, Vol. 1, p. 284, from Jean (John) Barbot.

97 See, for instance, Davidson, *Black Mother*; Mannix and Cowley, *Black Cargoes* Pope Hennessy, *Sins of the Fathers*; D'Auvergne, *Human Livestock*.

98 Davidson, *Black Mother*, p. 92, Jean Barbot, *A Description – Churchill's Collection of Voyages*.

99 Davidson, *ibid.*

100 Curtin, *The Atlantic Slave Trade: a Census*, pp. 272–3.

101 The story of the king of Annomaboe in the Gold Coast has been discussed elsewhere, see for instance *Gentlemen's Magazine*, Vol. 19, February 1749, pp. 89–90; also Vol. 20, June 1750, p. 272, and Vol. 21, June 1751, p. 331 for other Gold Coast potentates sending their eldest sons to England to be educated. Also see Davidson, *Black Mother*, pp. 235–6.

102 J. K. Fynn, *Asante and Its Neighbours*, London, 1971, pp. 86–7 and ch. 6; Alan Lloyd, *Drums of Kumasi*, London, 1964, pp. 75–6; J. D. Fage, *A History of West Africa: an Introductory Survey*, Cambridge, 1969, 4th edn., p. 110.

103 T. E. Bowdich, *Mission from Cape Coast to Ashanti in 1817*, London, 1819, p. 72.

104 Rodney, *Upper Guinea Coast*, pp. 114–16; Davidson, *Black Mother*, pp. 243–5; Geoffrey Bing, *Reap the Whirlwind*, London, 1968, p. 86.

105 Rodney, *Upper Guinea Coast*, pp. 113–14.

106 *Ibid.*, pp. 117–18, 177.

107 It has been suggested that rum was probably introduced to the African coast by interlopers who at the time were searching for a commodity which would be readily acceptable. See K. G. Davies, *The Royal African Company*, London, 1957, p. 115.

108 Lewis Tappan, *Life of Arthur Tappan*, London, 1870, Appendix 4, p. 419; also R. West, *Back to Africa*, London, 1970, pp. 148–9.

109 H. M. Waddell, *Twenty-nine Years*, p. 250. He referred to a non-drinking King Eyo, who saw drink as injurious to a man at the head of affairs and referred to one of the subordinate chiefs whose life was wasting by his excess consumption of alcohol. Drink was sometimes a matter of preference, as the reference to King Eyo shows, and sometimes a matter of habit. Some potentates in the slave-trading days delighted in receiving it. We have already quoted the visit of the king of Warri to his prospective in-law, King Pepple of Bonny, in this chapter.

110 Pope Hennessy, *Sins of the Fathers*, pp. 101–6. Pope Hennessy's doubts about the genuineness of Agaja's intentions are raised as the latter seemed disposed to sell slaves to Captain William Snellgrave and others. Yet, this portrayal of Agaja might have suited Snellgrave's propaganda as a slave dealer in order not to discourage other European slave traders from coming to the coast. Pope Hennessy, however, observed that the theory cannot now be either proved or disproved but the king's willingness to trade with these English captains makes its veracity improbable (Pope Hennessy, *op. cit.*, pp. 101–5).

111 Basil Davidson informs us that twenty-two of King Affonso's letters written between 1512 and 1540 are preserved in the Portuguese archives and had been written by a Congolese baptised as João Texeira, who showed a good command of the Portuguese language; *Black Mother*, p. 119.

112 *Ibid.*, pp. 138–9.

113 *Ibid.*, p. 139.

114 For the entire episode see Davidson, *Black Mother*, pp. 119–25; Birmingham, *Trade and Conflict in Angola*, pp. 21–5; Chancellor Williams, *The Destruction of Black Civilisation*, Dubuque, Iowa, 1973, pp. 160–6.

115 Birmingham, *Trade and Conflict in Angola*, p. 30.

116 Chancellor Williams, *Destruction of Black Civilisation*, pp. 169, 171.

117 Birmingham, *Trade and Conflict in Angola*, pp. 106–8.

118 *Ibid.*, p. 109. The Nzinga Mbande–Portuguese confrontations have been discussed extensively, see also pp. 30–1, 92–5, 98–103, 104–23, and Chancellor Williams, *Destruction of Black Civilisation*.

119 Birmingham, *Trade and Conflict in Angola*, pp. 92–3.

120 *Ibid.*, p. 114.

121 See n. 110 above.

122 See Karl Polanyi, *Dahomey and the Slave Trade: an Analysis of an Archaic Economy*, London, 1966, pp. 133–9.

123 Rodney, *Upper Guinea Coast*, pp. 90–1, and also his *West Africa and the Trans-Atlantic Slave Trade*, Dar es Salaam, 1967, p. 21, also his *How Europe Underdeveloped Africa*, pp. 90–1.

124 Compare with the seventeenth-century objections of the Sultan of Bantam and the Javanese refusal to allow the Dutch to establish a stone castle or fortified factory in any of their ports in case the Dutch followed the Portuguese precedent of gradual absorption of the territory around the fort, fears which proved to be justified. See C. R. Boxer, *The Dutch Seaborne Empire 1600–1800*, London, 1965, pp. 189–90.

125 W. W. Claridge, *A History of the Gold Coast and Ashanti*, reprinted London, Cass, 1964, Vol. 1, pp. 45–6. The speech was taken from De Barros and Faria. Also quoted in J. C. DeGraft Johnson, *African Glory*, p. 129.

126 DeGraft Johnson, *African Glory*, p. 130.

127 Attoh Ahuma, *Memoirs of West African Celebrities . . .*, Liverpool, 1905, pp. 15–17, 19–23, H. O. A. McWilliam, *The Development of Education in Ghana*, London, 1975, pp. 45–58; H. Lochner, 'Anton W. Amo: a Ghana Scholar in 18th-century Germany', *Transactions of the Historical Society of Ghana*, iii (1958), pp. 169–79; also Boxer, *The Dutch Seaborne Empire*, pp. 152–3.

128 Cugoano, *Thoughts and Sentiments*; Equiano (Gustavus Vassa), *The Interesting Narrative . . .*, London, 1789.

129 These two are discussed briefly in Chapter 12.

130 Dike, *Trade and Politics in the Niger Delta*, pp. 34–46.

131 Rodney, *Upper Guinea Coast*, pp. 200–22; K. Y. Daaku, *Trade and Politics on the Gold Coast, 1600–1720: a Study of African Reaction to European Trade*, Oxford, 1970.

132 There were many variants of this: creole-English (the so-called pidgin English) and creole-French are other examples of the languages evolved.

133 Rodney, *Upper Guinea Coast*, pp. 209–12. There was quite a Vaz community, all related.

134 Rodney, *Upper Guinea Coast*, pp. 216–19. Their role in the slave trade was immense.

135 See Davies, *Royal African Company*, pp. 280–1, 285, 288–9; Daaku, *Trade and Politics*, pp. 115–16; on Edward Barter see *ibid.*, pp. 98–9; William Bosman, *A New Account of Guinea and the Slave Trade*, London, 1705, pp. 26–7.

136 Daaku, *Trade and Politics*, chs 5 and 6; Margaret Priestly, *West African Trade and Coast Society: a Family Study*, London, 1969, contains an exposé on the family of

the Brews from their European ancestry to the Fante Brews and their descendants.

137 Reynolds, *Trade and Economic Change on the Gold Coast*, p. 112.

138 Fynn, *Asante and its Neighbours*, pp. 63–4. See also Bowdich, *Mission from Cape Coast to Ashanti*, and John Atkins, *A Voyage to Guinea, Brazil and the West Indies*, London, 1737, p. 188.

139 Rodney, *Upper Guinea Coast*, pp. 221–2.

140 See the humiliating treatment of a Baga king by a powerful mulatto, Don José Lopez, in the early eighteenth century in Rodney, *Upper Guinea Coast*, p. 215. Another, known as Pa Antonio in 1821, was a village chief in his own right in the Port Lako region of Upper Guinea, and many more captured power all along the West African region. The increasing importation of firearms to which they had access tipped the scales in their favour to the disadvantage of some traditional African rulers.

141 Rodney, *ibid.*, esp. pp. 121–4. See Atkins, *Voyage*, Vol. 1 p. 188, who said that a 'recent confrontation between the Asante and Fante had been caused by the activities of one John Konny, a mulatto'.

142 Rodney, *Upper Guinea Coast*, p. 208.

143 *Ibid.*, pp. 209–15.

144 *Ibid.*, pp. 236–40.

145 See Fynn, *Asante and its Neighbours*, pp. 128–9. The Anlo and Popo denied Danish suzerainty over them while the people of Keta remained unreconciled to the erection of the Danish fort, Prindsenstein, against their will. The Danes used armed men to supervise the construction of the fort. The encounter is full of Danish intrigue and African resistance.

146 *Ibid.*, p. 128.

147 Hopkins, *Economic History*, p. 103.

148 D'Auvergne, *Human Livestock*, pp. 31–2. D'Auvergne reminds us that those piratical acts took place daily and that sometimes Europeans went ashore to capture the inhabitants of Cape Roxo, burning and spoiling their town. At times Africans would turn on their European assailants with bows and arrows, often killing some.

4   Resistance in Africa and during the middle passage

African attitudes to enslavement before they reached the Americas is a subject that requires further research. Records are thin on the question, and much has to be gleaned from the observations of Europeans such as slave captains and doctors and slaves subsequently freed.[1] But it is clear from the records that slaves resisted their enslavement both on the soil of Africa and during the middle passage across the Atlantic Ocean. Those who tended to rationalise the enslavement of Africans used all sorts of excuses to justify slavery – the Ham theory, the docility of the African, Aristotelian assertions, and other forms of arguments, often absurd.[2] But they and their supporters went further to postulate the docility of the Africans. It is clear, however, that docility belongs more to the realm of fantasy than fact, and is not upheld by many of the accounts of Europeans who themselves traded on the African coast. Even in Africa, where the slave traders had to come to terms with warlike peoples before purchasing captives, they certainly could not count upon the docility of those conquered. Captains who experienced the middle passage knew that because of slave insurrections it was often more hazardous than was generally believed – so dangerous in fact that it became necessary for ships to take out a special insurance.[3]

One of the earliest forms of African resistance to enslavement was observed during John Hawkins' second slave-trading voyage to the Sierra Leone river in 1564. James Pope Hennessy, who has attempted to set the record straight, informs us that Hawkins' crew of Englishmen set out to go inland, against the advice of Hawkins, to interfere with the people. They were surprised by a band of Africans, who attacked them, wounded several and pursued them back to their boats, shooting at them with arrows and hacking to pieces those who floundered fully-armoured in the mud. By this time two hundred Africans had gathered on the bank. In the confrontation which ensued, seven of Hawkins' best men, including the captain of the *Salmon*, were killed and thirty more wounded. With tidings of further attacks in the offing to be mounted by the 'king of Sierra Leone', Hawkins beat a hasty retreat. Moreover, since his crew were sickly from the climate, he set sail at once for the West Indies.[4]

Commenting on this episode Pope Hennessy wrote: 'The coastal Negroes might not yet have firearms, but they had, as a first line of defence, their dreaded climate, and as a second, courage and poisoned arrows.'[5] There is also an interesting version of Hawkins' third slave-trading voyage. On the Senegal river the Jolof assailed his expedition with bows and arrows so that Hawkins' attack on them was a dismal failure; and the prospect that Africans were playing drums to alert the neighbourhood to imminent danger, and with the fear of possible attack, Hawkins decided to move further eastward to secure his cargo before heading for the Spanish Main, with the fatal results which are so well known at the Port of San Juan de Ulloa. James Pope Hennessy observed that not till well into the seventeenth century did Englishmen resume slave trading, and not by seizure but by purchase and negotiation.[6] On the ground, the activity of slave trading was of itself a hazard; aboard ship it was no better. The *South Carolina Gazette* of 7 July 1759 recounted an incident which was by no means unique in the annals of slavers on the West African coast:

A Sloop commanded by a brother of . . . Captain Ingledieu, slaving up the River Gambia, was attacked by a Number of the Natives, about the 27th of February last, and made a good Defence; but the Captain finding himself desperately wounded, and likely to be overcome, rather than fall into the Hands of such merciless Wretches, when about 80 Negroes had boarded his Vessel, discharged a Pistol into his Magazine, and blew her up; himself and every Soul on Board perished.[7]

However, more seasoned slave traders generally took precautionary measures against contingencies of the kind experienced by Joseph Hawkins, who left Charleston, South Carolina, on 1 December 1779 on the *Charleston* for the Guinea Coast.[8] On arrival the ship's captain attempted to buy a cargo of Igala or Igara (misnamed Galla, not to be confused with those in the neighbourhood of Kenya, Somalia and Ethiopia),[9] who had been defeated by the Igbo after a confrontation and captured. Hawkins had previously reproached himself for embarking on the slave trade but had found consolation in the belief that he had embarked on it through necessity and was undertaking an act of humanity in reducing the Igala captives to slavery.[10] Furthermore, he deluded himself with the belief that he had succeeded in persuading the captives that their lot would be better in America than in Africa. When he approached the place of embarkation he seemed impressed by the 'sullen melancholy and deep sighs of the Galla prisoners'. In order to assuage their anguish and elevate their spirits he offered them liquor, but as soon as the slaves were embarked aboard the sloop six of the captives who were allowed to stay on deck began a general revolt. Continuing, Joseph Hawkins explained:

> Two of them found means to jump overboard; a sailor who was in the small boat astern seized one of them by the arms, and the end of a rope being thrown to him, the slave was taken on board, though not without some difficulty. The others who had been at the oars, seeing their fellows, one of them seized, and the other struck on the head with a pole, set a scream, which was echoed by the rest below; those that were loose made an effort to throw two of the sailors overboard . . . they seized on the guns and bayonets that lay ready, and rushed upon the slaves, five of whom from below had got loose, and were endeavouring to set the rest free, while those we had to deal with above, were threatening to sacrifice us to their despair. . . . I had neither gun nor sword, and to retire in search of either, would have been to give slaves a decisive superiority; I laid hold of the pallon stick, and had raised it to strike one of them who had nearly wrested a gun from one of the sailors, but before I could give the blow, I received a stroke of an oar, which severed my little finger from my hand . . . the blow was broken that I had intended, but I renewed the effort, and with effect, for I levelled the fellow, and the sailor recovered his gun, whom I could not prevent from running the poor negro through the body; the hatch was open, and he fell among his fellows, who had, crowded, tied and ironed as they were, to assist as far as they were able, by holding our legs, encouraging their companions, and shouting whenever those above did any thing that appeared likely to overcome one or other of us. We at length overpowered them; one only having escaped and one being killed, the rest were immediately bound in double irons . . . . Five of the sailors were considerably but not dangerously hurt, and of the slaves, those who had been riotous above and below, nine were severely wounded.[11]

Accounts such as these testify to the resistance of some Africans in avoiding capture and in seeking to escape enslavement. During confrontations such as those narrated above casualties occurred frequently on both sides. The seventeenth and eighteenth centuries were noted for the recurrence of revolts against enslavement. The documentation of these incidents is better for the eighteenth and nineteenth centuries than for the earlier period. But it is possible that Portuguese and Spanish archives could yield a rich harvest of early attempts to resist enslavement. The *Boston Post Boy* of 13 August 1750 sounded a note of caution and vigilance to those engaged in the slave trade after narrating an incident in which the ship the *Snow Ann* experienced on 14 April 1750 an insurrection of about sixty Africans, who seized the powder and arms and began a revolt against the Europeans at 3 o'clock in the morning. According to the account they wounded all the crew except two, who were in hiding; they then ran the vessel ashore a little south of Cape Lopez and escaped. The vessel broke up, and while the crew reached for their boats one of them was drowned; the rest got ashore only with great difficulty. The captain, who had received serious wounds, died soon after reaching land. Six of the remaining crew headed for Mayumba (in Loango, Angola) where they were taken aboard an English vessel. Five of them, who were ill from wounds received in the confrontation with the Africans, were left behind. Those who set out for Mayumba lost one on the way and the remaining five arrived at Mayumba on 3 May 1750. Three boarded a vessel, the *Rider*, bound for Amsterdam, although one was seriously ill and had to be attended by a surgeon; the other two got on board the vessel *Hawk* under the command of Captain Waynman.[12]

Another incident occurred the following month, May 1750, when slaves on board the ship *King David* of Bristol rose at 5 o'clock in the morning, having carefully planned a revolt. The slaves being more numerous than the crew overwhelmed them, seizing the arms and killing the captain and five others. As resistance seemed impossible the European crew did not offer any. The Africans fastened the chief mate in irons and threw nine of the crew overboard also fastened in irons. They were about to throw out the chief mate when wise counsel prevailed and they preserved him so that the ship could be safely navigated back to land. Although the Gold Coast, Calabar and St Thomas were suggested as possible points of disembarkation, the difficulties made these destinations unattainable. The Africans, therefore, decided on a venue which would be free from the presence of Europeans. Having arrived at Desiada, two Europeans and four Africans were sent in a boat to spy out the land with the instruction that if any Europeans were found to be living there the searchers should return and kill the remainder of the crew. Rumour later had it that they did not find an island of their choice and that they fell into French hands. The fate of the Africans is not known.[13]

About thirty years earlier, John Atkins, who made a voyage to Guinea in 1721, recounts an incident in which a vessel, the *Robert* of Bristol, under the command of Captain Harding, purchased thirty slaves from Sierra Leone who soon afterwards rose in revolt under the leadership of a Sierra Leone potentate described in the account as 'Captain Tomba'. Donnan, who records the narrative of John Atkins, tells us that Tomba encouraged 'the accomplices with what he called the prospect of Liberty'. It is noteworthy that European recorders of such encounters persisted in referring to them as 'treacherous'. According to the record, the revolt was aided and abetted by an African woman. Tomba attacked the sailors who were sleeping in the forecastle. The incident, as narrated by Atkins himself, continues:

> He found three Sailors sleeping on the Forecastle, two of which he presently dispatched, with single strokes upon the Temples; the other rouzing with the Noise, his Companions seized; Tomba coming soon to their Assistance, and murdering him in the same manner. Going after to finish the work, they found very luckily for the rest of the Company, that these other two of the Watch were with confusion already made awake, and upon their Guard, and their Defence soon awaked the Master underneath them, who running up and finding his Men contending for their lives, took a Hand–spike, the first thing he met with in the Surprize, and redoubling his Strokes home upon Tomba, laid him at length flat upon the Deck, securing them all in Irons.

'The Reader', Atkins observes, 'may be anxious to know their Punishment: Why, Captain Harding weighing the Stoutness and Worth of the two Slaves, did, as in other Countries they do by Rouges of Dignity whip and scarify them only.'[14] The story is continued and we are told that the woman who gave Tomba assistance was hoisted on her thumbs and flogged, then slashed with knives till she died. The other conspirators were condemned to death – two of them compelled to eat the heart and liver of the first before they themselves were killed.[15] Such atrocities could hardly have made for affection between the enslaver and enslaved.

An English captain of a slave ship in the early eighteenth century, William Snelgrave, gives us a glimpse of the nature as well as the magnitude and frequency of slave revolts both in West Africa and on board ship. He argues that they tended to recur because of ill usage,[16] but he fails to see in one of the examples he cites that the African yearning for freedom was the reason for such insurrections. His example of the Coromantine[17] Africans is a case in point. In the year 1721, after a slave revolt, he questioned the slaves as to why they had dared to revolt, and in their reply they suggested that he was a 'rogue' for daring to purchase them from their homeland, intimating that they were determined to regain their freedom.[18] Three of the mutinies which he witnessed at first hand occurred in 1704 (one) and 1721 (two).[19]

The first of these revolts occurred on board the vessel known as the *Eagle Galley of London*, which was under the command of William Snelgrave's father and to which he was purser. The slaves had been bought from Old Calabar and the mutiny took place while the vessel was anchored in the Cross river. There were four hundred slaves on board and not more than ten white men able to do service since the rest of the ship's company had either died or were sick, and two of their boats had then gone ashore with twelve people to fetch wood. This afforded the Africans on board ship the opportunity to plan their mutiny, so Snelgrave informs us. They were able to do so at 4 o'clock in the afternoon when at supper. Three of the white men were still standing guard with cutlasses in their hands – one at the ship's forecastle was stout; suddenly he saw the Africans seizing the chief mate with a view to throwing him overboard. The English sentry used the flat side of his cutlass against the Africans and as a result they released their hold on the mate, who escaped and ran on the quarterdeck to obtain arms. William Snelgrave himself was unwell and lay in the great cabin. But on hearing the outcry of the slave mutiny he took two pistols and ran on deck, and there saw his father and the chief mate and handed them the pistols. The latter demanded the submission of the Africans, who ignored him as they were struggling with the chief sentry, who had earlier helped the mate to escape. It was Snelgrave's belief that they could have killed the sentry had they succeeded in wrenching his cutlass from him. Having failed in their effort to obtain his cutlass, they considered throwing him overboard but his resistance saved him. Captain Snelgrave's father, seeing the stout sentry in danger, fired his pistol over the heads of the rebellious Africans in order to frighten them, but a slave struck back at Snelgrave's father with a billet, in such a manner that the father was stunned; but a repeated attempt by the slave was halted as a young African of seventeen years, to whom the Europeans had allegedly been kind, put out his arm to stave off the blow and received, as a result of his bravery, a fractured arm. Simultaneously, the mate fired his pistol and shot the African who had struck at Snelgrave's father. This terminated the mutiny and all the Africans in revolt threw themselves on their faces and pleaded for mercy. Further cross-examination of the slaves revealed that only twenty had been involved and that the two ringleaders had slipped away, jumped overboard, and were drowned. Snelgrave himself, who was ill at the time, due to shock, recovered, and the young man who had shielded his father was granted freedom after being cured by a surgeon on their arrival in Virginia.

William Snelgrave was persuaded that kind treatment minimised the danger of slave mutinies on board ship. But he also believed that there were certain stout and stubborn people who could never be satisfied even with tenderness. Most of these were Coromantine slaves from the Gold Coast (modern Ghana). Thus, he observed a Coromantine revolt on board the vessel the *Henry of London* in 1721. Although the slaves were secured in irons and carefully watched, they still mutinied. At the time of the revolt Snelgrave was moored at a place on the Gold Coast known as Mumfort, having on board his vessel about five hundred African slaves, three hundred of whom were men. The ship's crew consisted of fifty white people, with good officers and all the fifty in excellent health. But Snelgrave was complacent. The mutiny, which began at midnight under the bright African moon, revealed an attempt by some of the Africans to seize cutlasses from the white sentries, but it failed because of the arrival of more white men on deck. In the meantime some of the Africans jumped overboard and clung to the ship's cables, but they were rescued. It was at this point that William Snelgrave sought to ascertain, through their linguist, the cause of what he described as 'the mutiny' and was told that Snelgrave was a 'great Rogue' to purchase them from their country and that they were resolved upon regaining their freedom.[20] According to his narrative, no sooner had they been pardoned than they were discovered a few days later to be plotting again. But even threats that they would be severely punished did not deter them from trying again.[21]

Commenting on the attitude of the slaves, Snelgrave felt some disquiet, and observed, 'I knew several voyages had proved unsuccessful by Mutinies; as they occasioned either the total loss of the Ship and the white Men's lives; or at least by rendering it absolutely necessary to kill or wound a great number of Slaves, in order to prevent a total Destruction.'[22] Furthermore, he was aware that many of the Coromantins despised punishment and even death itself. He observed that it had happened so frequently in Barbados and other West Indian islands that whenever an attempt was made to deal with them severely in order to break their stubbornness when they refused to work, twenty or more of them tended to hang themselves on the plantation at a time. But Snelgrave admits that slave revolts on board ship were numerous, often ending tragically.[23]

He relates another episode which had occurred on board a vessel known as the *Ferrers Galley of London*, under the command of one Captain Messervy. Ten days after the ship had left the coast of Guinea for Jamaica, the African slaves on board killed Captain Messervy by beating his brains out with little tubs in which they ate their boiled rice. The chief mate responded by discharging partridge shots into the crowd, resulting in the death of nearly eighty Africans, some of them by drowning when they jumped overboard after the shot was fired. The mutiny was contained but the surviving slaves on board remained sullen and many of them, accordingly, starved to death, having refused food. On arrival at Jamaica the slaves twice attempted to raise a revolt, even before they had been sold. Because the planters obtained intelligence of these 'unruly' slaves they were reluctant to buy them, so that they had to be sold at a lower price. From Snelgrave's account the venture proved a disaster, for the ship was detained for months in Jamaica because of the happenings; it was later lost in a hurricane.[24]

Captain Crow of Liverpool observed of the Quaws sold at Bonny that they 'were ever the foremost in any mischief or insurrection among the slaves, and from time to time many whites fell victims to their fury at Bonny.... The slave ships were always obliged to provide separate rooms for these men between decks and the captains were careful to have as few of them as possible amongst their cargoes.'[25]

But taking possession of slaves, either on African soil or on board the slave-trading vessels, was not of itself an assurance that the slaves would not be restive. John Atkins, Surgeon to the Royal Navy, who made voyages to Guinea and other parts of the world, including Brazil (1721 and 1722), stressed the fact that vigilance needed to be exercised on the voyages from West Africa to the Americas. He wrote:

> When we are slaved and out at sea, it is commonly imagined, the *Negroes* ignorance of Navigation, will always be a safeguard; yet, as many of them think themselves bought to eat, and more, that Death will send them into their own Country, there has not been wanting Examples of rising and killing a Ship's Company, distant from land, tho' not so often as on the coast; but once or twice is enough to show a Master's Care and Diligence should never be over till the Delivery of them. Some Negroes know well enough that the preserving one white man may answer their purpose in an exchange; however, generally speaking, we allow greater liberty in our Passage, as conducive to the Health; we let them go at large on the Ship's Deck, from sunrise to sunset, give such as like it, Pipes and tobacco, and clean and air their Dormitories every day.[26]

A number of issues emerge from the quotation. The first is that revolts by Africans against enslavement were recurrent, and were sometimes conducted some distance from the mainland, though risings and killings were more frequent on the coast. Furthermore, having experienced risings or attempted risings a few times, ships' captains and their crews became more conscious of the need for unending vigilance and more aware that Africans were not so stupid as to kill all their European captors in order to avoid the contingency of not getting safely back to land or to use them as hostages for purposes of bargaining. A battle of wits between the captured and their captors thereby emerged, each watching the other, the slaves looking for the opportunity to regain their freedom, while their enslavers took steps to prevent them from getting out of hand and possibly successfully achieving their liberation. But John Atkins also observed that most of the slaves he saw quartered in Sierra Leone and awaiting sale and transportation looked 'very dejected'.[27] Dejection did not indicate that enslaved Africans liked their new status; resistance showed itself in many forms. In Atkins' account of his visit to Guinea, he tells of the arrival of a Caboceer somewhere on the Grain and Malaguetta coasts who seemed shy to enter the European's ship, afraid of being kidnapped (i.e. panyarring). Atkins makes it clear that the Caboceer's towns-people had often suffered from the 'treachery of ships, and they as often returned it, sometimes with cruelty, which has given rise to the Report of their being savages and cannibals at several places; very unlikely any where, because they could not part with their slaves, which are but few, if they had this custom, nor could they have any trade or Neighbours. Their fears would make them shun the enemies (the rest of mankind) and all correspondence totally cease.'[28]

We get a glimpse of some of the factors responsible for revolt on board ship by reading Dr Alexander Falconbridge, another ship's surgeon, who also wrote on the slave trade of the Guinea Coast in 1788. He observes the method of forcibly feeding slaves who refused sustenance either from depression or because of the curtailment of their liberty, thus:

> Upon the negroes refusing to take sustenance, I have seen coals of fire, glowing hot, put on a shovel, and placed so near their lips, as to scorch and burn them. And this has been accompanied with threats, of forcing them to swallow the coals, if they any longer persisted in refusing to eat.[29]

These methods, he admits, generally worked, and he was also 'credibly informed' of a certain captain in the slave trade who poured melted lead on any Africans who obstinately refused their food.[30]

There was, of course, the practice of exercising the slaves in order to keep them in good health, this often being achieved by permitting them to appear on deck under favourable weather conditions to dance. Those who moved sluggishly were flogged with the cat-o'-nine tails. But Alexander Falconbridge writes:

> As very few of the negroes can so far brook the loss of their liberty, and the hardship they endure, as to bear them with any degree of patience, they are ever upon the watch to take advantage of the least negligence in their oppressors. Insurrections are frequently the consequence; which are seldom suppressed without much bloodshed. Sometimes these are successful, and the whole ship's Company is cut off. They are likewise always ready to seize every opportunity for committing some act of desperation to free themselves from their

> miserable state; and not withstanding the restraints under which they are laid, they often succeed.[31]

He gives information about other insurrections and attempted revolts which signify complete African opposition to enslavement. He narrates the incident of ten Africans being brought to a ship on which he was working one evening before their departure from the African shore and how one of the Africans jumped overboard and was said to have been instantly devoured by sharks. He records that during the whole time they were anchored in the Bonny river fifteen Africans belonging to a vessel from Liverpool found means of throwing themselves into the river; very few were saved, the remainder falling victim to sharks. He also observes a similar incident on a French ship moored there, and concludes, 'Circumstances of this kind are very frequent.'[32] He then recounts an incident on the coast of Angola at the Ambris river while his ship was anchored there. The crew erected a tent for sheltering themselves on land from the weather. Having spent several fruitless weeks trying to obtain slaves, and having failed because of the opposition of an English slave-trading vessel, they decided to leave the area. The night before their departure the tent was struck. Eighteen African women on board their vessel observing this threw themselves into the sea through one of the gun ports. They were all, with the exception of one, immediately picked up, and the missing slave was eventually found about a mile from the shore. Falconbridge's narratives are especially instructive. He recounts another incident in which an African woman, 'too sensible of her woes, who pined for a considerable time, and was taken ill of a fever and dysentry', declared that she preferred to die and refused all food and medical assistance, and was dead within a fortnight. On being thrown overboard, her body was instantly torn to pieces by sharks.[33] Then again there was the case of another enslaved African girl on board a vessel who fell into a deep depression and it was considered prudent to send her ashore to an African slave dealer so that she might recover. When she learned that there was the chance that she might regain her liberty, she revived and became very cheerful, but on learning accidentally that she would be taken aboard the ship again she hanged herself.[34]

Other Africans unable to tolerate their enslavement went mad, and Falconbridge records that many, especially women, died in that state. Observing the act of one woman who not only took a handful of her country's earth after being enslaved but also swallowed it in order to be at one with the soil from which she was being wrenched, Falconbridge wrote: 'the unhappy Africans are not bereft of the finer feelings, but have a strong attachment to their native country, together with a just sense of the value of liberty'.[35]

Captain Thomas Phillips of the *Hannibal*, who sailed in the years 1693 and 1694, stated in his journal that the dangers of revolt by enslaved Africans were greater when they were within sight of their own continent, and that once they had retreated from the shore on the transatlantic voyage the slave revolts tended to cease, for as he expressed it, 'Out of sight [was] out of mind'. Yet, in the same place, he indicates that Africans were 'loth to leave their country'.[36] This has led the authors of *Black Cargoes* to assert that 'as long as a vessel lay at anchor, the slaves could dream of seizing it. If they managed to kill the crew, as they did in perhaps one mutiny in ten, they could cut the anchor cable and let the vessel drift ashore. The opportunity was lost as soon as the vessel put to sea.'[37] What the authors have done is to miss an early statement by Thomas Phillips[38] in the same journal, which contradicts his later statement. For a proper understanding it is essential to include both citations, which, in some respects, have a few sentences which are similar, but there the similarities end. In his earlier statement, Phillips observed:

> When our slaves came to the seaside, our canoes were ready to carry them off to the long boat, if the sea permitted, and she convey'd them aboard ship where the men were all put in irons, two and two shackl'd together to prevent their mutiny, or swimming ashore. The Negroes are so wilful and loth to leave their country, that they have often leapt out of the canoes, boat and ship, into the sea, and kept under water till they were drowned, to avoid being taken up and saved by our boats, which pursued them; they having a more dreadful apprehension of Barbados than we can have of hell. . . .
>
> We had about 12 negroes did wilfully drown themselves and others starved themselves to death; for 'tis their belief that when they die they return home to their own country and friends again.[39]

In his second statement in the same narrative, Thomas Phillips wrote:

> When our slaves are aboard we shackle the men two and two, while we lie in port and in sight of their own country, for 'tis then they attempt to make their escape, and mutiny; to prevent which we always keep chest of small arms, ready loaden and prim'd constantly lying at hand upon the quarter-deck, together with some granade shells; and two of our quarter-deck guns, pointing on the deck thence, and two more out of the steerage, the door of which is always kept shut, and well barr'd; they are fed twice a day, at 10 in the morning and 4 in the evening, which is the time they are aptest to mutiny, being upon deck; therefore all that time, what of our men are not employ'd in distributing their victuals to them, and settling

> them, stand to their arms; and some with lighten matches at the
> great guns that yaun upon them, loaden with partridge, till they have
> done and gone down to their kernels between decks . . . . When we
> come to sea we let them all out of irons, they never attempting then
> to rebel, considering that should they kill or master us, they could
> not tell how to manage the ship, or must trust us, who could carry
> them where we pleas'd; therefore the only danger is while we are in
> sight of their own country, which they are loth to part with; but
> once out of sight out of mind: I never heard that they mutiny in any
> ships of consequence, that had a good number of men and the least
> care; but in small tools where they had but few men, and those
> negligent or drunk, then they surpriz'd and butcher'd them, cut the
> cables, and let the vessel drive ashore, and every one shift for
> himself.[40]

The statements appear identical but on closer examination they
mirror some contradictions. One of the statements tends to leave
the impression that once slaves were out of sight of their country
the danger of insurrection did not exist because 'out of sight out of
mind'. This was not the experience of other writers and, especially,
John Atkins, who reminds us that lack of knowledge of navigation
was no barrier to slave mutinies on board ship.[41] In fact, it is not
borne out by the assertion of the authors of *Black Cargoes* that
'There are fairly detailed accounts of fifty-five mutinies from
1699–1845 from passing references to a hundred others'.[42]

Other captains experienced African resistance to enslavement by
taking every available opportunity to throw themselves overboard
in the belief (which Phillips himself observed) that death translated
them back to their homeland. References to these actions by slaves,
not only on the home front, but during the middle passage as well,
are so ubiquitous that it would be superfluous to cite them all here.
If it were true that the slaves, once out of sight of their home
country, no longer mutinied, why was it necessary to employ some
thirty to forty Gold Coast slaves as mentioned by Thomas Phillips?

> . . . we have some 30 or 40 gold coast negroes, which we buy, and
> are procur'd us there by our factors, to make guardians and overseers
> of the Whydah negroes and sleep among them to keep them from
> quarrelling; and in order as well to give us notice, if they can
> discover any caballing or plotting among them, which trust they will
> discharge with great diligence.[43]

The prevention of the slaves from quarrelling among themselves
can be discounted as the least convincing reason for employing
thirty to forty extra hands. Rather, the second reason given by
Thomas Phillips seems nearer the truth, to give early warning of

118

any attempts by slaves to mutiny or seek their liberty. If ever there was a classic case of 'divide and rule,' something later fostered on the plantations in order to frustrate the cohesiveness of slave resistance, here it was. The process of conditioning Africans to accept slave status began even as they were leaving the shores of Africa; it was to be intensified in the form of psychological warfare on the far side of the Atlantic in the Americas, with adverse consequences for the slaves themselves. The evidence of a slave trader in the succeeding century presents a contrary viewpoint about resistance only at home and not elsewhere because 'out of sight out of mind'. John Newton, who engaged in the slave trade between the years 1750 and 1754, and who later took Holy Orders, becoming Rector of St Mary Woolnooth in London and author of the hymn 'How Sweet is the Name of Jesus', records instances of attempted revolts in his *Journal* as well as the general state of feeling on the possibilities of insurrections by slaves on board ship. In his *Journal* he writes on 26 April 1753:

> I was at first continually alarmed with their (African slaves) almost desperate attempts to make insurrections upon us . . . when most quiet they were always watching for opportunity. However from about the end of February they have behaved more like children in one family than slaves in chains and irons and are really upon all accounts more observant, obliging and considerate than our white people . . . it is true we are not wanting in such methods of guarding against them as custom and prudence suggests, but I hope I shall never be weak and vain enough to think such a guard sufficient: 'except the Lord keep the city the watchman waketh but in vain,' the same may be said of a ship in any circumstances and it is more observably true of a Guineaman.[44]

The above-quoted passage surely mirrored not only the anxiety and the strains which were involved in the hazardous traffic in Africans but the subtleties introduced by Africans into the situation in which they could make European slavers relax their guard, thus providing them with the opportunity to make a bid for freedom. The religious meditation might have been added into Newton's journal for good measure, but it emphasises the unending nature of vigilance and the absence of an assurance that something terrible would not occur. Newton also records an incident on 7 December 1753 in which a ship, *Adventure*, belonging to Beatson of London and which had been on the coast for five months, was run ashore one morning by slaves who had risen in rebellion. He goes on to record the loss of the vessel with all but one man killed and one wounded.[45] In Newton's *Thoughts Upon the Slave Trade* incorporated into his *Journal*, he wrote:

The risk of insurrection is to be added. These, I believe, *are always meditated*; for the men slaves are not easily reconciled to their confinement and treatment; and if attempted, they are seldom suppressed without considerable loss; and sometimes they succeed, to the destruction of a whole ship's company at once. Seldom a year passes, but we hear, sometimes of whites and blacks involved, in one moment, in one common ruin, but the gun powder taking fire, and blowing up the ship.[46]

Newton himself gives us an insight into another factor in African slave resistance. Many Africans, believing they were being taken away to be eaten, were alarmed by the thought, and as Newton states:

When a hundred and fifty or two hundred stout men, torn from their native land, many of whom never saw the sea, much less a ship, till a short space before they had embarked; who have, probably, the same natural prejudice against a white man as we have against a black; and who often bring with them an apprehension they are bought to be eaten: I say, when thus circumstanced, it is not to be expected that they will tamely resign themselves to their situation. It is always taken for granted that they will attempt to gain their liberty if possible. Accordingly, as we dare not trust them, we receive them on board, from the first, as enemies; and, before their number exceeds, perhaps, ten or fifteen, they are all put in irons . . . . That these precautions are so often effectual, is much more to be wondered at, than that they sometimes fail. One unguarded hour, or a minute, is sufficient to give the slaves the opportunity they are always waiting for. An attempt to rise upon the ship's company, brings on instantaneous and horrid war; for, when they are once in motion, they are desperate; and where they do not conquer, they are seldom quelled without much mischief and bloodshed on both sides.[47]

Others showed disapproval in other ways, as Wadström, Chief Director of the Royal Assay and Refining Office in Sweden, informs us. For those brought in as captives, both men and women and children too showed their dejection sometimes with shrieks and sorrows.[48]

There were other hazards which sometimes resulted from the impetuosity of European slave traders in seizing Africans in order to complete their cargoes. Such incidents, described as 'buckra panyarring or kidnapping',[49] were recurrent; but, as can be gleaned from the journals of slave traders, these were hazardous and tended to result in tragedy for innocent Europeans identified with the nationalities of those who had preceded them in kidnapping Africans. Nicholas Owen, an Irishman, in his *Journal of a Slave Trader*, recounts an experience in the eighteenth century on the coast of Guinea in which he and his brother were seized by the coastal Africans and confined for about four to five days in retaliation for the kidnapping of Africans by a Dutch captain.[50] The incident took place at Banana Islands in the Sierra Leone river and it is better to tell it in Owen's words, for they reveal the penalties for breaking faith or for infringing the rules of conduct established between Euro-African trading partners. Owen writes:

> The capt. and 5 hands went on shoar in order to trade, but upon our setting our selves on shoar we were secur'd by the natives, put into irons, and hove down upon the ground in a barbarous manner, stripping us of all our cloaths, and in short made a prize of us. We demand the reason of such usage and was answer'd that it was in revenge of a Dutch capt. who had forcibly detained some of their free people and used them ill, and aded that they would take our ships and cargo in revenge but would take our lives, as we ware Englishmen. This they readeley perform'd, our people on board makeing no resistance as being ignorant of our confinement. The people they bound with ropes and hauld our vessell ashoar, confistacateing our cargo, which consisted of the following goods – rum, tobacco, sugar, chocolate, snuff and household furniture – drank and eat until they were easey, rifleing our chests and plundering us of everything they thought proper. In this adventure we lost 4 years' pay all in gold, besides our venture which amounted to 40 or 50 dollars in New England, and consequently a great dail more in Africa. We ware detain'd in irons 4 or 5 days, when they let us have liberty to walk up and down the island for our recreation. In this manner we remain'd, until a certain gentleman named Mr Hall carried us of the island in his shalop, he being the same time bound the Cape de Verd islands, in order to buy Cloaths, such as I have spoken of before in the beginning of my Journal.[51]

The experience was hardly a cheerful one and the revenge appears to have been an attempt to excise a 'pound of flesh' from those who were held accountable for the actions of other Europeans, who broke the rules of conduct on the west coast. Seizure, as has been mentioned earlier, was common practice on the coast of Guinea, but it became the accepted norm that an African on the coast who considered himself injured by a European of any nation took his revenge on the next European who appeared a suitable victim, even if that European was quite unconnected with the crime.[52]

Wadström not only condemned the practice of kidnapping Africans by European traders, which he stigmatised as 'robbery',[53] but observed that the enticement of unsuspecting Africans on board

European slave ships in order to spirit them away was hardly consistent with 'civilised standards' of conduct. He notes that the relatives and friends of Africans kidnapped in this way would brace themselves for revenge. He then recalls an incident of kidnapping in 1787 by the captain of an English vessel in the Gambia river and how the captain of the vessel sailed away with the Africans but was soon forced to return and cast anchor. The Africans on the coast, bent on retaliation, not only boarded the vessel, but two other English vessels anchored there at the same time, and killed most of their crews; the few who escaped took refuge at a nearby French factory, from where they told their tale. Wadström commented: 'Thus did the innocent suffer the same punishment as the guilty.'[54]

There were other kinds of dangers on the Guinea coast which arose out of misunderstanding. The Dutch factor William Bosman recounted one such incident involving the English. At the time of their commencement of trade in Whydah, an English captain and his men, who had found a snake in their house, killed it and threw it out. The Africans, finding the snake, enquired after the culprits, but the English, unaware of the sacredness of the snake to the people, gleefully owned up to the affair. Whereupon the people attacked the English and killed them all and burned their house and goods. The incident struck terror into the English and for a long time they avoided trading in Whydah and operated elsewhere. At other times, however, Europeans perpetrated outrages on Africans, which evoked identical responses. Bosman notes a Dutch factor belonging to the Dutch West India Company, a Mr Bleedsnyder, who made himself odious to Africans in the Benin region through his brutality. The man seduced the wife of one of the governors of the area and thereby enraged her husband, who assailed Bleedsnyder with a number of armed men; the Dutchman, however, escaped, although when he got on board ship he died from a fatal wound inflicted by Africans. The Dutch Company sent armed men from Elmina to Benin to avenge the murder of their dead factor. According to Bosman, these soldiers 'so rigorously executed, or perhaps stretched, their Commission, that they killed, or took prisoner, every person of the village' who could not escape.[55] When the king of Benin was informed, in spite of the revenge which the Dutch had taken, he called the African who had been the occasion for the Dutch outrage and intervention, and had him and his entire family executed and their corpses thrown out to be devoured by wild animals; their home was also razed to the ground with instructions never to be rebuilt.[56] Clearly the king seems to have been preoccupied with the rules of hospitality, but he was also concerned to maintain trading and good relations with his European partners, and internal action which could interfere with those relations was frowned upon. Yet these slave traders accumulated many grievances among coastal Africans.

Bosman also tells of his arrival at Cape Mesurado (Mizurado) where he found that Africans refused to board his vessel, and, on enquiring why they were hesitant, was informed that two months previously the English had arrived in two large vessels and had 'ravaged the Country, destroyed all their Canoes, plundered their houses and carried off some of their people for slaves; upon which the remainder fled to the inland-country, where most of them were at present'.[57] As a result trade there stood still. Bosman then found two old men who pretended to be captains and obliged him to pay them seven pounds of copper as custom because of the injuries they had suffered at the hands of the English, but, being timorous, the Africans would not board his ship. Furthermore, the people were so conscious of European kidnapping that, if any one came on shore armed, they immediately fled. This hardly testifies to Africans being willing to be kidnapped or taken into slavery. According to Bosman, he was informed that the people in the area were at peace with their neighbours and had no notion of any other enemy except the English, and that the people had captured some Englishmen and had publicly declared that they would endeavour to capture as many Englishmen as the English had carried away in their vessels. Whether they did Bosman does not say, but he gleefully comments on the fate of those in the possession of Africans: 'These unhappy English were in danger of being sacrificed to the memory of the Friends, which some of their Nation carried off.'[58]

Elsewhere on the Gold Coast the people of Assin expressed their dissatisfaction with the French by refusing them even the right to fetch water from their neighbourhood.[59] Because of slave trading and slave kidnapping, the atmosphere at the coast could at times be charged, and tended to breathe suspicion. William Smith, a surveyor in the employment of the Royal African Company in 1726, observed in the Gambia region that Africans surrounded him and felt they would have killed him because they believed he was trying to bewitch them with his surveying instrument.[60] The return of Africans kidnapped by European slave traders, on the other hand, was an occasion for joy, as was noted in the journal of Nicholas Owen in May 1752, when a number of Africans were brought back by Captain William Morgan after they had been kidnapped by the Danes.[61]

Successful slave mutinies

As slave trading became widespread subterfuges were ingrafted on it, and the preceding examples are sufficient to demonstrate amply that Africans, who were being taken from their home country, began their resistance in Africa whenever it was possible to do so. That resistance then continued during the middle passage and was translated to the Americas. The middle passage has been observed in many tracts of the slave trade era and information on it is so ubiquitous as to warrant extended discussion. It was also the subject of a British parliamentary commission, from which numerous chilling revelations can be gleaned.[62] The mutiny of slaves and epidemics both contributed to heavy fatalities, and one of the dreaded diseases was ophthalmia, which contributed to blindness. Two successful revolts, in particular, are symbolic of the un-quenched spirit of African resistance to slave status, and they are also important because of their international implications. Both the revolts occurred after the English and the North Americans had officially abolished the slave trade, but this was also an era in which the clandestine slave trade continued unabated, especially among the Spanish, Portuguese, Brazilians and others.

The first revolt occurred in 1839 and was led by Joseph Cinque, an African aboard the Spanish vessel known as L'Amistad. Most of the slaves were newly imported Africans and were bound (so the Spanish claimed) for the Cuban port of Guanaja from Havana. Only one of the slaves was Cuban-born. Under the leadership of Cinque the slaves killed the captain and cook, sent two other sailors ashore, and ordered two of the European slave merchants to steer the vessel to Africa. As the story went, Cinque himself only knew that Africa lay to the east, observing it by day through the rising sun but, being ignorant of the movement of the stars at night, he could not be sure that the men were steering towards Africa. It was this trick that the two men employed to divert the ship to Long Island in the United States, for during the day they sailed eastward and at night they sailed north-westward. When the vessel ap-proached the United States it was impounded and the slaves were kept in custody, but their arrival stirred abolitionists and friends of the slaves into feverish action, and John Quincy Adams, the pro-minent North American lawyer and statesman, took up the cause of the slaves and by 1841 the U.S. Supreme Court was able to rule that the Africans had been illegally introduced into Cuba and so dis-allowed the claims of the Spanish government. Only the Cuban-born slave was liable to return as a citizen of Cuba, but to avoid this contingency the abolitionists spirited him away before he could be sent back to Cuba, employing the channel of the underground railroad to confound the slave catchers. Cinque and his associates were released and eventually sent back to Africa with a missionary in the hope that they would form an advance missionary vanguard, but it is said that Cinque himself drifted into slave trading.[63]

Spanish demands for compensation, however, continued for some years until the 1850s.

The second of the incidents occurred in November 1841 on board an American vessel known as the *Creole*. It had set out from Hampton in Virginia bound for New Orleans with a cargo of 135 slaves. Under the leadership of Madison Washington, an escaped slave who had returned to rescue his wife and was recaptured, the slaves rose in rebellion. In the rising a white man was killed and the crew of the *Creole* urged to sail to the harbour of Providence in Nassau (in the Bahamas), a British colony. With the slaves successfully landed there, England set them free, since it had abolished slavery. The incident caused an international furore between Britain and the United States governments.[64] The British refused the United States' demand for their return. The issue rankled for a while but was eventually settled as part of a general agreement, the Webster-Ashburton Treaty of 1842, which not only resolved a border dispute between the U.S.A. and British Canada, but also put the final seal by both countries on the determination to abolish the slave trade. As a result both countries mounted joint patrols in order to secure compliance with the treaties prohibiting the slave trade.[65]

Conclusions

In observing the numerous forms of African resistance before their arrival in the Americas some conclusions about African attitudes to their enslavement become inescapable. Some Africans on the mainland of Africa, even after capture, took advantage of any available opportunity to escape or drown themselves either at the port of embarkation or once at sea. Drowning became recurrent when there was no other escape route, and this attitude to death was rooted in the African belief that death translated a person back to the land of his forebears.

The violence of the African reaction on the west coast at the time of John Hawkins' second slave-trading voyage reveals a community that was prepared to rise to the occasion to forestall European threats to societal cohesiveness and local tranquillity. It showed to the English slave traders that the community could sometimes rise up to the challenge of depredations visited on them by outsiders, and that outsiders could not always expect to act with impunity. The ability to mobilise opposition to slave dealers was therefore possible, though it was not always sustained. As the coastal African middlemen became webbed into the Euro-African connection of the slave-trading business, so did their power of terror increase, and so were they able to diminish the effectiveness of locally organised resistance. If, therefore, there was resistance in one area rather than another it was not that Africans in general were willing to acquiesce in their enslavement; rather, it reveals that they were unduly circumscribed within an aristocratic and autocratic framework (forged out of the slave-trading connection), which developed over the period of slave dealing, and which made it only possible for the enslaved to await the time of their removal from the coast to the Americas. Furthermore, where there was religious sanction imposed in the enslavement of some, the African victims could hardly rebel against the power of the priests who in some societies commanded prestige and constituted a vital pillar of power that could not be ignored. The credulity of the people to their religious mentors can be seen in the general acquiescence to the awe-inspiring Aro-Chukwu Oracle.

Captain William Snelgrave, who suggested that 'ill-usage' was a factor in the unrest of slaves being taken from Africa, asserted that revolts were minimised by their kinder treatment. While this could be true, as it was in some cases, he misses the point that Africans could not tolerate the bare fact of their enslavement which, in essence, meant that they could not bear the denial of their freedom, and yet, in the next breath, he admits that it was an African impression that slave traders were 'man-stealers'. His acute sense was quick to detect that the so-called 'warlike' peoples did not brook the curtailment of their freedom, and they had numerous ways of demonstrating this. These included the refusal to eat as an act of defiance and the singing of melancholy songs which affected the sensibilities of their captors.[66] Such techniques of passive resistance on the part of slaves before their arrival in the Americas sometimes proved too costly for the slave-trading venture, for the loss of slaves through death in this manner not only dismayed the captain and put his employment in jeopardy, but also increased the dangers of financial losses to his employers in the metropolis. And there was an added burden: it limited the supply of slaves to the plantations and so raised the price of slaves in what was essentially a highly competitive and insatiable environment. Slave captains and their subordinates therefore found it necessary to use devices which would secure the conformity of slaves, such as bringing a piece of burning coal to the mouth of a slave who refused sustenance in order to induce the slave to open his or her mouth.[67]

It is also necessary to examine what lay behind these slave revolts before their arrival in the Americas. Part of the answer must be found in their spontaneity, and in others in the carefully calculated manner in which they were carried out. Next, they must also be observed in terms of the conception which the Africans had of themselves – in short, their notion of freedom and the perception of their dignity. While being put in chains severely limited their freedom of movement and action, yet ignorance of navigation was not such an important deterrent to mutiny as might at first be thought, and chains did not deter others from throwing themselves overboard and drowning or running vessels ashore. It becomes compelling to ascertain the factors that inspired African reactions. Those who have documented the incidents do not give much guide, although some unwittingly provide explanations without appearing to do so. Thus, we see in the accounts of Captain Crow and Alexander Falconbridge that, in spite of their divergent outlook, both could still arrive at the same conclusions about such incidents. What Crow wrote about the African idea of freedom Falconbridge confirmed, though their philosophies differed, the former being a slave trader and the latter a convinced anti-slaver following his experiences as a ship's surgeon.

Among the factors that weighed heavily in forms of resistance were the following: the resentment by Africans of the brutal manner of their capture; their storage like animals in a pen in barracoons during the waiting period before the transatlantic voyage began; and the unsatisfactory conditions of the middle passage engendered by overcrowding and inhuman treatment by the crew (who sometimes suffered disastrously when their guard was relaxed). There was also the overriding fact that their liberty had been curtailed. These were the preliminaries to the traumatic experiences which awaited the slaves once they were beached on the far side of the Atlantic, where brutality became the common experience.

The implications for the European slave traders were far-reaching. First, it became necessary for them to take precautionary measures, and resistance helped to usher in shipping insurances.[68] Second, plantation-owners began to express preferences for slaves from certain areas while rejecting those perceived to be more dangerous from other areas. Third, the fear of losses became an ever-present feature of the conduct of slaving, and traders fortified themselves against unforeseen contingencies, especially on board ship and by overcrowding their vessels. Fourth, and most ominous for slave traders, the revelations of African reactions became useful weapons in the abolitionist armoury in later times for intensifying their campaign against the trade.[69]

We now turn our attention to the introduction of Africans into the Americas, to plantation stratification and to the strategy employed by slave owners to maintain the slave system.

Notes

1 See O. Cugoano, *Thoughts and Sentiments on the Evils of Slavery*, London, 1787, p. 11, for the persistence of passive resistance; O. Equiano, *The Interesting*

Narrative of the Life of Olaudah Equiano (Gustavus Vassa) the African, London, 1789.

2 See John Cory, *Observations upon the Windward Coast of Africa 1805–1806*, London, 1807; new impression, 1968, pp. 72–3; John Atkins, *A Voyage to Guinea etc.*, London, 1735, pp. 177–8. Atkins observed these claims but was not a subscriber to them. F. P. Bowser, *The African Slave in Colonial Peru*, Stanford, Cal. 1974, p. 27; also Rev. Theo Thompson, *The African Trade for Negro Slaves Consistent with Principles of Humanity and with the Laws of Revealed Religion*, Canterbury, n.d. (18th century), pp. 8–31, esp. pp. 12 and 15.

3 B. Quarles, *The Negro in the Making of America*, p. 23; E. Donnan, *Documents Illustrative of the History of the Slave Trade to America*, Washington, D. C., Vol. 3, pp. 217–93, 352; also H. T. T. Catterall, *Judicial Cases Concerning American Slavery and the Negro*, Washington, D. C., Vol. 1, 1926, pp. 19, 22, 25, 28 (representative samples), Vol. 3, 1932, p. 568. See also contested cases of the slave ship *Zong* in F. O. Shyllon, *Black Slaves in Britain*, London, 1974, ch. 12. It provides interesting citations on the state of the law relating to insurance. Also see Thomas Clarkson, *History of the Abolition of the Slave Trade*, Vol. 1, pp. 95–7.

4 J. Pope Hennessy, *Sins of the Fathers: the Atlantic Slave Traders 1441–1807*, London, 1960, p. 62; for preliminaries, see pp. 58–61.

5 *Ibid.*, p. 63.

6 *Ibid.*, p. 64.

7 Donnan, *Documents*, Vol. 4, 1935, p. 374. But we see how the record observed Africans – we have both the postulates of prejudice as well as racism in the citations. It seemed improper for Africans to resist enslavement but seemed legitimate for Europeans to capture and enslave them.

8 *Ibid.*, as narrated in Joseph Hawkins; also Hawkins' *A History of a Voyage to Africa etc.*, New York, 2nd edn., 1797, pp. 146–9. Joseph Hawkins at the time was inexperienced. He had gone to Charleston from New York to seek employment and was hired to engage in the slave trade. It was his one and only voyage to the coast of Africa. This section and the entire orientation of the chapter has profiled from E. Franklin Frazier, *The Negro in the United States*, ch. 5.

9 The Gallas of eastern Africa are known severally as Borana, Wardeh, Oromo (Orma), or simply as Galla, but should not be confused with the Igara (Igala) of the Niger-Benue geographical region of Nigeria, mentioned in the quotation as 'Gallas'.

10 See Hawkins, *History*, pp. 146–9, and E. Donnan, *Documents*, Vol. 4, p. 496.

11 Donnan, *Documents*, Vol. 4, pp. 494–500, esp. pp. 498–9. The entire episode of Joseph Hawkins' voyage is in Donnan, pp. 494–500.

12 Donnan, *Ducuments*, Vol. 2, pp. 485–6, quoted from the *Boston Post Boy*, 13 Aug. 1750.

13 *Ibid.*, Vol. 2, pp. 486–7.

14 Atkins, *Voyage to Guinea*, pp. 71–3; *A New General Collection of Voyages and Travels. Europe, Asia, Africa and Americas, etc.*, London, 1745, p. 449; Atkins quoted in Donnan, *Documents*, Vol. 2, p. 266.

15 Atkins, *Voyage to Guinea*, pp. 72–3. What greater imposition of cannibalism than this could there have been on unwilling clients?

16 Captain William Snelgrave, *A New Account of Some Parts of Guinea and the Slave Trade*, London, 1737 and 1971, pp. 162, 166.

17 Coromantin was a misnomer for the Asante and other Gold Coast slaves named after the port of embarkation to the Americas at Koramantse.

18 Snelgrave, *A New Account . . .*, p. 170.
19 The second occurring a month after the Coromantin revolt at Mumford (Gold Coast).
20 Snelgrave, *Parts of Guinea*, pp. 168–72.
21 *Ibid.*, p. 173.
22 *Ibid.* This point receives confirmation in Dr Alexander Falconbridge, *An Account of the Slave Trade on the Coast of Africa*, London, 1788, pp. 19–32.
23 Snelgrave, *Parts of Guinea*, p. 185.
24 *Ibid.*, pp. 189–90.
25 *Memoirs of Captain Crow*, pp. 200–1.
26 Atkins, *Voyage to Guinea*, pp. 175–6.
27 Atkins in Churchill (ed.), *New General Collection of Voyages and Travels*, Vol. 2, London, 1745, p. 317.
28 Atkins, *Voyage to Guinea*, pp. 57–8. Atkins in another part of the book provided a strong argument to controvert the assertions of some slave captains and factors, like Bosman and Snelgrave, that Africans were cannibals. He argued that not one of those who had asserted that Africans were cannibals had ever seen them eat human flesh and that it was probably a way of inverting the African popular belief that they were being taken away to be eaten by Europeans (see pp. 122–32). It is a spirited defence which needs to be read.
29 Falconbridge, *Account of the Slave Trade*, p. 23. He also observed that when asked to sing, as was to be expected, their songs were generally melancholy lamentations on their exit from their native country (p. 23). This cannot indicate acceptance of slavery, rather the contrary. See also his testimony to the *House of Commons Committee on the Slave Trade, 1790*, Sheila Lambert (ed.), Vol. 72, Wilmington, Del., 1975, p. 595.
30 *Ibid.*
31 *Ibid.*, p. 30.
32 *Ibid.*
33 *Ibid.*, p. 31.
34 *Ibid.*
35 *Ibid.*, p. 32. Alexander Falconbridge in his submissions to the House of Commons Committee on the Slave Trade said that the melancholy songs were 'lamentations for the loss of their country'; see Lambert (ed.), *House of Commons Committee on the Slave Trade, 1790*, p. 595.
36 Thomas Phillips, 'Journal of a Voyage . . . to Cape Monseradoe in Africa, Guiney to Whidaw, Island of St Thomas and Barbados', in Churchill, *Collection of Voyages and Travels*, Vol. 6, p. 229.
37 D. P. Mannix and M. Cowley, *Black Cargoes: a History of the Atlantic Slave Trade, 1518–1865*, New York and London, 1962 and 1963, p. 111.
38 Phillips, 'Journal of a Voyage', p. 219.
39 *Ibid.*
40 *Ibid.*, pp. 229–30.
41 Atkins, *Voyage to Guinea*, pp. 175–60.
42 Mannix and Cowley, *Black Cargoes*, p. 111.
43 Phillips, 'Journal of a Voyage', pp. 229–30.
44 John Newton, *The Journal of a Slave Trader (1750–1754)*, together with *Thoughts Upon the African Slave Trade*, B. Martin and Mark Spurrell (eds.), 1962, p. 80.
45 *Ibid.*, p. 88.

46 *Ibid.*, p. 102. Note the emphasis on *always*. Italics not in original.

47 *Ibid.*, pp. 103–4.

48 C. B. Wadström, *Observations on the Slave Trade and a Description of Some Parts of Guinea during a Voyage Made in 1787 and 1788*, London, 1789, pp. 11–12.

49 Falconbridge, *Account of the Slave Trade*, p. 18.

50 Nicholas Owen, *Journal of a Slave Trader*, London, 1930, pp. 37–8.

51 *Ibid.*

52 *Ibid.* See also p. 112 n, and p. 115 n.

53 Wadström, *Observations*, p. 7.

54 *Ibid.*, pp. 19–21.

55 Bosman, *A New and Accurate Description of the Coast of Guinea*, London, 1705 and 1967, letter xix, p. 376 ff.

56 *Ibid.*, pp. 431–3.

57 *Ibid.*, p. 475.

58 *Ibid.*, p. 476.

59 *Ibid.*, p. 429.

60 William Smith, *A Voyage to Guinea*, London, 1744, 2nd edn., 1967, pp. 17–20.

61 Owen, *Journal of a Slave Trader*, p. 106.

62 See House of Commons, *Sessional Papers of the Eighteenth Century: George III: Minutes of Evidence on the Slave Trade, 1790*, Vol. 72, Part 2, Wilmington, Del., 1975, pp. 588–93, for the slave experience in the middle passage; also pp. 597–9, 630–1, evidence of Alexander Falconbridge.

63 There are many accounts of the *L'Amistad* affair and easily accessible in W. E. B. DuBois, *The Suppression of the African Slave Trade to America 1638–1870*; John Cromwell, *The Negro in American History*, Washington, D. C., 1914, Appendix D, 'The Amistad Captives', pp. 245–6; Mannix and Cowley, *Black Cargoes*, pp. 217–18; also Lewis Tappan, *Life of Arthur Tappan*, New York, 1871, pp. 317–18.

64 See *National Anti-Slavery Standard*, 18 Nov. 1841 p. 93, cols. 5–6; also 30 Dec. 1841, p. 118, cols. 1–6; 6 Jan. 1842, p. 121, cols. 1–6; 13 Jan. 1842, p. 125, cols. 1–6, p. 126, cols. 1–6. The case of the *Encomium* also occurred in 1834; see *Ibid.*, 6 Jan. 1842.

65 Mannix and Cowley, *Black Cargoes*, pp. 218–19. As subsequent pages of *Black Cargoes* show, the Americans did not discharge their own obligations wholeheartedly and continued through using the flag of convenience to aid and abet the Spanish slave trade, pp. 220–3. DuBois, *Suppression of the African Slave Trade*, pp. 142, 273. This incident is also narrated in many other places. It surfaced in the 1843 speech of the Rev. Henry Highland Garnet; see C. G. Woodson, *Negro Orators and Orations*, Washington, D. C., 1925, pp. 150–7. For an indictment by an American squadron commander (Commodore) in West African waters on US persistence in the trade, see A. H. Foote, Africa and the American Flag, pp. 151–6, 215–16, 219–20, esp. pp. 253, 259.

66 See House of Commons, *Evidence on the Slave Trade 1790*, evidence of Alexander Falconbridge.

67 *Ibid.*

68 See the case of the slave ship *Zong* cited in n.3 above, and Cugoano, *Thoughts and Sentiments*, pp. 111–12.

69 Any of the anti-slavery newspapers of the period would yield a wealth of information, but see the *Liberator* (Boston, Massachusetts) for various dates in the early nineteenth century, and especially the years 1831–43.

5   The plantation hierarchy

Introduction to the plantation

In the preceding chapter we saw the beginnings of African resistance to their newly imposed status of slave. We noted the hazards of slave-catching on the west coast of Africa and the difficulties experienced by some captains of slave ships. We mentioned, too, the experiences of the middle passage that led to numerous confrontations between African slaves and ships' crews which continued throughout the slave-trading era. These and other modes of resistance, both at home in Africa and on board ship during the middle passage, were but preludes to the greater eruptions that later plagued the plantations in the Americas.

In order to reinforce the factors which not only made for revolts but made them inevitable and contributed to the tenacity of the slave system in the New World, we must now turn our attention to the strategy of the slavocracy. The term 'slavocracy' corresponds to the slave-owning as well as cultivating aristocracy referred to as 'planters', or 'plantocracy', a term which broadened in time to include others such as merchants, brokers and other speculators in slave disposal, who acquired ownership of slaves and plantations by fair or foul means. But the term here is also used more expansively to include the subordinates who assisted in the development and maintenance of the slave system. By strategy we mean the methods, measures and techniques employed by slave holders and their supporters to sustain the slave system. Broadly, these methods of control were juridical, economic, political, military, social and psychological in character. The various methods employed by the slavocracy and their supporters ran together and combined to convert Africans into beasts of burden, to make them no better than the brutes of the forest. In this chapter we must also consider the reception accorded slaves on their arrival in the Americas, as well as their implanted attitudes and prejudices, the so-called 'laws' or regulations of the system, and the social norms and the methods of ensuring the continuation of slavery, since these too were an essential part of the entire strategy.

In discussing the question of strategy the impression should not be given that from the outset there was a uniform conspiracy,

131

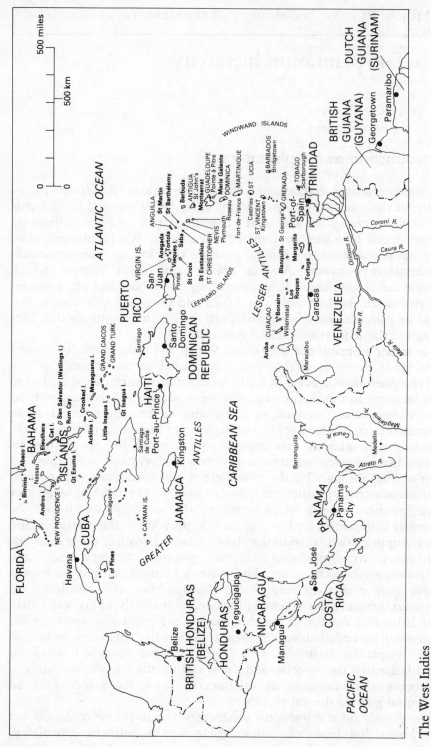

The West Indies

supported by rigid legislation, to create a slaving system by the slave holders, though in a later period it is possible to identify a conspiracy, which aimed to maintain the system that had developed against pressures from elsewhere.[1] It should not be implied either that all slave societies were uniform in character, though with the passage of time certain important common features emerged, and it is with these that we are primarily concerned.

In considering the evolution of the strategy of the slave holders in North America, Kenneth Stampp's observation that the south's 'peculiar institution in the early stages grew slowly and uncertainly',[2] is surely correct. Initially, much of the strategy evolved through practices and customs before it became known to law. The presence of the African slave in the Americas existed many years before the recognition of the legal status of chattel slavery. The Spanish colonies were the exception, and based their slave system on the *Siete Partidas*[3] of King Alfonso X, alias the Wise, codified in the thirteenth century. But a modern historian, F. P. Bowser, has reminded us that the *Siete Partidas* constituted more 'a statement of legislative intent and principles' than a rigid code. He has observed that initially the *Partidas* were intended to guide law-makers in the Americas and to enable slaves to achieve free status, but with time this freedom proved illusory for the vast majority, if not for the few.[4]

The *Partidas* elaborated the principle of recognition of the slave's personality and humanity, but there it ended. In its application, away from the metropolis, local practices were conditioned by expediency and a preoccupation with gain. The *Siete Partidas* were therefore increasingly set aside, unless there were clergy not so taken in by the slavocracy (some clergymen were slave owners in Latin America and elsewhere in the Americas) to mortgage their consciences, and who constituted themselves into the conscience of the Spanish outposts in the Americas. The transplantation of the *Partidas* had as its objective the minimising of abuses against slaves and also provided for state intervention in a conflict between master and slave but, with colonial society as it was and as it developed, harmonisation of these interests did not always take place. In fact local opinion very often conflicted with the intentions of the Crown at home. Local laws formulated on the spot soon began to supersede the *Partidas* and were based on the assertion that they were intended to cope with the daily problems on the spot. Although there was a consistency of laws emanating from the slavocracy, use of the *Partidas* as the guide, and the fact that local laws needed the sanction of the home government before being applied, guaranteed the slaves, in theory at least, certain rights which seemed inviolable. But in reality the laws enacted and implemented for the control of slaves and the coloured population were as harsh as those known in other theatres of slavery in the Americas. Furthermore, distance from the metropolis did not encourage the application of the spirit of the law as envisaged by the crown and evasions were not infrequent. It is in this light that one must view the practices of the plantations, regardless of their legal framework.

Within the New World slave societies that were being established, law and custom (the latter resulting from practice) helped to determine the strategy. While it is not the intention of this work to examine the many laws and facets of law which were enacted to control slave societies, their features are mentioned not only in this chapter but in other parts of the work as the need arises. Specific laws for the purpose of obtaining compliance of slaves are also mentioned. But the nature of some of the practices which helped to solidify the strategy are considered later. This, however, is not a subject which can be exhausted within the compass of a few chapters. Accordingly, only certain aspects of the strategy are examined. Among them are the gradations of slave societies, which helped to emphasise not only differences of status but also conditioned social relationships. The divisions based on other criteria, apart from occupation (i.e. the kind of tasks or division of functions performed), are considered. These relate to place of origin; prejudices; preferences; the criteria of colour, which were numerous in slave societies; religion; and the implications of all these for social cohesiveness and the legacy of this in the post-emancipation period. Also considered are the treatment of slaves and the stipulations imparting knowledge and religion to slaves and freemen of African descent, all of which were tantamount to a conspiracy by the slavocracy to keep the slaves and those descendants of Africa in 'darkness'. We look, too, at the conflicts arising therefrom. In short, the strategy in question was political, economic, social, psychological and juridical in nature. Sometimes the distinctions between these divisions were blurred. But first we must begin with the introduction of the Africans as slaves into the Americas both on the plantations and in other centres of activity. If the plantations are emphasised it is simply because the majority of Africans who came as slaves were taken to the rural areas, to work on farms (as in mainland North America), to labour on plantations, or to toil in mining areas. This, of course, does not ignore that there was an urban slave population. But the fact remains that much of the conditioning emerged initially from the rural environment, and the figures of urban slaves make them just a fraction, albeit a significant fraction, of the many whose lives were spent in the Americas. One must not ignore the fact that there were plantations in North America, or what later became the United States of America, and while farms were more numerous, large plantations were nevertheless known, though in comparison with other theatres of slavery they were fewer.

Arrival, disposal and the 'breaking in' of African slaves

In this chapter we are concerned with seeing how Africans were received in their new setting with a view to acclimatising them to conditions quite unlike those in Africa. Some apologists and protagonists during the slave-trading centuries, and in later writings, have tended to use the factor of the unsuitability of the New World climate to European settlement and exertion as their justification for the procurement of African labour. But in the light of our knowledge of European settlements, and taking account too of continued emigrations to tropical America and other areas, the theory stands discredited. Yet, from the time of the arrival of the Africans, measures were taken to ensure the permanence of their slave status unless released by death. The arrival, sale and the 'breaking in'[5] processes were all aspects of the same thing – that is, to secure compliance and conformity. Dr Alexander Falconbridge gives us a graphic picture of some slave arrivals in the New World and the way the welcome frightened the African slaves, but he also tells of one situation in which the slaves ran away naked into the town until they were apprehended.[6] The West Indian writer, C. L. R. James, has given us an example of the ceremonial arrival, disposal and breaking-in of Africans in Black Jacobins. While conceding that there were wide local variations as to practice, his account nonetheless typifies the kind of initial treatment meted out to the newly arrived slaves and is revealing of the methods employed very early to entrench the distinction between master and slave, lord and serf, violator and victim, oppressor and oppressed. Often in the Americas when the slave ships reached port their cargoes were brought on deck for purchase. Sometimes auctions were announced in advance for a later date, but once the sale commenced the purchaser examined the slaves for defects, and this they did with a curiosity similar to that which one might witness during a first encounter with a horse or mare or ox.[7] It was like a process of smelling out. Their teeth were examined, their skin pinched and, at times, their perspirations were tasted to ensure purity of the slaves' blood and to determine that their health was as good as their appearance. Africans were subjected to all these indignities and still more. Having done this the purchaser, once he decided on a purchase, sometimes slapped the slaves or, as James observes of St Domingue, spat on their faces, in order to establish the distinction which separated master and slave.[8] The scrutiny seemed necessary, for with the passage of time some not so good cargoes of slaves were on occasions passed for healthy slaves. The practice of plugging with oakum the bottoms of slaves suffering from the flux was sometimes carried out in order that they might appear healthy.[9] But the ceremonial receptions of slaves were common practice and can be gleaned from either the autobiographies of slaves[10] who later made good their escape from the citadel of slavery or secured manumission, or from the routine historical accounts of the period. The ceremonial reception was part of the seasoning process and of the psychological technique employed to break the spirit of resistance of the slaves; and seasoning, as a process of acclimatisation, took anything from one to three years. J. B. Moreton, an ex-Jamaican overseer, estimated and believed that about thirty thousand slaves died annually in the seasoning, apart from the high mortality rate known to have existed during the middle passage.[11]

Thus, from the above, we see that the welcome of the slaves began with examination, then sale, and then the 'breaking-in', intended to acclimatise them to the routine of their new environment. Extended, the welcome became seasoning. A rationale to seasoning was the practice of distributing the newly arrived slaves among veteran slaves, or putting them under their special supervision, so that they would soon master their assignments, become reconciled to the climate and food and understand the current language, and shed the propensity to commit suicide. If the slaves achieved this they became very valuable; if they did not they were useless.

Plantation life and hierarchy

Much of the cultivation which was carried on in the New World was based on the plantation, and out of this emerged the plantation system, though we must not forget that the early importers of slaves into the Americas, the Spanish, needed them to work the mines and till the land.[12] The use of slaves in mining did not cease, but the slaves were also necessary for the production of staples as well as food crops. There was no uniformity in the size of plantations in the Americas. While the West Indies and Brazil had large-sized plantations, those of North America were relatively small with slave populations ranging from twenty to fifty, though this did not rule out exceptions, some plantations having more than five hundred slaves.[13]

In the United States, with the cultivation of cotton on a large scale, it was observed that with about three-quarters of the slaves directly engaged in agriculture, mostly in the production of cotton, the 'typical life of the slaves was life on the plantation'.[14] In the

West Indies the slaves knew nothing else but the plantation, with the exception of the domestic slaves, who were in a different category in the differentiation of slave society, or the dockers and wharf hands.

Class and caste institutionalised

It is difficult to make a clear distinction between class and caste as they evolved in slave societies[15] of the Americas, but for the sake of precision we shall define *class* in terms of economic status and the kind of labour performed within the hierarchical arrangement, and *caste* in terms of shade gradations (the colour of the skin) making for social attitudes of exclusiveness and aloofness. But, all said and done, class and caste very often coincided, even with the progression of slavery and after its demise in the nineteenth century. The latter aspect has survived into the twentieth century and is one of the lasting legacies of slavery in the Americas.

In these social, class, racial, as well as colour, divisions in slave societies, local variations depended on numerous factors, one of them being the size of the population as well as the size of the plantations and estates cultivated. Nevertheless, with our present state of knowledge, we are able to assert that there were similarities in social divisions in all the Americas. These divisions were, and still are, more numerous in the West Indies than elsewhere in the Americas. Since Jamaica presented the fullest development of these distinctions, we should observe the very perceptive differentiations noted by the Reverend Caldecott and well-entrenched in the nineteenth century as the most representative form of social organisation on the plantations. He distinguished the following five groups: first, the ruling whites; second, the subordinate whites; third, the white bond servants; fourth, the coloured people and free blacks, and finally, the slaves. This was a kind of hierarchical arrangement reminiscent of the feudal system in medieval Europe. Although Caldecott quoted the economist, Alfred Marshall, who asserted that 'the two great forming agencies of the world's history have been the religious and the economic', Caldecott observed that in the West Indies (and we might say in the Americas) the economic was the ruling agency. That sentiment also sums up slavery on the plantations. For, where the paramountcy of economic gain ruled the hearts and heads of men, nothing else mattered and the end justified the means.

So, the plantation system settled the entire fabric of society. But these various categories distinguished on the plantations as distinct social groups, if not classes, were further subdivided. Thus, under the ruling white oligarchy were to be noted: planters, merchants, professionals, lawyers, doctors, clergymen, many as high government officials, and lastly, the governor and other high officials.

1a The planters   The planter was often landlord, farmer and manufacturer, owning the land, growing the cane and manufacturing the sugar, molasses and rum. All these activities were embodied in an 'estate'. An arrangement of this kind involved a large capital outlay and the small men stood little chance of competing effectively. Small men who tried with a few acres were easily devoured by the 'big men'.[16] Here are some figures. The first list is a breakdown of a typical West Indian plantation in the eighteenth century.[17]

Acreage	500
Devotion to sugar cane	150
Remainder devoted to provision	
of pasturage for estate consumption	350
African slaves employed	200
Required capital per acre	£80
Total capital needed	£40 000

Estimate of 'La Sucrerie Cottineau', St Domingue, 1784

	Number	Average Value	Total Value
Total acres	1560	£15.7s	£23 950
Acres under cane	453	£44.2s	£19 983
Sugar works			£9 593
Negroes	173	£48.14s	£8 423
Livestock	150	£16.4s	£2 427
Utensils, etc.			£774
Total			£45 167

St Domingue livres are converted into sterling at the ratio of 28.7:1. The figures relate to a single plantation in St Domingue, that of Cottineau, and help to demonstrate that the plantation was a large business undertaking.

Source: Gabriel Debien, *Plantations et Esclaves à Sa.Domingue*, Dakar, 1962, p. 18, reproduced in R. Sheridan, *The Development of the Plantations to 1750*, London, 1967, p. 54.

J. B. Moreton, an ex-West Indian overseer towards the end of the eighteenth century, observed not only the big business aspect of the sugar plantation but also the hazards that went with it.

Here let me observe the vast expence which attends establishing a sugar plantation, supposing keeping only one hundred acres constantly under canes. The mill, boiling and curing-houses, and distill-house, with all the conveniences belonging to them, such as coppers, still, vats, cisterns, reservoirs, tutters and pumps, manager's house, stores, etc. etc. will cost about £8000; one hundred and forty slaves will cost about £6000 more; and if there is not the convenience of water to the mill, and the plantation is far from the shipping-place, there will be forty good mules, and about one hundred oxen, always required on the estate, which will cost about £300 and will require a good convenient grass-penn to feed them; finding the slaves in food, and some sorts of cloathing, and keeping up their numbers still as they die, as also that of cattle and mules, and finding plantation implements, is attended with no small expence annually; say £800; supposing the plantation and penn to contain three hundred acres, at £30 per acre (which is very cheap) they will amount to £9000 more: all which sums amount to £26 000 at the lowest computation; (indeed, any sort of good plantation with slaves and stock, etc. will cost £30 or £40 000); which sum of £26 000 at 8 per cent interest is average one hundred and sixty hogsheads of good Muscovado sugar yearly and eighty puncheons of rum, the sugar to net at £15 sterling per hogshead, and the rum at £12 per puncheon, both will amount to £3360 sterling; from which, deducting the annual expence, the remainder is £480 in favour of the planter; which is by no means equal to the risque he runs of hurricans, droughts, etc. etc. so that in my humble opinion a sugar plantation should be no desirable object for a man to seek after. Any man with four or five thousand pounds may get possession of a plantation, slaves etc. by compounding to pay the remainder of the value in annual installments, and giving a mortgage by way of security on the estate; and after he had exhausted all his property thereon, it is taken from him or his heirs in the end, and sold to pay off debts: I say, there is very little difficulty in getting possession of an estate, but a great deal to keep it.[18]

According to Caldecott, at the time of high prosperity in Jamaica there were 700 such 'estates'. The planter lived like an English squire in a 'Great House', the equivalent of a medieval manor house. A good deal of his household provisions was supplied by the estate and usually forty African slaves were attached to domestic service. This was the picture during the early stages. Later, when the planter accumulated wealth, he often retired to the home country – Britain – leaving the estate in the care of agents. Thus, the planter or owner became an absentee landlord[19] and his agent assumed the title of attorney or factor. Thus even an inefficient agent could be put in charge of anything from ten to fifteen estates. He could reside on one of the estates, if not on his own, and from time to time receive reports from his overseers. Caldecott records that in 1796, out of 769 Jamaican proprietors, 606 were absentee.[20] The effect of this was calamitous. These absentee landlords at home were able to influence Parliament at Westminster and so secure their interests on the plantations, just as the planters of the American South, whose plantations determined the economy of the South, assumed the dominant influence in the government there and received representation in Congress sufficient that they were able to secure for a long time the maintenance of the slave system.[21] The writer of the *Journal of a Lady of Quality*, an eighteenth-century eyewitness of an impressionistic account, whose author was Miss Janet Schaw, left a fine but revealing repository of happenings in the slave islands of the West Indies; and, although she displayed little or no emotion about the evils of the slave practice, having herself accepted the norms and values of those societies, she was a perceptive observer and had something of interest to say on the practice of absentee landlordism. Writing of Antigua between 1774 and 1776, she showed how the basis of the practice was rooted in the despatch of children of planters to Britain at an early age to attend boarding schools, where they cultivated friendships, forming their outlook in Britain as well as beginning their early connections there, and left Britain, just at the time when they were at an age to enjoy it most, to return to the West Indies as 'banished exiles'. She saw this practice of sending children to Britain at a very early age as improper, for not only did she observe numerous instances of the failure of these children to adjust to their home environment in the West Indies, but felt their yearning for Britain resulted in many of them abandoning the islands (which she regarded as little paradises) to live extravagantly in Britain. This involved throwing away 'vast sums of money in London, where they are either entirely overlooked or ridiculed for an extravagance[22] which, after all, does not even raise them to a level with hundreds around them; while at the same time they neglect the cultivation of their plantations, and leave their delightful dwellings to overseers, who enrich themselves and live like princes at the expense of their thoughtless masters, feasting every day on delicacies, which the utmost extent of expense is unable to procure in Britain'.[23] She singled out Antigua as an exception to the rule, having more proprietors on it than any of the other islands, thus giving it, according to her, a greater superiority. Of St Christophers she recorded, on hearsay, that it was almost abandoned to overseers and managers, caretaking 'the amazing fortunes that belong to individuals, who almost all reside in England'.[24] In revealing some of the abuses to which absenteeism gave rise, she specifically mentioned a Mr Mackinnon, who had never been to his West Indian estate until circumstances compelled him; his overseer forgot he had any superior and had neither given account nor made any remittances to his master for over two years.

This was the factor which impelled Mr Mackinnon to visit his estate, where he was fortunate to find it in good order and to discover that the overseer had justified his trust. Nevertheless she observed that since Mr Mackinnon's constitution had then become entirely British he was much affected by the West Indian climate and was forced to think of wintering in New York for health reasons. As slavery progressed, the planters ceased to be men with independent capital, and because of mortgages, jointures, annuities to younger brothers and sisters, and other expenses, planters were induced to borrow and rely increasingly on loans; thus the margin of profit or income left to the nominal owner of an estate became smaller and smaller. For these reasons the estates were worked at high pressure with a view to securing quick, profitable returns, and the entire business became increasingly speculative, with estates often changing hands.[25]

1b The merchants Still in the top group of the plantation hierarchy were the merchants, whose duty it was to buy and export the products of the estates. In turn they imported foreign provisions, tools, clothes, hardware and luxury goods. British firms, as well as firms in other European countries, had agencies on the islands and thus began a system of consignment whereby a planter agreed to hand over his entire produce in exchange for the articles supplied by the firms. With the ascendancy of this kind of relationship the merchants soon made inroads into the erstwhile preserves and independence of the producer class, and indirectly, of the colonies as well.[26] Thus, after the failure of the firm of Higgensons of Liverpool, it was revealed that it had controlled one-third of the entire produce of Barbados. From this and other sources it can be gleaned that the resident merchants and their principal agents acquired the social status of planters and attorneys. In fact planters who retired to the metropolis became creditors and merchants, thus achieving for a while an uneasy merger between the planters and merchants.

Edward Long, author of a history of Jamaica, observing the situation in the eighteenth century, has demonstrated how merchants, through loans, made inroads into the preserves of the planters until they became overwhelmed or even displaced, or became increasingly dependent on them. The impression he left was that the merchants were hard 'task-masters' and that this produced a state of 'perpetual warfare' between them, and that it tended to destroy the mutual confidence which should have existed between merchants and planters. Through these proceedings planters were ruined by their creditors (merchants) and dispossessed of their property. Litigation became rife and this, in turn, unsettled the slaves as they were liable to be transfered to another owner with the minimum of warning. At times the planter was known to have barricaded himself within his estates with the support of his slaves, armed; and the slaves had sometimes refused to be sold elsewhere.[27] These conflicts were local, but Long suggested that it was better for the planters to redeem themselves by cultivating the friendship and 'support of honest wealthy merchants in Great Britain by the wisdom and efficacy of new credit laws' as the merchants of Jamaica were merely appendages to the merchants of Britain and depended on them, without whose assistance the merchants of Jamaica would have been nothing short of 'beggars'.[28] Long had recommended this, having observed that the planters of Antigua had done this through legislation, for he believed it would produce a salutary situation in Jamaica.

The conflicts which bedevilled the relations of the two groups among the slavocracy in the plantations were reflected in the founding of separate headquarters to discuss their interests in London. The Jamaica Coffee House, the first headquarters of the West India interest in London, consisted of merchants, mostly among the richest of plantation society, and functioned in England from 1674.[29] Later they were to coalesce with American mercantile interests, continuing to be separate from the Planters Club.[30] But with the commencement of meetings between planters and merchants from 1775 the unification of their interests could be said to have begun.[31]

It has been suggested that the American revolution affected planter prosperity in the West Indies, and that the need for solidarity between planter and merchants led to the formation of a common front.[32] But the British prejudice of the landed interests, the so-called gentlemen, for a time existed, as during the period of the English industrial revolution and down into the nineteenth century, when the squirearchy looked down on merchants and members of the commercial classes as upstarts with no tradition.

1c Men of the professions   This group consisted of professionals who were higher government officials, as well as lawyers, doctors and clergymen. Slightly apart were the governor and other high officials, the latter constantly sent from the metropolitan country. While the American colonies could boast during the colonial era of being able to elect their own governors, the West Indian colonies at no time came near to achieving this. These offices were very important and well remunerated. In Jamaica the colonial secretary, the provost-marshal, and the prothonotary[33] drew from £6000 to £9000 a year apiece. The entire system gave rise to abuse and often the appointments were conferred on court favourites (as they were too in the French, Spanish and Portuguese colonies). Other recipients were party supporters who neither went out to the plantations nor ever contemplated doing so. These 'patentees', instead of being on the spot, appointed permanent deputies and leased out the revenues of their offices. It was revealed, for example, that an office of £1050 was let for £840 a year, leaving £210 for the lessee who, in fact, did all the work.[34] This exploitation of the men on the spot in the colonies by those who took the lion's share as well as the prestige was long-standing, and from time to time it evoked the resentment and protests of the colonists and others,[35] but to no avail, for the practice of the mother country was in keeping with the mercantilist preoccupations of those times. Thus, the British Parliament would not recognise nor countenance Acts passed by the local legislatures in the years 1699, 1711 and 1715, which were intended to curb such abuses.[36] The leaseholders continued to squeeze out exorbitant fees and it was said that the 'controller of customs' at Kingston in Jamaica received fees on shipping five times those charged in American ports. Although Lord Lansdowne, the Secretary of State, in 1782, forbade the issue of patents, apart from residence, it took two generations for the reforms to be effective. It was known that in 1814 there were still ninety-four patents in the colonies held by fifty-five absentees (including all colonial secretaryships), of which ninety had been issued since 1782. But in 1834 the number had been reduced to six. The situation was not dissimilar to that prevailing in other colonies. In 1814 six Canadian offices were in this position. Yet, the American colony of Virginia for forty years experienced the imposition of a non-resident governor, the Earl of Oakney.[37]

Lawyers were required to have obtained qualifications at the English Bar, although the governor had the prerogative of sometimes issuing licences to some so that they might practise. Solicitors could either obtain their qualifications in England or serve articles in the colonies.

Many of the doctors were not properly qualified. Many were holders of a Certificate of Apothecaries.[38] The few who were properly qualified ranked as professional men. Long's highmindedness led him to suggest that Jamaica needed properly-trained physicians, surgeons and apothecaries to attend to slaves, many lives being annually lost because of 'dabblers' far from skilful.

Public affairs then were administered and monopolised by the planters, merchants and lawyers. The franchise qualifications were not only high (in terms of property and influence) but were encumbered in several ways with reservations to keep the local legislative assembly and local vestries entirely in the hands of the vested interests, who constituted the ruling oligarchy. It is from among them that the magistrates and the grand jurors and officers of the militia were recruited.

2 The subordinate whites   These formed the second major category in the plantation hierarchy in the slave societies of this period. Among them were, first, managers or overseers of estates, with salaries ranging from about £100 to £200 a year, some of whom aspired to the status of attorney. Secondly, there were the 'book-keepers'. They directed the operations in the fields and in the boiling house, earning about £50 to £80 a year and could graduate to overseers' status. Their mortality rate tended to be high and they rarely worked for more than five or six years, their deaths resulting often from disease or vice, and the rank and file were replenished by immigrants from Britain. By being peddlers of vice they constituted a distinct class. Their employers despised them as social inferiors. Many of them nurtured ambitions of working temporarily and eventually acquiring the money with which to become slave owners too. Since the assessment of capability was judged on the manager's ability to produce a bumper crop, the managers quite often tended to demonstrate that ability by driving the slaves to their utmost limit, and this often had fatal consequences on slaves and the land – much more so than had the owner been present. They were mostly young men, wild and easy-going, and lived as a barrack community with the overseers, and were not permitted to marry. It gave them reason to indulge their sexual passions, as Moreton and others observed.[39] Accordingly, only a negligible number of them lived to middle age. Third, there were a few master mechanics, some of whom worked independently, possessing ten to twelve slaves, while others worked on the estate. Fourth, there were the clerks in the offices and retail stores. In Jamaica the storekeepers were mostly Jews. As more mulattos were born in the community there arose a crop of 'coloured' persons and these in time wended their way into the clerkship and mechanical trades, as in another context they would fill intermediate roles.[40]

3a The white bond servants   Initially these were drawn from the criminals and political prisoners from the mother country.[41] They were indentured servants, some for life and others for a defined period, and were allocated to various estates. They also included thieves, vagrants and vagabonds, or those described as such in the mother country. Some were even abducted under the pretext of being convicts, a practice not dissimilar to the abduction of Free Negroes or coloured people in North America under the pretext that they had been slaves and had at a previous date run away from their masters. But even within this group there were immigrants who had come on their own initiative by offering themselves to be indentured as servants for a defined period. But this hardly improved their status and their treatment was no better than that of those stigmatised as criminals. They hardly experienced any relief until their period of indenture had been completely served. There were also settlements of poor whites occupying smallholdings, as in Barbados. But they were far from prosperous and constituted a community of outcasts. This latter group was largely recruited from a variety of sources which included such people as the earlier settlers of the islands; ex-officers and sailors; pirates; buccaneers in the Caribbean and the Spanish Main; a thousand Irish men and girls despatched during the reign of Cromwell; Cavalier refugees from Cromwell's rule; and Commonwealth men who fled Britain at the time of the Restoration of Charles II. They also included some émigrés from the British colony of Surinam[42] after the Dutch had received it in exchange for New Amsterdam (now New York) in North America in 1675, and some of the survivors of the Scottish fiasco on the Gulf of Darien (i.e. the Darien Scheme), together with Huguenot refugees from France who intermarried with English settlers. From the above we have gleanings of the disparate groups which formed this class in the plantation colonies of the British West Indies. But we must consider how the above two classes, i.e. subordinate whites and white bond servants, evolved.

3b Indentured European servants   It was observed in 1724 that there were three kinds of 'white' servants brought to the colonies, as follows: first, *contract labourers*, who were people who had agreed to be servants for a fixed period of time at a certain agreed wage;[43] second, *indentured labourers*, who were commonly known as 'kids', and their period of indenture was four to five years; third, *the criminal class* (the majority), who were made up of convicts and felons transported from the mother country. Many of them had been guilty of crimes such as murder. For Portuguese Brazil and other colonies of Portugal in Africa and Asia, these *degradados* consisted of rogues, vagabonds, 'sturdy beggars' exiled from Portugal to the colonial ports of Recife, Bahia, Luanda, etc. They contributed much to lowering the morality of those societies. The influence of many of them on other servants on the plantation or in the colonies was corrupting. It might well be that for some of them their transportation to the colonies was not really a worsening of their material condition. One writer ventured to assert that 'Their being sent thither to work as slaves for punishment is but a mere notion for few of them ever lived so well and so easy before, especially if they are good for anything [nothing]'.[44]

Among this criminal class the period of service ranged from seven to fourteen years. They and the indentured servants received an allowance of corn and clothes to start them off when they had completed their service. They came from all over Britain (England, Wales, Scotland and Ireland). Their lot was much better if they were under 'good' masters than if they were under bad ones. But these criminal types were among the villains, given to loose and riotous living. Accordingly, brutal methods were sometimes employed to tame them, and often unsuccessful attempts were made to curb them by law.

At the conclusion of their service opportunities were provided for some to work as free day labourers or to rent a small plantation for a paltry sum, or even to become overseers,[45] or, if they had acquired any skills in carpentry, as a blacksmith, in tailoring, sewing, bricklaying, as coopers or in any other trade, they were free to pursue this. Thus, their wages were deemed to secure them against complete destitution. The exceptions to this were the infirm, the lame, those worn out by age, deformities, accidents or some other incapacitating ailments. But this latter group became chargeable to the parish in which they resided. Where families with many poor children abounded, the vestry took on the responsibility of caring for them and apprenticed the children until they were able to support themselves through their own labour. It was felt that the latter arrangement prevented these pauper children from becoming vagrants, vagabonds and beggars. Furthermore, they were secured from abduction or arrest because they were in regular employment, for abduction or arrest would have placed them in a far worse plight than their existing one. Moreover, it enabled them to give an account of themselves should they be confronted with the charge of having run away from their masters, just as Free Negroes, who could not give an account of themselves, were deemed to be runaway slaves liable to arrest and enslavement. Moreover, such a situation would have made them very vulnerable since the financial inducements given to informers and catchers made the latter assiduous in the discharge of their duties of reporting on those servants or 'negroes' who could not produce identity cards to show where they were employed and the name of their owner. We can see that what came to be the 'pass laws', known in the colonial era in East and Central Africa, had their foundations in the slave societies of the western hemisphere. The fate of those so apprehended was often far from happy; for, apart from their chastisement, it involved them in the extension of their period of servitude, worked out sometimes in proportion to the expenses and inconveniences incurred in their recovery for what was deemed to be their gross dereliction of duty.[46] The pounds, shillings and pence of plantation inconveniences were often worked out in incredible detail.

But it was too easy to glamorise the lot of the indentured servants or the contract labourers. There were occasional revelations of their lot being very unsatisfactory. For example, a William Eddis described conditions he observed in London in 1792. He was at pains to emphasise that they were quite often brought to America under false pretences, a practice known as 'crimping', and that, contrary to the widely held notions of improvement, the 'indented servants and the convicted felons' were often treated alike and that both groaned beneath a system worse than 'Egyptian bondage'. Accordingly, attempts at escape by these servants were not infrequent, though, more often than not, they were unsuccessful, partly because the country was intersected by a network of rivers which barred the path of the escapers, and partly because the 'utmost vigilance' was exercised in halting people on the move under suspicious circumstances. In addition, there was the practice of advertising an escapee and promising a reward for his recapture. These factors tended to forestall those who intended to escape from a contract which proved to be no better than servitude. The writer asserted that 'the European servants were in a far worse plight than African slaves; for, since the masters recognised that servitude for the African was for life, the death or loss of a slave in the prime of life represented a financial loss, and they took care to exercise less severity than they would on those unfortunate European wretches'.[47] This assertion is certainly questionable, even if we do not dispute the better demeanour of some slave owners towards their slaves or their instructions for the handling of African slaves,[48] for, simply, in a choice between temporary servitude and perpetual servitude, the former is to be preferred, though no form of servitude is compatible with man's dignity and yearning for self-expression. Moreover, the assertion is insupportable by the high rate of slave mortality.

4a The coloured people   These were mainly the progeny of the cohabitation of a planter, manager, attorney, overseer or other free European with, often unwilling, African women slaves. With the growth of some free coloured women, the varieties of colour became more numerous. Their progeny sometimes were the inheritors of large bequests on the death of their white or coloured fathers. Edward Long implied that the practice was widespread in Jamaica and in the Spanish colonies as well. His arguments are not repeated here because they are long and tedious, typical of a man of rather illiberal instincts, racist in the extreme, and because they are an attempt to satirise what essentially was a pathetic problem which plagued slave societies. He even provided a diagrammatic representation of how the breed became more 'degenerate' or less so, and the manner in which the breed was improved. As has been observed in another context, the entire pattern of behaviour leaves one with a picture of inverted eugenics. He attributes this breed to 'intemperance and sensuality' and, according to him, they constituted a 'spurious offspring of different complexions,[49] the result of licentiousness'. Long was scathing about the liaisons of Europeans

147

and African women and even suggested the application of the principles of the 'Lombard law' to curtail the affinity which white slave owners showed for their female black and tawny slaves.[50] But Long was also concerned about the morals and chastity of the slaves; for, as he argued, while quoting Montesquieu with approval, 'slavery should be calculated for utility, not for pleasure. The laws of chastity arise from those of nature, and ought in all nations to be respected.'[51] In revealing his strong disapproval for the coloured progeny who littered the plantations, he wrote:

> On first arriving here, a civilised European may be apt to think it imprudent and shameful, that even bachelors should publicly avow their keeping Negro or Mulatto mistresses; but they are still more shocked at seeing a group of white legitimate, and Mulatto illegitimate children, all claimed by the same married father, and all bred up together under the same roof. Habit, however, and the prevailing fashion reconcile such scenes, and lessen the abhorrence excited by their first impression.[52]

But he was even more dissatisfied with the practice of bequeathing large legacies to these 'coloured' children, often in slavery, which he felt would disorientate the society, and he provided arguments against leaving large legacies to them and approved of the stipulation which limited the kind of inheritance that a slave should have as a bequest.[53] His principal argument was that the children were 'illegitimate' and, although he was willing for special concessions to be made in exceptional situations, these could only be done by an Act of the legislature.[54] According to him, the Jamaican Assembly in 1762 made enquiries as to the bequests made to mulatto progeny of their testators, and the amount was found to approximate to £200 000–£300 000, including 'four sugar estates, seven penns, thirteen houses, besides other lands unspecified'.[55] Turning to Spanish America, he wrote:

> Let any man turn his eyes to the Spanish American dominions, and behold what a vicious, brutal and degenerate breed of mongrels has been there produced, between Spaniards, Blacks, Indians, and their mixed progeny; and he must be of opinion, that it might be much better for Britain, and Jamaica too, if the white men in that colony would abate their infatuated attachments to black women, and instead of being grac'd with a yellow offspring not their own perform the duty incumbent on every good citizen, by raising in honourable wedlock a race of unadulterated beings.[56]

But, worse still, apart from facing up to the Europeans' handiwork,

Long could not be reconciled to the opportunities which were afforded these coloured progeny, male and female, to study abroad. In fact, he called them names which were uncomplimentary – 'young Fuscus', 'Miss Fluvia' – and on their return to the colony they had to live among their relations of 'unfortunate birth', such as 'Quashee and Mingo'.[57]

The implication in all this is that the more fortunate coloured progeny had a good start in life through manumission, through inheritance of a huge fortune to set up on their own, and through educational opportunities. The less fortunate ones still had advantages over others in that they became clerks, blacksmiths, masons and carpenters, and as skilled craftsmen they were a degree or two higher than the ordinary free blacks or even slaves, whose lot was to toil in the fields.

4b The free blacks   These are further subdivided into the *bozales* (i.e. those freshly imported from Africa), some of whom ran away from the plantations to form Maroon communities[58] until recognised by treaty or law; and the second group being Creole blacks who certainly were in the majority among the free blacks. It is not easy to compile their numbers in order to underline the differences. But some writers tend to imply that the differences between the two groups were so fundamental as to suggest that each was a class or special group apart.[59] Long's strictures on the 'Guinea Negroes' in contrast to the 'Creole Negroes' leaves the impression that the latter were to be preferred in the organisation of plantation hierarchy. The general impression seems to have been that the former, if not a 'brute', 'savage', 'degenerate', 'bestial', 'stupid', or 'vice-ridden' type was akin to a 'monkey', 'orangoutang' or was 'quadrumanous'[60] and was the very incarnation of the 'devil'. Such imagery had its functions within slave societies and survived the slave experience, as one of the unfortunate legacies bequeathed to mankind. At this point the question which Dr Eric Williams once raised looks as if it needs reappraisal. Williams wrote that 'Slavery was not born of racism but rather racism was the consequence of slavery'.[61] The point is that if the African was so considered by the imagery described above, it is no surprise that he was treated like a brute. This question of racism and slavery or the slave trade has been made by a modern European author[62] and needs to be taken more seriously than has hitherto been the case. But in order not to stray from the subject, these free blacks consisted in the main of manumitted African slaves (Creole and non-Creole) induced to purchase their freedom, or of descendants of free parents or a mother who was a free woman, as the status of the child tended to follow that of the mother and if the woman were a slave and the father a free man, then the child would be a slave according to the practices of slave societies. This was the so-called 'womb law'. Some of these free men[63] were outstanding and men of merit, in spite of Long's desire to deflate their achievements.[64] They were to be found in trades and stores, and very frequently they possessed a slave or two.[65] It is even suggested that in Brazilian society these free men had recognisable status.[66] In the United States the weight of prejudice led to its rationalisation and fear of competition on the part of 'mean' whites resulted in free blacks being regarded as a 'degraded class'. The possession of a slave or two tended to give them a vested, if negligible, interest in the institution of slavery. They could hardly have been of any consequence in the maintenance of slavery, but participation in the keeping of slaves was added ammunition for the Europeans, who saw nothing wrong in the institution of the slave trade when many of the Africans transported from Africa were allegedly slaves in their own country[67] (an untrue assertion on the Europeans' part). This group of people in the plantation hierarchy in a category or class of their own were removed from the higher classes and separated from the slaves who were the lowest in the hierarchy. They accordingly became the target for religious conversion and they seemed very receptive to the evangelisation which was directed at them during a later period. Jamaica, with some other slave communities, had its own peculiarity, namely the 'Free Negroes of the Mountains' or Maroons. These communities were initially formed from escaped Spanish African slaves and other slaves, who continued to flee the plantations until the demise of slavery. These Maroons intermittently disturbed the peace of mind of the planters (if there ever was any peace in a revolt-ridden and recurrent insurrectionary situation). They were eventually captured and deported in 1796 to Nova Scotia; later some of them were transported to Sierra Leone in West Africa.[68] The remnants of this group, after the abolition of slavery, became Jamaicans.

5 The slaves   The last group, but by no means the least important one, except in social status and influence, were the slaves, who, in terms of the production of wealth for the plantations and the mother country, were the most numerous in the community but the least organised, and consequently the least represented – if represented at all – in the councils of the plantation. They were disenfranchised. Even among them there were subdivisions according to occupation.[69] It has often been asserted that plantation tasks were graded according to sex, age and strength of members of the labour force, but Frances Anne Kemble, writing from Georgia in the U.S.A., denied this to be the case in many instances. On her husband's estate, on her first visit, she found men and women working as field hands with the same tasks to perform. She asserted that this was 'a noble admission of female equality'. But, in time, her husband diminished the quantity of work performed by women.[70] The four main divisions were:

a *Mechanics* – made up of carpenters and smiths (caulkers) on the estate, and stevedores.

b *Domestic servants (slaves)* – consisting of men and women, some of whom were among the privileged in the social setting; at least in having enough to eat in the household of the owners and inheriting the cast-off clothes of their masters and mistresses.[71] These again tended to include mulattos, often the progeny of the planters themselves, who were not recognised as their children.[72] These formed the ranks which divulged any attempts at escape or insurrection by slaves. They sought to ingratiate themselves with the master.[73]

c *Headmen* – these included herd drivers of cattle and mules and some were slave drivers, head watchmen and head boilingmen.

d *The field hands and the boiling hands*[74] – they were pace-setters and supervisors of small groups. These were the men and women who bore the 'burden and the heat' of the long and arduous years of slavery on the plantations, often working from sunrise to sunset. Their cabins were far from hygienic and lacked even rudimentary furniture. Food consisted of cornbread and bacon. Where a master was a little more considerate, he might allow the slaves some plot of land on which to cultivate vegetables and even keep a pig or some poultry. When this extra concession existed it was possible for the slaves to vary their diet. This category consisted of both predial attached and predial unattached.[75]

As for the division of duties on the plantations among the slave groups, it would appear that the American experience was not dissimilar to that of the West Indies. Most of the slaves – men, women and children – worked in the fields. The three ways in which work might be done on the plantations were, first, by the *task system*, in which work for a day was assigned to a slave, based on what was considered his ability to perform it. Or, according to Janet Schaw, 'They are sorted out to match each other in size and strength. Every ten being placed under a driver who walks behind them with a short whip and a long one.'[76] Secondly there was the *gang system*, in which the pace was set by a good slave driver and emulated by the rest of the gang. The third system was that whereby slaves proceeded to work on their own initiative: under such circumstances the chief motivator was fear of the whip. Divisions of gangs varied from three or four or more, according to the circumstances and size of the plantations or estates as well as the size of the slave population. When there were four gangs, they consisted of the Great Gang or First Gang, consisting of the majority of field hands, including the boiling hands. Members of the Second Gang, who, although regarded as inefficient and less powerful than those comprising the First Gang, were sometimes known to perform identical operations. The Third Gang, when there were only three gangs, was described as 'feeble' and consisted of children, the aged, infirm and pregnant. But when there were four gangs, then the Fourth Gang consisted of little children, sometimes known as the Grass Gang. Both the Third and Fourth Gangs performed such monotonous tasks as weeding, collecting wood, greenmeat and food for the livestock, but even their assignments were not as light as might be imagined. On the whole, the field hands had a hard existence, working very long hours, often from dawn to dusk and in the boiling house there were those who worked the night shift for twelve hours at a stretch. Such was the lot of the field hands, who bore the burdens of the plantations and slave societies.

These slaves were quartered in wooden huts, sometimes known as log cabins, which were massed together near the place of work, the large and thick plantation shielding them from the great house (or mansion) of the planter. The lot of these slaves was unlike that of the domestic slaves. They had to grow their own provisions and once a year clothes were doled out to them, often coarse and ragged.[77] Many of the field hands were familiar with the vicissitudes of starvation. There is no doubt that some slave owners took care to nourish their slaves in order to urge them to greater exertions. Likewise there were careless slave masters and overseers who overworked the slaves; in fact, they drove them hard, sometimes even on empty stomachs, and often with fatal results. The records of travellers and eyewitnesses, like Janet Schaw, tend to give the impression of 'well fed, well supported' negroes,[78] but this kind of evidence from someone who believed in the perpetuation of slavery can hardly be conclusive. A high mortality rate was known to exist on many slave plantations, though the fact that some deaths were due to illness can hardly justify the assertion that the slaves were well-fed. Of course, it is reasonable to suppose that some planters, anxious that the slaves should work well, might have taken pains to look into their welfare, especially in matters relating to food; but, in a highly speculative business, speculation which increased in intensity as the competition between the big and the small slave holders grew and as the quick-profit motive was a major factor in the speculative game, there is much room for scepticism about the notion of 'well-fed' and 'well-contented slaves', something which is not borne out by the autobiographies of slaves themselves.

The above structure of the plantations within the same zone, or even in different zonal locations, would repay further scrutiny.

Nevertheless, we cannot pursue this here since it is not relevant to the basic point of this study.

We have been at great pains to sketch, briefly, the types who populated the plantations and the hierarchical arrangements in order to demonstrate the numerous and varying types from which African slaves were expected to derive their values in a new environment. Their values were also expected to mould the African slaves into acquiescence in their altered status. As the arrangements into which these diverse types were thrown speak for themselves, it is not difficult to imagine the havoc wrought on the enslaved Africans' psychology in this long period of acculturation to the New World environment. It is, therefore, easy to understand the many and conflicting tendencies exhibited by Africans and their descendants in the diaspora resulting from centuries of sustained conditioning, propaganda, badgering and brutalisation. The arrangements were further complicated by the divisive techniques inherent in the institutionalisation of castes based on skin colour differentiations and gradations and induced preferences as well as other divisive criteria. This entire approach to the enslaved African by the slavocracy was to constitute, in large measure, the strategy of the slavocracy against which slaves, in time, were to evolve a counter strategy. The gradations by preference, class and colour in further encouraging divisions among Africans and their Creole counterparts now require attention.

Notes

1 See, for instance, *The National Anti-Slavery Standard*, 27 Jan. 1842, for the first pro-slavery convention in Annapolis (Maryland), which met on 13 Jan. 1842. Activities in the various parliaments, both local and national, would yield a rich harvest on this conspiracy to maintain the system.
2 Kenneth Stampp, *The Peculiar Institution*, New York, 1969, p. 21.
3 Elsa V. Goveia, 'The West India Slave Laws of the 18th century', in E. D. Genovese and L. Foner (eds.), *Slavery in the New World: a Reader in Comparative History*, N. J., 1969, pp. 113–37. For a more extended exposition of the *Partidas* see Herbert Klein, *Slavery in the Americas: a Comparative Study of Virginia and Cuba*, Chicago, 1967, pp. 57–85.
4 F. P. Bowser, *The African Slave in Colonial Peru, 1524–1650*, Stanford, Cal., 1974, pp. 273, 274; also see Klein, *Slavery in the Americas*, and Carl Degler, *Neither Black Nor White*, New York, 1971, pp. 31–4. The French promulgated a *Code Noir* (Black Code) in 1685. The English colonies neither in the Antilles nor on the mainland of America had a model, except perhaps that of villeinage and the common law.
5 U. B. Phillips (ed.), *Documentary History of American Industrial Society*, Cleveland, Ohio, 1910, Vol. 2, p. 31; also Bryan Edwards, *History, Civil and Commercial of the British West Indies*, London, 1819, Vol. 2, p. 340.

6 Alexander Falconbridge, *An Account of the Slave Trade on the Coast of Africa*, London, 1788, p. 34. He mentions the sale of slaves by scramble. See also his evidence to the *House of Commons Committee on the Slave Trade*, Sheila Lambert (ed.), Vol. 72, Wilmington, Del., pp. 595–6. In that account he cited two instances of this technique of disposal of slaves and how it frightened them.

7 Pope Hennessy, *Sins of the Fathers: the Atlantic Slave Traders 1441–1807*, London, 1970, p. 116; also Falconbridge, *Account of the Slave Trade*, p. 17, Slaves were checked for deformities.

8 C. L. R. James, *Black Jacobins*, London, 1938, p. 3.

9 Alexander Falconbridge, *Account of the Slave Trade*, p. 35.

10 A list of some slave autobiographies is given in the bibliography, but especially see Olaudah Equiano, *The Interesting Narrative of the Life of Olaudah Equiano or Gustavus Vassa, the African*, London, 1789.

11 J. B. Moreton, *West India Customs and Manners . . .* , London, 1793, p. 136. Whether Moreton's figure is exaggerated is difficult to say, but he was an overseer in one of the British plantations in the West Indies and certainly experienced slavery at close quarters as an overseer and had much to say about it. He seems to have been a man of humane consideration.

12 Note must be taken of Genovese's observation that half the slaves of the American South lived on farms, rather than plantations as defined by contemporaries – that is, in units of twenty slaves or more. He also argues that if a big plantation is to be defined as a unit of fifty slaves then only one quarter of the southern slaves lived on big plantations – see E. D. Genovese, *Roll Jord'n Roll*, New York, 1976, p. 7. Plantations were larger in the Caribbean than in the southern United States. Also F. P. Bowser, *The African Slaves in Colonial Peru*, pp. 12–24, 325. The African link with Peru had been forged by 1580.

13 E. E. Franklin Frazier, *The Negro in the United States*, New York, 1961, p. 7.

14 Harold Underwood Faulkner, *American Economic History*, 6th edn., 1949, p. 328.

15 The expression 'slave societies' as used here related to those societies in the Americas which were based on the use of slave labour in spite of the presence of a minority of free individuals. They therefore embraced freemen and slaves. The entire societal framework, whether the political, economic or social arrangement, was based on slavery.

16 Modern research indicates that by 1650 Barbados was suffering from the disappearance of the 'small landowner'; see Richard Pares, *Merchants and Planters*, London, 1960, p. 18. Large and small plantations had coexisted at the beginning, but from about 1640 (Barbados), 1670 (Antigua) and 1700 (St Domingue) the process of creating larger plantations was in the ascendant (*ibid.*, p. 19).

17 A. Caldecott, *The Church in the West Indies*, London, 1898, pp. 26–7. The information here is far from extensive but sheds light on the nature of slavery when it became 'big business'. Caldecott did not say whether the figures represented a constant factor, but nonetheless they help to demonstrate the power potential of the big estate against the small competitor in a business that was highly competitive. For a Latin American example, see N. Deerr, *The History of Sugar*, Vol. 1, p. 129, for the cost of running big sugar estates towards the end of the eighteenth century; total costs were £35 000, number of slaves 220, overheads £1200.

18 J. B. Moreton, *Customs and Manners*, pp. 57–8.

19 With the North American variant we are informed that 'absentee ownership

was not widely prevalent in the South, but where it existed it was a great curse, involving as it did the employment of a hired overseer. Good overseers were scarce'. See Faulkner, *American Economic History*, p. 328. See also F. L. Olmstead, *Journey in the Seaboard Slave States*, New York, 1856, pp. 45–7 (overseers are mentioned as unreliable). Also Lowell Joseph Ragatz, *Absentee Landlordism in the British Caribbean, 1750–1833*, p. 7. This held good for French planters as well. Moreton, an ex-overseer, states it explicitly, *op. cit.*, pp. 79–84, 88–91. Also see E. D. Genovese, *Roll Jord'n Roll*, pp. 12–13, where it is revealed that Georgia, Alabama and the Mississippi valley experienced much absenteeism while North Carolina and Louisiana lacked the phenomenon.

20 Caldecott, *The Church in the West Indies*, p. 27. It would be interesting to check comparable figures for the United States and for the other plantations of the Europeans engaged in the slave trade.

21 W. E. Dodd, *The South in the Building of the Nation*, Vol. 5, p. 74. Quoted also in Faulkner, *American Economic History*, pp. 68, 327. The politicians produced by the South reveal an example of a ruling minority (the planters) moulding public opinion. This interpretation needs to be taken with caution, for the West Indian planter was also adequately represented in Parliament and could not be ignored. But the observations are largely correct.

22 See L. J. Ragatz, *The Fall of the Planter Class in the British Caribbean 1750–1833*, London and New York, 1928, p. 50. It was recorded that during a visit to Weymouth, George III and William Pitt came upon a wealthy Jamaican planter with an impressive entourage of outriders and livery. The king's displeasure emerged in his effusion, 'Sugar, sugar, eh? All that sugar! How are the duties, eh Pitt, how are the duties?' Also see E. E. Williams, *Capitalism and Slavery*, Capricorn Books, 1966, p. 91, also ch. 4 for the displays and extravagances of the West Indian interests.

23 [Janet Schaw], *Journal of a Lady of Quality (1774–76)*, New Haven, Conn., 2nd edn., 1939, pp. 92–3. Here the point of view about the superiority of Antigua to other island colonies with reference to absenteeism is sustained even in the official records. See for instance, PRO, CO 152/54, Governor Ralph Payne of the Leeward Islands to the Earl of Dartmouth, 6 Oct. 1773.

24 *Journal of a Lady of Quality*, p. 93. Mr Mackinnon's case was not an isolated one. It was a widespread situation and even Mathew Lewis had a similar experience; see *Journal of a West Indian Proprietor*, and Moreton, *Customs and Manners*, pp. 50, 69–74.

25 See Ragatz, *The Fall of the Planter Class*, p. 10 and chs. 2 and 3.; E. Long, *History of Jamaica*, London, 1774, Vol. 1, pp. 398–9. Long indicated that many flourishing plantations were ruined as a result of this.

26 For a comparable situation in Cuba see Hugh Thomas, *Cuba or The Pursuit of Freedom*, London, 1971, pp. 82, 136. See the whole of his ch. 10 for the development of this tendency so that by 1850 mills were beginning to be owned by companies rather than individuals. An eighteenth-century traveller observed the planters' 'absolute dependence' on the merchants; Humboldt, *Travels*, pp. 280–1. The development of banking accelerated this in other slave theatres.

27 Long, *History of Jamaica*, Vol. 1, p. 395. This point is amply discussed in Ragatz, *The Fall of the Planter Class*.

28 Long, *History of Jamaica*, pp. 395–6. His arguments appear between pp. 391 and 402.

29 Lilian M. Penson, *The Colonial Agent of the British West Indies*, London, 1924, p. 181; also E. Brathwaite, *The Development of Creole Society in Jamaica 1770–1820*, Oxford, 1971, p. 111.

30 Penson, *Colonial Agent*, pp. 189–91.

31 *Ibid.*, pp. 205–7.

32 L. M. Penson, 'The London West India Interests in the 18th century', *English Historical Review*, xxxvi (1921), pp. 378–81.

33 'Prothonotary' or 'protonotary' is not a term in current use. Formerly in England it was a term used for the Registrar or Chief Clerk of Courts of Chancery, Common Pleas, or King's Bench. He was a sort of Chief Secretary or Chief Recorder.

34 Caldecott, *The Church in the West Indies*, p. 29.

35 See Herman Merivale, *Lectures on Colonisation and Colonies Delivered 1841–42*, London, 1928.

36 Long, *History of Jamaica*, Vol. 1, p. 80; also Spurdle, *Early West Indian Government*, New Zealand, 1962, pp. 200–2.

37 Caldecott, *The Church in the West Indies*, p. 29.

38 Long, *History of Jamaica*, Vol. 2, pp. 593–5. Long seemed to suggest that many of them were 'quacks'. Yet Brathwaite in his *Development of Creole Society* (pp. 144–5), states that the doctors were good. His evidence for this assertion does not surface. Captain Steadman had an unfortunate experience in Surinam with a doctor whom he referred to as a 'quack' and whose medication almost proved fatal. Steadman's animus for this man is spelled out in his account of the incident; see J. G. Steadman, *Narrative of Five Years among the Revolted Negroes of Surinam, 1772–1777*, Vol. 1, pp. 343–5, 353.

39 Moreton, *Customs and Manners*, pp. 77–8, 88–90, 97, 99, 122–33; Pares, *Merchants and Planters*, p. 14.

40 Klein, *Slavery in the Americas*, pp. 195–6, 259. Klein indicates that the situation in Cuba provided for economic and social mobility with 'whitening' being continuous – the mulatto, through wealth, being graded as white and the blacks as mulattoes – but with so much racial intermingling and intermarriage the whitening process continued. Mulattos worked in the economic sector ranging from unskilled operators to skilled operators but the colour criteria which were fashioned during the slave era became a legacy of the post-emancipation period. See also Donald Pierson, *Negroes in Brazil*, Chicago, 1942, pp. 68–70, 322–3.

41 See Sir William Besant, *For Faith and Freedom*, London, 1889, Vol. 3, pp. 21–38, esp. pp. 27–8, 31, 72, 94, 108–16; also Daniel Defoe, *Colonel Jack* and *Moll Flanders*, London, 1722.

42 This colony was successfully founded by Francis, Lord Willoughby of Farnham, in 1652, who had earlier, in the 1640s, espoused the parliamentary cause but had veered to the royalist side as a result of the excesses committed by the parliamentarians. He fled to Barbados in 1650 and, until the capitulation of Barbados to Cromwell, was governor there until 1652 when he fled to Surinam. See A. P. Newton, *European Nations in the West Indies*, p. 206.

43 Often these had been enticed to the plantations by true or false stories but with prospects of improving their economic and social status. Many in the earlier stages were of peasant stock, at least from France (Pares, *Merchants and Planters*, p. 14), followed later by townfolk.

44 C. R. Boxer, *The Portuguese Seaborne Empire*, London, 1969, pp. 314–16; U. B.

Phillips (ed.), *Documentary History of American Industrial Society*, Cleveland, Ohio, 1910, Vol. 1, p. 339.

45 They had aspirations even to became landowners once their period of apprenticeship was over, we are assured by the researches in the French archives of a modern historian; see Pares, *Merchants and Planters*, p. 14; also Moreton, *Customs and Manners*, p. 91–5, for his views on these ambitions.

46 Phillips, *Documentary History*, pp. 339–40.

47 *Ibid.*, pp. 343–4.

48 See, for instance, the instruction of Richard Corbin to his agent for the management of his plantations in Virginia in 1759, quoted in Phillips, *Documentary History*, Vol. 1, pp. 109–10. It showed a more humane consideration by a slave holder in terms of care of slaves than was generally the case. Also the 'Rulers for plantation management of a cotton estate in Mississippi Bottoms', instructions of a Mr J. M. Fowler to his overseers (1857), cited by Phillips, pp. 112–14. But the latter might be the instructions of an owner sobered by hard experience – if not his own, then, at least, by those of others.

49 Long, *History of Jamaica*, Vol. 2, p. 327.

50 *Ibid.*, p. 330. By the application of the principle of the Lombard Law, a slave and his wife would have become free if the master debauched the slave's wife.

51 *Ibid.*

52 *Ibid.*

53 *Ibid.*, p. 323.

54 *Ibid.*, pp. 324–7.

55 *Ibid.*, p. 323.

56 *Ibid.*, p. 327.

57 *Ibid.*, pp. 328–30, also pp. 404–44, esp. pp. 410–11.

58 Apart from the Maroon communities, not many of the *bozales* existed among the free blacks, except those who secured their manumission through purchase or by faithful service or through participating in the army in time of war, as occurred in the North American wars, especially the revolt against England.

59 Long, *History of Jamaica*, Vol. 2, pp. 351–78.

60 Fiction and imagination made up much of what Long wrote in this section, rather than fact. But what he expressed therein was embedded in common speech and thought concerning the Africans and their descendants. Long also suggested that the Negro from Guinea was brutish as the 'Hottentots' and yet Long had never encountered a 'Hottentot' (see his Vol. 2, p. 364). It is an indication of how fantasy assumed the respectability of truth.

61 Williams, *Capitalism and Slavery*, p. 280.

62 Pope Hennessy, *Sins of the Fathers*, pp. 57–8. By contrast with the received tradition see Capt. Steadman's favourable comment on the African physique.

63 In Jamaica, Long identified three classes of these freed blacks and mulattos, as follows: the lowest, those manumitted by will or instrument sealed and delivered in the toll book or the secretary's office: second, free born (with additional privileges, such as trial by jury); and third, those manumitted by Private Acts of Assembly (with rights approximating those of English citizens but with some disabilities such as disenfranchisement); Long, *History of Jamaica*, Vol. 2, pp. 286–320. As for methods of securing manumission, the following were listed: domestics secured it through long and faithful service; through commission of service for cash (reminiscent of medieval serfdom) – through

this means slaves hired their services and paid their owner a weekly or monthly sum, and were thus able to save and purchase their freedom. Furthermore, there were manumissions for the performance of some 'public duty', sometimes, as in Antigua, being accompanied by a grant of land to form their community. But where no land was given, such manumitted persons had to hire themselves to a family (the implication being to deprive the freeman of the right to be self-employed, and this, in fact, constituted slavery by the back door). Where land was plentiful, as in Jamaica, the position was otherwise; see Long, *History of Jamaica*, Vol. 2, p. 322.

64 See, for instance, what Long said about Francis Williams, *History of Jamaica*, Vol. 2, pp. 475–8.

65 Caldecott, *The Church in the West Indies*, p. 35; Moreton, *Customs and Manners*, pp. 133 ff., Carter G. Woodson, *Free Negro Heads of Families in the United States in 1830*, Washington, D. C., 1925, or the earlier work entitled *Free Negro Owners of Slaves in the United States in 1830*, Washington, D. C., 1924. Also see the *Frederick Douglass Papers*, Vol. 11, No. 18, Rochester, N. Y., 16 April 1858, for 'Negro Slaveholders in Louisiana', being descendants of former French and Spanish planters. See too Kenneth Stampp, *The Peculiar Institution*, New York, 1956, pp. 194–5.

66 See Tannenbaum, *Slave and Citizen: the Negro in the Americas*, New York, 1947, pp. 90–4. But this assertion is denied by Donald Pierson, who observed that the Free Negro, by virtue of his origin and by the association of his colour with servility, had an uphill struggle in groping for status and that his employment was commensurate with servile status or synonymous with hard work. Thus, in Brazil, he wrote: 'artisan labour was not for the black man', *Negroes in Brazil*, Chicago, 1942, pp. 48–70; also see William and Ellen Craft, *Running a Thousand Miles for Freedom, or The Escape of William and Ellen Craft from Slavery*, London, 1860, pp. 37–8, for the numerous disabilities suffered by so-called 'free coloured men' bolstered up by custom and various prohibitive Acts.

67 See letter to Peter Fontain, Jr., Westover, Virginia, 30 March 1757, printed in Ann Maury, *Memoirs of a Huguenot Family*, Williamsburg, Va., 1853, pp. 351–2.

68 R. C. Dallas, *The History of the Maroons*, London, 1803, Vol. 1, pp. i–xii, and Vol. 2, letters 12–16 inclusive. Also James Walker, *The Black Loyalists*, London, 1976.

69 See Aptheker, *American Negro Slave Revolts*, New York, 1944, p. 61. Hierarchy among slaves included personal servants, general domestic workers, drivers and field workers. This also had an inbuilt and developed system of rewards; see J. Winston Coleman, Jr., *Slavery Times in Kentucky*, Chapel Hill, N. C., 1940, pp. 48–51. Domestic slaves being encouraged to remain aloof from the field hands, sometimes (but not always) gave them possible identification with the household. The distinctions between *bozales* and *Creoles* were also maintained.

70 Frances Anne Kemble, *Journal of a Residence on a Georgian Plantation in 1838–1839*, London, 1863, pp. 29–30.

71 See Coleman, *Slavery Times in Kentucky*, p. 50.

72 The domestics in one household might approximate 20–40 in number, as follows: 1 butler, 2 footmen or waiting men, 1 coachman, 1 postillion, 1 helper, 1 cook, 1 assistant (cook), 1 key or storekeeper, 1 waiting maid, 3 house cleaners, 3 washerwomen, 4 seamstresses. Not only did the historian,

Long, observe that they constituted 'too numerous a tribe of domestic servants' on whom the owner reposed too much fidelity, but that extra hands were made available, if there were children in the family, providing each of them with extra indulgences with each child having a nurse, and each nurse an assistant, boy or girl; Long, *History of Jamaica*, Vol. 2, pp. 281–2.

73 See A. Steward, *Twenty-two Years a Slave and Forty Years a Freeman*, Rochester, N. Y., 1857 and 1859, p. 32. Also Henry Bibb, *Narrative*, New York, 1849 and 1850, p. 136.

74 Boiling of the cane sugar was a process of sugar production, and this phrase refers to people who worked in the boiling house.

75 Both were among the non-predial slaves referred to by Eric Williams in his *History of the People of Trinidad and Tobago*, p. 84.

76 [Janet Schaw], *Journal of a Lady of Quality*, pp. 127–28.

77 F. L. Olmstead, *Journey in the Seaboard Slave States*, New York, 1856, p. 47.

78 *Journal of a Lady of Quality*, pp. 103–4.

6   Divide and rule

Judgement on the new arrivals

Here we are concerned with another aspect of the complex stratification fostered on the plantations. The arrival of the slaves was an
occasion for moral and value judgements to be made on their
worth. These judgements were based partly on experience with
slaves from certain areas of Africa and, accordingly, they tended to
be graded as 'good', 'bad', 'indifferent', 'robust', 'lazy', 'intelligent',
'loquacious', 'stupid', 'warlike', 'mediocre', 'delicate' or 'disease-
prone'. These gradations in turn added to the complexities of the
differentiations on the plantations. At the inception of slavery it was
not known which slaves came from which community in Africa. It
is even doubtful whether towards the end of slavery this was
always known. Nevertheless, the tendency was to identify the
slaves with the port of their transhipment but it was found that
even this criterion was not itself adequate, for those brought from
the interior of the continent and sold on the coast might have
belonged, and very often did belong, to some other linguistic group
than the one with which they were identified in the Americas.

The slaves were brought in batches and distributed by sale to the
plantations. But it was still possible to put a certain term of
identification on groups of slaves. Accordingly, on the plantations
slaves came to be known as: Eboes, Congos, Tappas, Nagos
(Yorubas), Koromantees[1] (Coromantins) and Phantees (Fantees),
Mandingos and Foulahs (from the area of Senegambia), Hausa,
Minas, 'Ebbo-bees' (Ibibios), the latter sometimes known as
Mocos; Gaboons, Whidaws (Ouidahs) and Papaws (Popos), Ardras
and Chidaws from Dahomey. The area covered stretched from
Senegambia to Angola,[2] although slaves were also brought from
Mozambique and Madagascar.[3] These names varied from one area
of shipping the slaves to another, but, in the main, the above list
was more recurrent. Accordingly, distinctions were made about
them in terms of their adaptability or non-adaptability to slave
society. These distinctions were not only an induced class differentiation based on place of origin[4] but helped to entrench social
differentiation by occupations. It is not unreasonable that as slavery
progressed they were given work in accordance with assumptions

made of their 'national' characteristics. It is, therefore, necessary that we briefly observe some of their characteristics made by someone who was considered by Stedman as a 'professional planter' in 1803.

It was the belief of the planter that African slaves showed wide variations in habit, brought as they were from a very extensive continent, possessing soils varying widely in their fertility, and differing moral and physical systems, with wide variations in character and occupations. Some, he believed, were given to farming while others were not, some were warriors while others were hunters, and yet others idled away, merely subsisting on the bounty of mother nature and, therefore, were unaccustomed to hard work or indeed any work whatsoever, but given to 'animalistic' indulgences. He counselled, therefore, that they must be assessed as to their suitability for slavery by considering their places of origin, though he admitted that the latter could not be accurately ascertained since some of the slaves would have been captives of war and, therefore, not necessarily originating from their port of embarkation.

He observed that the inhabitants of the Gold Coast, described as the Koromantins, Phantees and Minas, being conditioned to war from their infancy, seemed to have imbibed not only an alert mind but also an alert body. They were 'hardy and robust' and came into slavery with 'lofty ideas of independence'. Accordingly, they were dangerous to the plantations, especially those of the West Indies, and particularly in Jamaica where they were instigators and leaders of recurrent revolts. They were persistent disturbers of the 'peace' on the plantations. The African slaves from the region of Senegambia, who included the Mandingos and Foulahs, were described as handsome with features resembling those of Europeans, tall and well-proportioned and that among them many were literate in the Arabic language,[5] and many could be described as scholars in it. These he felt were ill-suited to rough labour on the fields or plantations but made excellent domestic servants. Coupled with these were slaves brought from the region of the Congo, who were said to be also handsome and very dark and well-proportioned, but, apart from their sense of humour, they were unsuited to the rigours of field work, though, as domestic servants and tradesmen, they were reputed to be good. An additional note on the Mandingos, apart from their unsuitability for field work, was that they easily took ill but were reputed to be good as watchmen or suited to work in the distillery or in the boiling houses.

The Igbos and Ibibios (from what came to be latter-day Eastern Nigeria) were said to constitute the greater part of the cargoes brought from West Africa (or the Guinea Coast) and were known to be 'stubborn' and 'turbulent' and were very prone to commit suicide.[6] But apart from these characteristics they were a hardy people with their women much superior to the women of other nationalities and only slightly inferior to their own menfolk. It was felt that they responded well to good treatment and, if so treated during the initial seasoning period, they tended to make better slaves. The Gaboons or Gabonese slaves were deemed to be the worst of the slaves brought to the plantations and were, at the early stage of the slave trade, less expensive, but in the end proved to be good for nothing. Many captains without prior knowledge of their nature had purchased large numbers of them, but at a later stage they were sold through false declarations being made on their actual place of origin. They had such frail constitutions that many of them died, either during the middle passage or soon after their arrival on the plantations; and, furthermore, they were very prone to illness, which for the purchaser meant a substantial financial loss upon their demise.

Then from the region of Dahomey came the Whidaws and Papaws and Chidaws. The former were reputed to be among the 'best' Africans brought, and others known as Aradas were reputed to be even better still, and the few who were imported from this region were purchased by the French and were highly commended by them for their qualities, whereas the latter, the Papaws (Popos) and Chidaws were not so highly considered.[7]

What has been described above was merely one aspect of the 'divide and rule' principle built into the slave system in order to sustain it. Another aspect involved the separation of slaves from the same region of origin in order to forestall any attempts to plot revolts or insurrections.[8] As an actively pursued policy it contributed to slaves losing their mother tongue. There is the case of Trinidad during the slave era where proposals which had been advanced for coping with the pauperism prevalent among ex-slaves were objected to on the claim that 'by keeping the Africans together instead of scattering them, their use of their own barbarous dialects, customs and superstitions would be kept up'.[9] The stamping out of any traces of African culture, so deliberately and actively pursued by the slavocracy, was a major factor leading to the loss among the slaves of their original language. The process was one of deculturisation, although subsequently an acculturative process distinct from that of Africa was infused into slave society.[10] In its turn, it did not produce an equilibrium in West Indian culture. In an area where this kind of separation was not actively pursued, as in Brazil, the language of the Nagos (Yoruba) has not only survived to the present day, but occupies an important place in the university curriculum, especially in Bahia. It was not the only method employed to destroy these African languages; the method of violence discussed below was also valuable to the purpose of the slavocracy.

Closely allied with distinctions based on origin were the characteristic divisions between Creole-born black slaves and African-
born slaves. The distinction, which slave societies made between
Creole black slaves and *bozal* African slaves, penetrated the consciousness of both groups, affecting their relations as well as their
cohesion to undertake slave revolts.[11] The implications are too
numerous to mention, but one aspect of this is that they developed
stereotypes for one another, with the Creoles' contemptuous attitude to Africans (the *bozales*) being reflected in such terms as 'salt-
water negroes' and 'Guineybirds'.[12] There was a tendency for the
Creole blacks to lord it over the *bozales*.[13]

It therefore meant that, with the arrival of fresh hordes from
Africa with the slave ships, the Creole blacks were provided with
the opportunity to taunt and tease them and to express their
disrespect. The antagonisms were more pronounced in some slave
theatres and the slavocracy made the most of it, entrenching their
prejudices therein and so indicating their preferences; and, by so
doing, further complicating the divisions which already existed
among the slaves. It suited the slavocracy, for without the divisions
the slaves would have found a common enemy to contend with.
Thus we see two notorious slave owners and authors of a Jamaican
and West Indian history in the eighteenth century, Edward Long
and Bryan Edwards, revealing such prejudices. Bryan Edwards
wrote an opinion of the Creole slaves as exceeding the Africans in
'intellect, strength and comeliness',[14] whereas Edward Long suggested that differences between the Creole blacks and Africans, in
which the former came off better, was 'not only in manners, but in
beauty of shape, features and complexion'.[15] The divisions were
thus heightened not only by using the criterion of beauty to divide
them, but by separations between mannerless and courteous slaves.
The condemnation of all *bozales* into the category of 'bad' is too
facile to carry credibility. But yet in another context the slavocracy
would refer to the Creoles as possessing the smacking of every sin
that had a name – ranging from 'thieves' to 'knaves' – but there is
hardly much consistency in these categorisations. They seem to
have been made either at moments of indignation or with a view to
justifying the whites in their actions. Yet they served a useful
purpose within the compass of 'divide and rule'. Religion also
became a divisive factor. For instance, a French missionary in the
Antilles in the seventeenth century, Jean Baptiste Labat, recorded
that African slaves who had already been Christianised refused to
eat with new arrivals from Africa on the basis that the latter were
non-Christians.[16] In time the divergent Christian sects or denominations would entrench the divisions.

Another method of 'divide and rule' or 'subjugation' was that of
separating families. The method of capture and the disposal of

slaves from the coast of Africa was often the first step in this separation. We read in Equiano's narrative of the way he and his sister were separated during their initial capture and reunited before their ultimate disposal at the coast and final separation.[17] But the practice of separating families, once beached in the colonies, was a regular occurrence.[18] Even when families had been established in slavery, the slave owners had no qualms of conscience in disposing of one parent to one purchaser, the other parent to another bidder and children to another.[19] Of the callousness of this system, Wilson Armistead has recorded an incident which took place in Kentucky. There a slave owner had offered to sell a 'negro' woman and her blind child to another slave trader. The trader, however, declined to receive the boy, stating that he wanted slaves for stocking his plantation and that a blind one was useless to him. But the seller was anxious to dispose of the mother without the encumbrance of the child hampering the slaves. Both buyer and seller were relieved of their dilemma when a third person offered to buy the child for a dollar. A Mrs Bailey, a doctor in Cincinnati, acquainted with the incident, wrote a spirit-stirring poem on the event.[20] But the frequency of the practice, unparalleled in callousness anywhere since the dawn of human history, can be gleaned from the advertisements of slave owners themselves. Here is one example from what appears to have been an impoverished slave holder.[21]

> Negroes for Sale – A Negro woman, 24 years of age, and her two children, one eight and the other three years old. Said negroes will be sold separately or together, as desired. The woman is a good seamstress. She will be sold low for cash, or EXCHANGED FOR GROCERIES. For terms, apply to Matthew Bliss & Co., 1 Front Levee, (New Orleans Bee).

Here is an eye-witness account by Equiano (alias Gustavus Vassa) on the obnoxious practice of separating families:

> And at or after a sale it was not uncommon to see negroes taken from the wives, wives taken from their husbands, and children from their parents, and sent off to other islands, and wherever else their merciless lords choose; and probably never more during life to see each other. Often times my heart has bled at these partings. Nor was such usage as this confined to particular places or individuals; for, in all the different islands in which I have been (and I have visited no less than fifteen), the treatment of the slaves was nearly the same; so nearly indeed that the history of an island, or even of a plantation, with a few such exceptions, as I have mentioned, might serve for a history of the whole.[22]

Let us now consider the complexities of colour gradations.

Skin colour and shade complexes and conflicts

The institutionalisation of pigmentation and shade conflicts tended to conceal what was essentially a major divisive factor in the diffusion of power in slave societies. As an aspect of slavery it is one of the most enduring, apart from the creation of a mentality which could rightly be regarded as 'slavish' in the mental attitudes of the descendants of former slaves. It has become part of the worldwide complex of racism as well as colour, caste, prejudice and discrimination which inflame passions in the most unimaginable ways. But apart from racialism as a stark social fact, the West Indies and the United States are unique in that to them has been bequeathed not only racialism as a legacy of slavery but also 'the colour problem' which was concomitant with that system of the enslavement of the children of Africa and the indenturing of some of the children of Europe. Slavery provides the root cause for the survival of shade gradations, thus inducing social stratification as well as wide variations of economic power in the social structure. Colour differentiation was induced as part of the strategy which militated against the cohesion of the rank and file of all the oppressed peoples dwelling in slave societies.[23]

But the wide proliferation of colours among the very peoples on the plantations, and the mining areas as was the case in North and South America, was largely the result not only of immigration but also the result of miscegenation, which was so common in these societies. To this we shall return presently in this chapter. But from these associations, enforced as well as voluntary, have resulted the various kinds of coloured people differentiated as *mulattos, quadroons, quintroons, octoroons, mestizos (mustees), mustefinos* and *zambos*, not disregarding the predominant African group (or negroes as they came to be called) and those of European origin, designated 'whites'.[24]

The mulatto was the offspring of an African and European, or as indicated by colour between the black woman and the white man.[25] The quadroon was the progeny of white and mulatto parents. The octoroon was a person whose African (negro) ancestry was one-eighth. The mestizo (or mustee) was the offspring of white and quadroon parents. The zambo was a cross between an African and Amerindian. The cross between a white and mustee produced a mustefino. In the period of slavery, the children of a white and mustee were reckoned by law to be white and entitled to all the rights and privileges of whiteness. With these jealously guarded distinctions, people were higher in social gradation the farther away

165

they were from the African negroid complexion. It did happen that the mother of such 'white' persons could still be in slavery while her offspring were deemed to be free because of a peculiar colouration.[26] This fact has produced the phenomenon, not unknown in the West Indies and most of the Americas today, of families possessing different shades of colour with lightness in colour being more preferable, whereas the darker the skin colour, the greater the ostracism, even within family circles. If ever there was a classical case of a house divided against itself, this was it, and it had its very origins in the gradations of slave societies. But in the arrangement of the social hierarchy, the Europeans, 'whites', were at the apex of the economic and social pyramid (though we have earlier seen there were gradations even within this stratum), and the people of African origin (the so-called pure blacks)[27] were at the bottom. Here again we have distinguished the divisions between the 'free blacks' and the slaves, and also the divisions according to the occupations of the slaves, between the more privileged domestic slaves – taskmasters – on the one hand, and the field hands on the other; and as well as among the free blacks, the few who were owners of a few slaves and those who owned none. This was slavery, not only in its infamy but also in its ramifications.

Having by social custom affixed the insignia of slave on people of darker hue from Africa, the laws bolstered and institutionalised these practices and attitudes, conferring the peculiar label of slave on the colour 'black'. Yet, coloured slaves existed throughout the centuries of slavery. Because of this, the presumption of slavery fell on any 'negro', irrespective of whether he was a free person – a presumption which was extended to the 'mulatto'. In the eyes of the law those three steps removed from the African black in lineal descent were deemed to be white and those below this were considered mulattos, the so-called 'coloured' people.[28] The statutes of many slave states in North America embodied this presumption. As a result, any free 'negro' or 'coloured person' had thrust on him or her the onus of proving that he or she was a free person, and in those days, when greed of gain pervaded much of the thinking, this was no mean feat. In Maryland in 1717, for instance, free negroes or mulattos of either sex who intermarried with a white person automatically became slaves for life. In Virginia and Kentucky, however, the presumption of slavery was fixed on anyone possessing one quarter African blood.[29] It is easy to see why the system was able to persist a long time without the chains bursting asunder, for these divisive tendencies, based on colour criteria, tended to weaken the potential cohesiveness of slave societies.[30] Some members of the slavocracy were preoccupied with a racial purity that was no longer possible or realistic in slave societies as they evolved.[31] Thus, when emancipation of the slaves came, the change was merely juridical, as Eric Williams has ably argued.[32] It was neither an economic nor a social, nor for that matter a psychological, change. The preceding practice laid the basis of the present class structure in the West Indies and the rest of the Americas. This has been extended in the social relationships between peoples of different hues involving discriminatory practices in clubs, hotels and some public places.[33] The black man, who uplifted himself through education and wealth as well as intermarriage into a lighter caste, acquired the norms and attitudes of the lighter shades, who tended to occupy a middle stratum in the pyramidal structure. Thus, class differences were very often colour differences. But even black men and women who acquired wealth, thus enhancing their social status, tended to think of lighter persons in poorer circumstances as being 'black'.[34]

Just as under slavery, with opportunities for advancement being provided more for the light-skinned individuals, this factor, even after emancipation and into the 1950s, continued to operate to facilitate the acceptance of the former into employment rather than those who were darker. Such areas of employment included intermediate positions, such as shop assistants and secretaries in various offices, including banking. Each of these top grades in the hierarchy were imbued with the idea of their superiority over others, the octroon over the mulatto,[35] the octroon over the quintroon, the quintroon over the quadroon, and so on. Even the laws of slave societies, as well as the opinion of the ruling clique (what in default of a better word we might call public opinion), as well as custom, did not allow white fathers to acknowledge their coloured offspring, especially when under an existing condition of marriage with another white woman. It was customary for some considerate parents to open up social avenues for their children, thus conferring a greater advantage on their mulatto offspring[36] than the competition of the social system would have granted them. Thus, in time, they could rise in occupational as well as social status to a point not easily attainable by their black contemporaries. There are recordings of the promotion of private acts (often in contravention of the official stipulations and regulations) to enable some of the progeny of these white men in their dealings with African slave women to secure bequests.[37] This happened more often in the British West Indies than in North America. Although according to slave law the state of the child often followed the mother's status, yet, very often, the artisan class was recruited from the progeny of liaisons between white men and African or mulatto slave women. Often the progeny were manumitted by their fathers. Children of 'negro' women who were emancipated were free and their progeny with white men were sometimes sent to England or Europe to be educated. Yet the laws did set a limit to the amount of property which a coloured person might inherit.[38] But the distinctions in social rank based on shade were maintained, for such persons were not regarded as equals with the whites. They were middlings. As Charles Wesley rightly observed of North America, such attainments were not necessarily due to differences of ability 'but by the conditions which made the mulatto more acceptable than the black among the Americans in general.... It is common knowledge that, especially where resemblances were too evident, many of these children, with the help of an indulgent parent, were educated and sent to the Northern States, to Canada, and abroad.'[39] Wesley further maintained that

> These opportunities are occasioned by a social system which has given the best opportunities, in slavery as well as in freedom, to coloured Americans of mixed blood. The favoured class among the slaves was more often the mulattoes. They became intelligent because they were favoured and not *per se*, because of their blood.... But where conditions were made equal for both groups, the degree of attainment was the result of individual ability and not group ability based on colour purely. The house servants and the mechanics were selected from both the mulatto and the black groups, and under generous masters they would attain an equal rank in efficiency.[40]

While the puritanism of North America prevented the white fathers of children, whose mothers were either slaves or women of colour, from acknowledging them openly, these fathers sometimes degenerated in their manner of conduct in that they developed the habit of selling even their progeny into slavery,[41] an unnatural factor, far removed from the obligations of parental tenderness. In some cases the offspring of such loose associations, often initiated by the slave owner or planter, were quartered on the plantation to work as slaves. The West Indian planter parents, being of a different disposition, were not without their parental feeling towards their offspring and the mothers of these children. One way in which such planters revealed their associations with black slave women was by manumitting them and their offspring.[42] They tended to bestow pecuniary benefits on their 'mulatto' children obtained from slave mothers. In spite of the decree of the Jamaican Assembly of 1762 that a 'testamentary device' from a white person to a negro or mulatto not born in wedlock, exceeding in value £2000 currency, should be void and the property go to their heir-at-law, evasions of the statute were still possible through the promotion of private bills.[43] But these laws, often private acts, passed through the legislature with such regularity as to enable white fathers to make generous provisions for their mulatto offspring in spite of the existence of laws prohibiting the bestowal of extensive properties to such children. Typical private acts designed to make provisions for some of the progeny of white men with slave women were 'to entitle Francis Clarke, Shirley Clarke, Ann Clarke, Robert Pawlett Clarke, Thomas Clarke and William Clarke, the reputed children of Robert Clarke, of the Parish of St Catherine, Gentleman, by Charlotte Pawlett, a Free Mulatto Woman, to the same Rights and Privileges with English Subjects, under certain Restrictions'; and 'to authorise and enable William Wright of the Parish of Portland, in the County of Surrey, in this Island, Esquire, to sell and dispose of his Estate, both real and personal in this island, by Deed or Will, in such Manner as he shall think proper, not withstanding an Act of the Governor, and Council and Assembly of the Island, and 'An Act to prevent the inconveniences arising from exhorbitant Grants and Devices made by White Persons to Negroes and the Issue of Negroes and to limit and restrain such Grants and Devices'.[44]

The result was that in time the population of coloured people in the islands and the mainland of America increased considerably.[45] This class, resulting from the interbreeding of European men and African slave women, increased considerably in most of the islands from 1750 onwards.[46] Concubinage and licentiousness gave rise to more interbreeding and it soon began to give this coloured group occasional importance within the plantation community. It was even recorded of Barbados in the 1790s that 'a comely negress', during Governor Ricketts' administration in that island, 'reigned at government house, enjoying all a wife's privileges save presiding at his table'.[47] And Ricketts was not an exception, for some other high governmental officials, including governors, were not exempt from these habits. Governors like the Sixth Earl of Balcarres (Governor of Jamaica, 1795–1801) and the Duke of Manchester (Governor of Jamaica, 1808–11 and 1813–21) were notorious for the fathering of brown-skinned children resulting from their profligate habits.[48] Their acts were not without private censure from other self-righteous whites like the Nugents.[49] These pastimes contributed to ephemeral sexual relationships rather than to permanent ones through matrimony.[50]

The system of sex

Not only did the enslavement of man degrade him, but the pervading moral practices further added to this degradation. The societal arrangements gave every encouragement to licentious living and distorted the values known both in Africa and Europe whence these settlers came. For in these two continents marriage was a recognised, if not sacred, institution. On the plantations the legal stipulations made it almost impossible for slave marriages to secure legal sanction[51] or even to have any permanence, thus inducing the practice which paramours had of often discarding female partners and choosing new ones. The planters and the societies over which they were overlords encouraged unrestrained sexual appetites and licentiousness to an alarming extent for all grades of people on the plantations. Many planters hardly restrained their appetites.[52] Thus, Edmund D'Auvergne observed that 'The white man in the West Indies was not satisfied with one woman'.[53]

To understand the type of person who would have contributed to this state of affairs, it is necessary to consider the observation in the early nineteenth century of Sir Robert Schomburgk, who had some interesting points to make about the kind of European settler who came to the West Indies. 'If we consult the history of our colonies', he wrote, 'it will generally be found that the first settlers were of that class of society in which morals and virtue are seldom to be met with. Ruthless and unprincipled, it was not amelioration of their Christian virtues which led them to distant climes, but the desire of enriching themselves by any means at their disposal.'[54]

Another nineteenth-century commentator, observing the situation towards the end of the nineteenth century, asserted that 'the discouragement of marriage and the profanation of the Sabbath are models which the slaves can hardly be expected to improve'.[55]

The situation was, if anything, worse on the North American mainland. Here we see from the pen of a woman traveller and observer a very perceptive account of society in America in about 1837. The traveller, Harriet Martineau, stated that it was a well-known fact reverberating over the world at the time that violence of the most 'savage' kind was ever present in the southern states of the American Union.[56] She argued that whether such deeds were few or recurrent was beside the point, for the fact that they occurred at all testified to the existence of such hatred that made the unleashing of violence possible. Furthermore, she added,

> They arise out of the licentiousness of manners. The negro is exasperated by being deprived of his wife – by being sent out of the way that his master may take possession of his home.... If the negro attempts to retaliate, and defile the master's home, the faggots are set alight about him. Much that is dreadful ensues from the negro being subject to toil and the lash: but I am confident that the licentiousness of the masters is the proximate cause of society in the south and south-west being in such a state that nothing else is to be looked for than its being dissolved into its elements, if man does not soon cease to be called the property of man.[57]

The licentiousness of the kind described by Harriet Martineau was a source of endless conflict between master and slave, which often called forth the fury of the slave. Information on this state of affairs is ubiquitous.[58] An incident recorded on one of the West Indian islands is worthy of note and confirms the state of perpetual warfare. It was said to have occurred in 1800 when Molly, a planter's mistress or lover, 'held the candle while her negro lover murdered her master and paramour in his bed'.[59]

In her study of Africans in nineteenth-century Trinidad, Maureen Warner, by recalling the African family life in the parent continent, in which polygamy was the norm and where wives did not necessarily live in the same compound as their husbands,[60] introduces a corrective to the notion of wholesale and unrestrained licentiousness of Africans on slave plantations so characteristic of writers. This picture could be the logical conclusion of writers from societies in which the norm was monogamy, as was the case with missionaries in Africa in the nineteenth century, when they could not understand why their congregation could embrace Christianity and remain polygamists. But having said this, licentiousness was widespread, but it was not just an African pastime. In fact, it was the Europeans who set Africans the pattern, for it was they who forcibly, even from on board ship, took African women for pleasure,[61] and, with the emergence of a large progeny of coloured women, the coloured men were also forced into these relationships, while others were compelled to be prostitutes. These relationships were dissoluble at pleasure, in order to take up others. These examples, even by the highest dignitaries of the plantations – the governors themselves[62] – set the pace for the slaves. Not every slave fell for the bait in the same way as not every white fell for it (an early reference has been made to the self-righteous attitude of the Nugents[63]), but the vast majority was pressed into the situation either by coercion through the separation of partners by selling one of them in order to compel the other partner to take in another, or just by sheer observation and force of habit of contracting ephemeral unions. When the West India proprietor, M. G. Lewis, asked one of his slaves why he had not married a woman, he replied that if white men were not content with one woman, why should the poor slave be?[64] The answer was rather revealing. But the fact that some agencies acted as pimps[65] in the plantation setting for the procurement of women for the gratification of white men made licentiousness more certain. Another factor in the situation, which did not exist in the African social system in the parent continent and which was also an aspect of plantation morals, was that of polyandrous relationships in which many slave and free black and coloured women had many men. There were, of course, more lasting monogamous relationships, if not upset by the quick return preoccupations or just plain bloodymindedness of the planters and overseers; but these were more the exception. Licentiousness predominated; permanent relationships were rare and ephemeral unions the norm. They had maximum impact on the post-slavery psychology of ex-slave societies, especially in the West Indies.

Planters, inebriated with their right to do as they pleased with their property, which included slaves whose responses must be absolute submission, indulged their sexual appetites, while their laws guaranteed them this right to mishandle their 'property' at will. This over-indulgence proved a menace to the chastity of the African slave women brought under the charge of such owners. There is hardly any autobiography of a slave who later secured freedom which does not relate incidents of this nature, recurrent as they were in societies in which the chief pastimes of the upper classes were sumptuous revelry, banqueting, liquor imbibing – often consumption of the choicest wines as well as the local brew – and dancing. For the inferior white, however, drinking and card-playing and debauchery were their main pastimes. The slaves, for their part, found leisure only on Sundays (if ever) or during official holidays. The chastity of the slave women, until about fifty years before the abolition of slavery, was open to violation by the white man.[66] Some African slave women resented their coercion into such indulgences, while others took advantage of all that it entailed to entice their white suitors.[67] Thus, in the *Journal of a Lady of Quality*, it is recorded that 'The young black wenches lay themselves out for white lovers, in which they are but too successful. This prevents their marrying their natural mates, and hence a spurious and degenerate breed neither so fit for the field, nor indeed for any work, as the true bred negro.'[68] 'Besides', she continued, 'these wenches become licentious and insolent past all bearing, and as even a mulatto child interrupts their pleasures and is troublesome they have certain herbs and medicines that free them from such an incumbrance, but which seldom fails to cut short their own lives as well as that of their offspring. By this many of them perish every year.'[69]

The licentiousness of white men on the slave plantations was such that it was known and accepted that young men brought from Europe to the West Indies and other parts of the Americas as overseers often took black or coloured mistresses. An observer of the West Indians in the nineteenth century commented thus:

It is a well-known and notorious fact, that very few of the white men in the West Indies marry, except a few professional men and some few merchants in the towns, and here and there, in the country, a proprietor or large attorney. Most of the merchants and shopkeepers in the towns, and the whole of the deputy planters (viz. overseers) in all parts of the country, have what is called a housekeeper, who is their concubine or mistress, and is generally a free woman of colour; but the book-keepers, who are too poor and too dependent to have any kind of establishment, generally take some mulatto, or black female slave, from the estate where they are employed, or live in a more general state of licentiousness.[70]

The degeneracy of the society was complete. By forming such associations with either their masters, managers or overseers, these slave women had a temporary enhancement of their status and experienced a temporary respite from unrequited toil. As a boost to their morale and status they were addressed by the slaves through the courtesy titles of Miss X or Miss Y, as the case may be. They, in turn, identified themselves with the names of their lovers or paramours and so spoke of themselves as 'Mr A's love' or 'Mr B's love'. They became more privileged than other slaves being taken into domestic service. Their paramours made sure that they were secure from lashings, which would involve the bruising of their bodies, the intention being to keep them as attractive as possible. They were relieved from menial labours, which tended to have a debilitating effect on their physical condition. Their paramours bestowed small favours on them, such as providing them with cheap jewellery and other ornaments. The planter's wife, who was bound to find out about her husband's activities with slave women, was likely to show her reaction by taking it out on the slave herself, either through scolding or by administering some body and head blows on the slave.[71] But the moment of truth often arrived when the African slave woman no longer held glamour for the master and was then discarded, while the planter or owner sought a new partner. With her downgrading also went her self-respect, for she no longer enjoyed such sonorous titles as Miss X or Miss Y but was referred to as 'Mammy Strumpet' or 'Old Sam's Nan'.[72]

Spanish America

Spanish Peru produced its own variants in these racial contacts, thus producing *mulattos* – the offspring of Africans and Europeans – *zambos*, the offspring of Africans and Amerindians, and *mestizos*[73], the offspring of Spaniards (and Portuguese) and Amerindians. While the zambo was dreaded in colonial Peru as well as the metropolis[74], the contacts between the three groups could not be maintained effectively. Official policies attempted to curtail, especially, the contacts between the African slaves and the Amerindians,[75] just as it had attempted to adopt stringent measures to curtail Euro-Amerindian contact, but both failed dismally. The outcome was an outcrop of mixed types – mulattos, zambos, mestizos, quadroons and others. Moreover, since the zambos were often the progeny of male African slaves and the free Indian women, their progeny in theory would acquire their mother's status and, with that, the implication of the growth of a freed coloured population.[76] But, in spite of the Spanish male's assumption that the African and the Amerindian were two degenerate races, his proclivities for African women were far from limited. From such contacts there was a proliferation of mulatto children. While the lot of the Afro-Indian or zambo in the cities was far from pleasant because it meant having to make the best within a system of constraints and prejudices, modern research tells us that 'The fate of the mulatto and of the still lighter products of Afro-Spanish sexual unions was in many instances somewhat more pleasant.'[77]

In spite of the frequency of the alarm about Afro-Spanish sexual contacts, irrespective of Crown stipulations and prohibitions, liaisons between Spanish men and African women were widespread and persistent throughout the colonial period. It was asserted by a seventeenth-century observer that Spanish men preferred black women to their own, attributing this propensity to the fact that most of them had been suckled by African wet nurses.[78] But it would appear that both the black women and the mulattos had an overpowering attraction over their Spanish suitors and even over Amerindian men, and became the cause of numerous crimes of passion, resulting in the greater increase of mulattos.[79] Yet, the Afro-Peruvians or mulattos, being the offspring of African slave women, inherited the status of their mothers. Although the zambos[80] in theory and law were the progeny of free Amerindian mothers, in reality they rarely possessed the advantages of freedom.[81] The zambos' position was unsatisfactory if they either had to identify with their Amerindian mothers in the villages or with their African slave fathers. They were, therefore, in an awkward position in the hierarchical arrangement since they were still lower in status than the African slaves. If, therefore, they attempted to identify with their mothers, and therefore with the social standing of the Amerindian which was inferior to that of the African slaves, they were subjected to all sorts of vexatious experiences and obligations, such as payment of tribute and provision of labour imposed by the Spaniards. If, on the other hand, they abandoned the village for the larger Spanish world in the urban centres (and many of these zambos were urban-born), they entered it with a still more inferior status. So in opting for the urban centres they had to cope with the problems of adapting to the prejudices and constraints imposed by the Spaniards. Their situation remained inferior either in the village or in the urban centre, for they were the product of two of the most despised peoples in Spanish America.

Of the Afro-Peruvians or mulatto types, fathers sometimes freed them, so much so that the Spanish government in 1563 had no alternative but to accept, by promulgating a decree, the realities of racial admixtures in the colonial setting. By doing this they were merely conforming to the Peruvian practice which had existed from the earliest times of settlement when Spanish fathers of mulatto slaves freed them and provided for them.[82] In order to liberate their progeny, white fathers either did so by a letter of manumission, or by providing for this in their wills, or by recourse to other expedients. If, for instance, the child was begotten from the slave of another, the fathers made cash payments to the master of the slave, for a letter of manumission did not suffice in that case, and in extreme cases the fathers of such children threatened to sue.[83] But there were cases when Spanish fathers freed their progeny while refusing to recognise them as their offspring. Bowser records that in such cases the tendency was to remove the mother and child away from the locality, and he drew attention to a case in 1615 in which a cleric, Dr Bernardo Cavers, despatched a six-month-old mulatto boy and his pregnant mother to serve in the household of a friend in Panama.[84] It was remarkable that fathers of coloured children were embarrassed by their own handiwork and some preferred to remain anonymous while carrying out the task of manumitting their coloured progeny from slavery. There was also cited the case of a mulatto, Fransisca Rodrigues, and her month-old quadroon son, who were freed in 1630 after payment of 900 pesos to their master by a third party who preferred anonymity.[85] There were more complexities in the situation than meets the eye, and sometimes even slave fathers were unprepared to liberate their coloured progeny (as in other slave theatres) and the mother had to have recourse to more charitable patrons to achieve the end of manumission, such patrons becoming godfathers.[86] In cases where the colours and features of the children approximated to those of white fathers, the children were preferred and manumission was easier. A case was recorded in 1635 in which a nobleman (Don Pedro Ramirez de Valdes) and his wife freed the eighteen-month-old son of a slave, Maria Mulata, 'because he was white and blond and had a Roman nose'.[87] We are even made aware of the fact that the sexual attraction of the coloured woman for the Spaniard 'could impede rather than promote liberation if the jealousy of the white wives was sufficiently aroused'.[88]

The French colonies

On the French plantations, with St Domingue (later Haiti) as the most important, the circumstances of colour divisions were not very different, except that the colour prejudice and divisive tactics of the whites tended to generate hatred among the various colour groups. Thus, the whites hated the blacks but appear to have hated the mulattos even more. It produced a reciprocal response from the mulattos, who also hated the blacks and the whites alike. There was no love lost between the blacks and others.[89] Observing the complexity of these divisions in St Domingue, the West Indian historian, C. L. R. James, wrote that the divisions between the white and black and intermediate shades approximated 128. According to him: 'The true mulatto was the child of a pure black and a pure white. The child of a white and mulatto woman was a *quarteron* (the quadroon of the English- and Spanish-speaking societies) with 96 parts white and 32 parts black. But the quarteron could be produced by the white and *marabou* in the proportion of 88 to 40, or by a white and the *sacatra* in the proportion of 72 to 56 and so on all through the 128 variations. But the *sang-mele* with 127 parts white and one part black was still a man of colour.'[90]

In the last sentence we see an absurdity of the colour situation, for by definition the sang-mele would have been more a white person than a coloured or black one. Not only were the mothers of these mulattos in slavery in the colony but they had other half brothers there also. As in other theatres of slavery, the authorities strove to keep the colour groups apart, but with little success. Through their industry and frugality and avoidance of intoxicants, extravagance and profligacy, the mulattos, from small beginnings, sometimes rose to be property owners of wealth. Some who had acquired wealth sought to obliterate traces of their origin and sought high office in the militia.[91] But the whites discriminated against them in numerous ways.[92] First, they were not permitted to bear the names of their white parents.[93] The opportunity which they took to educate their children in the metropolis in France was later taken away from them by legal stipulation for, while free in France, on their return to the plantations of St Domingue, they experienced the harsh realities of constraints and numerous disabilities. These disabilities became so numerous that they were even forbidden to wear swords, sabres and European dress.[94] Rights of assembly for such occasions as weddings and feasts were denied them and they were not even allowed to play European games.

The insult was further extended when, in 1781, they were even denied courtesy titles such as *Monsieur* and *Madame* and, until 1791, even if they had a European guest at their home they could not dine with him from the same table.[95] Such were the absurdities of French society in the Antilles, and in their greatest colony from which the metropolis draw immense benefits, until the coloured population, buoyed up by its prosperity and its sensibilities, touched by the experience of education, began to find ways and means to respond to these humiliations. Thus, because of the prohibitions bolstered up by law and social custom 'the man of colour who was nearly white despised the man of colour who was only half white, who in turn despised the man of colour who was only one quarter white, and so on through all the shades'.[96] The consequences were devastating when the subject people of St Domingue in 1791 decided to bid for their freedom; and the distinctions which had been carefully fostered and foisted on the entire population survived into the post-emancipation period of modern Haiti.

Another feature of 'divide and rule' which appeared in St Domingue was fostered by the higher bureaucracy who, seemingly less prejudiced than the lower bureaucracy and planters, rendered some assistance to mulattos. In time, as many mulattos became large property owners, they tended to have a common bond with the higher bureaucracy, a fact which, at the time of the St Domingue (Haitian) revolution, left the higher bureaucrats with divided loyalties of race interests (with other Europeans) and class interests (with the mulatto property owners and wealthy bourgeousie).[97]

Like the Haitian coloured people, English West Indian coloureds educated abroad in England, on their return tended to demand civil, political, economic and social liberties; but their essential aspirations were to approximate to white status and share their identity of interests. But the laws and customs of St Domingue like those of Jamaica and elsewhere in the Americas, were contrived to maintain these distinctions between whites, coloureds and free blacks, as well as in the U.S.A. between the whites and everyone regarded as black.[98]

The Portuguese

The Portuguese variant, like the Spanish one, was not very divergent either. Stipulations, prohibitions, antipathies, legal enactments or decrees – none stemmed the process of hybridisation. Apologists[99] for Portuguese licentiousness and sexual liaisons with African and Indian women, who saw in them expressions of humane policies, were wide of the mark and seem to have ignored the Crown's condemnation of mixed associations and 'marriages'. Concubinage of the masters with the slaves was so widespread as to be condemned in 1705 by a Jesuit, Jorge Binci,[100] who also saw the exploitation of African women in prostitution, and recognised that the function of legislation was to uphold the classes and caste formations embodied in the master and slave arrangement entrenched in the Portuguese domination of the other colours.

These divisions ensured Portuguese dominance in the social setting. Miscegenation was a continuous and unrelenting process and the outcome was a whole series of colour differentiations consisting of metropolitan Portuguese, Creole Portuguese, *mamelucos*,[101] Africans from Africa, Creole Africans, Amerindians divided between those regarded as 'savage' Amerindians and the *caboclos* or catechised Amerindians, as well as attempts even to differentiate between Angolans, Congolese and *moleques*.[102] The imprint of these practices survived emancipation to plague societies in proportion to the strength of prejudice and feeling.

In his comparative study of Brazil and the United States of America, Carl Degler has called our attention to the variations in the intensity of racial prejudices in the United States of America as well as in Brazil, so that it can be inferred that its intensity was greater in one part of Brazil and the U.S.A. than in another, and the differing conclusions reached by various studies of slave societies in both countries mirrored the regional variations within them; but, in essence and in general, racial and colour prejudices and permissiveness existed in all slave theatres without exception.[103]

The interesting feature of this system is that, while the owners, overseers and managers, who sought these associations and pleasures with black women, kept a countenance of sternness and even exhibited attitudes of hatred and often contempt for Africans, they were not slow to take advantage of the cover of night to take up liaisons.[104] It was clear from these associations that the racial superiority and colour superiority which these white men peddled were merely palliatives for the actual reality of economic domination and the exploitation of human beings. The attitude of the white women was conditioned more often than not by the fact that they saw only the black 'wenches' as their natural rivals in situations in which the white women seemed temporarily relegated to the background, though they were the legally recognised spouses. Nonetheless, racism as an inbuilt factor continued to be an integral part of the slave system in the western hemisphere as well as in South Africa and the Portuguese plantations in Africa. The force of habit gave credence and power to racism. The cumulative effect of this mode of thought in which the racial veneer was superimposed on what was, in all essentials, naked economic exploitation, infused into the consciousness of both the victims and practitioners an attitude of mind which, after centuries of handing down, became a live virus separating peoples whose interests were not necessarily divergent. The race boost which Western Europeans gave themselves during the centuries of infamy in turn produced its own natural reactions from its victims. From mere rationalisations employed to justify the enslavement of one species of mankind by another, the Western Europeans bequeathed a tragic legacy to their descendants and to mankind at large.

Some of these black women made attempts to assert their dignity once drawn within the domestic orbit of the master. They showed their resentment to their debasement by disposing of the slave master either through poisoning (which was very common on the plantations)[105] or by other convenient methods. Many fatalities occurred this way. But while slave women formed an association with a slave owner, manager or overseer, it was she who often revealed to her master or mistress any attempts by the slaves at insurrection. Thus she sometimes became the agency of tragedy and a dangerous detractor to the revolt of human beings against a nefarious system. Modern research testifies that such black or coloured women acquired by white paramours became useful in 'the subtle control of plantation slaves'.[106]

Even at ports, slave girls were kept by inn-keepers, and prostitution was rife.[107] Often these hostesses were manumitted black or mulatto women, having been so released by their white masters whom they had favoured and some probably continued to favour. Ex-slave women kept as mistresses tended to exhibit considerable fidelity towards their keepers. Coloured young men had to be content with finding partners from among women who had been discarded or abandoned by the whites or among negro women. 'To the white man it mattered not at all whether the woman he fancied was esteemed the wife of a slave. She had to do his bidding. In some islands by a primitive law of hospitality, the white guest was furnished with a bedfellow. Slave women were flogged for refusing this office.'[108] The slave woman was always at the mercy of her owner's appetite or her keeper's right through the white hierarchy from the greatest to the least. An attempt was made in 1788 in Grenada to protect the slave woman from being debauched by the imposition of a fine on anyone who attempted to violate a slave's wife. The fine for a master committing such an offence was £165, for an overseer twice his salary, and £50 for a stranger. If the slave woman preferred to avoid the consequences of licentious living or enforced licentiousness by not procuring children, there were a number of factors which she took into consideration, such as that child bearing and rearing became an encumbrance which limited her pleasures; furthermore, that her beauty was likely to fade with child bearing, and once this happened she was no better than a discarded horse. In addition, the fear of bearing children that were likely to be sold into slavery away from her tender care by a capricious master made such a mother shudder or recoil from procreation. The incident was recorded at Kingston, Jamaica, of a mother whose two little boys were sold one after the other; she became mad as soon as the second sale had been accomplished.[109]

Such were the legacies bequeathed to the post-slave societies in the Americas. The differentiations according to colour mirrored a highly colour-conscious society with attendant consequences for their future cohesion. Such was the world created by the perpetrators of African slavery in the Americas, and these formed the collective experiences of African-derived peoples in the New World diaspora.

The implications of colour differentiation

The implications of colour differentiation were numerous and multifarious, but it is better to demonstrate this by reference to one typical slave society in the Caribbean, that of Jamaica, where the legacies of slavery still plague social relationships. This is not to say that they do not manifest themselves in other former slave societies, but Jamaica is used here in order to illuminate the complexities of the problem. In this respect, Fernando Henriques' study of 'colour'[110] is enlightening and many of his arguments are confirmed. Thus, we find that one of the lasting legacies of slavery in the West Indies, and to a limited extent in the United States and Latin America, but especially in Jamaica and Trinidad, is the evolution of numerous groups of people separated from each other by colour and social distinctions and prejudices. While no laws of segregation exist in the West Indies and Latin America today, the prejudices based on the colour arrangements persist, having been fostered by centuries of institutionalisation in customary practice. Colour dominates those social relationships in matters of employment and therefore social advancement; colour determines people's standing in the social hierarchy. This was, of course, truer for the 1950s and the 1960s than today, as corrective measures began to be introduced in the post-Second World War period, albeit slowly. Slavery, however, entrenched these differences in a manner in which the white colour was seen as a quality of excellence and the black seen as the quality of degradation, even that of the devil himself. Thus, the middlings (that is, those between them, variously called 'mulattos', 'brown men', 'red men' and 'high-yeller women' etc.) sought to emulate the whites and restricted their associations with blacks (at least openly) in order not to be despised. But, in spite of this, whites were still contemptuous of them. White opinion about them set the patterns of their behaviour and the supposed inferiority of the 'negroes' advanced by whites also became part of their customary belief. The U.S.A. produced its own peculiar phenomenon of 'passing', while in Latin America the mulatto type became the norm and the majority. But the immigration policies of the Latin American governments in the twentieth century in re-

stricting immigration mainly to people of European stock have re-
entrenched the colour factor in hierarchical gradations, which often
coincide with class as well. But these are not as pronounced as in
the West Indies.

According to this characterisation, all the evils imaginable and
unimaginable are associated with blackness, and all the good with
whiteness; thus, with the acquisition of characteristics approximating whiteness, people are assumed to have become better. This
has become part of the psychology of even the black people and their
mulatto half brothers and sisters as well, so that the tendency to
hair straightening is representative of this sometimes conscious or
unconscious effort to ape whiteness, while at the same time providing the hair straighteners with a booming trade. The mentality is
sometimes mirrored in black magazines and newspapers, which
often advertise potions for whitening the skin. It was this absurdity
which was ridiculed by the West Indian calypsonist, Lord
Kitchener, when, in one of his songs on the redhead lady, he spoke
of the blonde and brunette ladies 'using peroxide' in order to change
the colour of their hair. He called it 'false beauty'. Thus, through
this, the beauty parlours continue to entrench this mentality and
are, in fact, agencies of these endeavours to 'whiten the stock'.
When a man married a woman of a fairer complexion than himself,
or *vice versa*, this was regarded as an elevation. The implication is
that the children had greater prospects of a better chance in life
(irrespective of endowment or capability). Of course, in essence, it
tended to infuse self-hatred consciously or unconsciously. Those of
a fairer complexion who associated with the blacks in a marital
relationship believed that they were elevating the blacks or
degrading the white stock. There is real ambivalence here. The
greatest achievement of a black or coloured man, often the uneducated or the semi-educated type, was to marry a white woman,
and *vice versa*. Of course, it did exist among the educated classes
too. Such chances were believed to be enhanced abroad rather than
in the islands themselves. But often, the wife had to become
reconciled to the coloured friends of her husband and was very
likely shunned by the whites. Even Edward Long had cause to refer
to these problems of various colour breeds within the same family
brought about by the licentiousness of planters and their subordinates.[111] It was bequeathed as a legacy to the post-emancipation
period and has survived into the twentieth century. It happened
therefore that wealthy coloured men could take to wife poor white
women in the belief that they were enhancing their status in
society. Fernando Henriques observed that, apart from whites, all
groups in Jamaica accept the principle of a man marrying or
cohabiting with a woman fairer than himself.[112]

There are numerous manifestations of colour problems and prejudices beyond the scope of this work and we cannot deal at length with them. The colour problems enter into employment considerations with the fairer people being given the choicest positions in employment, as in the days of slavery. Thus, in the clerical posts and in banks and private firms, and as shop assistants and shopkeepers in the capital, Kingston, or in northern towns like Montego Bay, it is people of lighter complexion who fill these posts. This has not changed much in places like Montego Bay, which receives a frequent retinue of tourists from the American mainland, many of them southerners, with their racial prejudices. The policy of giving advantage to those of a lighter hue was also known in respect of government appointments till the constitutional reforms of 1944 in Jamaica altered the employment policy. Opportunities for promotion were based on whether one had the 'right colour'. Exclusive clubs tended to proliferate and discriminate as well. The north coast of Jamaica, with Montego Bay in the forefront, has been the centre of these practices. It became part of the psychology of women who tended to manifest it even more, and these prejudices were even extended into religious communities and practised by religious denominations. The orthodox bodies have been the worst offenders – these include the Anglicans, Methodists and Roman Catholics; whereas the unorthodox, such as the African Methodist Episcopal communities, are less prejudiced. Many orthodox church members tended to resent having their parishes placed under the charge of a black or coloured priest or clergyman, in spite of the disreputable records of many white clergymen in slave societies in the heyday of slavery. Even the 'brown man' (as he is sometimes called) has remained a victim of divided loyalty. Although he occupies a middle position between the white and black in the hierarchy of colour and class arrangements, yet, in spite of his awareness of white attitudes of superiority towards him, he still feels impelled towards the whites and, while also assuming a superior attitude towards the blacks, still feels a kind of kinship affinity with them. The prominent Jamaican brown man of the post–emancipation era, Edward Jordan, typified that attitude of mind. But there have been many more since emancipation.

One would find identical colour gradations in Trinidad, although the infusion of the Indian and Chinese elements has also complicated the arrangements, as in Guyana and Surinam as well. There are so many variants in the Caribbean area, including Guyana, which would repay study. That of Barbados, which has a large white minority in charge of sugar estates, approximates to the West Indies prior to the emancipation of slaves. Equally Barbados has produced the phenomenon of what in another context would be described as a degenerate group of whites, characteristically referred to as the 'Red Legs'. The polarisation between black and white still persists and this aloofness in outlook has implications for islands like the Bahamas and the Bermudas,[113] which, not emerging from this psychological void, found it necessary to remain aloof from the rest of the West Indies. Thus, both states did not join the erstwhile West Indian federation and often see themselves as of a different kind, distinct from other West Indians.

In order to sustain these divisions and stress distinctions, both custom and law were employed. But custom helped to inform law and was itself so powerful as to embody its force. An ex-slave, Lunsford Lane, who had obtained his freedom but had returned to the plantation in order to secure the purchase of his family from servitude, soon found this out. In his own words he repeated what had been said to him by his interrogator, the Mayor of Raleigh, thus:

> Mr Loring then spoke to me again and said that notwithstanding I had been found guilty of nothin' *yet public opinion was law*; and he advised me to leave the place the next day, otherwise he was convinced I should have to suffer death. I replied, 'not tomorrow, but today'.[114]

The incident narrated above occurred after he had returned to the city of Raleigh, North Carolina, where he had previously been a slave and after having been given the assurance that he was free to visit and execute his business. His account tells how he fell foul of 'public opinion' for having allegedly given abolitionist lectures in the state of Massachusetts.[115]

Notes

1 There are many variations of this word, e.g. Koromantins, Koromantynes.
2 Donald Pierson, writing about the African slaves in Brazil, noted others, such as Gêges (or Ewes), *Negroes in Brazil: a Study of Race Contact at Bahia*, Chicago, 1942 and 1947, pp. 31–5; while Gilberto Freyre in *The Masters and the Slaves (Casa-Grande and Senzala): a Study in the Development of Brazilian Civilization*, New York, 1946, pp. 301–6, esp. 302, n. 69, identified among others, Kanembus (from Bornu) and Bagami (from north-eastern Nigeria).
3 Slaves from Madagascar would have included those brought from the interior of East Africa and sold at various points on the coast and in the slave market of Zanzibar.
4 O. Patterson, *Sociology of Slavery*, London, 1967, p. 147; also Freyre, *The Masters and the Slaves*, pp. 302–3.
5 Captain Stedman observed the Coromantynes as 'the most esteemed' in Surinam while the 'Loango negroes' were reckoned to be the 'worst', Stedman, *Narrative of Five Years among the Revolted Negroes of Surinam, 1772–1777*, London, 1806, Vol. 2, p. 254. An example of one slave literate in

Arabic was Job Ben Solliman (anglicised as Solomon), son of the High Priest of Bondu, sold into slavery in North America but rescued and returned to his country. See Douglas Grant, *The Fortunate Slave*, London, 1968. Others are mentioned by Freyre and Pierson.

6 See some of the writings of slave-trading captains and surgeons, e.g. Joseph Hawkins, *A History of a Voyage to the Coast of Africa . . .*, 2nd edn., Troy, N. Y., 1787, pp. iii–iv, 87–90, 139–40, 142.

7 'Extract from Practical Rules for the Management and Medical Treatment of Negro Slaves in the Sugar Colonies by a Professional Planter', London, 1803, Part 1, ch. 1, quoted in U. B. Phillips, *American Negro Slavery*, New York and London, 1918, Vol. 1, pp. 127–33. See also Bryan Edwards, *The History, Civil and Commercial, of the British Colonies in the West Indies*, London, 1818–19, Vol. 2, pp. 88–90. Views here conflict, for Edwards contended that the Pawpaws were a docile lot, dutiful in the discharge of their responsibilities (pp. 87–8). Thomas Attwood, in his *History of the Island of Dominica*, published in 1791, suggested that Creole slaves were less stupid than newly imported Africans (the *bozales*), p. 267. Also quoted in Elsa V. Goveia, *A Study of the Historiography of the British West Indies*, Mexico, 1956, p. 36.

8 This was also Portuguese policy in Brazil; see Freyre, *The Masters and the Slaves*, p. 306.

9 G. R. Mellor, *British Imperial Trusteeship 1783–1850*, London, 1951, p. 434.

10 The fear was ever-present that slaves speaking a common language could more easily join together.

11 Maureen Warner, 'Africans in 19th-Century Trinidad', in *Bulletin of the African Studies Association of the West Indies*, v (Dec. 1972), p. 49. This was evident in the French Antilles from the seventeenth century. See Rev. C. Jesse, 'Du Tertre and Labat on the 17th-Century Slave Life in the French Antilles', in *Caribbean Quarterly*, vii, 3 (1961), p. 148.

12 Edward Long, *The History of Jamaica*, Vol. 2, London, 1772, p. 410.

13 *Ibid.*, p. 444. Long mentions how the Creoles tried to frighten the new arrivals into submission.

14 Edwards, *History, Civil and Commercial, of the British West Indies*, Vol. 2, p. 185.

15 Long, *History of Jamaica*, Vol. 2, p. 410.

16 Jesse, 'Du Tertre and Labat', p. 14.

17 Olaudah Equiano, *The Interesting Narrative of the Life of Olaudah Equiano or Gustavus Vassa the African*, London, 1789, Vol. 1, pp. 59–61, 61–2.

18 U. S. P. G Archives, London, Fulham Papers, Vol. 2, West Indies 1808–11.

19 This is contrary to Professor Blassingame's assertions in *The Slave Community*, New York, 1972, pp. 78–9. While admitting that the family of the slaves had no legal existence, he still maintained that it 'was in actuality one of the most important survival mechanisms for the slave'. Yet, in the same context Blassingame makes the admission that 'By all odds, the most brutal aspect of slavery was the separation of families' (p. 89), and that many were touched by this tragedy. The admission is made in subsequent pages of *The Slave Community* concerning the instability of families. See, for instance, his pp. 90–2. Both William and Ellen Craft saw both their parents separated and sold, a brother sold and a sister mortgaged (William and Ellen Craft, *Running a Thousand Miles for Freedom etc.*, London, 1860, pp. 9–11, 27). They also mentioned the practice of slave owners selling the children of parents already

disposed of and children of slave women and their slave-owning white fathers (pp. 2, 16). In fact, Ellen Craft's first master was her father and she was so white that she appeared like one of the approved children of the family and was often so mistaken by visitors to the home.

20 Wilson Armistead, *Five Hundred Thousand Strokes for Freedom*, London, 1853, Leeds Anti-Slavery Series, No. 26, Appendix 2.

21 Quoted in Frank Tannenbaum, *Slave and Citizen: the Negro in the Americas*, New York, 1947, p. 77.

22 Equiano, *The Interesting Narrative*, Vol. 1, pp. 220–30. This is evidence from the experience of the slave himself, more authentic than from the records of slave dealers.

23 F. P. Bowser in *The African Slave in Colonial Peru 1524–1650*, Stanford, Cal., 1974, p. 285, has a most telling statement on the use of this technique.

24 See Appendix 2.

25 There were occasions when the father was black and mother white. See, for instance, C. H. Wesley, *Negro Labour in the United States 1850–1925*, New York, 1927, p. 41.

26 This again is another paradox of the slave system, for according to one of the operational principles the status of slave followed that of the mother. Yet such progeny who could have been slaves by the status of their slave mothers escaped this servitude probably because they were the secretly acknowledged children of a plantation dignitary.

27 In Portuguese Brazil and Spanish America the Amerindian status was lower than that of Africans in the hierarchical gradations and the progeny of the Amerindian-African fusion, the zambos, occupied a lower place still.

28 See M. Lewis, *Journal of a West India Proprietor*, London, 1834 and 1929, p. 106, and Long, *History of Jamaica*, Vol. 2, p. 321.

29 Tannenbaum, *Slave and Citizen*, pp. 68–9.

30 E. Brathwaite, *The Development of Creole Society in Jamaica 1770–1820*, Oxford, 1971, p. 176.

31 Long, *History of Jamaica*, Vol. 2, p. 327.

32 Eric Williams, *The Negro in the Caribbean*, Manchester, 1942, pp. 12–13, 15.

33 See, for instance, the attitude of the British Parliament after they had been informed that a distinguished citizen of Guiana, Sir Frank McDavid, was refused accommodation in a hotel in Bermuda on the grounds of colour. House of Commons *Parliamentary Debates* (Hansard), Vol. 521, col. 239, Dec. 1953, written answer.

34 M. Kerr, *Personality and Conflict in Jamaica*, Liverpool, 1952, ch. 10, on 'class and colour', esp. p. 98, and on colour legacy, pp. 172–3.

35 Within these arrangements contradictions existed. In Jamaica, for instance, in terms of labour capability one Negro was regarded as more than equal to two mulattos (see M. G. Lewis, *Journal of a West Indian Proprietor*, London, 1834 and 1929, p. 95). This also involved the tenacity of the dichotomy between the domestic slaves who were often 'coloured' and the 'field slaves', most of whom were 'black'. See also the statement of Alexander Willocks to the House of Commons Commission of 1790 in which he said that a Creole Negro was equal to three African *bozales*.

36 Other white parents who indulged in the habit of selling their coloured children away into slavery not only failed to recognise the products of their endeavours in their association with black slave women but also rejected the

natural obligations of paternity. Whatever the consideration in acting thus, it scarcely showed a sense of responsibility, and slaves were expected to learn from such people.

37 See H. T. T. Catterall, *Judicial Cases etc.*, London, 1926 and 1968, Vol. 1, pp. 329, 364; Vol. 2, p. 6. Also see Long, *op. cit.*, Vol. 2, pp. 323–30.

38 See *Acts of Assembly passed in Jamaica from 1770 to 1783 inclusive*, Kingston, Jamaica, 1786, pp. 11, 30. Some private acts sought to establish equality with whites for some coloured persons.

39 Wesley, *Negro Labour in the United States*, p. 41. In the St Domingue situation it was not the white parents who sent their children to France for education but those mulattos themselves who had acquired wealth through their industry. See C. L. R. James, *The Black Jacobins, Toussaint Louverture and the San Domingo Revolution*, London, 1938, p. 40.

40 Wesley, *Negro Labour in the United States*, p. 42. We are assured by another writer that the distinction was of degree rather than kind in the 'coloured' part of the population – part of this population was brought closer to the master, apart from perpetuating social distinctions. Thus, in the British West Indies, it was customary not to deploy mulattos on the cane fields but rather to confine them to domestic service and enable them to acquire skill at a trade. It was expected of the white man to manumit his mulatto children and was regarded as detestable and disreputable if he did not do so. The opposite position was known to obtain in the United States. There, because of the strength of opposition to manumission, it was difficult in many states for a white father to set free his progeny even if he had the inclination. Yet some such children were freed, and there were many cases of litigation on inheritance of property by mulatto offspring of white fathers. See Tannenbaum, *Slave and Citizen*, pp. 122 ff. for a slightly divergent picture of the North American situation, where the terms 'mulatto' and 'mustee', although used, did not alter the fact that they were all classified as 'negroes', except in Georgia, which recognised them, and by a Law of 1765 encouraged their immigration into the state for reasons of expediency with further considerations of half-hearted integration. But the rigid polarisation between black and white led to the need for some kind of accommodation of the lighter-skinned mulattos into the white stratum, thus giving rise to what Winthrop Jordan called 'the silent mechanism of "passing",' *White Over Black*, pp. 167–70. For a fuller discussion of the North American variant see the entire chapter entitled the 'Fruits of Passion' for the dynamics of interracial sex, pp. 136–78.

41 Bowser mentions this with reference to Peru, *The African Slave in Colonial Peru*, p. 287, but examples are ubiquitous.

42 Yet in Spanish America, and notably in Peru, the sexual attraction of the coloured woman for the Spaniard could impede manumission if the jealousies of the white wives were sufficiently aroused. But often it was the women and children who benefited from manumission rather than males, estimated at 82 per cent female and 3 per cent male adults. Furthermore, urban slaves, as elsewhere, were greater beneficiaries than rural slaves, *ibid.*, pp. 287–98.

43 E. B. F. d'Auvergne, *Human Livestock*, London, 1933, pp. 100–5.

44 Quoted in L. J Ragatz, *The Old Plantation System in the British Caribbean*, p. 24, n. 116; *Acts of Assembly Passed in Jamaica, from 1770 to 1783 inclusive*, pp. 11, 30ff. Numerous Acts appear between these pages.

45 See PRO, CO 28/51 of 1768; CO 71/4 of 1773; CO 28/69 of 1802; and CO 71/4 of 1804.
46 In colonial Peru in 1650 they accounted for 10 per cent of the population (Bowser, *The African Slave in Colonial Peru*, p. 301).
47 John Poyer, *The History of Barbados*, London, 1808, pp. 639–40.
48 Sir Sydney H. Olivier, *Jamaica: the Blessed Island*, London, 1936, pp. 91–2. We learn that 'five bastards belonging to the Duke' (Olivier refers only to Manchester) were in school in Kingston. *Journal of Lady Nugent*, London, 1839, Vol. 1, pp. 38, 68, refers to the Duke of Balcarres.
49 Also Brathwaite, *Development of Creole Society in Jamaica*, pp. 110–11. General George Nugent was Lieutenant Governor of Jamaica (1801–6), and his wife Maria made a recording of her experiences in two volumes (see above).
50 J. B. Moreton, *West India Customs and Manners . . .*, London, 1793, pp. 124–5.
51 This in spite of what is said of laws guaranteeing slave marriages in Latin America. See, for instance Pierson, *Negroes in Brazil*, pp. 83, 94, 159; Bowser, *The African Slave in Colonial Peru*, p. 315; Degler, pp. 35–9. Also see *Fulham Papers*, Vol. 2, West Indies, Part 1 (1803–27), Rev. B. Byam to Lord Bishop of London, 4 Dec. 1820, pp. 23–6.
52 The picture was no different in Spanish America in spite of official efforts to prevent racial intermingling. It was proverbial that the black woman seemed to have had an overpowering attraction for the Spanish settler, Bowser, *The African Slave in Colonial Peru*, pp. 282–3, 287. It was the same in the Dutch and French colonies. While this may not have applied to the religious puritans who went to North America, this picture could be generally made for the various slave theatres for which the evidence is ubiquitous. See also C. R. Boxer, *The Dutch Seaborne Empire, 1600–1800*, London, 1965 and 1966, p. 241, and James, *Black Jacobins*, pp. 36–7.
53 D'Auvergne, *Human Livestock*, p. 100. This was not dissimilar to the practice in North America.
54 Sir Robert Schomburgk, *The History of Barbados*, London, 1848, p. 92.
55 A. Caldecott, *The Church in the West Indies*, London, 1898, p. 48. See also S. M. Elkins, *Slavery*, Chicago, Ill., 1959, pp. 50–2, on the disallowing of slave marriage. Also Thomas R. R. Cobb, *An Inquiry into the Law of Slavery in the United States of America*, Philadelphia, 1858, p. 246.
56 Harriet Martineau, *Society in America*, New York, 1837, Vol. 2, pp. 119–20, recorded knowing about the death of four men by summary burning alive within thirteen months of her residence in the United States.
57 *Ibid.* See criticism of Martineau by F. A. Kemble, *Journal of a Resident on a Georgian Plantation*, London, 1863, pp. 14–15, 28–9. Kemble did not say that Martineau misrepresented the situation but that she did not carry out her enquiries far enough and collected the views of those whose complacency to the institution of slavery was well known.
58 The autobiographies of ex-slaves are replete with these accounts. See also Kemble, *Journal*, pp. 10–12, 22–3, 169, 177, about the comings and goings, and even wife-grabbing by overseers from slaves.
59 D'Auvergne, *Human Livestock*, pp. 101–2.
60 Warner, 'Africans in 19th-Century Trinidad', pp. 27–59.
61 Falconbridge, *op. cit.*, p. 23–4; also Hawkins, *History of a Voyage to the Coast of Africa . . .*, pp. 156–8.

62 See *Journal of Lady Nugent* for her references to the mulatto progeny of the
    Earl of Balcarres, Governor of Jamaica; or the references to the Duke of
    Manchester, another Governor of Jamaica (see Olivier, *Jamaica: the Blessed
    Island*).

63 *Journal of Lady Nugent*, Vol. 1, pp. 66, 87–8.

64 Lewis, *Journal of a West Indian Proprietor*.

65 Patterson, *The Sociology of Slavery: an Analysis of the Origins, Development and
    Structure of Negro Slave Society in Jamaica*, London, 1967, pp. 160–2.

66 D'Auvergne, *Human Livestock*, p. 100.

67 *Journal of Lady Nugent*, Vol. 1, p. 26; [Janet Schaw], *Journal of a Lady of
    Quality*, New Haven, Conn., 1921, 1939, p. 112; Long, *History of Jamaica*, pp.
    327, 328–32; also Alejo Carpentier, *Explosion in the Cathedral*, London, 1963,
    pp. 32, 41.

68 Schaw, *Journal*, p. 112. Psychologically it was soon infused into the
    consciousness of the 'half breeds', by custom and praxis, that field work was
    degrading to them. This fact alone could make them feel unfit for such work.
    But it is not to be doubted that some were fragile, though this should not lead
    us to accept the notion. Frances Anne Kemble's *Journal*, for instance, revealed
    the 'unreasonable' request of a mulatto woman, Sally, on a Georgian
    plantation, who wanted to be relieved from field work because it was
    undignified for her, being a 'mulatto'. The revelation showed how colour
    consciousness had sunk deeply into its practitioners and victims. See Kemble,
    Journal, pp. 246–7, and Moreton, *Customs and Manners*, pp. 124–5.

69 [Janet Schaw], *Journal of a Lady of Quality*, pp. 112–13, stresses this aspect of
    the whites' licentiousness, calling the relationship 'unnatural' and Miss Schaw
    herself admits that the outcome was 'crowds of mulattoes' seen everywhere in
    the streets, houses and inside everywhere. Furthermore she said of the practice
    that it was a 'crime that seems to have gained sanction from custom, tho'
    attended with the greatest inconveniences, not only to individuals, but to the
    public in general'. In her footnote to this assertion she wrote, 'Many of these
    gentlemen – managers, as well as the overseers under them – contributed, in
    a great degree, to stock the plantation with mulatto and mustee slaves. It is
    important to say in what number they have such children, but the following
    fact is too often verified, "that as soon as born they are despised, not only by
    the very authors, under God, of their being, but by every white, destitute of
    humane and liberal principles", such is the regard paid to the hue of
    complexion in preference to the more permanent beauties of the mind'.

70 R. Bickell, *The West Indies as They Are: or a Real Picture of Slavery but more
    particularly as it exists in the Island of Jamaica*, London, 1825, p. 104. See also
    James, *Black Jacobins*, pp. 29–30, 32, 34.

71 The truculence of the slave woman here observed might, in part, have been
    due to her awareness that for once, by being the bedfellow of her master, she
    was put at par with the lawful wife, a fact which conferred on her the right of
    self-assertion and of equality with her mistress.

72 D'Auvergne, *Human Livestock*, pp. 101–5.

73 Bowser, *The African Slave in Colonial Peru*, p. 151. Apart from the mulattos
    and zambos, there were other variants including mestizos and quadroons (pp.
    154, 298).

74 *Ibid.*, pp. 151, 283–7.

75 We are also assured that these efforts to curtail the Afro-Indian contacts were a

technique of 'divide and rule' for the fear arose that this contact might lead to a union of Amerindians and Africans which could be dangerous to the Spaniards (Bowser, *The African Slave in Colonial Peru*, p. 151) and as a result the Crown's policy was to 'wall off the Indian in his remote village from all contacts with Spanish society and to breed divisions and mistrust between the races' (p. 285).

76 *Ibid.*, p. 286.

77 *Ibid.*

78 *Ibid.*, pp. 286–7. See James in *Black Jacobins* (pp. 36–7) for a comparable situation in St Domingue (Haiti) and that neither legislation nor race prejudice could destroy the attraction of the black woman, and later coloured, for the white man. Recordings abound. A French observer to Bahia (Brazil) between 1718 and 1719 felt scandalised by the preference of the local citizens for coloured women even when white women were available. As Professor Boxer has said: 'It is true that the sexual attraction of the *Mulatta* for the average Luso-Brazilian male is overwhelmingly evidenced by the accounts of foreign travellers, by complaints of colonial authorities, both ecclesiastical and lay, and by popular song and story.' C. R. Boxer, *The Colour Question in the Portuguese Empire, 1415–1825*, London, 1961, p. 132.

79 Bowser, *The African Slave in Colonial Peru*, pp. 151, 287.

80 The term *zambo* should be distinguished from Samboe, which in most of the West Indies and the slave colony of Surinam was a cross between a mulatto and a black, being of a deep copper-coloured complexion with dark hair that curls in large ringlets. Stedman observed that 'These slaves both male and female are generally handsome, and chiefly employed as menial servants in the planters' houses', see Stedman, *Narrative*, Vol. 1, pp. 326–7. This again emphasises that the house slave was always a cross-breed and seldom black. See also D. P. Mannix and M. Cowley, *Black Cargoes: a History of the Atlantic Slave Trade, 1518–1865*, New York and London, 1962 and 1963, p. 127.

81 Bowser, *The African Slave in Colonial Peru*, pp. 286–7.

82 *Ibid.*, p. 287.

83 *Ibid.*

84 *Ibid.*, p. 288.

85 *Ibid.*

86 *Ibid.*, pp. 288–9.

87 *Ibid.*, p. 289.

88 *Ibid.*, p. 297. Bowser gives examples of this in the seventeenth century, a rather complex arrangement.

89 James, *Black Jacobins*, pp. 42–3; also Edwards, *History, Civil and Commercial*, Vol. 3 (on Santo Domingo), p. 1.

90 James, *Black Jacobins*, p. 38.

91 *Ibid.*, pp. 39–40.

92 Edwards, *History, Civil and Commercial*, Vol. 3, pp. 10–15.

93 James, *Black Jacobins*, p. 39.

94 See Sir Alan Burns, *A History of the British West Indies*, London, 1954, pp. 561–2; also Stephen Alexis, *Black Liberator: a Life of Toussaint Louverture*, trs. William Stirling, London, 1949, pp. 20–2.

95 James, *Black Jacobins*, p. 41.

96 *Ibid.*, p. 43.

97 *Ibid.*, p. 44. But one must take cognisance of Elsa Goveia's point that all

whites, in spite of class divisions, were united by instinct and the opportunities for economic advancement also aided this in the Leeward Islands in the eighteenth century. See *Slave Society in the British Leeward Islands at the End of the 18th Century*, New Haven, Conn., 1965, pp. 205–8, 212–14. Also Edwards, *History, Civil and Commercial*, Vol. 2, pp. 7–8. There is an interesting statement about the attitude of even the poorest white who regards himself superior to others, the consideration being based on assumptions of the superiority of skin colour.

98 Brathwaite, *Development of Creole Society in Jamaica*, p. 178.

99 Freyre, *The Masters and the Slaves*, pp. 83–6ff., 261–5, 329, 395–9, 409; Pierson, *Negroes in Brazil*, pp. 70 n. 112, for dismissal of an Indian (Amerindian) officer for marrying a negro and thus soiling his blood and showing himself unworthy of his office.

100 J. H. Rodrigues, *Brazil and Africa*, Berkeley, Cal., 1965, pp. 58–9.

101 These being offspring of white–Amerindian cross breeding. See C. R. Boxer, *The Golden Age of Brazil, 1695–1750*, Berkeley and Los Angeles, 1962, pp. 16, 23, 300–1.

102 *Ibid.*, pp. 59, 107–8.

103 Degler, *op. cit.*, pp. 98–101.

104 See James, *Black Jacobins*, p. 37; also Brathwaite, *Development of Creole Society in Jamaica*, pp. 185–6. It must also be observed that in North America (later the U. S. A.) even white women (including married ones) sometimes had illicit sexual associations with black slaves; some revelations of these associations occasionally surfaced in divorce proceedings; see, for instance, James B. Johnson, *Race Relations in Virginia and Miscegenation in the South, 1776–1860*, Amherst, Mass., 1979, pp. 253–6.

105 James, *Black Jacobins*, p. 9. See also Abbé G. T. F. Raynal, *Slave Trade: a Full Account of This Species of Commerce, etc.*, 1792, p. 44. He stated that 'poison hath at different times been the instruments of their vengeance'.

106 Brathwaite, *Development of Creole Society in Jamaica*, pp. 100–5.

107 Freyre, *The Masters and the Slaves*, p. 455; Boxer, *The Golden Age of Brazil*, pp. 138, 165. Crown and official attempts to legislate against the practice of letting out slaves for prostitution proved abortive (Boxer, pp. 165–6ff). For further use of slave women in prostitution in North America, see William Goodell, *The American Slave Code in Theory and Practice*, New York, 1853, p. 304. He wrote, 'The slave may be used so as to be "used up" in seven years – may be used as a "breeder", as a prostitute, as a concubine, as a pimp, as a tapster, as an attendant at the gaming table, as a subject of medical and surgical experiment, and the legislature makes no objection against it but he may not be used as a clerk.' Also see F. Douglass, *My Bondage and My Freedom*, New York, 1968 (1st edn., 1855), p. 60. He revealed that 'the slave woman is at the mercy of the fathers, sons and brothers of her master'. Many slave autobiographies have variations on this theme of compulsion in handling slave women and a few examples will suffice, as evidence is ubiquitous. See Moses Roper, *A Narrative of the Adventures and Escape of Moses Roper from American Slavery*, London, 1840, pp. 24, 63–6; Henry Bibb, *Narrative of the Life and Adventures of Henry Bibb: an American Slave*, New York, 1849, pp. 98–9, 112–16.

108 D'Auvergne, *Human Livestock*, pp. 100–5.

109 See a comparable situation in Stedman's *Narrative*, Vol. 1, pp. 329–30, in which the anguish of a mother for the brutal drowning of her child head-downward in a river led her to fling herself into the river with a view to drowning. She was rescued and given between three and four hundred lashes.

110 F. Henriques, *Jamaica, Land of Wood and Water*, London, 1960, esp. ch. 6.

111 Long, *History of Jamaica*, Vol. 2, pp. 327–30.

112 Henriques, *Jamaica*, p. 130 and ch. 6.

113 See Eva N. Hodgson, *Second Class Citizens, First Class Men*, Bermuda, n.d. (1968?), esp. ch. 2.

114 Lunsford Lane, *Narrative . . .* , p. 41 in W. L. Katz (ed.), *Five Slave Narratives*, New York, 1968, Italics not in original.

115 *Ibid.*, p. 38.

7 The treatment of slaves

This subject is more complex than might at first appear. The treatment of slaves in any one location during the entire period of slavery could fill volumes and the account, because of the numerous plantations dispersed all over the Americas, would be impossible to compile within the compass of one chapter. What is necessary here is to sketch certain common characteristics which were, in fact, typical of the ways slaves were treated. It is necessary first to stress the almost universal role and use of violence as an ever-present weapon of slavocratic strategy employed for minor as well as major transgressions or even for gratifying the sadistic instincts of either the planter, the overseer or slave driver. This latter problem, however, belongs to the realm of psychology, and it might be necessary in time to see the production of texts which deal with the psychology of the handlers of slaves on the plantations. Secondly, closely connected with violence was the policy of separation, characteristically known in the imperial era as the policy of 'divide and rule' or 'divide and conquer'. It was a feature which helped to make the responses of the slaves to their enslavement less explosive than they might otherwise have been; but its purpose was to secure the slave system from total collapse with the attendant consequences of economic ruin for those who had staked all their fortunes in the business of slavery. Thirdly, there was the encouragement of licentiousness without the legal sanction and recognition of marriage. Fourthly, allied to this was the practice of slave breeding to which we shall return later in the work. Fifthly, there was the policy of quick return. The fatalities which resulted from these made the demand for slaves insatiable. Practices of ill-treatment and overwork leading to death may not have been universal since evidence exists of masters who took care of their slaves, but as the entire system was wasteful of manpower, of itself it kept the slave trade in being for a long time.

It is necessary to consider each of these broad headings in turn, for the amplification sheds some light on the cruel nature of the treatment meted out to the slaves. These headings are far from exhaustive but they give an insight into the revolts and the endeavours to defeat slavery made by its victims and their friends.

Violence and cruelty on the plantations

We have already seen the violence in the capture of the slaves and the nature of insurrection on board ship with their attendant consequences of more violence; but these were minor compared to the violence meted out to the slaves once they were beached on the other side of the Atlantic. From its inception violence was an element built into the slave system which was perpetuated in the western hemisphere. It was as much the weakness as well as the sustaining factor in the survival of the system for a long time, apart from the vested interest position of powerful interests both in the metropolitan countries and on the plantations themselves. Violence was ubiquitous and varied, and can be found by any seekers who endeavour to handle any manual of slavery whether it be the autobiographies of slaves; eye-witness accounts; journals of so-journers on the plantations; reports before parliamentary commissions; from anti-slavery literature (even governors' despatches); from the writings even of the supporters of slavery; or from legal trials and so-called laws, which governed the running of the slave societies. Most slaves' accounts are replete with instances of civil violence. We can therefore only mention some of the offences with examples without doing more than scratching the surface in cataloguing the violence on the plantations and an analysis of the violence. Nevertheless, what is ventured here must be seen as typical of a system which had such an inbuilt mechanism for the perpetuation of itself. Since we are concerned with violence during the entire period in which slavery was sustained in the Americas, it is necessary to cite from earlier as well as later accounts.

One of these instruments for inflicting violence on the slaves was the presence in most plantations of the 'militia', used for the pursuit of runaway slaves, or for quelling insurrections, or attempts at revolt or maintaining order. But they were by no means the only instrument, for the slave catchers and the slave drivers and overseers belong to the same category of those who dispensed violence. Yet the chaining of slaves, and the pillorying of them, were just as much 'legitimate' and well-attested means of violence known to the plantations and slave societies.

Even the prejudiced observation of the *Journal of a Lady of Quality* (whose acceptance of plantation slavery we have already noted in another context) is revealing, for not only did she reveal the groupings to which the African slaves were subjected, but she also drew attention to slave drivers holding short as well as long whips and the purpose of 'these weapons', she felt, could easily be surmised; but she continued by describing the operation as 'a circumstance of all others the most horrid'.[1] These slaves, both male and female, were naked down to the girdle and previous indications on their bodies of flogging could constantly be observed. She contended that, however dreadful this might appear to a humane European,

> I will do the creoles the justice to say, they would be as averse to it as we are, could it be avoided, which has often been tried to no purpose. When one comes to be better acquainted with the nature of the Negroes, the horror of it must wear off. It is the suffering of the human mind that constitutes the greatest misery of punishment; but with them it is merely corporeal. As to the brutes it inflicts no wound on their mind, whose natures seem made to bear it, and whose sufferings are not attended with shame or pain beyond the present moment.[2]

Other forms of punishment were applied whenever the use of the whip failed to make the slaves amenable. Runaway slaves when recaptured were 'mildly' chastised for a first offence but on a second and subsequent offence of the same kind they had a leg secured to a heavy log or had a collar with hooks fastened to their necks which tore their flesh whenever they bent their heads. Apart from the above quotation of Janet Schaw from the second half of the eighteenth century, when slavery and the slave trade were in full swing, it is a distortion of the facts regarding human feelings to a state which involved their debasement. Their acquiescence in physical violence of the kind mentioned and their mental immunity to this treatment, asserted by her, belong only to the world of make-believe and fantasy. They have no foundations in the records. We can hardly read the lives of ex-slaves, such as Frederick Douglass[3] or any of the other eighteenth- and nineteenth-century slaves previously mentioned in this work, or the fulminations of an ex-slave, the Rev. H. H. Garnet, without encountering a complete rebuttal of Miss Schaw's assertion regarding the punishment being 'merely corporeal'. But these justifications were often made by self-satisfied slave-owners and their defenders, evidence of which is ubiquitous. Earlier still, in 1676, an unsuccessful revolt of the Koromantees recorded in Edmund D'Auvergne's *Human Livestock* revealed the way in which these slaves were treated. The account showed that six of them were burnt alive.[4] We also get glimpses of cruelty of the kind in question while reading through the account of the pro-slavery 'Historian of the West Indies', Bryan Edwards, who was himself descended from slave owners. His account related to an abortive but formidable revolt in Jamaica in 1760.[5] Commenting on this, Edmund D'Auvergne wrote: 'The man who was burnt alive uttered not a groan, and saw his legs reduced to ashes with the utmost composure, seizing the opportunity, one is glad to hear, to dash a flaming brand in the face of his tormentor. Two others were hung upon a gibbet to die. They died, one on the eighth day and the other on the ninth day.'[6] We have another account of the eighteenth century at the time of the Mississippi Bubble (1718–20), when after the foiling of an attempt by slaves to rid themselves of their French masters and assume authority themselves, eight of them were condemned to be broken alive on the wheel, and the women involved in their scheme were compelled to watch the occurrence.[7] Another incident was recounted by the Charleston (South Carolina) *Evening Gazette* of 12 July 1785 in which a runaway slave belonging to a Mr Baron, who had rubbed himself with grease to make his body slimy and thus evade being captured, had taken refuge in a 'Negro quarter'. When his pursuers, Messrs Car and McKennon, entered the quarter and attempted to capture him by force, the slave drew out a knife stabbing and killing Mr Car, while at the same time inflicting severe gash wounds on his companion. Eventually he was captured and condemned to death. The *Evening Gazette* continued: 'He was immediately led to execution, and had his hand struck off, which he bore with an indignant firmness, but his mutilated bleeding stump being immersed in boiling pitch, he appeared to feel the torments of the damned, he was now thrown into the hot pitch and then hanged. Humanity recoils and sickens at such a horrid scene, the crime was great; so was the punishment.'[8]

But these practices did not abate at the turn of the eighteenth century or as the nineteenth progressed. In the nineteenth century another example of the absolutism which an owner exercised over his slave can be seen. This incident occurred in Virginia in which an owner, Mr Souther, killed his slave whose name was Sam. In the administering of punishment Souther escaped with a finding of second degree murder and was sentenced to five years in a penitentiary.

> The Negro was tied to a tree and whipped with switches. When
> Souther became fatigued with the labour of whipping him he called
> upon a Negro man of his, and made him cob Sam with a shingle. He
> also made a Negro woman of his help to cob him. And, after
> cobbing and whipping, he applied fire to the body of the slave; about
> his back, belly and private parts. He then caused him to be washed
> down with hot water, in which pods of red pepper had been steeped.
> The Negro was also tied to a log and to the bed post with ropes,
> which choked him, and he was kicked and stamped by Souther. This
> sort of punishment was continued and repeated until the Negro died
> under its infliction.[9]

Whether this was common practice or an isolated case as indicated in the judicial records is immaterial. What is important is that it happened and that it happened on one slave was a reason why all other slaves should have revolted against their enslavement. But it showed the methods of many slave owners, handlers and overseers with which the records are replete. From time to time attempts at justification were made; as, for instance, this extract from the rules of management in the sugar colonies shows. It read: 'Where slavery is established and the proportion of slaves outnumbers their masters ten to one, terror must operate to keep them in subjection, and terror can only be produced by occasional examples of severity.'[10]

Trivial offences were punished with much severity.[11] As Frederick Douglass observed, whipping could result from a 'mere look, word or motion – a mistake, accident, or want of power'. 'Does a slave look dissatisfied? It is said, he has the devil in him, and it must be whipped out. If he speaks loudly when spoken to by his master he is said to be getting high-minded and should be taken down a button-hole lower.'[12] For instance, allowing a mule to go astray would involve a protracted period of flogging with a cartwhip on the bare back and buttocks. This was a vicious instrument and every stroke of it drew blood from the slave. Even when the slaves protested with words such as: 'Think me no man?', meaning do you think I do not possess human feelings, they emphasised their humanity though degraded as slaves. The slave owners or overseers who ordered and watched the administering of such measures acted with such indifference as if they were paying the slaves their wages. An observer noted that, sometimes, slaves were flogged not so much because they had offended but to spite another book-keeper under whose charge the slaves were, because one overseer had a difference with the said book-keeper, or due to a difference of opinion between a proprietor and his manager.[13]

Thus, from the above, we see the African slaves in the western hemisphere suffered not only from the strains of overwork, which took its own toll on life; but they were also made to groan under the whip which taskmasters had no qualms in administering. Frances Anne Kemble, who spent the years 1838–9 on a Georgian plantation, recorded in her *Journal*: 'that the planters found it upon the whole their most profitable plan to work off (kill with labour) their whole number of slaves about once in seven years, and renew the whole stock'.[14] It is incontestable that there were wide variations in the treatment of slaves. But, as an author has observed, the consensus of opinion was that he fared best under the Portuguese, the Danes, the French and the Spaniards and worst under the Dutch and British. He might well have included the North Americans. He maintained that 'the abuses, the immoralities, the tortures practised upon the slaves, and the fierce outbreaks to which they occasionally gave rise, fill hundreds of volumes. They seem to have reached the height of their intensity in Dutch Guiana and the British West Indies.' 'For a hundred years', he observed, 'slaves in Barbados were mutilated, tortured, gibbeted alive and left to starve to death, burnt alive, flung into coppers of boiling sugar, whipped to death.'[15] Other forms of punishment 'legally' approved were as follows: cutting out of the tongue, pulling the eye out (blinding the slave), scalding, or deprivation of a limb. To these may be added others gleaned from British parliamentary papers. Such atrocities included the castration of some young Africans, cutting them to pieces and disembowelling them and burning their entrails.[16]

Revolts, or attempts at revolt, were severely punished and the cruel practices continued until the end of slavery in the West Indies and later in the United States of America. The fate of captured or defeated insurgents was ghastly, often culminating in death. Sometimes they were shot, at times hung on gallows in the market place by gibbet halter. Often the executions were summary after the pretence of a trial, and at times the person used for the role of hangman was another 'negro' who had become identified with the slave holders (though himself not a slave holder but just a 'privileged slave'). Here was an example of an induced element for dividing the rank and file of the oppressed. But the defiance of the insurgents was often commendable, even if their deeds were deemed despicable by the slavocracy. The observation of a missionary eye-witness of the Jamaican revolt of 1831–2, the last in the great series of revolts organised by West Indian slaves during the entire period of slavery, is quite revealing, if read completely.[17] This was the so-called 'Baptist War'. The Rev. Belby's revelations in that account could be generalised for other places and times during the centuries of slavery, but in a nutshell he rightly stigmatised the method of the execution of the slaves as a 'wholesale system of murder'.[18] It is a fitting note on which to conclude our coverage of the application of cruel violence.

We can now consider the practice of slave rearing which formed an essential part of the ill-treatment of the African slaves.

The practice of slave rearing

Allied to the licentiousness of the plantations was the practice of slave breeding and rearing. We have already seen that the mortality of African slaves on the plantations was high and that they had to be replaced by fresh cargoes imported from Africa. Some planters felt that one method of supplementing their slave numbers and consequently their working hands was through the encouragement of interbreeding among the slaves themselves.[19] With reference to Colonel Martin, one of the most comfortable estate-owners in Antigua in the eighteenth century, and a member of one of the most reputed and long-standing families on the island, the 'Lady of

197

Quality' commented on slave breeding. She attributed the bounteousness of the child crop to the benevolent treatment of the slaves by the planter. Thus, she asserted that

> the effect of this kindness is a daily increase of riches by the slaves born for upwards of twenty years, and that he had the morning of our arrival got the return of the state of his plantations, on which there then were no less than fifty-two wenches who were pregnant. These slaves, born on the spot and used to the Climate, are by far the most valuable and seldom take these disorders, by which such numbers are lost that many hundreds are forced yearly to be brought into the island.[20]

Or as Frances Anne Kemble wrote of Georgia in the nineteenth century: 'their lives for the most part were those of mere animals and their increase being identical with mere animal breeding to which every encouragement is given for it adds to the master's livestock, and the value of his estate'.[21]

On the cruelty of the system she observed: 'I find many women have bourne from five to ten children rated as workers, precisely as young women in the prime of their strength who have had more; this seems a cruel carelessness.'[22] Furthermore, as some slaves born on the plantations tended to endure well and become more acclimatised to climatic conditions than those freshly imported from Africa, the practice of slave breeding found another rationale. But one of the major factors responsible for this internal production of slaves was the acute labour shortage after the slave trade was abolished by Britain and the U.S.A. in 1807 and 1808 respectively. This, of course, did not put an end to the smuggling in of slaves from the west coast of Africa and between the plantations. Governor Buchanan of Liberia in 1839 was able to remark that 'The chief obstacle to the suppression of the slave trade on the coast [of Africa], is the *American Flag*. Never was the proud banner of freedom so extensively used by those pirates upon liberty and humanity as at this season.'[23] In fact, this kind of smuggling continued especially in North America until almost the outbreak of the Civil War. Although the official ending of the slave trade by the U.S.A. in 1808 contributed to the extension of the practice of slave breeding, and aimed at forestalling government interference with trading in slaves and the ordering of society in the south, it must be borne in mind that slave raising was in existence long before the abolition of the slave trade. The practice was universal in the West Indies. Barbados appears to have excelled.[24]

This aspect of plantation life is important because it enables us to understand some of the factors in the revolt of Africans on the plantations. Slave rearing involved the downgrading of the Africans

198

to the level of procreating beasts like cattle or horses. The system of slave rearing, like cattle rearing, became an important appendage of the plantation system supplementing numbers lost on the voyage to the Americas or augmenting the decrease in flow of slaves after the law decided to exercise vigilance on those who transgressed by attempting to import slaves. Yet in dealing with this aspect alone, we are made increasingly aware of an economic system which brought untold wealth to the plantation breeders but we are also shown the misery inflicted by the system and the depravity of the breeders. F. A. Kemble in her *Journal* recalled her meeting with one 'tall, emaciated-looking negress' who was ill and who unfolded to her a most distressing history of bodily afflictions. 'She was the mother of a very large family, and complained to me that, what with the child bearing and hard field labour, her back was almost broken in two'.[25] It was an inverted kind of eugenics. Indeed, we come up against the paradoxes of slavery, for while there were plantation breeders of slaves who took particular care to nourish their slaves to achieve their intentions of frequent procreations, in other plantations the slave was a victim of hunger. This one fact, among others, makes generalisations about slavery increasingly difficult. It would be more correct to observe that the system differed from state to state, island to island, plantation to plantation and even more from locality to locality.

The practice of slave breeding encouraged inter-state slave trading in North America or what has been called the 'domestic slave trade'. In the West Indies after the abolition of the slave trade, the inter-colonial slave trade under the pretext of 'domestic servants attending on their masters' was fostered.[26]

We are observing a system which provided its victims with no kind of decent family life; and when this was conceded, the family life was made indecent; for if the female member was not a victim of the planter, merchant, overseer or book-keeper, her offspring were often torn away from her and sold into servitude. A slave owner would often also sell his slaves separately, dividing members of 'families' from one another. Advertisements for sale were not infrequent and it seems monotonous to mention more than one of them, they are so ubiquitous and easily accessible in any documents or documentary evidence relating to the evolution of slavery in the West Indies and the Americas. There was very little consideration for the ages of those sold for they could be a year old or fifty years. Take, for instance, the prices that were fetched for domestic-bred child slaves in some parts of the southern states of America in May 1857:

Name	Age	Price
Jack	4	$376

Elvina   5 $400
Bettie   8 $785

In the same year in Maryland, a girl of about 14 fetched the price of $900; a small girl, $880; a small girl, $350. In Missouri, a girl of 9 fetched $805; boy aged 5, $487, boy aged 2½, $325.[27]

It is important to note that no kind of inheritance was allowed the slave except that of 'slave', which tended to follow the status of the mother and so the slave could not acquire property whether as a gift or through inheritance.[28] How could one described as slave in the laws of the slave states acquire property when in fact he or she was property? So the argument ran and others argued on the grounds that they were illegitimate. But the system was not simple; court decisions reinforced the chattel status of the slave and it is particularly interesting to note that the legal stipulations of the various slaveholding states did not suggest otherwise. Whatever the slaves acquired through their industry was deemed to belong to their master. It is not difficult to see how those stipulations would be generators of revolt, for though the slaves might be ignorant of the subtleties of the legal stipulations of the country, state, or country to which they belonged, they were not unaware of the natural laws of justice and injustice; and especially when injustice was so blatantly perpetrated upon themselves. In the case of the women it was worse still, for they were treated like mares hired out for the purpose of reproducing and their offspring automatically belonged to their owner. That this practice predates the abolition of the slave trade by the English is shown in the caption of the *Charleston City Gazette*, South Carolina, in 1796 advertising fifty prime negroes for sale:

> They are Negroes selected out of a larger gang for the purpose of sale but are prime, their present owner, with great trouble and expense, selected them out of many for their several years past. They were purchased for stock and breeding Negroes, and to any Planter who particularly wanted them for that purpose. they are a very choice and desirable gang.[29]

A major factor which continued to weigh heavily on the practice after the abolition of the slave trade was the expansion of the cotton culture. The invention by Eli Whitney in 1793 of a cotton gin made the demand for slaves insatiable. In Maryland, Virginia and Kentucky (real centres of breeding), where the ordinary labours of slaves were deemed less remunerative, slave rearing was a particularly important industry since their sale, or the sale of some of them, enabled owners to pay their debts, obtain money, or offer legacies to their children. Very often it was the young slaves who went, if part of the gang was to be disposed of. Bancroft gives a vivid account of the practice thus: 'The executor of A. T. Goodwyn held a public sale of all the decedent's crops, stock, household furniture and plantation utensils and some of the negroes – "20 Slaves, consisting of men, women, boys and girls, between 14 and 25 years of age, selected out of a lot of more than 100 Terms. Cash for the slaves, and a credit of 12 months for the other property, Petersbury, Va. Republican, 29 September 1847".'[30] The consequences for the enslaved African woman in such territories employing her as a procreating animal were tremendous. Judicially denied any personality in law, since as a slave she was regarded as property, by her being turned into a procreating beast she lost her moral personality as well, and both factors blocked the passage to manumission.

Profits for the owners of these slaves accrued phenomenally and Frederick Bancroft quoted Francis Corbin writing on Virginia in 1819 as saying:

> *Miserabile dictu* our principal profit depends on the increase of slaves and that a court case in Virginia revealed that 'the scantiness of net profit from slave labour has become proverbial, and that nothing is more common than actual loss, or a benefit merely in the slow increase of capital from propagation'.[31]

Even the protagonist of slavery, Professor Thomas Roderick Dew, who became President of William and Mary College in 1836, repeated in many parts of his dissertation on the 'Abolition of Negro Slavery' that the profits from slave rearing were phenomenal, and believing that 'the 6000 slaves which Virginia annually sends off to the South are a source of wealth to Virginia', warned the legislators of the state to beware lest in advocating colonisation for negroes away from America, 'this efflux, which is now so salutary to the State, and such an abundant source of wealth, be suddenly dried up'. He concluded that when slavery was destroyed 'no matter how, the deed will be done, and Virginia will be a desert'.[32] We get a glimpse from these citations that Virginia was the foremost breeder among the slave-breeding states and that Virginians raised them more cheaply than those obtained through the foreign supply system. Thus it can be inferred that the largest number of slaves exported from Virginia were of the domestic breed rather than imported ones from the west coast of Africa or elsewhere, but this was, of course, more so after the abolition of the slave trade. A modern historian informs us that in 1830 Virginia was credited with exporting 8500 slaves annually due to the breeding of slaves, like cattle, on the estates.[33]

According to Bancroft, Jesse Burton Harrison asserted that

The only form in which it can safely be said that slaves on a plantation are profitable in Virginia, is in the multiplication of their number by births. If the proprietor, beginning with a certain number of negroes, can but keep them for a few years from the hands of the sheriff or the slave trader, though their labour may have yielded him not a farthing of nett revenue, he finds that gradually but surely, his capital stock of negroes multiplies itself, and yields, if nothing else, a palpable interest of young negroes . . . . The process of multiplication will not in this way advance the master towards the point of nett revenue; he is not the richer in income with the fifty slaves than with twenty. Yet these young negroes have their value; and what value? The value of the slaves so added to his number is the certain price for which they will at any time sell to the southern trade . . . . An account, on which we may rely, sets down the annual number of slaves sold to go out of the States at six thousand, or more than half the number of births! . . . And will 'the aspiring blood of Lancaster' endure it to be said that a Guinea is still to be found in America, and that Guinea is Virginia?[34]

Yet there was a tendency for some of the prejudiced observers of the plantations during slavery to refer frequently to the licentious-ness of the negroes. The evidence was not that the negroes were licentious but rather that they were forced into relationships in which they were compelled to produce so many children within a definite period, all in the interest of profit. Inducements were even given to be more prolific.

But who were these people who sank so low as to practise plantation breeding and rearing? According to William Wells Brown, an ex-slave, author and later one of the leaders of the Afro-Americans, we learn that from his own knowledge of the state of Maryland, in which he had been previously enslaved, 'those who raise slaves for the market are to be found among all classes from Thomas H. Benton[35] down to the lowest political demagogue who may be able to purchase a woman for the purpose of raising stock, and from the doctor of divinity down to the most humble lay member in the church'.[36]

William Wells Brown informs us that it was customary among slaves to speak of marriage and that slaves did marry, or, at least, had the ceremony performed. Nevertheless there was no such thing as a slave being 'lawfully married' and there never occurred a case in which a slave was arraigned in court for bigamy. It was the convention within the slave system that a man might have as many women as he wished, and the women as many men as she desired, without the law taking cognizance of the behaviour of either party.[37] Furthermore, there were instances in which slave masters after disposing of the husband of a slave woman would compel her

202

to take another.[38] It is not hard to see the reasons for this encouragement of loose living; it was to gratify the aspirations of the slave owner's yearning for laboratory-bred slaves.

The Rev. William Davis, a clergyman in the Leeward Islands in a letter to Governor Hugh Elliot on 16 March 1815 written in order to vindicate himself of the charge of cruelty to slaves, wrote:

> We must however lay out a little money in the purchase of Negroes, in order to make up for our recent losses. In our list we have I suppose 50 to 60 women of the age for breeding, and yet it is strange we have seldom more than 7 or 8 infants born in a year.[39]

This again shows that the practice of slave rearing was deeply rooted, especially as the plea for the right to purchase slaves was being made six years after Britain had officially abandoned the slave trade. But the point of licentiousness in the refusal to grant permission for marriage by slaves was taken up in 1820 by a minister, the Rev. Byam, who had resided in the West Indies for some years. In a letter to the Bishop of London in December of that year he drew the attention of the Bishop to the question of marriage of the slaves in the West Indian colonies. He insisted that less was known on the subject in Britain and regretted that such a state of affairs should have existed in the nineteenth century. He then told the story that, while in Antigua the previous April, two persons of colour (mulattos about 'thirty years of age of respectable character and conduct') had applied to him to join them in marriage. The Rev. Byam secured the consent of the clergyman of the parish in question so that the marriage would be celebrated in church. This he observed was the result of his 'repeated remonstrances and exaltations' with slaves to turn aside from the 'usual system of cohabitation by mutual consent alone, and desoluble at pleasure'. Byam continued his story:

> Pleased of course at finding this result of my endeavour, and seeing the probability of their introducing with effect civilized and moral habits amongst the negroes, I applied immediately to the incumbent of the parish, and was gratified by an acknowledgement in reply of his ready acquaintance. The bands were consequently published in the parish church on the 16th, and again on the 30th of April; the third publication however, having been omitted, to my inquiry respecting the cause of such omission I received a reply of which the principle part was stated in the following words: 'consulted the law officers of the crown, and considering the yet religious slow acquirement of our slaves, and how likely they would have the breech of their marriage vows, and as during, my incumbency of near 40 years in St George Parish, I have never before been called

upon to marry slaves, they are of an opinion that I may act improperly by making a precedent that in the present state of the colonies might lead to a belief that it gave immunities it does not.

In another part of the same letter it is stated that 'having published the bands of marriage between the slaves [this] had been the subject of discussion and blame'. It is scarcely necessary to add that a stop was put to the marriage.[40] Even the new Governor of Antigua, Sir Benjamin D'Urban, who had not at the time arrived at his post when informed of the situation, expressed surprise and regret.[41] The Rev. Byam expressed the hope that the understanding of the Governor of Antigua would lead to more enlarged and more just notions becoming familiar among the white inhabitants than 'had ever been hitherto admitted in favour of the ignorant and degraded brethren'. He continued:

> From my own experience and observation I have no diffidence in declaring that the island's stand greatly in need of Your Lordship's inter-position. The solitary example from Antigua will suffice, though it may not be amiss to mention by the way that this is the very same island that has had the credit (See Walker's dedication of excellent letters to the planters of Antigua) of attending more to the moral improvement of the working classes than any other *English* Island in the West Indies. If so, my Lord (and, from all the information which I was able to collect, I am strongly inclined to believe his supposition to be correct) how dark and general must be the prejudice on the one side and the ignorance on the other![42]

The implications were clear in that even an 'enlightened' island like Antigua, supposed to be morally above the other plantation islands, had refused the marriage of slaves in an era of amelioration.

The quick return policy and its implications

This is not an attempt to enquire in detail into the profitability or otherwise of slavery. That economic considerations were motivating factors cannot be denied, and that individuals profited handsomely from the system is also easily shown, even though some may have lost in the venture. The journal of any West Indian planter is replete with the trappings of affluence. The work of assessing profitability in quantitative terms awaits further research.[43] From the past as well as recent researches of scholars, Professor Elkins admits to the validity of the thesis of profitability. He rightly observes, for instance, that 'Any enquiry must begin with Southern culture and its long-standing commitment to Negro slavery. It must assume all the arrangements of Southern life that somehow depended on and radiated from this commitment: not only a deep-rooted labour system, but a body of law, a system of race relations, a style of life.' It might be objected that such items are not 'economic'. But actually, Elkins argued, they are, and that 'any conceivable venture in large-scale agriculture had to proceed from there; any criterion of "profitability" would have to take all this as given; these arrangements made competition on any other basis out of the question.'[44] Elkins draws from past and contemporary sources to justify the argument of profitability in a quantitative sense and asserts that 'far from being a decrepit institution, the economic motives for the continuance of slavery from the standpoint of the employer were never so strong as in the years just preceding the Civil War'.[45] Quoting again from Conrad and Meyer (who shifted their emphasis away from the plantation to the slave himself, i.e. not necessarily to the agricultural management of the plantation but to the slave as investment, and who showed it was possible to make useful deductions about the economic soundness of the operation of slavery),[46] he asserts in terms of slave breeding that: 'Slavery was profitable to the whole south' and concludes that the 'continuing demand for labour in the Cotton Belt insured returns to the breeding operation on the less productive land in the seaboard or border states. The breeding returns were necessary, however, to make the plantation operations on the poorer lands as profitable as alternative contemporary economic activities in the United States.'[47]

But, as Elkins recognised, a fuller picture to give backing to the generalisation on the subject of profitability would need the assembly of much statistical data and much computation of the accounts to enable a broad picture of profitability to emerge. By dwelling on the question, however briefly, Elkins pointed to a valuable field of research for enthusiastic scholars on the economics of slavery. This section is intended to examine the implications of the 'quick return policy', whether enunciated by those who invested in the slave trade, or in the maintenance of plantations – individuals or corporations, both were locked in a common activity. Implicit in the minds of participants – both active and passive – was the quick return motive.[48] Those who piloted the ships to the slaving theatre on the coast of Africa were sometimes agents of larger concerns, but were themselves anxious to see that their ventures were not futile, for non-profitability implied that their own financial rewards from their employers would not amount to much. They therefore had to be crafty, sometimes flexible, and often ingenious, once they had arrived at the theatre of operation; for a false step could mean the failure of the venture or the prolongation of their stay on the west coast, an area allegedly infested with fever, and one which took its toll of European lives. Therefore, there was lurking at the back of the mind of every adventurer the need to secure slaves quickly and accomplish the necessary crossing to the Americas. The same element of expediency was also seen in attempts to overload slave ships or pack them in such a sardine-like manner that many men and women died before the journey was completed. The method of loading the vessels also contributed to the spread of infectious and contagious diseases, some of which resulted in the blindness of some slave ships' crews and even resulted in death.[49]

Once in slavery, the ill-usage of slaves which characterised some planters, attorneys and overseers (though it is not established that most planters behaved in this way) also contributed to the high mortality noted elsewhere in this work. But added to this was the induced factor of speculation which hardly helped the slave.[50] That slave prices fluctuated is also attested in the records; but, that obnoxious practice of slave breeding, of which Virginians were among the arch culprits, was based largely on the speculative principle. Thus, we can see from the above, that slave breeding was conditioned by the policy and hope of substantial return; in a sense, it could be said to be the exception in the 'quick return policy' because breeding took time, but the net result of the practice was the amassing of huge fortunes.[51] Nonetheless, in general, the plantocracy were preoccupied with their speedy returns and their enrichment to enable them to take up domicile in the mother country. Those who achieved this breakthrough often had with them money to be extravagant and profligate. We learn from more recent evidence that some of them not only entered the metropolitan parliaments but they exercised considerable influence there, especially on matters relating to the plantations. The West Indian plantocracy was represented in both Houses of the British Parliament either personally or by vocal representatives.[52] Compared to the English, the French sugar islands were reputed to be better managed.[53] The quick return policy had disastrous consequences, often self-defeating; for the slave commodity made wretched often failed to attain any worthwhile market value and at times the slaves died.[54] Dying was a regular occurrence known both to the middle passage and after installation on the plantations.

Official and unofficial attitudes regarding returns from slaving had serious implications for both the slave trade and slavery. Much of the intractability was allied to economics; the fear, real or imaginary, of economic ruin was always trotted out as an argument for its continuance. We have the celebrated statement of the Colonial Secretary, William, Earl of Dartmouth, to whom the slave girl Phyllis Wheatley ironically enough dedicated some of her poems. Lord Dartmouth had, on the eve of the American revolutionary war, quite bluntly stated (and in doing so spoke for many of the opponents of abolition), 'We cannot allow the colonies[55] to check or to discourage in any degree a traffic so beneficial to the nation.'[56] But the more telling statement is that of a twentieth-century British statesman, Winston Churchill, who, at the time of the Second World War, summed up the gains of the slavery connection as follows:

> Our possessions of the West Indies, like that of India, . . . gave us strength, the support, but especially the capital, the wealth, at a time when no other European nation possessed such a reserve, which enabled us to come through the great struggles of the Napoleonic Wars, the keen competition of commerce in the eighteenth and nineteenth centuries, and enable us not only to acquire this appendage of possessions which we have, but also to lay the foundations of that commercial and financial leadership which, when the world was young, when everything outside Europe was undeveloped, enabled us to make our great position in the world.[57]

Nevertheless, the implications due to the high fatalities induced in slave societies by the quick return policy made the appetite for more slaves insatiable, and as this was a wasteful usage of manpower, the importation of fresh slaves to meet the exigencies of labour shortage on the plantations itself helped to keep the slave trade and consequently slavery in being for a long time.

But the removal of able-bodied manpower also had implications for Africa. It was stultifying to local incentives for production of worthwhile commodities, for these became of secondary importance to the supply of slaves (often through warfare). Yet, prior to the commercialisation of slaves, areas of Africa affected by the trade (such as West and Central Africa) had produced gold, iron wares made from iron foundries and forges, ivory, varieties of art works,[58] textiles, varieties of grains, pepper and other spices. These industries suffered a serious setback when the transatlantic diaspora gathered momentum. Since the manpower exported from Africa constituted its capital, as Basil Davidson has rightly observed, and since the payments earned by potentates and prime merchants on the African coast were articles of self-glorification, as has been stated elsewhere in this work, economic stagnation occurred, no matter how disguised in modern scholarship.[59] Since Africa's capital (manpower) brought no returns in the form of capital goods but was attended by increasing misery for the Africans in general both at home and abroad, the slave trade and slavery constituted a double calamity.

Other aspects of cruelty

Apart from what has been observed previously there were miscellaneous aspects of cruelty which made slavery a nightmare for its victims. One feature of this cruelty endured by the slaves was the discipline of starvation due to under-feeding or bad food, or even deprivation of food. The situation went unnoticed in some slave theatres for years, and a year before the British abolition of slavery Governor Maxwell from St Christopher (St Kitts) in 1832 wrote to Lord Goderich as follows:

> I beg to state that the feeding and the nature of labour of the slaves in these islands has been notorious for many years and set forth in the Parliamentary papers, where it is clearly demonstrated that a systematic violation of the Leeward Island Amelioration Law of 1798 has prevailed . . . since its enactment. Indeed the important subject of feeding and regulating the labour of slaves until your Lordship took it up, has been almost unnoticed in almost all the official communications to the respective colonies, upon the attempts of the Legislatures to amend the Laws for the protection of slaves and in justice to myself I beg to say, that during my residence in England I mentioned the subject at the Colonial Office, but which did not receive that attention which I have always been convinced it deserved.[60]

Lord Goderich himself quoted the above statement of Governor Maxwell to Governor Will Nicolay on 5 April 1832.[61] He sought compliance with the amelioration measure of 1798, adding that because the Chief Justice of the island was himself a plantation proprietor he expected punctual obedience to the law which he was eminently engaged in compelling others to obey.[62] He sought a firmness against opponents by suggesting that such persons could not oppose and expect to be kept in government as the government's sincerity would be distrusted. But, when in sheer desperation, its victims unleashed ferocity in retaliation for the wrongs, which they experienced continuously, the privileged of the plantation societies in turn had a taste of their own medicine. It would be interesting to ascertain some of the factors which led to many of the sadistic displays which pervaded the centuries of slavery, but this must await the results of psycho-analytical data from similar and more recent occurrences, such as those of the concentration camps, or of the apartheid regime in South Africa, for only through comparative studies of this kind would it be possible to formulate plausible theories for the sadistic actions of many plantation taskmasters and slave-drivers, whose roles were no less analogous to those of the men who have been devising and operating the more modern institutions mentioned above.[63] Nevertheless, the factors of brutalisation, vindictiveness and even, ironically, reform, were present in slave societies both from within and from external pressures.

The axiom of stability was implicit in the concept of 'public order' emphasised in the laws and harsh customs of slave societies, for instability swung the pendulum forward and backward and seemed hardly conducive to the maintenance of slavery. Vindictiveness came readily either when slaves revolted, escaped, damaged property or took any other steps to assert their manhood. Some of the punishments were instituted by custom and usage; others were bolstered up by 'law'.[64] Thus we see in a Code of South Carolina that punishment was meted out as follows to any slaves offering violence to any 'Christian or white person'.[65] It was severe whipping for the first offence, branding (with a hot iron) for the second offence, and death for a third. These laws are parallelled in most of the slave theatres of one or other of the European slave-holding nations.[66] If the slave injured and maimed a white person summary execution followed. In the same code runaway slaves received whipping for a first offence, branding for a second, cropping of the ears for a third, castrating for a fourth.[67] The punishments varied from one slave theatre to another but they had common features of severity and brutality. Other forms of cruelty included the hounding of runaway slaves with dogs. Also slaves were staked to the ground, a punishment mentioned by Equiano, the ex-Igbo slave, in his autobiography. Sometimes slaves were hung by the wrists and thumbs in crucifixion (and sometimes in inverted crucifixion); at other times hooks were secured round the necks of the slaves so that they dug into the flesh whenever the slave moved and bent down. Among other forms of punishment was solitary confinement. These methods of brutality were multifarious and endless and no useful purpose would be served in extending the list. This aspect of cruelty meted out to the slaves was not to achieve reform of the slave system but rather to instil fear into other slaves so that they dared not attempt any insubordination or be guilty of any offence. It was partially successful in keeping temporary peace, but it was an uneasy peace, and it not only brutalised the slaves but failed to prevent their restiveness, ushering in numerous forms of slave resistance. That it kept some slaves down for a while is all that can be said for it, but this induced element of terror became in many ways self-defeating, even though terror tactics were employed until the demise of slavery in the Americas. The following example is a typical case.

An unusual case? Mr Hodge

On 8 May 1811 a slave owner of Tortola in the Leeward Islands, Mr Hodge, was hanged for numerous murders and cruelties to his slaves. The evidence presented against him came not only from slaves but from other white persons, who could have supported him by providing counter evidence but instead chose to put up evidence against him. That he was not supported indicated the party strife which was common in the plantations and bedevilled the relations of West Indian whites.[68] The cruelties were comparable to those by which Mr Overzee in North America killed his slave, as recounted above. Played out in a twentieth-century situation, Mr Hodge might have first been recommended for a psychiatrist's report. The peculiar case of Hodge became a matter for public concern, and it drew the attention of the British government because amelioration measures, as a result of the action of abolitionists,[69] had begun to be fostered on the plantations. It is quite conceivable, however, that there were many unrecorded Hodges in the treatment of slaves. Governor Hugh Elliot in a letter to the Earl of Liverpool seems to have been well aware of this, and of how the cause of justice must have been perverted over a long period.[70] In a setting in which violence and cruelty constituted the rule, rather than the exception, and in which force was needed to suppress the truculence of slaves who dared assert their humanity or resentment against mishandling, cruelty was all-pervasive. The records, as well as travellers' experiences and slave autobiographies, are far from silent on its ubiquity.

Here it is necessary to mention some of the crimes for which Mr Hodge was convicted and hanged. Hodge was portrayed as a person of 'a cruel malicious diabolical disposition and not having the fear of God before his eyes but moved and seduced by the instigation of the devil'.[71] Hodge killed two of his slaves, Margaret and Else, by brutal methods in each case; they were seized and pinned to the ground with their faces upwards and then Hodge ordered boiling water to be poured down their throats. It impaled them and they died as a consequence.[72]

The fact that Hodge was not brought to trial before 1811 shows the possibilities for evasion to which Hugh Elliot alluded in some of his despatches to the Colonial Office. The crimes for which Hodge was arraigned were committed between 1807 and 1811. Another slave, Cudjoe, was killed by pinning him to the ground face downward with his legs and arms extended and held down. After much flogging and laceration on his bare buttocks, the slave languished in pain and died. Another slave, Tom, was set upon, pinioned to the ground face downwards and was whipped with a cartwhip until he was bruised and lacerated, with Hodge in attendance. The flogging continued for upwards of an hour and Tom lived on in agony for four days before expiring.

Another revelation speaks for itself:

> That Bella a small mulatto child reputed to be the natural child of said Hodge by his female slave Peggy (then about eight years of age as this deponent believes) was repeatedly cartwhipped by order of said Hodge, and this deponent further said he hath more than once seen the said Hodge strike the child with a stick upon her head and break her head – and hath repeatedly seen him kick her so violently in the lower part of her belly as to send her several feet, on the ground from whence he this deponent thought she never again would rise.[73]

There were also cases of burning the mouths of slaves with hot iron, all resulting in death. Hodge's ill-treatment of his workers also extended to a freeman, Peter, whom Hodge put in irons and tortured till he died. The fastening of slaves in stocks was one of Hodge's pastimes. The number of slaves said to have been killed by his cruelty approximated sixty.

The trial of Hodge led to the assertion of a principle which was communicated to the Petty Jury by the Chief Justice, namely that:

> It is clear that the life and limb of a slave are not at the disposal of the Master, and, that however, an Owner might have a right to correct his slave at his discretion, yet, such correction must be presumed to be given for some fault or offence, and ought to be *limited* to the bounds of moderation; whenever that is exceeded, and death ensues, the master or party ordering, or directing it, is accountable.[74]

This statement of principle was the result of the adoption of measures of amelioration for improving the conditions of the slaves, notoriously bad throughout the slave-trading centuries. The application of the law on the side of the slave almost for the first time in this sphere revealed that some moral principles, even though fostered on the slave societies from without, were beginning to have a salutary effect on conditions. But it took centuries of intolerance and ignorance to arrive at such a stage. We now turn to consider the use of religion and the denial of education as further weapons in the armoury of the slavocracy to manipulate slave societies.

Notes

1 [Janet Schaw], *Journal of a Lady of Quality*, New Haven, Conn., 1921, 1939, p. 127.

2 *Ibid.*; also see E. B. F. D'Auvergne, *Human Livestock*, London, 1933, p. 96.
3 See, for instance, letters of Frederick Douglass to his former slave master, Thomas Auld, on the tenth and eleventh anniversaries of his escape from bondage, in Carter G. Woodson, *The Mind of the Negro as reflected in Letters written during the Crisis 1800–1860*, Washington, D.C., 1926, pp. 203–13. See *A Narrative of the Life of Frederick Douglass, an American Slave, Written by himself*, Boston, 1845, 4th edn., pp. 38–41, 47–8, 50. His reflection on the need to take his freedom on the shore of Chesapeake Bay is told on pp. 64–5. See also his resistance to Covey, pp. 71–2. Also his *Life and Times of Frederick Douglass 1817–1882*, Hartford, Conn., pp. 96–8.
4 D'Auvergne, *Human Livestock*, pp. 108–10. Another author records that after the failure of a revolt in Antigua in 1736 five African slaves were broken on the wheel, six hung alive in chains (one of these was eight days and nine nights dying) and fifty-eight were burnt at the stake. See A. C. Caldecott, *The Church in the West Indies*, London, 1898, p. 23.
5 Bryan Edwards, *The History, Civil and Commercial, of the British Colonies in the West Indies*, Vol. 2, London, 1818–19, pp. 77–9.
6 D'Auvergne, *Human Livestock*, p. 110.
7 U. B. Phillips *et al.* (eds.), *A Documentary History of American Industrial Society*, Cleveland, Ohio, 1910, Vol. 2, pp. 248–9.
8 *Ibid.*, pp. 117–18.
9 Original source Souther *v.* Commonwealth, 7 Grattan 673 (June 1851) quoted in H. T. T. Catterall, *Judicial Cases Concerning American Slavery and the Negro*, reprinted 1968, New York, Vol. 1, pp. 223–4. Very often such incidents were committed with impunity. It was not until the first decade of the nineteenth century with the introduction of Amelioration Acts that some cognizance began to be taken of such incidents. Reactions to them were often not similar. For instance, a Mr Hodge, who committed numerous cruelties on his slaves, was hanged. But when a few years later a Mr Huggins in Nevis was treated more leniently there was official reaction. Mr Huggins had ordered public floggings of his slaves in the market place in Nevis in 1810 and in spite of the presence of some magistrates who witnessed the floggings, approximating 100 lashes and repeated again and again, those magistrates did nothing to prevent or stop the proceedings. Lord Liverpool was indignant in a letter to Governor Elliot in which he stressed that the jury which had handled the case of Huggins were corrupted and thundered that the Prince Regent had directed that such magistrates and others involved be removed from office and that done publicly in order to express fully the disapprobation of his Royal Highness. See PRO, CO 153/34, Bathurst to Elliot, No. 10, 20 Feb. 1813; Liverpool to Elliot, 12 April 1811 and enclosures; Liverpool to Elliot, 20 April 1810; Elliot to Bathurst, No. 29, 28 Jan. 1813. Also see CO 239/29, Will Nicolay to Viscount Goderich, 23 Aug. 1832, which relates to the sins of the fathers being visited on the children twenty-two years later.
10 See also Edward Long, *The History of Jamaica: General Survey of the Ancient and Modern State of that Island with Reflections, etc.*, London, 1774, Vol. 2, p. 497, for his justification for brutality; and W. E. B. DuBois, *The Suppression of the African Slave Trade to the United States of America 1638–1870*, New York, 1896, pp. 5–6.
11 See Rev. Henry Belby, *Death Struggles of Slavery*, London, 1853, pp. 17–25, for the repression with which the slavocracy attempted to subdue the slave revolts in Jamaica in 1831–2 and 1837. Also see Stedman, *Narrative of Five Years among the*

Revolted Negroes of Surinam; London, 1796, Vol. 1, p. 346, for Surinam.
12 Douglass, *Narrative*, 1845, p. 79.
13 Belby, *Death Struggles*, p. 185. These may have been rare but they reveal the flimsy factors which could induce the perpetration of cruelty in slave societies, where instinct dictated conduct. William Wells Brown, an ex-slave, recounted another experience, see *Narrative of the Life of William Wells Brown*, London, 1850, pp. 27–8. See also Stedman, *Narrative*, Vol. 1, p. 346, where Stedman related how a manager on another estate flogged a slave messenger because he disliked the message conveyed by the slave from the proprietor.
14 William Goodell, *The American Slave Code in Theory and Practice*, New York, 1853, p. 304.
15 E. D. Morel, *The Black Man's Burden*, London and Manchester, 1919, pp. 21–2. The picture regarding cruelty could be generalised for other plantations, see also James Pope Hennessy, *Sins of the Fathers: the Atlantic Slave Traders 1441–1807*, London, 1967, pp. 146–8 for references to slaves being boiled in cane juice; and S. Alexis, *Black Liberator: the Life of Toussaint Louverture*, London, 1949, p. 20.
16 See *Parliamentary Papers*, Vol. 30, 1790. Castrating the slave was also a form of punishment; F. Tannenbaum, *Slave and Citizen: the Negro in the Americas*, New York, 1947, pp. 65–71; A. Benezet, *Some Historical Account of Guinea*, Philadelphia, 1771, p. 75. The French General Rochambeau used this method against the blacks in St Domingue, see C. L. R. James, *The Black Jacobins, Toussaint Louverture and the San Domingo Revolution*, London, 1938, pp. 359–60.
17 Belby, *Death Struggles*.
18 *Ibid.* See, for instance, pp. 29, 87, 103–6 *et seq*.
19 See PRO, CO 152/101, Leeward Islands, Vol. 1, 1813, letter of the Rev. William Davis to Governor Hugh Elliot, 16 March 1813. Davis himself carried out the practice but admitted that slaves acquired from breeding were insufficient so he advocated purchase; this request was being made by a clergyman six to seven years after Britain had abolished the external and domestic slave trade. Also CO 239/4, Probyn to the Rt. Hon. Earl of Bathurst, No. 76, 8 July 1818. In his testimony to the House of Commons Committee on the Slave Trade in 1790, Alexander Willock (pro-slaver) who had lived thirty-six years on the island of Antigua and had returned to England in 1781, in reply to the question when he conceived it more in the planter's interest to keep up his stock by breeding slaves, replied: 'We reckon one Creole Negro bred upon the estate to be worth three Salt Water Negroes (that is to say imported Africans)'. House of Commons, *Sessional Papers 18th Century: Reports and Papers, Slave Trade 1790*, Vol. 72, p. 346.
20 [Schaw], *Journal* pp. 103–4.
21 F. Kemble, *Journal of a Residence on a Georgian Plantation in 1838–1839*, London, 1863, pp. 152–3.
22 *Ibid.*, p. 152.
23 Commander Andrew H. Foote, *Africa and the American Flag*, London and Folkestone (1st edn., 1854), reprint 1970, p. 152, also quoted in DuBois, *Suppression of the African Slave Trade*, pp. 162–67, esp. p. 163.
24 O. Patterson, *The Sociology of Slavery: an Analysis of the Origins, Development and Structure of Negro Slave Society in Jamaica*, London, 1967, p. 145.
25 Kemble, *Journal*, p. 31.
26 See E. E. Williams, *History of the People of Trinidad and Tobago*, Port of Spain, 1964, p. 76.
27 See Weston, *Progress of Slavery*, pp. 116–17, quoted in Frederick Bancroft, *Slave*

Trading in the Old South, Baltimore, Md., 1931, p. 79; see also *The Liberator*, 27 July 1833, for a breakdown of 371 slaves reportedly imported into New Orleans principally from Virginia. For persistence of the domestic slave trade see *The Liberator*, 17 May 1834 and 24 May 1834; *National Anti-slavery Standard*, 22 July 1841, article by Dr Joseph Parish.

28 Thomas R. R. Cobb, *An Inquiry into the Law of Slavery in the United States of America*, Philadelphia and Savannah, Ga., 1858, p. 238. Some slave holders made some bequests to their coloured progeny, and evidence of this exists in wills of some plantation owners. Many private bills to achieve this end were promoted in Jamaica. See, for instance, *Acts of the Assembly passed in the Island of Jamaica from the year 1681 to the year 1769 inclusive, two volumes in one with an Appendix containing laws respecting slaves*, Kingston, 1787, Vol. 2. pp. 36–9. Also *Acts of Assembly passed in the Island of Jamaica from the year 1784 to the year 1788 inclusive*, Kingston, 1789; see also Edwards, *History, Civil and Commercial*, Vol 2, pp. 22–3; Long, *History of Jamaica*, Vol. 2, pp. 320–7; Catterall, *Judicial Cases*, Vol. 1, pp. 119–20, 228–9, 241–2.

29 Bancroft, *Slave Trading*, p. 68, cited from *Charleston City Gazette*, 10 March 1769, in Phillips *et al.*, *Documentary History*, Vol. 2, pp. 57–8.

30 See J. W. Coleman, *Slavery Times in Kentucky*, Chapel Hill, N.C., 1940, pp. 144, 145–52, 179–82. See his p. 152 for prices of domestic-bred slaves in southern markets for which they were bred; Bancroft, *Slave Trading*, p. 68.

31 Bancroft, *Slave Trading*, p. 68. The tailpiece of the quotation is from Catterall, *Judicial Cases*, Vol. 1, p. 215.

32 Bancroft, *Slave Trading*, p. 71.

33 Tannenbaum, *Slave and Citizen*, p. 80.

34 Bancroft, *Slave Trading*, pp. 72–3. Guinea (West Africa) was the chief source from which most of the African slaves were shipped to the western hemisphere, but as we have seen elsewhere in this work slaves came from central and eastern Africa as well.

35 Thomas Hart Benton was a distinguished Senator from Missouri whose Senate career spanned thirty years from 1820 to 1850 and terminated because of his opposition to a 'too generous concession to the secessionists' on the compromise of 1850 which led to their rejection of him. But having sought election to the House of Representatives he persisted in vain in his efforts to repeal the Missouri Compromise. He was an editor of the *Missouri Enquirer* from 1815, a friend of President Jackson and under him became Administrative Spokesman in the Senate. He had a lucrative legal practice in Missouri and his views on slavery changed over the period of his career in the Senate; but, essentially, he was a 'moderate' on the issue and, while an opponent of the extension of slavery in the latter part of his career, he was also an opponent of abolition. He was reputed to be an upholder of a sound money policy, and belonged to the 'hard' money faction as against the advocates of 'soft' money into which the Democratic party was split, and earned the nickname of the 'Old Bullion'. His authorship of *Thirty Years View* (1854–56) is regarded as one of the outstanding political autobiographies. *An Abridgement of the Debates of Congress from 1789 to 1856* (1857–61); see *Concise Dictionary of American Biography*, New York, 1964, pp. 69–70.

36 William Wells Brown, *Narrative of the Negro in American Rebellion*, Boston, Mass., 1867, pp. 82–3. See also Long, *History of Jamaica*, Vol. 2, p. 328.

37 Brown, *Narrative*, pp. 88–9; also W. L Katz (ed.), *Five Slave Narratives*, New York, 1968, pp. 88–9.

38 Brown, *Narrative*, pp. 87–8.

39 PRO, CO 152/101, Leeward Islands, Vol. 1, Hugh Elliot to the Hon. Earl of Bathurst, No. 35, 27 March 1813, and enclosures. Also attestations and statements submitted by the Rev. William Davis.

40 U. S. P. G., Fulham Papers, Vol. 2, West Indies Part 1, 1803–27. Rev. Byam, King's College, Cambridge, to the Bishop of London, 4 Dec. 1820, concerning slave marriages.

41 *Ibid.*

42 *Ibid.*

43 See, for instance, what S. M. Elkins in *Slavery: a Problem in American Institutional and Intellectual Life*, Chicago, 1959, said of the situation in his Appendix B, pp. 231–7.

44 *Ibid.*, p. 232.

45 *Ibid.*, p. 233, quoted from Lewis Cecil Gray, *History of Agriculture in the Southern States to 1860*, New York, 1933, Vol. 1, p. 476. That economic considerations were ever-present in the West Indian situation is seen in the arguments of the pros and cons of the abolition of slavery. Opponents of abolition continued to assert that the planters and the nation would be ruined. But even in official quarters one of the arguments for abolition was economic, *viz.* to make room for the new industrialism which had no need for chattel slave labour.

46 Elkins, *Slavery*, p. 235.

47 *Ibid.*, p. 236. Quoted from Alfred H. Conrad and John R. Meyer, 'The Economics of Slavery in the Ante Bellum South', *Journal of Political Economy*, 67 (April 1958), pp. 95–130.

48 Active participants here relate to slave captains, pirates and those who piloted ships to the coast of Africa and transported slaves to the western hemisphere. They also include all who contributed to the working of the plantation system with the exception of slaves, who had no say in the matter. Passive participants included the church (also an active participant because of prelates who owned and managed plantations (many religious orders as well as individual prelates owned slaves), the monarchies, financiers and those who provided material and moral assistance in aiding and abetting the slave trade and its corollary, slavery. Each of the latter constituted some vested interest, more often than not involving some financial reward. It is also difficult to read Dr Eric Williams' *Capitalism and Slavery*, New York, 1966, without seeing the paramountcy of economic considerations.

49 See, for instance, Joseph Hawkins, *A History of a Voyage to West Africa*, Troy, N. Y., 1787, pp. 177–9; also B. Quarles, *op. cit.*, pp. 22–3.

50 It was essentially these consequences that J. B. Moreton, an ex-overseer, was anxious to stress in his *West India Customs and Manners*.

51 See Bancroft, *Slave Trading*, p. 87.

52 This essentially related to the West Indian planters. One of the outstanding leaders of 'Negro' thought and action in the period of the anti-slavery crusade, Samuel Ringgold Ward, an Afro-American and a British citizen in Canada, who visited England to further the anti-slavery cause, wrote in his autobiography that 'The guilt of our colonies was endorsed at home; nay, the owners of colonial slaves were dwellers at the West End of London, our senators and our

Peers. Commoners who were planters, in London, Liverpool and Glasgow, rolled in untold wealth, the fruit of the Negro's unpaid toil. . . . A baronetcy or a peerage was scarcely more desirable or more honourable than to be known as a *great West Indian planter*, the owner of so many hundred slaves! Sometimes, indeed, baronet or peer, and planter, were associated titles of the same distinguished individual. These brought all the influence of wealth, name, position, patronage, and senatorial place, to bear upon the government, which but too easily winked at the wickedness and obeyed the demands of the then British slave power. Thank God I am writing *past* history; but history it is! S. R. Ward, *The Autobiography of a Fugitive Negro: His Anti-slavery Labours in the United States, Canada, and England*, London, 1855, pp. 291–2. Planters were also among the owners of 'pocket boroughs' in England which patronised parliamentary candidates. The pocket boroughs became casualties of the Act of 1832. Their French counterparts were not as powerful and well organised as the British slavocratic interests. See L. B. Namier, *England in the Age of the American Revolution*, London, 1961, p. 235.; R. I. and S. Wilberforce, *The Life of William Wilberforce*, London, 1838, Vol. 3, p. 183; B. W. Higman, 'The West India Interests in Parliament, 1807–33, I,' in *Historical Studies*, Melbourne, xiii, 49 (1967), pp. 1–19.

53 Basil Davidson, *Black Mother: Africa, the Years of Trial*, 1959, 1960, 1961, p. 81.

54 *Ibid.*, p. 97.

55 The colonies referred to here were the British West Indies and pre-revolutionary U.S.A.

56 Quoted by E. D. Morel, *The Black Man's Burden*, p. 21. Variations on this theme are ubiquitous among the anti-abolitionists.

57 Quoted in E. E. Williams, *The Negro in the Caribbean*, Manchester, 1942, pp. 12–13.

58 We assert with Dr Williams that 'slavery on the West Indian sugar plantations (or any plantation for that matter) allowed them neither time, nor scope nor encouragement to develop their native capacity and to reproduce their native arts and crafts'. Williams, *History of the People of Trinidad and Tobago*, p. 37.

59 Davidson, *Black Mother*, pp. 239 *et seq.* Authors who have not emphasised stagnation include A. G. Hopkins, *An Economic History of West Africa*, London, 1973, pp. 121–50, and J. D. Fage, 'Slavery and the Slave Trade in the Context of West African History', *Journal of African History*, x (1969), pp. 393–404; also Fage, *A History of West Africa: an Introductory Survey*, Cambridge, 1969, pp. 85–7. For an author who stresses this stagnation in the form of under-development, see Walter Rodney, *How Europe Underdeveloped Africa*, London, 1972, pp. 103–61. But the entire tone of the work rivets on this pattern of trading relationship which immensely contributed to African under-development. Also see G. N. Uzoigwe (ed.), *Anatomy of an African Kingdom*, New York, 1973.

60 PRO, CO 239/29, Slavery No. 83, Maxwell to Viscount Goderich, 30 Jan. 1832.

61 *Ibid.*, Goderich to Nicolay, 5 April 1832.

62 *Ibid.*

63 These impressions are gleaned from S. M. Elkins' *Slavery*, and although we are aware of the differences between the concentration camps and slave societies in the New World, the network seems to have been tighter with the concentration camps than with slave societies, for hardly any escape routes were possible in the former, while in the latter the mountain fastnesses and thick undergrowths, as

has been mentioned elsewhere in this work, provided slaves with places of temporary refuge and even a more permanent abode, as in the case of the Surinamese Maroons.

64 Elsa V. Goveia, 'The West Indian Slave Laws of the Eighteenth Century', in Foner and Genovese (eds.), *Slavery in the New World: a Reader in Comparative History*, Englewood Cliffs, N.J., 1969, pp. 113–37; also Pierre de Vassière, *Saint Domingue: la Société et la Vie Créoles sous l'Ancien Régime (1629–1789)*, Paris, 1909, pp. 181, 186–9.

65 See Goodell, *op. cit.*, pp. 305–7; Winthrop Jordan, *White over Black, American Attitudes towards the Negro 1550–1812*, Chapel Hill, N.C., 1968, pp. 106 *et seq.* The 'Christian' in the context used was synonymous with a white person. French excesses in St Domingue still continue to fill writers and scholars with amazement. Both Leclerc and Rochambeau remain inglorious names in the African experience in Haiti. There were similarities with other slave theatres of the rival European powers. The South Carolina law was comparable to that of the Danes in the West Indies; see, for instance, W. Westergaard, *The Danish West Indies under Company Rule (1671–1754)*, New York, 1917, pp. 158, 162ff.

66 In the French *Code Noir* of 1685 it was death for slaves striking their masters, mistresses or any of their children and drawing blood from them or for dealing any of them a blow to the face. The punishment was severe for striking any free person, with death as a possibility if deemed necessary. *Code Noir*, articles XXXIII and XXXIV. For an English translation of the *Code Noir* of 1685, see Long, *History of Jamaica*, Vol. 3, pp. 921–34, and for that of 1716 see pp. 934–41.

67 The case of Souther killing Sam has been mentioned in the early part of this work. Professor Aptheker also mentioned how a Mr Overzee killed a slave of his who dared defy slavery by hanging him by his wrists after being severely lashed. Later hot lard was poured over Tony, and three hours later he died. See H. Aptheker, *American Negro Slave Revolts*, New York, 1944, 1963, pp. 134–5. But one of the most atrocious forms of brutality from the West Indian island of Tortola occurred in the early part of the nineteenth century and for which the slave owner, Mr Hodge (quite an influential planter) was hanged in 1811. See below.

68 PRO, CO 152/97, Leeward Islands, Vol, 1, 1811, Hugh Elliot to Earl of Liverpool, No. 39, 9 May 1811 and enclosures.

69 See Lilian Penson for a contrary viewpoint in *The Colonial Agent of the British West Indies*, London, 1924, pp. 230–1.

70 PRO, CO 152/97, Leeward Islands, Vol. 1, 1811, Elliot to Earl of Liverpool, No. 39, 9 May 1811 and enclosures.

71 *Ibid.*, depositions.

72 *Ibid.*, see depositions 1808–11.

73 *Ibid.*, depositions.

74 *Ibid.*

8 Conflict between darkness and light

Educational and religious barriers

Both religious and educational barriers were used by slave owners to keep slaves in their assigned place in the social hierarchy. The maintenance of the slave system was based on ignorance. Although rationalisations such as 'civilising the negroes' and 'enlightening their benighted souls'[1] were often used, religion and education were two vital qualities denied to slaves. Efforts were made to thwart the endeavours of slaves or Free Negroes to educate themselves or to be assisted in their ambitions for knowledge through the help of white philanthropists and humanitarians. Many a slave, deprived of the opportunity, must have cursed the slave owners a million times for actively depriving him of his African cultural heritage while taking no positive steps to educate him in the culture of Europe from which most of the owners came. As a result masters contributed to bequeathing a legacy of ambivalence among slaves to both cultures. What was bequeathed was a slave culture which placed slaves at a great disadvantage when compared to free people.[2]

Samuel Ringgold Ward, who was born a slave in Maryland and whose parents escaped from bondage while he was but an infant, lamented the injustice which the policy of enslavement inflicted on Africans through denying them education. He wrote, 'Among the heaviest of my maledictions against slavery is that which it deserves for keeping my poor father – and millions like him – in the midnight and dungeon of the grossest ignorance. Cowardly system as it is, it does not dare allow the slave access to the commonest source of light and learning.'[3]

Ward's fulminations sum up the attitude of the plantation overlords, who saw quite clearly that enlightenment through education brought with it the critical mind which would unhesitatingly question the propriety for a man's enslavement and that of others like him. This questioning is nowhere more clearly revealed than in the autobiography of Frederick Douglass.[4]

But the education question was inextricably bound up with that of religion, and even in the evolution of negro education it was the 'Negro Church', as a social institution, which came to provide the first successful incentives. The religion of almost all the various Christian sects was proclaimed to be out of bounds to the slaves. In this the Spanish, French and Portuguese colonies (i.e. the Roman Catholic colonies) were more 'progressive', in theory at least, than the sects which had earlier challenged the rigid methods of Roman Catholicism. The interconnection between education and religion was no more clearly brought out than by slaves and ex-slaves cultivating the habit of reading the Bible. It was known that the Bible was the first among books which many slaves sought to read once they had learnt how to do so.[5] The slave owners were not themselves unaware of the connection between the two. But what seemed a tightly-knit framework of regulations and objections relating to the education of slaves was punctuated both by the attitudes and notions of some individuals and by organisations (black and white), for ways and means of circumventing legal stipulations concerned with maintaining negro ignorance were found.

One of the outstanding Afro-American scholars of the early twentieth century, Professor Carter G. Woodson, in his book *The Mis-education of the Negro*, stated that 'History does not furnish a case of elevation of a people by ignoring the thought and aspirations of the people thus served'.[6] Professor Woodson, who wrote a book on the *Education of the Negro prior to 1861* (in North America) divides the history of education of the *ante-bellum* negroes into two periods – the first from the commencement of slavery in North America to the 'climax of the insurrectionary movement' about 1835; and, the second, commencing therefrom to the outbreak of the Civil War. According to Woodson, in the first period the question of whether it was prudent that the negro should be educated or not was answered in the affirmative. But after the series of slave revolts in which the 'intelligent negroes' and abolitionists were allegedly implicated, the pendulum swung back against negro education. In fact, southern whites asserted that it was impossible to 'cultivate the minds of Negroes without arousing over much self-assertion'.[7]

The key to the objection lay in the expression 'over much self-assertion', for self-assertion of the kind envisaged was at the centre of the slave owners' fears. A similar situation existed in the British West Indies, where religious instruction to the slaves was regarded as a 'cloak for plots' against the existing order.[8] Often the blame for slave revolts was placed squarely at the door of the missionaries, who were said to imbue the slaves with the idea of insubordination.[9] Real or imagined, these revolts provided the plantocracy and local authorities with ammunition for denying slaves the opportunity to be Christianised and educated. A committee of the Jamaican House of Assembly appointed to inquire into the Jamaican slave revolt of 1831–2 cited religious teaching as one of the causes of the revolt. The committee observed the causes thus:

> ... from a mischievous abuse existing in the system adopted by different religious sects in this island ... by their recognising gradations of rank among such of our slaves as had become converts to their doctrines ... and lastly, ... the preaching and teaching of the religious sects called Baptists,[10] Wesleyan Methodists and Moravians (but more particularly the sect of Baptist), which had the effect of production in the mind of the slaves a belief that they could not serve both a spiritual and a temporal master.[11]

Professor Carter G. Woodson gave us some examples of slaves who within the framework of the church enjoyed for a time the boon of freedom and showed reluctance to give up that liberty when they were required to do so. There was the case of a black slave named Thomas Jones who escaped from Baltimore County in 1793. His master's account of the cause of the slave's flight is interesting: 'He was raised in a family of religious persons commonly called Methodists and has lived with some of them for years past on terms of perfect equality; the refusal to continue him on these terms gave him offense and he, therefore, absconded. He had been accustomed to instruct and exhort his fellow creatures of all colours in matters of religious duty.' Another slave named Jacob belonging to Thomas Gibbs of the same state escaped in 1800 with a view to enlarging his liberty as a Methodist minister. His master who advertised him as a runaway declared that 'He professed to be a Methodist and has been in the practice of preaching of nights'. In the same year another black preacher of the kind mentioned above, named Richard, escaped from Hugh Drummond in Anne, Arundel County, and another slave by the name of Simboe escaped shortly afterwards from Henry Lockey of Newbern, North Carolina.[12] They were all demonstrations of the self-assertion which many of the slave-holding communities feared; but they shed light on what enlightenment could do to the institution of slavery. Accordingly, the conspiracy to keep the slaves of African descent in perpetual ignorance was strong. It was enshrined in the laws of the various slave-holding communities as well as in their customs. The evidence is so voluminous that texts which yield much of the data are listed in the bibliography of this work.[13]

Attitudes and policies of the established churches

Differences among the slave systems of the New World were not only to be found in the divergencies of slave codes but also in the part played by the various Christian denominations in matters relating to the education as well as spiritual well-being of the slaves. In the English-speaking U.S.A. and West Indies Christianity was a luxury which the plantocracy could not afford to bestow on the slave. Contrasts between the British and Latin colonies showed themselves very early. The chief Protestant church which had severed its connection with the parent church of Rome was the Anglican church. It was for all practical purposes, in the British West Indies as well as in the American colonies, the established church.[14] Since, however, the early colonisers of the west were the Latin powers of Spain and Portugal, it is to them that we must first turn our attention.

Portugal and Spain, being the two great European Catholic powers of the fifteenth century, had their claims to the lands in the eastern and western hemisphere respectively demarcated by papal authority. Portugal had initiated the movement for international expansion and had asserted that these lands fell within the scope of the Papal Bull of 1455, which had authorised Portugal to reduce all 'infidel' peoples to servitude. Columbus's discovery of the New World on behalf of the Spanish government in 1492 heightened the rivalry and conflict between Spain and Portugal. This has already been mentioned in Chapter 2. Nevertheless, the Reformation in Europe gave other European nations the temerity to challenge both the authority of the Pope to parcel the world as he thought fit, and the monopoly of the high seas exercised by Spain and Portugal. These powers were led by England, Holland and France; the first two were Protestant powers, while France was a Catholic country.

The Roman Catholics

The Africans of the diaspora received their first experience of Christianity through slavery. This is not to say that the slave masters had any genuine consideration for the spiritual welfare of their slaves or with proselytisation. The attitude of conferring the benefits or privileges of the Christian faith differed from area to area.[15] We learn that one cause for the discovery of America was to translate into action the desire of European zealots to extend the Catholic religion into other parts.[16] The early converts of the Spanish and French missionaries were the Amerindians and Carib-Indians.[17] There was at the time no consideration of the African of the diaspora, or 'negro' as he later came to be known. Many colonists themselves saw the 'negro' as being 'outside the pale of Christianity'. Generally, descendants of Africa were stigmatised as 'infidels' and their suitability for Christianity was questioned. Therefore, proselytising the African slaves seemed unnecessary.[18] But Latin colonisation of the Americas was brutal and harsh to its indigenous population and had the terrible consequence of reducing their numbers. The fear of complete decimation tantamount to genocide through the rigorous conditions of labour which they imposed on the Indians accelerated the acute labour shortage and led them to consider the importance of African labour. The appeal of Bishop Bartolomé de las Casas, Bishop of Chiapas in Mexico, gave added weight to the deliberation to import African slaves. Therefore, with the arrival of the first group of these slaves from the west coast of Africa, the *bozales*, the missionaries were faced with the question of whether the newly imported 'heathen' ought to be considered fit for the Christianity that was offered to the Indians. The Portuguese maintained a farcical ceremony of baptism from the port of Luanda for three centuries.[19]

There was in existence the unwritten law that a Christian could not be held in servitude. This for the planters would have meant no slaves once they were baptised; accordingly, they opposed any moves to proselytise among the new arrivals and those who were yet to arrive in unending streams for centuries after.[20] They frowned on the introduction of Moorish slaves who might attempt to proselytise for Islam. Since freedom was automatic on the assumption of the unwritten law that Christians could not be slaves, the acute labour shortage would have been more acute. Earlier the European sovereigns, actuated both by religious scruples and humanitarian considerations towards the Africans, rejected their importation into the Americas. But these sovereigns eventually succumbed to pressures from various quarters and acquiesced in their importation, but added the proviso that those slaves should first embrace Christianity.[21] This capitulation of the sovereigns led to the promulgation of royal decrees by Spain and France providing that Africans enslaved in the Americas should merely be indoctrinated to the principles of Christianity. But these decrees, though possessing the force of law, became dead letters. The attitudes of slave holders inhibited progress.

Planters could not bring themselves to accept any sentiments which involved them in the humanitarian treatment of slaves. Those planters, not themselves motivated by any high considerations for religion, felt that too much enlightenment for the slaves might inspire them to entertain hopes of liberty and might even actuate them into bidding for the status of free men. These so-called 'just laws' were anything but complied with – but the colonial functionaries tended to give the home government the impression that all was well in the colonies and that the laws were being generally observed. It was easy for all the colonies to evade the laws or set them aside, as most of them did, since no inspection system for the commercial outposts were instituted and it was not easy for the home government to judge correctly the attitude of their subjects in the colonies concerning Christianising the bondsmen. But from time to time individual humanitarians protested against the negligence of duty and enormities committed by the plantation communities. Such protests were said to include those of Alonso (Alfonso) de Sandoval[22] in Cuba and two Capuchin monks, (among others) who were imprisoned in Havana because they inveighed against the failure of the planters to provide for the religious instruction of slaves. Such daring advocates of fair play, often in the minority, had their voices stilled through persecution. Persecution, as slavery progressed, was the experience of many missionaries, who failed to conform to the will of the plantocracy and slave societies.[23]

But there were more successful efforts elsewhere among the African slaves in Latin America. There, proselytising took place and recognition was granted them by the clergy. In what is now the United States of America, French and Spanish missionaries, who were in the main confined to the Atlantic coast, came into very little contact with African slaves. The Latin policy dominated the early colonial period in the West Indies, and even with the annulment of the unwritten decree and special statutes the planters were made to concede the need for religious instruction of the slaves. In this respect they complied with the instructions of the metropolis.

Maryland, earlier settled by the Catholics, seems to be the only colony on the Atlantic seaboard in which the opportunity was made available for Christianising African slaves. There was an initial resistance to the idea but the right to proselytise regardless of colour was conceded. An early Act of Maryland (1715),[24] and a similar one in South Carolina in 1711, allowed for slave baptism but also stipulated that 'such baptism shall not be construed to effect emancipation of any slave'.

The legislature of Louisiana enacted that it was the 'duty of every owner to procure his sick slaves all kinds of temporal and spiritual assistance which their situation may require'.[25] But these 'privileges' of Maryland and Louisiana of baptism at birth and extreme unction at death (Roman Catholic in origin) were considered to be a show of great kindness; but beyond that they were the 'alpha and omega' of the legal provision made for the slaves as religious beings, according to Goodell.[26] In short, the first priests and missionaries in Louisiana brought to it a crusading spirit and saw it as a necessary part of their task to make Christians of slaves and 'enlighten' them. The instructions they provided were made to meet the specification of the first ordinances of the Spanish and French sovereigns and later that of the French *Code Noir*, and the Spanish *Siete Partidas* relating to slaves in the Latin colonies. The French *Code Noir* of 1685[27] specifically stipulated that slaves should be made Christians. Yet the Abbé Raynal in 1792 could observe that 'The Catholics think themselves obliged to give them [slaves] instructions, and to baptise them; but their charity extends no further than the bare ceremonies of baptism, which is wholly useless and unnecessary to men who dread not the pains of hell, to which, they say, they are accustomed in this life'.[28]

The consequences of the church's championship of African slaves by embracing them in the Christian fold were tremendous and did contribute substantially to the emergence of a very different social setting from those of the British West Indies and North America.[29] The African slave was a human being and not only the 'property' which other slave societies made of him. Thus, in the early eighteenth century, there were black priests as well as bishops in Brazil, and according to one modern historian the Negro clergy seemed to 'have been more reverent, better living, more earnest than the Portuguese clergy'.[30] Tannenbaum contends that the African slave had a special place in the community, for he had simultaneously arrived on the South American scene with the white conquerors and had with facility become knowledgeable in the language of his master and adopted some of his habits and customs, which gave him an identity not distinct from his European master. Consequently he became an integral part of that community. Furthermore, his heroism was not unrecognised. One of Brazil's two national heroes, he continues, was 'Henriques Dias, a Negro hero whose fame dated from the early colonial wars against the Dutch'.[31] The negroes' formidable defence of the 'Negro Republic' of Palmares or Palm Forests (1630–97), which required an army six thousand strong and about seventy years to destroy, also helped to demonstrate the military capabilities and physical courage of negroes.[32] In most of Latin America the descendants of Africa have been part and parcel of the general process of evolution of those societies.[33] An Afro-Cuban general, Antonio Maceo,[34] among others, led the struggle for Cuban independence in 1895, and not only did many descendants of Africa fight in that war but they constituted the major part of the forces which participated and undertook the protracted war against Spain.[35] The armies of Simon Bolivar also knew many illustrious descendants of Africa. These activities, rather than the role of some in the Catholic church in emphasising the humanity of the African slave, made the task of securing his manumission, in theory, less ardous and more peaceful than was the case in the other colonies of the Americas. Public opinion, it is suggested, seemed more favourable in Brazil to the manumission of any slave requesting to purchase his liberty providing the fixed price was offered. It later became enforceable by law. Accordingly, a large number of slaves secured manumission between 1864 and 1870 after accepting service in the Paraguayan War.[36] But the championship of the church was not so thorough as

224

might be at first imagined. The clergy as a group were not ardent abolitionists. On the contrary, many priests owned slaves and were accused by abolitionists of practising on their slaves the same cruelty they decried elsewhere. Many of them justified slavery.[37] Nonetheless, in addition to the encouragement which a slave might be given to secure his freedom, according to the received tradition, no obstacles were placed in his path either for becoming a fully-fledged member of the community or for ascending the ladder of social progress. Having done much of the work in Brazil in the colonial period, the African slaves and their descendants came to be in possession of most skills, arts and crafts, and from their ranks and those of mulattos have sprung many sculptors and artists. The mulatto progeny of rich Brazilian planters, as well as those of St Domingue (later Haiti), were educated abroad – those of Brazil in Lisbon and those of St Domingue in France. Here some writers have claimed that there was no denial of education for the negro.[38] An American historian has even recorded that a planter (far from being the ignorant kind known to most of the plantations in the Americas) trained a private band of musicians through educating some of them in Rio and others in Lisbon.[39] The question that arises is how significant were the numbers?

It was also observed that religious orders played a prominent part in evangelisation and education. The Franciscan and Dominican orders of priests and friars, as well as the Jesuits and others, owned large plantations in Brazil with large slave populations of African origin, whose treatment it was claimed, with much exaggeration, was 'humane' compared to other plantations. Some historians have gone on to say that the slaves of these religious orders were almost never sold. Donald Pierson has observed that the plantation slaves did not see themselves as belonging to the friars who supervised them but rather to the saint whose name the orders bore.[40] But none of these must leave the reader with the false impression of the humanity of slavery even in the Portuguese territory of Brazil. It was far from humane, and brutality and cruelty were ever present.[41] But Pierson makes the controversial point that in the Spanish and Portuguese colonies the laws forbade cruelty and brutality (though slave societies hardly ever admitted to cruel practices), and that occasionally brutalities were punishable by law. The implication of Pierson's observations was that, compared to the United States and the British West Indies, these brutalities might have been fewer and probably less frequent. But a reading of Professor C. R. Boxer hardly makes this credible. Boxer wrote:

> Apologists for slavery, who still exist in surprising numbers, commonly claim that allegations of ill-treatment must be exaggerated, since owners would not willfully reduce the value of

their own property by working their slaves to death in a few years, or by deliberately starving them. This, however, is just what many proprietors did do, in the belief that it was more profitable to get everything out of adult slaves in a few years and then replace them by *Negros bocais* or raw hands.[42]

Boxer discounts the common belief that the Brazilian was an exceptionally kind master and says that this was applicable only to eighteenth-century slavery under the Empire, and is contradicted for the colonial period by the testimony of numerous reliable eyewitnesses from Vieira to Vilhena, to say nothing of the official correspondence between the colonial authorities and the Crown. He calls attention to the evidence of a doctor-surgeon, Luis Gomez Ferreira, who lived for more than twenty years in Minas Gerais in Brazil during the first half of the eighteenth century and whose experiences were documented in a book on his return to Portugal. In it he admonished slavocrats of the Minas Gerais to treat sick slaves kindly, to house them warmly and well, and generally to take a personal interest in their welfare, adding that in such matters slave owners 'commonly sin greatly, for which they will have to account to God ... and thus for their own profit as from a sense of duty, they should treat their slaves well when they are healthy, and better when they are sick, not depriving them of what they need'. Elsewhere in the book he 'denounced them for the cruel treatment of slaves whom he felt they ought to cherish as their children'. Again Professor Boxer adds: 'Naturally, there were some humane owners, and several of them figure honourably in the pages of *Erario Mineral*, but they were clearly the exception rather than the rule.'[43] Furthermore, as their death rate was very high, their reproduction rate was very low, and this resulted in a rapid turnover of slaves and put further strains on Africa to supply slaves.[44]

The Protestants

Although we observed that the attitude of the early Catholic colonists was not very favourable to the evangelisation of the slaves from Africa, that of the Protestants in the English colonies was anything but helpful in this matter. Here colonists lacked the missionary spirit of the Latins and were more preoccupied either with the establishment of new homes or with economic gain in the Americas. Their attitudes to the African-derived people did not lead them to consider their wards as people on whom Christian philanthropy could be bestowed; rather they saw them as tools to gratify their yearnings for economic gain. It was, therefore, no surprise that since the economics of slavery was the paramount consideration, the spiritual needs of the slaves meant little to the colonists and planters.[45] This was even more so when confronted with the unwritten law that a Christian could not be held a slave. The Anglican church ignored the slaves and coloured freemen and only towards the end of slavery in the West Indies, less than two decades from the end, did its members begin to consider it necessary to impart some form of religious teaching, a failure for which Lord Olivier in a later period castigated them,[46] and for which others at the time made representations to the Bishop of London and the governments of some of the West Indian islands.[47]

Some religious prelates provided the slavocracy with justifications for their spiritual neglect of the slaves. For instance, the Rev. George Bridges in his *Annals of Jamaica*, written in 1828, not only tried to justify slavery on biblical authority, but claimed that negroes lacked the 'intellect' that was a prerequisite for Christianity.[48] He seems to have so endeared himself to the planters that the Jamaican Assembly voted him a sum of £700 in appreciation of his support.[49] Some evangelical work was carried out among the Indians of North America. In the West Indies – Barbados, Jamaica, Antigua, and many more islands – the 'narrowing influence of industrial exigency soon mastered the colonial mind'. For a century and a half the doors of the established churches were closed to the hundreds of thousands of heathens by whose physical labour the colonial structure was upheld.[50] Yet this was the era in which the religionists, in justifying the enslavement of the children of Africa, claimed, hypocritically, to be bringing the 'heathen' to Christ.

It has been suggested, rather misguidedly, that the Society for the Propagation of the Gospel in Foreign Parts, founded in London in 1701, was a notable exception to the indifference which characterised the thinking of the Protestant sects.[51] As a society organised for the purpose of carrying the word to the 'heathen' – the Amerindians and the Africans – the objects of its 'philanthropy' were meant to bring to them a 'proper' understanding of the doctrine of the church and knowledge of man's relationship with God. Operating through branches of the established church its areas of ministration were, at first, limited. They included New York, Virginia, Maryland, Boston and Philadelphia. It conceived of its conversion of the children of Africa abroad with much enthusiasm, as it laboured for the conversion of Indians and Europeans. Among its distinguished prelates were Bishops Lowth, Fleetwood, Williams, Sanders, Butler and Wilson, who persistently urged this duty on their subordinates.[52] Bishop Fleetwood, in this keenness in 1710 to bring three hundred negroes whom the Society had inherited on two Codrington estates in Barbados into the Christian fold, urged that 'if all slaves throughout America and every island in those seas were to continue infidels forever, yet ours alone must be Christians'.[53] But contrary to the exaggerated claims for Anglican humanitarianism made by Professor Klingberg[54] on behalf of the Codrington estates, the facts were otherwise. The Codrington experiment was not only a dismal failure but attempted, as modern research indicates, to reconcile Christianity and slavery by making both compatible. The aim of the experiment indicated in the bequest of Colonel Christopher Codrington was that a college be established on the estates and negroes there educated, instructed and converted. It was hoped that the experiment would persuade the slavocracy to allow the benefits of religious instruction to their slaves by producing at Codrington model slaves of exemplary character. But the Society could not bring itself to forgo the profits that accrued from its possession of the estates; nor could it ignore the prejudices of the local planters in relation to the enlightenment of Africa's descendants. By hiring agents to run the estates on their behalf the entire experiment collapsed and the Society made no black converts between 1717 and 1726.

Indeed, as Professor J. H. Bennett, Jr reminds us, attempts were made to interpret the Codrington bequest as being intended for the education of whites rather than blacks.[55] When the college buildings were eventually completed in the 1740s it was white children who were admitted. The descendants of Africa on the estates had to wait over a hundred years before they received any benefits from the inheritance. When in 1793 the Society in London sought to ascertain from its managers on the estates their success in converting negroes they drew a blank. But before the eighteenth century was over the Society was being assailed for its belief that Christianity could be made compatible with slavery. The attacks by Bishop William Warburton in 1766 and Antony Benezet in the 1770s are cases in point. The Society's response was nonetheless feeble.[56] There was also a more sordid side to the Society's experiment. Between 1712 and 1761 the estates received 450 Africans free of charge, but the mortality rate was high, and far from ameliorating the conditions of its slaves to bring down the death rate, the estates instead resorted to the expedient of slave breeding to replenish their supplies. With badly kept records and no stated opinions on slave marriages, and with its failure in operating the estates to secure observance of the sabbath, it could hardly be considered motivated by humane considerations. Towards the end of the century it had trained no more than three blacks to read, these men being elderly and scarcely literate.[57]

The slavocracy resuscitated the old Roman practice of excluding the slave from religion. In spite of the existence in the West Indies of the Jamaican Slave Code of 1696, which allowed for the instruction of the slaves in the principles of the Christian faith, the slavocracy ingeniously set the law aside. Paramount in their considerations were the profits from the sugar plantations and industry.

They feared that slaves once accepted into the Christian fold might automatically gain their freedom and therefore cease to be property, since the teachings of Christianity were deemed incompatible with slavery. Throughout the seventeenth century this view was ever-present. Those who thought in this manner failed to see the implicit contradiction, for while they asserted on the one hand that Africans were incapable of appreciating Christianity because they lacked the necessary mental equipment to do so and therefore should remain unenlightened as slaves, on the other hand the principles of Christianity maintained that all men were brothers and children of God and therefore equal in the sight of God. In order to circumvent such dilemmas, and at the same time to assuage their consciences, the ingenuity of the clergy of the established church was brought to bear on the situation to twist the teachings of Christianity to fit the circumstances of slave holding. It became possible thereafter to assert that Christianity and slavery were not incompatible. Thus we find a law in Virginia of 1667 stating that baptism did not lead to enfranchisement.[58] An Act of Barbados of 1676 forbade religious instruction to slaves on the grounds that it would lead to 'notions of equality'.[59] We can see then that there was no uniformity in thinking, much less in practice, but the net result was a conspiracy to keep peoples of African descent out of reach of Christian principles. Yet in the neighbouring French and Spanish colonies, religious teaching was at least legal in theory, even if not enforced.

Many devious arguments were advanced in the English colonies to debar African slaves from Christian teaching, arguments such as slaves lacking the mental capacity to comprehend the complexities of Christianity. They even denied the humanity of slaves.[60] But Bishop Butler took an opposing view and asserted that 'Despicable as they [the African slaves] may appear in our eyes, they are the creatures of God, and of the race of mankind for whom Christ died'.[61] However, those who persisted in their arguments against imparting knowledge and Christianity to their unfortunate and wronged victims sometimes sought inspiration from the Old Testament to bolster up their arguments. The Africans were regarded as the Canaanites of old, driven out of the land, hence 'The heathen are driven out and we have their lands in possession; they are numerous and we are few; therefore hath the Lord done this great work to give his beloved rest'.[62] Others even tried to justify leaving out the slaves entirely by hypocritically suggesting that enforced conversion of the slaves to Christianity was shameful and inconsistent with 'true worship'. The fact was that so long as it suited the plantocracy and their adherents to deprive Africans of the teachings of Christianity they did so; when it suited them to behave otherwise and admit Africans to worship they acted differently. This conversion depended on self-interest prevalent at the time –

self-interest being the chief motivator of the planters. It is easy, therefore, to see how for a hundred and fifty years most of the slaves of the West Indies, and especially those of the British colonies, were deprived of Christian and religious teaching.

Pioneers of evangelisation among slave communities

We have noted that in effect the established church in the Protestant colonies, the Anglican church, took no interest in the thousands of slaves its own nationals brought to the West Indies and to the American colonies.[63] It was to the nonconformist and dissident churches that the task of converting Africans of the diaspora devolved. Their task was scarcely made tolerable by the many difficulties they experienced. The legal stipulations barring or restricting them, the ridicule which they experienced, their being hounded out of the islands and the localities in which they sought to operate, and even recurrent threats on their lives, all made their operations an arduous task and only in time did they bear fruit. These nonconformists, who included the Quakers (or Friends), the Methodists, Baptists, and Moravian Brethren (or *Unitas Fratrum*), operated under the most strenuous conditions imaginable. But even here we must beware of running away with the impression that these sects were not in their evolution associated with slave holding. William Goodell quoted the Rev. James Smylie, of the Amite Presbytery, Mississippi, as confirming that three-quarters of all the Episcopalians, Methodists, Baptists and Presbyterians, in eleven states of the Union were in full fellowship with those who bought, sold and apprehended runaway slaves for sale. He also stressed that these sects in the Free States were in full fellowship with those of the South, that the majority of them made no remonstrations against slavery, and that the few who took a stand were regarded as 'fanatics' and 'disturbers of the peace of the Church'.[64] Thus we see that the nonconformists only after owning slaves eventually began evangelising among them. In essence they were poachers turned gamekeepers.

Nonconformity unveiled

During the late seventeenth and throughout the eighteenth centuries, the Methodists and Baptists emerged in the United States as an evangelical force appealing to the untutored mind. They were able to make inroads into black communities and within a short time were able to set the direction for the spiritual development of most of the blacks in the United States. Both these sects, and the Scottish-Irish Presbyterians, we are assured, 'imbibed more freely

230

than other denominations the social compact philosophy of John Locke and emphasised the doctrines of Coke, Milton and Blackstone as a means to justify the struggle for an enlargement of the domain of political liberty, primarily for the purpose of securing religious freedom denied them by the adherents of the Anglican Church'.[65] We learn, however, that the interests of both the Methodists and Baptists did not initially centre on blacks; rather they attempted to steer between Scylla and Charybdis because, although forbidden to hold slaves, they were expected to promote the moral and religious improvement of the slaves without, in the main, either publicly or privately disturbing the civil order. Thus, one of the missionaries who devoted twenty years of service to the West Indies aptly remarked that

> For half a century from the commencement of Methodism the slaves
> never expected freedom, and the missionaries never taught them to
> expect it; and when the agitation of the later years unavoidably
> affected them more or less, as they learnt chiefly through the violent
> speeches of their own masters or overseers what was going on in
> their favour in England, it was missionary influence that moderated
> their passions, kept them in the steady course of duty and prevented
> them from sinning against God by offending against the laws of
> man.[66]

Directly and indirectly the policies of the missionaries helped to sustain slavery. The outstanding exceptions were the few individuals who refused to sacrifice principles and many of these were hounded out of the plantations, rough-handled, imprisoned, killed by mob violence, or ill-treated so badly that they died from the after-effects. Among them were black ministers of religion.

Dr Thomas Coke, celebrated as having brought Methodism to the West Indies, revealed in his writings that the progress of Christianity would enhance social stability. He wrote in one of his volumes that 'To submit to dispensations the most painful and afflictive, without murmuring against that hand which administers, or arraigning that justice which distributes, is perhaps the greatest evidence of divine grace that we can expect from God, on this side of the eternal state'.[67] Coke made it clear in his work, in three volumes, that, in converting the slaves, obedience and subordination were as vital as Christian virtues,[68] and the implication is clear that the religious groups were not out to destroy slavery but make it more secure by conditioning the slave to tolerate it by conformity. Although some of these prelates, Coke not excepted, thought that Christianity was not compatible with slavery, they nonetheless wallowed in contradictions and encouraged attitudes of subservience into slave-consciousness.[69]

It was not all smooth sailing, for even the venerated Bishop Asbury recorded in his *Journal* in 1776 that he met black people some of whose masters forbade them to attend classes in religious instruction.[70] Although the nonconformity of the dissenting churches radiating from England, Germany and North America possessed the markings of their distinct social milieu, they were similar in their features, their practices and their experiences, whether in the West Indies or in North America. Essentially, the aim of these churches was a thorough indoctrination of the slaves; it was not in the first instance to teach them a religion of fellowship in which slavery had no place.[71] From merely being houses of worship and places where prayers such as the Lord's Prayer were recited, the churches nonetheless soon began to become places of instruction for negroes. Of course, attendance at church services provided solace from unrequited toil. Some slaves through this channel learned to read and write, a dangerous development for the slave holders. Those slaves who acquired the rudiments of education passed on their knowledge to others, but their numbers were negligible compared to the many who remained illiterate. There was a touch of irony in the activities of those who sought to save the souls of African slaves but were not prepared to save their bodies as well. The attitude of the planters was ambivalent: at some stages they viewed religious teaching with suspicion; on other occasions they saw religion as a means of conditioning African slaves to accept their lot as bondsmen.[72] These conflicting postures pervaded the thinking of the slavocracy as slavery evolved, especially in the eighteenth and nineteenth centuries, and remained until its demise.

The Quakers   Professor Woodson detected a genuine interest in the evangelising activities of the Quakers in their approach to the negroes. Being friends of humanity, they accepted and asserted the equality of people no matter what their pigmentation, and they denounced the false religion of other colonists, thereby bringing down upon themselves the wrath of public functionaries on the plantations, many of whom prohibited the attendance of negroes at Quaker meetings. The opposition to the Quakers became more vehement when two Quaker stalwarts undertook activities which involved, as the slave holders thought, the undermining of the slave system. George Keith in 1693 began the promotion of religious training for the slaves as the necessary prerequisite for their emancipation; while William Penn (the leading name in the foundation of the colony of Pennsylvania) actually advocated the abolition of slavery and sought to commit the entire Quaker sect to returning negroes to Africa so that they could Christianise the whole continent.[73] We must observe this as one of the earliest of the 'African return' notions which were to become more persistent in the nineteenth and early twentieth centuries. Such was the situation in the North American colonies.

The position in the British West Indies was somewhat similar. In Barbados Sir Robert Schomburgk noted the benevolent sentiments of the Quakers, who he believed were assiduous in their endeavour to Christianise the African slaves. They were naturally seen as dangerous to the community by the white oligarchy, since it was felt that they propagated notions of equality, which were hardly conducive to stability and 'good order' in slave societies. Accordingly, they were so persecuted and prosecuted in Barbados that 'many had to leave the island'. Many of them who fled to Jamaica in 1658 received the welcome of General D'Oyley. But the laws of Jamaica were soon to assail them. On 21 April 1676 the Barbados Council passed an Act forbidding negroes from attending Quaker meetings and from 8 June 1681 the legislation was put into operation. The preamble to that Act read: 'Whereas of late many Negroes have been suffered to remain at the meetings of the Quakers, as hearers of their doctrine, and taught in their principles, whereby the safety of the island may be much hazzarded'. The Act prohibited negroes from attending any meeting house under penalty of being forfeited if belonging to any of the Quakers, half the money to go to the informer, the other half to the public use of the island. The same Act contained a clause which forbade dissenters instructing any pupils or keeping schools upon the island.[74] The Quakers were therefore compelled to leave Barbados, and Schomburgk himself noted in 1848 that he was not aware of the existence of any member of the Quaker sect on the island (even though the Act was later repealed in 1810). The vacuum created by the Quakers' departure was filled by the Moravians.

The Presbyterians   The attitude of the Presbyterians is also of interest, especially as the question of the abolition of slavery in North America was coming to the fore just before the colonists seized their independence from Britain. In 1774 it seemed as if abolition would be linked with the then current advocacy of the rights of man. The Presbyterians being requested to institute action in this direction found themselves, on the recommendation of Dr Ezra Stiles and the Rev. Samuel Hopkins, considering the idea of sending two 'natives of Africa' on a mission to propagate Christianity in Africa. This, of course, compelled the Presbyterians to discuss many aspects of negro slavery, and the debate which ensued led to the commissioning of a report upon it. In the light of the report the Presbyterian Assembly accepted proposals to send missionaries to Africa but postponed further consideration of the question of slavery.

Later the Presbyterians and the other nonconformist sects such as the Methodists and Baptists became imbued with the struggle for the rights of man, and increasingly they came to accept the idea of equality of the negro in church, although they were not always spirited in their denunciation of slavery.[75] But the effects of this shift in emphasis were becoming apparent. Congregations came to accept negroes and the opportunity gave them a platform which they had hitherto been denied and their 'light soon shone among men'. They demonstrated remarkable powers of oratory in expounding the scriptures and unusual interest among whites was shown in their deliveries. But the liberalism of the dissident sects caused offence to the aristocracy of the established church (the Anglicans), and to minimise the odium which might be incurred these dissidents failed to live up to the principles which they had earlier proclaimed of granting negroes unfettered freedom of participation in church activities. With black preachers coming to the fore and attracting wide attention, the Anglican church felt moved to demonstrate its offence by pointing to long-established laws which prohibited negro ministers from preaching. While the negroes confined themselves to limited local areas, the established authorities paid little attention to them; but, when their oratorical powers assumed apocalyptic proportions in which they captivated both the blacks and whites and appeared to be the voices heralding the new day of Western man's redemption, the white opposition became more vehement, even after the North American colonies had obtained their independence. Attitudes were different before the attainment of independence, since at the time, as British subjects striving to break away from British control, they were more inclined to be tolerant of negro sentiments expressed through the church. It could then be said that their struggle was one – for liberty. But after independence many white Americans forgot the road on which they had previously travelled and were inclined to frown on black aspirations. As Professor Woodson aptly put it: 'The attitude of most Americans then, unlike that of some of the British, seemed to be that the good things of life were intended as special boons for a particular race.'[76] This attitude was persistent. Frances Anne Kemble, who between 1838 and 1839 resided in Georgia, recorded in her *Journal* that an overseer flogged a slave man for getting his 'wife' baptised.[77]

Nonconformity in the West Indies

The Moravian Brethren   The tasks of nonconformists in the West Indies were no easier than those of their counterparts in North America. The *Unitas Fratrum* or United Brethren, commonly known as the Moravian Brethren, from Germany, were present in the Caribbean in the eighteenth century, at the time when the Methodists from England and the Baptists from America were also operating. Even the Moravians supported themselves partly by the labour of slaves whom they owned.[78] They began their operations on the Danish island of St Thomas in 1732; they reached the British West Indies in 1754, first Jamaica,[79] then Barbados (1765), but by 1790 they had only forty Africans on their communicants' roll. Ultimately they were more successful in Antigua, where in 1812 there were 8994 members of the Moravian community.[80] With their arrival the slaves also began to receive the gospel from the Protestant sects. Mission stations sprang up elsewhere and it was observed that by 1788 there were such stations in Jamaica, Antigua, St Christopher and Barbados. But opposition to the preaching of the gospel remained unabated into the nineteenth century and well beyond the passing of the Act in 1807 abolishing the slave trade.[81] The response of slaves was unenthusiastic, for at the turn of the century they could boast of no more than a thousand converts in Jamaica.

The Wesleyan Methodists   Although it was Mr Gilbert, Speaker of the Antiguan Assembly, who, through contact with John Wesley in England, introduced a modicum of Methodism into the area, which was later continued by an immigrant Methodist shipwright, John Baxter, it was not until the accidental arrival of Dr Coke in 1787 as General Superintendent of Wesley's missionary work, driven by a storm to the island on his way to America, that Methodism began to take firm roots in the West Indies. Thus by 1793 there were 6570 Methodists in Antigua, the vast majority of whom were slaves. But they met stiff opposition in Jamaica, where a newspaper controversy and a riot resulted from their conversion of a house to a chapel. They were restricted to preaching after dark, when the slaves were done with their work, and even this privilege was soon taken away. The Methodists were thereafter restricted to Sundays only for their religious activities, but found even this was in conflict with the intentions of the planters, who regarded Sunday as the day when slaves should cultivate their own plots of land.

Dr Coke[82] visited Jamaica on three occasions (the other dates were 1791 and 1792); his adherents were mainly coloured people and Free Negroes. Thus at the end of the eighteenth century there were only about 600 Methodists on the island (of whom some were white). In Barbados there was hardly much success, for a riot occurred after the building of a chapel, and as the jury of planters and officials failed to convict the instigators the magistrates later closed it down in 1801. Three years later there were only forty-nine members and in 1812 there were only thirty, comprising eleven whites, thirteen Free Negroes, and six slaves.

The Baptists   The Baptists were probably the most successful of the nonconformist sects which came to the British West Indies. They were from the United States of America and the pioneers of this missionary movement were Afro-American ex-slaves. The two most outstanding ones were George Lisle,[83] a Baptist deacon from Virginia, and Brother Moses Barker. After the American revolution some Empire Loyalists quitted the United States for Jamaica, and Lisle, who had been indebted to a Colonel Kirkland, accompanied him there. He established a chapel at Kingston and embarked on the work of evangelisation, having previously demonstrated his skill as a preacher in the country from which he was now a fugitive. Initially he did not find the task easy. It is even said that he was aided by some whites such as Bryan Edwards (author of *History, Civil and Commercial, of the British Colonies in the West Indies*). Distrust nevertheless existed among the white community, but some of the slaves found the new religion to their liking and Lisle achieved conversions. But Lisle was well aware that his work would not find easy acceptance because of the atmosphere of hostility to missionaries which pervaded the island. He was imprisoned several times on the flimsiest of pretexts, yet he was undaunted and persisted. His measure of success is shown in the fact that he was able to establish, with the assistance of thirteen schoolmasters, a school for the instruction of negro children. Moses Barker was another immigrant to Jamaica, and achieved success with smaller congregations.

Until the turn of the eighteenth century both men continued their pioneering efforts unaided from either England or North America. But they succeeded in training what were known as 'class leaders', some of whom in time were to become the initiators of independent churches, becoming revivalists[84] of sorts by infusing certain African elements into their beliefs and practice. In 1813 John Rowe arrived from the London Baptist Missionary Society to aid the pioneers.

In spite of their achievements they were greeted with hostility by the plantocracy and the privileged of the islands. With the further agitation of the slave question by abolitionists and their adherents many of these missionaries came to be viewed with suspicion; they were seen as the friends of the slaves, if not agitators, whose activities were supported by political liberals in the mother country. It was observed that

> the suspicion soon hardened into definite animosity. The planters feared the influence of such leaders of the Negroes, and the

missionaries became identified in their minds with agitators against the social system of the colonies. Their plan was to tolerate but frustrate evangelisation: to grant licences, but to do so under such conditions as rendered them almost useless, such as forbidding any preaching wherever owners and attorneys did not themselves invite it, preaching after sunset and baptising without notice and permission.[85]

Some of the missionaries demonstrated their resistance to regulations which sought to curtail their activities and in their refusal to conform they suffered imprisonment and banishment with threats to their lives if they dared to return. The first missionary to Barbados could not preach for years and was only allowed to keep a day-school. Apart from assaults on missionaries and illegal imprisonment, churches were also sometimes burned down. Although the early missionaries appeared to achieve very little, their presence nonetheless testified to the evangelical spirit that was astir. While the upper classes ignored them, some slaves saw them as harbingers of a future hopeful day, and their activities laid the foundation for future evangelisation.

As late as 1802 Acts of the Assembly of Jamaica were still being passed forbidding preaching to slaves. Nevertheless, when the pressure of the emancipation movement gathered strength, that fact and the protests of the Methodist Missionary Society in England made it possible for the British Parliament to disallow such legislation.

Evangelisation, which at an early stage in the development of slave societies was seen as dangerous for African slaves and their progeny, came later to be viewed as capable of instilling docility, though this point of view was by no means shared by all planters. Until the end of slavery there were planters afraid of its influence. Nevertheless, by 1815 the Jamaican legislature accepted the right of slaves to be instructed. The effect, however, was minimal, since the motives for the enactment were far from honest. But it was through a little evangelisation here and a little there that a few slaves came to be literate. Thus while in 1816 a Moravian missionary in the West Indies could mention with glee that he had met for the first time a black man who could read,[86] the planters and slavocracy trembled at the thought of any such achievement by the slaves – and even much more so in the United States' plantations.[87]

The enhancement of missionary work

It could be said that missionary work in the British West Indies, partly aided by the activities of the abolitionists, began to achieve success by leaps and bounds between 1800 and 1833. In November 1818 the Combermere Charity School[88] was founded in Barbados for coloureds and negroes; thirty-two out of the eighty-nine scholars were children of slaves. The following year in the same island a Central School for children of subordinate whites was founded. But essentially missionary activities were restricted to mitigating the problems of deprivation. In spite of this opposition was not unknown. The burning down of a Wesleyan chapel in Bridgetown (Barbados) in 1823 is a case in point. The culprits were never detected or brought to justice. But the growth of evangelisation was accompanied by the establishment of theological colleges such as St Augustine's, Canterbury, the Theological College of Wells and Codrington College. In British Guiana in 1824 endowments were made to three established churches – the Church of England, the Scottish Presbyterian and the Dutch Reformed.[89]

Moravian missionaries also founded schools, but difficulties persisted. The first of their day schools founded in Jamaica in 1826 was abandoned. The rigorous adherence to custom as well as the arm of the law conspired to render their achievements negligible. Even the rector of St Lucy, Barbados, was found guilty of misdemeanour, fined a shilling and received Royal pardon for the alleged offence of inculcating the notion of 'equality' in his teaching.[90] The assertion that the missionaries were inculcating the notion of equality into their flock was never absent from the minds of opponents of evangelisation, as shown in the findings of the Committee of the Jamaica Assembly Report against dissenting missionaries in 1828.[91] As a result of the revolt shortly afterwards some who had been incensed by it constituted themselves into what they called the Colonial Church Union in 1832.[92] From its activities, it had the makings of a nineteenth-century 'Red Hand'.[93] It burned down churches, assaulted and illegally imprisoned missionaries, and even burned the rector of Hanover's parish. Two hundred slaves were killed in an open field; elsewhere five hundred others were executed.[94]

Yet these acts of insane ferocity did not deter the Baptists. They led a deputation to London in 1833 to agitate the question of speedy emancipation and were warmly received by some of the leaders of the abolitionist movement, including Wilberforce and Thomas Fowell Buxton, and it might be said that their contribution, among others, speeded up the passing of the Emancipation of Slavery Act of that year.

In spite of what has been said above, nowhere was irreligion more glaring than on the plantations of the British West Indies and in the North American colonies. The Rev. George Bridges, who as rector of St Anne's parish in Jamaica was a champion of the plantocracy and opponent of the dissenting missionaries, and founder of the pro-slavery Colonial Church Union and 'its most energetic leader',[95] commented thus at the turn of the nineteenth century:

> Empty churches, the unhallowed burial of the dead, in fields and gardens, the criminal delay of baptism; the discouragement of marriage, and the profanation of the Sabbath, are models which the slaves can hardly be expected to improve. Fraught with pernicious consequences to the whole community, it is in vain that the clergy from eight-and-forty pulpits zealously denounce the wrath of heaven, and the loss of men, while some attend to hear them; for it cannot be expected that the heathen, or the neophyte, will approach an altar which seems despised, or neglected, by the presumed superiority and high attainments of his temporal master.[96]

The persistence of African religious forms

There was one aspect to the African religious experience in the Americas which has not been given sufficient attention and remains a subject for more systematic study. Some *bozal* Africans, denied their master's religion, clung tenaciously to their own belief systems brought from Africa. These religious practices have been variously called Voudon (Voodoo) in Haiti,[97] and Obeah and Myalism in the British West Indies. Some Africans were not so anxious to embrace the Christian religion as might have been expected, and among those who were admitted to it there was the intermingling of African symbols and rituals with Christian ones.[98] There were also African slaves who were already Muslims before their admission to the plantations and who embarked on proselytising through the numerous slave revolts noted in Brazil. But, in the main, the vast majority of the slaves, and especially the Creole blacks who knew nothing of African religious beliefs, were denied any guiding moral principles by being denied Christianity and accordingly, until almost the end of slavery, they groped for values. The denial of religious teaching, which was associated with education in slave societies, was essentially to maintain the slaves in the darkness of ignorance because it suited the slave system, since enlightenment and religious teaching might have led to rebellion. Even the *Code Noir* of 1685, which in the French colonies conceded baptism and Christian indoctrination to the African slave, prescribed severe penalties for Africans who after being baptised persisted in the religion of their continent of origin. But these harsh penalties did not prevent Africans from persisting in Voudon and other forms of belief.

This is neither the place nor the time to expatiate on the nature of persistent religious forms, but their tenacity and widespread nature, as noted by many writers and observers of slave societies often with hostility and misunderstanding, conspired to confuse the issue. Evidence suggests that the more they were forbidden the more they were merely driven underground and strengthened. Edward Long, historian of Jamaica, bitterly and ungraciously commented on the persistence of Obeah in Jamaica thus: 'Few, if any, of the African natives will listen to any proposition tending to deprive them of their favourite superstition and sensual delight.'[99] Long also wrote that Creole slaves only wished to be baptised to be protected from the Obeah-man's 'witchcraft' or 'pretended sorcerers'. He asserted that their minds were too steeped in superstition.[100] Official attempts to destroy them were indications of the hold they had on people's minds, and their value in slave revolts have been noted elsewhere.[101] Stedman noted in Surinam that African religious meetings were deemed dangerous as 'their "Sybil" [a prophetess] who deals in oracles, sagematrons, enjoin their followers to destroy their masters or desert to the woods and so the practices are prohibited in Surinam'.[102] In spite of the law and the severity of the punishment, Stedman admitted that it was 'often practised in private places and is very common amongst the Owca [Aucanners] and Seramica [Saramacca] negroes'.[103]

Yet, in spite of the misunderstanding with which observers discussed the subject of Obeah, there were those who saw its religious content. Martha Beckwith in the twentieth century has portrayed Obeah as 'the religion of the shadow world, the religion of fear, suspicion and revenge'.[104] This of course ignores the fact that fear is not characteristic of African religions or belief systems alone, since most religions, not excluding Christianity and Judaism, incorporate such an element as well. The counter-cult to Obeah, Myalism,[105] was also observed by Martha Beckwith: 'Various religious sects have flourished from time to time in Jamaica who claimed the power to remove the spells of Obeah, but always through counterspells of their own based upon the same idea of spirit possession.'[106] But the most telling observation which demonstrates the tenacity of African religions and religious forms on the plantations comes from Joseph J. Williams, who in 1932 quoted from Dr Nassau thus:

> The evil thing that the slave brought with him was his religion. You do not need to go to Africa to find the fetich. During the hundred years that slavery in our America held the Negro crushed, degraded and apart, his master could deprive him of his manhood, his wife, his child, the fruits of toil, of his life, but not deprive him of his faith in fetich charms. Not only did the religion of the fetich endure under

slavery – it grew. None but christian masters offered the Negro any other religion; and by law, even they were debarred from giving them education. So fetichism flourished. The master's children were infected by the contagion of superstition; they imbibed some of it at the Negro foster-mother's breasts. It was a secret religion that lurked thinly covered in slavery days, and that lurks today beneath the Negro's Christian profession as a white art, and among slaves of far distant plantations, with words and signs – the lifting of a finger, the twitch of an eyelid — that telegraphed from house to house with amazing rapidity (as today in Africa) current news in old slave days and during the late Civil War, suspected, but never understood by the white master; which, as a superstition, has spread itself among our ignorant white masses as the 'Hoodoo', Vudu, or Odoism, is simply African fetichism transplanted to American soil.[107]

In fact, belief in Obeah in the post-emancipation period was extended to people of East Indian origin, and an interesting case in the former British Guiana (currently Guyana), in 1918, revealed how the daughter of the Dutch owner of Plantation Hoitgedacht, one of the two coffee or cocoa estates remaining in Canal No. 1, had been allegedly killed by Obeah in what was essentially a remote district.[108]

Williams also recognised that the religious priests or diviners were members of an elite, since they were assumed to have the power to control good and evil. The pull of Voudon, Williams observed, was magnetic. There is a similarity between the New World religion stigmatised as Voudon and that of Whydah (in what was formerly Dahomey but now known as the Republic of Benin) whence it had come to the Americas.[109] Penalties were severe for openly professing such practices. Masters who allowed their slaves to participate in such ceremonies were also deemed guilty and punishable as heretics. The restrictions extended to any meeting of slaves of different masters and a police order in Port-au-Prince in 1772 prohibited Free Negroes and coloured people from dancing the *calenda*, considered to be profane.[110]

The persistence of religions brought by the enslaved from Africa remains a fact in New World societies, even in large areas where syncretism has been observed, whether in Brazil, Cuba, the West Indies or North America. The persistence of these forms calls for more understanding and sympathetic studies than has hitherto been the case, for the current belief, which has been widespread, is that African religious forms, made synonymous with 'witchcraft' and 'pretended divination', were submerged by an all-powerful Christian prejudice.

Recapitulation: the strategy of the slavocracy

What has been observed in the preceding four chapters amounts to the techniques which slave owners and their associates devised over time to keep the slave system in being. We can gain a clear impression of how the techniques worked in practice by referring to the writings of Frederick Douglass, himself an ex-slave, who documented some of his own experiences. Here we see the subtleties of the strategy that were intended to make slavery durable. Douglass, who maintained that 'to enslave men successfully and safely it was necessary to keep their minds occupied with thoughts and aspirations short of liberty', argued that a certain degree of attainable good must be kept before them.[111] He demonstrated how periodic holidays, especially the Christmas holidays, were employed to manipulate the slaves in favour of the system. For with these holidays went pleasures and sports and excessive drinking; when the short-lived pleasures were gone the memories survived and sustained the slaves in their hardship. Even the prospect of an impending holiday and the pleasures it promised gave rise to anticipation. According to Douglass:

> These holidays were also conductors or safety valves, to carry off the explosive elements inseparable from the human mind when reduced to the condition of slavery. But for these the rigours of bondage would have become too severe for endurance and the slave would have been forced to dangerous desperation.[112]

He went on to describe the nature of the songs and dances which emanated during the period, some of which became popularised on the plantations and which reveal the ways the slaves perceived their condition. One song satirising the meanness of slave owners went like this:

> We raise de wheat,
> De gib us de corn;
> We bake de bread,
> Dey gib us de crust;
> We sif de meal
> De gib us de huss;
> We peel de meat,
> De gib us de skin;
> And dat's de way
> De take us in;
> We skim de pot
> Dey gib us de liquor,
> And say dat's good enough for niggers.

242

Walk over! walk over!
Your butter and de fat;
Poor nigger you can't get over dat
Walk over.[113]

Even those of rebellious spirit like Douglass were encouraged to drink. Douglass added, 'Everything like rational employment was frowned upon; and only those wild and low sports peculiar to semi-civilised people were encouraged. The licence allowed appeared to have no other object than to disgust the slaves with their temporary freedom, and to make them as glad to return to their work as they were to leave it.'[114] The slave was not only slave to his master but also to intoxicants such as whisky and rum. There were, of course, slaves who took advantage of the opportunity to do something more constructive for themselves, but the vast majority became victims of the dupe practised on them. As Douglass said: 'When the slave was drunk the slave holder had no fear that he would escape to the North. It was the sober, thoughtful slave who was dangerous, and needed the vigilance of his master to keep him a slave.'[115] He further observed that when a slave asked for hours of 'virtuous liberty' a cunning master would take advantage of his ignorance and cheer him with a revolting brew artfully labelled 'liberty'.[116] Douglass concluded: 'I believe those holidays were among the most effective means in the hands of slave holders of keeping down the spirit of insurrection among the slaves.'[117] They were, in fact, devices for mitigating the severity of slavery, but Douglass saw them as a 'fraud instituted by human selfishness, the better to secure the ends of injustice and oppression. The slave's happiness was not the end sought, but the master's safety.' 'Not to be drunk during the holidays was disgraceful,' he added.[118]

In tidying up what has so far been observed about the strategy of the slavocracy, it can be said that judicial, economic, political, military, social and psychological methods of control were involved. These aspects of the control of slaves were in keeping with the prevailing concepts of public order. The juridical aspect of the strategy was bolstered up by draconian laws.[119] Legislation was framed to impose absolute control on the actions of slaves. There were a few exceptions here and there but they were few and far between. Furthermore, theory tended to diverge from practice, for in spite of the existence of stipulations in some slave states for the proper handling of slaves, evasions were the rule since proper monitoring by the distant metropolitan powers was difficult to achieve. When the home governments eventually assumed the role of watch-dogs certain abuses were unmasked, but this only happened very late in the day.

Closely allied to the judicial control system was the economic, the basis of slavery in the Americas. Under the techniques of economic control the slave was expected to surrender his labour completely for no reward whatsoever; in time, the practice of hiring slaves with much of the earnings belonging to the lord and master was developed, and even later they were paid considerably less than comparable poor whites, a practice which continued into the post-emancipation era. The advertisements of runaway slaves containing promises of reward were a bait for those in a poorer economic condition; mercenary types even encouraged slaves to run away and then later attempted to recapture them for a reward.[120] It was also a divisive factor for it divided people into slave escapees and slave catchers and informers. Escapes constituted one of the most nagging problems of plantation operators, and the entire coercive machinery of the state was used in order to track down transgressors. Since the entire system was rooted in profitability, economic considerations were paramount.

Next to the economic aspect of control was the political one. In the main, it involved the use of all-embracing political power by the planters, merchants and their supporters, both within and without the assemblies in the colonies and states and in the plantations, as well as in organisations and interest groups like the West India and American Planters Clubs and later the Planters and Merchants Clubs and the Massiac Club in Paris (an organisation of wealthy colonial planters). The clubs in turn had supporters inside the national assemblies of the metropolitan countries, representing their case forcefully and ensuring that their interests were safeguarded. Another weapon of political control was the total disenfranchisement of the slaves. Even after they had secured manumission and had become freemen many of their disabilities remained because of the overwhelming influence of the planters. Occasionally conflicts existed between high government officials on the spot, being appointees of the metropolitan government, and the local plantocracy, but these moments were few, and, more often than not, there was identity of interest.

The military aspect was also allied with political control for it gave support to the political order. Both the military (as in the United States) and the militia were used to maintain order and safeguard against, and on occasions quell, slave revolts. The activities of the militia were extended to slave catching and punitive expeditions. The militia existed in most of the colonies and they were made up of the able-bodied among the free whites; only in exceptional circumstances did they contain coloured and black freemen. In the use of this technique not even the United States federal authorities stood exculpated since federal troops were also stationed in parts of the South and very often supported the slavocracy; they were used in the Seminole Wars, which essentially were wars for the entrenchment of slavery. It was always argued that federal authorities were bent on upholding the constitution, but they were also used to suppress revolts.

The social aspect of the strategy was based on habit, attitudes and customs built up over time until they became ingrained and often carried the force of law. They were laced with prejudices, objections, fears and even superstitions, and they were widely diffused through the press, pulpit and through folklore. They tended to deflate the position of the freed negroes and the freed coloured population so that their status was indistinguishable from that of slaves. These attitudes and practices were closely allied with stratification, and various techniques of psychological warfare were employed to implement them.

Thus we come to the final weapon in the armoury of the slavocracy, the psychological. There were various ramifications of this and the techniques were so numerous that they could sometimes be elusive. The seasoning of slaves and the kind of welcome they received on arrival at the plantations were some of the initial techniques used to condition slaves to accept their new and degraded status. Even the trial and execution of slaves in the presence of others was designed to serve as a warning to refractory and insubordinate fellow slaves. The drilling of the notion of inferiority and instilling it from a very tender age was another technique. It was extended to the imposition of small white slave masters over small black or coloured slaves who were made to act the donkey or respond in an animal manner to the passions of the former. There was also the role of slave-holding and slave-owning religious prelates, who employed the Bible to rationalise their actions while claiming justification and Biblical authority for slavery and the assumed 'inferiority of the negro'. This also resulted in pseudo-science being used in support of the (unprovable) notion of 'negro inferiority'. Even the works of so-called anthropologists, who devised false theories of race and racial capabilities, became entrenched.

The social customs, practices and laws conspired to keep the African from acquiring enlightenment through denial of education and the practice of any form of religion. Despite the pitting of this full apparatus of the state and social system, some slaves found ways to instruct themselves, as the autobiographies of former slaves show. They also formulated their own religious practices based on the beliefs they brought with them across the ocean, and in some slave theatres, such as Brazil, the practice of Christianity was deeply influenced by African religious rites and symbols. Having studied the strategy of the slavocracy, we must now turn to consider the strategy of the slaves.

245

Notes

1 See the strictures of Lord Sydney H. Olivier on these pretensions in *Jamaica: the Blessed Island*, London, 1936, pp. 85–107, and especially p. 87, for his reference to the government as a 'negrophobic plantocracy with the sympathy of the established clergy'; and p. 88, where it is said that the clergy sent were 'much better qualified to be retailers of salt fish or boatswains to privateers than ministers of the gospel'. This citation derived from Edward Long, *The History of Jamaica: General Survey of the Ancient and Modern State of that Island with Reflections, etc.*, London, 1774, Vol. 2, p. 238. See also Olivier, *Jamaica*, pp. 89–90, 91–4; and John Barbot, 'A Description of the Coast of North and South Guinea' in (J. W. Churchill), *Collection of Voyages and Travels etc.*, London, 1774–8, 1752, Vol. 5, pp. 270–1.

2 See the statement of F. A. Kemble, *Journal of a Residence on a Georgian Plantation in 1838–1839*, London, 1863. pp. 164–5, on this ambivalence. Also D. B. Davis, *The Problem of Slavery in Western Culture*, Ithaca, N.Y., 1970, Vol. 1. pp. 192, 195. The Free Negro was only nominally free. Most of the laws and customary practices of slave societies acted as restraints on his freedom, making that freedom illusory.

3 S. R. Ward, *The Autobiography of a Fugitive Negro: His Anti-slavery Labours in the United States, Canada, and England*, London, 1855, p. 6. Also see Lunsford Lane, 'Narrative' in W. L. Katz (ed.), *Five Slave Narratives*, New York, 1968, p. 20, in which he indicated that he was never permitted to learn to read. Also see Jacob Stroyer, 'My Life in the South' in Katz, p. 31, showing that it was contrary to law for a slave or negro to obtain education. Note too the fulminations of J. W. Pennington in 'The Fugitive Blacksmith', also in Katz, pp. 43, 56–7. Ellen Craft, *Running a Thousand Miles for Freedom*, London, 1860, pp. 32–3, for punishment inflicted for teaching a slave to read even the Bible.

4 F. Douglass, *The Life and Times of Frederick Douglass 1817–1882*, John Lobe (ed.), London, 1882. See also *Narrative of Frederick Douglass, an American Slave, written by himself*, 4th edn., Boston, Mass., 1845, pp. 33–4, 36–9.

5 Frederick Douglass, an exceptional slave, read the 'Columbian Orators', a popular school text, at the age of thirteen. But in St Domingue one slave, if not many others, was able to read books dealing with notions of freedom which helped to mould his revolutionary outlook – that slave was Toussaint L'Ouverture, whose name is immortalised as the leading Haitian revolutionary of the late eighteenth and early nineteenth centuries.

6 Carter G. Woodson, *The Mis-education of the Negro*, Washington, D. C., 1933, p. 24. But Woodson's point was far from being universally true; slavery throve on ignorance, and from the beginning the education of the African slave was out of the question, whether in Spanish, Portuguese, French or British America.

7 Carter G. Woodson, *The Education of the Negro Prior to 1961*, London, 1915, p. 2.

8 Alan Burns, *History of the British West Indies*, London, 1965, p. 594.

9 *Ibid.*, pp. 616–18. The contradictory opinion of making the slave docile through religious teaching is expressed on pp. 635–6, but this was a later development.

10 *Jamaica: report of a committee of the House of Assembly appointed to inquire into the cause of and injury sustained by the recent rebellion, 1832*, Parliamentary Papers 1831–2 (561), Vol. xivii, pp. 3–4. Also in V. Harlow and F. Madden, *British Colonial Development: Select Documents, 1774–1834*, London, 1953, pp. 584–5. It is necessary to observe that the first Baptist missionaries to Jamaica were Afro-American ex-slaves. They were David Lisle and Moses Barker. This religious sect more than any other appealed to the slaves and, in fact, Baptism emerged as the religion of the masses. Later their work was aided by the Baptist Missionary Society of London. But a schism developed within the community in which some in their endeavour to Africanise their sect asserted independence by the formation of independent churches.

11 *Ibid.*

12 Carter G. Woodson, *The History of the Negro Church*, Washington, D.C., 1921, p. 72.

13 As an example, see what Edward Long termed the 'Jamaican *Code Noir*', Long, *History of Jamaica*, Vol. 2, pp. 485–92.

14 Maryland was begun by Roman Catholic colonists under the leadership of Sir George Calvert. Other colonies established, especially in the New England area, were the products of nonconformity among the Protestant sects. Then we must not forget that colonies changed hands both in the West Indies and North America between contending European powers who represented different Christian persuasions. Both the Dutch and English were Protestants, the Spanish, the Portuguese and French were Catholics. The outcome of the struggles was that the British acquired most of the colonial possessions, displacing their rivals by relegating them to tiny enclaves. First, they dislodged the Dutch in the Dutch Wars in North America; later the French, after the Seven Years War. Spanish and French possessions were captured at various times in the evolution of the colonies between the seventeenth and nineteenth centuries. Thus the British eventually gained Trinidad and Jamaica from the Spanish. The process of eliminating rivals that was taking place on the West African coast was also occurring in the western hemisphere. The outcome was that some features of the religious attitudes adopted by one power towards their slaves survived. The Portuguese remained in Brazil and the Spanish in most of South America till their various colonies achieved sovereignty in the early nineteenth century and Cuba towards the end of that century.

15 Long, *History of Jamaica*, Vol. 2, pp. 428–31. Also see pp. 440–1 for his rationalisation against granting the Africans Christianity and for his strictures against the Roman Catholics (Portuguese, Spanish and French) for attempting to bestow superficial Christianity on the blacks. He ridiculed and belittled the efforts of these Catholics.

16 Woodson, *History of the Negro Church*, p. 1.

17 PRO, CO 71/4, William Young to the Earl of Hillsborough, 28 July 1772.

18 We must observe that this related to the slaves taken directly from Africa to the western hemisphere. Those who found themselves translated to metropolitan Portugal or to Spain or Italy found Christianity early. They were set apart from the main body of slaves carried to the Americas. They intermarried with the Europeans and many into the nobility. Some of this negro blood extended to Albania and Austria. See Mary Wilhelmine Williams,

'Slavery' in the *Encyclopedia of Social Science*, New York, 1934, Vol. 14, p. 80. Also mentioned in W. E. B. DuBois, *The World and Africa*, New York, 1947, 1965, p. 47.

19 A bishop's chair laid in marble survived the slave-trading centuries. The bishop is said to have sat on this and blessed African slaves on their way to the slave ships.

20 See U. B. Phillips, *American Negro Slavery: a Survey of the Supply, Employment and Control of Negro Labor as Determined by the Plantation Regime*, London, 1918, pp. 48, 99; also Davis, *The Problem of Slavery in Western Culture*, p. 206.

21 See S. M. Elkins, *Slavery: a Problem in American Institutional and Intellectual Life*, Chicago, 1959, pp. 67–8. See also 'Resumé of the Origin of the Introduction of Slaves into Spanish America' (1685), quoted in Elizabeth Donnan, *Documents Illustrative of the History of the Slave Trade to America*, Washington, D.C., 1965, Vol. 1, pp. 342–6; F. P. Bowser, *The African Slave in Colonial Peru 1524–1650*, Stanford, Cal., 1974, pp. 27–31, 37.

22 The impression of Alonso (Alfonso) de Sandoval as a humanitarian has derived from a number of writers and is misleading. Among them are C. G. Woodson, *History of the Negro Church*, p. 3; C. R. Boxer, *Four Centuries of Portuguese Expansion, 1415–1825: a succinct survey*, Johannesburg, 1961, p. 69; and H. S. Klein, 'Anglicanism, Catholicism and the Negro Slave', in Foner and Genovese (eds.), *op. cit.*, p. 142, n. 14. D. B. Davis has introduced a corrective to this misleading viewpoint to show that Boxer erred in 'thinking largely of the blistering indictment' by Sandoval of the slave traders and had wrongly pictured him as 'one of the most eloquent critics of slavery prior to the British abolitionists of the late-eighteenth century'. Sandoval only attacked abuses of the slave trade and not the trade itself; see Davis, *The Problem of Slavery*, Vol. 1, p. 191, n. 57.

23 Although their treatment varied from one locality, colony or slave theatre to another, they often mirrored severities. See for instance. H. M. Waddell, *Twenty-Nine Years in the West Indies and Central Africa*, London, 1970, pp. 68–9; 70–4, 76–9 for activities of the Colonial Church Union in Jamaica; A. Caldecott, *The Church in the West Indies*, London, 1898, pp. 75–6, 92, 94–5; Woodson, *History of the Negro Church*, pp. 131–5; S. R. Ward, *Autobiography of a Fugitive Negro*, London, 1855, pp. 64–66.

24 An earlier Act of 1671 in Maryland, while allowing for the 'importation of Negroes' stipulated that even if baptised slaves and their progeny were to remain slaves. See Donnan, *Documents*, Vol. 4, pp. 9–10.

25 Quoted in William Goodell's *The American Slave Code*, p. 300.

26 See also Woodson, *The History of the Negro Church*, pp. 4–5.

27 Neither Brazil nor Portugal adopted a Black Code; see D. Pierson, *Negroes in Brazil: a Study of Race Contact at Bahia*, Chicago, 1942, 1947, p. 88; also see n. 66 in the previous chapter. Article II of the French *Code Noir* allowed for Christianisation as an obligation. Article III forbade any religion other than Catholicism in the islands. The first fourteen articles of the Code relate to the slaves and Christianity, pp. 421–41.

28 Abbé Raynal, p. 25. Church intervention was to have a slow impact, but in time the Christian negro slave in Latin America was considered 'axiomatic'.

29 Pope Urban VIII in July 1639 invested four Dominican missionaries to go to the French West Indies with the duty of exerting themselves to satisfy the spiritual needs of the inhabitants and to aim at converting the Indians and

'infidels', George Breathett, 'Catholic Missionary Activity and the Negro Slave in Haiti', *Phylon*, xxiii, 3 (1962), p. 278.

30 F. Tannenbaum, *Slave and Citizen: the Negro in the Americas*, New York, 1947, pp. 90–1.

31 *Ibid.*, pp. 91–2; also D. Pierson, *Negroes in Brazil*, pp. 91–2. Henriques Dias was a Pernambucan slave who aided the Portuguese in the seventeenth century to drive the Dutch out of Pernambuco. He was showered with honours and placed in charge of a negro regiment. Tannenbaum's theories have been increasingly challenged (see Carl Degler, *Neither Black Nor White: Slavery and Race Relations in Brazil and the United States*, New York, 1971, pp. 19–21, 34–9).

32 Tannenbaum, *Slave and Citizen*, pp. 91–2; R. K. Kent, 'Palmares, an African state in Brazil', *Journal of African History*, vi, 2 (1965), pp. 161–75. Also see Pierson, *Negroes in Brazil*, p. 50, n. 62.

33 Pierson, *Negroes in Brazil*, pp. 90–1. But this could be said for all slave societies.

34 See Hugh Thomas, *Cuba or The Pursuit of Freedom*, London, 1971, ch. 20–22, for an earlier Afro-Cuban attempt at independence, national in scope, but ultimately betrayed and chs. 25, 27, 28 and 29 for subsequent events. Also see J. M. Figueredo, *La Revolución de Yara*, 1880, and R. Guerra y Sanchez, *Guerra de los Diez Años, 1868–1878*, 2nd edn., 1900.

35 Thomas, *Cuba*, pp. 323–6.

36 Pierson, *Negroes in Brazil*, pp. 51–2.

37 *Ibid.*, pp. 54–5, 83–5.

38 Pierson, *Negroes in Brazil*, pp. 83, 92; also Tannenbaum, *Slave and Citizen*, p. 63. But the assertion is hardly credible since the education of mulattos in St Domingue was a source of conflict with the whites.

39 Pierson, *Negroes in Brazil*, pp. 92–3; also Tannenbaum, *Slave and Citizen*, pp. 91–2.

40 Pierson, *Negroes in Brazil*, p. 87, n. 62.

41 C. R. Boxer, *The Golden Age of Brazil 1695–1750: Growing Pains of a Colonial Society*, Berkeley, Cal., 1962, p. 173. While one would not assert that the numerous slave revolts known to the Brazilian slave theatre were due solely to the brutality of the system, yet that severity was also a factor in the revolts. Donald Pierson exaggerates when he asserts that the recurrence of these slave revolts did not mean slavery was severe in Brazil, *Negroes in Brazil*, p. 45. While severity was not the only factor in those revolts, severity is nonetheless confirmed. Boxer wrote: 'The mixture of races among Negroes in Minas Gerais and elsewhere was the chief safeguard of their masters against slave revolts which were planned at various times and places.' He then recalled the notification of the Crown in 1719 by the Count of Assumar of one particularly widespread plot which had envisaged a general massacre of all whites on Good Friday while they were attending church, but how the plot was revealed as a result of the struggle for supremacy between the Minas (i.e. West Sudanese) and Angolans (i.e. the Bantus) for supremacy as to which of them should assume the kingship after the overthrow of their masters, pp. 176–7. Thus, judging from other theatres of slavery, evidence abounds that the violence of the system produced counter-violence from the slaves. Pierson contradicts himself even on the same page by admitting the presence of atrocities and rigours of the plantation. See also his p. 47 where he

admits that the kings of Portugal, made aware of the 'hardships inflicted on Negro slaves in Brazil, exhorted them "to put a stop to such crying inhumanities"' (p. 47). There was the case of the negro in Rio Grande do Sul whose wrists were tied above his head and, after honey had been poured over his nude body, was left to the insects; the raping of small children, fracturing of teeth with a hammer, use of stocks, filling of razor slashes with salt, castration of males, amputation of the breasts of females, and the murder of African slaves, these barbarities were not unknown or infrequent (Pierson, *Negroes in Brazil*, pp. 47–8). These could be multiplied for other theatres. After recounting these, one fails to see how these acts would not be generative of many slave revolts. The Pierson thesis stated above is only acceptable if one accepts any state of slavery as humane. The evidence of other historians runs counter to his assertion. See. S. J. Stein, *Vassouras: a Brazilian Coffee County 1850–1890*, New York, 1974, pp. 134–7, 139–41; Degler, *Neither Black Nor White*, pp. 31–9; Arthur Ramos, *The Negro in Brazil*, Washington, D.C., 1939, pp. 34–5; Marvin Harris, 'The Myth of the Friendly Master', in Genovese and Foner (eds.), *op. cit.*, pp. 38–59. This friendliness of the master has been the stock in trade of the greatest propagandist for Portuguese colonialism so far, Gilberto Freyre, *The Masters and the Slaves: Casa Grande y Senzala*, New York, 1946, pp. 4, 181–2, and taken up by Pierson and Tannenbaum. But the Tannenbaum thesis, in spite of its contribution to the study of comparative slavery, is now in the main discredited.

42 Boxer, *The Golden Age of Brazil*, p. 174.

43 *Ibid.*

44 *Ibid.*, pp. 175–6.

45 See the reply of Robert Robertson, 'A Letter to the Rt. Rev. the Lord Bishop of London from an inhabitant of His Majesty's Caribbean islands containing some consideration of his Lordships two letters of 19 May 1727', London, 1730. Also Edmund Gibson, *Two Letters of the Lord Bishop of London*, London, 1727, the first to the masters and mistresses of families of the English plantations abroad; the second to the missionaries there and his insistence on the conversion of African slaves.

46 Olivier, *Jamaica*, pp. 87, 91–4.

47 Fulham Papers, Vol. 2, Circular of Rev. McNeil, Rector of Manchester, Jamaica, to Duke of Manchester, Governor of Jamaica, 3 Sept. 1817; and Robert Adam to Bishop of London, 6 May 1823.

48 G. W. Bridges, *The Annals of Jamaica*, London, 1828, Vol. 2, p. 430. His blatant racism spans the entire length of his concluding chapter, pp. 398–436.

49 F. Cundall, *Historic Jamaica*, Kingston, Jamaica, 1915, p. 327.

50 Caldecott, *The Church in the West Indies*, p. 3.

51 This was Carter G. Woodson's viewpoint in *History of the Negro Church*, shared by Caldecott and Klingberg.

52 Woodson, *op. cit.*, p. 65.

53 Annual sermon of Bishop William Fleetwood, 16 Feb. 1711, in Frank J. Klingberg. *Anglican Humanitarianism in Colonial New York*, Philadelphia, 1940, pp. 210–11. The complete sermon appears on pp. 196–212. Also in F. J. Klingberg, *Codrington Chronicle: an Experiment in Anglican Altruism on a Barbados Plantation, 1701–1834*, Berkeley and Los Angeles, 1949, p. 4.

54 Klingberg, *Codrington Chronicle*, p. 4.

55 *Ibid.*, pp. 85–103. See also J. H. Bennett, Jr., *Bondsmen and Bishops: Slavery and*

Apprenticeship on the Codrington Plantations of Barbados, 1710–1838, Berkeley, Cal., 1958, pp. 5–10, also p. 1.

56 Bennett, *Bondsmen and Bishops*, pp. 1–3, 3–5, 82–5.

57 *Ibid.*, pp. 4–9, 22–9, 35, 75–86, 98; see also pp. 106–7, 44–74, 89–90, 116–22. This book is an essential corrective to Klingberg's exaggerated claims for Codrington as representing Anglican humanitarianism guided by the Society for the Propagation of the Gospel. These revelations merely indicated that slavery tainted or poisoned whatever it touched.

58 Caldecott, *The Church in the West Indies*, p. 67. See also H. T. T. Catterall, *Judicial Cases Concerning American Slavery and the Negro*, Washington, D.C., 1968, Vol. 1, p. 12, for the 1729 decision of the English Attorney, that baptism did not confer emancipation and that merely bringing a slave to England did not confer freedom. This position had been implied two years earlier by the Bishop of London. See Edmund Gibson, *Two Letters of the Lord Bishop of London*, pp. 10–11. See also William R. Riddell, 'The Baptism of Slaves in Prince Edward Island', *Journal of Negro History*, vi (July 1921), p. 308. This relates to Negro and mulatto servants imported into this part of Canada as slaves and the fact that baptism did not dispose of the status. It was a measure passed in 1781.

59 Woodson, *History of the Negro Church*, pp. 25–6.

60 *Ibid.*, pp. 26–7. Yet the trials of slaves for certain offences were an indirect confirmation of the slaves' humanity, but the slave masters did not see the contradiction between their assertions and praxis.

61 *Ibid.*

62 *Ibid.*

63 See Olivier, *Jamaica*, pp. 87, 91–4, for his attack on Anglicans' negligence and their pro-slavery role. The implication was that being pro-slavery they could hardly be regarded as friends of the slaves.

64 William Goodell, *American Slavery: a Formidable Obstacle to the Conversion of the World*, New York, 1854, pp. 17, 23, 24.

65 Woodson, *History of the Negro Church*, pp. 25–60.

66 See H. M. Waddell, *Twenty-nine Years in the West Indies and Some in Central Africa*, quoted in Woodson, *ibid.*, pp. 26–7.

67 Rev. T. Coke, *A History of the West Indies etc.*, Liverpool and London, 1808, Vol. 1, p. 28.

68 *Ibid.* See, e.g., pp. 27–38.

69 See Coke's Vol. 2, ch. 33, for the effect of conversion of slaves in Antigua. He observed that 'Many [slaves] who have been turbulent lions, were now become peaceable lambs'. It made conversion fraudulent. Here was a missionary who could not employ the tenets of his faith to inveigh against an obnoxious system. See also the pointed comments of Elsa Goveia, *A Study of the Historiography of the British West Indies, to the End of the 19th century*, Mexico, 1956, pp. 92–3. Coke was not hostile to the planters, and in fact was reassuring to them; he was even in agreement with their confrontation with the Caribs in the eighteenth century. His only criticism of them arose when they persecuted the dissenting missionaries on the issue of religious toleration, pp. 93–4.

70 Woodson, *History of the Negro Church*, pp. 17–18. See Woodson's *The Education of the Negro Prior to 1861*, New York, 1915, p. 14, for a confirmation of this point. See also F. A. Kemble, *Journal of a Residence on a Georgian*

Plantation in 1838–1839, London, 1863, pp. 164–5. She observed that some kinder or cowardly masters, in order to evade the charge of keeping their slaves in brutish ignorance, permitted only what they assumed and hoped would be a little harmless religious enlightenment but intermingled 'with much religious authority on the subject of submission and fidelity to the masters, they trust their slaves may swallow without its doing them any harm, i.e. that they may be better Christians and better slaves'. She saw dangers in this half-hearted concession.

71 Woodson *History of the Negro Church*, pp. 7–8, 26–7.
72 Woodson, *The Education of the Negro Prior to 1861*, p. 14; Kemble, *Journal*, pp. 164–5.
73 Woodson, *History of the Negro Church*, pp. 17–18.
74 William Sewel, *History of the Rise, Increase and Progress of the Christian People called Quakers*, London, 1772, p. 535. Also quoted from Sir Robert H. Schomburgk, The *History of Barbados*, 1848, pp. 94–5.
75 Woodson, *History of the Negro Church*, p. 41.
76 *Ibid.*, p. 41.
77 Kemble, *Journal*, p. 212. She recorded repeated pleas addressed to her to intercede with the master so that some slaves could be baptised.
78 Caldecott, *The Church in the West Indies*, p. 72.
79 Frank Tannenbaum in his *Slave and Citizen* records that the first Moravian settlements were made in Jamaica in 1732 (pp. 82–4). Sir Harry Johnston wrongly recorded that the Moravians began operations in the Danish island of St Thomas in 1733, *The Negro in the New World*, London, 1910, p. 347. Both Tannenbaum and Johnston were wrong – the date was 1732 in the Danish island of St Thomas; see J. H. Buchner, *The Moravians in Jamaica*, London, 1854, pp. 63–7.
80 Schomburgk, *History of Barbados*, p. 95.
81 Tannenbaum, *Slave and Citizen*, p. 84; Caldecott, *The Church in the West Indies*, pp. 63, 82, 92, 94–5. See Fulham Papers, Vol. 2, Part I, 1803–27, West Indies, Thomas Moody to the Bishop of London in November 1820; also Meeting and Resolution of W. India Planters and Merchants, 23 July 1823, which reveals the slowness in accepting the religious instruction of slaves. Although the resolutions in 1823 appear to give approval, the old suspicions on the function of religion remained. See also Fulham Papers, Vol. 3, Part II, 1810–26, West Indies, Rev. William Davies, Rector of St Peter's Bassaterre and St John Capisterre, to Lord Bishop of London, 1 May 1821. Although the letter indicated that the 'ancient prejudices with respect to the black and coloured population . . . had in some measure subsided', the letter is revealing of the mood of the slavocracy. Davies had preached a sermon to convince them of the necessity for religious instruction of the slaves but calculated to placate the slavocracy. The sermon slanted the facts and tended to impose the blame of previous non-instruction on the brutality of the slave condition and on the slaves themselves and not on the masters – a sermon hardly sincere in the Christian spirit to suggest convincingly that there was even a change of heart from the rank and file of the clergy of the established church.
82 See Thomas Coke, *History of the West Indies*, 3 vols., London, 1808, Liverpool, 1810, London, 1811. His first visit was in 1784.
83 Olivier, *Jamaica*, p. 99.
84 *Ibid.*

85 Caldecott, *The Church in the West Indies*, pp. 75–6.

86 *Ibid.*, p. 86.

87 See what Frederick Douglass said about his efforts to read and write when discovered by his slave master, *Life and Times*, pp. 51, 62–3, 122–4; pp. 66–7 for his organisation of a school to teach slaves to read. The laws also were designed to fashion non-literate slaves, while others forbade the use of slaves as scribes. See also F. A. Kemble's unsuccessful efforts to discover how a slave named London had learnt to read and write, and how she continually received the evasive reply, 'Well, missis me learn, well, missis, me try,' and finally, 'Well, missis, me 'spose Heaven help me', to which she replied that she knew Heaven was helpful, but hardly to the tune of teaching folks the letters. She obtained no satisfaction, *Journal*, pp. 168, 199–200.

88 The school was named after Lord Combermere who, as Governor of Barbados, took an active interest in promoting the Central School for children of poor whites in Bridgetown (the capital) as well as the Colonial Charity School for children of the African and coloured population. The aim here was to teach the children the three Rs – reading, writing and arithmetic. The girls were also taught needlework. There was also a fourth R, religious instruction, for the moral well-being of the children. When the first annual report on the Charity School was issued, it was shown to contain 89 children of both sexes, 57 of whom were free and 32 children of slaves. The maintenance depended on voluntary contributions (at home and abroad) as well as subventions from the Church Missionary Society. Thus Bishop Coleridge, at the beginning of 1825, was able to observe the number of schools in Barbados connected with the church (and these were very few indeed) for the religious instruction of the poor: six for white children, one for coloured and one on Codrington College property for slaves; Schomburgk, *History of Barbados*, pp. 105–6. Schools were situated near churches or chapels or were chapel schools – i.e., held in the same building. When Sunday schools began to be attached to nearly all churches, adults also attended.

89 Caldecott, *The Church in the West Indies*, p. 92.

90 *Ibid.*, p. 93.

91 See Harlow and Madden, *Select Documents*, Oxford, 1953, pp. 484–5.

92 Waddell, *Twenty-nine Years in the West Indies*, pp. 76–82; Olivier, *Jamaica*, pp. 92–9; also Caldecott, *The Church in the West Indies*, pp. 94–5. The Colonial Church Union was declared an unlawful organisation and its existence ended as quickly as it had emerged, but not before it had persecuted a number of dissenting missionaries.

93 See V. B. Thompson, *Africa and Unity: the Evolution of Pan-Africanism*, London, 1969, p. 397.

94 Caldecott, *The Church in the West Indies*, pp. 94–5; Olivier, *Jamaica*, pp. 76–83.

95 Olivier, *Jamaica*, p. 92. The Colonial Church Union aimed at defending the interests of the colonists – in short, maintaining slavery, delaying emancipation and silencing dissenting missionaries.

96 Bridges, *Annals of Jamaica*, London, 1828, Vol. 2, pp. 4–5.

97 Jean Price-Mars, 'Trans-Atlantic African Survivals and the Dynamism of Negro Culture', *Présence Africaine*, Nos. 8–10 (June–Nov. 1956), First International Congress of Negro Writers and Artists, pp. 281–2; Jacques Stephen Alexis, 'Of the Marvellous Realism of the Haitians', *Présence*

Africaine, Nos. 8–10 (1956), p. 261. Also Janheinz Jahn, *Muntu: an Outline of Neo-African Culture*, English translation, London, 1961, ch. 2, esp. pp. 29–33, 51–2.

98 Price-Mars, 'Trans-Atlantic African Survivals', p. 28; Jahn, *Muntu*, pp. 33, 41–5, 53–6.

99 Long, *History of Jamaica*, Vol. 2, p. 428. See also J. J. Williams, *Voodoos and Obeahs: Phases of West Indian Witchcraft*, London, 1932 and 1970, p. 137, for a confirmation of the unsympathetic attitude.

100 Long, *loc. cit.*

101 Long, *History of Jamaica*, Vol. 2, pp. 451–2, with reference to the Tackey revolt in Jamaica in 1760; also C. L. R. James, *The Black Jacobins*, pp. 18–21, 85–7, with reference to Voudon in the Haitian slave revolt; and William Suttles, Jr., 'African Religious Survivals', Journal of Negro History, vol. lvi, No. 2 (April 1971), 97–104; and Degler, *Neither Black Nor White*, pp. 56–7; also Pope Hennessy, *Sins of the Fathers*, pp. 150–2.

102 Stedman, *Narrative*, Vol. 2, p. 262.

103 *Ibid.*, p. 263.

104 Martha W. Beckwith, *Black Roadways*, Chapel Hill, N.C., 1929, p. 106.

105 *Ibid.*

106 *Ibid.* J. J. Williams quoting from G. DeLesser suggested that Myalism was the old religion of the Asante; Williams, *Voodoos and Obeahs*, p. 145.

107 Williams, *Voodoos and Obeahs*, pp. 51–2.

108 PRO, CO 2416, CO 111/623, Governor Collett to Viscount Milner, 7 March 1919.

109 Williams, *Voodoos and Obeahs*, pp. 69–70.

110 Jahn, *Muntu*, pp. 32, 33, 41–5, 53–6.

111 Douglass, *Life and Times*, p. 118.

112 *Ibid.*, pp. 118–19.

113 *Ibid.*, p. 118.

114 *Ibid.*, pp. 119–20.

115 *Ibid.*, p. 120.

116 *Ibid.*

117 *Ibid.*, p. 119.

118 *Ibid.*, p. 118.

119 See Elsa V. Goveia, *Slave Society in the British Leeward Islands at the End of the Eighteenth Century*, New Haven, Conn., ch. 3. Also Jordan, *White over Black*, pt. 2, ch. 3, esp. pp. 103–22.

120 See Douglass, *Life and Times*, p. 65.

9   African resistance to slavery in the Americas

This chapter focuses on some of the techniques and practices which Africans, carried away as slaves to the Americas, evolved for accommodating to their new status. Until recently the general picture of slavery surviving through four centuries left the impression that slaves accepted their status, and that even after emancipation many of them preferred their previous condition of bondage to liberty. Since there are now many studies that deal with the resistance of African slaves, both collectively and individually, no useful purpose would be served by trying to encompass the reactions of slaves in all the various theatres of enslavement. However, some general observations need to be made, for in reality slaves not only rejected their bondage but developed complex mechanisms for cushioning themselves against the worst excesses of the economic system of which they were a part.

Until Professor Herbert Aptheker pioneered his studies on the slave revolts within the United States,[1] the tendency had been to portray Africans in the New World as docile,[2] in spite of the testimony of travellers' journals which commonly referred to uprisings.[3] Four years later, in 1941, Professor Melville J. Herskovits also drew attention to the phenomenon of slave resistance.[4] The view that their works challenged is typified in the following quotation from Harriet Martineau, who visited the United States during the 1830s.

> There is no reason to apprehend serious insurrection; for the negroes are too degraded to act in concert, or to stand firm before the terrible face of the white man. Like all deeply-injured classes of persons, they are desperate and cruel, on occasions, kindly as their nature is; but as a class, they have no courage. The voice of a white, even of a lady, if it were authoritative, would make a whole regiment of rebellious slaves throw down their arms and flee.... They will never take the field, unless led on by free blacks.[5]

Present-day critics of Aptheker's approach to the question of slave resistance are apt to forget that his study was the logical outcome of the desire to refute the current and accumulated myths surrounding the subject that had fossilised into dogma.[6] However, one person

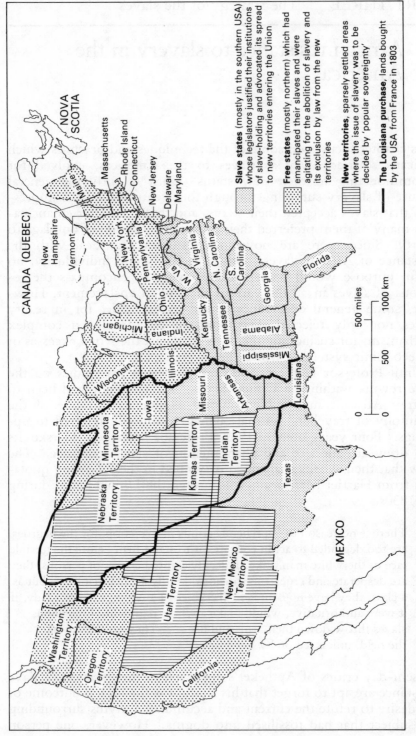

Slave states (mostly in the southern USA) whose legislators justified their institutions of slave-holding and advocated its spread to new territories entering the Union

Free states (mostly northern) which had emancipated their slaves and were agitating for the abolition of slavery and its exclusion by law from the new territories

New territories, sparsely settled areas where the issue of slavery was to be decided by 'popular sovereignty'

The Louisiana purchase, lands bought by the USA from France in 1803

The United States of America before the Civil War, showing slave-owning and free states who had previously refused to accept such dogma (and that as early as the closing years of the nineteenth century) was Dr W. E. B. DuBois, the distinguished Afro-American scholar and spokesman for his people. According to DuBois the 'docility of the Negro was a myth'. He wrote:

> Crucifixion, burning, and starvation were legal modes of punishment. The rough and brutal character of the time and place was partly responsible for this, but a more decisive reason lay in the fierce and turbulent character of the imported Negroes. The docility to which long years of bondage and strict discipline gave rise was absent, and insurrections and acts of violence were of frequent occurrence.[7]

Our concerns in this and subsequent chapters are with some of the questions which surround the subject of African slave resistance in the Americas. We shall consider the characteristics of resistance; the measure of their success and failure; some of the falsehoods on the subject that periodically surface in print; the role of domestic slaves in revolt compared to that of field slaves; the Maroon communities in the slave theatres; and the special case of St Domingue.

Characteristics of slave revolts

While Professor George P. Rawick is a strong critic of the Elkins 'Sambo syndrome', supposed to represent a docile slave who had been conditioned by the slave experience not to resist the institution, he warns that Aptheker's work needs to be handled with caution because

> ... it needlessly exaggerated the incidence of slave revolts, relies heavily on rumour, and seems to suggest that resistance to slavery could be best demonstrated by portraying black slaves as virtually always on the barricades. If black slaves in North America, faced with a huge expanse of territory, controlled by a white majority, faced with overwhelming odds, had engaged in the large number of extensive slave revolts that Aptheker suggests they did, they would not have been brave, but foolhardy and absurd. Indeed, it would have been childlike behaviour.[8]

In his objections to this line of approach, which gave the impression that the state of slavery was so bad that slaves were 'almost always either plotting insurrection or actually at the barricades', he questioned the claims made for hundreds of slave rebellions, and the assertion that American negro slaves had 'a heroic record of rebellion against overwhelming odds'. If this were so, he asked, why were 'these rebellions so universally unsuccessful if they were so ubiquitous, and why did the slaves foolishly revolt so often without a chance of victory?'[9] The question of revolt, of course, centred on treatment and the response to it, but not only on this but on other considerations as well. In an earlier chapter we indicated how the yearning for freedom was itself a factor inducing revolt, even at home and on board ship. It is further made as a consideration for the Nat Turner revolt, which Aptheker stresses in spite of his critics.[10] Rawick's choice of sources (slave narratives) leaves one with some doubt about the criteria he used in reaching his conclusions. While it is true that 'the views of the ex-slaves as presented in their narratives and interviews enable us to see the conflicts between master and slave that took place day by day, and how these developed over time',[11] in spite of their shedding light on the nature of brutality and harshness of societies, they also certainly provide us with the rationale for slave rebellion when slaves felt that they had suffered enough of the brutalities perpetrated on them. Aptheker noted:

> Vengeance did not sleep. Bourbon historians, who have made slavery idyllic and the slave an inferior people, have little place in their works for accounts of this vengeance – this heroic anti-slavery struggle of the Negroes.

There is no doubt that the slaves and the slavocracy (and this term is used in the broadest sense to include those who helped to sustain the slave system in the plantations) interacted as Rawick insisted, but we are not to be led to the conclusion that they were often of a beneficial kind. Slave societies, in the main, were not humane societies and were, in fact, the negation of them, and since actions produced reactions, brutality was of itself bound to produce brutality, and where kindness was shown it was possible to obtain reciprocity of kindness; but this did not mean that slaves liked the situation and would not seize a chance to escape from it. Frederick Douglass observed: 'Give him [a slave] a bad master and he aspires to a good master; give him a good master, he wishes to become his own master.'[12] This was a very telling statement of the kind of sentiments and emotions pulsating within the slaves' breasts; but apologists of slavery tended to gloss over this. In another context Douglass wrote prior to his escape from slavery:

> I have observed this in my experience in slavery, that whenever my condition was improved, instead of its increasing my contentment it only increased my desire to be free, and set me to thinking of plans

to gain my freedom. I have found that to make a contented slave it is necessary to make a thoughtless one.[13]

Douglass might have been an exceptional slave but such sentiments must have welled up in the minds of many more slaves,[14] as the poems of George Moses Herton, the slave poet of North Carolina, showed.[15] If slaves, therefore, revolted by violent means a number of factors must have been taken into consideration so that they were left with no alternative but to use this technique in calling attention to their grievances. Second, since many of them, as we have been assured by slave captains, would rather die than brook the status,[16] the propensity to kill themselves through suicides was great, and on board ship many of them died by throwing themselves over-board with the belief so ubiquitously noted that death translated them to their country of origin. Third, they must have felt that revolt would provide them with the opportunity to move away from the scene and establish isolated areas of liberty without the burdens of servitude – this factor lay behind the establishment of Maroon communities and *quilombos* in the Americas and these were in existence from the second half of the sixteenth century. Fourth, where the revolts were better organised, they had hoped, albeit naively, to overturn[17] the system and establish a more tolerable society. These are by no means all the considerations but recurrent failures (not on the same plantations) could not prevent others elsewhere from trying in case they succeeded, and, in fact, the success of the Haitian revolt gave heart to some slave rebellions and frightened the slavocracy of neighbouring theatres of slavery.[18] These rebellions were not asinine or puerile in spite of what Rawick[19] said of the Aptheker approach.

However, before observing the nature of resistance we must look for causes. They were numerous and it is difficult to unravel all of them. From Aptheker's text and from the writings of many ex-slaves we find some of the following among the reasons for revolt. The first was cruelty, something that went far beyond physical brutality. Second was malnourishment, which can also be con-ceived as an aspect of cruelty. Third, economic depression not only affected the planters but the slaves too. Many of the pleas from the West Indian slavocracy to the British Parliament for relaxing re-gulations prohibiting the import of provisions tended to mention the distressed conditions of the slaves consequent on destruction brought about by hurricanes, shortages due to lack of imported provisions or other causes. Fourth, the growth of the slave popula-tion might have given its members confidence in a society in which they considerably outnumbered whites. It was a factor in the imposition of what are called the deficiency laws.[20] DuBois observed this situation in North America thus:

> Again and again the danger of planters being 'cut off by their own
> negroes' is mentioned both in the islands and on the continent. This
> condition of vague dread and unrest not only increased the severity
> of laws and strengthened the police system, but was the prime
> motive at the back of all the earlier efforts to check the further
> importation of slaves.[21]

The fear that the importation of a great negro population might
endanger the safety of the colony of South Carolina was expressed
as early as 1698. It led to the legislative encouragement of white
servant immigration. At the time the British secured the *Asiento* the
colony enacted two heavy duty Acts because the number of blacks
had increased so considerably in the province. The importation of
African slaves reached such a magnitude in 1734 that the colonists
wrote to the British government:

> We must therefore beg leave to inform your Majesty that, amidst
> our other perilous circumstances, we are subject to many intestine
> dangers from the great number of negroes that are now among us,
> who amount at least to twenty-two thousand persons, and are three
> to one of all your Majesty's white subjects in this province. Insurrec-
> tions against us have often been attempted.[22]

But efforts to balance their numbers with the importation of whites
were to no avail; in 1740 the colony experienced the revolt of a
slave known as Cato, and the consternation occasioned by it led to
the imposition of a duty of £100 for every slave brought into the
colony, but this only acted as a temporary halt. The colony felt
compelled in 1760 to order a total prohibition of the slave trade,
though this was disallowed by the Privy Council, and the governor
reprimanded. The colony complained that 'an importation of
negroes, equal in number to what have been imported of late years,
may prove of the most dangerous consequence in many respects to
this Province, and the best way to obviate such danger will be by
imposing such an additional duty upon them as may totally prevent
the evils.'[23]

Fifth, revolts or attempted revolts often earned the odium of the
slavocracy and led to more severity by the authorities, which could
have the effect of generating further plans for rebellion. Such
tendencies were known in the West Indies, notably in Jamaica.
Sixth, revolts could be incited by the observation of other revolts.
A revolt which seems to have had much impact on slave societies,
both on the restiveness of slaves and the slavocracy, was that of St
Domingue in 1791, about which more will be said presently.
Seventh, the prevalence of revolutionary philosophies and activities
associated with the French Revolution undoubtedly influenced the

260

Haitian revolt.[24] Eighth, there was the belief by slaves in some instances that their emancipation had been authorised and that they were therefore being unlawfully kept in bondage.[25] This occurred in Virginia in 1730 with the landing of a new provincial governor from England. A ninth factor had to do with the spread of various philosophical ideas, more general than those directly emanating from the French Revolution. For instance, between the years 1770 and 1783 the prevalence of a revolutionary philosophy and the spread of ideas of an equalitarian religion such as Methodism (from 1785 to 1805), or ideas against a foreign power (as for instance during the years 1812–15 when England and the U.S.A. were at war), or even parliamentary or congressional or national assembly debates, or even open public campaigns by abolitionists, could incite slave revolts. After the Nat Turner revolt most Southerners blamed the abolitionists for the disturbance. It is this latter aspect which Marion D. deB. Kilson referred to as access to external sources of communication.[26] Tenth, there were, of course, revolts which assumed the character of evangelistic crusades, such as the recurrent revolts, especially those led by the Hausas in Brazil, which had proselytising as their aim.[27]

In his study of Jamaican slave resistance Dr Orlando Patterson, like Aptheker before him in the study of North American resistance, distinguished two principal types of resistance, namely passive resistance and violent resistance. He further subdivided the passive type into the following: (i) refusal to work, general inefficiency and deliberate laziness; (ii) satire; (iii) running away; (iv) suicide. Violent resistance was subdivided into two – individual violence and collective violence.[28] These divisions in many respects coincide with those of Aptheker.[29]

That the lines between individual and collective forms of resistance are blurred is suggested by another author, Rawick, who analysed actions within the framework of the slave community or slave communities. Seen within the context of these communities the acts of resistance constituted the interactions which were taking place between the actions of the slavocracy and the slaves. In spite of that author's criticism of Aptheker's approach to the entire question, he admits its obvious merits by saying that 'while it is currently fashionable in some circles to attack Aptheker's *American Negro Slave Revolts*, which clearly is often very wrong, nevertheless I must insist that its bias is preferable and has been more fruitful for serious scholarship than that of those scholars who have emphasised the "docility" of the black slaves in North America'.[30] But the same author proceeded to introduce his corrective in considering individual resistance by observing that:

The mechanisms of individual acts of resistance, as well as those of

261

collective actions, become clear if we focus upon the slave community. People do not individually resist in any significant degree without some sort of support and social confirmation from a community. There must be ways whereby individual acts of repression become known throughout the community, ways whereby individuals learn from each other that resistance is legitimate, and ways whereby individuals learn from each other of particular ways to resist. In order for large numbers to resist with any degree of success, slaves had to know that other slaves resisted, and how this was accomplished.[31]

Rawick then proceeded to discuss the various networks of communications by which slaves transmitted information to one another. His approach has obvious merits and is attested to in the records. For instance, the transmission of information relating to individual acts of repression, or of unfair dealings by masters to their slaves, became generally known and led in some cases to slave satire.

Mathew Lewis in the nineteenth century recorded a song which was sung by slaves on a Jamaican plantation concerning a slave owner who, when his slaves had become old and infirm, tended to cast them away to die at a place called the 'Gulley'. The song, we are informed, was very popular among the Jamaican slaves and it ran like this:

> Take him to the Gulley! Take him to the Gulley!
> But bringee back the frock and board.
>
> Oh! massa! massa! me nodeadee yet!
> Take him to the Gulley! Take him to the Gulley!
> Carry him along!'[32]

The song in fact referred to a transaction which took place towards the end of the eighteenth century on an estate in a neighbourhood called Spring Garden, where there was a cruel proprietor named Bedward. It was customary that when an infirm black slave was pronounced incurable Bedward ordered that the unfortunate victim be taken to a solitary vale upon his estate called 'the Gulley' where the unfortunate person was thrown down and left to the fate of being devoured by Johncrows before he died. Through this method the greedy proprietor evaded expenses for maintaining slaves during their fatal illness; he also insisted that the frocks and clothes of the dying person be returned, together with the board on which the person was carried. Thus the abandoned slave was left naked.[33] On one occasion a black slave who was being taken to 'the Gulley' pleaded that he was still alive and begged to be spared, but his pleas were ignored by Bedward, and the slaves being much affected by the case rescued him the same night, concealed him in their village and nursed him back to recovery, after which he left the estate undiscovered. Suddenly one day his master came face to face with him in Kingston and, recognising him immediately, seized him as his slave. But the victim's cries attracted a crowd and after they had heard his pitiful story, and sympathetic to the manner in which the slave had gained his freedom, they became indignant and Mr Bedward, ashamed of himself, was glad to get away and made no further attempt to reclaim his erstwhile slave. The story reads like that of David Lisle (master) and Jonathan Strong (slave) which eventually led to the Somersett case in 1772.

Nevertheless the slaves' capacity for satire was amply demonstrated in the song, and the popularity of it showed their capacity for transmitting information relating to the cruelty of masters. The technique was one of resistance, which paid dividends. We get insights into the reactions of Jamaican slaves repeated elsewhere, when an ex-West Indian overseer of the eighteenth century observed that slaves sang while hard at labour and, although their songs had neither 'rhyme nor measure', he found them 'witty and pathetic' and often laughed heartily and had sometimes been struck by the 'deep melancholy of their songs'. He gave an instance of a song about the 'barbarity' of an overseer as conveyed by the slaves:

> Tink dere is a God in a top,
> No use me ill, Obisha!
> Me no horse, me no mare, me no mule,
> No use me ill, Obisha!

Another such song ran like this:

> If me want for go in a Ebo,
> Me can't go there!
> Since dem tief me from a Guinea,
> Me can't go there!
>
> If me want for go in a Congo,
> Me can't go there!
> Since dem tief me from my tatta,
> Me can't go there!
>
> If me want for go in a Kingston,
> Me can't go there
> Since massa go in a England,
> Me can't go there!

The mention of the yearning for the Igbo country and the Congo as contained in the same song testifies to a kind of evolving consciousness of oneness in oppression, even though the slaves originated from divergent parts of Africa with differing tongues. The society itself was conditioning its collective outlook and was to produce in time what DuBois described as Africans from various parts united in experience and beginning to 'think of Africa as one idea and one land'.[34]

However, the impression must not be created that because both the slaves and the slavocracy found means of cushioning the slave system in order to absorb the periodic shocks which slavery entailed, that slaves did not, even by methods which they regarded as those of passive resistance, use the method of confrontation. The slave laws were in the main harsh and left the impression of confrontation at the barricades. The daily battle of wits between slaves and their handlers reflected these confrontations which, if they sometimes did not lead to outright violence, did not make the slave system any less violent, for it was a cardinal principle of slave handlers that severity was a vital factor in maintaining slavery.[35]

While it might not have been frequent, it occasionally happened that some unhappy slaves in a state of starvation became desperate at their fate and 'resolved to redress their wrong, and gain their freedom, or perish in the contest'. Accordingly, they formed themselves into strong parties to 'kill their task-masters, and burn and destroy houses and canes; and at the last, when they are too closely pursued, kill themselves also'.[36] Moreton, whose words these are, further recorded that it frequently happened that when slaves were too 'cruelly treated, after their supplicating the Deity in the most humble and affecting manner, "Oh! good God in a top! – Oh! good God of ebrey world! – look down and pity your poor black negro", – they hang themselves, cut their throats, or stab themselves.'[37] He then related an experience in which a rude and uncultivated slave by the name of Hector, a head cooper on a plantation in the parish of Clarendon and reputedly a good workman, failed to make the number of puncheons required by the overseer. As a result Hector was tied hands and feet to a ladder and flogged. Some time later, when Hector was at work, the overseer came again and addressed Hector thus, '"You scoundrel, I'll cut your backside to pieces if you don't make more puncheons!" Hector replied: "Hecta don't regard him life – kill Hecta one time! Hecta nebba will make puncheon for you, Obisha!" At which he took the axe in his left hand, and with a stroke chopped off his right hand!"' Commenting on this Moreton pondered, 'What must the feelings and agitations of poor Hector's heart have been to commit such a desperate act on himself? What a brave general, or valiant admiral, might that man have made, had his intellects been properly cultivated from his youth, and trained to the army or navy.'[38] But even Aptheker recognised that resistance did not always involve confrontation when he wrote that, 'between 1720 and 1865 in the United States there was a regularity in the recurrence of slave revolts and the fact that many Negroes always fled served as a safety-valve and diminished the number of slave revolts'.[39] Yet there is validity in the argument of Aptheker applicable in other slave theatres apart from the United States in his observation that,

> During slavery the South was a dictatorial oligarchy which terrorised
> the slaves and suppressed their frequent insubordination and
> revolts.[40] . . . The fear of such rebelliousness was a persistent factor
> in the life of the South which has too long been overlooked by social
> historians. The facts presented here certainly refute the stereotypes of
> docile Negro slave; the American Negro consistently and
> courageously struggled against slavery in every possible way and he
> must continue in this tradition if he is to break the barriers of
> discrimination today.[41]

This fear was noted by other writers for the West Indies as well. DuBois quoted a governor of Barbados who observed that 'the public mind is ever tremblingly aware to the dangers of insurrection', and went on to add that the statute books all over the territory testified to this fact.[42] The ferocity of those confrontations between slavocracy and slaves was confirmed in the writing of Bryan Edwards, himself a slave owner and later an absentee landlord, when he noted that the Maroons in Jamaica 'continued to distress the island for upwards of forty years, during which time forty-four Acts of Assembly were passed, and at least £24 000 expended for their suppression'.[43]

The implications of Aptheker's arguments about slave revolts were that they were more often successful than had been generally admitted. Although they singularly failed to overturn the system as in St Domingue (modern Haiti), they nonetheless achieved certain limited objectives whether conducted individually or collectively.[44] Frederick Douglass wrote that by intimidating a cruel slavemaster, Covey, he was able to prevent the latter striking him again.[45] Douglass's action heartened the slaves and also made the overseer generally more cautious in his application of the whip. Scattered throughout some of the autobiographies of slaves can be found similar examples of resistance by individuals. The biography of Harriet Tubman[46] gives us another example of such action until she finally escaped from slavery to return and disturb the peace of mind of the slavocracy by spiriting slaves away from the south of the United States. Although most of the collective slave revolts resulted in the promulgation of draconian laws for their control, imposing severe restraints on the movements and actions of slaves as well as the imposition of severe punishments to warn others against such insurrections, these measures constituted bad advertisements for the slave owners' case and were often seized upon by their enemies to discredit them. Thus after the Nat Turner revolt of Southampton County, Virginia, in 1831, William Lloyd Garrison, the distinguished abolitionist and founder of *The Liberator*, assailed the Southern slavocracy in strong words and warned them of the dangers consequent on slave holding.[47] Each revolt, and especially if it was a major insurrection, had the effect of drawing the attention of the public to the issues involved and created crises of conscience among the public, which in time were to give the crusades against slavery the gravity they deserved.

Aptheker, who noted about 250 revolts in the North American experience, argued that the figure 'demonstrated that "organised" efforts at freedom were neither "seldom" nor "rare", but were rather a regular and ever-recurring phenomenon in the life of the old South'.[48] This observation has been attacked on the grounds that it entrenched the portrait of constant confrontations at the barricades.[49] But the picture, observing both the West Indian and Latin American plantations and notably Brazil, often on a large scale, revealed the recurrence of these revolts.[50] It is, of course, a pertinent argument that some of the revolts were ill-organised, while others were spontaneous, but some of the celebrated ones like those of the 'Famous Republic of Palmares', and those of Gabriel Prosser, Denmark Vesey, Nat Turner and Samuel Sharp in Jamaica, the Maroons and Tackey, and Mackandal in St Domingue, had competent planning at their base. Even in the act of running away from the plantations, regarded as a type of passive resistance, we find that the 'barricade' was close by, so that when a runaway slave was cornered he at times took the grave step of killing his assailants.[51] By contrast, the number of large-scale slave rebellions in the United States seems fewer than those of Latin America.

In spite of Donald Pierson's observation of numerous and persistent slave revolts in the Latin American theatre, and in spite of his statement that in the *Archive Publico* at Bahia there were four volumes of 'police documents covering the revolts of this period', with 'each volume containing from a thousand to twelve-hundred sheets of long-hand which for their age are fairly well preserved',[52] Pierson supplied the faulty judgement that 'the number and persistence of these slave insurrections may suggest that slavery in Brazil was unusually severe'. The reverse seems to be the fact, even by his own evidence. Insurrectionists were unassimilated Free Negroes and semi-independent slaves, morally isolated from the Europeans. Although the hardships incidental to a plantation system obviously existed, and atrocities occurred here as elsewhere, the slavery involved . . . was ordinarily a mild form of servitude.'[53] The evidence for this is inconclusive. In spite of the existence of more days of rest in the Catholic plantations (because of fast days and attitudes towards the sabbath), the slaves still felt the need to rebel against the status imposed upon them. In spite of the time they had to 'work for their own profit', the difference between Brazilian (and Latin American) slavery and that of other theatres is merely one of degree rather than kind. Slavery involved constraints; and constraints by the master meant the right of the latter to impose his will rather than allow the exercise of the free choice of the former. The evils and severity of slavery were prevalent, for even in the early years of Portuguese colonisation in Brazil, the letters of Jesuits had many references to Indian slaves 'tortured and branded in the face'.[54] Pierson's arguments seem rather contradictory; for in spite of observing the importation of numerous Yorubas, Geges and Hausas, the latter being Muslims who converted many of the former to the Islamic faith, he saw them as 'shrewd and intelligent, being at times superior in cultural equipment to their masters', for many of them were literate, and some were said to have written Arabic with great facility. Often they combined to plan a revolt, or purchase the freedom of a favourite friend, or to 'work under a leader for the liberation of all' and some whose manumission they secured they sent back to Africa paying the cost of the fares. Furthermore, he argued that the Hausas principally spearheaded the numerous slave revolts with the result that in the period under consideration Europeans lived more or less in a state of alarm.[55] He continued by noting that the tendency to class some blacks as docile was hardly tenable and, although we are accustomed to hear of 'warlike Keromantynes or Gold Coast Negroes', Koster nonetheless attributed 'the relative peace of Pernambuco compared with Bahia' as due to the fact that fewer of the Gold Coast types, reputed to be firm in mind and body and ferocious in disposition, were imported into the former than the latter.[56]

The records testify to vengeful slaves, as Aptheker noted. Slavery was a vindictive system with all manner of means available to punish those who sought to undermine it, whether by the purchase of freedom, by running away, by incendiarism, by suicide, by self-mutilation or self-immolation, by aiding and abetting the escapes of slaves, by returning to slave citadels to assist in the spiriting away of slaves, and by killing personnel identified with the institution, from book-keepers to proprietors. The ubiquity of violence made violent resistance common. It was recorded in the United States of America in 1799 that a group of blacks who were being transported through Southampton County, Virginia, killed two whites in their attempt to escape, and in 1826 seventy-five slaves mutinied on a Mississippi river steamer, killing five white men on board and escaping to Indiana.[57] As Aptheker observed, slaves living close to swamps, or impenetrable forests, or frontier areas, tended to combine to act against slavery. The 'barricades' were ever-present judging from the merciless responses of slave holders to slave rebellions.

Domestic slaves and field hands

The respective roles of these groups in slave resistance revolves around dichotomy instituted into the slave system. There seems to be a need for reappraising the roles of both groups. The generally accepted view is that the domestic slaves fared better than the field hands, that often they shrank away from revolts, and that, more often than not, they played the role of informers.[58] The issue focuses on the treatment of the domestic slaves *vis-à-vis* that meted out to the field slaves; how different was their treatment and to what extent did it act as a catalyst or brake on resistance? Equally, in a society which was highly colour-conscious, the issue of the role of mulattos *vis-à-vis* the blacks also needs to be considered. Writing of the dichotomy between domestic slaves and field hands Orlando Patterson wrote:

> The common view concerning social divisions among the slaves held both by contemporary and modern historians is that the household slaves formed a kind of slave aristocracy as opposed to the field Negroes who, it is claimed, envied the lot of the former. This viewpoint is both crude and erroneous.[59]

Frederick Douglass also made some interesting observations on domestic slaves:

> The servants constituted a sort of black aristocracy. They resembled the field hands in nothing except their colour, and in this they held the advantage of a velvet-like glossiness, rich and beautiful. The hair, too, showed the same advantage. The delicately formed coloured maid rustled in the scarcely-worn silk of her young mistress, while the men were well attired from the overflowing wardrobe of their young masters, so that in dress, as well as in form and feature, in manner and speech, in tastes and habits, the distance between these favoured few and the sorrow and hunger-smitten multitudes of the quarter and the field was immense.... Viewed from his table, and not from the field Colonel Lloyd was, indeed, a model of generous hospitality. His house was literally a hotel for weeks during the summer months. At these times, especially, the air was freighted with rich fumes of baking, boiling, roasting and broiling....
> Viewed from Colonel Lloyd's table who could have said that his slaves were not well clad and well cared for?... The poor slave, on his hard pine plank, scantily covered which his thin blanket, slept

more soundly than the feverish voluptuary who reclined upon his downy pillow.[60]

The question of the support or non-support of domestic slaves for revolts depended on many factors apart from merely being confined to the home, or the loyalty which they owed or allegedly owed to the master. Some domestic slaves also played prominent parts in slave revolts; examples included Tackey in Jamaica (1760) and Toussaint L'Ouverture[61] in St Domingue (1791–1802), but other factors helped to condition their consciousness. Nevertheless, the general picture that emerges from reading the records is that domestic slaves, if not participants, sat on the fence to see how things were shaping up; those of them who played a part against the rebel slaves tended to be brutal against them, qualifying themselves for rewards for their 'loyalty' to the slavocracy, in some cases being manumitted.[62] Thus we see how, through inducements, slaves could be encouraged to be opportunist. But equally some of the slaves from the fields might have revealed plans of revolt in anticipation of receiving some reward.[63] The records are silent on this, and although accounts of slaves who betrayed plans to revolt are numerous, those involved are not usually identified as domestic slaves or field hands. Yet the frequent references to them as mulattos,[64] as well as the method of narrating their role, tends to leave the impression that many of them must have been domestic slaves.[65] Moreover, since they tended to view themselves apart, either by caste, occupation, or origin (Creole-born),[66] distinctions of which the slavocracy made so much and which boosted the egos of the mulatto and coloured slaves, their willingness to cooperate with the rebel field slaves might appear more frequently in doubt than if certain induced antagonisms between them and the field slaves did not exist.

It is ubiquitous in the records that many of the revolts were staged by newly-imported Africans, the *bozales*, or by those who had not assimilated to the plantation system. If one is to take this at its face value the implication is that Africans fresh from the continent refused to accept the status of slave, whereas those who had acclimatised acquiesced in it. When it is remembered that other slave rebels had resided within the plantation colonies for some while, often long before staging revolts, the tendency to pin the revolt only on new arrivals needs modification. The propensity to revolt might have been greater for new arrivals, but those who had become settled also took part in revolts in all the major slave societies.

A factor which sometimes made for solidarity in slave revolts was that of religion. Certain elements surviving in African religious beliefs, to which the plantation's slaves adhered but simplistically designated 'Obeah', did bring even Creoles into the ranks of rebel slaves because of their awe of the 'Obeah priests' or because the entire belief system had a hold on them.[67] If we consider one major slave rebellion comparable to most of the major revolts which occurred in each of the slave theatres, that of Jamaica in 1760 led by the house slave, Tackey, who must have had many domestic slaves as adherents, among others, we note that, although the revolt was principally led by the Coromantins (Akan), there were also involved slaves imported from French Guadeloupe[68] and sold in Jamaica to a Captain Forrest, slaves who had been in the West Indies for some time, knew the use of arms, and had previously participated in military engagements. Edward Long described them as the 'most dangerous'. But equally we observe that twenty slaves from the estate of a 'gentleman proprietor', even though Coromantins, when given arms to defend his home, joined the rebels, though they spared their master's life in view of his reputation for being humane.

What happened in the revolt was, first, there was a conflict of loyalties since it was a Coromantin-led revolt, the question of ethnic solidarity becoming a factor; secondly, there must have been differing perceptions of loyalty to the planter in spite of his alleged humanity;[69] third, concerning the aim of the rebellion, it is clear that it was intended that in the end the island might belong to the rebels who would acquire a status of freedom comparable to that of the Maroons.[70] Fourth, the factor of colour must also have been present, for Edward Long makes several references to mulattos killing 'negroes' in the confrontation, the mulattos becoming involved on the side of the slavocracy.[71] There must have been many other factors which conditioned the revolt, unascertained and unascertainable but easily surmised. The dichotomy between domestics and field hands might have been a consideration, but this belongs to the realm of conjecture. Another complication in attempting to postulate a dichotomy between the roles of the house and field negroes in slave revolts is the contribution of Free Negroes, some of whom, like Denmark Vesey, led slave revolts. In sum, it is probably not entirely correct to assert that the domestic slaves were at all times the betrayers and the field hands at all times the fighters, but the evidence tends to point in this direction because of other elements inherent in the practice of 'divide and rule' so entrenched in the strategy of the slavocracy. We find the point raised again by the late Afro-American scholar, E. E. Franklin Frazier, who in discussing the 1822 revolt of Denmark Vesey wrote:

> The faithful house servants were often bound, as we have seen. One of the heroic figures in the Vesey conspiracy recognised this fact

when he informed his lieutenant: 'But take care and don't mention it [the plot] to those waiting men who receive presents of old coats etc. from their masters, or they'll betray us'.[72]

In reinforcing the point making for the distinction between the domestic slave and the rest, Professor Franklin Frazier went on to indicate that in the Charleston conspiracy the leaders were often those having no loyalty and sentimental attachments to the masters, and their followers often porters, labourers, stevedores, dairymen, carters and slaves from the surrounding neigbourhood.[73]

An added difficulty in analysing the respective roles of domestic and field slaves arises when we consider that Christianity provided a motive force for some slave revolts, as in the case of Nat Turner, or that of Samuel Sharpe in Jamaica in 1831–2. A blend of African religious usages and Christian usages occurred in the revolt of Denmark Vesey, whose lieutenant, Gullah Jack, was reputed to be a 'sorcerer'. In the South American situation, and especially in Brazil, Islam was a dominant and unifying factor in slave revolts, in which the distinction between the role of domestic slaves and field slaves does not surface. We merely see Muslims rebelling in what essentially were religious crusades, and the crusaders made no distinction in their proselytising activities. Professor John Hope Franklin has drawn attention to risings led by scholars in Arabic and Islamic doctrine, whose crusades were directed against infidels as well as against the slave system.[74]

Dr Orlando Patterson quotes J. Stephens as indicating that

> It has been the common lot of agricultural slaves to endure more labour than other bondsmen; it has, on the other hand, been their privilege, not only to be less exposed than domestics to the personal caprice and ill-temper of a master, but to have a far greater stability of situation, and a surer possession of their families and of the property they have been permitted to acquire.[75]

Yet it was also the experience of the field hands to be exposed to the choleric tempers of managers, overseers, book-keepers and others, and to have the stability of their family lives interfered with, as recounted by J. B. Moreton, himself an ex-West Indian overseer.[76] It is difficult to argue that the lot of one was better than the other, though there might have been cases where the burden was unduly borne by the field hands and boiling hands, who sometimes worked such long hours that they lost concentration and strength and fell into the boiling copper. Lady Nugent observed the overwork of the boiling hands, writing in her *Journal*:

> I asked the overseer how often his people were relieved. He said

every twelve hours; but how dreadful to think their standing twelve hours over a boiling cauldron, and doing the same thing; and he owned to me that sometimes they did fall asleep, and get their poor fingers into the mill; and he showed me a hatchet, that was always ready to sever the whole limb, as the only means to saving the poor sufferer's life! I would not have a sugar estate for the world![77]

In the divisions between domestics and field hands, as Patterson admits (and this could be generalised for many slave theatres), the colour factor was present. Patterson wrote that it was unusual for any household slaves to be pure black,[78] and went on to stress that field hands hardly ever aspired to be domestic servants[79] if they were black, rather choosing to become tradesmen.[80] He continues:

One important aspect of these divisions among the slaves was the correlation of colour and status. We have already pointed out that most of the house servants were coloured slaves and that among them the darker paid deference to the light shaded . . . . Colour then – and this point cannot be over-stressed – was only of psychological significance to the coloured group and while it operated objectively to the Negroes' disadvantage, it, nonetheless, tended to remain subjectively meaningless to them . . . . High or low status among them was merely a reflection of the attitudes and estimation of the master.[81]

When therefore it came to revolt it was the element of severity that inflamed the slaves against the slave system, as was shown in a number of slave revolts, such as that of 1831–2 in Jamaica and elsewhere.[82]

Yet if we look superficially into one of the Latin American slave theatres, that of Brazil, we find distinctions between urban slaves, slaves who worked in the mines, and the vast majority of field workers constituting some five-sixths of the whole, who, according to Professor Franklin, 'fared worst'. But we learn that the lot of the urban slaves, who mostly worked as servants in the town homes of the planters, or in shops at the docks, was not too difficult compared to the circumstances of the field hands. Professor Franklin observed the situation thus:

There was a tendency for the urban owner to maintain too large a staff of personal servants, a practice which led one mistress to assert that she had nine lazy servants for whom there was not enough employment.[83]

The way owners overcame the problems of having too many servants was to hire them out as 'freelancers' or negros de ganho. The field hands, by contrast, worked from 'sunrise to sunset'. They were supervised by white stewards, 'whipped, threatened, intimidated and tortured', and laws introduced for their protection were often ineffective.[84] These examples only serve to stress the differences between domestics and field slaves, but the subject needs more detailed study. At this point we shall turn to consider the role of the Maroons in slave societies.

The Maroons

The term 'Maroon' is used here to embrace not only the celebrated Maroons of Jamaica but also to denote similar communities in the United States and Latin America. Significantly the word itself derives from the Spanish, even though the prominence of the Jamaican Maroons only came to light following the British capture of Jamaica from the Spanish in 1655. Edward Long in the eighteenth century described them as 'Wild Negroes',[85] but this definition is scarcely helpful. The *Shorter Oxford English Dictionary* suggests that the term derives from the Spanish *cimarron*, meaning wild and untamed, and that it related to 'one of a class of fugitive slaves living in the mountains and forests of Dutch Guiana and the West Indies'.[86] The point implicit in the concept of Maroon is that the person or persons concerned lived in isolation from other communities. Some were fugitives from slavery, others were fugitives from enslavement. By this token we realise that there were many Maroon communities in the New World during the slave era. In Jamaica they were known as Maroons, Hog Hunters or Negroes of the Mountains; in Dutch Guiana they were called 'Bush Negroes'; in Brazil they constituted themselves into the *quilombos*, the greatest being that of the 'Famous Negroes of the Palm Forests or Palmares or Alagoas'; and in Florida they were known as the Seminole Indians. There were in fact Maroon communities too numerous to mention. We cannot discuss these major communities in terms either of origin or organisation, but we should observe the role they played in resistance to slavery. In Cuba *Cimarrone* communities formed villages known as *palanques*. The island of St Vincent had its own peculiar feature of the 'Black Caribs'. These communities were, with the exception of the Seminole and Black Carib communities, formed by rebellious slaves who ran away from slave estates to create independent communities of their own.

The Cimarrones

Running away began early in the slave experience in the New World, and by the seventeenth century a number of Maroon communities had come into existence, constituting a thorn in the flesh of the communities of slave holders. A historian of colonial Peru has written:

> Of all the crimes committed by the black slave population of Peru, few were more serious and none more widespread than flight from the master's service. The master lost a sizeable investment when a runaway black made good his escape; and recapturing a runaway often involved considerable trouble and expense. Further, runaway slaves, called *Cimarrones* by the Spanish, tended to band together for companionship, greater security in the countryside, and many such bands became a menace to agricultural pursuits and to trade and communication along the highways.[87]

But unlike in Cuba, Panama, the West Indies and Brazil, the development of huge *Cimarrone* communities in Peru was inhibited by certain factors, one of them being the absence of lush tropical vegetation. Their concentration in urban centres was also a discouragement, and their conspicuousness among Indian communities remained a serious drawback too. But in spite of these impediments they were not deterred from taking the risk of running away, thereby becoming a matter for serious official attention. As Bowser observed:

> *Cimarrones* were a source of concern almost from the very beginnings of Spanish Peru. As early as 1544 runaway blacks were 'assaulting and killing' men and robbing farms on the outskirts of Lima and Trujillo.[88]

This encouraged the Governor of Lima, Gonzalo Pizarro, to proceed in 1545 against a community of 200 *Cimarrones* who were well entrenched and organised in a settlement a few miles from the coast. These blacks had accumulated large quantities of Spanish weapons and ammunition, and rumour had it that they had a 'king' and were determined to overthrow the Spanish and assume the government of the Indians.[89] Since their settlement was inaccessible, the *Cimarrones'* Spanish assailants had to dismount to confront them in hand-to-hand combat, and in the encounter the Spanish lost some of their men, including important dignitaries. This for a while minimised the dangers from *Cimarrones* on any large scale, but their activities were not eliminated for small encounters were not unknown in places of sparse settlement.[90] As in other theatres of Maroon activity the *Cimarrones* continued to augment their numbers by natural increase as well as by the arrival of escaped slaves. Escape from slavery remained an endless problem for the Spanish, as it was for other slave societies. In Peru, as elsewhere, stringent measures were instituted for dealing with those likely to harbour slaves, such as free persons of colour, and apart from 'bounties' there were also penalties for harbouring escapees. To these were added the use of the *Santa Hermandad*, or constabulary, created for the express purpose of controlling the slave population in the rural areas and arresting runaway slaves. The force's inefficiency, corruption and bickering limited its effectiveness, however.

The control of the Peruvian Maroons consisted of a combination of efforts, both voluntary and official, through bounties paid by slave owners, by the imposition of laws, and by the use of slaves and free persons of colour employed because of their knowledge of the countryside and their linguistic abilities.[91] Part of the government's failure to control the *Cimarrones* was the result of a 'tendency toward overbureaucratisation compounded by maladministration'.[92] As the slave population grew the problems of the government were compounded. As in other theatres, these *Cimarrones* committed outrages and depredations on others, among whom the Indians were particular sufferers.

In his comparative study of slavery in Virginia and Cuba, Herbert Klein draws our attention to the fact that one of the earliest problems to plague the settlers was the '*Ladino-bozales* problem', the fusion between escaped Africans and the Indians to whom they escaped. As early as 1526 it was observed that many slaves were escaping inside Hispaniola and the other islands and forming turbulent *Cimarrone* communities sheltered by mountain fastnesses.[93] As in other places then and later, the *Cimarrones* not only appeared as a threat to the settler communities but the assistance they gave the enemies of Spain,[94] such as buccaneers, pirates and 'freebooters' who roamed the Caribbean, demonstrated how dangerous they were. The problem lasted until the demise of slavery, despite various attempts by European settlers to eliminate, control or disorganise *Cimarrone* communities.

The Spanish *Cimarrones* established village communities, known as *palanques*, and lived by cultivation and hunting, even though earlier on, as in most of the Maroon theatres of operation, they had lived by raiding the local communities and plantations. They barricaded themselves within inaccessible regions surrounded by swamps or by thick vegetation or walled by mountains. In order to avoid being tampered with they often moved inland, providing havens for fugitive slaves, especially *bozales*. Legislation which began during the first half of the sixteenth century, as in Jamaica, proved ineffectual. One of the stipulations debarred negroes from entering cities or villages at night. The authorities identified *Cimarrones* as 'makers of mutinies, seditions and rebellions, highway robberies and other thieveries'.[95] The Cuban authorities in the 1530s instituted the voluntary constabulary, the *Santa Hermandad*, to

275

curb them and recapture fugitive black slaves. As this was inadequate, a class of professional slave catchers known as *rancheadores* was formed; the methods they used were so brutal that in 1540 Crown intervention became necessary to debar them from castrating captured fugitive negroes, and they were also ordered to refrain from molesting free persons of colour.[96] But the preoccupation with subduing the *Cimarrones* lasted throughout the slaving centuries in spite of the use of experienced military fighters against them. Even though penalties were imposed on runaways if captured, slaves continued to escape to join and form Maroon communities. Initially, in Cuba, escape for four days earned fifty-five lashes, for more than eight days one hundred lashes, and after six months, if escapees were captured among the ranks of *Cimarrones*, they were hanged.[97]

In spite of extremely harsh measures against Free Negroes abetting the *Cimarrones*, which included the death penalty, the communities nonetheless survived. They were also found in Jamaica, Guadeloupe, Martinique, Cuba, Panama, Mexico (along the coastal belt), Puerto Rico, Dominica, St Vincent and even Brazil. Unlike their counterparts in the temperate parts of America like Virginia (where the climate conspired against the permanent formation of Maroon communities), the *Cimarrones* generally occupied more tropical regions which aided them in their confrontations with the slavocracy of the Americas.[98] *Cimarrone* villages sprang up, as well as much smaller settlements consisting perhaps of only a couple of huts. We learn that in the Cuban situation masters later tried to make concessions for the voluntary surrender of slaves and allowed legal loopholes to exist for slaves to return. But few runaways returned for, as Klein states, 'slaves who took the expedient of running away were those who refused to adjust themselves to the plantation system'.[99]

The Black Caribs

While it would appear that the Arawaks generally accommodated to European colonisation, the Carib Indians remained turbulent for a considerable period, killing Englishmen who landed both in St Lucia and Grenada and harassing settlements in Guadeloupe and Martinique. The most turbulent Caribs, who feature so much in English records, were those of St Vincent. They have sometimes been referred to as the 'Black Caribs', for many were an admixture of Carib Indians and African escapee slaves, who continued to increase their ranks and fuse with them. Their resistance was so persistent that even at the time of the outbreak of the Seven Years War in 1756 the so-called 'Neutral Islands', consisting of St Lucia, St Vincent, Dominica and Tobago, although having both English and French settlers, were still in the control of the Caribs. At the start of the war the French occupied the islands but were subsequently dislodged by the British, and in the final settlement of the war in 1763 British tenure was recognised by the Treaty of Paris.[100] Yet, for over nine years after the signing of the treaty the Caribs of St Vincent remained unreconciled to their coming under British jurisdiction. A letter written by Governor William Young from St Vincent in July 1772 to the Earl of Hillsborough, the Secretary of State for the Colonies, emphasises the difficulties with the Black Caribs.[101] The Governor, after paying a courtesy call on the French General and Commander-in-Chief at Martinique to discuss French attitudes towards reducing the Black Caribs to obedience, wrote:

> I am persuaded of his sincerity [Count de Nosiere] and candour on the subject of our discourse, yet whenever a war may happen between the two Nations [England and France], it cannot be doubted but that the Caribs, who have a strong and natural attachment to the French, will be ready to unite and cooperate with them, were they to remain in the present temper and uncontroul'd situation. This will not appear strange, when we reflect that they have been long connected by trade and interest with the neighbouring French islands, and regard the English settlers here as bold intruders. All the better sort of them speak French, and are Catholics; the lower class of our people (unaccustom'd to sacrifice to the graces) do not treat the Charibs with the same gentleness and attention they are usually accustomed with by our politer neighbours and the claims of the British Crown to the sovereignty and Domain of the island, never openly asserted by the French king add to the completion of their jealousy and distrust of us. For these reasons they never can be ours by inclination: Fear and apprehension only can controul them: This is a heavy calamity to a young colony, and I conceive must afford by an unpleasing speculation to the Crown: To be compelled by force of arms to reduce or perhaps to extirpate a small handful of Men, the last who bear the name of Charibs and who dare assert their Rights and Freedom among islands ourselves call Charibbean, or on the otherhand to trespass against sound policy, and leave in a little spot, along with savages, our own subjects neglected, and exposed to their jealousy and revenge, whenever fit occasion shall present itself, are shocking alternatives.[102]

In the letter Governor Young goes on to intimate that there were some among the settlers who were convinced that nothing less than total removal of the Caribs from the island would leave the colony safe.

The Governor hoped that mere threat rather than the use of force might persuade the Caribs to yield their position, but their resis-

tance was persistent as the Governor himself observed when he
wrote:

> But I am sorry to inform your Lordship that notwithstanding this,
> and that much pains have been taken to persuade the Charibs, the
> critical moment of their fate is at hand, and that everything depends
> on their obedience, and submission to an excellent King and Father,
> they have not hitherto discovered the heart of gratitude or sensibility
> of His goodness; On the contrary, they esteem the pretentions of
> the Crown, and unwarranted usurpation of their Rights, not to be
> justified but by Superior Power, and they say they are resolved to
> dispute them by force of arms.[103]

The Governor still hoped that when troops from North America
arrived and the Caribs saw 'the regular forces as assembled against
them and in motion, they will be led to think differently of their
condition; or perhaps they may at first hazard a small opposition,
by which they will be convinced that the King's Troops are really
empowered to act, and so feel the wisdom and necessity of submission'. But he hoped that they would not persist in their perverse
obstinacy for this would lead to their own destruction 'which
mercy would forbid', and yet in the meantime the colony would be
thrown into confusion and the task of their 'final reduction, and
removal, not so easily effected as some have imagined'.[104]

The Governor then outlined some of the dangers which might
inhibit progress, for with the rainy season approaching the climate
would be favourable to the Caribs and against the British, and he
stated that 'Soldiers newly arrived, and engaged against such
enemies, must fall if the business is protracted; and in a cause where
no honour can be gained, every loss is the more to be regretted'. He
was still hopeful of persuading the Caribs but added that,

> In the meanwhile it is natural for them to put the best face on things
> they can, and to wish to intimidate, and discourage all attempts of
> reducing them to dependency. But when they are really convinced
> this is not a private undertaking, and actually see a power against
> them they despair successfully to oppose, I am much mistaken if
> they do not assume the wiser part. Many of their Chiefs are very
> sagacious and sensible, and the interruption they have hitherto given
> to the King's Sovereignty ought not to be attributed to their
> ignorance, but their dissatisfaction to comply with any proposition
> which may subject them to Government, and produce a change in
> manners. They had long flattered themselves no regular force would
> be exerted against them, and that a war would soon arrive, which
> might prove successful to France, and drive us from the country,
> before their own subjection could be effected, but this hope may in a

few weeks prove delusion, and their conduct be changed with the principle that influenced it.[105]

In another part of the letter Sir William Young wrote:

> At present we have no communication or intercourse together, and alth' alarmed, and suspicious of approaching danger. They keep at a distance and seem indifferent of parly. We remain on our settlements, carrying on the business of our plantations as usual, without extraordinary apprehension of danger or incursion; not from their love, but because we think them too wise to commence hostilitys, at a time we are prepared under such circumstances, would be to curt their own ruin. The cause of defence would be best supported by argument, and plead for them some forgiveness: Besides if they really mean (what I do not believe) an obstinate perserverance, their best defence will be in delay, and the shelter of their woods and mountains. Their numbers are very differently represented and not easy to guess at, as we are not permitted to have access to the Quarters they inhabit.[106]

These extended but interesting citations show just how tenacious the resistance of the Caribs was.[107]

The Jamaican Maroons

Without going into detail about the origins of the Jamaican Maroons, it is clear they had come into being under Spanish rule. At the time the English, effecting Cromwell's Western Design, dislodged Spain from Jamaica in 1655, there were about 1500 enslaved Africans, most of whom on the surrender of their masters retreated to the mountains from where they made frequent excursions to harass the English conquerors. Their activities, unlike those of their counterparts elsewhere in the Americas, involved depredations and killings and terror, and although one group of them surrendered to the British under their leader Juan de Bolas, who was later to become a Colonel of the Black Regiment, the vast majority of the slaves refused to surrender. When Juan de Bolas was then sent by the English to reduce the Maroons to submission they ambushed him and cut him to pieces. Forces sent against them under Captain Colbeck in March 1664 were no more successful. According to Bryan Edwards, 'They continued to distress the island for upwards of forty years, during which time forty-four acts of Assembly were passed, and at least £240 000 expended for their suppression'.[108]

Both the Jamaican historians, Edwards and Long, give their versions of the Maroon–British confrontations, and a version of the conflict was also given by Dallas.[109] But this study is not concerned with the whole of British–Maroon relations and the various causes of conflicts, except to portray the role of the Maroons in slave resistance. We are informed that they were African slaves who had not assimilated to the plantation system and that there were many Coromantins in their rank and file.[110] Like other Maroons they disturbed the slave settlements and plantations, taking every opportunity to destroy its peace by setting fire to canefields and outhouses, killing cattle and carrying away slaves. Although Bryan Edwards insisted on calling their actions 'dastardly',[111] within the context of guerrilla warfare their activities were legitimate and the Maroons simply repaid in kind the surprise attacks which the British levied against them. Their familiarity with the terrain of the country was a valuable asset, enabling them to evade capture and making it possible for them to divert their attacks to other sections of the country, robbing and killing their 'enemies'. They presented so formidable an opposition that some plantations had to be abandoned.[112] Two Maroon wars were fought, the first between 1725 and 1740 (which has been regarded as one of the three major slave revolts and the most serious on the island),[113] and the second in 1795–6. At the conclusion of the first series of British–Maroon confrontations a treaty was concluded assigning them some portions of Jamaica, but the treaties between the Maroons of Trelawney and those of Accompong and other subordinate Maroons included a number of clauses that were to become sources of conflict in the future. The Articles of Pacification signed on 1 March 1738 consisted of:

> Article 7: They were to assist in repelling foreign invasion. Article 9: They were to assist with the return of runaway 'negro' slaves to their owners, were to receive a premium of thirty shillings for each fugitive slave returned to his owners by them, besides expenses.[114]

The result of the second stipulation was that the Maroon communities in Jamaica, which hitherto had been a haven for fugitive slaves, were pressed into action on behalf of the slavocracy with a view to serving the ends of the slave system. Accordingly, the Maroons were very active as slave catchers during numerous slave revolts. Before their pacification the British had employed the Mosquito Indians to achieve the end of reducing the Maroons to submission. One revolt in which the Maroons played a leading part in suppressing was that of 1760[115] (regarded as another of the major Jamaican slave revolts). Commendations for their contribution to the defeat of the rebels were given by the Jamaican Assembly.[116] Yet, ironically enough, Maroon inspiration had been an important factor in inspiring the revolt in the first place, as Long suggests.[117]

History contains such parallels, and one is reminded of the effect which Martin Luther's pronouncements had on the European peasantry, but how when they were inspired he took fright at the formidable nature of their strength and urged their suppression.[118]

The Jamaican Maroons therefore played the role of slave catchers and suppressors of slaves, unlike Maroons in other theatres. Yet there were indications that Maroons sometimes discharged their duties in a half-hearted way. Bryan Edwards tells of an incident in which Maroons were sent to catch a party of fugitive slaves, but instead of pursuing them they plucked the ears from the bodies of some dead slaves and returned with the ears to inform the slavo-cracy that they had killed the slaves, providing the ears as testi-mony.[119] Long also draws attention to initial Maroon reluctance during the rebellion of 1760, claiming they had not been paid their commission for previous services rendered.[120] This being done, the Maroon performance was far from satisfactory. While Long asserts that the Maroons adhered to the letter of the treaty,[121] Dallas maintains that the provisions were never adhered to and[122] that this resulted in the second Maroon War (1795–6), in which one section of the Maroon community was defeated and removed from the island to Nova Scotia. A factor in their defeat was their disunity, but as Dallas wrote:

> Some may be inclined to think a Maroon insurrection a petty
> warfare of unskilled negroes: but I believe the officers who served in
> this campaign will allow that the events of it, and the tactics
> opposed to them, if not so grand as those that fill the Grecian and
> Roman pages of history were at least as singular and embarrassing as
> any that were presented to the mind by the enormous armies that,
> about the same time, extended from one end of Europe to the other.
> A small body of negroes defied the choicest troops of one of the
> greatest nations in the world, kept an extensive country in alarm,
> and were at length brought to surrender, only by means of a
> subvention still more extraordinary than their own mode of
> warfare.[123]

The Maroons of Suriname

We cannot discuss the resistance of the so-called 'Bush Negroes' of Suriname or Dutch Guyana in detail, but as the most tenacious of Maroon communities in the Americas those of Suriname merit some discussion. The phenomenon of *marronage* began with the inception of the colony, first founded by Lord Francis Willoughby of Parham in 1650. Later it became Dutch. By this time *marronage* had become such a menace as to threaten the very survival of the Surinamese settlement and it became necessary in the late eighteenth century to despatch troops to the colony from the Netherlands to attempt to eradicate them. The activities of Dutch troops was the subject of a book by Captain Stedman,[124] from which we can glean a good deal of information about Maroon activities. Like most of the other colonies the various Maroon communities which emerged in Suriname augmented their numerical strength both by natural increase and by receiving fugitives from the plantations. Furthermore, whenever they made incursions into plantations of the colonies they captured people whom they took to enlarge their community, and there were many occasions when slaves on the plantations offered them no resistance. The Surinamese Maroon phenomenon survived beyond the post-abolition period and still survives into our day. Such major communities as are distinguishable today were also known in the eighteenth century and include the Djukas (otherwise known as the Aucanners or Aucans, dwelling on the upper Marowyne river; the Saramaccas (or Saramaccaners, living on the banks of the Suriname river); the Matuari (dwelling along the Saramaccan river); and, a later discovery, the Boni, or Bonny, Maroons (who might have been the result of a combination of three or more Maroon communities, and who for a time occupied the Cottica and later Lawa rivers and, at the time of their tutelage under the Djukas, lived on the lower Marowyne river). These were by no means all the Maroon communities but they fell within the province of what one writer has described as *grand marronage*.[125]

The Maroons' survival also bears testimony to their strength, and attempts to assimilate them into modern Surinamese society have not been completely successful. They have continued to organise themselves according to what they have tried to preserve of their ancestral pattern of organisation, and this in spite of the presence of a government agent dwelling among them, the *Postholder*. While they have developed an appetite for some European goods, and have even welcomed the establishment of schools among them, they have jealously guarded against any wholesale attempt to assimilate them into the wider society, and against being absorbed into the labour market as a source of cheap labour.[126] Although there are now town Maroons in Paramaribo, who mingle with the local people, the bulk of the communities are only accessible after hazardous journeys along rivers full of rapids. Their survival reveals the unbeatable spirit of African resistance to the system of slavery in an earlier age.

Observing the nagging problem the Maroons presented to the plantation settlements in the late eighteenth century, and the abortive forages made by armed soldiers from the colony in pursuit of them, Stedman wrote: 'These frequent miscarriages evince how difficult it is for European troops to carry on a war in the forests of South America.'[127] But wherever contact was made and some members of the Maroon community were captured, European vindictiveness matched Maroon vengeance for brutality, and led Stedman to suggest that 'every spark of feeling and humanity was extinct'.[128] Between 1760 and 1767 the Dutch were forced to sue for peace with three of the major Maroon communities.[129] The treaty itself, modelled on the Jamaican Maroon treaty of 1739, did not at once dispose of the problem of *marronage* or the periodic conflicts which arose between the settlers and Maroons. But the Surinamese Maroons, like *grand* Maroons elsewhere in the Americas, often quartered themselves in inaccessible parts of the territory surrounded by thick forest growths and marshes or behind river rapids. Occasional difficulties still arose because the European signatories to the treaty were not forthright in adhering to their spirit. But the treaty only came after an abortive attempt to build a cordon round the Maroons in order to cut them off from the settlements, but they continued their depredations on the plantations, often reaping a rich harvest in terms of provisions, arms and ammunition, and personnel, including women. Attempts by the colonies to put the Amerindians against them failed. The terms of the treaty included not only the undertaking to return fugitive slaves and to prevent the fostering of new Maroon communities, but they were also not to engage in any combination whatsoever; in fact, this last element entrenched one operational principle in the plantations of the Americas, the principle of 'divide and rule' or 'divide and control'. It almost proved fatal to the Maroons. Thus we see that the settlement adopted convenient temporary expedients till they could gain an additional supply of troops from the metropolis. Yet the Surinamese Maroons were in no way deceived.

One of the Maroon groups which the Surinamese colonists refused to recognise and bring into a treaty arrangement until late in the century was the Boni under their leaders Boni, Baron and Joli Coeur. Boni, the most prominent and tenacious leader, proved elusive to his assailants and for a spell between 1776 and 1788 he and his followers took refuge in Cayenne. But, confronted by both the French and the Dutch on both sides of the border, he retreated into Suriname along the lower Marowyne and he and his followers resumed their attack on the plantations between 1788 and 1793. Their tactics of waging a guerrilla war unfamiliar to the hordes of troops imported from Europe proved very successful. The colonists were not often appreciative of the exertions of the troops sent to pursue the Maroons. The military campaigns waged against the Boni up to 1778 brought the colony to the verge of financial ruin. The colonists' policy of divide and rule paid dividends, however, when in October 1777 the Djuka Maroons attacked the Boni, taking with them a number of prisoners, some of whom they killed. But soon afterwards the Djuka and Boni reached some kind of accord which especially alarmed the colonists since such an agreement was contrary to the treaty which they had concluded with the Djukas in 1760. The Boni refrained from attacking the plantations only until 1788. Boni continued to elude his European assailants, but the colonists' persistence in trying to play off the Boni against the Djuka was again rewarded when in February 1793 a party of seventy Djuka in a surprise but retaliatory attack on Boni himself killed him. Boni's son, Agossu, escaped first into Cayenne and later into Brazil. Subsequent treaties with the Djukas in 1791 and 1809 put the Boni Maroons under Djuka tutelage, and they continued uneasily under this arrangement until 1860.[130] But efforts to destroy Maroon communities or prevent their growth proved abortive.[131]

The Seminoles

The term 'Seminole' (an Indian word meaning runaway)[132] was initially used for both Indians and fugitive African slaves, but in time its use became limited to Indians. Accordingly, in order to distinguish runaway Seminole Indians from fugitive negroes the latter came to be called 'Exiles of Florida'. But both groups lived in close proximity, interacted and even intermarried, and their interests became united to the extent that they fought several times as a united group against the onslaughts made upon them by the states of the South such as Georgia, South Carolina and Tennessee, and against troops of the United States of America. Having fled into the Spanish territory of Florida they became free citizens, but the attempts by slave hunters and slave owners in the United States to re-enslave them and to force their descendants into slavery led to two major Seminole wars. These resulted in much bloodshed and carnage, and in the end, after one hundred and fifty years resisting subjugation, the remaining Seminole groups retreated into Mexico.

The Seminole fugitives rapidly grew in number during the period in which Florida was held by Spain, and in 1736 they were even formed into companies for the defence of the territory.[133] The exiles continued to enjoy their liberty until the time of the American Revolution. When the U.S.A. acquired Florida from the Spanish in 1819 arrangements were put in train with a view to enslaving the exiles as well as their descendants. The exact numbers of 'negro' fugitives is not easily ascertainable, but in 1836 it was estimated that there were probably about 1400 negroes dwelling among the Seminole Indians, of whom about two hundred were 'slaves'. Dr Kenneth Porter maintained that 'Not only were the Seminole slaves not slaves in the usual sense of the word; they might even lay claim to being the true rulers of the nation'.[134] Some of them had been purchased from the Spaniards, others had previously belonged to the English, and therefore they had 'a better knowledge of the white man and his custom than did their masters, and were indispensable as go-betweens and interpreters whenever an occasion arose for negotiations between their old master and their new'.[135] That both the first and second Seminole wars were not just wars against Indians alone is attested in the records as well as in the statements of certain American generals who were involved in them. In reference to the first Seminole War, General Andrew Jackson referred to the conflict as 'this savage and Negro war'.[136] The Seminole Wars took the form of slave hunts as well as punitive encounters, for as Porter observed, 'It seems clear that the wars were almost entirely due to the position held by Negroes among the Seminoles, and that the invasion of Florida was almost as much a slave-hunting as it was a punitive expedition.'[137] Although the confrontations resulted in much bloodshed, the negroes as well as the Indians fought with determination not to be enslaved, retreating to the swamps to which the United States' troops could not follow. Although the U.S.A. could not correctly estimate the number of negroes among the Seminoles, their agent in Florida in 1821 observed of them:

> They fear being again made slaves, under the American government and will omit nothing to increase or keep alive mistrust among the Indians, whom they in fact govern. If it should become necessary to use force with them, it is to be feared the Indians would take their part. It will, however, be necessary to remove from the Floridas this group of lawless freebooters, among whom runaway negroes will always find refuge. It would, perhaps, be possible to have them received at St Domingo, or furnish them with the means of withdrawing from the United States.[138]

The above quotation testifies to the tenacity of the ex-slaves and their descendants as well as revealing the despair of their opponents. In spite of the strictures against these people, they were not just 'freebooters' but sensible people who highly prized the freedom they enjoyed and who did not see the wisdom of succumbing to enslavement to meet the labour demands of their assailants.

Nevertheless, in spite of the various agreements attempted between the United States government and the Seminoles, the preoccupation of the government was with fugitive slaves entering the territory and it was clear that the United States and the slavocracy had no intention of abiding by the terms of any peace.[139] The Seminole Wars turned out to be much more formidable than the United States at first thought. In the second Seminole War the reverses suffered by the United States were colossal and the resistance of the Seminoles showed not the profligacy of 'savage freebooters' but rather the spirit of men so imbued with the sense of their worth and their freedom that they were prepared to sell their lives dearly for it. Among the outstanding Seminole negroes were Louis Pacheo, who spoke English, Spanish, French and the Indian language, all with great facility; he was an indispensable person to the Seminoles, and on one occasion led Major Dade into an ambush in which the Americans' rank and file were depleted.[140] 'Negro Abraham' made a deep impression on whites, who described him as 'one of the most remarkable men that his race had produced in North America up to that time'.[141] Other leaders included John Caesar and Inos, who both fought bravely in the second Seminole War for the defence of their community. During the second war General Jessup rightly concluded that, 'This, you may be assured, is a negro, not an Indian war; and if it be not speedily put down, the South will feel the effects of it on their slave population before the end of the next season'.[142] This comment was made in spite of the presence of an Indian leadership too, including Powell, alias Osceola, Micanopy, Philip and Cooper. In fact, Osceola and his followers were surprised in 1837 and destroyed with the exception of three, the chief escaping. The defeat resulted in the capture of some negro prisoners, among whom were women and children, and led to the treaty of Fort Dade in 1837 which provided for the removal of Seminoles and negroes.

At the time General Jessup was deeply anxious to ensure that the so-called peace did not collapse:

> The Negroes rule the Indians and it is important that they should feel themselves secure; if they should become alarmed and hold out, the war will be renewed.[143]

The slave hunters, seeing the capitulation of Fort Dade, thought it would give them the opportunity to practise their pursuit, but it merely hardened the Seminole Indians and negroes in their resistance, and rather than succumb they fought to the death, and even after the capture of Osceola, Cooacooches and 'Wild Cat' escaped and continued the war. But General Jessup's attempt to make the negroes desert the Seminole Indians did not influence the majority of them to abandon their freedom; instead they preferred freedom to empty promises. An important point to remember is that many of the Seminole resistance fighters were of the younger generation and had never known slavery. A few negroes nonetheless guided the invading troops, and as in other theatres of slavery there was always a willing negro to betray the rest. The names of the collaborators were Morris, Sampson, Sandy, Gopher John, Ben

Wiggins and Jim Boy, the last a Creek chief of negro blood who allied seven hundred of his warriors to the government forces.

The cost to the United States was tremendous, the expenditure being estimated at $32 million, involving the lives of six hundred soldiers and twenty-eight to thirty officers. Although the war is regarded as 'the most serious Indian war in the history of the United States', Kenneth Porter suggests that 'it should rather be described as a Negro insurrection with Indian support'.[144] Having failed to dislodge the Seminoles from Florida, the U.S. finally concluded some form of peace with the remaining Seminoles and, although they were persuaded to leave Florida and settle in Indian territory among the Creeks, they did not overcome their suspicion of the Creek Indians. The Fugitive Slave Law of 1850 made their position insecure and untenable and started them on another move, and making their way through Texas they entered Mexico as free people. Their subsequent history does not belong to this work.

The Republic of Palmares

The discussion of Maroon communities in slave theatres would not be complete without some mention of the 'Famous Republic of Palmares'. From the earliest days of their colonisation of Brazil the Portuguese and their Dutch rivals experienced the escape of slaves from the plantations to form village communities or *quilombos*. Dr Irene Diggs, while admitting that the most famous of the *quilombos* was that of 'Os Palmares', informs us that 'the *quilombo* of Os Palmares... for a time constituted an independent state of black men (and women) similar to those which existed at the time in Africa'.[145] The implication in the statement is that the fugitive slaves formed communities along lines familiar to them in their original homeland in Africa. The Republic[146] lasted from about 1630 to 1697. The early *quilombos* in Brazil were formations of fugitive African slaves who had been arriving in Brazil from the 1530s. It was estimated that the number entering Pernambuco in 1630 amounted to 4000 annually.[147] The exact date of the origin of the *quilombos* remains shrouded in mystery, but at the time of the Dutch advent in Brazil in 1630 African slaves had begun to organise themselves in such settlements. In that year there occurred a bold move by forty African slaves imported from Guinea, who fled from Porto Calvo to Os Palmares, about 30 leagues into the interior from Pernambuco. They not only barricaded themselves but began thereafter to harass the surrounding communities of Porto Calvo, Alagoas, Rio Grande, São Francisco and Serinhaem. Like other Maroons they chose inaccessible zones for their habitation protected by mountains and steep and precipitous slopes, but their name derived from the coconut-palm tree which grew in abundance around them, *palmera pindoba* – hence Palmares and Negroes of the Palm Forests. They became settled cultivators, like the Seminoles, and produced not only maize but fruits, and supplemented their food supply with domesticated animals, fishing and hunting. Some became traders in gold and skins, while others were artisans and blacksmiths who helped to forge the weapons which they used for their defence. We are assured that 'Neither medicine nor witchcraft were permitted'.

The people of Os Palmares organised a government with clearly defined rules of conduct, and punishments were prescribed for offences, such as the death penalty for murder, adultery, stealing or desertion.[148] Each of the towns, known as *mocambos*, was under the control of a potentate, and in times of crisis they all came together in the central *Casa del Consejo* (Council House) in Macaco. Accounts vary about the actual size of Palmares, whose population has been variously estimated at between five or six thousand and thirty thousand.[149] One important function of Os Palmares was that it was a refuge for fugitive slaves. Those who came of their own volition were given complete freedom, but those captured from the neighbouring plantations (*fazendas*) had to earn their freedom by bringing in other captives. Running away from Palmares was treated with great severity, and the Palmerenos (that is, the inhabitants of Palmares) not only harassed the outlying plantations by incendiarism and pillage but also made away with women (including white women)[150] and children to augment their population. The community organised its own intelligence service. Other *quilombos* of note were those of Sierra del Cubato, São Paulo, Leblon, Rio de Janeiro, Maranao and Mato Grosso.[151] The *quilombo* of Rio de Janeiro, which persistently disturbed the outlying plantations, was eventually destroyed in 1650, forty-seven years before the destruction of Palmares. Expeditions sent by both the Portuguese and the Dutch against Palmerenos were singularly unsuccessful. The Palmerenos' outstanding leader, Zumbi, fought valiantly and set his followers a brave example during the final assault on the settlement, becoming a legendary figure. Both the Dutch and Portuguese in their expeditions had negroes in their ranks, but Palmares endured until 1697 when the onslaught on it with the use of advanced technology and the cutting off of the food supply of the Palmerenos led to a fierce struggle for survival. Rather than succumb to slavery Zumbi and his followers fought to the death and committed mass suicide.[152] As Irene Diggs has observed, although Palmares was destroyed, 'There remains of their struggle and heroism a name, Zumbi of Os Palmares, sonorous as the *tambores* (drums) that in the night brought to those still in slavery the rebellious message of their free brothers of the *quilombo*.'[153] But the destruction of Palmares was not the end of slave rebellions in

Brazil, for many more occurred in the eighteenth and nineteenth centuries, such as the celebrated *Guerras Santas* of the nineteenth century led by Muslim Hausa slaves.[154]

Recapitulation

By way of summarising what has been noted so far about the conduct of the various Maroon communities, the first point to make is that they almost all shared in common the retention of much of their cultural heritage from Africa, and even the Seminoles and Black Caribs assimilated a good many African customs and values. Another feature of the communities was their cohesiveness and unity of purpose in action. They organised government either in a rudimentary way, like the Jamaican Maroons, or in a more sophisticated manner, like the Palmerenos. Their spirit of independence was revealed in their flight from the plantations in the first place and later by their continued resistance to enslavement. Initially most of the Maroon groups attacked the slave communities for sustenance and to increase their numbers with both males and females; but in time most of them became sedentary cultivators, while other members traded or became artisans. The Maroons of Jamaica were forced to agree by treaty to return fugitive slaves, but it is by no means clear that they always observed the stipulation. They also assisted the slavocracy to defeat slave revolts and in this were an exception among Maroon communities; by contrast other Maroons were prominent in resistance, if not actively then indirectly, their presence being an inducement to slave restlessness. The Maroons were hunted communities and were often brutally assailed, but though campaigns occasionally depleted their numbers they were never defeated except in Jamaica and Palmares. Indeed the heroes and heroines of Palmares never accepted defeat but fought on to the bitter end, losing their king, when he threw himself over a cliff, and subsequently committing mass suicide, like the people of Numantia before them. Rather than be captured alive, by their action they 'earned for Palmares the nomenclature "Negro Numantia"'. In the end, of course, the Maroons were often compelled to leave their territory; many of the Jamaican Maroons were deported to Nova Scotia, while the Seminoles retreated to Mexico rather than succumb. Under astute and brave leadership the Maroons made their own contribution to the resistance of slavery in the Americas.

Success or failure of resistance

At this point it is necessary to make a few pertinent remarks about the notion of success or failure of the slave revolts, a question that is in general need of reappraisal. In one sense most of the revolts failed, yet in another sense they succeeded. If we are to look for some of the reasons why, with the exception of the Haitian rebellion, they singularly failed, the following considerations come to mind. The technique of 'divide and rule', which has been discussed in the preceding pages, inhibited cohesion, and slaves therefore found their unity of action impaired by ephemeral considerations such as skin colour or the perceived advantages to be gained by not participating. In spite of the presence in plantations of determined slaves – individualists prepared to risk even their lives for freedom and who provided the motive force behind insurrections, and sometimes the leadership – the weaknesses of the slaves in slave societies rested, in the last analysis, on their lack of unity. Slaves who hesitated or held aloof from insurrections did so often from fear of the consequences in an environment dominated by draconian laws.[155] Among other considerations was the fear of transportation which was often applied to slaves who were not sentenced to death. This is ubiquitous in the records.[156] A notable place of slave transportation was Honduras, but at times they were sold to other countries and so slaves passed from one European slave-holding community to another, where they were known to continue to generate revolts. There was also the consideration that banishment took one away from a master whom one knew to another and probably much worse task-master, and the fear of leaving dear ones and friends for an unknown destiny acted as a further deterrent.

We have already mentioned the role of the proverbial domestics or 'faithful' house slaves, those who acted in hope of enhancing their status and respectability within the slave system or felt they were doing some good by saving their master. In the United States the fact that slaves were distributed over a wide expanse of land in small communities tended to inhibit communication, and if this did not act as a deterrent to revolt it made failure a certainty. Christianity acted as an opiate. Initially it was not permitted because of the fear that it might lead slaves to self-assertion and to question their status. In the Catholic communities it was decreed that it should be permitted but the planters were able to evade the regulations, and even the religious communities, with the exception of the Dominicans in Haiti and some Jesuits in Brazil, did not act assiduously in the discharge of their religious obligations. But once Christianity began to take root it tended to condition slaves into submissiveness. It sometimes worked. The Rev. Hope Waddell, a Scottish missionary to Jamaica, implied that the slave revolt of 1831–2 in Jamaica was not supported by certain of the slaves who had received the faith,[157] though it is equally true that some of the slaves who took part were Christians, Baptists in the main, and hence the revolt was sometimes referred to as the 'Baptist War'.

Yet, among leaders of slave insurrection, some used even their Christianity to guide them; the references to Nat Turner and Denmark Vesey are examples. But where slaves employed their own African religious usages, as in Haiti, or even in the Jamaican revolt of 1760, which was ostensibly led by Tackey, an Obeah priest,[158] some cohesion was found. Moreover, in the Denmark Vesey revolt there emerged a combination of Christianity and traditional African religion in that Vesey's lieutenant, Gullah Jack, was reputed to be a 'sorcerer'.[159] Also, African slaves who led revolts in Brazil, in what essentially were Muslim *jihads*, brought the religion from their African homeland. It seems that there was a much greater prospect for cohesion when slaves used their own religion and religious practices brought from Africa than when they embraced Christianity. Even the revolt of the Jamaican Maroons, so much celebrated, rested on the solidarity which their African heritage imparted.[160]

On another level the slave revolts succeeded. The general viewpoint on the slave rebellions is that they singularly failed. But that they did not overturn the system is not enough justification for suggesting failure. Not all revolts had the intention of overturning the system, as we are reminded by Marion D. de B. Kilson, even though by repeated assaults on it some slaves must have hoped that the system would collapse. The extent to which slave revolts helped to determine the final demise of slavery in all its theatres has yet to be determined, though W. E. B. DuBois asserted it very early, and undoubtedly revolts in one area tended to create restiveness among slaves in others – a notable example being the Haitian revolt, which preoccupied North and South America and the whole of the West Indies with the fear that events there might be repeated elsewhere. The spectre of Haiti especially haunted the West Indies and led Governor Eyre of Jamaica to persuade the island to abandon government by a constitutionally elected assembly for autocratic rule by the governor following the so-called 'Morant Bay rebellion' of 1865,[161] which took place more than a generation after the official ending of slavery by the British. The fact that this situation persisted until almost the end of the century bears testimony to the influence that slave revolts exercised on the minds of policy makers, on public opinion and on the home governments. Moreover, the activities of abolitionists in giving publicity to slave revolts – as, for instance, William Lloyd Garrison did in the case of the Nat Turner revolt of 1831 – is another example of the way resistance was used to try to bring an end to the slave system.

The extent to which recurrent revolts influenced official decision making needs to be demonstrated, but to dismiss insurrections as having no impact would be grossly misleading. In suggesting this we do not discount the other factors which aided ultimate emancipation, but it seems that the revolts also qualify to be placed beside the many other influences. From the aspect of passive resistance of slave revolts running away – we have observed that desertion contributed to the ruination of some planters, especially on the North American continent where the Underground Railroad became a major channel of escape from the citadel of slavery. In a theatre in which labour scarcity was the general cry, running away made the problem more acute than ever. Suicides, self-immolation and mutilation certainly deprived the owners and their adherents of working hands. This was sabotage and tended to frustrate owners' hopes and expectations. There were other subtle ways of resistance too, of which only two will be mentioned. One related to the way slaves gained the confidence of their owners who then trusted them to run errands.[162] With this trust firmly entrenched the slave took the first opportunity to escape; the lament of the master often appeared in advertisements which contained the sad comment that the slave had no reason to run away for he had been kindly treated. The records are replete with such statements and sentiments. The second type of resistance is mentioned by Orlando Patterson. Sometimes the slaves deliberately provoked a quarrel in which the master, attorney or overseer wasted many hours trying to make peace. The slave recognised this as a sort of sabotage, for valuable working time was lost in resolving such disputes.[163] The many expedients to which the slaves had recourse cannot be discussed in a work of this size. It is of itself deserving of another volume.

In this brief consideration of slave resistance during the centuries of slavery in the Americas we see that resistance, whether formal or informal, constituted a continuous battle of strategies between slave holders and slaves. Sometimes one got the upper hand of the other, and *vice versa*, but the fact that slavery proved tenacious was indicative of the fact that the slavocratic strategy dominated the relationship. That the slave system collapsed in the long run, resulting in emancipation, showed that the strategy, though evolved piecemeal and accompanied by draconian stipulations and regulations, was not foolproof. It is at this point that we need to examine the special case of St Domingue.

Notes

1 H. Aptheker, 'American Negro Slave Revolts', *Science and Society* (Summer 1937).

2 See, for example, Harriet Martineau, *Society in America*, 3 vols., New York, 1837, Vol. 2, pp. 330–1.

3 See F. A. Kemble, *Residence on a Georgian Plantation in 1838–1839*, London, 1863, p. 244.

4 M. J. Herskovits, *The Myth of the Negro Past*, New York and London, 1941, pp. 88ff.

5 Martineau, *Society in America*. She was criticised by Kemble for basing her assessment of North America on suspect and unbalanced evidence.

6 H. Aptheker, *Essays in the History of the American Negro*, New York, 1945 and 1964; see his reference to Ulrich B. Phillips, John D. Hicks and G. Randall as proponents of the myth of rare slave insurrections. Also U. B. Phillips, *American Negro Slavery: a Survey of the Supply, Employment and Control of Negro Labor as Determined by the Plantation Regime*, New York, 1918, for the expression of views of docility and submissiveness, what Basil Davidson in another context has referred to as the 'cheerful school' of African colonial history; see Basil Davidson, *The Africans: an Entry to Cultural History*, London, 1969, pp. 313–14 *et seq*. Phillips was in fact one of the pioneers of the idyllic and distortionist school of American slavery against which Aptheker contended, especially because Phillips tended to portray American slavery as humane and benevolent. But those who assail Aptheker do so because of his committed scholarship to which most scholars are prone according to their biases and ideological stances, but to which they seldom admit. See Aptheker, *Essays*, pp. 3–4, 7–8.

7 W. E. B. DuBois, *The World and Africa*, New York, 1947, p. 62, and *The Suppression of the African Slave Trade to the United States of America, 1638–1870*, New York 1896 (Schocken edn., 1969), p. 6.

8 George P. Rawick, *The American Slave – a Composite Autobiography: from Sundown to Sunup, the Making of the Black Community*, Westport, Conn., 1972, pp. 74–5, n. 3. Aptheker did refer to constant escapes by slaves from slave citadels, though Rawick seems to have over-dramatised the issue of confrontation. Aptheker aimed to show that actual confrontations occurred. Aptheker in *Essays*, p. 209, in which he provided a 'chronology of slave revolts' had written: 'Alleged revolts referred to in secondary works are not given here because the references were erroneous or doubtful. Censorship was rigid at that time and it is highly probable that some of the revolts were never reported. At times, too, slave disaffection was reported in such general terms that it is difficult to know whether concrete revolts were behind the generalities.'

9 *Ibid.*, p. 54.

10 H. Aptheker, *Nat Turner's Slave Rebellion*, New York, 1966, pp. 45–6.

11 Rawick, *The American Slave*, p. 55.

12 F. Douglass, *My Bondage and My Freedom*, New York, 1855, p. 263.

13 Douglass, *Narrative of the Life of Frederick Douglass, an American Slave, Written by Himself*, Boston, Mass., 1845, p. 99.

14 From autobiographies of ex-slaves could be gleaned numerous expressions of hope to achieve freedom by diverse means but principally by the expedients of resistance and running away. Planning for this was also evident. See Lunsford Lane, *Narrative of Lunsford Lane, Formerly of Raleigh, North Carolina*, Boston, Mass., 1842 and 1848, pp. 7–8; Austin Steward, *Twenty-two years a Slave and Forty Years a Freeman*, Rochester, N.Y., 1857 and 1859, pp. 76–8, 106–15; William Green, *Narrative of Events in the Life of William Green*, Springfield, Ohio, 1853, pp. 9–14; Elijah P. Mass, *Life and History*, Louisville, Ky, 1885, p. 11–16; Jacob Stroyer, *My Life in the South*, Salem, Mass., 1890, 4th edn., 1898, pp. 24–9; Louis Hughues, *Thirty Years a Slave*, Milwaukee, Wis., 1897, pp. 98–114; Josiah Henson, *The Life of Josiah Henson*, Boston, Mass., 1844, p. 25. We also know from slave narratives that there were slaves who spoke of

'rebelling and killing', while others felt an increasing desire to be insubordinate after being initiated into military training. See Steward, *Twenty-two Years a Slave*, pp. 77–8. Also *William Webb*, Detroit, Mich., 1873, p. 13.

15 See George Moses Horton, *Hope of Liberty (Poems)*, 1829, reprinted as *Poems of a Slave*, 1837.

16 See Chapter 4 above; also House of Commons Sessional Papers: Slave Trade, 1790, Vol. 72, 18th Century: Reports and Papers – Evidence of Alexander Falconbridge; also Falconbridge, *op. cit.*, p. 30.

17 Marion D. de B. Kilson, 'Towards Freedom: Analysis of Slave Revolts in the United States', *Phylon*, xxv, 2 (1964), p. 175.

18 Bryan Edwards, *The History, Civil and Commercial, of the British Colonies in the West Indies*, London, 1818–19, Vol. 3, pp. 430–1. The entire volume deals with St Domingue (Haiti); H. Aptheker, *American Negro Slave Revolts*, pp. 27, 42–44 *et seq.*, 96–100; DuBois, *Suppression of the African Slave Trade*, ch. VII, pp. 94–5; Lady Maria Nugent, *A Journal of a Voyage and Residence in the Island of Jamaica . . .*, London, 1839, Vol. 2, pp. 28, 197–8, 201–2.

19 Rawick, *The American Slave*, p. 75, n. 3. DuBois in another context observed in his book on John Brown that 'one thing saved the South from the blood sacrifice of Haiti – not, to be sure, from so successful a revolt, for the disproportion of races was less, but from a desperate and bloody effort – and that was the escape of the fugitive'. See W. E. B. DuBois, *John Brown*, Philadelphia, Pa., 1904, pp. 82ff.

20 Slave owners whose incomes were dependent on the value of the crop tended to urge the slaves to greater exertions. Sometimes it led to the sale of slaves involving separations, and these would produce individual revolts.

21 DuBois, *Suppression of the African Slave Trade*, p. 6.

22 *Ibid.*, p. 10.

23 *Ibid.*, pp. 10–11.

24 Edwards, *History, Civil and Commercial*, Vol. 3, pp. xii, xviii, 43–5; 89–95; 103–8, 112–13 *et seq.* Edwards contends that it was the ideas of the French Enlightenment which sparked off the revolution. Facile as this assertion is, it was a necessary concomitant to the other factors in the harsh realities of St Domingue which generated the revolt of the oppressed slaves and discriminated against mulattos, culminating in the revolution and the expulsion of the French from the island.

25 This factor was present in the Jamaican slave revolts of 1807 and 1831–2.

26 Kilson, 'Towards Freedom', pp. 175–87.

27 Donald Pierson, *Negroes in Brazil: a Study of Race Contact at Bahia*, Chicago, Ill., 1942, 1947, pp. 39–45; Gilberto Freyre, *The Masters and the Slaves (Casa Grande and Senzala)*, New York, 1946, pp. 298–9.

28 Orlando Patterson, *The Sociology of Slavery: an Analysis of the Origins, Development and Structure of Negro Slave Society in Jamaica*, London, 1967, pp. 260, 261–73.

29 Aptheker, *American Negro Slave Revolts*, ch. VI.

30 Rawick, *The American Slave*, p. 75, n.5.

31 *Ibid.*, p. 107.

32 M. G. Lewis, *Journal of a West India Proprietor*, London, 1834, p. 90; also *Journal of a Residence among the Negroes of the West Indies*, London, John Murray, 1845, pp. 141–2. The practice of mistreating slaves who had become old and dispensable was not confined to the West Indies alone. It was

ubiquitous. J. G. Stedman during his stay in Suriname referred to it and observed the situation thus: 'Whereas the old ones [slaves] had long been disfigured, worn out and almost unfit for any service; nay that killing them altogether would be a benefit to the estate.' *Narrative of Five Years among the Revolted Negroes of Surinam, 1772–1777*, London, 1796, Vol. 1, p. 346.

33 Moreton, *West India Customs and Manners*, London, 1793, pp. 152–3. See another almost identical situation which occurred in Columbia, South Carolina, and is recounted in Martineau, *Society in America*, Vol. 2, p. 113.

34 DuBois, *The World and Africa*, p. 7.

35 Moreton, *Customs and Manners*, pp. 88–9.

36 *Ibid.*, pp. 147–8.

37 *Ibid.*, pp. 148–9.

38 *Ibid.*, p. 140. This incident upholds Aptheker's thesis of vengeance as a factor in slave revolts. For this act of defiance by Hector was also vengeance against the entire slavocracy by being thus deprived of a hard worker after the latter felt unjustly treated.

39 Aptheker, 'American Negro Slave Revolts', p. 514.

40 *Ibid.*, p. 536.

41 *Ibid.*

42 DuBois, *The World and Africa*, p. 62.

43 Edwards, *History, Civil and Commercial*, Vol. 1, p. 525.

44 Monica Schuler, 'Akan Slave Rebellions in the British Caribbean', SAVACU, (a Journal of the Caribbean Artists' Movement) Jamaica, i, 1 (June 1970), p. 27 (entire article on pp. 8–31) had erroneously suggested, despite the brilliance of her article, that these revolts made no significant contribution to the eventual abolition and emancipation. Contrast her views with DuBois' argument more than two generations earlier and his evidence in respect of Haiti in 1896 as a factor among others in the suppression of the slave trade. See his *Suppression of the African Slave Trade*, pp. 94–5 (1969 edn), also *The World and Africa* (1947), pp. 65–6. Compare with Elsa V. Goveia, *Slave Society in the British Leeward Islands at the end of the Eighteenth Century*, New Haven, Conn., 1965, p. 337.

45 Frederick Douglass, *The Life and Times of Frederick Douglass 1817–1881*, London, 1882, chs. 15–17, esp. ch. 17; also *Narrative of Frederick Douglass*, ch. 10, esp. pp. 58–65, 65–75.

46 Sarah Bradford, *Harriet Tubman: the Moses of her People*, New York, Corinth Books, 1961; and her *Scenes in the Life of Harriet Tubman*, Auburn, N.Y., 1869.

47 *The Liberator* (Boston), i (3 Sept. 1831), p. 143.

48 Aptheker, *Essays*, p. 11.

49 Rawick, *The American Slave*, pp. 74–5, n. 3.

50 Pierson, *Negroes in Brazil*, pp. 39, 41, 45, 74.

51 William Still, *The Underground Rail Road*, Philadelphia, 1872. Accounts are too numerous to mention but see, e.g., pp. 240–2, 348–57, 423–4; also William and Ellen Craft, *Running a Thousand Miles for Freedom or The Escape of William and Ellen Craft from Slavery*, London, 1860, pp. 12–80. Still, *op. cit.*, pp. 368–77; J. Henson, *Life*, pp. 40–58; John Anderson, *The Story of the Life of John Anderson, a Fugitive Slave*, London, 1863, pp. 8–126.

52 Pierson, *Negroes in Brazil*, p. 39, n. 33.

53 *Ibid.*, p. 45.

54 Ibid., p. 46–7.
55 Ibid., pp. 39–40.
56 Ibid., pp. 41, n. 38, and 44, n. 47.
57 Aptheker, American Negro Slave Revolts, pp. 218–29, 276–9. See also 'Sarah, a Fugitive Slave', in Coleman, op. cit., p. 233.
58 Captain Steadman, writing of eighteenth-century Surinam, implied that this was the case. See his Narrative, Vol. 2, pp. 359–60. He suggested that, of the estimated slave population of Surinam of about 80 000, nearly 30 000 were kept in idleness. This was his reference to domestic slaves. On p. 361 he referred to them as a 'superfluous number of idlers'. Since most of the domestics were Creoles, it is reasonable to assume that the divisions and lack of co-operation between the Creoleblacks or mulattos and bozal Africans were maintained. This point need not be pressed too far as Creole slaves sometimes took part with other African-derived peoples in slave revolts.
59 Patterson, Sociology of Slavery, p. 57.
60 Douglass, Life and Times, pp. 32–3.
61 But even Toussaint had worked in the fields and knew the field conditions at first hand. See Edwards, History, Civil and Commercial, Vol. 5, pp. 112–13.
62 Edward Long, The History of Jamaica: General Survey of the Ancient and Modern State of that Island, London, 1774, Vol. 2, p. 463.
63 Betrayals were as frequent as plans for revolt. See Long, History of Jamaica, pp. 454–5, for how three negroes betrayed the Coromantin planners of St John who had fixed a date on which to attack Mr Langher's house, and also how another Caffee of the parish of St Thomas sat periodically in the 'private cabals' of Coromantins and betrayed their entire plan.
64 Ibid., Vol. 2, pp. 450, 454, 461.
65 Ibid., pp. 449.
66 See Coleman, op. cit., chapter entitled 'Massa's People'.
67 William Suttles, Jr., 'African Religious Survivals as Factors in American Slave Revolts', Journal of Negro History, lvi, 2 (April 1971); also C. L. R. James, The Black Jacobins: Toussaint Louverture and the San Domingo Revolution, New York and London, 1963, p. 56; Long, History of Jamaica, Vol. 2, pp. 451-3, 463.
68 Long, History of Jamaica, pp. 452–3. This mention of so-called French Negroes contradicts his assertion of rebels being only newly imported. These might have even been Creoles.
69 Ibid.
70 Ibid., pp. 444, 452.
71 Ibid., pp. 450, 454, 461. One mulatto man slew three rebel slaves; another behaved with 'great bravery' for, leaping on the breastwork, he assaulted the rebels, sword in hand.
72 E. Franklin Frazier, The Negro in the United States, New York, 1957, rev. edn., 1961, p.90.
73 Ibid.
74 J. H. Franklin, From Slavery to Freedom: a History of Negro America, New York, rev. edn., 1969, pp. 123–5.
75 Patterson, Sociology of Slavery, p. 57.
76 Moreton, Customs and Manners, pp. 77–8, 79–84, 88–90.
77 Nugent, Journal, Vol. 1, p. 141.
78 Patterson, Sociology of Slavery, pp. 61–2.

79 Even in North America, Frances Anne Kemble appears to have observed the same thing, for she recorded the case of one mulatto woman, Sally, who pleaded with her that she might be taken off field work and attached to the home as it was degrading for her being a 'mulatto woman,' and found the request strange (see *Journal*, pp. 246–7).

80 Patterson, *Sociology of Slavery*, p. 62.

81 *Ibid.*, pp. 64–5.

82 See Henry Belby, *Death Struggles of Slavery* . . . , London, 1853, ch. 12; Hope M. Waddell, *Twenty-nine Years in the West Indies*, London, 1970, pp. 66–7.

83 Franklin, *From Slavery to Freedom*, rev. edn., p. 121.

84 *Ibid.*, pp. 122–5.

85 Long, *History of Jamaica*, Vol. 2, p. 445; also Edwards, *History, Civil and Commercial*, Vol. 1, pp. 522–45 *et seq.*

86 *The Shorter Oxford Dictionary*, Vol. 1, p. 1208.

87 F. P. Bowser, *The African Slave in Colonial Peru*, Stanford, Cal., p. 187. The author discusses the control of Africans in subsequent pages, pp. 187–211.

88 *Ibid.*, p. 187.

89 *Ibid.*, pp. 188–8.

90 *Ibid.*, pp. 188–9.

91 *Ibid.*, pp. 196–9, 201–5.

92 *Ibid.*, pp. 220–1.

93 H. S. Klein, *Slavery in the Americas: a Comparative Study of Virginia and Cuba*, Chicago, Ill., 1967, pp. 68–9.

94 Bowser contends that in spite of the Afro-Peruvians' hatred of the Spaniards, they 'seemed to have plotted few acts of rebellion and did not flock to the standards of foreign invaders', *The African Slave in Colonial Peru*, p. 220.

95 Klein, *Slavery*, p. 70; Bowser, *The African Slave in Colonial Peru*, pp. 187, 189.

96 Klein, *Slavery*, p. 71; Bowser, *The African Slave in Colonial Peru*, p. 212. In 1617 and 1619 the idea of instituting the *rancheadores* on the Cuban model was suggested for Peru, but it fell through. Demoticus Philalotes (pseud.), *Yankee Travels through the Island of Cuba or The Men and Government, the Laws and Customs of Cuba as Seen by American Eyes*, New York, 1856, letter 8, pp. 38–42. He describes a hunting down of *cimarrones* resulting in the capture of six runaways.

97 Klein, *Slavery in the Americas*, p. 71. The penalties in Peru appear to have been even more severe. There, for three days' absence, the punishment was a hundred lashes and a day in the stocks; a return within ten days but in which it was proved that sexual relations with a black or native woman motivated him, his genitals were publicly removed; and if he had not returned within twenty days death was the penalty when recaptured. A master could file legal objections to prevent death. For running away a second time the ten-day punishment of the first offence applied, and execution was the penalty for a third offence (see Bowser, *The African Slave in Colonial Peru*, pp. 197–8).

98 Klein, *Slavery in the Americas*, p. 72.

99 *Ibid.*, pp. 155–6.

100 J. H. Parry and P. M. Sherlock, *A Short History of the West Indies*, London and New York, 1966, p. 171.

101 PRO, CO 71/4, Sir William Young to the Rt. Hon. the Earl of Hillsborough, 28 July 1772.

102 *Ibid.*

103 *Ibid.*

104 *Ibid.*

105 *Ibid.*

106 *Ibid.* This volume contains more correspondence relating to the resistance of the Caribs of St Vincent, and together they constitute an interesting chapter in the colonial confrontations.

107 Yet in 1895 at the time of the St Domingue revolt they were being urged to revolt against the British, and did revolt. They were finally removed in 1797 to Honduras. For their subsequent history in their new environment see D. M. Taylor, *The Black Caribs of Honduras*, New York, 1951.

108 Edwards, *History, Civil and Commercial*, Vol. 1, p. 525,

109 R. C. Dallas, *History of the Maroons*, London, 1803, 2 vols.

110 Long, *History of Jamaica*, Vol. 2, pp. 302–45; Edwards, *History, Civil and Commercial*, Vol. 1, pp. 523–35; Dallas, *Maroons*, Vol. 1, pp. 22–55, esp. pp. 29–30, 33.

111 Edwards, *History, Civil and Commercial*, Vol. 1, p. 527.

112 *Ibid.*, p. 528.

113 Long, *History of Jamaica*, Vol. 2, p. 462.

114 *Ibid.*, pp. 445, 450–51, 454; Edwards, *History, Civil and Commercial*, Vol. 1, pp. 532–5.

115 Long, *History of Jamaica*, Vol. 2, pp. 445, 450–1, 454; Dallas, *History of the Maroons*, Vol. 1, pp. 101–3 *et seq.*

116 *Ibid.*, p. 462.

117 *Ibid.*, Vol. 2, p. 444.

118 E. G. Rupp and Benjamin Brewery, *Martin Luther: Documents of Modern History*, London, Edward Arnold, 1970, reprinted 1979, pp. 121–6 (Open University set book); also Ronald H. Bainton, *Here I Stand: a Life of Martin Luther*, New York, New American Library, and London, New English Library Ltd, 1950, ch. 16, esp. pp. 209–21.

119 Edwards, *History, Civil and Commercial*, Vol. 1, p. 544.

120 Long, *History of Jamaica*, Vol. 2, p. 451.

121 *Ibid.*, pp. 451–2.

122 Dallas, *Maroons*, Vol. 1, pp. 124–5, 127–8.

123 *Ibid.*, p. 122–3.

124 Stedman. *Narrative.*

125 Gabriel Debien, 'Marronage in the French Caribbean', translated from the original entitled 'Le Marronage aux Antilles Françaises au XVIII siècle', *Caribbean Studies*, vi, 3 (1966), pp. 3–44, also reproduced and re-edited in *Maroon Societies: Rebel Slave Communities in the Americas*, Richard Price (ed.), New York, 1973, pp. 107–42.

126 Silvia W. de Groot, *Djuka Society and Social Change: History of an Attempt to Develop a Bush Negro Community in Surinam 1917–1926*, Assen, Netherlands, pp. 47–55, 68–84, 85–9, 90, 94.

127 Stedman, *Narrative*, Vol. 1, p. 366.

128 *Ibid.*, Vol. 1, pp. 254–5.

129 *Ibid.*, Vol. 1, pp. 80–3 *et seq.*; Vol. 2, pp. 187–214. Also de Groot, *Djuka Society and Social Change*, pp. 11–16. The entire book deserves to be read; also Silvia W. de Groot, 'Van isolatie integratie De Surinaamse Marrons en hun a fatammelingen Officiele documenten betreffender de Djoeka's, 1845–1863', *Ver handelingen van het koninklijk Institut voor Taal-landen*, Volkenkunde del.

41,' s–Gravenhage, Martinus Nijhoff, 1963. (Its appropriate English title is: 'From Isolation to Integration: the Surinam Maroons and their Descendants: Official Documents Concerning the Djuka Tribe 1845–1863.) There is an English summary at the end. See also S. W. de Groot, 'The Boni Maroon War 1765–1793, Suriname and French Guyana', in Stichting, Suriname Museum, Zorgen-Hoop, Zeelandia, *Bibliotheek Archeologie en Natuur-Histoire*, Paramaribo, Suriname, pp. 6–23; reproduced from *Boleti de Estudios Latino Americanos y de Caribe*, No 18 (June 1975), paper first presented to the 41st International Congress of Americanists in Mexico, 1974. The treaties were concluded as follows: with the Djukas (1760), Saramacca (1762) and with the Matuari (1767).

130 De Groot, 'The Boni Maroon War', pp. 22–3.

131 Stedman, *Narrative*, Vol. 2, p. 214.

132 Joshua R. Giddings, *The Exiles of Florida*, Columbus, Ohio, 1858, p. 3. Giddings assures us that the term 'Seminole' was all-embracing to incorporate Indians led by Seacoffee and African fugitives, even though it was later narrowed down.

133 *Ibid.*, p. 2. There is even evidence that the fugitive tendency had been a long-standing one. See K. W. Porter, 'Relations between Negroes and Indians within the Present Limits of the United States', *Journal of Negro History*, xvii (July 1932), pp. 316–67; also 'Florida Slaves and Free Negroes in the Seminole War, 1835–1842', *Journal of Negro History*, xviii (1943), pp. 390–421.

134 Porter, 'Relations between Negroes and Indians', p. 325.

135 *Ibid.*, p. 326

136 *Ibid.*, pp. 333–4; also Giddings, *Exiles of Florida*.

137 Porter, 'Relations between Negroes and Indians', p. 334.

138 Quoted in Porter, *ibid.*, p. 334.

139 See Seminole Treaty at Fort Moultrie (1823) for return of fugitives entering the territory. The Seminoles reacted, resulting in a seven-years' war. But negro opposition to this was strong and the treaty could not operate among the Seminoles. (There was an earlier treaty between the Creek Indians in 1790 for return of runaway negroes.) Later, escaped negroes could not return to their erstwhile masters so they and their brethren resisted the agreements. Like those of Cuba they were sedentary cultivators, not hunters. Negro resistance is well attested, and negroes refused to follow their masters or Indians if they acceded to the request to move to the Creeks (Porter, 'Relations between Negroes and Indians', pp. 336–7). The crucial point in their refusal was their adherence to independence.

140 *Ibid.*, p. 338–9.

141 *Ibid.*, p. 340.

142 *Ibid.*, p. 341.

143 *Ibid.*, p. 342.

144 *Ibid.*, p. 347.

145 Irene Diggs, 'Zumbi and the Republic of Os Palmares', *Phylon*, xiv, 1 (1953), p. 69. Kent, in his article, regarded it as an 'African State in Brazil', and so entitled his paper (*Journal of African History*, vi, 2 (1965)).

146 *Ibid.* Chapman described it as a 'strange republic', for the republic embodied monarchical and republican features. The head of the republic was a king. See Charles E. Chapman, 'Palmares, the negro Numantia', *Journal of Negro History*, iii (Jan. 1918), pp. 29–32.

147 *Ibid.*; Diggs, 'Zumbi', p. 62.
148 See Kent, 'African State in Brazil'; Diggs, 'Zumbi'.
149 *Ibid.*
150 Pierson, *Negroes in Brazil*, pp. 50, 62.
151 Kent, 'African State in Brazil'; Diggs, 'Zumbi'.
152 Diggs, 'Zumbi', pp. 66–8.
153 *Ibid.*, p. 70.
154 *Ibid.*, pp. 64, 68.
155 See, for instance, *Acts of the Assembly passed in the Island of Jamaica from 1776 to 1785.*
156 See Long, *History of Jamaica*, Vol. 2, pp. 462–3 and notes.
157 Waddell, *Twenty-nine Years in the West Indies*, pp. 51–3, 55–7, 61–4.
158 Long, *History of Jamaica*, Vol. 2, pp. 451–2.
159 Frazier, *The Negro in the United States*, p. 93.
160 See Suttles, 'African Religious Survivals as Factors in American Slave Revolts' *Journal of Negro History*, lvi (April 1971), 97–104.
161 Ansell Hart, Jr., *The Life of George William Gordon*, Kingston, Institute of Jamaica, 1972, p. 135. The entire book contradicts the received view that the riot of 11 October 1865 was a 'rebellion'.
162 Coleman, *op. cit.*, pp. 100, 232.
163 For other techniques of resistance see Aptheker, *American Negro Slave Revolts*, ch. 6, esp. p. 140; also Kenneth M. Stampp, *The Peculiar Institution*. New York, Vintage Books, 1956, ch, 3, 'A Troublesome Property', mirrors many variations of this kind of behaviour. See his p. 106, for instance. Patterson, *Sociology of Slavery*, ch. IX.

10   The Haitian Revolution: first phase

In our consideration of the techniques of resistance evolved by African slaves to defeat the slavocracy the case of St Domingue, which became the modern state of Haiti, merits particular attention – for at least seven reasons. First, it was the only successful slave revolt in the Americas to overturn the system and, in fact, the only recorded one in modern history. Second, its impact on other slave theatres was dramatic; the spectre of revolution that it created continued to haunt slave societies long after the demise of slavery.[1] Third, it had inspirational value for the black peoples throughout the Americas.[2] Fourth, it had some effect, too, on the psychology of European slave holders whose attitudes to the descendants of Africa were, in the main, contemptuous. Fifth, the reasons behind the success of the revolt which became a revolution help us to understand more fully why the slave revolts in other theatres failed. Sixth, it is important because it enables us to study the colour divisions in one of the slave theatres and to focus on their implications which notably affected the fortunes of the revolution in its initial stages, in its developmental stage too, and which still continue to plague Haitian society to this day. Seventh, the revolution had an international dimension because of the conflicting interests of European and American powers, which further complicated the course of events. In studying the Haitian Revolution there is a temptation to write a history of all the developments until the attainment of sovereign status by the island. However, a full account is undesirable here as there are many interesting texts[3] available which provide a valuable history of the experiences of the Haitian people.

Background to the revolution

There was both an external and an internal background to the St Domingue revolt, external because the fervour of the French Revolution for 'Liberty, Equality and Fraternity' eventually reached the French colony. Furthermore, big power intrigues, ambitions and duplicity in dealing with the Haitians added a new, dangerous dimension to the islanders' struggles and left the slaves in the long term with no alternative but to make a determined bid for the liberation of the country from the slave owners. The complexity of these conflicting interests needs briefly sketching in order to illuminate the nature and character of the evolution of events. Internally the revolution must be placed in the context of the state of society in the colony, which had progressed from bad to worse as a result of the arrogance of the planter class, the mistreatment of African slaves and mulatto freemen and the unseemly treatment of the lower orders by the so-called *petits blancs*, or poor whites. The colour division of St Domingue and the disabilities under which the various groups suffered, with, of course, the exception of the ruling whites, accumulated over a long period of time, to provide the major causes of the revolt. Many writers on St Domingue from the eighteenth to the twentieth century are generally agreed that the plantocracy of the colony constituted a law unto themselves. A twentieth-century writer has stated that they were very rich and 'flushed with opulence and dissipation', depraved in manners and treated the slaves with a harshness, brutality and vileness unknown in the English and Spanish islands.[4] Although the statement is that of a former British colonial governor, there is some accuracy in it, in spite of the English bias which it represents; within slave plantations no one power had the monopoly of cruelty or benevolence, for cruelty, as we have seen in these pages, was ingrafted early on the slave system. But while it is true that racism on most of the plantations existed, that of St Domingue was unique. An example is to be found in the hatred which developed between the whites and coloured population of the island, known variously as *l'Affranchis* or mulattos or *gens les couleurs*. The educational and social opportunities which the latter found for advancement and the opportunities for acquiring enlightenment in the metropolitan country, France, placed many of them in a group superior in intellect and achievement to many of the whites and, especially, the *petits blancs*. Yet the disabilities of the coloured people were immense. While in France they could exercise the rights of free men and women; in their homeland, St Domingue, their rights did not amount to much and they suffered many vexatious restraints. In the colony the metropolitan whites and the Creole whites insisted on stressing their superiority, in spite of the fact that some of the mulattos were property and slave owners. These differences were extended in the manner of dress to styles which the coloured people were expected to wear.[5]

The whites of St Domingue possessed considerable leisure time, and a comfortable life which reached its apogee in the eighteenth century.[6] According to the modern Haitian historian, Jean Stephen Alexis, 'life possessed an unimaginable splendour in which all that Nature and man could contrive to delight the senses was entirely at the disposal of the great planters. As they indulged in all the excesses of unbridled luxury, their moral sense was completely perverted.'[7] This over-indulgence blunted the whites' moral senses, and in their over-exuberance they came to take up certain sadistic pastimes. Jean Stephen Alexis continues his observation thus:

> In particular, the Marquis of Caradeux, the Count of La Toison-Laboule, and the Viscount of Flonc, carried human wickedness to its uttermost limits. On the slightest pretext Negroes would be thrown alive in cauldrons of boiling sugar. Others would be buried alive in a standing position, with their heads above the ground, which would then be smeared with syrup to whet the appetites of the ants, so that the wretched victims were glad to be stoned to death by their own compassionate comrades. Another torture was the 'four stake death', from which not even pregnant Negresses were exempt. Each of the four limbs was attached to a post while the victim was flogged to death. Many slaves were hung up by the ribs and left to die, such cruelties being daily occurrences.[8]

In spite of these excesses, the English historian of the West Indies Bryan Edwards, himself a slave owner, was to assert that the conduct of the whites towards negroes was not 'in general reprehensible . . . but lenient and indulgent as was consistent with their safety'.[9] Yet, on the same page, he contradicted himself by writing that the mulattos directed the same kind of indignities received at the hands of the whites at the blacks, and referred to the mulattos as 'hard-hearted taskmasters'.[10] The implication of the first citation was that the master class and the whites did not practise cruelty, yet in the second citation we learn that the mulattos, who were themselves victims of white excesses, extended these excesses to the black slaves. It makes Bryan Edwards an unreliable reporter of the Haitian situation; some of his facts were accurate but his interpretations are tainted with both his racial prejudices and the prejudices of his class of slave owners. But the harsh realities of St Domingue were not in accord with the complacent attitude of Bryan Edwards. Among those whites who occupied a lower stratum of the social hierarchy of St Domingue the element of jealousy was ever-present in their attitude to the mulattos; conscious of the fabulous wealth and the grand airs assumed by the land-owning slavocracy towards their inferiors, the *petits blancs* vented their frustrations on the mulattos and African slaves by recourse to ill-treatment. We learn that the subordinate whites were not all French in origin. Some of them were Italians, Greeks, Portuguese and Spaniards, most of them were 'escaped gallows birds', and their presence constituted a 'constant threat of anarchy and disorder in the colony'[11] In spite of their education and opulence, the mulattos were still the victims of

the 'universal scorn and contempt of the whites', and being excluded from vital public offices and constantly insulted they found
an added grievance against the whites. Thus, in a society in the
main based 'on racial discrimination, the mulattos hated all whites,
not excepting their own fathers'.[12] It is easy to understand their
anger when in the streets they would often be forced to make way
for the most humble of white men, and at theatres and at church they
had to accept segregation. All these indignities also hardened them
against the descendants of Africa, the so-called negroes, whom
they despised. But it is observed that their own colour prejudice
extended in subdivisions among themselves, divisions already
alluded to in this work. The degradation of the blacks and the
mulattos was both physical and moral. Thus, from above, we can
see that St Domingue, in the late eighteenth century just before the
eruption, was a heterogeneous society in which the class struggle
was given a thick gloss of colour. The plantocracy, on the one
hand, was determined to maintain its privileges, even at the risk of
severing its ties with the home regime. Immediately below it were
the subordinate whites, consisting of craftsmen, artisans, overseers
and many of the lower orders of the plantation society, who also
staked some claim to the spoils of the colony, and who seemed
prepared to take over from the planters, if need be. They constituted a formidable opposition to the improvement of the status of the
freemen. The free coloured population, the mulattos, and a few free
blacks resented the restrictions imposed on them and seemed prepared when the situation became ripe, to obtain their political rights
by seizure, if need be; but in their own preoccupation they had no
regard for the rights of slaves. Last, but not least, were the African
slaves, though for a long time inarticulate (and that is not to say
that many slave revolts had not occurred prior to 1791), they were
poised on dissolution of the slave system, when the time arose, and
by blood, if need be. As Alexis has commented:

> Saint Domingue was thus a mosaic of races, a society sated with
> wealth, vice, suffering, vanity, misery and indulgence – a melting
> pot of contrasts in which various irreconcilable forces were bound in
> the end to flare up into a vast conflagration, even without the spark
> of the year 1789 to set it off.[13]

In 1789 St Domingue was also the greatest supplier in the world of
sugar, coffee, cocoa, cotton, spices and precious wood, and vessels
of various nations visited and traded with the colony, the turnover
amounting to two-thirds of France's overseas trade.[14]

The implication of Alexis's above-quoted remark relating to the
year 1789 is important and worthy of consideration. Bryan
Edwards, commenting on the situation, attributed the major cause

of the revolt to the influence of the French *Philosophes* and the revolutionary fervour which made the explosion inevitable. Alexis provides a corrective to this simplistic viewpoint. There is even a greater implication for the Edwards' point of view. Having earlier asserted that the French planters were lenient and indulged the slaves, and that cruelty was generally absent from their handling of them, the inference is to be made that the slaves had no reason to revolt and would not have revolted of their own accord. Referring to the mulatto revolt, which was led by Vincent Ogé in 1791, he asserted that both the mulatto and black insurrections had the same origin, and asserted that:

> It was not the strong and irresistible impulse of human nature, groaning under oppression, that excited either of these classes to plunge their daggers into the bosom of unoffending women and helpless infants. They were driven into these excesses – reluctantly driven – by vile machinations of men calling themselves philosophers (the proselytes and imitators in France, of the Old Jewry associates in London) whose pretences to philanthropy were as gross a mockery of human reason, as their conduct was an outrage on all the feelings of our nature, and the ties which hold society together.[15]

While this statement revealed an awareness of the impact of the external factor flowing from the French Enlightenment, it showed complete disregard for the day-to-day happenings in human relationships which could be productive of conflict, as was the case in slave societies. Having himself been impressed with the fact that most of the slave revolts of the many West Indian islands often originated from *bozal* Africans who had not acclimatised or had time to adjust to slave conditions, he still observed that in St Domingue 'a very considerable part of the insurgents were not Africans but Creoles, or natives. Some of the leaders were favoured domestics among the white inhabitants, born and brought up in their families. A few of them had even received those advantages, the perversion of which, under their philosophical preceptors, served only to render them pre-eminent in mischief; for, having been taught to read, they were led to imbibe, and enabled to promulgate those principles and doctrines which led, and always will lead, to the subversion of all government and order.'[16] Yet, in the next breath, he seems to contradict himself by stating that 'unquestionably, the vast annual importations of enslaved Africans into St Domingo, for many years previous to 1791, had created a black population in the French part of the island, which was beyond all measure, disproportionate to the whites; the relative numbers of the two classes being as sixteen to one. Of these circumstances the

305

leaders of the rebels could not be unobservant, and they doubtless derived encouragement and confidence from it.'[17] What this statement fails to make explicit is whether the revolt was a combination of *bozal* Africans and Creoles of African descent, which it was.[18] Merely to suggest that the Creole leaders took advantage of the presence of numbers is to deflate what must have been a carefully planned operation and what even the superior armed forces of three European powers, France, Spain and England, could not destroy. But the viewpoint mirrored that bias against the people of African descent so characteristic in the writings of Bryan Edwards and others who shared his prejudices, prejudices which became so much of the stock in trade of racial supremacists and their adherents.

The uniqueness of the Haitian uprising needs to be considered and is observed in the eulogistic work of the Afro-American prelate, the Rev. Theodore J Holly, who wrote that:

> This revolution is one of the noblest, grandest, and most justifiable outbursts against tyrannical oppression that is recorded on the pages of the world's history . . . the Haitian Revolution is also the grandest political event of this or any other age.[19]

The Rev. Holly first argued that a race of men almost dehumanised by the excesses of slavery and its oppression rose up from what amounted to ages of slumber and redressed after three centuries the wrongs inflicted on them. Apart from seeing it as providential design, he argued that it surpassed the American Revolution by an 'incomparable degree', for the American Revolution was a revolt of a people already 'comparatively free, independent and highly enlightened. Their greatest grievance was the imposition of three pence per pound tax on tea, by the mother country without their consent. But the Haitian revolution was a revolt of an uneducated and menial class of slaves, against their tyrannical oppressors, who not only imposed an absolute tax on their unrequited labour, but also usurped their very bodies.'[20] But the oppressors against whom the Afro-Haitians contended were not only the mother country, as was the case of the American revolutionaries, but unlike and more fearful than this revolt, the colonial government of Haiti was also thrown in the balance against the Afro-Haitian rebels turned revolutionaries. While the American insurrectionists had their colonial government in their own hands together with their individual liberty at the commencement of the revolution, the black insurgents, by contrast, in Haiti had 'yet to grasp both their personal liberty and the control of their colonial government, by the might of their own right-hands when the heroic struggle began'. In contrasting the obstacles to be surmounted by both the American and Haitian revolutionaries, he likened that of the Americans to a mere 'tempest in a teapot', while that of the Haitians he likened to the 'dark and lurid thunder storm of the dissolving heavens'.[21] Holly, therefore, concluded on the uniqueness of the Haitian Revolution in these words:

> Never before, in all the annals of the world's history, did a nation of abject chattel slaves arise in the terrific might of their resuscitated manhood, and regenerate, redeem, and disenthral themselves: by taking their station at one gigantic bound, as an independent nation, among the sovereignties of the world.[22]

On the contrary, he likened the American revolutionaries to the French revolutionaries who, in spite of their proclamation of the principles of liberty, equality and fraternity, had no intention of conceding these to the despised African peoples, whom they had enslaved.[23] That point is important because, when the Haitian revolt was in progress in its first year, even President George Washington, the champion of American liberty, not only supplied arms and ammunition to the French to suppress the African revolt, but expressed his sentiments in a letter of 27 December 1791, in which he lamented the spirit of revolt demonstrated by the 'Blacks'.[24] It was a rather telling letter for one so celebrated as the champion of liberty and for one who had just fought for liberty, but it did show the preferences of the men of European origin, and if it did not express a racial bias then it expressed a class one, or even both.

At this initial stage, the United States of America supplied the following to the French:

1000 muskets and bayonets
110 musket cartridges
10 barrels of musket powder and ball
Cartridge paper and thread to make up the cartridges
5000 flints
500 gun screws
1000 brushes and priming wires
1000 cartridge boxes and belts

It was regarded as a singular opportunity for the people of the United States 'to manifest their zeal to repay in some degree the assistance afforded them during the perilous struggles of the late war'[25] (i.e. war with Britain for independence). But American involvement and racial prejudices were more blatant under President Jefferson and his Secretary of State, James Madison, and when the latter in due course became President. These involvements complicated the problems of Haitian independence, but the black revolutionaries found themselves caught in the maelstrom of big power controversy and ambitions, and it is appropriate to examine the dimension of international relations of the revolution.

That the French Revolution had its impact on the mood of St Domingue – involving Europeans, mulattos and Afro-Haitians – goes without saying. That the divisions of the white colonists between royalists and republicans remains a truism, and that the mulattos were among the first to demand their rights and sparked off an abortive revolt in 1791 under Vincent Ogé, does not need recounting; but that their preoccupations were with their own interests and not with those of the slaves, and that they sought to approximate the whites in status and, in some respects, be in alliance with them against the best interests of the slaves, also made the revolt of the slaves inevitable. For a good while the mulattos, preoccupied with their own importance, would not unite themselves with the African and black Creole slaves and so made the struggles between these groups for mastery of St Domingue ferocious, the scars of which have remained among the Haitians to this day. That it also shaped the course of events in the island is well attested in records and the numerous texts which have appeared on the struggles of that unhappy island. That European perfidy added to the ferocity of the struggles again remains an indelible part of the records, but the perfidy of the French was even more damnable, for even the pro-European, Bryan Edwards, who also advocated assistance to the planters, was to write, after the abduction of Toussaint in 1802, that by their perfidy the French forfeited their claims to any sympathy.[26] The perfidious treatment of the blacks by both General Leclerc and his successor, Rochambeau, enshrines their inglorious names in the annals of Haitian experience. Yet, in the initial stages and for a long period during the confusion that engulfed the entire island of St Domingue, Edwards observed that mulattos were still seeking to unite their interests with those of the whites against the blacks. The Concordat of 11 May 1791, was a case in point.[27] Bryan Edwards himself was to assert that European perfidy destroyed any meaningful alliance.[28] But, like some others, sensing the danger which a successful slave revolt in St Domingue would represent to Jamaica and other British dependencies, he hoped that with the restoration of peace between England and France and the incorporation of the mulattos into French citizenship, the latter would be converted into friends, with a view to suppressing the rest of the revolt, and so instead of the mulattos being enemies they would be accepted as friends.[29] The sentiment was significant, for it expressed a colour-class bias against the blacks. With these intrigues and suggestions it is still a great surprise that the Afro-Haitian revolution succeeded. Yet, in another context, Edwards observed that Rigaud, the mulatto leader, saw the situation clearly, that there would never be peace till 'one class had exterminated the other'.[30] Such was the dress rehearsal, when the curtain was raised for the black slave revolt in St Domingue in August 1791.

The mulatto revolt in St Domingue

With the proclamation of the revolution in France and the fall of the Bastille, the Assembly found itself confronted not only with the problems of domestic France but with those of France overseas as well. One of the issues which intruded on their preoccupations was the question of whether their declared principles of liberty, equality and fraternity extended to the mulattos and African slaves in the Antilles. The point was forcibly brought home to them by the appearance of Vincent Ogé, a young quadroon from Dondon in St Domingue, who was in France at the time of the revolution and took advantage of his association with the members of *les Amis des Noirs* to advance the plea for the revolutionary benefits to be extended to the mulattos and for all disabilities against them to be removed. During the discussion the issue of the slave position was raised, but the assembly shelved it. Accordingly, the French National Assembly promulgated decrees in recognising the full rights of the free coloured men of St Domingue whereby they were supposed to acquire the same status as white men. They therefore deputed Ogé as their Commissioner to the Assembly of St Domingue to represent the decrees of the revolution; in short, he was the chief delegate of the freemen to the St Domingue National Assembly. Ogé arrived back unannounced in St Domingue on 21 October 1790, and two days later appeared before the National Assembly of the colony to present his case. An unpleasant argument ensued and the Assembly refused to recognise any such decrees from France. As a result of Ogé's humiliation by the Assembly he embarked on revolt. Although advised by his mulatto compatriot, Jean Baptiste Chavannes, to concert his efforts with the blacks in order to ensure their support, Ogé arrogantly insisted that he would have nothing to do with the blacks, and that the National Assembly decree in France made no reference to 'Negro' slaves. Ogé's ill-considered and ill-prepared revolt with a small force was easily routed by the colonial Assembly and he, together with Chavannes and other mulatto leaders, escaped into the Spanish part of the island (Santo Domingo), but they were handed back by the Spanish Governor, Joaquim Garcia. A tribunal of landowners soon pronounced a death sentence on Ogé and his associates and condemned them to be broken on the wheel, and on 25 February 1791 Ogé and Chavannes, watched by the Assembly at the Place d'Armes, were broken on the wheel, and it is indicated that, while Chavannes was contemptuous of the whole operation and died bravely, Ogé screamed and begged for mercy while the wheel crushed their bones.[31] The Haitian historian, Alexis, observing the Ogé episode, wrote:

> The Ogé episode reflected the ambivalence from which the mulattos suffered; it showed the aspiration of the mulatto to identify with the whites in spite of the latter's contempt for them. They found themselves unable to identify with the degraded African (Negro), their illiterate brothers. The nature of colonial society provided part of the explanation for this ambivalence in trying to escape the other nature to which the mulatto owed his origin. In a society in which custom had become unwritten law in which the colour of the skin decided the superiority and inferiority of people, the mulatto was in the hierarchical arrangement superior to the Negro and by custom he was supposed to be liberated at the age of 24. In 1675 the King of France had decreed that 'all children of slaves are slaves'.[32]

In spite of this, the mulattos continued to enjoy the privileges conferred on them by their white fathers, who provided them with opportunity for advancement through education, through land grants and through their protection, with the result that they became the middle class of St Domingue society, but it was a middle class based on colour.[33] It is easy to see why the mulattos were unwilling to be associated with the slaves apart from the psychological infusions and the manner of conduct; they owned about one-third of the slaves of the colony and in spite of Abbé Gregoire's pleas to them to take account of the slaves in granting them full civil rights, the mulattos seemed unwilling to make concessions to the blacks.[34]

The blacks' revolt

The fervour of the French Revolution reached the Antilles rather early, for even in 1789 slaves had revolted in Guadeloupe and Martinique, but their revolts were suppressed. But between 1789 and 1791 the slaves of St Domingue initiated their plans and held nocturnal meetings in the forests. Nevertheless, they bided their time while they observed their masters engage each other in an internecine struggle. Furthermore, revolutionary literature was circulating among them.[35] While the slaves worked and kept their counsel, they also observed many disputes and arguments continuing between conflicting tendencies among the white hierarchy of St Domingue. As the historian C. L. R. James observed, some of the men who were to lead the revolution had not yet stirred. Dessalines was still a slave to a black master; Christophe, who worked in a hotel, listened to the discussions and worked, while Toussaint read Abbé Raynal.[36]

The arrival of the French troops from revolutionary France to carry out the wishes of the revolution in March 1791 saw the colonial whites divided between royalists and revolutionaries. The troops, on landing, embraced mulattos and blacks, indicating that the French Assembly had conceded equality to all. Slaves in the neighbourhood of Port-au-Prince seized arms and revolted, but they were easily crushed by the Marquis de Caradeux, commander of the National Guard and himself a wealthy planter.[37] But the colonial *bourgeoisie* refused to accede to French government requests to enfranchise the mulattos and lynched them instead. The colonists now established a new Assembly at St Marc, to supersede an erstwhile Assembly that had crumbled, in order to proclaim their independence from France. In their attempt to move the Assembly to Le Cap (later Cap Haitien), then the seat of the Governor, some of them were killed by slaves who were in revolt in the north of the island.[38] Although the whites were becoming conscious of a slave rising, they continued to disparage them, feeling that they were too disunited to revolt effectively.[39] They were wrong, however. When, therefore, on the night of 22 August 1791, the leaders of the revolt, under the leadership of the Voodoo priest, Boukman, assembled at the Morne Rouge, a mountain overlooking Le Cap in a thickly forested place, where Voodoo incantations were used and a prayer chanted, it was the signal that the revolt of the descendants of Africa in St Domingue had begun. C. L. R. James has rendered the words of the prayer to us:

> The God who created the sun which gives us light, who rouses the waves and rules the storm, though hidden in the clouds, he watches us. He sees all that the white man does. The god of the white man inspires him with crime, but our god calls upon us to do good works. Our god, who is good to us, orders us to revenge our wrongs. He will direct our arms and aid us. Throw away the symbol of the god of the whites, who has so often caused us to weep, and listen to the voice of liberty, which speaks in the hearts of us all.[40]

If, therefore, the confrontations became ferocious, it was in response to the severity with which the whites treated their captured black prisoners. Some free blacks joined the revolt and we learn that even some mulattos, on seeing the slaves in arms on a grand scale, persuaded some of their rank and file from Le Cap and its neighbourhood to join their 'hitherto despised' brethren and 'fight against a common enemy'.[41] Later they were to be joined by

311

Toussaint, Dessalines and Christophe, but the mulattos, who did not wish to be under the command of a black leader, followed the mulatto leaders, Rigaud and Pétion, to form a second front of opposition to the French. The course of the St Domingue revolt has been discussed in too numerous texts to warrant recounting here. C. L. R. James's is still one of the classic pieces and a good guide to other texts. With the line-up as it was in St Domingue, it is now time to examine the external aspect of the revolt, stemming from the presence of European troops and trading relations with North America.

St. Domingue in the maelstrom of European and American rivalries

The early years of the St Domingue revolt proceeded against a background of estranged Anglo-French relations, as well as deteriorating Franco-American relations, and the background to this development is necessary. The fervour of the French Revolution had alienated some sections of opinion in England and had produced opponents.[42] The death of the French king at the hands of the revolutionaries did not improve matters. The Revolutionary and Napoleonic Wars, which spanned the years 1793 to 1815, with only a short intermission, signified by the Peace of Amiens in 1802, were the outcome of the French revolutionary fervour and England's reaction to it.

For the North Americans contact with St Domingue had been established while the North American colonies were still under the control of England, and this contact too was reinforced during the War of American Independence, in which the North Americans and the French were in alliance against the British. When it is borne in mind that the American Revolution also had its impact on the French Revolution, then we are made aware of the transmission of ideas from which the colony of St Domingue could not be immune. These cross-currents add to the complexity of the situation which later developed in St Domingue. The rising of the Afro-Haitians and the mulattos was further complicated by the complex international relations of the powers surrounding the colony, of which the rebels knew little concerning their nature and magnitude, for the diplomacy had important secret aspects.

Great power diplomacy regarding Haiti continued even into the second half of the nineteenth century, for France never lost hope of trying to regain the old colony, either by subterfuge, by direct means or through the back door. The policies of the United States fluctuated from one side of the pendulum to the other, mirroring an ambivalence from a nation which had proclaimed itself the champion of liberty and had enunciated it in the preamble of its constitution. Its policies were less than liberal and they were conditioned by the fact that it was still a slave-holding state up to the 1860s. England, having failed by direct military intervention to dislodge the French[43] or subjugate the Haitians, sought ascendancy by other means and tried to obtain the most favourable conditions for the exercise of its influence in the territory. Its trade agreements, its diplomatic activities through its trade consuls and its consciousness of its societies in the Caribbean based on slave labour, led it to pursue policies which were often contradictory. It was out of this confusion that the people of St Domingue emerged triumphant in 1804, when they proclaimed their state independent.[44]

The island on which the struggles took place in the late eighteenth and early nineteenth centuries was originally known to its Indian inhabitants as Haiti, but had been named by the early European colonisers, the Spanish, Hispaniola. The Peace of Ryswick of 1697 had confirmed the French hold on the western part of the island, which they named St Domingue and was known as San Domingo to the English, while the other part to the east remained Santo Domingo, to the Spanish. As has been indicated in an earlier chapter of this work, the European powers, preoccupied with mercantilist interests, imposed restrictions on trade between their colonies and outsiders. North America had earlier established contact with St Domingue and had continued to supply it with provisions and slaves as well, but the ascendancy of mercantilist doctrines led the English to impose further curbs on the activities of its colonies. The Board of Trade in London, conscious of the activities of these North Americans with St Domingue, attempted to restrict the contacts by instructing their governments in the colonies to adhere strictly to the Navigation Laws and laws restricting trade with outsiders. This proved a herculean task. The French government, aware of the English prohibitions in 1767, decreed that Môle-Saint-Nicolas be a free port in St Domingue in order to enable foreign vessels to dispose of their wares there, if they wished. Accordingly, foreign vessels were able to purchase lumber, dyewoods, livestock, raw and tanned hides, furs, grapes and tar and, in return, receive molasses and rum. Even this did not meet the requirements of the French colonists of St Domingue, who were anxious to secure food and provisions which a distant France could not always supply them with, and saw the necessity for the removal of import restrictions. Periodically, as with the English colonies, it was emergencies which compelled the restrictions to be lifted, as was the case in St Domingue in 1769, when the ports were opened to allow for the importation of flour, which was added to the list of articles enumerated above.

The period of the American revolt against England strengthened

313

these American ties because of the alliance of France and the American insurgents, and so the colonial ports of France were laid open to American merchant shipping from 1778 until the emergence of the North American colonies as the United States of America in 1783. Thereafter the French, because of the clamour of mercantile and agricultural interests in France, were compelled to abrogate the agreement and, while there were those like Lafayette (who had also fought on the side of the Americans against England) who pleaded the cause of the Americans, the prevailing climate of opinion was in keeping with the mercantilist demands to exclude them. Yet, in August 1784, the French, by the Arrêt du Conseil d'Etat du Roi, allowed for the establishment of seven free ports in its colonies in the Caribbean, with three in St Domingue. The three ports in St Domingue were Cap Français, Port-au-Prince, and Cayes-Saint-Louis. The enumerated list of 1767 was extended to include coal, salt beef, salt fish, rice, maize and vegetables as part of the imports, while the exports were still restricted to molasses and rum. It showed the persistence of the agrarian and mercantile interests in France. But the pressure from this quarter was so unabating that the French government decided to backslide on its policy of liberalisation of trade in relation to the Caribbean. The result was that smuggling became the order of the day and it became difficult to prevent this. Then came distress and food shortage in St Domingue in 1788 and this compelled the governor of the colony to reopen the ports of the island to provide the inhabitants with bread and grain, and allowed for the free importation of the colony's products. The North Americans, while taking advantage of this, found that France, because of pressure at home, would not countenance this, and the Minister of Marine in France annulled the measures of the Governor of St Domingue, M. de Chilleau, and replaced the Governor with a hard-liner. The action resulted in an open confrontation between the colonists and the metropolitan government, as represented by the Governor. The refusal of the colonists to accede to the restrictions led the Governor to dissolve their Assembly. Americans, however, who regarded the trade with French St Domingue as vital, sent Sylvanus Bourne as their Consul to Cap Français, but on his arrival in 1791 Bourne received a cool reception, and after months of evasion and non-recognition he departed from Haiti in July 1791, and tendered his formal resignation in December of that year.[45]

At the time of his departure, Bourne had observed that tension between whites and mulattos was reaching fever pitch, and this eventually exploded later that year. With the rise of the blacks in August 1791 the United States found itself drawn into the controversy by the appeal made from the colonial administration, which sent delegations to the various parts of the Americas and England.

One reached the island of Jamaica to solicit the assistance of Lord Effingham, Governor of Jamaica.[46] With these appeals being made by the colonists, the French government became suspicious of American intentions in St Domingue, and Jefferson was at pains to emphasise that America had no interests in conquests and that the American government was anxious to act in concert with the wishes of the French government with a view to harmonising the policy of the French colonists with that of metropolitan France, and to demonstrate this the U.S. extended help to the French through payments in settlement of the national debt owed to France. Its effectiveness was noted by the diplomatic historian, Professor Tansill, who observed that, but for this United States assistance, 'It would have been almost, if not quite, impossible for the French Administration to have sustained itself in Santo Domingo during the early days of the revolution'.[47] As events developed in St Domingue and the relationship between the powers altered, this lack of ambition on the part of the new United States changed. But, as Tansill rightly observed, the United States 'was not the only nation to lend aid to intervention by military force – intervention that resulted in little achievement and serious loss both in prestige and manpower'. The importance of this West Indian misadventure is now clearly recognised by historians, and Sir John W. Fortescue even went so far as to maintain that the real secret of British impotence against the arms of France from 1793 to 1799 might be found in the 'two fatal words, St Domingue'.[48]

Any reader of Bryan Edwards on British involvement in St Domingue would be under the impression that it was with reluctance that Britain went into the colony and engaged in the struggle against both the French and the St Domingue blacks on the side of the colonial planters. But this is far from representing the British official position, and the records of the British despatches are eloquent.[49] They reveal an active interest to supplant the French and it was only after the circumstances of war, the combined pressure of the blacks and mulattos under the respective leadership of Toussaint and Rigaud, the loss of many troops through yellow fever and other ailments, and the home government's desire to scale down the cost of the operations and make financial economies, that the situation became so hopeless that Britain, through the efforts of Colonel Thomas Maitland, counselled a less dishonourable retreat. It was not an act of benevolence, nor was it the result of wise statesmanship. It had become expedient because Britain's existence on the island was no longer tenable and the concentration of British troops would have been hard pressed to cope with the combined black and mulatto forces that were closing in on them. The fact will be revealed as the St Domingue drama unfolds.

The colonists fled in all directions, some to Cuba, some to the

United States, while others fled to South America. While it might be true that some of the colonists, who fled to neighbouring British plantations such as Trinidad and Jamaica, had hinted that Britain might assume suzerainty over the colony – and this might have been so for people with royalist sentiments opposed to the takeover by republicans – Bryan Edwards gives too simplistic a picture of the French settlers requesting that Britain might assume control of the island, and this without any British interest.[50] Yet Edwards, wallowing as he did sometimes in contradictions, was to provide some of the reasons why the British would be actively interested in gaining ascendancy over the island. With British and French relations strained as a result of the French Revolution and the execution of the king in Paris, with the revolutionary fervour spreading to the French Antilles with attendant consequences for the British Antilles, with the rivalries between them undiminished, it is difficult to accept Edwards' facile explanation, but the Foreign Office and Colonial despatches reveal an active interest. Yet Edwards did appreciate one factor conditioning British policy, when he spoke of Lord Effingham's response to the request by the Commissioners sent from St Domingue to solicit help from the Jamaican government, by writing that 'he [Effingham] saw, in its full extent, the danger to which every island in the West Indies would be exposed from such an example, if the triumph of savage anarchy over all order and government should be complete'.[51] Effingham at first promised some arms and ammunition and provisions, while not able to offer troops initially, but considered the possibility of sending one or more English ships with the hope of intimidating the 'insurgents'.[52] When the British landed their superior forces it did not intimidate the slaves, but rather drove them to greater exertion. They were made aware of the fact that imperialism could be international. But, by the year 1793, with the landing of British troops at St Domingue, Britain had already become an active participant in the war to supplant the French and seemingly to restore slavery. This factor made the war more ferocious. That the white French colonists wished to transfer their allegiance to the British, having become incensed by the two decrees of the French government of 15 May 1791 and the law of 4 April 1792, which enfranchised the mulattos and the free blacks, is hardly credible. That they were disgusted with the metropolitan government, and especially those of them who had royalist leanings, there is no doubt; but for the weakness of their position they would have preferred not control by the British but independence, and this fact continued to rankle with them as the fortunes of war altered. Even when, opportunistically, some of them sheltered under Toussaint's banner, they nurtured hopes of their own eventual triumph. Having despatched the small British force which seized the harbour of Jérémie, the Môle-Saint-Nicolas and then, on 4 June 1794 securing the surrender of Port-au-Prince, they achieved nothing more. Thereafter they suffered reverses. As Professor Tansill has remarked:

> The capture of Port-au-Prince marked the high tide of British good fortune in Haiti. Recession began when the mulatto general, Rigaud, took the offensive in the summer of 1794, and soon Leogane was in his hands. And although Toussaint failed in his assault upon Saint-Marc in September of that year, he was rapidly learning the art of war from these defeats even as the Russians learned the same lesson from the reverses they suffered at the hands of Charles XII of Sweden.[53]

But from 1793 the complication had begun, for American vessels were in danger of being seized by both the French privateers and the British, and especially those trading with St Domingue and the French Antilles. By a decree of the French National Assembly of 9 May 1793 any neutral vessels taking provisions to the 'enemy' (i.e. the rebels) were to be detained, although payment was to be made for the provisions and freight and demurrage paid to the owners of the vessels. Only American vessels were excepted. The British, on 8 June 1793, passed an Order in Council along similar lines. In order to prevent American vessels trading with the French Caribbean ports, the British issued another Order in Council on 6 November 1793 authorising commanders of British warships to 'detain all ships laded with the produce of any colony belonging to France, or carrying provisions or other supplies for the use of such colony'.[54]

As the result of these measures American vessels discontinued trading with the Caribbean until assured of the safety of their vessels, and this resulted in the Jay Treaty of 19 November 1794, which helped to harmonise relations between Britain and the United States, but in turn produced difficulties for the United States in its relations with France. But, prior to this, by an embargo of Bordeaux, the French had attempted to limit considerably commerce in the Caribbean and had detained some American vessels, and a Directory Decree of 2 July 1796 set aside the Franco-American treaty, insisting that thenceforth American vessels were to be restricted on the same conditions as British vessels, and the attempt by the agents of the French Directory in St Domingue to apply the provisions of the decree resulted in disaster for American shipping in Caribbean waters. French privateers captured numerous American vessels and the American Congress was forced to adopt retaliatory measures, and from June 1798 commercial relations between the United States and France, as well as its possessions, were suspended. Thus, the existing commercial treaty with France was abrogated and the United States created a Navy Department.[55]

It was at this time that President John Adams began to think that it might be 'expedient' to have the French islands 'free and independent, in close alliance and under the guarantee of the United States'.[56] Alexander Hamilton was also thinking along similar lines and wanted the Adams administration 'to be committed to a policy which favoured Haitian independence', although we are assured that Hamilton and his federalist party were interested in Haiti principally for the expansion of trade and suppression of privateering.[57] The American Secretary of State, Henry Pickering, appears to have expressed the nation's viewpoint, or at least a section of it, that a policy of peace might ensue between Toussaint and the British, as well as the Americans, and he thereupon embarked on his own initiative to court Toussaint. At the time Pickering spoke of Toussaint in glowing terms, regarded him as 'amiable and respectable', and saw him as 'the Commander-in-Chief'. Pickering was of the opinion that Toussaint had not compromised his position with the British.[58]

In this aspiration lay the seeds of trouble and disagreement which were later to occur between the British, the Americans and the Haitians. The peace which they sought for British dependencies and the United States was to prevent the spread of revolution among the black slaves of their respective territories. The French Agent of the Directory, General Hedouville, who arrived in Haiti about this time, saw 'a most sinister aspect' behind the amiability and respectability of Toussaint observed by Pickering. But when Hedouville landed in St Domingue in April 1798 he realised that Toussaint was 'the supreme power' in the territory and returned to France after six months. Toussaint's major task was to defeat the mulatto leader, André Rigaud. In order to be sure of this, Toussaint saw the need to cultivate the friendship of the United States. He was also aware of the fact that Rigaud had previously spoken of possible commerce with the United States and, anxious that America did not become an active supporter of Rigaud, he wrote to President Adams on 6 November 1798 regretting the fact that American vessels were no longer visiting St Domingue and promised safety and protection to them; he also expressed willingness to pay for American produce. He followed this by sending his personal representative, Joseph Bunel, to Philadelphia in December. This led to Congressional approval in February 1799 for the resumption of trade with St Domingue. President Adams sent out Mr Edward Stevens as Consul-General and his success with Toussaint has been discussed at length by Professor Tansill.[59]

But Stevens also tried to harmonise British and United States policy in terms of commerce in the area. Jefferson, who was to succeed Adams as President, was expressing the opposing viewpoint. He was not only fearful of British ascendancy and domination of St Domingue instead of French dominance, but he also wanted to see prevented the ascendancy of regimes of coloured peoples in the Caribbean which would have implications for the United States, and he wanted to forestall this, if at all possible.[60] Apart from his racial bias against the blacks, Jefferson's fear was that an independent black or coloured Haiti was a bad example, and he forcibly expressed it both in his pronouncements and in his correspondence; and, while favouring trade with France, he was not prepared to countenance St Domingue hiving off from French control. In his letter to James Madison dated 12 February 1799 relating to Congressional approval of resumption of trade with Toussaint, he sarcastically noted that

'Toussaint's clause' had received the approval of both houses of Congress; even South Carolinas in the H. of R. voted for it. We may expect therefore black crews, and supercargoes and missionaries thence into the southern states; and when that level begins to work, I would gladly compound with a great part of our northern country, if they would honestly stand neuter. If this combustion can be introduced among us under any veil whatever, we have to fear it.[61]

The ground was being prepared for the diplomatic activities and agreements which were further to confuse the St Domingue situation. Rigaud's offensive against the British took place from the end of 1794, and with it also the reverses of the British continued. It was now another formidable foe which intervened on behalf of the Haitians. From the beginning of 1795 an outbreak of yellow fever began to decimate British troops and they soon became bogged down. Bryan Edwards gives us a glimpse of the toll of lives taken within so short a time, observing that British troops on 1 January 1795 amounted to 1490 on the Island of St Domingue, and that 738 of these were ill from the disease; by the summer the number of sick had increased and ten weeks later, after the further landing of the 81st Regiment of 980 men, 630 of them were dead. By June 1795, out of a total of 3000 British soldiers, only 1300 were fit for duty.[62]

The year 1795 found Britain in the Caribbean experiencing much turbulence, which some attributed to the ill winds blowing from the St Domingue slave revolt. Britain had to confront the Maroons in the second Maroon War (1795), which eventually led to the defeat of the Maroons of Trelawny and their removal to Nova Scotia. Simultaneously Britain engaged in a final confrontation with the Caribs of St Vincent (1795–6), who had continued to harass the Caribbean settlements for over a century, and this also led to their removal to Honduras. Britain also preoccupied itself with the seizure of French territories, namely Martinique, Guadeloupe[63] and St Lucia,[64] and was at the time endeavouring to quell a slave revolt in early 1795 in Grenada. The slaves in the British island of Dominica had revolted in 1791 and Lord Grenville in London consulted the Committee of West India Planters and Merchants as to the amount of additional forces to be sent to the island.[65] In referring to these incidents, the aim is not to exonerate the British, but merely to show how Britain's activities were so far flung as to involve divided attention. This is not to belittle the formidable nature of the confrontation which Britain faced in St Domingue. But these and other factors contributed to the ineffectiveness of British attempts at military subjugation of St Domingue. Britain had failed to learn the lesson of the American Revolutionary War by endeavouring to supplant the French in Haiti and suppressing the Africans and coloured people who had raised the banner of revolt. One of the reasons given by some British historians for the loss of the American War of Independence was that the country was 'unfamiliar to the invader'. Be this as it may, here was a country unknown to the British invader and the invader was endeavouring to wrest it from the very people who knew and worked its terrain, the Haitians. The tragedy of yellow fever which struck recalls the story of the Spanish Armada in which the defeat of the Armada was celebrated in England with the saying 'Flavit Deus et dissipati sunt', implying that the 'Winds of God blew and they (the enemy) were dispersed', shortened to read 'God blew and they were dispersed'. The tragedy of the St Domingue affair was that God, at that material time, was no longer on the side of the English and so his epidemic took so many of the lives of the invaders, and by dispersing the enemies of the Haitians the incident became reminiscent of the destruction of Sennacherib.

When the year 1796 began the island of St Domingue had the British holding on to the western part, while the southern part was under the command of Rigaud, and the north under Toussaint's leadership. A mulatto/black confrontation took place when Toussaint, by his appearance at Cap Français, relieved the beleaguered French Governor, General Leveaux, who was surrounded by the mulatto forces, and put the mulattos to flight. This resulted in Governor Leveaux bestowing on Toussaint the title of Lieutenant-Governor of the colony and promising to follow Toussaint's advice. Professor Tansill, commenting on this measure of legitimacy which the French Governor had conferred on Toussaint, wrote, 'Such conduct spelled the "end of white prestige and the beginning of black rule" '.[66]

In May 1796 the Directory Commission of Five, sent to the island of St Domingue under the leadership of Sonthonax, arrived.[67] French intrigue at its worst showed itself even in the handling of the Commission by its leader. Its failure to make an impression to secure St Domingue for France was shown by the fact that Sonthonax, wishing to advance the cause of the blacks against the mulattos, seemed enthusiastic for Toussaint's faction, leading to the return of Giraud to France, while Roumé constituted no problem, as he lived in the Spanish part of the island, Santo Domingo; Leblanc died of poisoning; and Raymond felt powerless to oppose Sonthonax. Governor Leveaux was sent to France as Deputy from St Domingue. Toussaint thus had his chance to compel Sonthonax to embark for France on 5 August 1797.

Toussaint next directed his energies to the expulsion of the English, who were still entrenched in Jérémie, Port-au-Prince, Saint Marc and the fortress of Môle-Saint-Nicolas. Rigaud also co-operated in this endeavour to remove them from the island. In the meantime, on 20 April 1798, General Hedouville arrived in St Domingue as an Agent from the French Directory. Toussaint accorded him a welcome and some display of deference. But Hedouville, conscious of the fact that he had no army, had also to behave in accordance with the wishes of Toussaint, while biding his time, and so he acquiesced in the effort to expel the British from the island.

Prior to the arrival of Hedouville, however, the British troops in the island were beginning to be weary of the misadventure into which they had been led by the plea of the St Domingue planters and by their own ambitions to seize the island from the contending parties. Their expenditure had increased immensely and by 1796 the annual appropriations had reached £2 million; in the month of January 1797 alone the British had incurred debts of $700 000 and the British Treasury was becoming understandably restive. The British government appointed Major-General Simcoe to the High Command of the British forces in St Domingue, but he was also to endeavour to scale down the expenses to an annual outlay not exceeding £300 000 and British troops were only to be concentrated in Môle-Saint-Nicolas. Simcoe was hoping to occupy the island of Tortuga, near the Môle, and use it as his base of operations against St Domingue, but on his arrival at the Môle on 20 February 1797 he found the British forces in desperate straits and unable to engage in any serious operations. In March Toussaint's forces pushed the British troops in the west back upon Port-au-Prince, and the situation was becoming clearer that the British could not hold out much longer. Accordingly, in July, Simcoe, with his most able officer, Colonel Maitland, left for England to represent the situation, while leaving the command in the hands of Major-General Whyte.

The British War Office, despite Simcoe's report of the hopelessness of the situation, seemed unaware of the danger the British troops were in and appointed Major-General Nesbitt to take over command, but preceding him was Colonel Thomas Maitland, with a copy of the instructions given to Nesbitt. Both Toussaint and Rigaud were scoring successes against the British and the latter were hard pressed when Maitland arrived back in St Domingue in 1798. The relations between him and his superior officer, Major-General Whyte, belong not to this work but to British military history, and are not discussed here. With Maitland assuming authority, General Whyte handed over his command and left for England. Maitland withdrew a large section of his forces to Jérémie from Port-au-Prince as a prelude to the evacuation of Port-au-Prince, St Marc and L'Archaye, in accordance with the instructions given to General Nesbitt.[68] Then he attempted to negotiate with Toussaint the terms for British withdrawal in order to reduce the misfortunes of war, with requests that Toussaint should agree to protect and confirm the property owners of the areas that were being evacuated. Once the details had been agreed upon[69] Maitland withdrew to Jérémie and the Môle as the prelude to the eventual evacuation of St Domingue. Maitland then wrote to the British government doubting the wisdom of clinging to the fortified posts in St Domingue and preferring an honourable withdrawal for the English rather than a forced one.[70] He also saw the futility of the expense that would be involved. Maitland also wrote to the Earl of Balcarres, Governor of Jamaica, to persuade him to cultivate the friendship of Toussaint in order to guarantee the safety of Jamaica, which he feared was threatened.[71] The visit of Toussaint to the British camp at Môle-Saint-Nicolas on 31 August 1798, and the 'royal honours' accorded him by Maitland, provided both of them with the opportunity to sign the agreement for the final evacuation of the British.

It was this that became the Toussaint-Maitland Secret Treaty which was to cause its own problems, both for the British in their relations with the Americans and for Toussaint in that it caused embarrassment for him and rendered him suspect in the eyes of the French. In this agreement the British sought exclusive right to control the trade of St Domingue, while they urged Toussaint to proclaim himself King of Haiti, with the promise of British support from their squadrons stationed in his ports. Observing this agreement, the American historian, Tansill, wrote:

> Toussaint had not imbibed so freely that he had lost his usual cunning in state craft. The secret treaty that he signed on 31 August 1798 gave no exclusive trade advantages to England. The parties agreed upon a policy of non-interference, both political and military, in certain territories belonging to each other. England promised to adopt a 'hands off' attitude towards any part of the island of Santo

Domingo under the control of Toussaint, and the black general gave a pledge that he would adopt a similar attitude towards the island of Jamaica. Maitland also promised to send to Toussaint certain supplies which would be paid for in colonial produce.[72]

We can see from the kind of agreement that the British tried to foist on Toussaint that they were trying to exercise control through the back door by stationing squadrons of warships in Haitian ports. This would have been tantamount to what, in modern parlance, is known as 'neocolonialism'. Maitland then wrote to the Earl of Balcarres[73] in order to assuage the fears of Jamaica and to encourage correspondence with Toussaint, and indicating the provisions which Toussaint would need from the British or American importers in the future. He then left for England to report his actions.

Having secured the conditions for complete British evacuation, Toussaint took the opportunity in October 1798 to hasten the departure of General Hedouville for France. Before his departure the latter urged Rigaud to take up arms against Toussaint, allegedly asserting that Toussaint had been bought by the English, the émigrés and the Americans.[74] Toussaint then took the opportunity to promote his friendship with the English and the Americans, having handled the entire situation with consummate skill. The British government then prepared the Maitland mission to Philadelphia and then to St Domingue.

According to Tansill, the background to that mission dated back to the signing of the Jay Treaty of 1794, and the treaty itself was a consequence of the strained relations which existed between France and the United States which, by January 1797, seemed to be heading for a war. Here the British government, through diplomatic activity, wanted to ensure that there was some kind of alliance between Britain and the United States. While diplomatic channels were busy working out these arrangements, it is from these sources, consisting of the pronouncements of heads of states and governments, or their foreign ministers or other ministers of state and their ambassadors, that one gets a glimpse of the ambitions in the Caribbean, and sometimes the lack of sincerity of their policies towards St Domingue and towards Toussaint. They reveal not only the racial preoccupations of those involved, but their lurking fears of French ascendancy; all these things were unknown to the black leader of Haiti, who acted, for his part, with great sincerity, which even the despatches of these countries admitted.

Such was the tragedy of the St Domingue situation, which certainly provided a curtain-raiser for latecomers to the international scene as to the nature of trust which could be put on such diplomatic activities in the jungle of international relations. One can only use a few citations to indicate the complexities, for the documents themselves tell their own story, which cannot be dealt with adequately in this chapter.

While wooing America for unified action against the French, it was Liston, the British Minister in America, who, taking soundings from America, on 2 May 1798, retailed them to Lord Grenville in London, thus:

> At the same time I perceive that the American Ministers have their views fixed on the conquest of the Floridas and Louisiana for themselves and the acquisition of St Domingo (if not of the other French islands) by Great Britain.... I asked one of the ministers jocularly (taking it for granted that if they assisted us to take the French West India Islands and we assisted them to get possession of Louisiana and the Floridas, matters might be considered as pretty nearly balanced between us on that score) what return they were to make for all the care we took and were likely to take of their shipping in every part of the world? He said that as we defended the Americans at sea they must endeavour to defend us by land.[75]

While Lord Grenville seemed favourably inclined towards the idea, he replied in the following vein:

> Any proposals for concert and co-operation will be cordially received here and this not more on account of the direct advantage, whatever it may be, which this country may derive from them, than from the interests which we feel in contributing to enable the United States to defend themselves against the prevalence of the principles of anarchy which would inevitably follow any submission on their part to the insolence of France.... The conquest of Louisiana and Florida by the United States instead of being any cause of jealousy, would certainly be a matter of satisfaction to this Government, and in that state of affairs, it is also easy to see the advantage which America would derive from seeing St Domingo in the hands of His Majesty rather than of any other European Power.[76]

But before Liston had received Lord Grenville's communication he wrote again to him, expressing surprise at the *volte face* by members of the Adams administration concerning St Domingue. The administration, he wrote, appeared within a few days to have altered their ideas with regard to the island of St Domingue, and perhaps, with regard to the other possessions of the French in the West Indies. 'What I ventured to throw out in a former letter of the probability of their readiness to co-operate in throwing those colonies into the possession of His Majesty, I derived from the conversation I had recently had on the subject with the Secretary of State.... But Colonel Pickering now hints at a plan on the part of the blacks to declare themselves independent and to erect the island into a sovereign state, to which he seems to think it would not be inconsistent with the interests of America to consent.'[77]

On receipt of that despatch, Lord Grenville was upset, especially by the fact that the Haitian blacks were intending to declare themselves independent and a sovereign people. His 'horror' was expressed to the American Minister in London, Rufus King. But it became clear that both John Adams and Alexander Hamilton favoured the independence of French colonies in the Caribbean 'under the guarantee of the United States'.[78]

Then came an added complication when the French colonists in St Domingue communicated with the American representative in Cap Français, Jacob Mayer, indicating their willingness to cut off their links with France and declare themselves independent. This was probably done to prevent a possible declaration of independence by the blacks and recognition by the United States. Again President Adams, by September 1798 was inclining to the view that the French would never regain the colony and that a declaration of Haitian independence would be acceptable to the United States, but he held back from doing so because he did not wish to offend England, which held a divergent point of view on the island.[79] Here it appeared that the President was backsliding and seemed not to have had the courage of his convictions. Diplomatic activity continued in order to harmonise British and United States policies both in their dealings with France and with St Domingue. The discovery by the U.S. Minister in London of the secret British Treaty between Maitland and Toussaint and the diplomatic activities and representations which followed have been described by Professor Tansill and do not warrant recounting here.[80] However, negotiations between the British and the Americans centred on a number of issues. First, the Americans were concerned about the consequences which the provisions of the secret Treaty would have on American commerce in the Caribbean, and sought its revision. Furthermore, they were concerned that Toussaint's vessels did not tamper with American commerce as a result of the Maitland agreement and requested the insertion of the proviso that no privateers were to be pitted by Toussaint from St Domingue ports against vessels of the United States and that these were not to be confiscated.[81] Maitland's objections to these, however, were based on the fact that to incorporate them into an agreement with Toussaint would give the latter the impression that it was within his power to interfere with British and American shipping whenever he considered it necessary.[82]

Maitland explained the principle which guided the conclusion of his secret treaty with Toussaint as the desire to 'crush if possible [the influence of] the French Agent [Hedouville], to preserve the

325

tranquillity of those who have been under the British Government, to secure the peace of the island of Jamaica and as far as is compatible with these essential points to throw into the channel of British commerce as large a portion of the produce of Saint Domingo as possible'.[83]

Using some of Maitland's statement, Professor Tansill commented on the predicament of St Domingue thus:

> It should be clearly understood, however, that this inclination towards Toussaint was not based upon any 'personal predilection for any one of the Chiefs in the Island of Saint Domingo'. If Rigaud had been on a plane of equality with Toussaint he would have met with 'similar treatment'. In conclusion, Maitland advised the War Office to instruct any agent sent out to Haiti to keep constantly in mind the fact that he should never hold out to Toussaint 'any prospect of a connection' that would make his situation a 'matter of discussion when His Majesty's Ministers may think fit to treat for a general Peace'. The black dictator was merely a pawn in the complicated game of politics in the Caribbean, and no British advantage should be lost through deference to mere sentiment.[84]

The policies being pursued were designed to undermine Toussaint. He was to have the illusion of sovereignty while at the same time he would be discouraged from having his own navy.[85] Yet, even at that point Maitland was still of the opinion that Americans would benefit from the commerce in the zone rather than the British. Yet the British decided to proceed with Maitland's mission to Toussaint by way of the United States. Paramount in the consideration of the British War Office was the safeguarding of 'colonial possessions against the danger with which they are threatened by the present political and military state of Saint Domingo . . . and the next (a consequence and a principal security to the former) is to exclude other Nations (the United States excepted) from participating in any commercial advantages that can be derived from an intercourse with the Island'.[86] It conceived of the danger from the state of St Domingo from two points of view:

> 1st As Arising from the possibility of an open attack being made from that island upon any of the Possessions either of this Country or America.
> 2nd As likely to be produced by the example and description of the Military Authority existing in Saint Domingo, upon every country of which the principal population consists in slaves, assisted by means of influence and seduction that will be most actively exerted among such Slaves in the British Colonies and the Southern States of America, unless the utmost precautions are

> taken on the one hand, by ... destroying the authority of France
> in Saint Domingo, and ... by placing all intercourse with the
> Island under ... severe checks and control.[87]

It was also aimed at binding Toussaint to an undertaking 'in the strongest manner not to fit out any expedition, or to give any assistance or countenance to any hostile operations against the Territories of His Majesty or the United States'. The British War Office hoped that with America's agreement both of them would concert their efforts to impose these restraints on Toussaint not so much to the advantage of Toussaint and his followers but rather to gratify either the greed of gain or to satisfy the political ascendancy which one or other of them wished to have attained. But they were also anxious not to arouse Toussaint's suspicions about their intentions, even though these were subversive. But, as has been observed earlier, while Maitland was on his way to Philadelphia the U.S. sent out its own Consul, Edward Stevens, to St Domingue in response to Toussaint's request after securing Congressional approval in February 1799 for the resumption of trade with the island. The United States initiatives had been conditioned by the rumours which were circulating about the previous secret treaty concluded by Maitland with Toussaint in August 1798. Neither the British nor the Americans were anxious to allow Toussaint to have his own fleet. Secretary of State Pickering, while in favour of trade with Toussaint and feeling that this trade should be with all the world, believed it would be a mistake to allow him to have any ships under his control, and thought he should be forbidden to send out 'a single boat, unless with a view to go from one port of the island to another'.[88]

Another factor which emerged at the time of Maitland's arrival in Philadelphia on 2 April 1799 was the divergence which he observed concerning the policies of both the governments of the United States and Britain, and aptly summed it up thus:

> Our policy is to protect, theirs to destroy the present Colonial
> System. Our views only go to a partial, theirs to a compleat opening
> of Saint Domingo Market. We are willing to submit to a temporary
> Evil to avoid a greater; they see no Evil and some of them much
> good in the present situation of Saint Domingue.[89]

His dislike for the American system of government and their preoccupation with making money are spelled out in his despatch. While the negotiations were going on between Maitland and the American government, British circles still suspected America of urging the blacks to declare Haiti independent,[90] a fact which the British themselves had previously contemplated and attempted. But

327

Stevens, while deploring the notion of Haitian independence, believed it was inevitable and all that America had to do was to seize the opportunity 'with as little hazzards as possible to the Southern parts of the Union'.[91] However, President Adams' views on independence diverged from those of Secretary Pickering, for while the President favoured the view of Haitian independence, his Secretary shuddered at the danger that it might constitute to the United States.[92] Even at this point Maitland still felt uneasy that the United States might conclude a separate agreement with Haiti, but what eventually emerged in the Anglo-American agreement was intended to supplant the French and exclude them entirely from St Domingue. British delaying tactics in ratifying the Maitland-Toussaint treaty of 31 August 1798 led Toussaint to negotiate with Stevens. Toussaint was peeved by the fact that the British had not even attempted to implement some of the provisions of the treaty relating to supplies of provisions from Jamaica; the 'conduct of British warships in Haitian waters because of their disrespect and hostility was giving rise to suspicions in Toussaint's mind'.[93]

It was at this point that Maitland arrived at Cap Français on 14 May 1799, afraid that America might in fact have secured more favourable terms of trade than the British sought to secure. In attempting to secure terms as favourable from Toussaint, he threatened that Britain would continue the existing blockade of all Haitian ports and, in spite of friendly relations between the U.S. and Britain, no American ships would be allowed to discharge cargoes in St Domingue.[94]

Here was a crisis looming large, which was only averted by the fact that Stevens was a better diplomat than Maitland, and but for Stevens, Toussaint would have been unwilling to continue any negotiations with Maitland. It was Stevens who smoothed things over and enabled Toussaint to concede that he would prevent any attacks from his country to any part of the U.S.A. or any British possessions and he agreed that Cap Français and Port-au-Prince should be the ports of entry for trade goods. But these were the preliminaries to more substantial requirements. With rumours that Rigaud was planning to invade the coast of Jamaica, Toussaint's disinclination to continue negotiations with the English also manifested itself; for the news of the secret treaty which had become public abroad filtered back to St Domingue and Toussaint felt embarrassed and refused to receive Colonel Grant as the resident British Agent on the island. Maitland therefore had to be content with Stevens overseeing British interests till Toussaint could be persuaded to receive a British Consul.[95]

The resumption of negotiations with Maitland culminated in the signing of another secret treaty on 13 June, extending that of 1798, and while Edwards was not a signatory, he signified the United

States' concurrence in adhering to its provisos. With that treaty hostilities were to be suspended between Britain and that part of Haiti under Toussaint and the latter undertook not to fit out any expeditions to either American territory or British possessions.[96] Protection against the attacks of French corsairs was also to be assured. Yet the racial overtone and selfish economic considerations, apart from the protection of British possessions from possible revolutionary activities emanating from St Domingue, were uppermost in Maitland's mind. His letter to the new British Consul, Colonel Grant, was even more revealing and is an example of that perfidy which had dogged British-Haitian relations. Some of the contents of this letter need to be stated because they also shed light on Britain's later policy towards Haitian sovereignty after the signing of the Treaty of Amiens. Maitland expressed the view that it would not 'ever suit the character of the British Nation to enter into any further agreement with a Person of Toussaint's description',[97] even though Maitland admitted that Toussaint had scrupulously carried out the provisions of the treaty of 31 August 1798. Grant was to play the role of spy in Toussaint's domain, for he was to take care to prevent any attempts by St Domingue to invade British possessions, and was to keep a close watch on the size of Toussaint's fleet of coasting vessels. While he suggested that it would be highly dangerous to permit this fleet to serve as a 'nursery' for a formidable Haitian navy, a judicious use of the passport system should be used as a way of effectively checking and controlling the growth of Toussaint's naval forces, and the passport system should also be used to prevent the emigration of Haitian undesirables. Furthermore, Maitland favoured the continuation of chaos in St Domingue as he felt it served British interests, and so instructed Grant to do nothing which would favour the reconciliation of Toussaint with Rigaud. Here was the classic case of 'divide and rule', and, looked at from this point in time, it was certainly an unkind cut for the Haitians, who were engaged in a fratricidal battle which had been induced into that society by the policies of other Europeans and sustained over time so as to become the custom and the norm. Thus, Grant was to endeavour to 'prevent any amicable arrangement taking place between Rigaud and Toussaint'.[98]

Maitland aimed at keeping Toussaint friendly to Britain while he was in difficulty with the Agent of the French Directory and with Rigaud. But it also suited British interests while Toussaint was in rebellion against the French Directory, but were the French Directory to begin to gain 'ascendancy in the Island', Colonel Grant was to induce Toussaint to declare the independence of the colony, but he was not to hold out to Toussaint 'the smallest appearance of any further protection, or countenance from our Government'.[99] Yet, when independence came they held back recognition of the regime for many years. This method of conduct of international relations could hardly be regarded as honest. Nevertheless, these were the circumstances in which the slaves who had revolted against servitude were placed and hoped to find some assistance, and trusted in agreements forged by their leader with perfidious Europeans and Euro-Americans. Grant was advised to attempt to act in concert with America in matters relating to Toussaint.[100] But Maitland continued to reveal that the political goal was more to be desired and that he expected the trade with Haiti to be beneficial to none other than the United States and not Britain.[101]

He wrote to Lord Balcarres in neighbouring Jamaica asking him to supply provisions to Haiti, since on the supply depended the fate of Toussaint's cause.[102] In a second letter, written the same day to Lord Balcarres, he asked him to supply Toussaint with 100 barrels of gunpowder, 200 stands of arms and a 'few flints'. He was sure that these would be of 'infinite use to the black general'.[103] Maitland wrote again to Lord Balcarres on 20 June 1799 to apprise him of the fact that Toussaint was

> in a situation extremely unpleasant. Rigaud is already in motion and has put to death a very considerable number of White Inhabitants both at Jeremie and Aux Cayes, and universally to a man at Petit Goaves, which place he has made himself master of, and here he has murdered man, woman and child. I find Toussaint is in very great want indeed of Provisions, so much so that his Troops are at a stand for want of them . . . . The whole aspect of things here shows the crisis of this Island to be at hand, and at present though the chances are in Toussaint's favour, still there is not anything like certainty as I apprehend the other is considerably before him in his preparations for attack. Every hour convinces me more of the propriety of my advice to Your Lordship of not opening the Ports generally to English Vessels even after the first of August.[104]

Maitland also wrote to Admiral Sir Hyde Parker on 20 June 1799 and urged that provisions be sent at once to Toussaint and that the ports under Rigaud's control should be kept in 'the strictest blockade'.[105]

Even at this late stage the Americans were also more concerned to maintain harmony in policy with the British than to carry on any trade with St Domingue, and President Adams, in a letter to Secretary of State Pickering, expressed his sentiments in the following words:

> Harmony with the English, in all this Business of St Domingo is the thing I have most at heart. The Result of the whole is in my mind

problematical and precarious. Toussaint has evidently puzzled himself, the French Government, the English Cabinet and the Administration of the United States. All the rest of the World knows as little of what to do with him as he knows what to do with himself. His example may be followed by all the Islands French, English, Dutch, and Spanish and all will be one day played off against the US by European Powers.[106]

This was the situation by the middle of 1799. But more was to come. Looking at the activities of two years alone between 1798 and 1799, one still marvels that the Haitian revolt succeeded, but in these happenings were to be found the seeds of discord which plagued the country into the twentieth century.

The conclusion of this secret treaty led to the proclamation of President Adams on 26 June 1799 which led to the resumption of U.S. trade with St Domingue, with Cap Français and Port-au-Prince being opened only to British and American trade. America took advantage of the situation to send its warships into Haitian waters on the grounds of protecting American interests.[107] Much of the cordiality of the relationship between American and Toussaint's St Domingue was the work of Stevens, the Consul-General on the spot, who believed that in the confrontation between Rigaud and Toussaint the latter would triumph, and he urged his country to support Toussaint by legal measures.[108] It was this friendly feeling of Stevens towards Toussaint which led the latter to write to President Adams and then follow it up with a visit to his personal representative, already mentioned.

The American administration seems to have attached much importance to this establishment of good relations and hoped for mutual advantages from the commercial relations of the two countries. Stevens, having assured the State Department that American citizens and property in St Domingue were perfectly secure, then informed Toussaint in a communication that 'the American Government had an exalted opinion of his character', and expressed the view that the Adams administration had the 'unequivocal desire to maintain the harmony' existing between the two countries.[109] The American historian, Tansill, describing this harmony, wrote:

> The expressions of good faith and friendship between Toussaint and the representatives of the American Government were distinctly lacking in the relations that existed between the negro leader and the agents of Great Britain. Lord Balcarres (Governor of Jamaica) and Admiral Sir Hyde Parker were not entirely convinced that it was good policy to maintain intimate relations with Toussaint and these suspicions were reciprocated by the black dictator.[110]

331

For a while even, Toussaint's suspicions fell on Stevens, but this was soon cleared up, due to Stevens' competent handling of the situation and Toussaint himself, conscious of the fact that friendliness to America would assist him in the handling of the British in the Caribbean. Stevens strove to cement a cordial relationship. Then Admiral Sir Hyde Parker seized six of Toussaint's armed vessels that were about to attempt a blockade of Jacmel in their final assault on Rigaud. There again followed diplomatic activity between the United States and Britain. Pickering informed the British Minister in America, Liston, of the consequences which might occur from such attempts to seize any more of Toussaint's vessels, and Grenville in London was so informed.

America, now in open co-operation with Toussaint, employed their warships in Toussaint's waters and began capturing vessels *en route* to the ports under Rigaud's control. Definite orders were sent to the American Captain Christopher Perry of the frigate *General Greene* to 'assist in securing the convoy against the Boats of Rigaud' and to 'intercept them as much as possible'. He was, however, not to do anything to disturb the harmony which existed between Toussaint and the people of the United States.[111] This U.S. intervention on behalf of Toussaint and against Rigaud ultimately led to the triumph of Toussaint over his rival. As Stevens then saw the situation, the blockade would soon lead to Toussaint controlling the entire country and this would ultimately lead to the severance of the link with France and the formal proclamation of independence by the Haitians. However, American naval forces went on to bombard the forts guarding the entrance to Jacmel. Besieged this way, Rigaud and the elite corps of his army cut their way to safety.[112] On 11 March 1800 Toussaint's troops captured Jacmel and this paved the way for Toussaint's victory over the south. Toussaint was profuse in his gratitude to the American government for their assistance and then proceeded to move against the Agent of the French Directory, Roumé, resident in the Spanish sector, by inviting Roumé to assist in the campaign against Rigaud. Roumé's initial refusal earned him imprisonment in order to save him from the physical violence of the people. Roumé then agreed to co-operate, but Toussaint, conscious of the possibility of intrigues, kept Roumé in close confinement. This spell of imprisonment broke Roumé's spirit and he demonstrated willingness to co-operate with Toussaint and reluctantly conceded the occupation of Spanish Santo Domingo by Toussaint's troops, the territory having previously been ceded in 1795 by the Treaty of Basle to the French.[113]

While Toussaint was about to embark on the occupation of Santo Domingo, commissioners arrived from France with a view to mediating between Toussaint and Rigaud, but Toussaint immediately returned one of them to France. Directing his energies against Rigaud, Toussaint soon achieved a more ferocious confrontation in these fratricidal engagements. It is too easily assumed that the basis of the confrontation was colour, that is, the colour differences between the groups led by the two contenders.[114] But C. L. R. James calls our attention to the denial of this by both Rigaud and Toussaint.[115] What was essentially a class struggle accordingly had the colour factor infused into it in order to make it more formidable, and James puts the blame squarely at the door of the 'enemies' of the country who had earlier infused it into the relationships of these people. Furthermore, Rigaud claimed that it was the mutual enemies of both who were contributing to the diminishing friendship which would have bound both leaders together.[116] When we take account of the instruction given by Maitland to Colonel Grant not to do anything which would bring the two warring leaders together, then Rigaud's statement, as quoted by James, bears testimony to the intrigue by outsiders. There are many more letters of this kind in the records.[117] Blacks and mulattos were to be found in the armies of both Toussaint and Rigaud. In the north, where free blacks fought for Rigaud against Toussaint, the class struggle mirrored itself. But Pétion's defection from Toussaint to Rigaud mirrored not only the class but the colour considerations as well. Yet, when Toussaint made a bid to separate the mulatto Beauvais from Rigaud by praising the former and condemning the latter in the initial stages of the conflict, when both colour and class considerations were minimal, Beauvais, unable to decide, instead abandoned his command and sailed for France because, according to James, he was 'unable to take sides in this fratricidal struggle maliciously kindled by the eternal enemies of peace in San Domingo'.[118] James quoted the Haitian historian, Pauleus Sannon, who wrote:

> Without doubt the susceptibilities, the jealousies born of the differences of colour, manifested themselves sometimes to an unreasonable degree, but the exigencies of the service and a severe discipline had more than ever fused the three colours in the ranks of the army. The same state of things existed in the civil administration and this was one of the happiest consequences of political equality consecrated by the principles of the revolution. The rivalries of colour were not then the initial cause of the conflict which was beginning. They complicated it and became one of its elements, when many officers of colour, in several parts of the country, took Rigaud's side, and Toussaint had to treat them as traitors.[119]

The psychology of the mulattos as an intermediate group is lightly touched on as representing a factor in their instability.[120] But while

Rigaud looked up to France for assistance, Toussaint anticipated nothing from that country.[121] Directing his attention against Rigaud with greater energy, Toussaint was able, at the end of July 1800, to drive Rigaud from the island, and on 1 August 1800 Toussaint triumphantly entered Les Cayes.

Notes

1 One excuse employed by Governor Eyre to suspend constitutional rule in Jamaica after the so-called 'Morant Bay Rebellion' of 1865 was the play on the fear that a revolt on the lines of that of Haiti remained a possibility unless measures were taken in advance to forestall it. See Bernard Semmel, *The Governor Eyre Controversy*, London, 1962, pp. 46–7, 53, 55.

2 An example can be found in a book written by the Afro-American prelate, the Rev. James T. Holly, entitled *A Vindication of the Capacity of the Negro Race for Self-Government and Civilized Progress*, New Haven, Conn., 1857. This was the outcome of a lecture which the Rev Holly prepared and delivered to a Literary Society of Coloured Young Men in New Haven, after his return from Haiti in 1855. He repeated the performance in Ohio, Michigan and Western Canada, in the summer of 1856. When it was published in 1857, he dedicated it to the Rev. William C. Munrow, Rector of St Matthew's Church, Detroit, Michigan.

3 Outstanding texts are as follows: C. L. R. James, *The Black Jacobins, Toussaint Louverture and the San Domingo Revolution*, London, 1938, and many reprints; Stephen Alexis, *Black Liberator: the Life of Toussaint Louverture*, trans. from the French by William Stirling, London, 1949; Pierre de Vaissière, *Saint Domingue: la Société et la Vie Créoles sous l'Ancien Régime (1629–1789)*, Paris, 1909; H. Cole, *Christophe, King of Haiti*, London, 1967.

4 Alan Burns, *History of the British West Indies*, London, 2nd rev. edn., 1965, p. 561.

5 *Ibid.*; also James, *Black Jacobins.*, pp. 36–42. See also Bryan Edwards, *The History, Civil and Commercial, of the British Colonies in the West Indies*, London, 1818–19, Vol. 3, pp. 9–12 for some disabilities suffered by mulattos in St Domingue; and Ralph Korngold, *Citizen Toussaint*, London, 1945, pp. 25–7, for stipulations about dress.

6 Alexis, *Black Liberator*, p. 20.

7 *Ibid.*

8 *Ibid.* For further examples of almost unimaginable cruelty, not confined only to the French islands, see Spencer St John, *Haity or the Black Republic*, London, 1884, pp. 31–2. For the Dutch colony of Suriname, see a few representative samples in J. G. Stedman, *Narrative of Five Years among the Revolted Negroes of Surinam, 1772–1777*, London, 1796, Vol. 1, pp. 107, 126–7, 340; Vol. 2, pp. 25–7, 208–10, 215–17, 258–78, 290, 293–8. In Vol. 1, p. 126, he recorded how a Jewess, impelled by jealousy, plunged a 'red-hot poker' into the body of a quadroon girl.

9 Edwards, *History, Civil and Commercial.*, Vol. 3, p. 88. For a contrary view, see Spencer St John, a former English diplomat to Haiti, who described as 'harsh a [system of] slavery as ever disgraced the worst system of servitude' *Hayti.*, pp. 29, 30–1ff.

10 Edwards, *History, Civil and Commercial*, Vol. 3, p. 88.

11 Alexis, *Black Liberator*, p. 20. This confirms James's assertion that most of the earlier settlers were, in fact, the 'sweepings of Paris'.

12 *Ibid.*, p. 21.
13 *Ibid.*
14 Alexis, *Black Liberator*, p. 20; James, *Black Jacobins*, pp. 41–51; R. B. Sheridan, *The Development of the Plantations to 1750, an Era of West Indian Prosperity 1750–1775*, Barbados, 1970, p. 46.
15 Edwards, *History, Civil and Commercial*, Vol. 3, p. xviii, preface to 1st edn. He accused the *Amis des Noirs* of influencing the revolt, see his pp. 43–5. He also implied the complicity of the British Association for the Abolition of the Slave Trade because of its association with the French *Amis des Noirs* (pp. 89–95) and referred to their pamphleteering activities (pp. 112–13).
16 *Ibid.*, p. xix.
17 *Ibid.*, pp. xix–xx. Such a presentation of the situation is mere hair-splitting.
18 See Alexis, *Black Liberator*, p. 36, where he indicates that many of the slaves who formed the revolutionary army to expel the French from St Domingue came from various parts of the African continent, as follows: Congos, Senegales, Dahomeans, Lybians, Abyssinians, Bambaras, Pheuls, Ibos, Yolloofs, Guineans, Aradas, Touaregs, Moroccans. Toussaint forged his army from these heterogeneous groups.
19 Holly, *Vindication*, reproduced in H. Brots, *Negro Social and Political Thought 1850–1920: Representative Texts*, London, 2nd edn., 1966, p. 143.
20 *Ibid.*
21 *Ibid.* See an identical sentiment in W. Jordan, *White Over Black: American Attitudes towards the Negro 1550–1812*, London, 1968, pp. 376.
22 Holly, *Vindication*, p. 144.
23 *Ibid.*, p. 145.
24 See J. C. Fitzpatrick, *The Writings of George Washington, 1931–40*, Vol. 31, pp. 375, 453. Washington died on 14 December 1799, more than eight years after the St Domingue revolt began.
25 *Ibid.*, p. 375. The later change in American policy towards Haiti is briefly examined in the pages which follow.
26 Edwards, *History, Civil and Commercial*, Vol. 3, pp. 96–7 for other manifestations of French perfidy; Vol. 5, pp. 145–9; esp. pp. 148–9 also James, *Black Jacobins*, pp. 96–7.
27 Edwards, *History, Civil and Commercial*, Vol. 3, pp. 84–6, 96–8.
28 Even so racially biased a writer as Bryan Edwards had to admit that the French, by their treachery, had 'forfeited all claim to pity'; *ibid.*, Vol. 5, p. 150.
29 Edwards, *ibid.*, Vol. 3, pp. 430–1. A similar viewpoint was expressed in Spencer St John, *Hayti*, in Sir John Fortescue, *A History of the British Army*, London, 1899–1930, and in the War Despatches, especially those of the Earl of Balcarres.
30 Edwards, *History, Civil and Commercial*, Vol. 3, pp. 49–50.
31 The reactions of the French National Assembly to the colonial question are discussed in James, *Black Jacobins*, pp. 75–81. The Assembly itself vacillated on the question of slavery. According to James, 'reaction triumphed. But phases of a revolution are not decided in parliaments, they are only registered there' (p. 81).
32 Alexis, *Black Liberator*, p. 25.
33 *Ibid.*
34 *Ibid.* p. 24.

35 James, *Black Jacobins*, p. 82.

36 *Ibid.*

37 *Ibid.*, pp. 83–4.

38 *Ibid.*, p. 84.

39 *Ibid.*, p. 87. Boukman's background is also interesting. He originated from Jamaica and, while some people often referred to him as a 'sorcerer', he was, in fact, a High Priest of the Voodoo religion. He not only became a runaway slave who killed his master, but while continuing in hiding harassed the plantations by raids and by his activities, terrorising the slavocracy through incendiarism, as well as killing people and beasts and then disappearing.

40 *Ibid.*, p. 86.

41 *Ibid.*, p. 89.

42 See, for instance, Edmund Burke, *Reflections on the French Revolution*, 1791. By contrast see the jubilant position of Charles James Fox and his speeches in Parliament on the subject in the same period.

43 Yet in the early stages of the St Domingue revolt not only did the British send a squadron to aid the women and children to be evacuated from the country, but the French National Assembly expressed its gratitude to both the British and Jamaican governments. See T. Southey, *Chronological History of the West Indies*, London, 1827, Vol. 3, p. 61.

44 See *Proclamation of Independence*, 23 Nov. 1803, signed by Dessalines, Christophe and Clerveaux in Marcus Rainsford, *An Historical Account of the Black Empire of Haiti*, London, 1805, pp. 439–41.

45 C. C. Tansill, *The United States and Santo Domingo, 1789–1873: a Chapter in Caribbean Diplomacy*, Baltimore, Md., 1938. pp. 1–7.

46 Edwards, *History, Civil and Commercial*, Vol. 3, pp. iv–vi.

47 Tansill, *United States and Santo Domingo*, pp. 8–9.

48 Fortescue, *British Army*, Vol. 4, p. 325.

49 *Ibid.*, p. 326.

50 Edwards, *History, Civil and Commercial*, Vol. 3, pp. x, xxv–xxvi; also his ch. 10.

51 *Ibid.*, p. v. In his response to the planters' request, Lord Effingham saw himself as a kind of Messiah for them. But above all, St Domingue was a coveted prize, the richest sugar colony at the time of the revolt.

52 *Ibid.*, pp. v–vi. The French National Assembly later expressed its gratitude and appreciation to both the British government and the government of Jamaica for sending a British squadron from Jamaica to St Domingue, supposedly in defence of the French, and which helped in the evacuation of women and children. See Southey, *Chronological History*, Vol. 3, p. 61.

53 Tansill, *United States and Santo Domingo*, p. 10.

54 *Ibid.*, pp. 10–11.

55 *Ibid.*, pp. 11–13.

56 *Ibid.*, p. 13.

57 *Ibid.*, pp. 14–15.

58 *Ibid.*, p. 14. Quoted from Secretary Pickering to the American Consul at Cap Français, Jacob Mayer, 30 Nov. 1798.

59 *Ibid.*, pp. 16–18.

60 Library of Congress, Jefferson Papers, Vols. 90, 97, letters to James Madison, 13 April 1794, and James Munroe, 14 July 1793. Also in *ibid.*, p. 10.

61 Tansill, *United States and Santo Domingo*, p. 18, n. 65.

62 Edwards, *History, Civil and Commercial*, Vol. 3, pp. 180–8, esp. notes on pp. 181, 182; also pp. 408–31, esp. pp. 408–10.

63 The French recaptured Guadeloupe from the English in 1794 with the help of the slaves because of the French decree of 1794 conceding liberty to them. This, according to Elsa Goveia, altered the balance of power in the West Indies. See Goveia, *Slave Society in the British Leeward Islands at the End of the Eighteenth Century*, New Haven, Conn., 1965, p. 252. It was the revolutionary fervour and the exigencies of war which compelled the French to make the proclamation.

64 St Lucia, held by the British, was wrested from them by the blacks in what the British called the 'Brigands' War'. See Fortescue, *British Army*, Vol. 4, Bk. I, Bk. XI, chs. XIV, XVI, XVII. The British recaptured St Lucia by 1796 but gave up the attempt to recover Guadeloupe. See Goveia, *Slave Society*, p. 253.

65 See L. M. Penson, *The Colonial Agent of the British West Indies*, London, 1924, p. 207.

66 Tansill, *United States and Santo Domingo*, p. 20.

67 The other members of the Commission were Roumé, Leblanc, Giraud and Raymond.

68 PRO, WO 1/69, Duke of Portland and Secretary Dundas, draft instructions to General Nesbitt, 1 Jan. 1798 (Secret). The expression 'reducing the burthens of war' appeared in these instructions.

69 PRO, WO 1/69, Maitland to Dundas, 10 May 1798.

70 PRO, WO 1/68, Maitland to Dundas, 6 July 1798; also 1/70, Maitland to Earl Balcarres, 24 Aug. 1798.

71 PRO, WO 1/70, Maitland to Lord Balcarres, 31 Aug. 1798.

72 Tansill, *United States and Santo Domingo*, p. 29. See copy of secret treaty in letter to Dundas, 31 Aug. 1798 in PRO, WO 1/70. A copy of the treaty can also be found in PRO, FO 115/6 in the letter and enclosures sent by Lord Grenville to Robert Liston, 11 Dec. 1798.

73 PRO, WO 1/70, Maitland to Lord Balcarres, 31 Aug. 1798.

74 Tansill, *United States and Santo Domingo*, pp. 30–1.

75 PRO, FO, 5/22, Liston to Grenville, 2 May 1798.

76 Library of Congress typescript, Grenville to Liston, May 1798; Tansill, *United States and Santo Domingo*, p. 33; Grenville to Liston, 8 June 1798.

77 PRO, FO 5/22, Liston to Grenville, 12 June 1798.

78 Tansill, *United States and Santo Domingo*, p. 33.

79 PRO, FO 5/22, Liston to Grenville, No. 56, 27 Sept. 1798.

80 Tansill, *United States and Santo Domingo*, pp. 36–45.

81 PRO, WO 1/71, Rufus King to Henry Dundas, 8 Dec. 1798.

82 PRO, WO 1/70, Maitland to Dundas, 26 Dec. 1798, and WO 1/71, Maitland to Dundas, 5 Jan. 1799.

83 PRO, WO 1/70, Maitland to Dundas, 26 Dec. 1798.

84 Tansill, *United States and Santo Domingo*, pp. 38–9. For Maitland's sentiments see PRO, WO 1/70, Maitland to Dundas, 26 Dec. 1798.

85 PRO, WO 1/71, Maitland to Dundas, 5 Jan, 1799.

86 PRO, WO 1/74.

87 *Ibid.*

88 PRO, FO 5/25, Robert Liston to Grenville, No. 13, 18 Feb. 1799.

89 PRO, WO 1/71, Maitland to Dundas, 3 April 1799. He commented that it was not likely that Americans would agree cordially with the British view.

90 PRO, WO 1/71, Maitland to Dundas, 20 April 1799.
91 Tansill, *United States and Santo Domingo*, p. 58.
92 *Ibid.*, p. 73.
93 *Ibid.*, p. 60.
94 *Ibid.*, p. 61.
95 PRO, WO 1/71, Maitland to Col. Grant, Secret No. 2 (p. 399), 17 June 1799.
    He gave Grant reasons why he could not be admitted as agent immediately.
    Also in the same volume, Col. Grant to Henry Dundas, Jamaica, 7 Oct. 1799,
    and Col. Grant to Henry Dundas, 24 Oct. 1799.
96 PRO, WO 1/71, text of the Convention of 13 June 1799, and sketch of
    proposed regulations, pp. 223–5. The actual convention appears in French on
    pp. 371–83.
97 *Ibid.*, Maitland to Col. Grant, Secret, 17 June 1799, pp. 340–1, 337–68.
98 PRO, WO 1/71, Maitland to Grant, Secret, 17 June 1799, p. 357.
99 PRO, WO 1/71, Maitland to Grant, 17 June 1799.
100 *Ibid.*
101 PRO, WO 1/71, Maitland to Balcarres, No. 3, June 1799, contains requests for
    supplying Toussaint with provisions, pp. 431–8.
102 PRO, WO 1/71, Maitland to Balcarres, No. 2, 17 June 1799, pp. 425–8.
103 *Ibid.*
104 PRO, WO 1/71, Maitland to Lord Balcarres, 20 June 1799.
105 PRO, WO 1/71, Maitland to Hyde Parker. No. 2, 20 June 1799. In Maitland's
    letter three days earlier, 17 June 1799 (No. 1), he used the expression 'should be
    kept in a perfect state of blockade', Maitland to Hyde Parker, 17 June 1799.
106 Tansill, *United States and Santo Domingo*, p. 69.
107 *Ibid.*, p. 70.
108 *Ibid.*, p. 71.
109 *Ibid.*, pp. 71–2.
110 *Ibid.*, p. 72. The expression 'black dictator' is the only one which mars Tansill's
    account. The book abounds with this phrase. See PRO, WO 3/74, for a series
    of exchanges between the British Agent, Wigglesworth, and the Earl of
    Balcarres, Admiral Hyde Parker, Cathcart and Edward Robinson.
111 *Ibid.*, p. 73.
112 *Ibid.*, pp. 73–4.
113 *Ibid.*, pp. 75, 279–81. Toussaint's forces routed the Spanish troops' resistance
    on 21 Jan. 1800, and the Governor formally handed over the colony to
    Toussaint. He was now master of the entire island (see James, *Black Jacobins*, pp.
    238–9). The aim was to end slavery in the other part of the island.
114 See, for example, Edwards, *History, Civil and Commercial*, Vol. 3, pp. 413–15,
    419–20, 429–31.
115 James, *Black Jacobins*, pp. 229–31.
116 *Ibid.*
117 *Ibid.*, pp. 228–9. Maitland's letter to Col. Grant, quoted above, to do all in his
    power to keep Toussaint and Rigaud from reconciliation is an example of this.
118 *Ibid.*, pp. 229–30, 231.
119 *Ibid.*, p. 230. Quoted from Pauleus Sannon, *Histoire de Toussaint l'Ouverture*,
    Vol. 2, p. 140.
120 *Ibid.*, pp. 230–1.
121 *Ibid.*, p. 231. Later Rigaud was to report to Napoleon after leaving the island for
    France (pp. 234–5).

11 The Haitian Revolution: second phase

The Americans had continued to help Toussaint while he was still carrying out his offensive against Rigaud.[1] Relations between the Americans and Toussaint were still good after Rigaud's defeat, but were soon strained. Part of the blame must go to Toussaint who, having triumphed over Rigaud, imposed a heavy tariff on exports and imports which led Consul Stevens to point out that they would have an adverse effect on American trade; yet, in spite of Stevens' plea, Toussaint refused to repeal them or make concessions to the Americans. It was, therefore, left to be implied that Toussaint, having acquired mastery over St Domingue, was then in a position to dictate his own terms. If this was the case then it was a miscalculation on his part, for Toussaint had not understood that he was circumscribed by the cast-iron laws of *realpolitik* and this was to undermine his country far into the present century. But since this is a one-sided picture observed from American reaction, it is possible that the records relating to St Domingue under Toussaint would yield some explanation for his action. It is quite possible that Toussaint might have noted other factors in his relationship with America which he felt would undermine the sovereignty of St Domingue. In fact this was to come soon after. Already the strained relations between America and France looked like improving and here Toussaint had not reckoned with the vicissitudes of politics, for the re-establishment of an *entente cordiale* would mean a cooling off of relations between America and Britain, and simultaneously between America and Toussaint.[2] This was what happened.

The Treaty of Mortfontaine of 30 September 1800, whereby France and America decided to end previous hostilities, introduced a new factor into the St Domingue theatre. Moreover, the agreement by which President Adams had developed the policy of cooperation between America, Britain and Toussaint's St Domingue, and by which the British and Americans had prohibited intercourse with France and its colonies, was due to expire on 3 March 1801. Also, with a new administration under Jefferson, hostile not only to Toussaint's regime but also to the existence of any black regime in the Caribbean, the likelihood of renewing it was dimmed. Difficulties had already intruded on the situation even by November

1800, when, contrary to the spirit of the Toussaint-Maitland Treaty of 13 June 1799, the British Agent in Port-au-Prince seized American vessels trading with Jacmel and denied them access to the port. The details have been discussed elsewhere.[3]

By March 1801, after Jefferson had become President, the situation was complex indeed. He and his Secretary of State, James Madison, did not relish the Toussaint-Maitland Treaty which had made for the co-operation of the previous Adams era, and the new administration was prepared to abrogate it. Jefferson, having provided the French with the green light, found them making overtures towards greater amity with the U.S.A. and assiduous at discouraging any trade contacts with the blacks. Jefferson seemed to indicate that he was interested in preserving 'perfect neutrality',[4] but it was in fact a pro-French posture that he took. He replaced Stevens with a new consul, Edward Lear, without giving him any necessary letters of accreditation, and Toussaint was not slow to observe this change of policy, and although it annoyed him[5] he strove to preserve some semblance of good relations with America. The British themselves were not slow to notice that the new American administration was willing to see St Domingue restored to France.[6] Jefferson was even more emphatic in informing the French envoy in America that America would not entertain the ambitions of Toussaint. But Jefferson also saw the necessity of France making its peace with England in order to be able to 'reduce Toussaint to starvation' through the use of their army and fleet.[7] Jefferson was sure that the British would acquiesce in the undertaking to suppress Toussaint, especially because of British fears that Toussaint's example might spill over and disturb British colonies in the Caribbean.

Toussaint was being engulfed, and while observing the changed situation in his relations with the U.S. he continued to press for good relations, but his exertions did not earn him much American consideration. He was aware that he needed America for his supplies, both for war materials and provisions. America's policy from that time, however, was hostile to St Domingue. Even the Agent of the French Directory, General Hedouville, informed Napoleon Bonaparte on 1 November 1801 that 'twenty-five thousand muskets, sixteen pieces of artillery, and an immense amount of war material had already started for San Domingo' through the agency of private U.S. merchants.[8]

It was at this juncture that the British decided on extending the spirit of the Toussaint-Maitland Treaty by the conclusion of another convention on 16 November 1801 between Joseph Bunel (acting on behalf of Toussaint) and Edward Corbet, the Agent for 'British Affairs in Saint Domingo'.[9] This agreement imposed on Toussaint the duty of protecting French émigrés from 'Santo

Domingo' then resident in Jamaica and was to enable them to regain their property – in short, to assist their reinstatement. Furthermore, it was stipulated that the Governor of Jamaica was to have the right to appoint agents to reside in the ports on the island of St Domingue which were open to trade, and protection was to be extended to British merchants and their properties there. It also had a proviso for coasting trade from Cap Français and Port-au-Prince to other ports open to commerce. The convention seemed more like an imposition on a beleaguered Toussaint rather than terms of friendship. What were the concessions for Toussaint and his people?

In observing the situation, Professor Tansill has stated that

> These earnest efforts of Toussaint to conciliate Great Britain and America were all in vain. Jefferson was committed to a policy of cooperation with France against the black dictator, and the Department of State permitted our official relations with Santo Domingo to decline to a vanishing point. The significance of this official silence was not lost upon Lear, who wrote to Madison to complain that for months there had been 'not a single line of intercourse between the Government of the US and this – not a single line of communication from my Government (on which head I have been often questioned; and have been obliged to exercise my utmost ingenuity to parry the question) – no public ships or Vessels of the U.S. on the coast or in the harbours as heretofore'.[10]

Clearly there was perfidy in dealing with Toussaint. Powers which had emerged on the predication of lofty principles were unprepared to concede those principles to others like them – the U.S. predicated on its principles of all men being created equal and endowed with certain unalienable rights such as liberty and the pursuit of happiness, and the French and their proclamation of liberty, equality and fraternity; these principles became hollow when descendants of Africa and their coloured half-brothers were involved.

Professor Tansill has aptly observed that

> Toussaint's growing anxiety about the intentions of the American Government was well founded. Jefferson had little liking for the negro dictator and he had no scruples about laying plans for his destruction. If Napoleon wished to restore the French empire in the Caribbean, he would have no more sincere well-wisher than Jefferson, who failed to see that these French colonial possessions in the old Spanish Main were linked inextricably to Louisiana. In the event that a French armada crushed Toussaint it would not be long before a formidable French military establishment was set up in the Mississippi Valley.[11]

341

What was more perplexing about Jefferson's policy was not that he and Madison and their administration were the heirs of the revolution which brought freedom to the United States except for its enslaved African descendants, but they were the signatories of the freedom charter itself. Yet, in indicating their stance on St Domingue, they demonstrated their racial and class preferences towards others who, like them, had become preoccupied with freedom as a fact. Had Napoleon succeeded in his designs, the Americans would have been hard put to retain their liberty. From all appearances Napoleon had hoped to use Louisiana as the 'granary for St Domingue' and, pressurised by vested interests, among whom were the ruined planters of St Domingue and his wife Josephine, herself a Creole by birth, he surged forward towards the eventual restoration of French hegemony in St Domingue, and with it slavery. It turned out to be a misadventure of the greatest magnitude.[12]

The prelude to his expedition was the warning he sent to Toussaint on 4 November 1800 not to interfere with Spanish Santo Domingo. With the preliminaries for the Peace of Amiens signed on 1 October 1801 he prepared instructions for General Leclerc, his brother-in-law, to lead the fatal expedition to St Domingue. Jefferson had given *carte blanche* to Napoleon, and advance plans of the so-called 'punitive expedition' to St Domingue were supplied to the British Foreign Ministry and, on request, to the Governor of Jamaica. The latter was to provision the French fleet and 'Leclerc was to be regarded as heading a crusade against barbarous blacks that were a growing menace to all whites, whether European or American'.[13] If there was any doubt that the French, with the connivance of Britain and America, were embarked on a racial war and on one which spelled extermination or genocide for the blacks and their half brothers, the mulattos, here was the evidence.

But these preliminaries were not lost on Toussaint, for he became disillusioned after Britain and France had signed the Treaty of Amiens (1802). As an indication of Britain's change of policy the Lieutenant-Governor of Jamaica, Brigadier Nugent, withdrew the British Agent from St Domingue, which ran contrary to the stipulations of the Maitland-Toussaint Treaty. England's policy had all along been opportunistic; its attempt to dissuade Napoleon from the attack was brushed aside by an outburst from France's leader before his Foreign Minister, Talleyrand:

> Inform England that in taking my decision to liquidate Toussaint
> Louverture's government in Saint Domingue I have not been guided
> by commercial and financial considerations so much as by the need
> to stamp out in every part of the world any kind of anxiety or
> trouble. The freedom of Negroes, if recognised in Saint Domingue

and legalised by France, would at all times be a rallying point for the freedom-seekers of the New World.[14]

The sentiment expressed what every European and American slave-holding society feared but was blatantly racist in overtone. In brushing aside the request not to invade St Domingue Napoleon was hopeful for American support, as had been indicated by Jefferson, but another feature of Napoleon's insincerity in his international relations emerged from this temporary linkage with America. The perfidy emerged from the instructions which he issued for the guidance of Leclerc, who was specifically directed to admit American commerce to St Domingue during the action against Toussaint, but once this was over he was to reimpose the old regulations.[15] But these facts were concealed from the Americans, prompting Professor Tansill to speculate that 'If Jefferson had known of these instructions and of the real purpose behind the Leclerc expedition he would have taken immediate steps to reverse his friendly policy towards France. As it was, his programme of co-operation with Napoleon had dangerous implications for America, and had it not been for the valour and military skill of Toussaint, together with the decimation of Leclerc's legions by yellow fever, both Louisiana and Santo Domingo would soon have been French.'[16]

The fact that the old trading regulations were to be reinstated by Napoleon showed also the tenacity of mercantilism and the strength of the French mercantilist interests. In a footnote, Professor Tansill observed that 'It is of importance to note that, as far as Louisiana was concerned, the only reason why General Victor did not occupy it early in 1803 was that the fleet on which he was to have sailed was ice-bound in Dutch harbours'. In this regard, Professor Lyon, in his monograph *Louisiana in French Diplomacy, 1759–1804*, remarks: 'It is very probable that the ice of the Netherlands in the winter of 1803 rendered the United States a favour comparable to that which the Channel winds have often bestowed on the British Isles. Had it not been for the ice of January and February, Victor would have sailed for Louisiana, and the effective military occupation of New Orleans might have changed the subsequent destiny of the Mississippi Valley.'[17]

But it is doubtful that Jefferson could have championed Toussaint against France had he known the true situation. Jefferson's racism and opinions against the blacks were well known and ubiquitous, and so much a question of conviction. Jefferson himself was also a slave owner, and the persistent fear, expressed by the slave-owning territories, of the dangers to their societies of an independent black republic was passionately felt and expressed by him. Had he reversed his friendly policy towards France it would not necessarily have meant friendship to Toussaint or black Haiti. Here were the double standards of international conduct of the time, which still plague international relations in our world. There were other possibilities. Both America and England could have combined to seize and partition the island but this could have led to a confrontation with its inhabitants, the outcome of which would have been uncertain, but it would have resulted in even more suffering and bloodshed.

While Leclerc's expedition was still headed for St Domingue the American government counselled its agent in St Domingue, Edward Lear, to engage in duplicity. Although Lear knew that the expedition was on its way to destroy Toussaint and his compatriots and reimpose French control on the colony, he treated Toussaint with the utmost cordiality. The complicated story of this double dealing is discussed at length in Tansill and does not need reproducing here.[18] But even this gesture of American friendship to France was not reciprocated by Leclerc after his occupation of Cap Français on 6 February 1802. It was another indication of that perfidious dealing with which the entire episode, from the commencement of the revolution of the African slaves, is replete. This activity also merges with the preparations of the black Haitians to resist. To this we shall return presently.

But Leclerc, having attempted to force American merchants to sell him their cargoes, and having failed, described the American merchants in a letter to the Minister of Marine and Colonies as being as avaricious as 'Jews with whom it is impossible to deal'.[19] Here was another racial preoccupation of the era. Then followed a series of diplomatic representations and exercises, and these are detailed in Tansill.[20] Leclerc had later, in April 1802, revoked the recognition of the American Consul, Edward Lear, after having previously recognised his presence on landing.[21] Even the American envoy in Paris was subjected to humiliations and vexatious proceedings. French highhandedness only led to alienation between France and America. It became clear that with the French having a foothold on St Domingue they felt the Americans had become dispensable.

Leclerc's expedition of 20 000 veterans of the European war had appeared off Cap Français on the afternoon of 2 February 1802. The expedition had in its rank and file the mulatto leaders who had quitted the country at the time of Rigaud's defeat.[22] Among them were Pétion (who was Rigaud's lieutenant in the earlier confrontation), Villatte, Quayer-Lariviere, Leveille, Boyer, Birot, Borno Deleart, Nicolas Gaffrard and others. But other mulattos, like Clairveaux, clung to the banner of Toussaint and fought valiantly. When the French expeditionary force was first sighted on 29 January off Cape Samana on the eastern coast of the island

Toussaint was dismayed, but he simply said, 'We must perish, all France has come to St Domingue'.[23] It meant that the Haitians were to die fighting rather than yield to slavery. The preparations made by Toussaint and his lieutenants, Christophe, Dessalines, Clairveaux and Paul L'Ouverture, are too well known to require recounting here, but they testify to the epic nature of the resistance to foreign invasion and remain among the brightest constellations in the annals of African resistance to enslavement in the Americas. French ascendancy was not achieved by its prowess for it failed to defeat the determination of the blacks and later the mulattos. In the instructions which Leclerc had received, he was to employ the mulatto leaders in the war of extermination and subjugation of the blacks and later to deport them to Madagascar or another French island. The black generals were also to be so apprehended and transported to France, and slavery was to be reimposed. It showed quite clearly that Napoleon, even as heir to the French Revolution, was not prepared to tolerate the freedom of the blacks. His racism was manifest in his pronouncements.

Leclerc, in his attempt to land at Cap Français, met the determined resistance of Christophe, who, in accordance with the plans sketched out by Toussaint, used scorched-earth policies, burning the town as he retreated into the interior. While the names of Dessalines, the fearless Clairveaux and Christophe shine out among the defenders of the freedom of the country, the role of the blacks themselves in fighting for their own liberty has been submerged under their names. Yet the fact was that the generals would have achieved nothing but for the mass support and the determination of their followers never again to be enslaved. The masses needed the generals and the generals needed the masses and the combination proved so daunting to the French that in the end Leclerc, with a considerable loss to his forces both through fighting and the ravages of yellow fever, decided to use the technique of subterfuge to gain his end. Many historians and writers testify to the perfidy which this entailed, and the activities which resulted from it remain some of the most shameful in the annals of military confrontations. It was at this point that Leclerc employed the tactics of attempting to convince the Haitians that France had sent him to restore their liberty, assuring them that slavery would not be reimposed. Toussaint himself, full of doubt and a philosopher at the moment when action was demanded, was inclined to hearken to this and, while sure that slavery could not be restored, felt that his people could not survive without French assistance.[24] He did not wish to break entirely with France and this attitude of mind almost proved fatal to the revolution. Toussaint, a very trusting soul, had not taken into consideration the fact that the whites, whom he had protected under his banner, did not prove loyal when Leclerc's expedition arrived. In fact, they welcomed the expedition and clamoured for the restoration of slavery. The vacillation of Toussaint in declaring the country completely independent dismayed his followers and especially Dessalines and Christophe, but they remained within his ranks. Nevertheless, the events which succeeded were to convince the leaders that only total expulsion of the French would guarantee them their freedom.

In the meantime a truce was arranged in which Leclerc and Toussaint in conclave were able to agree that the fighting be stopped and that Toussaint's generals were to be incorporated into Leclerc's army and that the liberty and equality of everyone was guaranteed. Toussaint was offered the post of Lieutenant-Governor of the colony but he declined and preferred to return to his home in Ennery as a private citizen, believing that his work was done and that the freedom of his people would be guaranteed. He was wrong, however, and although he felt that the people would rise again to a man should the French institute subterfuge, he was not aware of the fact that he had fallen a victim of subterfuge. The French, using General Brunet, invited Toussaint to a conference, and Toussaint, unwisely but trusting to the end, found himself ambushed and arrested, hurried on board a vessel, the *Creole*, which was moored in readiness for the capture, and spirited away with his family to France. The incident occurred on 7 June 1802. Writers, including the most conservative and racist, agree that this was an act of 'treachery'.[25] Be that as it may, it was only a matter of time before the scales would fall from the eyes of the leaders who had decided to serve under the French banner in St Domingue, both blacks and mulattos. Among the black leaders who were still in the service of Leclerc were Dessalines, Christophe, Maurepas, and Laplume.[26] As Toussaint embarked for France, he told the French:

> In overthrowing me, they have felled in Saint Domingue only the trunk of the tree of Negro liberty; it will shoot forth from the roots, because they are deep and numerous.[27]

The removal of Toussaint did not mean the end of the revolution; on the contrary, it gave the revolutionaries greater force to die for their liberty. On his arrival in France, Toussaint was separated from his family, hurried across the Alps, and incarcerated in the fortress Château de Jeux on the French–Swiss border (in the Jura mountains) where, through ill-treatment and starvation, his death was hastened on 7 April 1803.

While Toussaint was on his way to France the St Domingue situation was fast deteriorating. Leclerc had begun his game of treachery and tried to use mulatto and black leaders to disarm the mass of their people. While succeeding in some places the endeavour failed in others. The relations between America and France also deteriorated. On the night of 2 November 1802, after writing many of his distorted half truths, falsehoods and absurd letters to Napoleon, Leclerc died of yellow fever. His successor, General Rochambeau, had also inscribed his name in the book of infamy. He deserved the title of 'Butcher of Haiti' and 'Savage Murderer of Haitians' for he was much more brutal than Leclerc and many writers are agreed that he had more brute force than wisdom. Professor Tansill struck the note when he wrote of Rochambeau: 'General Rochambeau maintained for a while in Santo Domingo a regime at whose record of bloodshed and wanton massacre historians still shudder.'[28]

But Rochambeau, while butchering the blacks in Haiti, was also harassing the Americans, as his predecessor had done. He imposed forced loans against American merchants and citizens on the island and imprisoned some of those who opposed his depredations. The Americans, as private citizens, found their redress by supplying arms and ammunition to the blacks, who were now ever more determined to rid their country of the French. This supply of arms also featured in diplomatic circles, and in representations made by France to America it was said that the Americans were supplying arms to the black insurgents. American merchants nonetheless continued the clandestine trade with St Domingue. American vessels suffered depredations and pillage at the hands of French corsairs whose headquarters were in Cuba, and as a result the U.S. merchants found it necessary to arm themselves against such attacks, evoking the protest of France who argued that America was carrying out a 'private and piratical war against a Power with which the United States is at peace'. These activities, which almost brought France and America to the brink of war, were ultimately resolved diplomatically, for France was anxious that American merchants should not give the blacks of St Domingue decided advantage over France by the sale of arms, and the American administration was still toying with the notion of restrictive policies which would enable France to overwhelm the black regime in St Domingue. Even John Wayles Eppes, a Virginian Congressman (1803–11) and a nephew of Thomas Jefferson, was prepared to pledge the treasury of the United States to ensure the destruction of the 'Negro' government.[29] The events in Franco-American relations relating to Haiti were continued after the declaration of Haitian independence and will be mentioned presently.

Writers on St Domingue and Toussaint are, in the main, agreed that Toussaint provided his people with leadership second to none. He built a disciplined army from the rank and file of degraded and brutalised slaves from the time of rising in 1791 until his abduction in 1802. It was not possible for the kind of fighting force he had created to succumb to attempts by the French or other Europeans to reimpose slavery. Leclerc had used the black generals against one another, but some premature events, such as Rigaud's deportation to France by Leclerc, the capture of Toussaint and his abduction to France, and attempts by the French to reimpose slavery in the whole of the Caribbean were to convince both the black and mulatto generals that their hopes lay not in service within the French army but with their people, who had already begun a revolt which was growing by leaps and bounds, to Leclerc's dismay.

According to C. L. R. James, it was the lesser-known leaders, not the men serving in Leclerc's army, who raised the banner of revolt,[30] and they must not be deprived of their honour in the entire struggle for the liberation of Haiti. Many of them are so far unrecorded but there is need for them to be better known in this event of epic proportions. Two, however, remain a credit to the heroism of the Haitian people: the black leader, Capois Death, whose real name was François Capoix [nicknamed La Mort] and the mulatto, Clairveaux. They were joined later by Christophe, Dessalines and Pétion, and the others who hesitated before returning to face their destiny. The tactics of 'hit and run' and guerrilla warfare had its pride of place and dismayed the French invaders. One by one the black and mulatto generals, who had taken service in Leclerc's army, defected, and with them their followers. With Christophe joining Pétion and Clairveaux on 14 October the rank and file of the blacks and mulattos were becoming unified. Rochambeau, as successor to Leclerc, was puzzled by the unification which had taken place among the ranks of blacks and mulattos. Dessalines was recognised by the Haitians as Commander-in-Chief, and Pétion as his 'unofficial second in command'. The French in St Domingue were at once in a quandary because Leclerc had not confided his instructions to his lieutenant, Rochambeau, and so the latter had to seek further instructions from France.

In the meantime he began his war of extermination against the mulattos which eventually drove them into the rank and file of the blacks and made the struggle more ferocious. C. L. R. James gives an account of a bizarre and lurid incident which occurred at Port-Republicain at a ball given by Rochambeau at which he invited mulatto women to officiate at the funeral of their husbands. This incident is worthy of recording for it represented that continuation of the carnage which both Leclerc and his successor, Rochambeau, brought on innocent people who dared to strike for their freedom. It was called 'civilisation' but in essence it was 'civilised barbarism' and words are inadequate to describe it. The records, however, are quite eloquent. This is how C. L. R. James recounted the incident:

Rochambeau hated the Mulattos more than the blacks. One night at

Port-Republicain he gave a great ball to which he invited several of the Mulatto women. It was a magnificent fete. At midnight Rochambeau stops the dancing and begs them to enter into a neighbouring apartment. This room, lit by a single lamp, is hung with black draperies in which white material figures as skulls; in the four corners are coffins. In the middle of their horrified silence the Mulattos hear funeral chants sung by invisible singers. Dumb with terror they stood rooted to the spot, while Rochambeau told them: 'You have just assisted at the funeral ceremonies of your husbands and your brothers.'[31]

From that moment the mulattos were in full revolt, in what was now 'a war with the racial divisions emphasising the class struggle – blacks and mulattos against white. Leclerc had proposed a war of extermination, and Rochambeau waged it.'[32] What followed thereafter is recounted in the records. It was a war of tigers, and the heroism of the blacks and mulattos was matched by French cruelty, sadism and brutality. Dessalines' handling of the crisis proved fatal to the French and it gives him an unsurpassed position in the history of the revolution of St Domingue. On 18 May 1803 at a conference of his commanders at Arcahaye, he tore out the white from the French tricolour of red, blue and white and from that moment unfurled the symbol of Haitian independence. He then intoned the chant 'Liberty or Death' and had it inscribed on the new Haitian flag. French attempts to regain St Domingue had dismally failed. The failure of the Peace of Amiens to subsist led to an outbreak of hostilities again between Britain and France by 1803. The blockade which the British imposed on Rochambeau also helped the Haitians to pin him down and render his struggle futile. The Haitians had triumphed. As James has rightly observed, the English role in the final stages of the Haitian contest was opportunistic.[33]

On 29 November 1803 Dessalines, Christophe and Clairveaux (Pétion was ill in bed) issued the preliminary proclamation of independence,[34] but the actual independence day was 1 January 1804. Before this, on 19 November 1803, Rochambeau, whose forces had been driven back to only two positions, Cap Français and Môle-St-Nicolas, signed a truce with Dessalines for the evacuation of Cap Français. The French garrison at the Môle surrendered a few days later and Rochambeau himself and those who opted to accompany him surrendered to the British at sea and became their prisoners.[35] Thus ended one of the most despicable expeditions ever undertaken by masters against their slaves; the scars survive to this day.

In 1803 the Americans had proposed to the French government the purchase of New Orleans and were surprised to find that the

French were willing to sell Louisiana as well. The St Domingue revolt, which became the Haitian Revolution, had also driven the French from North American soil. But the intrigues against the new state of Haiti were to continue unabated and to disturb its peace and tax its capacity for growth and development. The European world had not accepted the independence of descendants of Africa (or Afro-Haitians) in Haiti and was not prepared to recognise it for a long time (in fact Haitian independence was not recognised by the U.S.A. until 1862). There are many points of similarity between the Haitian and Russian revolutions, but this is not the place to discuss them.

The American government of Jefferson eventually, in 1805, passed a bill prohibiting any armaments trade with St Domingue, but this measure had come too late to undermine the revolution of the Haitians. American objections to the new black Republic of Haiti from 1804 continued beyond 1806 and, in fact, into the twentieth century. But worse still, France refused to recognise what was already a *fait accompli*, and continued its intrigues against the young republic and even harassed it with questions of reparation, to which one of its weak leaders, President Boyer, succumbed and, though it was never fully paid, the young country was saddled with unnecessary debt which inhibited its growth among the community of nations.[36] All these played their parts in the plight of Haiti through the years. It is still a wonder that the nation survived, but not until it had been brutalised again by the United States invasion and occupation in the twentieth century, and after it had resisted attempts to make it a new colony by the United States, France and Britain. It did not succumb. It chose poverty with dignity rather than enslavement for a mere morsel. That people have retained their sanity within the context of the nation is a source of endless wonder, but only sincere policies towards it would relieve it of the spectre of domination by outsiders which hangs over many client states of the twentieth century. But, as Theodore Holly reminds us, 'freedom and independence are written in the world's history in the ineffaceable characters of blood; and its crimsoned letters will ever testify to the determination and of the ability of the Negro to be free, throughout the everlasting succession of ages'.[37] This is the appropriate point at which we need to examine, briefly, reasons why the revolution succeeded, the only successful slave revolt in modern times.

Some reasons for success

From the above some conclusions can be arrived at as to why the St Domingue slave revolt succeeded while most of the others singularly failed to overthrow the slave system in the Americas. The points that are being made here are by no means exhaustive but help to focus on some of the reasons why revolts failed in other theatres. The first reason relates to leadership; foremost among the leaders was Toussaint L'Ouverture, who, in a space of ten years, converted slaves into one of the most effective of fighting forces, second to none in valour, discipline and consciousness of the cause for which they fought. They were, therefore, able to continue the struggle after their leader had been abducted, under new leaders thrown up by the revolution. Although Toussaint had failed his followers by not carrying the revolution to its logical end, his successors, and especially Dessalines, had no illusions about what had to be done to complete the process. He gave blow for blow, destroying whites equally as Rochambeau destroyed blacks. He employed ruthlessness and a scorched earth policy which, in less than a year, contributed to the capitulation of General Rochambeau.

The second factor rested on the organising genius of the leaders, first of Toussaint, and later of others. Their soldiers avoided rushing headlong, but instead used careful tactics of confronting the enemy in groups, sheltering under cover in the woods, and ambushing the enemies' troops, and developed guerrilla warfare to a fine art in what was essentially a life and death struggle. There were, of course, more open confrontations with the French as well, even more so after the abduction of Toussaint.

The third factor in success arose from the divisions in the rank and file of slave owners as well as their ambivalence to France, Britain and the Haitians. But their class and ideological prejudices did not help to unify their ranks. Some left the island, others fought with the British, some sought shelter under the blacks and mulattos, but when the expeditionary force came with Leclerc in 1802 they unashamedly rejoiced and abandoned the blacks.

Fourth was the division among the commissioners and troops despatched from France in the early days of the revolutionary struggles. There were divisions between revolutionaries and royalists which also complicated the situation and inhibited unity of action. The divisions in revolutionary France between Girondins and Jacobins were also reflected in the Haitian situation.

Fifth, there was the factor of European national rivalries which has been discussed at length in this and the previous chapter, with England seeking to supplant the French, and English and American interests diverging at times. These divergencies had implications for the development of the slave revolt. But even after 1805, while the Americans were withdrawing from the scene, the British, preoccupied with trade, were seeking to drive a wedge between France and Haiti to prevent any reconciliation.

Sixth, the confrontations which had taken place between the

English and the French in what were known as the Revolutionary and Napoleonic Wars interrupted the despatch from France of troops and the resumption of war after the uneasy peace of Amiens. The new war proved disastrous for the French, who were unable to send another expeditionary force when the forces they had sent to St Domingue were devastated both in combat and by yellow fever.

Seventh, yellow fever deserves its own role in decimating English and French troops. At the end of the confrontation the French had lost about 560 000 lives. Yellow fever also decimated the rank and file of the British troops who intervened in St Domingue, and the loss of lives among their rank and file eventually compelled them to negotiate an honourable withdrawal, rather than suffer a humiliating defeat by Toussaint.

Eighth, the French attempt to pursue a war of extermination drove the mulattos into the ranks of the blacks to unify the struggle and, in spite of their initial support for France, the mulattos later knew that there was no hope of peace until they had triumphed over France.

Ninth, following from the previous factor was the general belief among the Europeans and French Creoles that the Haitian blacks were too stupid to embark on any effective revolt. This attitude of mind also lured them into false hopes and proved their undoing, for when the blacks fought with ferocity to preserve the freedom they had won by their own efforts, the French were struck with disbelief. The slaves' consciousness of the fact that if they failed in their endeavours slavery would be reimposed with greater harshness elevated their cause to the level of a crusade. For those who spoke of the blacks as 'savages' it must be remembered that both Leclerc and his successor, Rochambeau, carried cruelty to excess. Leclerc had drowned over a thousand blacks in the harbour of Le Cap at one stroke, and he intended to carry out a war of extermination but became a victim of yellow fever. Such determination to carry out extermination of both blacks and mulattos was bound to make the revolutionary struggle more ferocious.

Finally, what proved most decisive above all in this success story was the resolute determination of the Afro-Haitians and their mulatto brothers and sisters never again to be enslaved by France or the British. The war had become a people's war and this was crucial to its success. They carried out their exploits against the French on land and sea and thence have been aptly described by C. L. R. James. James's book remains a classic and an epic account of the revolution. It was clear towards the end of 1803 that the slave revolt, which became the revolution, had triumphed over the slave owners. But the question remained whether the black hegemony in the midst of slave societies was to be allowed to survive. That story does not concern us here, but clearly it had raised the spectre of black revolution in slave societies and the slavocracy in the Americas was ill at ease. France, Britain and even the United States nurtured dreams of attempting to subdue or subjugate this black hegemony, and for most of the nineteenth century and part of the twentieth century the new state suffered both internally as well as threats from external sources, which were designed to keep it in a state of ferment. It is still a wonder that the revolution succeeded and survived, even if Haiti's economic development has been grossly retarded.

This is an appropriate point at which to consider means other than violence employed to bring about the demise of the slave system in the Americas.

Notes

1 C. C. Tansill, *The United States and Santo Domingo, 1798–1873: a Chapter in Caribbean Diplomacy*, Baltimore, Md., 1938., p. 75.
2 *Ibid.*
3 *Ibid.*, p. 76.
4 *Ibid.*, pp. 77–8.
5 See PRO, FO 5/32, Thornton to Hawkesbury, 2 June 1801, for a British version of the arrival of Lear.
6 See PRO, FO 5/32, Thornton to Hawkesbury, 2 June 1801, and CO 137/107, Thornton to Edward Corbet, 18 June 1801.
7 Tansill, *United States and Santo Domingo*, pp. 79–81.
8 *Ibid.*, p. 84.
9 See PRO, WO 1/71, for a copy of the Convention of 16 Nov. 1801.
10 Tansill, *United States and Santo Domingo*, p. 85, quoted from Lear to Madison, 9 Nov. 1801.
11 *Ibid.*, p. 85.
12 By the end of the confrontation in 1803 France had lost about 60 000 men.
13 Tansill, *United States and Santo Domingo*, pp. 86–7.
14 Stephen Alexis, *Black Liberator: the Life of Toussaint Louverture*, London, 1949, pp. 174–5. C. L. R. James wrote that 'Bonaparte boasted that England had shown some inclination to oppose the expedition, but when he threatened to clothe Toussaint with unlimited powers and acknowledge his independence, the British kept silent' (*op. cit.*, pp. 271–2). Yet, when Napoleon was in exile on St Helena he regretted not having ruled St Domingue through Toussaint. It was a case of acting in haste and repenting at leisure.
15 Tansill, *United States and Santo Domingo*, p. 87.
16 *Ibid.* This is a more correct assessment of the situation. See C. L. R. James, who wrote: 'To read English and French accounts of their operations in San Domingo one would believe that but for yellow fever they would have been easily victorious. But up to April there had been no yellow fever' (*The Black Jacobins, Toussaint Louverture and the San Domingo Revolution*, London, 1938, p. 323). The war of extermination had already failed by March. See subsequent pages. The valour of the blacks and mulattos who were steadfast

are forever enshrined in the annals of this resistance of the Haitians. Some notable examples of the lesser-known leaders whose resistance won Haiti for the Haitians were Clairveaux and 'Capois Death'. See James, *Black Jacobins*, pp. 367–8.

17 Tansill, *United States and Santo Domingo*, pp. 87–8, n. 51.

18 *Ibid.*, pp. 88–9.

19 *Ibid.*

20 *Ibid.*, pp. 89–96.

21 *Ibid.*, pp. 89, 92.

22 Shortly afterwards Leclerc deported Rigaud to France, where he was imprisoned in the same fortress that Toussaint was later to inhabit until he found his way back to Haiti in 1811. See James, *Black Jacobins*, p. 322.

23 E. L. Griggs and C. H. Prator (eds.), *Henry Christophe – Thomas Clarkson: a Correspondence*, Berkeley and Los Angeles, 1952, pp. 22–3. Also Rev. T. J. Holly, *A Vindication of the Capacity of the Negro Race for Self-Government and Civilized Progress*, New Haven, Conn., 1857, p. 159.

24 James, *Black Jacobins*, p. 290.

25 Bryan Edwards, *The History, Civil and Commercial, of the British Colonies in the West Indies*, London, 1818–19, Vol. 5, pp. 145–50; Spencer St John, *Hayti or the Black Republic*, London, 1884, pp. 67–8; James, *Black Jacobins*, p. 333–35; Tansill, *United States and Santo Domingo*, p. 96; Griggs and Prater (eds.), *Henry Christophe*, p. 28.

26 James, *Black Jacobins*, p. 357, indicated that Laplume 'remained faithful to the end'.

27 Griggs and Prater (eds.), *Henry Christophe*, p. 28. Holly; *Vindication*, p. 161. The French version is rendered as follows and was said to Savary, Chef de Division: 'En me renversant on n'a abattu à Saint Domingue que le tronc de l'arbre de la liberté des noirs; il repoussera, parceque les racines en sont profondes et nombreuses.'

28 Tansill, *United States and Santo Domingo*, p. 97; also Ralph Korngold, *Citizen Toussaint*, London, 1945, pp. 255–7, for some of the atrocities of Rochambeau on blacks – including drowning, burying alive, asphyxiating with sulphur fumes, and many other sadistic practices.

29 Tansill, *United States and Santo Domingo*, p. 105. For the development of Franco-American diplomatic activities and reactions, see especially his pp. 97–105.

30 See James's ch. 13 (*Black Jacobins*) entitled 'The War of Independence' and esp. pp. 337–55. The big black generals only defected later; Pétion and Dessalines reached an understanding for concerted action in August 1802 (p. 346). The little local leaders, as James called them, gave no peace to the army of the invaders (pp. 346–7). For arrest of Rigaud and family and deportation to France by Leclerc, see p. 322.

31 *Ibid.*, pp. 358ff. The source is Sannoun.

32 *Ibid.*, pp. 359, 360–2.

33 *Ibid.*, pp. 365–6.

34 See ch. 10, n. 44.

35 PRO, WO 1/910, George Montague to William Marsden, 2 Feb. 1804, signed by Capt. W. Lock.

36 It was Pétion who first proposed reparation to the French in the hope that it would assuage their wounded pride. Christophe would not hear of it, although

his correspondent and confidant in London, Thomas Clarkson, suggested it as a way of securing French recognition for Haitian independence. Yet it was their successors who had to be saddled with the payments that the French did not deserve. Of course only a part was paid. See Spencer St John, *Hayti*, pp. 79, 82–3. The French government in 1825 imposed a blockade on Haiti in order to secure compliance with its claims to reparation. The French demanded an indemnity of £60 000 000 reduced to £3 600 000 and later reduced to £2 400 000 to be paid in annual instalments over thirty years of £80 000. Such was the tragedy of Haiti, helpless and yet bullied by a colonial power determined either to reimpose slavery on unwilling subjects or to practise backdoor methods no less objectionable than banditry. In the face of this the Haitians suffered in silence while the other slave-owning powers, Britain and the United States, did nothing to restrain their partner in crime.

37 Holly, *Vindication*, p. 162.

12 Anti-slavery

The importance of this chapter lies in the fact that it represents another aspect of the strategy to defeat the slave trade and slavery in which the slaves and people of African origin in the diaspora played a prominent part. For those who have been nurtured in the traditional school of British anti-slavery studies the prominent names are familiar: William Wilberforce, Thomas Clarkson, Granville Sharp, Jeremy Bentham, James Ramsay, Zachary Macaulay, Sir Robert Stephens and many more. The traditional approach to anti-slavery, however, is no longer adequate. Many people, for example, are not aware that there were French abolitionists, North American abolitionists, Canadian abolitionists, Brazilian abolitionists and 'black abolitionists' that is to say – abolitionists of African origin in the diaspora. Although the white American abolitionists will be familiar to some American students, and probably the French abolitionists to French students, except in some Afro-American and Afro-Caribbean scholarly circles not much was said until recently about the part played by descendants of Africa in the anti-slavery movements, both independently and in combination with white abolitionists.

Benjamin Quarles' *Black Abolitionists*,[1] relating to the black contribution in the United States, introduced the vital corrective necessary to reappraise the anti-slavery movement. The book was a pioneering monograph which it was hoped would encourage studies of individual black contributions as well as follow-up works on certain aspects of the collective black effort. Quarles put to the fore the names of prominent Afro-American abolitionists such as Robert Purvis, Frederick Douglass, Henry Highland Garnet, Charles Lennox Redmond, Samuel Ringgold Ward, Austin Steward, William Wells Brown, Theodore Parker and many others. The aim here, however, is not to repeat Quarles's work or to attempt to summarise his book.[2] Our consideration in this exercise is rather to draw the strands together in terms of the black contribution to this vital crusade at a time when heavy prejudices weighed against them. We also need to bring in the contributions of other blacks from the British anti-slavery movement, thereby sketching in outline the black role within a much wider international framework.

With the growth of slavery studies since the Second World War, and especially since the 1960s, more and more books about the anti-slavery movement have been published. Writers have taken pains to correct some of the mistakes made by previous authors, and many books published in recent times may be said to belong to a humanitarian school of scholarship.[3] Many studies also relate either to the British anti-slavery campaign or to the American anti-slavery movement. Competent as these works are, there is still a need to reappraise the contribution of members of the African diaspora, and this from a variety of perspectives. Considerations that need investigation include the nature of black anti-slavery journalism, black people's tradition of opposing slavery, the elements of internationalism in the black anti-slavery effort, and a host of other subjects. It is, therefore, the purpose of this chapter to describe the efforts of the diaspora, while not entirely disregarding the white effort. Some attention must also be paid to the much less well-known anti-slavery campaigns in other European countries which contributed to anti-slavery either in thought or action, or both.

Although the slave trade was officially abolished in the British empire in 1807 and in the United States in 1808, other nations continued to trade in African slaves. Worse still, slavery persisted in all the Americas except Haiti. The struggles against slavery can broadly be examined either by theatre or by phase. If considered from the latter perspective the struggles were concentrated in two campaigns, as follows: first, for the abolition of the slave trade; and second, for the abolition of slavery or for what is generally termed 'emancipation'. The idea of combining both a regional and temporal approach is attractive since all theatres did not achieve their abolition and emancipation simultaneously, and this course is followed here. We have already noted in another context[4] that there is the need to reappraise the contribution which slave revolts made to the abolition of the slave trade and emancipation. Be that as it may, Britain's abolition of the slave trade followed by that of the United States, and the exertions of the British government to secure bilateral agreements with other nations engaged in the commerce had an important part to play in the termination of the trade,[5] (Denmark withdrew from the slave trade as early as 1792).[6] But through Britain's adoption of abolitionism as an aspect of its foreign policy, other nations followed in time, though with some defaulters. Sweden abolished the trade in 1813, Holland and France officially in 1814. Although the latter was achieved as a result of a treaty with Britain, the treaty did not come into full operation until 1 June 1819.[7]

Spain agreed to abolition in 1820, but the problem of Spanish involvement in the slave trade continued to divide Britain on the one hand and Spain and its colonies in the Americas on the other.[8] Spain in fact continued the trade with increased intensity, and revelations continued to be made of slavers leaving Havana in Cuba for the West African coast. In 1835 the British and Spanish governments agreed on the 'Equipment treaty', which gave Britain and Spain reciprocal rights to search and impound slave ships and condemn them in either the courts of Sierra Leone or Havana. But American assistance given to Britain was half-hearted, and the Spanish found loopholes in the agreement by using flags of convenience, either American or Portuguese; the United States also refused to concede to Britain the right to search its own vessels flying its flags.[9] The entire exercise proved difficult for Britain, and even brought British warships to Cuban waters in 1841. The United States co-operation with the British government remained half-hearted. The slave-trading activities merged with the era of revolutionary activities against Spain in the 1850s, but the slave trade persisted while the problems of Cuba became entangled with U.S. imperialistic designs and were only stemmed by the outbreak of civil war there. It was not until 1862 that the American President, Abraham Lincoln, conceded the right to search slave ships to the British.[10] But evidence suggests that the British failure to terminate both the Spanish and Portuguese slave trade was due to British economic interests.

Before 1842 the British could not act against Portuguese slave traders because its treaty with Portugal concerned the North Atlantic and did not cover the South Atlantic region from which Portugal was still drawing a substantial number of slaves. But after that date Britain persisted in its efforts to compel the Portuguese and Brazilians to abandon the trade and, ultimately, succeeded in 1851–2 (though a clandestine trade continued).[11] The tenacity of the opposition to the termination of the slave trade mirrored the strength of feeling among vested interests in the respective metropolitan countries as well as on the plantations themselves. Since abolitionism began with the British West Indian colonies, it is to them that we must now turn our attention.

British pioneers of anti-slavery

Like the struggles for abolition in the United States, the British abolition and emancipation movements had two distinct phases: the first from the 1770s to 1808, when the slave trade was abolished in the British empire, and the second phase from 1808 until the 1840s. Thereafter the British effort was diverted to giving moral and material support to other emancipation theatres, such as the U.S.A., or acting as counsellors to those who sought them. It was also the period in which the British, by international agreement, sought to commit other nations both to the abolition of the slave trade and to emancipation. It also saw British efforts on the high seas (very often thwarted) to arrest the clandestine slave trade, which assumed gigantic proportions, especially among the Portuguese-Brazilians, the Spanish-Cubans, and United States citizens acting on behalf of Cuban slave traders as well as themselves.

As two modern historians rightly observe, 'The initiative for abolition of the slave trade came from within English society, and not from within West Indian society.'[12] Initially, many in Britain saw the necessity for a systematic approach to these issues and felt that the abolition of the slave trade was the prerequisite for the emancipation of slaves. The initial fight was therefore to secure the first objective, and once this was secured the second was pursued with vigour.[13] But there were also those who saw both the abolition of the slave trade and emancipation as interlinked and advocated both simultaneously. Moreover, since the belief was rife at the time that the activities of the anti-slavers were also direct incitements to slave revolts, it seemed impossible to insulate the slaves from the activities which were being carried out on their behalf. In this respect we must not deflate the role of slaves through their revolts or attempted revolts in the overall contribution to the termination of the slave trade and slavery. Some of those who argued for the stoppage of the slave trade, even within the plantations themselves, were frightened by the overwhelming numbers of black slaves, and these fears were expressed both in the West Indies and North America. Numerical strength, it was argued, gave the slaves added confidence to revolt.[14]

Although the British anti-slavery movement was essentially a European affair, there were some individuals of African origin within its rank and file, of whom two were among the most outstanding.[15] Their contributions were in terms of propaganda as well as the moral arguments against the trade and system of the enslavement of man. These leaders were Ottobah Cugoano (christened as John Stewart) and Olaudah Equiano (alias Gustavus Vassa). Cugoano's *Thoughts and Sentiments of the Evils of Slavery* (1787) and Equiano's *Interesting Narrative*, published two years after Cugoano's book in 1789, complemented each other and arrived on the English scene at the time of the formation of the British Anti-Slavery Society and as the campaign for abolition was intensifying within the British Parliament and having an influence on British public opinion. Clarkson's publication, *The Impolicy of the Slavery Trade* (1788), was also on the scene, and these tracts continued to reinforce one another in the struggles for abolition. Apart from the arguments contained in them, both Cugoano's and Equiano's books were autobiographical, bringing into the debate against the slave trade and slavery the experiences of these descendants of Africa, who had been enslaved in the Americas and had later achieved manumission. They also acted as petitioners to the highest legislature in the land, the British Parliament, and it was even more explicit in Equiano's book, which he addressed to the House of Commons and the House of Lords in Parliament assembled. In Thomas Clarkson's book we get a glimpse of efforts made by the Committee for the Abolition of the Slave Trade to enlist the support of imported dignitaries; Cugoano's book ranked on the same level, drawing its inspiration from the essay with which Thomas Clarkson won fame as an anti-slaver. Clarkson sought to enlist the support of the very influential in society and abroad. In demonstrating the international dimension of the movement Clarkson wrote:

> But the committee in London, while they were endeavouring to promote the object of their institution at home, continued their exertions for the same purpose abroad within this period.
>
> They kept up a communication with the different societies established in America.
>
> They directed their attention also to the continent of Europe. They had already applied, as I mentioned before, to the King of Sweden in favour of their cause, and had received a gracious answer. They now attempted to interest other potentates in it. For this purpose they bound up in an elegant manner two sets of the Essays on the Slavery and Commerce of the Human Species and on the Impolicy of the Slave Trade, and sent them to the Chevalier de Pinto, in Portugal. They bound up in a similar manner three sets of the same, and sent them to Mr Eden (now Lord Auckland), at Madrid to be given to the King of Spain, the Count d'Aranda, and the Marquis del Campomanes.[16]

Anti-slavery texts provided numerous and damning evidence for the abandonment of the slave trade and servitude in the West Indies. Both Cugoano and Equiano were associated with the Sierra Leone venture for the resettlement of manumitted slaves, and although Equiano disagreed on some points with the organisers and thereafter had no further dealings with them, Cugoano took part in the venture to Sierra Leone, after which we lose track of his life.

The nature of opposition to anti-slavery in the British West Indian colonies at the time made any advocacy of abolition and emancipation dangerous in the extreme, as some of the dissenting missionaries were to find to their cost.[17] Much that could be done was only accomplished by petitions to Britain supplying evidence, enlisting the support of influential people, and seeking to influence public opinion. Even the celebrated Mansfield judgment in the Somerset Case of 1772 was not the result of organisational and protest activity in the West Indies but was in the main the work of the humanitarian spirit in England. But contrary to the exaggerated claim given to the Mansfield judgment that it abolished slavery in Britain,[18] recent research, based on careful examination of legal documents, official papers and newspapers, has revealed that this point of view is misleading.[19] Dr F. O. Shyllon in his admirable book has exploded the myth and discounted the claim that the judgment freed black slaves in Britain from their bondage. The merit of Shyllon's book is that it cites many examples of slaves brought to England and taken back to the colonies without their slave status being changed, and that when efforts were made to have their status either altered or redefined the English courts upheld their existing status as slave. Another merit of the book is that Shyllon points out that there was a misunderstanding by some contemporary observers (not least by some judges) who believed that the Mansfield judgment did, in fact, set the seal of doom on slavery. The misunderstanding was passed on through the generations who further perpetuated the myth which has plagued historical writing on slavery with dogmatic inaccuracy.[20] This for a long time obscured the real position. Quoting Dr Eric Williams, who had observed the hitherto widely accepted interpretation as 'poetic sentimentality translated into modern history',[21] Shyllon has rescued historical truth from romantic fiction and his research is a major contribution to the reconstruction of the events of that period, distorted as they were by the enthusiasm of the humanitarian school and entrenched in contemporary textbooks concerned with English abolitionism.[22]

There is another dimension to the anti-slavery activities in Britain. Hitherto too much emphasis has been put on the humanitarian aspect of it.[23] Later writers, beginning with Eric Williams, have assailed conventional notions. The debate initiated by Eric Williams with the publication of his book *Capitalism and Slavery* in 1944 has continued to rage with great intensity, one of his main critics being the late Professor Roger Anstey,[24] who in various publications reinforced the humanitarian argument. Williams, while emphasising the economic argument earlier elaborated by Professor L. J. Ragatz,[25] made a distinction between genuine[26] humanitarians as represented by Granville Sharp, and other abolitionists, whose considerations were far from humanitarian. Without wishing to be drawn into that debate in this work, as space does not permit, it is essential to indicate that the arguments are still continuing.[27] But the fact that the Williams thesis continues to be assailed without completely disposing of it testifies to its tenacity and strength. One modern historian[28] has attempted to suggest that the truth might lie somewhere between the humanitarian thesis of Professor Reginald Coupland and his disciples on the one hand and the economic thesis of Williams and his followers on the other.

Turning from the metropolis, where much of the abolitionist efforts were concentrated, there was also a minority of dissenting ministers, Quakers, Methodists and Baptists, active in the West Indies in the 1820s with the aim of securing not only the amelioration of the conditions of the slaves but the end of the system. Free coloured people in the colonies also clamoured for their disabilities to be removed in order that they might share identical rights with white people in slave societies; but mostly they were concerned with their own privileges rather than with the bondaged status of slaves. Although they secured full rights in Grenada by 1823, Jamaica and Barbados still resisted the demands of free coloured people so that they were compelled to put their case before the British Parliament. With equal force the slaves from the 1820s were demanding their emancipation and were showing a greater tendency to rebelliousness, one notable example of revolt for emancipation being recorded in British Guiana (present-day Guyana) in 1823.[29]

A notable exception to the mulatto indifference to the plight of the vast majority of the slaves was that of a coloured man of Jamaica, Edward Jordan, who was born in 1800 and by 1820 had thrown himself into the fray to seek civil rights for his own free coloured people as a prerequisite to seeking the freedom of slaves.[30] The Civil Rights Organisation of Free Coloured Jamaican Men which was formed had for a time to remain secret and underground, for the Caribbean societies had become nervous following the beginning of the Haitian Revolution and the proximity of Haiti to the remaining slave-holding colonies caused every criticism in the islands to be regarded as an incitement to insurrection. While at the time of the coloured organisation's formation no coloured person seemed willing to assume the post of secretary, Edward Jordan readily accepted the role. The organisation preoccupied itself with love of country, liberty and justice, principles to which Edward Jordan adhered to the end of his life. The championing of such causes in the islands in this period was tantamount to 'treason' in the eyes of the slavocracy, if not in Britain. In 1823 the society presented its petition to the Jamaican House of Assembly for the right of full participation by free people of colour in the political life of the island.[31] Although the plea was rejected, certain concessions were made to the free coloured people, but with their aspirations unsatisfied they nonetheless found it expedient to send emissaries, Richard Hill and Alexander Dawson Simpson, to present the original petition to the British Parliament. These men eventually were heard at the bar of the House of Commons in 1827, but the British Parliament carefully avoided taking any action. Edward Jordan, in collaboration with another coloured man of note, Robert Osborne, succeeded in establishing a newspaper, the *Watchman*,[32] which circulated twice weekly and was used as the focal point of their campaign.

Jordan's activities now set him on a collision course with the slavocracy, who imposed the death penalty for any publication which they considered to be 'dangerous or seditious'.[33] As this was always the technique used in slave societies to stifle the voice of abolitionism and civil rights, Jordan and Osborne had to tread warily, and although the articles contained in the paper were usually anonymous, those of Jordan were easily recognisable. From 1829 members of the slavocracy sought unsuccessfully to incriminate Jordan for his publications and pronouncements on the subject of civil rights, and they were supported in their efforts by pro-slavery papers like the *Chronicle* and the *Courant*, which expressed the prejudices of their readers and tried to suggest that the journalism of the *Watchman* was seditious, treacherous and insidious. Jordan, however, was not deterred from his chosen path to exercise the rights of free publication and discussion to champion the cause of freedom. In one of the issues of the *Watchman* Jordan wrote:

> We have been repeatedly taunted with being opposed to the *best interest of the island*. If to stand boldly forward as the consistent advocates of the rights of humanity – if to put forward our best energies to stem the torrent of the heartless and revolting oppressors of the wretched defenceless slaves, and hold them up to the execration of the virtuous and humane – if to do this be really in contravention of the *best interests of the island*, we at once plead guilty to the charge; and we further declare, in the most unequivocal manner, that we shall not fail, as often as opportunity may serve, to repeat these 'high crimes and misdemeanors'.[34]

The editor (Jordan) further directed his attack at that 'heterogeneous combination of intolerance, arrogance and imbecile folly – that many-headed monster, begotten by the far-fetched Parson B'.[35]

This was an obvious reference to the Rev. George W. Bridges, Rector of St Ann's, who had founded the pro-slavery Colonial Church Union, the organisation which had burnt down the churches of dissenting ministers after the Jamaican slave revolt of 1831–2. But all the attempts made by the slavocracy to arraign and convict Jordan proved in the end abortive; once Jordan was convicted for 'libel' and sentenced to twelve months' imprisonment together with a fine of £100, but this judgment was reversed on appeal in 1831 when Jordan had served only six months of the sentence.[36]

From that moment Jordan's secret organisation for advocating civil rights surfaced. His campaign for the removal of restrictive laws, the abolition of disabilities against coloured people, and the

363

conceding of political equality became unrelenting, and he even threatened a possible rising of the entire coloured population if the reforms were not conceded. Jordan continued his advocacies, but by 1833 the Act for the abolition of slavery passed by the British Parliament had reached the Jamaican Assembly, and its members were left with no alternative but to approve it (though only after much wrangling).

Thereafter, the emancipation Bill was ratified from 1 August 1834, emancipating children from the age of six years downwards while apprenticing the field hands for six years[37] and the domestic slaves for four years. The discrimination which had previously operated at work was thereby re-entrenched. Jordan as well as many dissenting missionaries rejected the apprenticeship system, stigmatising it as slavery under another name. His efforts were, therefore, directed towards its abolition. He himself became a member of the Jamaican Assembly in 1835 and used it as a forum for assailing the apprenticeship system. The decision for abolishing the system was taken on 1 August 1838; by 1840 it was gone. Jordan's complaint against the apprenticeship system was later confirmed by Eric Williams in his observation about emancipation. Williams wrote:

> Emancipation of the Negro was a juridical, a social and political change. In the eyes of the law the slave, formerly the property of his master, a human beast of burden completely in the power and at the discretion of his owner, became free, with all the rights and privileges and pre-requisites pertaining thereto. But emancipation was not an economic change. It left the new freeman as much dependent on and at the mercy of his King sugar as he had been as a slave. It meant for him not the land, which was incompatible with the requirements of the capitalist sugar industry. It meant a change from chattel slavery to peonage, or as has been said in another connection a change from the discipline of the cart-whip to the discipline of starvation. The slave was raised to the dubious dignity of a landless wage labourer, paid at the rate of twenty five cents a day in the British Islands. Sweet are the uses of emancipation! To free the Negro it was necessary not so much to destroy slavery, which was the consequence of sugar, as to alter the method of production in the sugar industry itself. This simple point is essential to an understanding of the situation of the Negro population in the Caribbean today. The black man, emancipated from above by legislation or from below by revolution, remains today the slave of sugar.[38]

After the abolition of the apprenticeship system the rest of Jordan's life until his death on 8 February 1869 was devoted to championing constitutional government, especially after the Jamaica Assembly had agreed to the plan of Governor Eyre, whose inglorious record culminated in the so-called Morant Bay Rebellion of 1865. The 'rebellion' and its aftermath remain a blot on British administration in that unhappy island.[39]

In the abolitionist agitation within the West Indian colonies the colour differences encouraged as a divisive factor appear to have exerted their influence. Thus, the majority of the coloured men sought privileges and aimed at approximating their interests to those of the ruling whites; only after their hopes were frustrated did they side with the dissenting missionaries and free blacks to exert pressure for abolition. In this effort it was Edward Jordan who most demonstrated steadfastness of mind and consistency of action in the crusade against the slave trade and slavery. Nevertheless, the greatest of the battles was to be fought in the metropolis, where the two former slaves, Cugoano and Equiano, allied their efforts with those of the British abolitionists to secure the ultimate objectives of the British Society for the Abolition of the Slave Trade. The society had been founded in England in 1787 and continued its existence until abolition reached the statute book in 1807. Its activities were continued by the African Institution, formed in 1807 and disbanded in 1827. In 1823 the Society for the Mitigation and Gradual Abolition of Slavery throughout the British Dominions, better known by its alternative name, the Anti-Slavery Society, was formed.

Anti-slavery in the United States

In spite of the effort to delineate the contributions of the African diaspora to the abolitionist endeavours, this cannot be entirely divorced from the general movement involving Afro-Americans and Euro-Americans or from its international connections. There is still the need to illuminate some of the less-known contributions of the African diaspora while bearing in mind the existence of extensive documentation on the Euro-American effort. Anti-slavery, for example, cannot be divorced from the thoughts of the Quakers, or from eminent names of white leaders such as William Lloyd Garrison, Thaddeus Stevens, Wendell Phillips, Lewis and Arthur Tappan and many others. The aim here must be to marry the black contributions with those of the whites while not deflating the role of the blacks. In considering the abolitionist efforts in the United States we must again distinguish two distinct phases: first, the early abolitionist movement before 1830; and second, the later abolitionist movement from 1830 to the end of the Civil War.

As in England, France and some of the West Indian territories, there were individual abolitionists with whom we are not at present concerned but whose contributions place them in the same tradition of struggle. The tendency to consider the black contributions as an appendage of the white American abolitionist crusade is often so misleading that Professor John Hope Franklin has reminded us that 'strong abolitionist doctrine was preached by Negroes long before Garrison was born'.[40] Nevertheless, in asserting this we should not disregard the individualist efforts of Quakers such as George Fox, who in 1671 urged his brethren in the West Indies to treat their slaves well and manumit those who had served long and well.[41] As an ardent believer in the equality of man he advocated the preaching of the gospel to all races.[42] Among other early Quaker anti-slavery stalwarts were Joseph Wood and Anthony Benezet.[43] But the Quakers of Germantown in Pennsylvania showed even greater zeal in the seventeenth century for the abolition of the slave trade as well as of the institution of slavery, and by 1783 were attempting to influence their British counterparts to urge Parliament by means of a petition to declare the trade illegal.

Early pioneers

The pre–1830 activists included Chief Justice Samuel Sewall[44] (in Calvinist Massachusetts), and John Woolman,[45] a Quaker who, together with Anthony Benezet, was an anti-slavery propagandist in North America in the eighteenth century. The organisation of the first anti-slavery society took place in Philadelphia in 1775. Other organisations followed, such as the Pennsylvania Society for Promoting the Abolition of Slavery (1795), and an organisation which sought The Relief of Negroes Unlawfully Held in Bondage, and for Improving the Conditions of the Race. A New York Anti-Slavery Society was formed in 1785 under the leadership of John Alexander Hamilton, and was followed by others in New Jersey, Delaware, Maryland, Connecticut, Rhode Island and Virginia. It was delegates from five of these groups who assembled in Philadelphia in 1794 and constituted themselves into a national organisation in a loose confederation with the name of the American Convention for Promoting the Abolition of Slavery and Improving the Condition of the African Race.[46]

These early abolitionists in the U.S.A. had a certain characteristic outlook quite distinct from their successors of the 1830s. Among their notable features were first, their religious orientations; second, their desire for conciliation; third, their gradualist tendencies; and fourth, their refusal to admit women to their ranks. In their approach to the issue they were utopian, believing that sentiment would move against slavery, encouraging it to wilt away. Moreover, they were not strictly speaking agitators, more moral suasionists and believers in compensated emancipation; their position seemed to reassure the Southern slavocracy that they would not tamper with the rights of property,[47] and they refrained from using invective and vitriolic language.[48] Furthermore, they do not appear to have had many blacks in their ranks, only admitting one light-skinned Afro-American, Robert Purvis, between 1775 and 1839. But the society showed a desire to aid the education of black people and especially in the maintenance of the African Free School, which in 1834 was incorporated into the city-supported system after forty-seven years of existence. The failure of the early abolitionists lay in the fact that they were not successful in creating a general climate of opinion against slavery, as their successors were to do. Economic considerations were also evident in their failure, for the expansion of cotton production was taking place in the South-west, and the strength of the Southern slavocracy was only too evident in the House of Representatives. The invention of the cotton gin in 1793 by Eli Whitney contributed to the expansion of cotton culture and to the tenacity of slavery in the U.S.A. Another factor which became important was what has been termed the Missouri Compromise of 1820, by which the slave state of Missouri was admitted into the Union. The early movement became less ardent in its endeavours, its meetings became irregular after 1832 and the society was finally wound up in 1834 after existing for forty-four years. Its intentions were good but it failed dismally to achieve concrete results.

In the light of what has been said above, Mary Stoughton Locke's assertion about the early abolitionist movement in her admirable study[49] needs some qualification. She makes a convincing argument that the early abolitionists' endeavours were intended to 'express the national disapprobation on the trade as an infringement of the rights of man, and the principles of the federal government'. She also argues that though its direct results 'were of no great importance', it accomplished 'much more than its immediate objective', for it aroused 'the Abolition Societies to something beyond their local interest and gave them greater breadth of purpose; it united them in a common cause, and led to the formation of an association which continued its activity until a new era of state and national anti-slavery Societies for which the earlier societies had prepared the way; above all, it furnished a legitimate outlet for anti-slavery energy in connection with a national cause'.[50] It is also her thesis that the activities of the earlier abolitionists awakened the national conscience into a greater awareness of the preoccupations of anti-slavery advocates, which leads her to deduce that:

> Abolitionists of the earlier day had seen the truth as clearly and
> spoken it as boldly as any of the later generation. If their language
> was usually more temperate it was not from timidity or indifference,
> but because they believed that persuasion was more effective than

provocation. They did what they did to save their country from the doom they foresaw, it was not the insufficiency of their zeal nor the defects of their organisation that made it impossible to avert that doom.... They formed the Abolition Societies and propagated anti-slavery ideas through their agency. They produced a constant outpour of anti-slavery pamphlets, orations and newspapers and magazine articles. In these ways they laid the foundations of the work of Lundy and Garrison and the Anti-Slavery Societies; and made possible the petitions presented by John Quincy Adams and the development of the Liberty, Free Soil and Republican parties.[51]

Although this is the appreciation and eulogy of a sympathiser, there is some truth in Professor Locke's observations, though a number of questions remain. For instance, why did the early abolitionists not have more than one coloured man in their rank and file? It is clear, too, that they lacked the breadth of vision of later abolitionists.

Abolitionists from the 1830s

These were men and women of a different stamp, who once they had begun their activities campaigned for uncompensated emancipation and pinned their struggles on the immediate abolition of slavery. They nonetheless consisted of moderates and radicals, and a cleavage occurred within their ranks in 1840, separating the gradualists from the immediatists. The later abolitionists were not so religiously orientated as were their predecessors, though they had religious men in their ranks; and, while possessing an elitist leadership, the movement was much more 'grassroots' centred and more broadly based. Furthermore, they also employed shock tactics and vitriolic language to describe slave holders, referring to them as 'man-stealers'.[52]

The American Anti-Slavery Society came into being on 4 December 1833; Garrison's declaration of intentions has been described by Benjamin Quarles as its 'Magna Carta'.[53] The declaration broadly revolved around the determination to secure entire abolition for the whole of the country and to elevate the condition of the people of colour. Many blacks became active members of the organisation, including James G. Barbados, James MacCrummell, Robert Purvis, John B. Vashon, the Rev. Peter Williams of New York, and Abraham D. Shadd of Chester County, Pennsylvania. The Massachusetts Anti-Slavery Society emerged the following year in succession to the New England Anti-Slavery Society, which had been founded in 1832. Among other blacks who became stalwarts of the Anti-Slavery Society were James T. Forten, John C. Bowers and Charles W. Gardner, a Presbyterian Pastor of Philadelphia. Initially women were encouraged to form their own anti-slavery society but according to Quarles, in 1839 they became incorporated into the male organisation.[54] A Juvenile Anti-Slavery Society was founded soon after the parent body in 1833.[55] Anti-slavery in North America was not a genteel affair; the violence unleashed by the slavocracy against advocates of anti-slavery and their sympathisers is revealed extensively in records and publications and needs no further recounting here. The pro-slavery groups often hired mobs, and both blacks and whites suffered from their excesses.[56] Some of the victims were mutilated or maimed, while others lost their lives. A notable example was the murder in November 1837 of the white clergyman, abolitionist and publicist, the Rev. Elijah Lovejoy, editor of the journal *Aulton Observer*.[57] Before this Lovejoy's press had on three separate occasions been thrown into a river. The murder of Lovejoy produced a white martyr for the abolitionist cause, and from that moment co-operation between blacks and whites was less hesitant and contributed immensely to making the struggle more cohesive and effective.

This was so much the case that when the abolitionist movement split in 1840 the division was based on deeply held convictions rather than along colour lines, for in both the organisations that emerged, the previous American Anti-Slavery Society led by William Lloyd Garrison, which eschewed political action, and the new organisation, the American and Foreign Anti-Slavery Society (May 1840), led by Arthur and Lewis Tappan, and which advocated political action, blacks were present. At this time there were admittedly some blacks who felt that they should go it alone and form their own black organisation, but they were discouraged from doing so by some of their black leaders, notably Robert Purvis, William Whipper and Frederick Douglass.[58]

In spite of this not all black or coloured people were abolitionists. Some, in fact, held pro-slavery sentiments, others owned a few slaves, while still others owned large plantations, were as affluent as the white Creoles of their class, and lived in some style.[59] Quarles aptly represented the situation when he observed that 'To be a coloured man is not necessarily to be an abolitionist'.[60] But among the black abolitionists were outstanding men and women, many of whom became popular celebrities on anti-slavery platforms. They included names like Henry Bibb, William Wells Brown, Frederick Douglass, Charles Lennox Redmond, Henry Highland Garnet, Sojourner Truth, J. W. Pennington, Austin Steward, Robert Purvis, Samuel Ringgold Ward, David Ruggless and many more.

Blacks in the crusade against slavery

Some retrospective glance at the contribution of members of the diaspora is necessary to substantiate the already quoted assertion of Professor J. H. Franklin about blacks and the early abolition movement. In assessing the contributions of blacks to the abolitionist movement before and after Garrison's organisation came into being, the following considerations are crucial. Among them were individualists who, like their white counterparts, sent out petitions[61] against slavery, in some cases anonymously. Some of their publications, beginning with newspapers, were carriers of anti-slavery sentiments, and the autobiographies of ex-slaves which became prominent in the nineteenth century were positive contributions to anti-slavery literature. Without white assistance or promptings they organised their own Vigilance Societies to resist the work of slave catchers.[62] Their National Conventions, which began from 1830, were preoccupied with anti-slavery and the future destiny of the coloured population of the United States. They assisted white abolitionists by subscribing to their newspapers. By their organisational efforts they began to preoccupy themselves, long before the abolition question got under way, with the question of education. One such example was the school established in 1797 for both blacks and whites by Paul Cuffee, a black Bostonian shipowner.[63] They showed themselves capable of black–white co-operation in the adroit way in which the Underground Railroad was organised which enabled slaves to escape from slave states to the free states and sometimes to Canada.[64] They also were active not only on anti-slavery platforms but were ardent in fund-raising to meet the expenses of the activities aimed at destroying the slave system. Added to this some of them maintained homes for escaped slaves as a sheltering point before their departure to a freer haven. Furthermore they, like their ardent white counterparts, experienced the rigours of mob violence and the anger of the pro-slavery barons and their protégés. These points need further amplification.

The names of Prince Hall (the Barbadian who founded the first black masonic order in the U.S.A.),[65] Benjamin Banneker (the almanac-maker, mathematician and astronomer),[66] and the Reverend Absolom Jones (founder of St Thomas Episcopal Church) and Bishop Richard Allen (founder of the African Methodist Episcopal Church) are often mentioned in the front rank of black abolitionists of the late eighteenth and early nineteenth centuries. These men, like their white associates, were to use petitions and the language of moral suasion to appeal to the slavocracy and the ruling authorities. The publication in 1789 of an anonymous pamphlet, *On Slavery*, by an Afro-American freeman[67] in the U.S.A. has been credited to

Benjamin Banneker, who is said to have addressed a letter in 1791 to Thomas Jefferson.[68] M. J. Bucher has written:

> The little-known but significant exchange of correspondence (for Jefferson replied civilly and sympathetically,) stating that he had sent a copy to M.de Condorcet, Secretary of the Academy of Sciences at Paris and a member of 'The Philanthropic Society,' 'because I consider it a document to which your whole colour had a right for their justification against the doubts which have been entertained of them') may have had much to do with Jefferson's doubts and fears about the rectitude and wisdom of slavery. Negro protest continued bravely but sporadically until it climaxed a generation later in the noteworthy collaboration of men like Samuel Ringgold Ward, Charles Lennox Redmond, Henry Highland Garnett, and Frederick Douglass.[69]

Bishop Richard Allen issued 'An address to Those Who Keep Slaves and Approve the Practice'[70] in 1794. Most of the black petitioners were moral suasionists who expected their petitions to prick the consciences of slave keepers and encourage a change of heart in them, and especially to influence people in high ranking positions in public life to institute policies or action for emancipation. In this respect they were not different from the Euro-American abolitionists before the 1830s.

But the black contribution was not confined only to petitions issued by prominent individuals. Other forms of attack were directed against the system through the pages of black and white abolitionist newspapers, through letters to newspaper editors, in books written by blacks and in numerous autobiographies of ex-slaves. These books became vital to the movement in the heyday of the second-phase anti-slavery crusade. The year 1829 was notable for the publication of three books. The first was perhaps the most vitriolic of the anti-slavery tracts designed to disturb the complacency of the slavocracy.[71] It was published by a coloured man originally born in North Carolina but then residing in Boston. His name was David Walker. The book was entitled *An Appeal to the Coloured Citizens of the United States*,[72] and became known as *The Appeal*. It showed a remarkable understanding not only of the United States but of events in the West Indies and in Europe. The important point of Walker's argument was that slaves should rise up and break off their shackles, and unless white Christian Americans changed their ways disaster would eventually overtake them. The second publication of note was that written by a house slave, George Moses Horton, *Hope for Liberty*, a book of poems.[73] The third was known as the *Ethiopian Manifesto in Defence of the Black-*

371

man's Right in the Scale of Universal Freedom[74] by Robert A. Young, who prophesied that a Messiah would arise to liberate his people. Of the three it was Walker's *Appeal* that kept the slavocracy on edge and uneasy. The book was vigorously attacked and numerous penalties threatened against those found carrying it or disseminating its arguments. In 1830 Walker died in mysterious circumstances, his death attributed by some to foul play.[75]

Before the publications of 1829 there were newspapers in existence run by free blacks, the first of them known as *Freedom's Journal*, published by John Russwurm (the first Afro-American college graduate) and the Rev. Samuel B. Cornish, often referred to as the 'Presbyterian Minister'.[76] In 1829 Russwurm left the U.S. and emigrated to Liberia. The paper was taken over by Cornish, who renamed it *Rights of All*. Another free coloured man, David Ruggles, a genius at biting sarcasm, founded the first black magazine, *Mirror of Liberty*. These publications were short-lived, but were followed by the celebrated anti-slavery publication of William Lloyd Garrison, *The Liberator* (founded in January 1831). Black newspapers were part of the Afro-American effort to influence the thought and action of the anti-slavery movement. Other such newspapers run by Afro-Americans later came on the scene, one of the most prominent being Frederick Douglass's *The North Star* (1847), which he edited with Dr Martin Robinson Delany,[77] who was later to become Douglass's arch-opponent concerning the destiny of Afro-Americans. *The North Star* was later renamed the *Frederick Douglass Paper* (1850)[78] and was published in Rochester, New York. The *Frederick Douglass Paper* was a real crusader and put the entire anti-slavery struggle within a wider international framework. Not only was it the aim of the paper to assail slavery in its columns but also to advocate universal emancipation. Domestic issues as well as international ones appeared on its pages. In 1837 there appeared another paper edited by Cornish entitled *The Coloured American*, but its span of life was only four years. Other newspapers by blacks were G. Allen and Henry Highland Garnet's *The National Watchman* in Troy, New York, and Martin Delany's *The Mystery*, published in Pittsburgh (1843–47). There was also *The Elevator* in Albany, New York. Syracuse saw the appearance of *The Imperial Citizen* established by Samuel R. Ward in 1848, and three years later L. H. Putnam produced in New York City *The Colored Man's Journal*. Then came *The Philadelphia Freeman, The Philadelphia Citizen, The New York Phalanx, The Baltimore Elevator*, and the *Cincinnati Central Star*. Thomas Hamilton[79] in 1859 published the *Anglo-African* from New York, and was succeeded as editor by Robert Hamilton and Henry Highland Garnet.

Of the papers in existence in the early 1850s were *The Colored American* (becoming *The Colored American Advocate*), which commenced publication on 4 March 1837 (its proprietor was Phillip A. Bell and editor Samuel Cornish); *The Ram's Horn; The Demosthenian Shield; The Mirror of Liberty* (edited by David Ruggles); *The Pittsburgh Mystery; The Palladium of Liberty; The Disfranchised American; The Colored Citizen; The National Watchman* (Troy, N. Y., 1842); *The Excelsior; The Christian Herald; The Farmer; The Impartial Citizen; The Northern Star of Albany; The North Star* (later the *Frederick Douglass Paper); The Mirror of the Times*, San Francisco (1855); *The National Reformer* (Philadelphia, edited by William Whipper), *The Christian Recorder*, Philadelphia, 1856 (editor Jabez Campbell); and *The Alienated American*, Cleveland, Ohio, 1852 (edited by W. H. H. Day). There is need for a closer study of these papers in an intense period of anti-slavery endeavour.

The early nineteenth century saw the appearance of many auto-biographies by ex-slaves and also a collection of slave biographies, one example being that collected by William Still, who was one of the black operators of the Underground Railroad.[80] Early in the nineteenth century a spate of autobiographies and biographies of ex-slaves came on the market. One of the earliest which had its impact on anti-slavery activity was *The Narrative of Frederick Douglass: an American Slave* (1845), broadened out ten years later into *My Bondage and My Freedom* (1855). Although Douglass was an exceptional slave, other narratives were nonetheless very informative, such as those of the Rev. J. W. Pennington, *The Fugitive Blacksmith* (Pennington later received a Doctor of Divinity degree at the University of Heidelberg), the Rev. Samuel Ringgold Ward's *The Autobiography of a Fugitive Negro and his Anti-Slavery Labours*, and the *Narrative of William Wells Brown*. These publications came at a time when the anti-slavery movement in the U.S. was entering its crucial and decisive stages.

The Afro-Americans fulfilled numerous roles. Notice began to be taken of many of the freemen and escapees and they were recruited into the anti-slavery rank and file. Blacks shared the same platforms as their distinguished white counterparts. Some of them became travelling agents for the Anti-Slavery Society. Others were show-pieces for 'doubting Thomases' who either did not believe that slavery was cruel or did not believe that the ex-slave was capable of rising to dignity and excellence. On their own initiative blacks mobilised their communities against slavery, ensuring that they attended anti-slavery conventions and organising support, both material and intellectual, for the defeat of slavery in North America. Thus, some Afro-Americans were the earliest subscribers to Garrison's *Liberator*, and blacks lent their support to the movement by organising fund-raising activities for the anti-slavery campaign. Some, like David Ruggles, the Reverend J. W. Loguen, and William Still,[81] organised guest houses for fugitive slaves travelling on the Underground Railroad, while others, like Harriet Tubman, unsure of total white support in her commitment to the liberation of her people, took her escapees all the way until satisfied they were out of harm's way.

Others still organised vigilance groups to forestall the schemes of slave catchers. This was an important anti-slavery activity in that it not only aimed at preventing escapee slaves being taken back into slavery, but also sought to prevent frauds involving the abduction of free coloured people into slavery as a consequence of the passing of the Fugitive Slave Act of 1850, which replaced the ineffective Fugitive Slaves Act of 1793.[82] Examples of the consequences of slave catching are numerous in the newspapers of the time and in ex-slaves' autobiographies and biographies. A notable example of the disaster attendant on slave catching was that referred to as 'The Christiana Affair' in 1858, which resulted in the death of a master slave catcher, Mr Gorschurch. The experiences of ex-slaves like Austin Steward read like adventure stories when read today.

It is clear that the record of blacks in the United States in the anti-slavery crusade was no less creditable than that of Euro-American abolitionists, and that the activities of both black and white in the crusade against slavery merged into one broad front, interracial and international in scope. We have seen that blacks initiated their own movement in the pre-Garrisonian era; they were not necessarily inspired by whites, nor were they appendages of the white movement. Thus the names of individuals like Prince Hall, Benjamin Banneker, the Rev. Absolom Jones and Richard Allen, among others, stand out among the advocates of abolition. Among other names of blacks in the anti-slavery movement were those of Frances Ellen Watkins, William and Ellen Craft[83] (who had earlier escaped through disguise by the channel of the Underground Railroad), and activists such as Sojourner Truth (alias Isabella) and Harriet Tubman, each in her contribution to the Underground Railroad and during the Civil War. We have also seen the importance of publications initiated from the black quarter, including newspapers, broadsheets, pamphlets, magazines, printed sermons, books and letters to the black and white press. Of the numerous publications that sprang up during the anti-slavery campaign many were short-lived, but they were part of a whole corpus of anti-slavery literature. The interracial and international nature of the second phase of U.S. abolitionism has been alluded to. Yet, in spite of what has been noted above, it is not often sufficiently emphasised that in these efforts blacks worked under numerous disabilities.

The publication by Frederick Douglass in 1847 of his own newspaper (Douglass by this time had emerged as the front-line leader of the coloured community in the U.S.) showed the parting of the ways with Garrison (who eschewed direct political action) and demonstrated his ability to act independently. Before the establishment of the paper he had considered the possibility of reinforcing one of the existing anti-slavery newspapers rather than embarking on a separate venture. However, his speeches abroad in England and Ireland, as well as his international contacts and those of other coloured people, helped to mobilise British opinion against North American slavery. His speech to the World Temperance Convention at Covent Garden in August 1846 was an example of that international spirit which characterised the anti-slavery movement. In summarising Douglass's speech the following points are crucial. He called attention to the fact that those who should have elected him as an official delegate to the Convention were still in slavery, and that there were also 400 000 free but disenfranchised people of colour; he therefore found himself unable to share in the patriotism expressed by white American delegates. He graphically outlined previous efforts made by black people 'free and intelligent, sober and benevolent' in Philadelphia to forge a Temperance Society, their efforts thwarted by white mob violence in 1842 during a procession. Douglass's skill in linking the breaking up of the temperance procession of coloured people on the anniversary of England's emancipation[84] of 800 000 slaves in the West Indies was a master stroke in establishing a vital correlation between movements and events, and Douglass's speech had the desired impact on the Convention.

As the nineteenth century progressed the slavery question was kept alive by the recurrent slave revolts, such as those of Gabriel (1800), Vesey (1822) and Nat Turner (1831). But even earlier still the establishment of Garrison's *Liberator* in January 1831 was a great event and a feather in the cap of the anti-slavery agitators. Then there was the murder in August 1837 of the white publicist and owner of the abolitionist paper the *Aulton Observer* (Illinois),[85] the Rev. Elijah Lovejoy, already mentioned; and, earlier still, the formation of the American Anti-Slavery Society in 1833, followed by a succession of incidents such as the two slave revolts on board ships, the *Amistad* (1839) led by Joseph Cinque,[86] and the *Creole* (1847)[87] under the leadership of Madison Washington. The Fugitive Slave Law of 1850, stigmatised as the 'Man-Stealing Act' or the 'blood-hound bill', the Kansas-Nebraska Act (1854) which repealed the Missouri Compromise of 1820, the Dred Scott Decision of Chief Justice Taney (1857), John Brown's execution (1859) and, last but not least, the election of Abraham Lincoln from the border state of Illinois to the U.S. presidency, culminating eventually in the Civil War, all these factors kept the flame of anti-slavery burning.

Another phenomenon in the interracial combination of anti-slavery in the U.S.A. was the Underground Railroad with its 'notorious' record of spiriting away slaves from the citadel of slavery to relatively freer territory within the Union and sometimes beyond.[88] Not only did the railroad evolve its own methods of operation but also its own language[89] of conduct as well as nomenclature for its operators and their depots.[90] A feature of its operation was secrecy, aided by Afro-American Secret Societies such as 'The Order of the Men of Oppression and Order of Emigration'.[91] All these helped to warn escapee slaves of the impending activities of slave catchers and often helped to forestall the abduction of fugitive slaves by spiriting them away to safer havens. This was an area in which the black-white combination was at its best. The number of slaves who passed into freedom through the channel of the Underground Railroad remains a matter for dispute. Nevertheless, the operation of this complex organisation disturbed the tranquillity and complacency of slave holders (as the newspapers of the era reveal by offers of rewards for recovery as well as against operators of the system) and consequently was a contribution to anti-slavery.

But the South was not idle. While the anti-slavery North formed Vigilance Committees to counteract the activities of the pro-slavery South, slave owners in the South formed their own Vigilante Committees which often engaged in the hot pursuit of slaves into free territory. While violence was not adopted as the policy of the anti-slavery conventions, more and more abolitionists with the passage of time became converted to the belief that slavery could not be abolished without the use of force.

The American South passed various stringent measures against the emancipationists, through stern laws,[92] the imposition of prizes on the heads of those aiding and abetting slave escapes, and severe punishments on those allegedly and knowingly inciting slave escapes and revolts. Many of the leaders of anti-slavery at one time or another had a prize on their heads for capture dead or alive.[93] Techniques of intimidation were employed by the pro-slavery South, mirroring the desperation of the Southern slavocracy and their Northern adherents. The records are replete with stories of terror tactics as well as terrorist methods for sustaining the slave system and for inveighing against anti-slavery advocates. They extended their activities beyond the confines of the South by pursuing fugitive slaves into Northern states of the Union, sometimes employing disguises as Quakers and even infiltrating anti-slavery ranks.[94] The Fugitive Slave Law of 1850 gave comfort to the Southern slavocracy while galvanising the anti-slavery advocates into further action in order to undermine the system. Slave-catching expeditions were not often attended by happy results, even for the pursuers.[95]

Thus, we see that the abolitionist crusade was conducted against a tide of prejudice and opposition, but its adherents and exponents persisted, though many of them held differing opinions. Those who crossed the Atlantic from the U.S.A. to Europe – that is, into Britain, France and Germany – were both white and black and spoke on platforms not as black or white abolitionists but rather as fighters for a great cause which fundamentally affected humanity. The names of these official as well as unofficial delegates are many, and some of them have left accounts of their visits and experiences.[96] Others wrote about anti-slavery activities elsewhere.[97] As the anti-slavery crusade neared its climax in 1850 more converts were drawn into its orbit, and a historian has noted that Boston, which had been hostile to anti-slavery in 1835, had reversed this policy by 1849 and from that year the New England Anti-Slavery Society was holding its annual convention at the same Faneuil Hall which in 1835 had been the venue at which abolitionism was denounced.[98]

The abolitionist campaign was elevated from its local beginnings to the national and then international scene. Professor Burgess notes that it is no exaggeration to assert that the entire course of the internal history of the U.S.A. between 1836 and 1861 was determined by the struggles in Congress over abolition petitions and abolition literature.[99] It was during this period that Southern congressmen sought within the National Legislature to curtail or eliminate the activities of abolitionists altogether. They complained about the Underground Railroad, which, it was then estimated, was responsible for the loss of about 2000 slaves annually.[100] Even in 1850 many Northerners frowned on abolitionist methods and even those not allied to them were able to observe that 'the present wide diffusion of anti-slavery sentiment in the United States is, in no small degree, owing to their [abolitionists'] exertions'.[101] Yet 1850 was a turning point in the anti-slavery crusade in the United States, and even the publication of Harriet Beecher Stowe's *Uncle Tom's Cabin* was another effort to assail the Fugitive Slave Law of 1850. Since the effects of the Fugitive Slave Law spilled over into Canada, or what was then British North America, one needs now to consider the anti-slavery there.

Anti-slavery in Canada

Anti-slavery here did not take the form of the large public campaigns known to England and the United States but rather was instituted through the Assembly and by court decisions. Professor Robin Winks in his admirable book, *The Blacks in Canada*,[102] has amply demonstrated that the initiative came from law officers, judges, chief justices, a former governor, J. G. Simcoe, and some attorneys, even a former Attorney General. Accordingly, Professor Winks notes, 'The heroes of abolition in British North America were its judges, men who by judicial legislation moved against an institution that still retained sufficient public support in Nova Scotia, New Brunswick, and Lower Canada to prevent popularly elected assemblies from abolishing slavery themselves.'[103] But in spite of this, slavery remained legal until 1834, although its growth had been severely limited by a combination of legislative and judicial actions, and Winks argues that had it not been for the Act of the imperial Parliament of 1833 Canada would have harboured a residue of slaves into the 1850s, and perhaps later.[104]

When anti-slavery became organised in British North America, emancipation had already been achieved by the Act of the imperial Parliament, so that activities there were primarily intended to reinforce American efforts to achieve abolition. The first anti-slavery society, in Canada West, had a dual purpose, first to combat prejudices locally, and second to assist the efforts of abolitionists in the United States and to reinforce British efforts to influence American affairs. The organisation came into existence on the initiative of the Brown family, George Brown (the leader), his brother Gordon, father Peter, and his sister Isabella, who constituted themselves into the nucleus of an anti-slavery society. The Toronto *Globe* (1844) was their organ for espousing the anti-slavery cause. Interest in American anti-slavery activities, however, predated their organisation. Thus, the editors and founders of the Afro-American paper *Freedom's Journal* (1827), John Russwurm and Samuel B. Cornish, sent agents to Canada to solicit support. Blacks in Windsor (Ontario) established a short-lived anti-slavery society; another was established in Upper Canada[105] under the leadership of John Roaf, a Congregational minister who in 1837 had attended a temperance convention in Saratoga Springs, New York, at which he made contacts with many American abolitionists. Another was the Rev. Ephraim Evans, a Wesleyan Methodist minister and editor of the *Christian Guardian*, who formed an Upper Canada anti-slavery society in Toronto late in 1837.

Robin Winks has so admirably described Canadian anti-slavery links with the United States that no useful purpose would be served by recounting them here. Canadian abolitionists were essentially gradualists, although the passing of the Fugitive Slave Act in the United States in 1850 as well as the influence of Frederick Douglass encouraged a more radical stance.[106] Other forums which influenced their actions were the negro conventions, one such convention being held in Toronto in September 1851 with fifty delegates signifying their approval for killers of slave catchers and asking Henry Bibb, the black journalist from Windsor, and J. K. Fisher and J. D. Tansley of Toronto, to prepare an appeal to negro residents in Canada West to found an agricultural league similar to the struggling land societies.

Anti-slavery activity in Canada was further given a boost by the arrival of Harriet Tubman at St Catherine's in Canada, where she spent seven years bringing fugitives from the United States to Canada. The Canadian Anti-Slavery Society was founded on the principle of abolishing world slavery in February 1861 at a public meeting at the City Hall in Toronto under the chairmanship of the mayor. The organisation was launched with a view to terminating the 'common guilt of the civilised and Christian world'.[107] The society appointed a committee to correspond with anti-slavery societies in the U.S.A. and Britain, and a constitution and bylaws were adopted. The new society possessed distinguished people in its ranks, and its composition again emphasised the white – black co-operation typical of efforts to abolish slavery. Of the blacks in the forefront of these activities were Henry Bibb, A. Bickford Jones, Wilson Abbot, George Brown, John Roaf and Samuel Ring-gold Ward. The first three were among the fourteen vice-presidents, while Ward was on the committee and Charles Stuart a corresponding secretary. The society agreed to make contact with John Scoble, then the Secretary of the British and Foreign Anti-Slavery Society, Lewis Tappan, Secretary of the American Foreign and Anti-Slavery Society, and Sydney Howard Gay of the American Anti-Slavery Society. The society was on several occasions addressed by black anti-slavery speakers from the United States who included Frederick Douglass, the Rev. Samuel J. May, Jr., and by Britain's chief Garrisonian spokesman and the impetus behind Edinburgh's Society for the Abolition of Slavery, George Thompson. Abolitionists from the U.S. pleaded with those in Canada to help in their efforts. Samuel R. Ward travelled through the province of Ontario on speaking tours. Some Canadians wrote articles for British anti-slavery journals, while others, like Willis, attended the 1858 meeting of the British and Foreign Anti-Slavery Society in London. The annual reports of the Canadian Society were circulated in the United States.

Yet the Toronto Society had little impact outside the city confines. With the exception of a few, Canadian abolitionists seemed cut off from the mainstream of other abolitionist societies. According to Winks, anti-slavery journalism in Canada far from aided the abolitionist cause because of its simplicity, quarrelsome nature and frequent lack of intelligence. Publications included The True Royalist; Bibb's Voice of the Fugitive (Windsor, 1851–3); its competitor, Abraham Shadd's Provincial Freeman (Toronto, and from 1855 in Chatham); and Linton Stafford's The Voice of the Bondsman, distributed free. The True Royalist and Weekly Intelligencer (Windsor, 1860) published by the Rev. A. R. Green did not last out the next year. The chief protagonists of anti-slavery in Canada West were ministers of religion, but their quarrels often crippled the society and the newspapers reflected their numerous problems. There were times, too, when the effectiveness of anti-slavery activities was diminished by anti-Americanism,[108] and according to Professor Winks, 'The Canadian abolitionist movement, like the American, was in fact several movements which from time to time seemed to confuse lesser issues with greater.'[109] But more devastating is Winks's judgement on the tenor of their activities when he wrote, 'the Canadian anti-slavery movement suffered from cupidity, false ambition, inefficiency, and dishonesty'.[110] Winks then describes how some of the prominent leaders fell from grace, among whom were Josiah Henson, S. R. Ward and John Scoble, and he proceeds to conclude that 'much of Canada's participation in the abolitionist movement resulted from geographical proximity rather than from ideological affinity', and that after 1861 Canadians lost interest in fugitive slaves. Because Canada was also in North America its interest in the slave question went beyond the period of British emancipation in 1833. A factor responsible for this was the continued interest in the influx of refugees from the United States, and, especially after the passing of the Fugitive Slave Act, the stream of refugees into Canada continued until the 1860s. Escape from the U.S.A. to Canada seems, as Professor Winks has observed, to have created a legend of 'liberal Canada' which does not fit the facts. But while the myth persists Canadians tend to congratulate themselves upon being upholders of the liberty of slaves and providers of succour for fugitives. But the strength of opposition to anti-slavery in Canada almost until the emancipation, and the expression of strong pro-slavery opinions, reveal the hollowness of the claim to Canada having had a consistent and tenacious anti-slavery tradition.

Anti-slavery in Brazil and South America

Unlike in England, France and the United States, there was no anti-slavery crusade of the same scale in South America, except in Brazil, and even here it was carried out on a much more modest basis and only really began in a small way in 1868, gaining ground by 1879 and culminating in the final abolition decree of 13 May 1888. Nonetheless stirrings against slavery and efforts to achieve emancipation were noted from about the second decade of the nineteenth century, although the one notable feature in the endeavours to abolish the institution of slavery and the slave trade was the persistence of slave revolts, which were earlier in time than the abolitionist stirrings and were persistent until the final demise of slavery in South America. In fact, one modern historian has suggested that 'The tardy spirit of emancipation was frequently jolted by the organised revolts of the Negroes'.[111] Between 1820 and 1822 quite a number of slave risings occurred in the region of modern Colombia and Venezuela with slaves refusing work. Simon

Bolivar, celebrated as the Great Liberator in South America, had conceived of the notion of drafting the slaves into the armed forces, but mining interests (the minocracy) objected strongly to such a step. Such a move by Bolivar did not, of course, make him an abolitionist. As a 'white supremacist' his move was one of expediency because he believed that if many African or black slaves survived the war of independence they could constitute a destabilising element in the body politic. Yet Bolivar's 'liberalism' convinced him that slavery was incompatible with natural law and with republican principles and so in 1819 he was encouraged to propose the complete abolition of slavery to the Constituent Congress Assembly at Cucuta. It is significant that this proposal was made before the English movement for the emancipation of slaves had gathered momentum. Although the Assembly did not approve the request, on 21 July 1821 it promulgated the 'free-womb law',[112] whereby the children of slave mothers were freed and machinery for implementing the law set up. It is significant that such a law was not passed in Brazil until 28 September 1871, about fifty years later. But the entire exercise savoured of gradualism, a feature which also characterised the Brazilian abolitionist movement in its early stages. Ever present in the objections of the minocracy were the fears which often gripped the plantocracy in other theatres of slavery in terms of agricultural labour, for they feared that the absence of forced labour would result in the abandonment of the mines and depression, either because of shortage of labour or the refusal of the freemen to labour there.[113]

However, it became impossible to implement the law of 21 July 1821, as those who were to implement it were slave owners. With the awareness that 52 per cent of a reported slave population of 46 829 were in the gold fields, resistance to Simon Bolivar's proposals for emancipation was sustained.[114] Furthermore, sectionalism within the state of Colombia led ultimately in 1830 to the break-up of the Colombian state and Bolivar's resignation from the presidency of the country. This also led to the issue of emancipation being shelved. But it continued to be evident in Colombia that with 55 per cent of the 38 940 slaves of Colombia in the gold mines, the minocracy could not accept any suggestions which they felt would interfere with gold production. Civil war intervened in 1839 and the slavery issue became enmeshed with other issues plaguing the country. But in 1842 and 1843 slave revolts also affected the gold fields in the region of Cauca. The slavocracy obtained from the President the right to sell their slaves to Peru and no fewer than 800 were sold before the practice was eventually terminated in 1847. Nevertheless, with the revolutionary fervour in Europe in 1848 liberal ideas were in the ascendant in Colombia and the coming to power of men with a reforming zeal began to put slavery under a

381

cloud. Denunciations of the practice became insistent and persistent, and by 1850 only legislation was needed to confine the institution to the past. In May 1851 all slaves in Colombia were manumitted, and on 1 January 1852 all servitude was abolished. The Colombian government agreed to compensate slave owners, but, as also in Ecuador, it does not appear that the government was ever sincere about this.[115]

In Venezuela, which hived off from the Colombian republic after the rupture of 1830, emancipation was a presidential initiative,[116] and not achieved without resistance. In Cuba the abolitionist struggle merged with the wars of independence, including the Ten Years War (1868–78), but the emancipation issue was not the most prominent. In short, the states of Central and South America showed no keen crusade against slavery and their achievements were not made without external pressures.[117] Yet the Brazilian crusade against slavery was of such a kind that it merits special consideration, as some of its features were similar to those in the United States.

Brazil revealed some peculiar features during the entire period of slavery. It was also one of the last countries officially to abolish the slave trade (1850) and slavery (1888). Some of the factors in this belated move are not difficult to find. Stated simply, the institution of slavery was deeply embedded in the economic and social structure of the society, and a mere juridical act could not dispose of it. But, as has been observed earlier, among the first to launch the anti-slavery crusade in Brazil were the slaves who persisted in their revolts and in the establishment of Maroon communities like the celebrated *quilombo* of Palmares celebrated as 'The famous Negroes of Palmares,'[118] which, to this day, remains one of the finest examples of the yearnings and determination of African slaves to ensure their freedom. There were of course in Brazil individual acts of manumission noted by many authors.[119] Such assertions have led to rather simplistic conclusions about the ease with which slaves obtained their freedom.[120] But as the records show, these assertions do not fit the facts and, while theoretically correct, in terms of the planters' visualisation of the economy manumission would have been disastrous. Some have even suggested that Brazilian emancipation did not assume the gigantic proportions of that of the United States because it was not felt that emancipation threatened the existing order, and some have gone so far as to say that this prevented in Brazil a bloody confrontation like that which eventually terminated the status of slave in the United States.

But other ways in which slaves attempted to undermine the system in Brazil were features common to the other theatres of slavery; these included flight from the plantations and mines and the formation of *quilombos*, suicide and service in the army.[121] Yet it was not with slavery but with the slave trade that the strength of slavocratic opposition was revealed. It crystallised when the Brazilian government enacted, on 7 November 1831, that 'All slaves entering the territory or ports of Brazil, are free'.[122] But in spite of this it was not until 1850 that it became effective, when legislation piloted by Ezebio de Queros, a minister of the Brazilian imperial cabinet, finally terminated the slave trade. But behind this Act, as well as behind the final abolition of slavery, external pressures were crucial. Among those who tried to exert influence was Britain, who in 1826 signed an agreement with Brazil to end slave trading four years later.[123]

There was also external pressure on the question of emancipation, first by the French Emancipation Committee who, in 1826, had written to Dom Pedro requesting that Brazil abolish slavery, and later in 1862 following Abraham Lincoln's Emancipation Proclamation in the United States. But the entire abolition programme in Brazil centred on gradualism and proceeded in stages. The first was achieved on 28 September 1871 when Brazil passed the *Ventre Livre*, or Free Birth Law, which conceded liberty to all children born of slave women. This was followed, on 28 September 1885, by the *Lei dos Sexagenarios*, or Law of Sexagenarians, which conceded liberty to slaves of sixty years and over.[124] But before the enactment of this law the movement for abolition had gained momentum largely as a result of impatience with gradualism. The Brazilian movement was first galvanised into action by the initiative of Joaquim Nabucco. It gained further ground as a result of the patronage of Dom Pedro II and activities of ardent black Brazilian abolitionists, whose contributions to anti-slavery in Brazil have yet to be fully assessed. Outstanding among black Brazilian abolitionists was Luiz Gonzaga Pinto da Gama, whose mother had taken an important part in the slave insurrections of Bahia in the 1830s; although he died in 1882 before emancipation had been completely secured in Brazil he, nonetheless, remained an inspiration to the movement. Other black leaders included Antonio Bento and José Ferreira de Menezes; the publicists José do Patrocinio and André Pinto Rebouças; the mulatto Carlos Gomes, the composer of the *Opera O Guarani* and reputed to be the 'creator of Brazilian music'; and the coloured Professor Alvares dos Santos, a mathematician at Bahia, and a patriot and organiser who gained the Alumni of the Faculty of Medicine of the *Sociedade Libertadora 2 de Julho* in Bahia in 1852. It is said that for twenty-five years Professor Alvares dos Santos supported the abolitionist movement through the holding of annual banquets, on 2 July, for his students, many of whom he organised into a 'patriotic battalion'.[125]

The Brazilian Anti-Slavery Society came into being in the home of Joaquim Nabucco on 28 September 1880, with Nabucco as president and André Rebouças as treasurer. This development gave rise to other emancipation societies throughout Brazil whose objectives included the protection as well as the ransoming of slaves. The rank and file of abolitionist societies, as with their counterparts in the United States, were at first largely composed of those who believed in peaceful propaganda and legal means for achieving the objective of emancipation. In time some, like Antonio Bento, were to become impatient with the legal approach. The cities of São Paulo, Rio de Janeiro and Santos, as well as the provinces of Bahia and Ceara in the north, felt the impact of the abolitionist crusade. Their publications, like those of their counterparts in other countries, were ardent and advocated immediate change. The earliest spokesman for abolition, Luiz Gama, rejected gradualism as well as the appeasement of slave owners in their 'criminal' acts and he was for a while the lone voice crying in the wilderness, asserting still the 'illegality' of slavery and clamouring for its eradication from society. By joining with Ruy Barbosa and other abolitionists to publish the newspaper *Radical Paulistano*, he reinforced the general efforts and many of his articles on abolition before his death on 24 August 1882 were published in the newspaper. But the campaign against slavery was undiminished by his death.

Another stalwart arose in the person of Antonio Bento, who had lost faith in the use of legal methods to terminate slavery, He gave a fresh impetus to anti-slavery in becoming celebrated as the person who inaugurated the Brazilian version of the Underground Railroad, what had previously been thought to be a peculiarity of the United States. But by organising such a complex network of escape techniques and routes he systematised the flight of Brazilian slaves from servitude. He received the financial assistance of a number of men prominent in public life, and this gave a boost to his struggles. He was fortunate in having the Underground Railroad operated by ardent and devoted workers, who spirited away many slaves. But he had an additional boost to his campaign when some slave owners liberated their slaves and threw in their lot with his efforts to persuade slaves to flee from the plantations. His activities spanned the entire country and he travelled extensively, aided by assistants. He was joined by people from various walks of life – politicians, professional people, engineers, academics, students, tradesmen, workers, artisans and street vendors. Although the mission was not without its hazards, the organisers of the Underground Railroad persisted. The escape of slaves in large numbers to the city of Santos in São Paulo, then under the name of Jabaquara, led to their organisation into villages known as *quilombos (Quilombo de Jabaquara)*. In these endeavours some exslaves demonstrated their capacity for leadership.

As an added boost to their campaign there were abolitionist publications in the form of broadsheets, newspapers, speeches, plays, pamphlets and books, including the publication of *Uncle Tom's Cabin* and Patrocinio's slavery novel, *Motta Moqueiro, On a Pena de Morte* (1877, second edition 1890). Novels and plays were often written under pseudonyms, and all assisted in keeping the country alive to the anti-slavery campaign. Among the papers of note were *A Redemmpçao*, edited by Antonio Bento; the periodical *Gazeta da Tarde*, founded by José Ferreira de Menezes on 10 July 1880 in Rio de Janeiro and circulated in the provinces; *Folha Nova, Jornal do Comercio; Novo Mundo*, the monthly organ of the movement organised by André Rebouças, *O Abolicionista*; and *Cidade do Rio*, a militant abolitionist paper launched by Patrocinio on 1 September 1887 just as the abolition campaign was reaching its climax. All proved to be valuable instruments for focusing attention on the abolitionist cause. In this respect, the anti-slavery crusaders were like their counterparts in the United States, Britain and France.

The Brazilian movement also was allied to international forces and demonstrated the necessity to consult abolitionists abroad and be informed about their techniques and methods. By comparing notes and through visits to Europe, Brazilian abolitionists were able to invigorate their own campaign at home. Thus, again, like their counterparts in the U.S.A., Brazilian abolitionists such as Patrocinio, Joaquim Nabucco, Carlos Gomes and André Rebouças (the last two of whom travelled in Europe), were able to attest that the anti-slavery movement was conceived within the framework of a wider internationalism. Their methods in many respects were identical, beginning modestly with the organisation of the first emancipation conference by Rebouças and Carlos Gomes at the São Luiz Theatre on 25 July 1880, leading to a proliferation of emancipation associations, and ultimately to the organisation of an Abolitionist Confederation by Patrocinio on 13 May 1883. Although the confederation had paid officials, much of its activities were secretly undertaken, emphasising the hazardous nature of its activities in Brazil as elsewhere. Secret agents, as in the U.S., became involved in spiriting away slaves and resettling them elsewhere. The movement, like other movements, had in its rank and file orators, journalists and popular writers. Patricinio and Rebouças as leaders complemented each other well. Meetings were often difficult to arrange and halls refused them by the authorities. Even funerals became the occasion for expressing abolitionist[126] sentiments. By 1877 the campaign attained a crescendo. Its success was seen in the fact that even the king, Dom Pedro II, and his reluctant queen, became converted to abolitionism. On 7 March 1888, José Alfredo Corres de Oliveira, a conservative, was appointed Prime Minister in order to carry through the emancipation measure. On the next day his Minister of Agriculture introduced the abolition legislation to Parliament, and on 13 May 1888, in the absence of the king, the

Princess-Regent Doña Isabel signed the emancipation decree liberating over one and a half million slaves. But the abolition campaign had as one of its casualties the monarchy, for republicanism gained the upper hand, ultimately leading to the abdication of Dom Pedro II.

In the anti-slavery crusade Afro-Brazilians were very prominent; unlike coloureds who were few in number. Indeed, in 1882 Rebouças expressed regret and his 'greatest sorrow' that only three mulattos were in the abolitionist party.[127] Earlier still it had been observed that some men of colour who were slave holders seemed unconcerned with abolition and were ardent opponents, and an instance was cited in 1884 in which a mulatto candidate for the Bahia Chamber openly proclaimed himself a pro-slavery candidate.[128] The role of coloured people in Brazil in anti-slavery was not very different from that revealed in the British West Indies during the abolitionist campaign.

The combination of elements which aroused and channelled public opinion against slavery came from divergent sources, such as literature, law and government, economics and religious and humanitarian sentiments. All these compounds made for the effectiveness of the anti-slavery crusades, with their effectiveness greater in some areas and countries than in others.[129] But as far as blacks were concerned anti-slavery provided a platform for leadership, a platform upon which future leaders were to build.

Notes

1 B. Quarles, *Black Abolitionists*, New York, 1969. References to black contributions began to appear in many texts in the 1960s.

2 The author is grateful to Dr Cyril Griffiths, who called his attention in 1969 to Benjamin Quarles's book.

3 A more recent example of the humanitarian school is the monumental work of the late Professor Roger Anstey, *The Atlantic Slave Trade and British Abolition, 1760–1810*, London, 1975. The initial basis for this work was laid in an earlier critique of Eric Williams: see R. Anstey, 'Capitalism and Slavery: a Critique', *Economic History Review*, xxi (1968), pp. 307–20. Of this earlier critique another author on the politics of liberation had written of the attacks on Williams as 'hit and run tactics' with negative results and that the Williams thesis continued to ride high. See J. U. J. Asiegbu, *Slavery and the Politics of Liberation, 1787–1861*, London, 1969, pp. xv *et seq.*

4 See Chapter 9.

5 See Suzanne Miers, *Britain and the Ending of the Slave Trade*, London, 1973. While the French navy did nothing to suppress the illegal slave trade, the government 'contented itself with passing ineffective legislation', p. 15. When the Bourbons fell in 1830, abolitionists came to power and new laws were passed in 1831, and France, by treaty with Britain, accepted a limited right of

search. The trade nonetheless increased and continued as a large-scale operation.

6 As the pioneer of abolition (apart from the vacillations of revolutionary France which had shown signs of this in 1792 but had later relented), Denmark's decree of abolition was to be enforced within its dominions at the end of ten years, in 1802.

7 In 1831 the French instituted harsher measures against slave-trading nationals of France. Suzanne Miers' work reveals the contrary view that France remained a defaulter, pp. 12–13, 15, 16–23.

8 See Hugh Thomas, *Cuba or The Pursuit of Freedom*, London, 1971, pp. 200–6, for his consideration of the politics of abolition. See also Miers, *Britain and the Ending of the Slave Trade*, pp. 19–20, n. 68.

9 See *National Anti-Slavery Standard*, 18 Nov. 1841, for the substance of a protest by the U.S. government through its Envoy Extraordinary and Minister Plenipotentiary to Viscount Palmerston, 13 Nov. 1840 on what the U.S. regarded as 'another unwarrantable search, detention, and ill-usage of an American vessel and her crew, on the coast of Africa, by one of Her Majesty's Cruisers employed for the suppression of the slave trade'. The U.S. protest was considered to be a legitimate one deserving 'satisfactory retribution'. Also the reply of Viscount Palmerston to Mr Stevenson, dated Foreign Office 8 Dec. 1840. The U.S. regarded the incident as dishonouring the American flag by British interference. The correspondence was not the first of its kind between the two governments and was not to be the last. The real point at issue was that the U.S. declined to be a party to treaties with other nations for suppressing the slave trade and accordingly opened itself to suspicion of aiding and abetting the slave trade. Moreover, it gave U.S. citizens the leeway to persist in the slave trade.

See also *National Anti-Slavery Standard*, 8 and 15 July 1841, containing revelations of numerous American vessels, American-built vessels and nationals as well as Cuban slavers using the U.S. flag for slave trading. Also the *New York Chronicle*, 13 March 1858, reported a Southern states' revival of the slave trade contrary to the national law for abolition early in the century. The *National Anti-Slavery Standard*, 9 Dec. 1841, estimated that, since the official abolition by the U.S. in 1808, the following slaves had been transported from Africa to the following places: Brazil, 2 420 000; Cuba and Puerto Rico, 1 020 000; French Colonies, Mexico and the U.S., 303 000; captured and liberated, 140 000; total, 3 860 000. From the computation it deduced that the slave trade doomed to the horrors of slavery annually 120 000 under Christian powers and 50 000 under Muslim powers, amounting to a total of 170 000. It estimated that 280 000 were destroyed annually in the procurement effort making a total of 450 000, or more than 1 200 a day.

Also quoted in *The Liberator* from the British *Foreign Anti-Slavery Reporter*. See also Commander A. H. Foote, *Africa and the American Flag*, p. 152, especially for Governor Buchanan's report of 1839; see also his pp. 153–6, 215–16, 219–20, 253, 259 for incidents confirming the assertion derived from a sentiment of Governor Buchanan of Liberia. Also W. E. B. DuBois, *The Suppression of the African Slave Trade to the United States of America, 1638–1870*, Cambridge, Mass., 1896, pp. 162–7, esp. p. 163.

10 Thomas, *Cuba*, p. 231. As the continuing slave trade was clandestine, it was not easy to ascertain that it had ended by this date. Some authors maintain that it

THE STRATEGY OF THE SLAVES

continued beyond 1865. See J. H. Parry and P. M. Sherlock, *A Short History of the West Indies*, London, 1966, pp. 185–6; for others to the end of the century, see Miers, *Britain and the Ending of the Slave Trade*, p. 20, n. 68.

11 Thomas, *Cuba*, p. 201. The suggestion here is that the Brazilian abolitionists, who became numerous, were themselves conscious of the 'spectre of Haiti' and wished to restrict the importation of Africans into Brazil. Thus we see that abolition again in this respect was not humanitarianism but an act of expediency.

12 Parry and Sherlock, *West Indies*, p. 177.

13 See *The Antigua Free Press*, 27 Aug. 1830, for a pro-slavery commentary on the activities of the British anti-slavery movement dated Saint John, 16 July 1830, castigating the Chairman of the Association, William Wilberforce, and accusing him of a *volte face* for instigating the movement to press on with the struggle for emancipation after previously giving assurances, in the early years of the endeavour to abolish the slave trade, that abolition was his only intention and nothing more. According to the commentator, 'Mr Wilberforce, himself avowed that the abolition of the slave trade was all that he desired, and denied any idea of intending to press for Negro emancipation.' But the commentator missed the point relating to the strategy adopted in the struggle to fight step by step.

14 Bryan Edwards, *The History, Civil and Commercial, of the British Colonies in the West Indies*, London, 1818–19, on Haitian revolt; DuBois, *Suppression of the African Slave Trade*, pp. 9–15, 22.

15 These books on the slave trade and slavery were published in 1787 and 1789 respectively.

16 Thomas Clarkson, *The History of the Rise, Progress and Accomplishment of the Abolition of the African Slave Trade by the British Parliament*, 2 vols., London, 1808, Vol. 2, pp. 30–1. The text on Slavery and the Commerce of the Human Species was, in fact, written by Thomas Clarkson in 1785 in Latin and won him first prize at the University of Cambridge. Cugoano, who wrote in 1789, prefixed his book with the phrase, 'Thoughts and Sentiments of the Evil and Wicked Traffic of the Slavery and the Commerce of the Human Species'.

17 Among dissenting missionaries who suffered the wrath of the slavocracy and their persecution, the following were prominent: William Knibb in Jamaica, William Shrewsbury in Barbados and the Rev. John Smith in British Guiana. The latter was sentenced to death for his alleged role in the East Demerara slave insurrection of 1823. Although he was to be reprieved he died in prison in February 1824 and was therefore regarded as the 'Demerara Martyr'. But the fate of Smith was not unlike that of other missionaries in the West Indies who suffered harassment.

18 This has been the stock-in-trade of numerous scholars. See any textbook of the recent past.

19 F. O. Shyllon, *Black Slaves in Britain*, London, 1974. This book is an admirable expression of painstaking scholarship. Another modern scholar had earlier spotted the exaggerated interpretation credited to the Mansfield judgment when he wrote, 'While public opinions and not a few antiquarians and local historians have held that slavery was illegal in the whole of British North America after the Summerset case, this was not so; for Lord Mansfield's decision, whatever it may be that he said, had no legal effect within the colonies.' Robin Winks, *The Blacks in Canada: a History*, Montreal, New Haven, Conn., and London, 1971, 1972, p. 26.

20 See for instance Richard West, *Back to Africa: a History of Sierra Leone and Liberia*, London, 1970, pp. 14–15, 20.

21 Quoted in Shyllon, *Black Slaves in Britain*, p. 170; also see E. E. Williams, *Capitalism and Slavery*, Chapel Hill, N. C., p. 45.

22 Miers more recently repeats the myth (*Britain and the Ending of the Slave Trade*, p. 4).

23 The principal exponent and pioneer was Reginald Coupland, *The British Anti-Slavery Movement*, London, 1933, which gave the efforts a moral twist. See also F. J. Klingberg, *The Anti-Slavery Movement in England; a Study of English Humanitarianism*, New Haven, Conn., 1926.

24 Anstey, *The Atlantic Slave Trade and British Abolition*, esp. chs. 4–11 inclusive and his conclusion, chs. 17 and 18. See also Seymour Drescher, *Econocide: British Slavery in the Era of Abolition*, Pittsburgh, 1977.

25 L. J. Ragatz, *The Fall of the Planter Class in the British Caribbean 1763–1833*, London and New York, 1928.

26 Williams, *Capitalism and Slavery*, pp. 179–86.

27 See H. Temperley, *British Anti-Slavery 1833–1870*, London, 1972; also Seymour Drescher, 'A case of Econocide: British Abolition and Economic Development'; Miers, *Britain and the Ending of the Slave Trade*, preface, p. xiii.

28 Asiegbu, *Slavery and the Politics of Liberation, 1787–1861*, p. xvi.

29 Parry and Sherlock, *West Indies*, pp. 185–6; also V. T. Daley, *A Short History of the Guyanese People*, London, 1975, pp. 164–5.

30 See W. Adolphe Roberts, *Biographical Sketches of Six Great Jamaicans*, Kingston, Jamaica, 1952, p. 5. Whether this is a rationalisation of Jordan's position only further research will tell, but in the light of present-day knowledge he might have seen the necessity for this step-by-step approach: first, the complete liberation of the free coloureds, and then the slaves. This was a piecemeal approach.

31 *Ibid.*, p. 6.

32 *Ibid.*, p. 8. The exact date of the establishment of the newspaper is not ascertained, but it is generally believed that it came into being between October 1828 and July 1829; by September 1829 the paper was known as *The Watchman and Jamaica Free Press*, although the *Free Press* designation was later dropped.

33 Roberts, *Biographical Sketches*, pp. 10–11.

34 *Ibid.*, p. 11.

35 *Ibid.*, p. 12.

36 *Ibid.*, pp. 12–14. The nationalism of the presiding Irish judges helped to prevent Jordan escape from the machinations of his enemies, the slavocracy.

37 There was here an element of discrimination in favour of the domestics: it was still 'divide and rule'. Since the Jamaican rebellion of 1831–2 had been commented on by Edward Jordan in the newspaper, his remarks were taken as treasonable. The point Jordan was emphasising was that the browns and the blacks were no longer divided because the 'divide and rule' policy of the whites had compelled the two groups to join together.

38 E. E. Williams, *The Negro in the Caribbean*, Manchester, 1942, pp. 12–15. In our own day, Cheddi Jagan's *Forbidden Freedom*, London, 1959, sheds light on the operation of the 'sugar empire' in the contemporary world.

39 See Bernard Semmell, *The Governor Eyre Controversy*, London, 1962, and Sir Sydney Olivier, *Jamaica: the Blessed Island*, London, 1936, ch 3. See also

Governor Eyre's opening address to the Jamaican General Assembly on 7 Nov. 1865, quoted at length in Ansel Hart, Jr., *The Life of George William Gordon*, Cultural Heritage Series, Vol.1, Institute of Jamaica, n.d., Kingston, Jamaica, pp. 113–15.

40 J. H. Franklin, *From Slavery to Freedom: a History of Negro America*, New York, 1948, 1967, pp. 249–50.

41 Parry and Sherlock, *West Indies*, p. 175.

42 Winthrop Jordan, *White Over Black: American Attitudes towards the Negro 1550–1812*, London, 1968, p. 194.

43 Joseph Wood was the author of *Thoughts on the Slavery of the Negroes;* Anthony Benezet produced *Caution and Warning,* as well as *The Cause of our Fellow Creatures the oppressed Africans.*

44 Author of an anti-slavery publication in 1700, *The Selling of Joseph.*

45 Author of an anti-slavery tract, *Some Considerations on the Keeping of Negroes,* 1850.

46 Quarles, *Black Abolitionists*, p. 9.

47 This assurance was to be given in the early part of the succeeding century by the adherents of the American Colonisation Society.

48 Quarles, *Black Abolitionists*, p.11.

49 Mary Stoughton Locke, *Anti-Slavery in America from the Introduction of the African Slaves to the Prohibition of the Slave Trade (1619–1808),* Boston, Mass., 1901, see esp. pp.142–3, 155–6, 191–7.

50 *Ibid.*, pp. 155–6. For a contrary viewpoint see Quarles, *Black Abolitionists*, pp. 11–12. He argued that the earlier movement had not succeeded in creating even a general sentiment against slavery. Also see Jordan, *White Over Black*, pp. 343–73, for limitations of early anti-slavery.

51 Locke, *Anti-Slavery in America*, pp. 191–7.

52 See, for example, *The Liberator,* 31 Aug., 12 and 19 and 26 Oct. 1833; *Frederick Douglass Paper*, 16 April 1858, and some other editions of both papers and *The North Star*. An examination of a few issues of Garrison's *The Liberator* and Douglass's *The North Star* and the *Frederick Douglass Paper* would yield results.

53 See Quarles, *Black Abolitionsts*, preface, p. viii.

54 Yet in the *Frederick Douglass Paper*, 16 April 1858, the following statement appeared to testify to the existence of a female anti-slavery society: 'We call attention to the Annual Report of the Rochester Ladies' Anti-slavery Society which we publish elsewhere in our column. It is a document which will be read with interest and profit.' Below that was an advertisement indicating 'the regular meeting of the Rochester Ladies' Anti-slavery Society, at the house of. . . . on Monday Evening April 19, at 6.30 o'clock p.m. . . .' On the fourth page appeared the Seventh Annual Report of the Rochester Ladies' Anti-Slavery Society.

55 This, too, was an attempt to imbue the young with anti-slavery ideas at an impressionable age.

56 See, for instance, when abolitionists the Rev. Charles Torrey and Joshua Leavitt attempted in January 1842 to cover the first Pro-Slavery Convention at Annapolis, Maryland, they were not only prevented from doing so but Leavitt was arrested by the police as an 'abolitionist incendiary' and lodged in gaol. He was released on 19 January on his own recognisance for $500 and those of S. S. Alexander and Joseph M. Palmer for $250 for his court

appearance the following April at Anne, Arundale County Court and for his 'good behaviour' in the meantime. *National Anti-Slavery Standard,* 27 Jan. 1842. See J. W. Coleman, *Slavery Times in Kentucky,* Chapel Hill, N. C., 1940, pp. 295–6, 299–300, 302–6, 310–16, 321–3. One uses this example because Kentucky was said to have the 'mildest' type of slavery in North America. See also Henrietta Buckmaster, *Let My People Go: the story of the Underground Railroad and the Growth of the Abolition Movement,* New York, 1941, pp.88–90, for some of Garrison's own experiences. Also, Benjamin Lundy, *Life, Travels and Opinions of Benjamin Lundy,* pp. 280–2, and *Genius of Universal Emancipation,* July 1834, for incidents on the nights of 9 and 10 July 1834. Lewis Tappan, *Life of Arthur Tappan,* New York, 1870. As a result of these hostile campaigns, towards the autumn of 1835 the Northern press was generally hostile to the abolitionists; see Lundy, *Life, Travels and Opinions,* p. 283.

57 Buckmaster, *Let My People Go,* pp. 103–5; Lundy, *Life, Travels and Opinions,* pp. 295, 297. He gives two accounts.

58 Quarles, *Black Abolitionists,* p. 56.

59 See, for instance, a leader in the *Frederick Douglass Paper,* 16 April 1858, on 'Negro Slaveholders in Louisiana'. The extract is from F. L. Olmstead, *A Journey in the Seaboard Slave States* New York, 1856.

60 Quarles, *Black Abolitionists,* p. 56.

61 An example of the petition was presented to the Senate of Massachusetts House of Representatives in February 1782 as the 'Petition of an African' and was signed by Belinda. This petition was published in Matthew Carey's *American Museum,* I, June 1787, pp. 463–5, and was one of the earliest indictments against slavery by an Afro-American. See also Vernon Loggins, *The Negro Author: His Development in America to 1900,* 1931, later edn. 1959, Port Washington, N.Y., pp. 34–5; or the petition of Equiano to the British Parliament in his dedication to the edition of 1790 of *The Interesting Narrative.*

62 W. Wells Brown, *Narrative of the Life of William Wells Brown: an American Slave, Written by Himself,* London, 1850, pp. 112–13; S. R. Ward, *The Autobiography of a Fugitive Negro,* London, 1855; A. Steward, *Twenty-two Years a Slave and Forty Years a Freeman,* Rochester, N.Y.

63 Rev. Peter Williams, Jr., *A Discourse Delivered on the Death of Captain Paul Cuffee,* 21 Oct. 1817.

64 Williams Wells Brown, himself an ex-slave, was proud to record in his autobiography his anti-slavery activities and stated that between 1 May and 1 December 1842 he had conveyed 69 fugitives over Lake Erie to Canada and had even visited Upper Canada in 1843, where he encountered in the village of Malden seventeen ex-slaves who owed their escape to his 'humble efforts'. See *Narrative of the Life of William Wells Brown,* p. 110, in *Five Slave Narratives.*

65 W. E. B. DuBois, *The Gift of Black Folk: the Negro in the Making of America,* New York, 1975, pp. 81–2.

66 He is credited with laying the plan for the U.S. capital of Washington, D.C.

67 This work had first appeared in the November and December issue of *American Museum* in 1788 as 'An Essay on Slavery' in two parts, 10 May and 23 May 1788, respectively. See *American Museum,* iv, pp. 414–17 and 509–12 (Nov. and Dec. 1788). *American Museum* was edited by Matthew Carey.

68 M. J. Bucher (ed.), *The Negro in American Culture,* based on materials of Professor Alain Locke, New York, 1956, p. 19.

69 *Ibid.*

70 See A. Singleton, *Life Story of the Rt. Rvd. Bishop Richard Allen:* also C. H. Wesley, *Richard Allen: Apostle of Freedom,* pp. 237–8.

71 William D. Parish (ed.), *Life, Travels and Opinions of Benjamin Lundy,* Philadelphia, Pa., 1847, pp. 222–3, reproduced from *the Raleigh Register,* North Carolina (containing extracts from the *Genius of Universal Emancipation* published in 1825 and edited jointly by Lundy and Garrison).

72 H. Aptheker, *One Continual Cry: David Walker's Appeal to the Colored Citizens of the United States,* New York, 1965.

73 G. M. Horton, *Hope of Liberty,* 1829, republished, Raleigh, N.C., 1837, as *Poems of Slave.*

74 Franklin, *From Slavery to Freedom,* p. 250. This writer has failed to locate Young's pamphlet.

75 B. Lundy, *The Genius of Universal Emancipation,* 3 Aug. 1831; also in *Life, Travels and Opinions of B. Lundy,* pp. 237–8. Lundy, though an abolitionist, rejected the spirit of Walker's *Appeal* and set the 'broadest seal of reprobation' on the pamphlet, because he felt it was calculated to 'rouse the worst passions of human nature and influence the minds of those to whom it is addressed'. Also *The Liberator's* deprecation of the *Appeal: The Liberator,* 1 Jan. 1831 and 29 Jan. 1831.

76 Although that paper was published before Garrison's *The Liberator,* in 1825 Garrison and Benjamin Lundy (a Quaker) had begun editing *The Genius of Universal Emancipation,* first as a monthly in the autumn of that year, and later as a weekly. Russwurm was not the first; graduating eleven days before Russwurm in 1826 was Edward Jones.

77 William C. Nell was also associated with *The North Star* at its inception. But even at its inception Douglass had difficulty maintaining the paper. It obtained financial assistance both from English abolitionists and also from an English woman abolitionist, Julia Griffiths, who in 1853 and 1854 published in the U.S.A. an anti-slavery annual, *Autographs for Freedom.* Her assistance emphasised the international character of the abolitionist crusade (see Vernon Loggins, *The Negro Author: His Development in America to 1900,* New York, 1964, p. 153).

78 In 1860 this was merged with *Douglass's Monthly* which had come into existence in 1858 for circulation in England. The *Frederick Douglass Paper* in the evening of its existence became a monthly.

79 This Afro-American founder of the literary magazine *Anglo-African* (see Loggins, *The Negro Author,* pp. 209–11) should not be confused with the white medical doctor-planter, later a State Senator in Georgia, observed as 'A gentleman of the Old South', who used a slave, and probably many more, for experiments in a manner reminiscent in our own day of the Nazi doctor Joseph Mengele. For more on this white Doctor Hamilton, see F. N. Boney, 'Doctor Thomas Hamilton: Two Views of a Gentleman of the Old South', *Phylon,* xxviii, 3 (1967), pp. 288–92.

80 See William Still, *The Underground Rail Road,* Philadelphia, Pa., 1872. William Still established a boarding house at No. 384 South Street below 9th South Side in Philadelphia which received the commendation of *The Liberator* in 1858. See *Frederick Douglass Paper,* 16 April 1858.

81 See *Frederick Douglass Paper,* 16 April 1858.

82 Douglass referred to this law of 1850 as the 'Blood Hound enactment' (see *ibid.*).

83 William and Ellen Craft told the story of their escape in a publication in England in 1860, *Running a Thousand Miles for Freedom or The Escape of William and Ellen Craft from Slavery*, London, 1860. Also see Still, *The Underground Rail Road*, pp. 368–77.

84 See *The Life and Times of Frederick Douglass 1817–1882*, Boston, 1882, pp. 215–16.

85 Buckmaster, *Let My People Go*, p. 103–5.

86 See Chapter 4 above.

87 *Ibid.*, n. 64 above, and Marion Gleason McDougall, *Fugitive Slaves (1619–1865)*, Fay House Monographs No. 3, prepared under the direction of Albert Bushnell Hart, Boston, Mass., Ginn and Co., 1891, pp. 25 *et seq.*, also Chapter 4, n. 64 above.

88 See Winks, *The Blacks in Canada*, ch. 6.

89 J. R. Coleman, *Slavery Times in Kentucky*, p. 226.

90 Buckmaster, *Let My People Go*, p. 216.

91 Franklin, *From Slavery to Freedom*, p. 256; Coleman, *Slavery Times in Kentucky*, pp. 226–7.

92 Often legislation was fashioned to prevent any free blacks from remaining within the confines of some Southern states; they were compelled to drift northward or westward, thereby reinforcing the rank and file of Northern abolitionists. An example was the 1839 Act of Maryland which imposed the following fines on free blacks entering the state: $20 for a first offence; $500 for a second with sale into slavery for failing to pay the fine. But free men of colour in the North constituted a job threat.

93 In 1831 Georgia's legislature offered a price of $4000 for the arrest of William Lloyd Garrison. Macon County placed a prize of $12 000 on the head of Arthur Tappan and New Orleans a prize of $20 000, while the pro-slavery South Carolina Vigilante Committee offered a prize of $1500 for any distributor of either David Walker's *Appeal* or Garrison's *The Liberator*. Sometimes Southern violence broke bounds and official places such as post offices were broken into in order to confiscate anti-slavery newspapers and make bonfires of them, as happened in July 1835 at Charleston, South Carolina. This often had the effect of intimidating Southern postmasters who considered it prudent to disallow abolitionist literature in the mail. See Franklin, *From Slavery to Freedom*, pp. 263–4.

94 See Franklin, *From Slavery to Freedom*, p. 264.

95 See some slave autobiographies – e.g. Austin Steward, *Twenty-two Years a Slave and Forty Years a Freeman*; and Ward, *Autobiography of a Fugitive Negro Slave*. The Christiana Affair was one such unhappy incident in which a slave owner in pursuit of escaped slaves was fatally wounded. See Still, *The Underground Rail Road*, pp. 348–57, for a record of this incident. Also F. Douglass's eulogy in his *Life and Times* on the occurrence, pp. 245–6.

96 See, for example, William Wells Brown, *Three Years in Europe: Places I have Seen and People I have Met*, London, 1852, and enlarged in 1854; also his play, *The Escape, or A Leap for Freedom*, 1835.

97 W. W. Brown, 'St Domingo: Its Revolution and Its Patriots', 1835, a pamphlet. It emerged out of speeches previously delivered in London and

Philadelphia on the rise and fall of Toussaint L'Ouverture, unmistakably an anti-slavery advance.

98 H. A. Herbert, *The Abolition Crusade,* New York, 1912, p. 98.

99 *Ibid.,* p. 102, quoted from J. W. Burgess, *The Middle Period of American History.*

100 *Ibid.,* p. 103.

101 *Ibid.,* pp.105-6. The statement was credited to one L. W. A. Johnston.

102 Winks, *The Blacks in Canada,* ch. 4.

103 *Ibid.,* p. 110.

104 *Ibid.,* pp. 110–11.

105 Upper Canada had the distinction of having passed legislation to abolish slavery long before the imperial Act of emancipation; see Winks, *The Blacks in Canada,* pp. 96 *et seq.*

106 *Ibid.,* pp. 253–4.

107 *Ibid.,* p. 255.

108 *Ibid.,* pp. 261–2.

109 *Ibid.,* pp. 262–4.

110 *Ibid.,* p. 265.

111 Dorothy B. Porter, 'The Negro in the Brazilian Abolition Movement', *Journal of Negro History,* xxxvii, 1 (1952), pp. 4–80, esp. p. 59. In subsequent pages the author lists a number of slave revolts beginning in 1719 with black slaves in Minas Geraes, slaves who, when their conspiracy was discovered, fled into the *sertao.* But she lists other revolts and the names of some of the leaders – such as the Bahian rebellion of 1798, followed by another uprising in Recife in 1823 under the leadership of Captain Pedro de Fonseca da Silva Pedrosa, a popular man of colour. There were also a series of religiously inspired revolts in Bahia between 1831 and 1837, the so-called Male or Muslim revolts in which one of the inspirational elements was the mother of Luiz Gama (Senhora Luiza Mahin) one of the greatest of the Brazilian abolitionists. See also p. 60 of the above-quoted article.

112 L. B. Rout, Jr., *The African Experience in Spanish America, 1502 to the Present Day,* Cambridge, 1976, pp. 237–8.

113 *Ibid.,* also Donald Pierson, *Negroes in Brazil: a Study of Race Contact at Bahia,* Chicago, Ill., 1942, 1947, pp. 51–4.

114 Rout, *The African Experience,* p. 238.

115 *Ibid.,* p. 240. The sum agreed on was 2 million pesos for slaves ranging in number between 16 000 and 20 000, either still in bondage or manumitted after July 1850; by 1883 only 25% of the agreed sum had been paid.

116 Rout, *The African Experience,* p. 251.

117 Thomas, *Cuba or The Pursuit of Freedom,* pp.281 *et seq.*

118 For a detailed discussion of this 'Famous Republic of Palmares', see R. K. Kent, 'Palmares, an African State in Brazil', *Journal of African History,* vi, 2 (1965), pp. 161–75; also Irene Diggs, 'Zumbi and the Republic of Os Palmares', *Phylon* (Atlanta University), xiv, 1 (1953), pp. 62–70.

119 Pierson, *Negroes in Brazil,* pp. 51–4; Robert Walsh, *Notices of Brazil in 1828 and 1829,* London, 1830, Vol. 2, p. 391; Daniel P.Kidder and James C. Fletcher, *Brazil and the Brazilians Portrayed in Historical and Descriptive Sketches,* Philadelphia, 1857, p. 135; F. Tannenbaum, *Slave and Citizen: the Negro in the Americas,* New York, 1947, pp. 50–65, 91; H. S. Klein, *Slavery in the Americas:*

a *Comparative Study of Virginia and Cuba*, Chicago, Ill., (Quadrangle Books, 1971) pp. 200–1 and notes. For the theory, pp. 62–5, 194, 196.

120 Tannenbaum, *Slave and Citizen*, pp. 53–8, 61–2, 65, 69, 105–6; Pierson, *Negroes in Brazil*, pp. 331, 346.

121 It is said that the assistance given by African slaves in the second part of the seventeenth century under the leadership of Henrique Dias to the Portuguese in order to dislodge the Dutch who had captured Brazil from the Portuguese converted the status of slave participants into that of Brazilian soldiers and patriots. See Dorothy B. Porter, 'The Negro in the Brazilian Abolitionist Movement', *Journal of Negro History*, xxxvii, 1 (1952), p. 58. It was also suggested that service by black slaves in the Paraguayan War (1864–70) also had this effect, for other slaves joined the ranks when they understood that Dom Pedro II, the anti-slavery king and resident of Brazil, encouraged the freeing of slaves to become volunteers to fight against Paraguay. *Ibid.*, pp. 58–9; Pierson, *Negroes in Brazil*, pp. 51–2.

122 *Ibid.*, pp. 10–11. Quoted from Charles W. Turner, *Ruy Barbosa, Brazilian Crusader for the Essential Freedoms*, New York, 1945, p. 193.

123 Miers, *Britain and the Ending of the Slave Trade*, p. 48; Thomas, *Cuba*, p. 231. The equipment treaties were foremost in the efforts to end the Latin trade, but the endeavour was long-drawn-out, as the records reveal.

124 Porter, 'The Negro in the Brazilian Abolitionist Movement', p. 61.

125 *Ibid.*, p. 69.

126 *Ibid.*

127 Pierson, in *Negroes in Brazil*, p. 66, observed their indifference and in some cases opposition.

128 *Ibid.*, p. 72.

129 See Pierson, *Negroes in Brazil*, p. 64, for factors contributing in Brazil to eventual success, among which he lists the decay of the sugar industry.

Epilogue   Character and preoccupations of leadership

The dispersion of Africans into the Americas and their experiences there threw up leadership of varied kinds, styles and persuasions. Since the planned second volume of the diaspora deals with the growth, nature and character of that leadership from the beginning of the dispersion, though principally from the eighteenth century when a definite pattern began to emerge, what is attempted here merely provides a bird's-eye view of the content of the first few chapters of that volume. It is not a substitute for the work itself. It is only intended to provide a lead into it.

The importance of leadership for a down-trodden people cannot be overstressed, and quite early such leadership evolved, despite efforts by the slavocracy to thwart its growth. The leadership that emerged was conditioned both by environmental factors and by the psychology engendered by the system of slavery. Some leaders saw no way out of the system except by outright confrontation. Others sought ways of scoring occasional victories against it in what they perceived as a Sisyphean undertaking, and so enunciated moral guiding principles often derived from an understanding of religion. There were those who drew their inspiration from ancient heroes and from the memory that was preserved of their African background. These were few and far between but their influences differed markedly from area to area, depending on the degree of socialisation of the slaves as well as free people. But these sometimes exerted immense influence. Others still tried to master the language and methods of their enslavers in order to confront them with the logic of their arguments. Men like Frederick Douglass belong to this genre of leadership. Such leaders often placed emphasis on organisation.

Leadership in the first phase crystallises into three broad categories; first, those who, for want of a better term, constituted a kind of 'physical force' leadership; second, there were moral suasionists; and, finally, those who often employed organisation and platforms to agitate a burning issue with a view to reaching a wider audience and, thus, inducing change. These were the activists. While these categories are arbitrary and sometimes overlap one another, they are useful for tidying up a complex phenomenon, which developed steadily, but, sometimes, unobtrusively. They were the forerunners

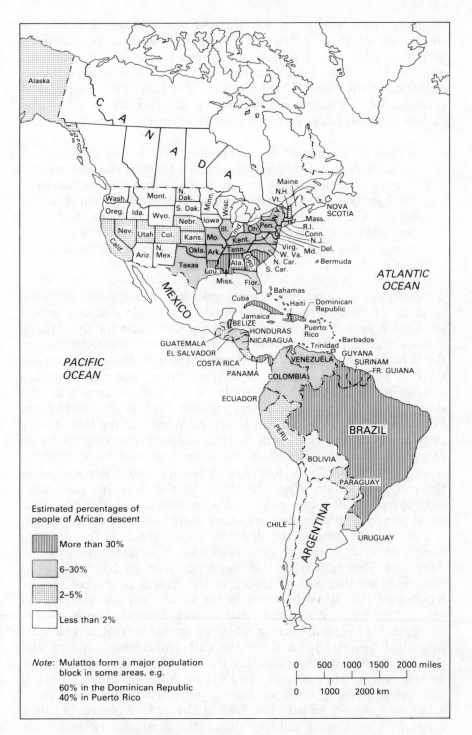

Distribution of people of African descent in the Americas today

397

of leaders who have become household words in our day. But the emergence of these outstanding men and women in a difficult period revealed their strength of character in the face of enormous odds, and they have been immortalised in the annals of descendants of Africa in the New World diaspora. For they were people who emerged out of struggle and the tone of their endeavours was set by no less a person than Frederick Douglass himself, who observed:

> If there is no struggle there is no progress. Those who profess to favor freedom and yet deprecate agitation are men who want crops without ploughing up the ground; they want rain without thunder and lightning. They want the ocean without the awful roar of its waters. This struggle may be a moral one, or it may be a physical one, and it may be both moral and physical, but it must be a struggle. Power concedes nothing without a demand. It never did and it never will.[1]

This handful of outstanding men and women compared with the majority of their brethren represented a leadership that was typical and which periodically arose to indicate directions for the African diaspora, principally in North America and to a limited extent in the West Indies and Brazil. In selecting a few to illustrate the trend there is an element of bias in their selection, but not in such a manner as to prejudice the study or to fail to emphasise the categories of leadership at a very difficult time in their evolution. For instance, the Rev. Samuel Ringgold Ward and the Rev. Henry Highland Garnet were both activist stalwart contemporaries of Douglass, sharing many ideas and aspirations and often speaking from the same platform, so it would be superfluous also to discuss them in great detail. What this study highlights is that full-length biographies of all these leaders are long overdue, and while some are at present available there are many more that need to be written.

The activists among the descendants of Africa in the diaspora were persistent in the general endeavour to defeat slavery in the Americas. This leadership was more persistent in North America than in other theatres of slavery in the Americas, except for the handful of Brazilians discussed in the section on anti-slavery and those Afro-Latin Americans who championed the cause of the struggles for independence or rallied to the banners of several wars unleashed against Spain from the early nineteenth century and thereby secured manumission for themselves and others in similar circumstances. They all combined the attributes of leaders of moral and physical force with an activist role. They were all deeply religious and seem to have had faith in Divine Providence, but their religious convictions did not blind them to the necessity for employing other measures, for example violence, to defeat slavery.

Even some, like Sojourner Truth, who belonged to the Garrisonian school of non-resisters at the time of the Civil War, by her own contributions to the Civil War effort, came to accept the logic of violence to attain the goal of emancipation in the land she had been forced to adopt. Nevertheless, their techniques of agitating the question marked them out as distinct from the other two categories of leaders. But, in the long term, the divisions are arbitrary and have merely been employed for analytical purposes.

In visualising this early leadership before 1850 less emphasis has been laid on the technique of brief biographical sketches simply because of their cumbersome nature, and this has only intruded incidentally when considering some specific roles and contributions in facing up to the issues which they considered crucial for themselves and which were destined to sustain them and their brethren. Their leadership claims are, therefore, deduced from the above-mentioned categories *vis-à-vis* themselves as a whole with the rest of their communities and their society at large, especially by their suggestions of limited and long-term goals as ideals to be striven for. It is in this regard that an attempt has been made to evaluate the early leadership among peoples of African descent in the diaspora in the Americas as they set the pace and tone for the succeeding half century.

The emphases of leadership altered as circumstances changed, but these leaders based their words and actions on their perception of the limited alternatives open to them and their brethren or those who looked up to them for guidance. Thus the issues which impinged on their consciousness and on which they had to decide were identical to those which confronted later generations of leaders and which still rankle within the leadership rank and file and among their followers. The most burning issues centred on the question, After freedom what? In attempting to answer this rhetorical question, while still fighting for the emancipation of all their people still under bondage and those who suffered numerous disabilities under nominal conditions of freedom, three alternatives suggested themselves: first, to be integrated and assimilated in the wider society in which they lived; second, to emigrate either within the confines of the nation to an area not yet densely settled or beyond the frontiers of the nation including emigration to Africa; and third (this was a later consideration), by expressing their separate identity within the wider framework of the same society. The latter, in more recent times, has been called 'nationalism'. But the latter phenomenon is not as recent as people have suggested; this identity has continued to be expressed since the founding of African and Negro churches from as far back as the late eighteenth century, and this yearning for independence as well as a spirit of independence has been extended to other spheres, albeit unsuccessfully in some instances. But for those who do not see this idea as a separate category in their consideration, this aspect became lodged into the second, i.e. emigration, becoming segregation. By this criterion the alternatives were twofold: integration or segregation. Even if this categorisation were to be accepted there is the need for a distinction between segregation within the confines of, for example, the United States, and segregation outside it. The latter, even in the heyday of the controversy about the destiny of peoples of African descent in the nineteenth century, was not described as segregation but rather as colonisation, emigration and, by opponents, transportation.

Yet, each of the three issues preoccupied the early leadership, sometimes creating polarities in the opinions of leaders. That the issues were unresolved, except by individuals who struck out on their own, and were bequeathed to succeeding generations of leaders, mirrored the dilemma of the situation as well as the complexities of questions posed by the envisaged destiny for descendants of Africa in their contact with descendants of Europe in the New World diaspora. The initial priority of this early leadership was to dispense with slavery. The other preoccupations came second but were just as vital. The leaders believed in a step-by-step approach, for it was felt that the other issues would become prominent once the stultifying institution of slavery was destroyed. But the leadership did not feel it had to wait for this to happen and so both issues were agitated simultaneously. Leaders realised that co-operation on as broad a front as possible was essential. It was such preoccupations which, in the early twentieth century, gave rise to organisations such as the National Association for the Advancement of Colored Peoples, the Urban League, the American Negro Academy, and various study groups for historical research; and also earlier such preoccupations initiated movements for emigration by men like Paul Cuffee, the Afro-American Bostonian shipowner who in his life-time made two voyages to the coast of Sierra Leone and on one of the trips took with him thirty-eight settlers.

Ideas of black co-operation were championed throughout the nineteenth century by leaders whose names have become household words, such as the Rev. Theodore Holly, Dr Martin Delany, Bishop Henry MacNeal Turner, the Rev. Alexander Crummell and their West Indian counterparts, John Henry Ellis, Albert Thorne, George Alexander Macguire, Henry Sylvester Williams, and many more. These men were the forerunners of the movement led by Alfred C. Sam (1917) and the mammoth movement of the great West Indian Marcus Garvey in the 1920s. But it was also felt among some of the leaders that those who had achieved liberation from slavery had to set the pace and be guided by certain principles; only through those principles could the struggles, whether for elevation or for civil rights, be seen in clear perspective.

In observing this early leadership the discussion has not been confined only to the characteristics and beliefs which these leaders had in common, but rather attention has also been focused on the differences in their approach to the alternatives posed by the societies in which they lived. It is, therefore, no surprise that their assimilationist aspirations led straight into the North American civil rights agitation that became prominent in the post-Civil War era and which spilled over into the twentieth century. In the West Indies and Brazil black efforts on a more modest scale settled for integration, which was more or less conceded with the passage of time. But here class divisions were crystallised which sometimes expressed themselves along colour lines. In the rest of South America there are numerous variations in assimilation, extinction and segregation which have been adopted to resolve colour problems. The nature of those societies inhibited the emergence of a leadership of peoples of African descent demanding their rights, except in Brazil, where after the demise of slavery there began a limited exodus of people of African origin from the Bahia region to West Africa, where they became assimilated into West African societies. These returnees emphasised the link between Africa and the diaspora. But in terms of sustained black leadership in Brazil, once the abolition of slavery had been achieved, the record is negative, though there is a sense in which the 'African personality' survives in Bahia in Brazil and in parts of the New World diaspora in its cultural expressions and in religious ritual.

What, therefore, has been attempted in this work is to make intelligible from a mass of widely diffuse and complex material this forging of an African diaspora in the Americas, through the activities of slave traders and external interests, which did not necessarily coincide with African interests. As it was not the African who instituted the diaspora he was not in a position to continue its progression once the external partners had embargoed the trade and were no longer willing to continue along the old lines of an established Euro-African partnership. The African potentates and prime merchants, the culprits in the dispersion, were able to continue the enslavement of others internally within the continent until imperial ascendancy terminated their initiative, even though they re-entrenched it under numerous colonial devices such as forced labour, migratory labour and the so-called 'contract' labour system of the Portuguese. But this belongs to another study.

Our chief purpose has been to establish the slave trade as a major factor in the creation of an African diaspora in the Americas, owing to the massive transplantation of people from Africa, and later to show that this dispersion had its own implications for Africans carried into the Americas in terms of the policies that were fostered on them through the ordering of the plantation societies to which they came and of which they became the mainstay, with its cruelties, subtleties and techniques of ensuring conformity. The responses to these various modes of handling have been considered in what has been broadly called slave strategy, even though it overlaps with other efforts to bring slavery to an end. We have seen how these activities helped the emergence of an early leadership in the period before the American Civil War which set the pattern for a later generation of leaders together also with dilemmas of accept-ance and rejection which have scarcely been resolved but which at various times have seen a change of emphasis. The problems confronted by that leadership set patterns, tones and goals for the future, and the conclusion reached is that the leaders who emerged immediately afterwards assimilated the tradition from which their predecessors had come in order to cope more effectively with the nagging question of their destiny in the Americas. This situation of ambivalence towards the New World on the one hand and Africa on the other still pervades their thoughts.

This study has not only attempted to encourage a new interpreta-tion of the slave trade and slavery, it has also attempted to achieve some historical sequence for the stages in the making of this African diaspora in the Americas, bearing in mind that even in that new world the African was not, as is often assumed, a *tabula rasa* on which all sorts of imprints could be made. Clearly, the imprints have left their lasting legacies and scars and have even blighted fundamental aspects of African culture in some places and led to the inversion of some in others; in yet others they have been merely fragmented; and in others again, such as in Haiti and Bahia (Brazil) and among the 'Wood Negroes' – the so-called 'Bush Negroes', of Suriname – the erosion of African culture and values has been minimal. Indeed syncretism has been a ruling element in most of the former slave theatres, and the African element has shown its impact on many aspects of the New World and European cultural life – for instance, in Brazil in dieting, music and in religion; hence the resurgence of the African (Yoruba) god of war, Ogun, as St George, and sometimes as St Anthony. In Cuba Ogun became St John. Side by side with this West African version of religion was also the 'Congolese cult'. These survivals point to the need for more fundamental studies in places like Bahia in Brazil, Suriname, Gasprillo (Trinidad), Dominica, Haiti, the Dominican Republic and, not least, on the west bank of the Demerara and on the east coast of Berbice in Guyana.

Attention has been drawn to some of the neglected features in the conceptualisation of the African diaspora even by some of its leaders. The reactions, values and ideals which have intermingled during four centuries of dominance of African life in the Americas mirror the numerous contradictions of the societies as well as their leaders' ambivalence to their own proclaimed principles of conduct. It is not surprising that the dominant or ruling members of the respective societies have reacted, not once favourably, to the conflicting alternatives and ideals which descendants of Africa have striven to attain.

The diaspora put the African in a position of inferiority, and only in the post-colonial period, in the West Indies, is this stigma being partially eroded because descendants of Africa in those parts constitute the majority. In the U.S.A., where they remain a minority, albeit a large minority, the stigma remains. The various nations of South America have tried to resolve the problems of the African presence in their own areas by recourse to various and often contradictory expedients. These expedients have varied from legislative enactments prohibiting persons of African origin from settling there to encouraging an influx of persons of European origin in order to reassert white control and preponderance in numbers. In others elimination has been allowed to continue. In some places descendants of Africa have remained a minority and, while not fully assimilated, have no voice whatsoever in the councils of the nations. In other areas, assimilation has established the mulatto as the dominant element. In yet other regions, where there is a sizeable African presence, even though again as a minority, there has been mental and spiritual assimilation accompanied by problems of poverty, discrimination and depression.

Even within the United States, where the 'black power' issue has been insistent, there still remains an ingrained ambivalence towards Africa. Nowhere is this more clearly expressed than in the conclusion to a recent book by Dr Rout: 'if there are Pan-African congresses and conferences, why have there been no such meetings exclusively for those who share both African origin and a common heritage of slavery in the Americas?... Peoples of the African diaspora... might discover that they have as much, or more, in common with each other than they have with Africans in Africa.'[2] Such an observation poses a problem for proponents of pan-Africanism within the United States and brings them into conflict with middle-class integrationists. These polarisations further compound the problems.

Detailed discussion of the African diaspora and its emergent leadership has not been extended beyond the period succeeding the American Civil War. This limitation has been by deliberate choice, imposed not only by the size of the present volume but also due to the author's perception; as, in this author's view, the latter period sees the shifts and strains in the stabilisation of leadership and deserves separate and more exhaustive treatment. This author's text on leadership is, therefore, a complementary volume to the one now released. Nevertheless, both periods form part of a continuum in conceiving the experiences and responses of the African diaspora in the Americas during the core period of this diaspora. The aim of this book, as indicated at the beginning, was to help illuminate aspects of the making of this African diaspora in the Americas.

Notes

1 Quoted in P. S. Forner, *The Voice of Black America: Speeches by Negroes in the U.S., 1797–1971*, New York, 1972, pp. 197–203; and Forner, *The Life and Writings of Frederick Douglass*, New York, 1950, Vol. 2, *Pre-Civil War Decade, 1850–1860*, pp. 426–39.
2 Leslie B. Rout, Jr., *The African Experience in Spanish America, 1502 to the Present Day*, Cambridge, 1976, p. 322.

Appendix 1 *Asiento* licences, 1518–1805

Dates of Contract	Duration	Recipients, Contractor or Nationality	Annual shipment envisaged	Total anticipated/ or supplied	Outcome
1518	4 years *asiento de negros*	Lorenzo de Garrevod, Duke of Bresa: Garrevod was Major-domo of the Royal Household.	4000 *bozales* to the Indies and the mainland	No figures	Excluded other dealers without Crown permission to ship slaves to Spanish colonies for 4 years. The monopoly sold to Genoese merchants for 25 000 ducats as Lorenzo had no ships – also sold in turn to Portuguese slave-trading captains.
1521	8 years	Garrevod	4000	Never delivered	Abruptly cancelled in 1523; 4000 slaves never delivered.
1528–32	4 years	Heinrich Ehinger and Hieronymus Seiler of the German Banking House of Welscher.	4000	Never delivered	Neither Charles nor the Germans seemed enthusiastic for renewal of contract.
1532–37			*Asiento* in abeyance		
1537		Cristóbal Francisquime and Domingo Martinez (Sevillians)	1500 *bozales*		
1537–86		Charles I's suspension of *Asiento* for 50 years			

Appendix 1 *Asiento* licences, 1518–1805

Dates of Contract	Duration	Recipients, Contractor or Nationality	Annual shipment envisaged	Total anticipated or supplied	Outcome
1586		Gaspar Peralta, Portuguese but Spanish subject	2800	No figures	Required payment for the privilege, 84 000 ducats.
1595	9 years	Pedro Gomez Reynal	4250	38 250 anticipated at end of period	Annual payment of 100 000 ducats. Death of Reynal (1600), contract terminated.
1601–09	Same terms as predecessor	Juan and Gonzalo Rodrigues Cutino	4250	No figures	This was the real first slave-trade monopoly.
1610–22		Antonio Rodriguez de Rivas (Delvas)		29 574	
1623–31		Antonio Manuel Rodrigues Lamego		No figures	
1631–40		Melchior Gomez, Angel and Cristobal Mendez de Sossa		No figures	
1640–62	*Asiento* in abeyance		Period of clandestine slave trading involving English, French, Dutch and others. No figures available but trading was greater than under the contract system.		

1662–71–73	7 years	Domenico Grillo and Ambrosio Lomelin (Lomelin died 1668)	English to supply 3500 at Barbados and Jamaica. Another author puts figure at 5000.	Unfulfilled	Contract uncompleted. Through Grillo the English and Dutch became subcontractors.
1674–76	5 years	Antonio Garcia and Don Sebastian de Silica (Siliceo); Garcia imprisoned in 1676. Garcia used Dutch as subcontractors involving Balthasar Coymans.	4000 pieces (peças) annually		
1676–81	5 years	Consulado de Sevillia (Council of Seville). Merchants later vested in the Dutch West India Company.			Returned privilege to the Crown in 1679.
1682–85	5 years	Don Nicolas Porcio with power of attorney for Don Juan Barroso y Pozo		Not more than half the number contracted.	
1685–87	2 years remaining and 2 years extending it to 1689	Don Balthasar Coymans (Death of Balthasar Coymans, 1686)			Split *Asiento* between Pórtio's faction and the Dutch firm of Coymans.

Appendix 1 *Asiento* licences, 1518–1805

Dates of Contract	Duration	Recipients, Contractor or Nationality	Annual shipment envisaged	Total anticipated or supplied	Outcome
1689		English Royal Africa Company contracted with the former Agent of Porcio in Jamaica (St Jago de Castillo or Santiago Castillo).			The split *Asiento* – the Coymans part to Guzman (a Portuguese), Bernardo Martin de Guzman.
1696–1703 1697		Portuguese Company of Cacheu with English as their subcontractors.		9853 (between 1698 and 1702)	Lisbon advanced Madrid a loan of 200 000 pesos. Portuguese made English subcontractors.
1701	Over 10 years	French *Asiento* – French Royal Africa Company of Guinea	4800	Total anticipated 48 000	
1713	Concluded for 30 years	English *Asiento* – South Sea Company	4800	Total anticipated 1 440 000	
1730	48 years	Guipúzcoa (Caracas company)	Thousands		
1740–60	20 years	Royal Havana Company		Between 4000 and 11 000 shipped into Cuba	Smuggling also continued.

1765–72	10 years 4 years' extension	Dom Miguel de Uriate (power behind was La Compañia Graditana later known as Compañia General de Negros).		
1784	2 years	Limited *Asiento* to British firm, Peter Baker and John Dawson Ltd of Liverpool	4000 to Venezuela and Trinidad	
1786		Same English firms as above	5000–6000 to Venezuela and Cuba	
1795 and 1805		Edward Barry (Irishman)		4000

Notes

The list omits many *licencias* granted by the Spanish monarchs during periods of suspension of the *Asiento*. In 1789 Spain made the trade in slaves free and the monopoly system came to an end and so the problem of contraband was no longer a preoccupation. It was common practice to sell the *asientos* to the highest bidders. There were three periods of suspension of the *Asiento* and three periods of its revival. The years of suspension were: 1532–37; 1537–86; 1640–62. Between 1540 and 1586 licences were awarded to an assorted group of individuals but in the period much contraband traffic continued and was far from satisfactory to the Spanish government. After the death of King Sebastian of Portugal in 1578, Philip III of Spain in 1580 acquired the Portuguese kingdom and in seeking to restore Portuguese loyalty revived the *Asiento* and he hoped that in granting the concessions to the Portuguese for conveying slaves, the Spanish colonies would also be supplied with the slaves they desired. The general terms of the contract were similar, the exception being the concession to Reynal and Juan Roderigues Cutinho to use the port of Buenos Aires, a privilege not conceded to later acquisitors of the *Asiento*. The preferences were in the entire control of Genoese bankers. The leading entrepôts for slaves were Cartagena (Colombia) or Porto Bello. Although Buenos Aires could have been used as an entrepôt – contraband slaves entered through this latter port and were then sold to overland traders – the Spanish government's endeavours to arrest the contraband trade proved abortive.

Portuguese slave trade to the Spanish Indies was terminated when Portugal broke off from Spanish rule. This, of course, created a dilemma for Spain as to who were to supply its colonies with slaves. The choice was to be out of the English, Dutch (both heretics) and the French (who were enemies of the Habsburgs). Till 1700 Spain was unable to establish African depots as it was engaged in European wars; also, as a result of the previous Papal Bulls which excluded Spain from the African zone and with no navy, had to swallow its pride.

Thrice in the period when the English held the *Asiento* the Spanish attempted to revoke the contract. The years were 1718, 1727 and 1739, and thrice the British persuaded Spain to relent in separate treaties in 1721 (Treaty of Madrid), 1729 and 1748 (Treaty of Aix-la-Chapelle). But it was finally revoked in 1750 with a compensation paid to the British of £100 000. Many of the *Asientos* were not legally fulfilled, and so much illicit trade and smuggling of slaves pervaded the entire period.

Sources: E. Donnan, *Documents Illustrative of the Slave Trade to America,* 5 vols., Vols. 1 and 3, Leslie Rout; Jr., *The African Presence in Spanish America*, London, 1976; C. H. Hering, *The Spanish Empire of America*, New York, 1963.

Appendix 2 Colour hierarchies in New World slave societies

1 Hierarchy in eighteenth-century Dutch Suriname

White planters
Equivalents in other parts of the Antilles and Brazil

Embryonic middle class
White overseers, clerks, merchants

Free blacks and free coloureds
The latter offspring of white fathers and black or mulatto mothers

Slaves
Africans and Creoles including mulattos

Amerindians
A class apart as they retreated into the interior

Note that class and colour divisions combine here. There were numerous subdivisions – the mulatto, quaderon, mestice, samboe and mongro were all known in the Dutch colonies. The social distance between each group was conspicuous in theory, though account must be taken in practice of the sexual proclivities of the dominant group in seeking liaisons with African slave women and coloured women. Colour gradations were also noted by Captain Steadman (see below).

2 Colour gradations observed by Captain J. C. Steadman in eighteenth-century Suriname

Before 1775 the inclusion of Amerindians further complicated the picture.

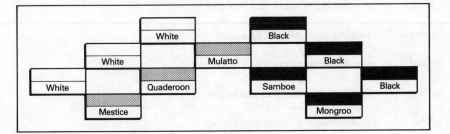

From Steadman, *Narrative*, Vol. 2, opposite p. 98.

3 Hierarchy in French St Domingue (representative of French Antilles)

Governor
Representative of France

Royal officials
Government agents of France, administrative and other officials including civil servants

Grands blancs
Equivalent to absentee landlords

Wealthy white planters
Seigneurs in St Domingue
Messieurs in Martinique
Bourgeoisie in Guadeloupe

Creole planters
Locally-born whites with complete attachment to the colony controllers of Le Cap and Port-au-Prince

Petits blancs
Poor whites, derisively called *les petits colons blancs*

Free blacks and mulattos
The latter known as *gens de coleur* or L'Affranchi; some were plantation owners.

Slaves (blacks, mulattos – *bozales* and Creoles)
Nègres ouvriers – negro field slaves
Nègres de jardin – negro domestic slaves

Note that class and colour are combined here. There were numerous subdivisions among the mulattos; the following table is adapted from Pierre de Vassière, *St Domingue*, Paris, 1909, pp. 217–20.

quadroon	cross between white and mestiço
mestiço	cross between white and mulatto
quateron	cross between white and mestif
mestif	cross between white and le capre
le capre	cross between mulatto and negro
griffe	cross between le capre and negro

According to C. L. R. James colour gradations and nomenclatures ran to 128 divisions. Though the divisions were rigidly maintained the passions they evoked resulted in numerous antipathies and hostilities so that the society was divided against itself. The real *grands blancs*, according to Professor Gabriel Debien, were permanently absent in France and knew nothing of St Domingue and the plantations, except that they drew their living from them.

4 Hierarchy in Colonial Spanish America

Spanish government and Catholic church

Iberian merchants
Landed interests and mine owners, sometimes incorporating the nobility

Criollo
Locally-born Spaniards, who had fewer opportunities for politics and administration but were members of the *cabildo* or town government

Castas

The castas contained numerous colour divisions among the lower orders, though some found themselves upgraded in the hierarchy through inheritance, manumission or military service. Castas included mulattos, negros, Amerindians and zambos. According to F. Tannenbaum (*Ten Keys to Latin America*, p. 72, and the source of the above diagram), Mexico had about 20 different types. These lower orders were further graded and local variations existed too.

The government would consist of the governor and officials from the metropolis, , the Council and the Assembly (from which Criollos were for a long time excluded). Among the higher officials in the administration would be registrars, legal officers, customs and tax collectors, military and naval men, priests and clergymen. Such people would belong to the upper middle class, whereas overseers constituted a lower middle class. There were no Spanish American equivalents to the white indentured servants of the British and French colonies.

Edward Long in his *History of Jamaica* (Vol. 2, pp. 260–1) identified the following classes in the Spanish territories: creoles or native whites, blacks, Indians and their 'varieties'; Europeans and other whites; and imported African slaves. On intermingling he noted the following:

white man	=	negro woman
white man	=	mulatta
white man	=	terceron
white man	=	quateron
white man	=	quateron
		white

Mediate or stationary
　quateron　=　terceron

　　　tente-enel-ayre

Retrograde
　mulatta　=　terceron　　　　negro　=　mulatto

　　　saltaras　　　　　　　　sambo de mulatta

　Indian　=　mulatta　　　　　negro　=　Indian

　　　mestize　　　　　　　　　sambode
　　　　　　　　　　　　　　　　Indian

　　　　　　　　　　　　　　　=　sambode
　　　　　　　　　　　　　　　mulatta

　　　　　　　　　　　　　　　givero

Long's book contains a full discussion of the various subdivisions and their implications in society, some of it rather misconceived.

5 Hierarchy in post-independent Latin America

Criollo
White creoles

Mestizo
Middle class approximating white in the colour gradation

Negro and mulatto

Amerindians

The last two categories constituted the mass. There were also numerous subdivisions, though their usage was more common during the colonial period.

6 Hierarchy in the British West Indies (especially typical of Jamaica)

Whites
Ruling whites
Subordinate whites
White bond servants

Mustifino (mustiphini)
Progeny of white and mustee, reputed to be 15/16 white; seems to coincide
with sang-mêlé of French St Domingue

Mustee
Coincides with mestizo, mestiço, or mustice of Spanish, Portuguese or Dutch
colonies. Progeny of white and Amerindian or quadroon.

Octoroon
Progeny of white and mulatto, possessing 1/8 negro blood

Quintroon
Progeny of white and mustifino, 1/5 negro.
Not a common type, more a product of mathematical precision.

Quadroon
Progeny of white and mulatto, though strictly speaking white and octoroon

Mulatto
Progeny of white and negro

Sambo(e)
Progeny of mulatto and negro

Negro
Descendant of Africa. No distinction as in French Antilles between negro and
marabou (moor)

1 The quadroon in the English plantations coincided with the French quadroon,
the progeny of white and mulatto (mestiço) parents. Some contemporary
observers suggested octoroon and quadroon were not divergent names, but in a
highly colour-conscious society, in which the criterion of colour was the
barometric measure for social advancement, the distinction was maintained and
was important, however arbitrary it might seem.

2 The absurdity of the situation can be seen by the fact that a quadroon could be
96 parts white and 32 parts negro, the sum total of white/negro combinations
therefore coinciding with the 128 colour divisions known to the French colony
of St Domingue. There, as C. L. R. James tells us (p. 38), the quateron could be
produced from a white and marabou (i.e. moor) in the proportion of 88:40
respectively, or from a white and sacatra in the proportion of 72:56 respectively,
and so on through 128 variations. A sang-mêlé was supposedly 127 parts white
and 1 part negro.

3 Although there appears to be similarity between the mustifino of the British
West Indies and the sang-mêlé of the French Antilles, the distinction ends there.
James reminds us that in spite of all the niceties of colour gradation in St
Domingue the sang-mêlé was still a man of colour subject to many disabilities
universally experienced by the coloured people of the French Antilles, whereas,
in the British West Indies, the mustifinos were granted the privileges of

415

whiteness. The implication is that the phenomenon known elsewhere as 'passing' for white sanctioned by custom did not apply in the French colonies. It should be no surprise, therefore, that French rigidity also welded the coloured population into one hostile and resentful group and class simultaneously. By contrast in the British plantation societies in the West Indies, by legal stipulations and custom, the mustifinos acquired the privileges of whiteness.

4 Another note of caution is necessary in regard to the term 'sambo(e)', which needs to be distinguished from the term *'zambo'* in Spanish America. The term, even if it resembles and derives from the Latin usage, did not coincide with the term, for in the latter case it related to the progeny of the African and Amerindian. Moreover, while sambo could often be a slave in the other colonies, the *zambo* in Latin America, being the progeny of a free Amerindian woman, had the status of a freeman, even if he were looked upon as socially inferior to the African by the ruling group. Bowser says of the *zambo* that he was dreaded in Spanish Peru, and attempts to prevent associations between Africans and Amerindians, which often resulted in numerous *zambo* offspring, proved abortive. But there is an additional aspect of the sambo usage peculiar to North America (its British West Indian equivalent is quashie) to designate the slave who allegedly is said to love the master and had other compliant characteristics as well. See J. W. Blassingame's *Slave Community*, chapter 5, for his critical approach to the sambo and other stereotypes.

7 Hierarchy in Portuguese Brazil c. 1750

Brancos
Whites or persons socially accepted as white

Pardos
People of mixed descent including mulattos, sometimes classified separately

Pretos
Negroes, whether bonded or free

Christianised Amerindians

There were numerous subdivisions as well. The implication is that non-Christianised Amerindians were beyond the pale. For a numerical breakdown of the populations of the various regions of colonial Brazil see Boxer, *The Golden Age of Brazil*, pp. 23, 301, and *The Portuguese Seaborne Empire*, pp. 171–3.

8 Some Current Guyanese Variants on Colour Distinctions

1 **Buck**
Guyanese Indian (Amerindian).

2 **Half–Buck**

Sometimes referred to as Buck and People; mixture with an Amerindian or Half-Amerindian.

3 **High Colour**

(used for ladies, and relates to colour approximating white).

4 **High Yeller**

as above, and again represents a lightness of colour.

5 **Coloured**

could be the result of any mixtures of various races and their progeny.

6 **Puttagee**

supposed to represent a kind of Portuguese colour. The concept here relates to a sallow complexion. In Guyana the Portuguese have never been highly regarded compared to other Europeans even if they are the commercial class and wealthy. The term itself is one of disdain.

7 **Fair Skin**

not very black but a degree higher than the Red Man or Red Woman.

8 **Red Man and Red Woman**

a specific type of coloured man or woman also light in complexion.

9 **Sallow Complexioned**

like the Portuguese above but resulting from a combination of other colours, most probably through generations of intermingling of colours.

10 **Negro**

anyone tracing ancestry to Africa even if born locally.

11 **Half–Negro**

implies what it says. Note that it does not say 'Half-African', as the thinking is in colour waves.

12 **Douglah**

progeny of an Afro-Guyanese and an Indo-Guyanese (East Indian). The latter came to the colony in the post-emancipation period as indentured labourers although some men of means also came in the period and often initially without their women. The term as understood and employed by descendants of East Indians means a 'slave'.

13 **Bouvianda**

(pronounced 'Boufiander') – progeny of Afro-Guyanese and Amerindian-Guyanese).

N.B. *These societies from slavery times have moved in waves of colour differences which are still socially expressed at least in private. The mentality is one of the lasting legacies of slavery in the Americas.*

Appendix 3 Sugar production in the American tropical colonies, 1741–5 and 1766–70

Table 1 Annual Averages (tons)

	1741–5	1766–70
French	64 675[2]	77 923[3]
British	41 043	74 452
Portuguese	34 000[3]	20 400[4]
Danish	730[5]	8 230[6]
Dutch	9 210[7]	6 800[8]
Spanish	2 000	5 200[9]
Totals	151 658	193 000

Notes: [1] The quantities shown in Tables 1 and 2 are the legal imports into the metropolitan countries. Colonies which exported less than 1000 tons annually are omitted.

[2] See Table 2, notes 1,2,3,6,7.

[3] 1760.

[4] 1776.

[5] 1775.

[6] 1770.

[7] 1740, 1745.

[8] 1765, 1770.

[9] 1764–8.

Source: Noel Deerr, *History of Sugar* (1949), Vol. 1, pp. 112, 131, 193–8, 235–6, 245; John Campbell, *Considerations on the Nature of the Sugar Trade* (1763), p. 54; David MacPherson, *Annals of Commerce* (1805), Vol. 3, p. 262; R. M. N. Panday, *Agriculture in Surinam 1650–1950* (1959), p. 19; Jacobo de la Pezuela, *Diccionario . . . de la Isla de Cuba* (1863), Vol. 1, p. 62.

Cf. R. B. Sheridan, *op. cit.*, Table 1, p. 22.

Table 2 Sugar production of the ten leading Caribbean islands, 1741–5 and 1766–70 (annual averages in tons)

	Area (sq. miles)	1741–5	1766–70
St Domingue (French)[9]	10 714	42 400[1]	61 247[2]
Jamaica (British)	4 411	15 578	36 021
Antigua (British)	108	6 229	10 690
St Christopher (British)	68	7 299	9 701
Martinique (French)	425	14 163[3]	8 778
St Croix (Danish)	84	730[4]	8 230[5]
Guadeloupe (French)	583	8 112[6]	7 898[7]
Barbados (British)	166	6 640	7 819
Grenada (British)	120	—	6 552
Cuba (Spanish)	44 164	2 000	5 200[8]
Totals	60 843	103 151	162 136

Notes: [1] 1742.
   [2] 1767, 1768.
   [3] 1741, 1744, 1745.
   [4] 1755.
   [5] 1770.
   [6] 1730, 1761.
   [7] 1767.
   [8] 1764–8.

[9] St Domingue was still the greatest producer between 1760 and 1770, with Jamaica coming second. By the beginning of the nineteenth century Cuba had become the greatest sugar producer in the Americas.

Cf. R. B. Sheridan, *op. cit.*, Table 2, p. 23. His source same as for Table 1.

Bibliography

Guide

1 *Unpublished primary sources from British archives:*
PRO (Public Record Office), CO, FO, WO, and HO, also T
2 *Printed primary sources*
  a Autobiographies and biographies of ex-slaves
  b Published documents consisting of   (i) Official (British Parliamentary papers, Command papers and Church records)   (ii) Unofficial
3 *Secondary sources*
  a Books: contemporary and recent (in English)
  b Non-English texts   (i) French   (ii) Spanish   (iii) Portuguese
  c Articles in learned journals, reviews and books
4 *Unpublished theses*
5 *Journals*
6 *Newspapers and magazines*

1   *Unpublished primary sources from British archives (Manuscripts) Public Record Office (PRO)*

These consist of a selection of papers and correspondence for the contemporary situation from the British Public Record Office concerning acts and activities of the Colonial, Foreign, Home, Treasury and War Offices. These are indicated as follows respectively: CO, FO, HO, T, and WO.

Bahamas

CO 23/14 Negro trouble — Letter from Fitzwilliam.
    23/62 No. 17 of 9 May 1815 — Relative to Sale of American Negroes in Bahamas.

Barbados

CO 28/18 List of Negroes imported between 1707 and 1726.
CO 28/40 (1728–40) Address of President of the Council of Barbados to the King requesting that importation of foreign sugar into Ireland and the plantations be forbidden except re-exportation from Great Britain, etc.

CO 28/51   Account of slaves imported 27 May 1767–27 Jan. 1768.
CO 28/56   State of feeling in the islands.
CO 30/1   Sixteen Acts of Barbados, 1643–1762 [Laws].

Dominica

CO 72/8   Operation of Act for prohibiting commerce with rebellious colonies, 17 May 1776.

Grenada

CO 101/1   Letter from Brigadier-General Rufane, Acting Lt.-Governor of St Vincent, on conditions on island.
CO 101/13   Disturbance by Caribs who feared being deprived of land.
CO 101/14   Memorial of proprietors of St Vincent now in London, asking for assistance against Caribs, who still hold nearly two-thirds of best lands, 22 June 1770.
CO 101/15   Dangers from Maroons to Owners of Plantations in Grenada. Slave Insurrection in Tobago, 14 Nov., 3 Dec., 1770.
CO 101/16   See especially Hillsborough to Leybourne on Caribs. Caribs to be retained in islands on terms of agreement similar to those made with Maroons in Jamaica, 18 April 1772. Also letter from Leybourne: preparation for expedition against black Caribs, 18 June 1772.
Lord Dartmouth to William Pulteney — troubles with Maroons and Caribs.
Papers on expedition against black Caribs, 1772.
CO 101/17   (1772–4) Papers on black Caribs.
CO 101/18   Mention of ignorance of Assembly of Caribs — papers on grant of land.
CO 101/19   Rivalry and jealousies of competing European powers.

Jamaica

CO 137/11   (1715–16) Papers on the enforcement of Acts of trade, etc.
CO 137/20   (1732–3) Account of the Negro Insurrection.
Papers on Acts regulating slaves and rendering free Negroes and mulattoes more useful.
CO 137/21   (1733–5) Letters, petitions and other papers on levy of duties on Negroes.
CO 137/22   Papers on discrimination against Jews.
CU 137/64   Papers on retention of fugitive slaves in Cuba, 1769.

Leeward Islands

On various subjects such as absenteeism and the role of prelates of the Established Church in the Caribbean as well as the Caribs and cruelty to slaves.
CO 71/4   Memorial from the Island of Dominica through Ag. Governor to Lord

North, First Lord Commissioner of H. M.'s Treasury, and William, Earl of Dartmouth, First Lord of Trade and Plantations and Principal Secretary of State for the Colonies, No. 2, 1 March 1772.

William Steward, Ag. Governor of Dominica and enclosure cited above, containing the 'Humble Memorial of the Commander in Chief and the Council and Assembly of His Majesty's Island of Dominica'.

CO 152/34   Extract of Letter from Governor Burt of Antigua to Lord George Germain, 1 Nov 1777.

CO 71/4   Sir William Young to Rt. Hon. the Earl of Hillsborough, His Majesty's Principal Secretary of State, 28 July 1772 (Comment on Caribs of St Vincent).

CO 71/4   William Steward, Governor of Dominica to William Earl of Dartmouth, 10 March 1773.

CO 78/51   (On absentee landlordism). Petition of the Assembly of Barbados delivered by Agent for the Island, Mr Walker, to the King.
Earl of Hillsborough to Mr Rous, President of the Council of Barbados, Whitehall, 31 Jan 1768.

CO 152/34   William Burt, Governor of the Leeward Islands (St Christopher) 7 May 1779.

CO 101/42   A. C. Ayde, President of the Council of Grenada, to Hon. Earl of Camden, 13 Feb. 1805.

CO 137/128   (Vol. 1 of 1810) Duke of Manchester, Governor of Jamaica, to Rt. Hon. the Earl of Liverpool, 27 May 1810.

CO 152/97   (Vol. 1 of 1811) Hugh Elliot, Governor of the Leeward Islands, to Rt. Hon. the Earl of Liverpool, 9 May 1811, and previous correspondence (on the slave master Hodge, his conviction and execution), 17, 18 May 1811, and enclosures.
Liverpool to Elliot, 12 May 1811 (case of Mr Huggins and cruelty to slaves); also Liverpool to Elliot, 7 Nov. 1811, 27 Jan. 1812.

CO 152/101   Elliot to Earl of Bathurst, 28 Jan. 1813 (on Huggins).

CO 152/101   (Vol 1 of 1813) Elliot to Earl of Bathurst, 27 March 1813, and enclosures concerning the cruelty to slaves by the Rev. William Davies.

CO 153/34   Bathurst to Elliot, 20 Feb. 1813 (concerning the murder of a Negro by Mr E. Huggins, Jr.) in which Bathurst insisted that the trial of Huggins should be beneficial; upholding the principle that the death of a slave, whether a Negro or a freeman, is equally a subject of legal investigation and deserving of the most exemplary punishment.

CO 239/4   General Probyn to Rt. Hon the Earl of Bathurst, 18 March 1818 (concerning cruelty to slaves by the Rev. Mr Rawlins); also Probyn to Bathurst, 21 March 1818.

CO 239/4   Thos. Probyn (Governor) to Mr President Mills, 28 Sept. 1818, and J. C. Mills to Probyn, 2 Oct. 1818 (dealing with the abduction of a freeman into slavery in which the government's disapprobation was expressed, resulting in the man's release.

Reverends and absenteeism in the Caribbean

CO 101/42 of 1805, Governor Fred. Maitland of Grenada to Rt. Hon. Lord Castlereagh, 3 Nov. 1805.
CO 71/43, Governor Barnes to Lord Castlereagh, 8 Dec. 1808.
CO 152/97, Governor Elliot to Earl of Liverpool, 15 May 1871.

Britain and St Domingue

HO 30/2 relating to British dealings with St Domingue.
WO 1 (Several volumes already listed in the body of the work.)
FO 5/25A
CO 318/17
CO 318/20

Treasury Records

T.70/57 folios 45, 45d.
T.70/82, folios, 61, 62, 66d.

2 Printed primary sources

a Autobiographies and biographies of ex-slaves

There is no certainty about the numbers of these ex-slave autobiographies and biographies and they are widely diffused. It has been impossible to locate them in one place and searching for them has involved travel over considerable distance. But as the authentic accounts of those who experienced slavery, they constitute a vital primary source. There is need for two kinds of research: first, to locate as many as are traceable; and second, to use them to evaluate the African diaspora exclusively from the slave perspective. Such studies would provide material for a comparative study of the generally received version of slavery from the perspective of outsiders as against the experience from the perspective of insiders. Far from quoting extensively (with a few exceptions) from these autobiographies and biographies (the latter containing the narratives of ex-slaves as recorded by others), it is an impressionistic gleaning which has been employed in this work to avoid encumbering this volume with quotations from these no less valuable sources. Both the autobiographies and biographies are mixed without subsectional headings.

Alexis, Stephen, *Black Liberator: the Life of Toussaint Louverture* (translated from the French by William Stirling), London, Ernest Benn Ltd, 1949. Numerous biographies of Toussaint exist, but in order to avoid overloading this section the rest have been put in the general bibliography of books. What has been done here is a matter of preference.

Anderson, John, *The Story of the Life of John Anderson, a Fugitive Slave*, London, 1863.

Ball, Charles, *Slavery in the United States: a Narrative of the Life and Adventures of Charles Ball, a Black Man who lived Forty Years in the Navy with Commodore Barney During the Late War. Containing an Account of the Manners and Usages of the*

Planters and Slaveholders of the South; a Description of the Conditions and Treatment of the Slaves; with observations upon the State of Morals Against Cotton Planters and the Perils and Sufferings of a Fugitive Slave, Who twice escaped from Cotton Country, New York, John S. Taylor, 1837; Pittsburgh, J. T. Shyrock, 1853.

Bibb, Henry, *Narrative of the Life and Adventures of Henry Bibb: an American Slave*, New York, 1849 (with an introduction by Lucius C. Matlack); also 1850.

Bradford, Sarah, *Scenes in the Life of Harriet Tubman*, Auburn, N. Y., W. J. Moses, 1869.

—— *Harriet Tubman: the Moses of Her People*, New York, Corinth Books, 1961 (with an introduction by Butler A. Jones).

Brent, Linda, *The Deeper Wrong: Incidents in the Life of a Slave Girl Written by Herself* (L. Maria Child, ed.), London, Hodson & Son & Tweedie, 1862.

Brown, Josephine, *Biography of an American Bondsman (William Wells Brown) by His daughter*, Boston, Mass., R. F. Wallcut, 1856.

Brown, Henry Box, *Narrative of Henry Box Brown, Who Escaped from Slavery Enclosed in a Box 3 Feet Long and 2 Wide. Written from a Statement of Facts Made by himself with Remarks Upon the Remedy of Slavery*. Recorded by Charles Stearns, Boston, Mass., Brown and Stearns, 1849.

Brown, William Wells, *Narrative of the Life of William Wells Brown: an American Slave, Written by Himself*, London, Charles Gilpin, 1850, W. Tegg and Co., 1853.

Craft, William and Ellen, *Running a Thousand Miles for Freedom or The Escape of William and Ellen Craft from Slavery*, London, Strand, William Tweedie, 1860.

Cugoano, Ottobah (*alias* James Stewart), *Thoughts and Sentiments on the Evil and Wicked Traffic of the Slavery and the Commerce of the Human Species humbly submitted to the Inhabitants of Great Britain*, London, 1787.

(Charlton, Dimmock,) *Narrative of Dimmock Charlton, a British-Subject. Taken From the Brig 'Peacock' by the U.S. Sloop 'Hornit', Enslaved While a Prisoner of War, and Retained Twenty-five Years in Bondage*, London, 1859.

Davis, Noah, *A Narrative of the Life of Rev. Noah Davis, a Colored Man, Written by himself at the Age of Fifty-four*, Baltimore, Md., 1859.

Douglass, Frederick, *Narrative of the Life of Frederick Douglass, an American Slave, Written by himself*, Anti-slavery Office, preface by William Lloyd Garrison, Boston, Mass., 4th edn., 1845.

—— *My Bondage and My Freedom, with an introduction by Dr James M'Cune Smith*, New York and Auburn, N. Y., Miller, Orton and Mulligan, 1855.

—— *The Life and Times of Frederick Douglass 1817–1882*, John Lobe, ed., London, Christian Age Office, 1882; another edn. produced by George L. Ruffin of Boston; Hartford, Conn., Park Publishing Co., 1882.

Drew, Benjamin, *The Refugee; or The Narrative of Fugitive Slaves in Canada Related by Themselves, with an Account of the History of the Condition of the Colored Population of Upper Canada*, Boston, Mass., John P. Jewett and Co., 1856.

Equiano, Olaudah (*alias* Gustavus Vassa), *The Interesting Narrative of the Life of Olaudah Equiano or Gustavus Vassa, the African, written by himself*, 2 vols. Jointly bound, London, 1789; and several other edns.

'Mr Fisher' (fictitious name), *Slavery in the United States: a Narrative of the Life and Adventures of Charles Ball, a Black Man Who Lived Forty Years in Maryland, South Carolina, and Georgia as a Slave*, Lewistown, Philadelphia, John W. Shugert, 1836.

Gilbert, Olive, *Narrative of Sojourner Truth: a Bondswoman of Olden Times . . .*

emancipated by the New York Legislature in the early part of the present century with a
history of her labors and correspondence drawn from her 'Book of Life', Battle Creek
Mich., 1878; published New York, Arno Press and the New York Times, 1968.

Grandy, Moses, Life of Moses Grandy, A Slave in the United States of America, Boston,
Mass., Oliver Johnson, 1844.

Green, William, Narrative of Events in the Life of William Green, Springfield, Ohio,
1853.

Griffiths, Mattie, Autobiography of a Female Slave, New York, Redfield, 1857.

Henson, Josiah, The Life of Josiah Henson, formerly a slave, now an inhabitant of
Canada, Boston, Mass., 1844.

—— Father Henson: Story of his Life, (introduced by Walter Fisher), New York,
Corinth Books, 1962.

Horton, George Moses, Hope of Liberty (Poems of George Moses Horton), 1829; later
reprinted as Poems of a Slave (a reprint of Hope of Liberty), Raleigh, N. C., Gales
and Sons, 1838.

Hughes, Louis, Thirty Years a Slave, From Bondage to freedom. The Institution of
Slavery as seen on the plantation and in the home of the planter. Autobiography of Louis
Hughes, Milwaukee, Wis., H. E. Haferkorn, 1897.

Jackson, Andrew, Narrative and Writings of Andrew Jackson of Kentucky; Containing an
Account of His Birth, and Twenty-six years of his Life While a slave: His Escape, Five
Years of Freedom, together with anecdotes relating to slavery; Journal of one year's
Travels, Sketches, etc. Narrated by Himself; Written by a friend, Syracuse, N.Y.,
Daily and Weekly Star Office, 1847.

Jacobs, Mrs (Harriet Brent), Incidents in the Life of a Slave Girl Written by Herself
(L. Maria Child, ed.), Boston, Mass., 1861.

James, Mrs (Mary Prince), The History of Mary Prince, a West Indian Slave. Related
by herself. With a Supplement by the Editor (T. Pringle) To Which is Added, the
Narrative of Asa-Asa, a Captured African, 3rd edn., London, F. Westley and
A. H. Davis, 1831.

Jones, Thomas H., The Experience of Thomas H. Jones, Who was a Slave for Forty-three
Years. Written by a Friend, as Given to Him by Brother Jones, Boston, Mass.,
D. Laing, Jr., 1850.

Lane, Lunsford, Narrative of Lunsford Lane, Formerly of Raleigh, North Carolina,
Published by Himself, Boston, Mass., J. G. Torrey, 1842 and 1848.

Louguen, Jeremain Wesley, The Rev. J. W. Loguen, as a Slave and as a Freeman, A
Narrative of Real Life, Syracuse, N.Y., J. G. K. Truair and Co., 1859.

Mass, Elijah P., Life and History, Louisville, Ky, 1885.

Montejo, Esteban, The Autobiography of a Runaway Slave, translated by Jocasta
Innes, London, Penguin, 1968; also 1970 and 1971.

Neilson, Peter, The Life and adventures of Zamba, an African Negro King, and His
Experience of Slavery in South Carolina, Written by Himself, corrected and
arranged by P. Neilson, London, Smith and Elder and Co., 1847.

Northrup, Solomon, Twelve Years a Slave, Narrative of Solomon Northrup, a Citizen
of New York, kidnapped in Washington City in 1841, and rescued in 1853, from a
Cotton Plantation Near Red River in Louisiana, Buffalo, N.Y., Derry, Orton and
Mulligan, 1853; London, Sampson, Low & Co., 1853 (D. Wilson, ed.).

—— Twelve Years a Slave; the Thrilling Story of a Free Colored Man, Kidnapped in
Washington in 1841, Sold into Slavery, and After Twelve Years' Bondage, Reclaimed
by State Authority from a Cotton Plantation in Louisiana, Philadelphia, Pa.,
J. E. Potter and Co., 18 ?

Pauli, Hertha, *Her Name Was Sojourner Truth: the Thrilling Story of the Famous Slave-born woman who pioneered the fight for human dignity*, New York, Camelot Books; London, Avon.

Pennington, J. W. C., *The Fugitive Blacksmith: or Events in the History of James Pennington, Pastor of a Presbyterian Church, Formerly a slave in the state of Maryland, United States*, New York and London, Charles Gilpin, 1850, 3rd edn.

Pickard, Mrs Kate E. R., *The Kidnapped and the Ransomed. Being the Personal Recollections of Peter Still and His Wife 'Vina' after Forty Years of Slavery*, with an introduction by Rev. Samuel J. May and an appendix by William H. Furness, Syracuse, N.Y., W. T. Hamilton, 1856.

Pierson, Mrs Emily Catherine, *Jamie Parker, The Fugitive*, Hartford, Conn., Brockett, Fuller and Co., 1851.

Platt, Smith H., *The Martyrs, and the Fugitive; or, A Narrative of the Captivity, Sufferings, and Death of an African Family and the Slavery Escape of their Son*, New York, D. Fanshaw, 1859.

Randolph, Peter, *Sketches of a Slave Life*, 1854.

Roper, Moses, *A Narrative of the Adventures and Escape of Moses Roper, from American Slavery*, Preface by Rev. T. Price, D. D., Philadelphia, Pa., Merrihew and Gunn, 1838.

———— *A Narrative of the Adventures and Escape of Moses Roper from American Slavery*, London, 1840.

Singleton, George A. *The Life, Experience and Gospel Labors of the Rt. Rev. Richard Allen, to Which is Annexed the Rise and Progress of the African Methodist Episcopal Church in the United States of America, Written by himself and published at his request*, n.d., New York, Nashville, Tenn.; Abingdon Press, 1960 (re-issue).

Steward, Austin, *Twenty-two Years a Slave and Forty Years a Freeman*, Rochester, N.Y., William Alling, 1857 and 1859.

Still, William, *The Underground Rail Road, Record of Facts, Authentic Narratives, Letters &c. Narrating the Hardships, Hair-breadth Escapes and Death Struggles of the Slaves in their efforts for Freedom as related by themselves and others or witnessed by the author*, Philadelphia, Pa., Porter and Coates, 1872.

Stroyer, Jacob, *My Life in the South*, Salem, Mass., 1890.

Thompson, John, *The Life of John Thompson — A Fugitive Slave, written by himself*, Worcester, Mass., 1856.

Titus, Frances, W., *Narrative of Sojourner Truth*, Boston, Mass., Yerrington, 1850.

Ward, Samuel Ringgold, *The Autobiography of a Fugitive Negro: His Anti-slavery Labours in the United States, Canada, and England*, London, J. Snow, 1855.

Watkins, James, *Narrative of the Life of James Watkins, Formerly a 'Chattel' in Maryland, U.S., Containing an Account of His Escape from Slavery. Together with an Appeal on Behalf of Three Millions of Such 'Pieces of Property', Still Under the Standard of the Eagle*, Bolton, Lancs., Kenyon and Abbatt, 1852.

Watson, Henry, *Narrative of Henry Watson, A Fugitive Slave*, Boston, Mass., Bela Marsh, 1848 (2nd edn., 1849; 3rd edn., 1850).

Wheatley (afterwards Peters), Phyllis, *Poems on Various Subjects Religious and Moral. By Phillis Wheatley, Negro Servant to Mr. John Weatley, of Boston in New England*, London, A. Bell, 1773.

Williams, Isaac, *Aunt Sally; or The Cross the Way to Freedom. A Narrative of the Slave-Life and Purchase of the Mother of Rev. Isaac Williams, of Detroit, Michigan*, Detroit, Mich., also Cincinnati, Ohio, 1858.

b   *Published documents*

(i) Official (British Parliamentary Papers)   **These consist of both House of Commons and House of Lords Sessional Papers containing reports, enactments in the colonies and their application.**

House of Commons Sessional Papers of the Eighteenth Century, Sheila Lambert, ed.; George III: published by Scholarly Resources Inc., Wilmington, Del.; Irish Universities Press, 1975.

Vol. 67: George III: Slave Trade 1788–1790 — Containing 'Copies of Several Acts for the Regulation of Slaves passed in the West India Islands, Ordered and Printed, 1 May, 1789'.

Vol. 68: Minutes of Evidence on the Slave Trade 1788 and 1789 before a Committee of the Whole House.

Vol. 69: Report of the Lords of Trade on the Slave Trade, 1789, Part I.

Vol. 70: Laws at Large respecting Negroes in the West India Islands.

Vol. 71: Minutes of Evidence on the Slave Trade, 1790, Part I.

Vol. 72: Minutes of Evidence on the Slave Trade, 1790, Parts I and II.

Vol. 73: Select Committee on the Slave Trade — Evidence (1790).

House of Commons Sessional Papers, 1696–1834, especially vols. 61–80.

House of Lords Sessional Papers, especially vols. 2, 4, 6, 11, 13, 15, 18, 19, 33 and 34. (Papers concerned with amelioration, compulsory manumission, relations between masters and slaves, the role of the 'West India' lobby in the British Parliament, and emancipation.)

Command Papers

Cmd 7977: Africa No. 3 (1896), Kirk, Brass, The 1895 Revolt — Report of Disturbances (incorporating Correspondence of Chiefs of Brass to Sir C. MacDonald, Nimbe, Brass, dated 14 Feb. 1895).

United Society for the Propagation of the Gospel (U.S.P.G.) London Archives

Fulham Papers, vols. 1 and 11 (covering the eighteenth and nineteenth centuries and containing correspondence and representations to the Bishop of London concerning the religious welfare or lack of it of slaves, 'slave marriages' and reports concerning the high-handedness of the slavocracy extending beyond the period of emancipation).

Parliamentary Papers

Reports from Commissioners of Inquiry on the Administration of Civil and Criminal Justice in the West Indies and South American Colonies, 1825–9:

First Report, 1825, Vol. XV

Second Report, 1826, Vol. XXVI

Third Report, 1826–7, Vol. XXIX.

Published: Irish Universities Press on the West Indies and Administration of Justice.

Acts of the Assembly Passed in the Island of Jamaica from the year 1681 to the year 1769 inclusive, Kingston, 1787, 2 vols.

Acts of the Assembly passed in the Island of Jamaica from the year 1784 to the year 1788 inclusive, Kingston, Jamaica, 1789.

Acts of the Assembly passed in Jamaica from 1770 to 1783, Kingston, Jamaica, 1786.

Parliamentary Papers, Vol. XXX (30), 1790; Forms of cruelty to slaves.

Parliamentary Papers, 1831–2, No. 561, Vol. XLVII — 'Report of a Committee of the House of Assembly Appointed to Inquire into the Cause of and Injury Sustained by the Recent Rebellion, 1832 (Jamaica)'.

Parliamentary Papers, Vol. XXII — Flags of convenience in the clandestine slave trade (1827).

(ii) Unofficial

Aptheker, Herbert (ed.), *A Documentary History of the Negro People in the United States*, New York, Citadel Press, 1951.

Blake, J. W., *Europeans in West Africa, 1450–1560, Documents, etc.*, London, Hakluyt Society, 1942, 2 vols.

Brots, Howard M., (ed.), *Negro Social and Political Thought 1850–1920: Representative Texts*, New York, London, Basic Books Inc., 1966.

Catterall, Helen T. T., (afterwards Mrs Ralph C. H. Catterall), *Judicial Cases Concerning American Slavery and the Negro*, Washington, D. C., Carnegie Institution, 1926–37; reprint, Octagon Press, U.S.A., 1968; also Dublin, Irish Universities Press, 5 vols.

(Churchill, John Walthoe) *Collection of Voyages and Travels etc.*, London, 6 vols., 3rd edn.; John Osborne, London, 1744–8, 6 vols.; another edn., 8 vols.; Thomas Osborne, London, 1752.

Cunard, Nancy (ed.), *Negro Anthology etc.*, London, Wishart and Co., 1934.

Cundall, Frank, and Pietersz, Joseph Luckert, *Jamaica under the Spaniards. Abstracted from the archives of Seville*, Kingston, Jamaica, Institute of Jamaica, 1907.

Diop, Alioune (ed.), First International Congress of Negro Writers and Artists, Presence Africaine, June-Nov. 1956, Paris.

Donnan, Elizabeth, *Documents Illustrative of the History of the Slave Trade to America*, Washington, D. C., Carnegie Institution, 1930–35; reprint New York, Octagon Press, 1965, 4 vols.

Fitzpatrick, J. C. (ed.), *The Writings of George Washington*, Vol. 31, Washington, DC., 1939.

Foner, P. S. (ed.), *The Life and Writings of Frederick Douglass: Pre-Civil War Decade, 1850–1860*, New York, New World Paperbacks, 1950 and 1967, 4 vols.

—— *The Voice of Black America: Speeches by Negroes in the U.S. 1791–1797*, New York, 1972.

Fyfe, C. (ed.), *Sierra Leone Inheritance*, London, Oxford University Press, 1964.

Griggs, E. L. C., and Prater C. H. (eds.), *Henry Christophe – Thomas Clarkson: a Correspondence*, Berkeley and Los Angeles, University of California Press, 1952 (original in French in the Manuscript Department of the British Library).

Harlow, V. T., and Madden, F., *British Colonial Developments 1774–1834: Select Documents*, Oxford, Clarendon Press, 1953.

Hodgkin, Thomas Lionel (ed.), *Nigerian Perspectives: an Historical Anthology*, London, Ibadan, and Accra, Oxford University Press, 1960.

Jameson, J. F. (ed.), *Privateering and Piracy in the Colonial Period: Illustrative Documents*, New York, Macmillan, 1923.

Jefferson, Thomas, *Notes on The State of Virginia . . . in 1781 etc.*, London, J. Stockdale, 1787.

Katz, William Loren (ed.), *Five Slave Narratives*, New York, Arno Press and New York Times, 1968.

Lundy, Benjamin, *The Life, Travels and Opinions of Benjamin Lundy, including His Journeys to Texas and Mexico, with a Sketch of Contemporary Events, and a Notice of the Revolution in Hayti*, Philadelphia, Pa., 1847.

Parish, William (ed.), *The Life, Travels and Opinions of Benjamin Lundy with a sketch of contemporary events, and a notice of the Revolution in Hayti*, Philadelphia, Pa., 1847; reproduced from the *Raleigh Register*, North Carolina, containing extracts from the *Genius of Universal Emancipation* published in 1825 and edited jointly by Lundy and Garrison.

Phillips, Ulrich B., *et al.* (eds.), *A Documentary History of American Industrial Society*, Arthur H. Clark Co., Cleveland, Ohio, 1910, 10 vols., Vols 1 & 2 entitled *Plantation and Frontier 1649–1863*.

Still, William, *The Underground Rail Road*, Philadelphia, Pa., Porter and Coates, 1872.

Thorpe, Earl E., *The Negro in American History: a Taste of Freedom 1854–1927*, II, Encyclopaedia Britannica Education Corp., 1969.

Tragle, Henry Irving, *The Southampton Slave Revolt of 1831: a Compilation of Source Material*, Amherst, Mass., University of Massachusetts Press, 1971.

Wesley, Charles H. (ed.) *The Negro in American History: Slaves and Masters 1567–1854*, Vol. III, Encyclopaedia Britannica Educational Corp., 1969.

Wilberforce, R. I. and S., *The Life of William Wilberforce by his Sons, with Extracts from his Diary, Journal and Correspondence*, London, John Murray, 1838, 5 vols.

Woodson, Carter G., *Negro Orators and their Orations*, Washington, D. C., Associated Publishers, 1925.

—— *The Mind of the Negro as reflected in Letters Written during the Crisis 1800–1860*, Association for the Study of Negro Life and History, Pennsylvania, 1926.

Wright, I. A., *Spanish Documents concerning English Voyages of the Caribbean, 1527–1568, Selected from the Archives of the Indies at Seville*, London, Hakluyt Society, 1929.

—— *Documents concerning English Voyages to the Spanish Main, 1569–1580*.
1. Spanish documents selected from the Archives of the Indies at Seville:
2. English accounts; 3. 'Sir Francis Drake Revived' and others, reprinted, London, Hakluyt Society, 1932.

3 Secondary sources

a Books: contemporary and recent (in English)

These books were written originally in English or translated into English from the original French, Portuguese, Spanish or Dutch by writers whose first language was one of these from which the texts were translated. Earlier and later works are all included in this list without any attempt to separate contemporary from later works.

Adams, Alice Dana, *The Neglected Period of Anti-slavery in America 1808–1831*, Boston and London, 1908.

Adamson, A. H., *Sugar Without Slaves: the Political Economy of British Guyana 1838–1900*, New Haven and London, Yale University Press, 1972.

Ahuma, Attoh, *Memoirs of West African Celebrities, Europe & Co., 1700–1850: With special reference to the Gold Coast*, Liverpool, D. Marples and Co, 1905.

Aimes, Hubert S., *A History of Slavery in Cuba 1511–1868*, New York and London, G. P. Putnam's Sons, 1907; reprint New York, Octagon Books, 1967.

Ajayi, J. F. A., *Christian Missions in Nigeria 1841–1891*, London, Longman, 1965.

BIBLIOGRAPHY

Ajayi, J. F. A., and Crowder, M. (eds.), *History of West Africa*, London and Harlow, Longman, Vol. 1, 1971; Vol. 2., 1974.

Anstey, R. T., *The Atlantic Slave Trade and British Abolition, 1760–1810*, London and Basingstoke, Macmillan Cambridge Commonwealth Series, 1975.

Aptheker, H. A., *American Negro Slave Revolts*, New York, Columbia University Press, 2nd printing, 1944; also, New York, International Publishers, 1963.

_____ *Essays in the History of the American Negro*, New York, International Publishers Inc., 1945 and 1964.

_____ *'One Continual Cry': David Walker's Appeal to the Colored Citizens of the World (1829–30), Its Setting and Its Meaning Together with the full text of the Third and last Editions of the Appeal*, New York, Humanities Press for A.I.M.S., 1965.

_____ *Nat Turner's Slave Rebellion: the Environment, the Event, the Effects, together with the full text of the so-called 'Confessions' of Nat Turner Made in Prison in 1831*, New York, Humanities Press, 1966.

Armistead, Wilson, *A Tribute for the Negro: Being a Vindication of the moral, intellectual and religious capabilities of the coloured portion of mankind*, Manchester, William Irving, 1848.

_____ (ed.), *Five Hundred Strokes for Freedom: a Series of Anti-slavery tracts etc*, Leeds Anti-Slavery Series, No. 26, London, W. & F. Cash, W. Tweedie, 1853.

Asiegbu, Johnson U. J., *Slavery and the Politics of Liberation 1787–1861: a Study of Liberated African Emigration and British Anti-slavery Policy*, London and Harlow, Longman, Green and Co., 1969.

Atkins, John, *A Voyage to Guinea, Brazil and the West Indies in His Majesty's Ships, the Swallow and Weymouth*, London, Vol. 1, 1735; Vol. 2, 1745

Atwood, Thomas, *History of the Island of Dominica*, London, J. Johnson, 1791.

Azurara, Gomes Eannes de, *The Chronicle of the Discovery of Guinea*, English translation by Charles Raymond Beazley and Edgar Prestage, London, Hakluyt Society, 1896, 2 vols.

Bainton, Roland H., *Here I Stand: a Life of Martin Luther*, New American Library, New York, and Scarborough, Ontario; New English Library Ltd., London, 1950.

Balandier, Georges, *Daily Life in the Kingdom of the Kongo from the 16th to the 18th Century*, translated by Helen Weavery, London, George Allen and Unwin Ltd., 1968.

Barbot, Jean (John), 'Description of the Coast of North and South Guinea', in A. and J. Churchill, *Collection of Voyages and Travels*, Vol. V (1682), London, 1732.

Beard, J. R., *The Life of Toussaint L'ouverture, the Negro Patriot of Hayti*, London, Ingram, Cooke and Co., 1853.

Beazley, Raymond C., *Prince Henry the Navigator: the Hero of Portugal and of Modern Discovery with an account of Geographical Progress Throughout the Middle Ages as the Preparation for his Work, 1394–1460 A.D.*, London and New York, G. P. Putnam's Sons and the Knickerbocker Press, 1895.

Beckford, William Thomas, *Remarks upon the situation of the Negroes in Jamaica, impartially made from a local experience of nearly thirteen years in that island*, London, T. & J. Egerton, 1788.

_____ *A Descriptive Account of the Island of Jamaica: with remarks upon the cultivation of the sugar-cane . . . also observations and reflections upon what would probably be the consequences of an abolition of the slave trade, and of the emancipation of slaves*, London, T. & J. Egerton, 1790, 2 vols.

430

Beckwith, Martha Warren, *Black Roadways: a Study of Jamaican Folk Life*, Chapel Hill, University of North Carolina Press, 1929.

Beer, George Louis, *The Commercial Policy of England toward the American Colonies*, New York, Columbus College (Studies in History, Economics and Public Law, Vol. 3, No. 2), 1893.

―― *British Colonial Policy, 1754–1756*, New York, Macmillan Co., 1907.

―― *The Origins of the British Colonial System, 1578–1660*, New York, Macmillan Co., 1908; Peter Smith, Gloucester, Mass., 1959.

―― *The Old Colonial System, 1660–1754*. Part I, *The Establishment of the System, 1660–1688*, New York, Macmillan Co., 1912, 2 vols.

Belby, Henry, *Death Struggles of Slavery: being a Narrative of Facts and Incidents, which Occurred in a British Colony During the Two Years Immediately Preceding Negro Emancipation*, London, Hamilton, Adams and Co., 1853.

Benezet, Anthony, *A Caution and Warning to Great Britain and her Colonies in a short Representation of the Calamitous State of the Enslaved Negroes in the British Dominions (Collected from Various Authors)*, Philadelphia, Pa., Henry Miller, 1766.

―― *Some Historical Account of Guinea . . . with an inquiry into the rise and progress of the slave trade etc.*, Philadelphia, Pa., Joseph Cruikshank, 1771, 2 parts.

―― *The Case of Our Fellow Creatures, the Oppressed Africans*, London, Friends Society, 1783·and 1784.

Bennett, George W., *A History of British Guiana: Compiled from various authorities*, Georgetown, Demerara, L. M 'Dermot, 1875.

―― *An Illustrated History of British Guiana*, Georgetown, Demerara, Richardson & Co., 1866.

Bennett, J. H., Jr., *Bondsmen and Bishops: Slavery and Apprenticeship in the Codrington Plantation, 1710–1838*, Berkeley, University of California Press, 1958.

Besant, Walter, *For Faith and Freedom*, London, Chatto and Windus, 1889, 3 vols.

Bickell, R., *The West Indies as They Are: or a Real Picture of Slavery but more particularly as it exists in the Island of Jamaica; . . . with notes*, London, J. Hatchard & Sons, 1825.

Birmingham, David, *The Portuguese Conquest of Angola*, London, New York, Institute for Race Relations, Oxford University Press, 1965.

―― *Trade and Conflict in Angola: the Mbundu and their Neighbours under the influence of the Portuguese 1483–1790*, Oxford, Clarendon Press, 1966.

Blake, J. W., *European Beginnings in West Africa 1454–1578: a Survey of the First Century of White Enterprise in West Africa with a special emphasis upon the Rivalry of the Great Powers*, London, Royal Empire Society Imperial Studies, No. 14, 1937.

Blassingame, J. W., *The Slave Community: Plantation Life in the Ante-Bellum South*, London, New York, Toronto, Oxford University Press, 1972.

Boahen, A. A., *Topics in West African History*, London, Longman, Green and Co. Ltd., 1966 (Forum Series).

Bosman, Wilhelm, *A New and Accurate Description of the Coast of Guinea*, London, J. Knapton, 1705, 2nd edn., midwinter 1721; a modern version by Frank Cass, London, 1967.

Bourne, E. G., *Spain in America 1450–1580*, New York and London, Harper and Bros, 1904; also New York, Bannes and Noble, 1962.

―― (ed.), *Narrative of the Career of Hernando Soto and the Conquest of Florida as told by a Knight of Elvas and in a relation by L. Hernandes de Biedma,* translated by Buckingham Smith, etc., New York, A. S. Barnes and Co., 1904, 2 vols.

Bovill, Edward W., *Caravans of the Old Sahara: an Introduction to the History of the Western Sudan,* International African Institute, London, 1933.

_____ *The Golden Trade of the Moors,* London, Oxford University Press, 1958; 2nd edn., rev. and with additional material by Robin Hallett, London, Oxford, New York, 1970.

Bowdich, T. E., *Mission from Cape Coast Castle to Ashantee 1817, etc.,* London, John Murray, 1819.

Bowser, F. P., *The African Slave in Colonial Peru 1524–1650,* Stanford University Press, Cal., 1974.

Boxer, C. R., *Salvadore de Sa and the Struggle for Brazil and Angola, 1602–1686,* London, Athlone Press, 1952.

_____ *The Dutch in Brazil 1624–1654,* Oxford, Clarendon Press, 1957.

_____ *Four Centuries of Portuguese Expansion 1415–1823: a Succinct Survey,* No. 3, Johannesburg, Witwatersrand University Press, 1961.

_____ *The Colour Question in the Portuguese Empire, 1415–1825,* London, 1961.

_____ *Race Relations in the Portuguese Colonial Empire 1515–1825,* Oxford, Clarendon Press, 1963.

_____ *Portuguese Society in the Tropics: the Municipal Council of Gao, Macao, Bahia and Luanda 1510–1800,* Madison, University of Wisconsin Press, 1965 .

_____ *The Dutch Seaborne Empire, 1600–1800,* London, Hutchinson and Co., 1965 and 1966.

_____ *The Portuguese Seaborne Empire 1415–1825,* London, Hutchinson & Co., 1969.

_____ *The Golden Age of Brazil 1695–1750: Growing Pains of a Colonial Society,* London, Berkeley and Los Angeles, University of California Press, 1962, 4th printing, 1973.

Brathwaite, Edward, *The Development of Creole Society in Jamaica 1770–1820,* Oxford, Clarendon Press, 1971.

Brawley, Benjamin Griffith, *A Social History of the American Negro, being a History of the Negro Problem in the United States, including a History and Study of the Republic of Liberia,* New York, Macmillan Co., 1921.

Bridenbaugh, Carl, *The Beginning of the American People. No Peace Beyond the Line: the English in the Caribbean, 1624–1690.*

_____ and Robert, *Vexed and Troubled Englishman, 1590–1642,* New York, Oxford University Press, 1968.

Bridges, G. W., *The Annals of Jamaica,* London, John Murray, 1828, 2 vols.

_____ *A Voice From Jamaica: in Reply to William Wilberforce,* London, Longman & Co., 1823.

_____ *Emancipation Unmask'd: In a letter to the Rt. Hon. the Earl of Aberdeen,* London, Edward Churton, 1835.

Brown, E. J. P., *Gold Coast and Asanti Reader, Book 1,* Crown Agents for the Colonies, London, 1920.

Brown, William Wells, *The Escape, or A Leap for Freedom (A Play),* 1835.

_____ *Narrative of William Wells Brown, an American Slave,* London, Charles Gilpin, 1850.

_____ *Three Years in Europe: Places I have Seen and People I have Met, etc.* C. Gilpin, London, 1852.

_____ *The Negro in American Rebellion, His Heroism and His Fidelity,* Boston, Mass., 1867.

Bryant, Joshua, *Account of Insurrection of Negro Slaves in the Colony of Demerara which broke out on the 18th of August, 1823*, Demerara, A. Stevenson, 1824.

Buchner, J. H., *The Moravians in Jamaica: History of the Mission of the United Brethren's Church to the Negroes in the Island of Jamaica from the year 1754 to 1854*, London, Longman & Co., 1854.

Buckmaster, Henrietta, *Let My People Go: the Story of the Underground Railroad and the Growth of the Abolition Movement*, New York and London, Harper and Bros., 1941.

—— *Out of the House of Bondage*, London, Victor Gollancz, 1943.

—— *The Seminole Wars*, New York, Macmillan; London, Collier-Macmillan, 1966.

Burke, Edmund, *Reflections on the Revolution in France and other Writings*, London, New York, Toronto, Oxford University Press, reprint in the World's Classics, 1950 (first version 1790–91).

Burns, Sir Alan C. M., *History of the British West Indies*, London, George Allen and Unwin Ltd, 1954 and 1965.

Butcher, Margaret Just, *The Negro in America Culture, based on materials of Professor Alain Locke*, New York, Alfred. A. Knopf, New American Library, Mentor Books, 1957.

Caldecott, Alfred C., *The Church in the West Indies*, London, S.P.C.K., New York, E. & J. B. Young and Co., 1898.

Campbell, R., *A Pilgrimage to My Motherland: or Reminiscences of a Sojourn among the Egbas and Yorubas of Central Africa in 1859– 60*, London, W. J. Johnson, 1861. Reprinted and ed. by Howard H. Bell as *Search for a Place: Black Separatism and Africa*, 1860; Ann Arbor, Mich., Ann Arbor Paperbacks, University of Michigan Press, 1971.

Canot, Capt. Theodore, *Twenty Years of an African Slaver (also Revelations of a Slave Trader: or Twenty Years Adventures of Captain Canot*, London, Richard Bentley, 1854; reprints 1855, 1856, 1928.

Carpentier, Alejo, *Explosion in the Cathedral*, translated by J. Sturrock, London, Victor Gollancz, 1963 (a novel).

—— *The Kingdom of This World*, translated from the Spanish by Harrier de Unis, London, Victor Gollancz, 1967; Harmondsworth, Penguin Books, 1975.

Charmilly, Coe, Venault de, *Answer by way of letter to Bryan Edwards Esq . . . . a refutation of his Historical Survey of the French Colony of St Domingue*, London, 1797.

Clairmont, F., *Economic Liberalism*, New York, 1960.

Claridge, W. W., *A History of the Gold Coast and Ashanti: Europeans in West Africa, 1450–1560*, (introduced by Sir Hugh Clifford), London, John Murray: 1915, 2 vols; reprinted with new introduction by W. E. F. Ward, London, Frank Cass, 1964.

Clarke, J. H. (ed.), *William Styron's Nat Turner: Ten Black Writers Respond*, Boston, Mass., Beacon Press, 1968, 3rd printing.

Clarkson, Thomas, *An Essay on the Slavery and Commerce of Human Species Particularly the African translated from a Latin dissertation etc.*, London, T. Cadell, J. Phillips, 1786.

—— *An Essay on the Impolicy of the African Slave Trade*, J. Phillips, London, 1788.

—— *The History of the Rise, Progress and Accomplishment of the Abolition of the African Slave Trade by the British Parliament*, London, Hurst, Rees and Orme, 1808, 2 vols.; also Longman and Co.

Cobb, Thomas R. R., *A Digest of the Statute Laws of Georgia in form prior to General Assembly of Session 1851*, Athens, Ga., Christy, Kelsen & Burke, 1851.

―――― *An Inquiry into the Law of Slavery in the United States of America*, Philadelphia, Pa. and Savannah Ga., 1858.

Coffin, Levi, *Reminiscences of Levi Coffin (An Abolitionist) . . . being a brief history of the labours and lifetime in behalf of the Slave etc.*, Cincinnati, Ohio, Western Tract Society, 1876; London, Dyer Bros., 1877; reprinted London, August M. Kelbey, 1968.

Cohen, Chapman, *Christianity, Slavery and Labour*, London, issued for the Secular Society by the Pioneer Press, 3rd edn., 1931.

Coke, Thomas (Rev.), *A History of the West Indies etc.*, Liverpool and London, Nuttal Fisher and Dixon, 3 vols, 1808–11.

―――― *The Case of the Caribbs of St Vincent (containing a short history of the Caribs by George Davidson)*, London, 1787.

―――― *A Journal of The Rev, Dr Coke's Visit to Jamaica, and the Third Tour on the Continent of America*, London, 1789.

Cole, Hubert, *Christophe, King of Haiti*, London, Eyre & Spottiswoode, New York, Viking Press, 1967.

Coleman, D. C. (ed.), *Revisions in Mercantilism*, London, Methuen and Co., 1969.

Coleman, John Winston, *Slavery Times in Kentucky*, Chapel Hill, University of North Carolina Press, 1940.

Collins (Dr), *Practical Rules for the Management of Negro Slaves in the Sugar Colonies*, London, 1803 and 1811.

Cooke, Frances, E., *An American Hero, the Story of William Lloyd Garrison, written for young people.*, London, Swan Sonnenschein, 1888 and 1910.

Corwin, A. F., *Spain and the Abolition of Slavery in Cuba 1817–1886*, Austin, Tex., and London, University of Texas Press (Latin American Monograph No. 9), 1967.

Cory, John, *Observations Upon the Windward Coast of Africa 1805–1806*, London, 1807; new impression, 1968.

Coupland, Reginald, *Wilberforce: a Narrative*, Oxford, Clarendon Press, 1923.

―――― *The British Anti-Slavery Movement*, London, Thornton Butterworth (Home Universities Library), 1933.

Cromwell, J. W., *The Negro in American History: Men and Women Eminent in the Evolution of the American of African Descent*, Washington D.C., The American Negro Academy, 1914.

Crow, Capt. Hugh, *Memoirs of the late Captain Hugh Crow of Liverpool etc.*, London, Longman, Rees, Orme, Brown and Green, 1830; London, Frank Cass, 1970.

Cundall, Frank, *Historica Jamaica*, Kingston, Jamaica, Institute of Jamaica, 1915.

Cunningham, John, *The Quakers From their Origin till the Present Time: an International History*, Edinburgh, John Menzies & Co., 1868.

Curtin, P. D., *The Atlantic Slave Trade: a Census*, Madison, Milwaukee and London, University of Wisconsin Press, 1969.

―――― *Two Jamaicas: the Role of Ideas in a Tropical Colony 1830–1865*, New York, Atheneum, 1970; originally published Cambridge, Mass., Harvard University Press, 1955.

―――― (ed.), *Africa Remembered etc.*, Madison, University of Wisconsin Press, 1967.

Daaku, K. Y., *Trade and Politics on the Gold Coast, 1600–1720: a Study of African Reaction to European Trade*, Oxford, Clarendon Press, 1970.

Dallas, R. C., *The History of the Maroons; from their Origin to the Establishment of their Chief Tribe at Sierra Leone including the Expedition to Cuba and the State of the Island of Jamaica for the last ten years with a succinct History of the Island previous to the period*, London, T. N. Longman and O. Rees, 1803, 2 vols (bound in one).

D'Auvergne, E. B. F., *Human Livestock*, London, Grayson and Grayson, 1933.

Davidson, Basil, *The African Awakening*, London, Jonathan Cape, 1955.

—— *Report on Southern Africa*, London, Jonathan Cape, 1952.

—— *Old Africa Rediscovered*, London, Victor Gollancz, 3rd impression, 1961 (1st and 2nd impressions, 1959 and 1960).

—— *Black Mother: Africa, the Years of Trial*, London, Victor Gollancz, 1961.

—— *The African: an Entry to Cultural History*, London and Harlow, Longman, 1969.

Davies, K. G., *The Royal African Company*, London, Longman, Green and Co., 1957.

Davis, D. B., *The Problem of Slavery in Western Culture*, Ithaca, N.Y., Cornell University Press, 1966; Cornell Paperbacks, 1970.

Davy, J., *The West Indies Before and Since Slave Emancipation*, London, F. G. Cash; Dublin, J. M. Glashan & J. B. Gilpin; Barbados, J. Bowen, 1854.

Deerr, Noel, *The History of Sugar*, London, Chapman and Hall, 1949, 2 vols.

Defoe, Daniel, *Colonel Jack: the History of a Boy That Never Went to School*, London, 1813, 3rd edn.

—— *The Fortunes and Misfortunes of the Famous Moll Flanders Who was Born in Newgate*, London, Westminster Hall, 1722.

Degler, Carl N., *Out of Our Past: the Forces that Shaped Modern America*, New York, Harper and Bros., 1959; revised edn., New York and Evanston, Harper and Row, 1970.

—— *Neither Black Nor White: Slavery and Race Relations in Brazil and the United States*, New York, Toronto, Macmillan Co., 1971.

Delany, M. R., *Official Report of the Niger Valley Exploring Party*, Leeds, J. B. Barry; London, Well and Millington & Co.; 1861; reprinted under the title *Search for a Place: Black Separatism and Africa*, Ann Arbor, Mich., 1971.

Dew, Thomas Roderick, *The Great Question of the Day*, Washington, D.C., Thomas Allen, 1840.

Dike, K. O., *Trade and Politics in the Niger Delta 1830–1855*, Oxford, Clarendon Press, 1956.

Dobson, Narda, *History of Belize*, Harlow, Longman Caribbean, 1973.

Dodd, W. E., *The Old South*, New York, Macmillan Co., 1937.

—— *The Cotton Kingdom*, New Haven, Conn., Yale University Press, 1920 and 1921 (*Chronicle of America* Series No. 27).

Douglass, Frederick, and Ingersoll, R. C., *Proceedings of Civil Rights Mass Meeting held at Lincoln Hall, Oct. 22, 1883, Speeches of Hon. Frederick Douglass and Robert G. Ingersoll*, Washington, D.C., C. P. Farrell, 1883.

Drake, St Clair, *The Redemption of Africa and Black Religion*, Chicago, Ill., The World Press, Institute of the Black World.

Drescher, Seymour, *Econocide: British Slavery in the Era of Abolition*, Pittsburgh, Pa., University of Pittsburgh Press, 1977.

Drewry, W. S. *Slave Insurrections in Virginia 1830–1865: a Dissertation*, Washington, D.C., Neale and Co., 1900.

435

Duberman, M. (ed.), *The Anti-slavery Vanguard: New Essays on the Abolitionists*, Princeton, N.J., Princeton University Press, 1965.

DuBois, W. E. B., *The Suppression of the African Slave Trade to the United States of America, 1638–1870*, Cambridge, Mass., Harvard University Press, 1896, and several edns. For this work Schocken Books, New York, 1969, introduced and ed. by A. Norman Klein.

_____ *Black Folk Then and Now: an Essay in the History and Sociology of the Negro Race*, New York, H. Holt & Co., 1940.

_____ *The Gift of Black Folk: the Negro in the Making of America*, introduced by E. F. McSweeney, Boston, Mass., Stratford Co., 1924; reprint New York, Millwood, 1975.

_____ *The World and Africa*, New York, Viking Press, 1947; reissue, New York, International Publishers Inc., 1965.

_____ *John Brown, the America Crisis Biographies*, Philadelphia, Pa., 1904.

_____ *Dusk of Dawn: an Essay towards an autobiography of a Race Concept*, New York, Harcourt, Brace and Co., 1940.

_____ *Souls of Black Folk: Essays and Sketches*, Chicago, A. C. McClury & Co., 1903, 2nd edn., several edns.

_____ *Black Reconstruction: an Essay towards the History of the Part which Black Folk played in the attempt to Reconstruct Democracy in America, 1860–1880*, New York, Harcourt, Brace & Sons, 1935.

Duffy, James, *Portugal in Africa*, Harmondsworth (Penguin African Library No. AP3), 1962.

_____ *Portuguese Africa*, Cambridge, Mass., Harvard University Press, 1959.

Dumond, D. L., *Anti-slavery Origins of the Civil War in the United States*, Commonwealth Foundation Lectures, University College, London, 2nd term, 1938–9; Ann Arbor, University of Michigan Press; London, Oxford University Press, 1939.

_____ *Anti-slavery: the Crusade for Freedom in America*, Ann Arbor, University of Michigan Press, 1961.

Dunn, Richard S., *Sugar and Slaves: the Rise of the Planter Class in the English West Indies 1624–1713*, London, Jonathan Cape, 1973.

Edwards, Bryan, *Observations on the Maroons etc.*, London, 1796.

_____ *An Historical Survey of the French Colony of St Domingo etc.*, London, 1797.

_____ *A Historical Survey of the Island of St Domingo*, London, 1801.

_____ *The History of the Island of St Domingo* (abridged), Edinburgh, 1802.

_____ *The History, Civil and Commercial, of the British Colonies in the West Indies*, London, 1818–19, 5 vols.

Elkins, Stanley M., *Slavery: a Problem in American Institutional and Intellectual Life*, Chicago, Ill., University of Chicago, 1959.

Estwick, S., *Considerations on the Negro Cause commonly called Address to the Rt. Hon. Lord Mansfield by a West Indian*, (i.e. Sommerset v Knowles and others), London, 1772, 2nd edn., 1773.

Fage, J. D., *A History of West Africa: an Introductory Survey*, Cambridge University Press, 1969; 4th edn. of *An Introduction to the History of West Africa*.

_____ and Oliver, R., *A Short History of Africa*, Harmondsworth, Penguin, 1962.

Falconbridge, Dr Alexander, *An Account of the Slave Trade on the Coast of Africa*, London, J. Phillips, George Yard, Lombard Street, 1788.

Falconbridge, Anna Maria, *Narrative of Voyages to the River Sierra Leone During the Years 1791–1793*, London, 1802, 2nd edn.

Faulkner, Harold U., *American Economic History*, New York, London, Harper Bros., 1949, 6th edn., first published 1921.

Ferris, W. H., *The African Abroad or His Evolution in Western Civilization*, New Haven, Conn., Turtlem Morehouse and Taylor Co., 1912, 2 vols.

Flinter, G. D., *The History of the Revolution of Caracas, with a description of the Llaneros, or people of the plains of South America*, London, 1819.

Floyd, T. S., *The Anglo-Spanish Struggle for Mosquitia*, Albuquerque, N. M., University of New Mexico Press, 1967.

Fogel, R. W., and Eagerman, S. L. (eds.), *The Re-interpretation of American Economic History*, New York, Evanston, San Francisco, London, Harper and Row, 1st edn., 1971.

—— *Time on the Cross: the Economics of American Negro Slavery*, Boston, Toronto, Little Brown and Co., 1974, 2nd printing.

Foner, Laura, and Genovese E. D. (eds.), *Slavery in the New World: a Reader in Comparative History*, Englewood Cliffs, N.J., Prentice-Hall Inc., 1969.

Foote, Commander Andrew H., *Africa and the American Flag*, Folkstone and London, Dawsons of Pall Mall, 1970 reprint; 1st edn., 1854.

Fortescue, Sir J. W., *A History of the British Army*, London, Macmillan and Co.; New York, Macmillan Co., 1899–1930, 13 vols.

Franklin, J. H., *From Slavery to Freedom: a History of Negro America*, New York, Alfred A. Knopf, 1948; 1st printing, 1947; 3rd edn., Vintage Giant, 1967.

—— *The Militant South 1800–1861*, Cambridge, Mass., Belknap Press of Harvard University Press, 1956.

—— *The Emancipation Proclamation*, Edinburgh, Edinburgh University Press, 1963.

Frazier, Elihu (Daggs, R.), *Fugitive Slave Case. District Court of the United States, for the Southern division of Iowa, Burlington, June Term, 1858; R. Daggs Vs Elihu Frasier et alls. Trespass on the Case Reported by Geo Frazee*, Morgan and M'Kenny, Burlington, Iowa, 1850.

Frazier, Franklin E., *The Negro in the United States*, New York, Macmillan Co., 1957.

—— *The Negro Church in America*, New York, Schocken Books, 1963.

Freidenthal, Richard, *The White Gods*, translated from the German by Charles Hope Lumley, New York and London, Harper and Bros., 1931.

Freyre, Gilberto, *The Masters and the Slaves (Casa-Grande y Senzala): Study in the Development of Brazilian Civilization, translated from the Portuguese by Samuel Putnam, 4th edn.*, New York, Alfred, A. Knopf, 1946.

Fyfe, C., *A History of Sierra Leone*, London, Oxford University Press, 1962; reprinted, 1968.

Fynn, J. R., *Asante and Its Neighbours 1700–1807*, London, Longman and North Western University Press, Legon History Series, 1971.

Gara, Larry, *The Liberty Line: the Legend of the Underground Railroad*, University of Kentucky Press, Lexington, Ky., 1961.

Garrison, W. L., *An Address on the Progress of the Abolition Cause delivered before the African Abolition Freehold Society of Boston etc.*, Boston, Mass., 1832.

—— *Thoughts of African Colonization, or an . . . exhibition of the principles and purposes of the American Colonization Society etc.*, Boston, Mass., 1832.

_____ 'An Address delivered at the Broadway Tabernacle, New York, August, 1838', Boston, Mass., 1838.

_____ 'West India Emancipation: a Speech delivered at Abington, Massachussetts etc.', Boston, Mass., 1854.

Garrison, W. P. G. and F. J. G., _William Lloyd Garrison 1805–1879, the Story of his Life told by his Children_, New York, Century and Co., 1883, 2 vols.

Genovese, E. D., _The Political Economy of Slavery: Studies in the Economy and Society of the Slave South_, New York, Pantheon Books, 1965: London, MacGibbon and Kee, 1966, 1967.

_____ _In Red and Black: Marxian Explorations in Southern and Afro-American History_, London, Toronto, New York, Allen Lane: Penguin 1971; originally published New York, Pantheon Books, 1971.

_____ (ed.), _The Slave Economy of the Old South: Selected Essays in Economic and Social History_, Baton Rouge, Louisiana State University Press, 1968.

_____ _The World the Slave Holders Made: Two Essays in Interpretation_, London, Allen Lane: Penguin, 1970; New York, 1969.

_____ _Roll Jordan Roll: the World the Slaves Made_, New York, Vintage Books, 1976.

Gibson, Edmund, _Two Letters of the Lord Bishop of London_, London, 1727, 1729.

Giddings, J. R., _Exiles of Florida or The Crimes Committed by Our Government Against The Maroons who fled from South Carolina and other Slave States Seeking Protection Under Spanish Law_, Columbus, Ohio, Follett, Foster and Co., 1858.

Goodell, William, _The American Slave Code in Theory and Practice. Its Distinctive Features Shown by Its Statutes, Judicial Decisions and Illustrative Facts_, New York, American & Foreign Anti-slavery Society, 1853, 2nd edn.; also several other publications.

_____ _American Slavery: a Formidable Obstacle to the Conversion of the World_, New York, American & Foreign Anti-Slavery Society, 1854.

Goveia, Elsa V., _A Study of the Historiography of the British West Indies to the End of the 19th Century_, Instituto Panamericano de Geografia e Historia, Commission de Historia 78, Mexico, 1956.

_____ _Slave Society in the British Leeward Islands at the End of the Eighteenth Century_, New Haven, Conn., and London, Yale University Press, 1965.

Graham, Maria (afterwards Calcott), _Journal of a Voyage to Brazil and residence there during . . . the years 1821–1823_, London, 1824.

Grant, Douglas, _The Fortunate Slave: an Illustration of African Slavery in the Early Eighteenth Century_, London, New York, and Toronto, Oxford University Press, 1968.

Gray, L. C., _History of Agriculture in the Southern United States of America to 1860_, Washington, D.C., Carnegie Institution, Publication n. 430, 1933.

Greenidge, C. W. W., _Slavery_, London, George Allen and Unwin, 1958.

Groot, Silvia W. De, _Djuka Society and Social Change: History of an Attempt to Develop a Bush Negro Community in Surinam 1917–1926_, Assen, Netherlands, Van Gorcum and Co., Dr H. J. Prakke and H. M. G. Prakke, 1969.

Harlow, V. T., _A History of Barbados, 1625–1685_, Oxford, Clarendon Press, 1926.

Harper, Lawrence A., _The English Navigation Laws: Seventeenth Century Experiment in Social Engineering_, New York, Columbia University Press, 1939.

Hart, Ansel, Jr., _The Life of George William Gordon_, Cultural Heritage Series, Vol. 1, Kingston, Jamaica, Institute of Jamaica, 1972.

Hawkins, Joseph, _A History of a Voyage to the Coast of Africa and Travels in the_

Interior of that Country — Containing descriptions of the Climate and Inhabitants and interesting particulars concerning the Slave Trade, Troy, N.Y., Luther Pratt, 1787, 2nd edn.

Hazard, Samuel, *Santo Domingo: Past and Present with a glance at Hayti*, London, Sampson and Low, Marston, Low and Searle, 1873.

Heckscher, Eli F., *Mercantilism*, 2 vols, translated from the German by Mendel Shapiro, revised by E. F. Soderland, London, 1951, 1955, 1956.

Henriques, Fernando, *Jamaica: Land of Wood and Water*, London, MacGibbon and Kee, 1960.

Henry, H. M., *The Police Control of the Slave in South Carolina, a dissertation etc.*, Emory, Va, 1914.

Herbert, H. A., *The Abolition Crusade and Its Consequences*, New York, Charles Scribner's Sons, 1912.

Herskovits, M. J., *The Myth of the Negro Past*, New York and London, Harper and Bros., 1941.

—— *Life in a Haitian Valley*, New York, Alfred A. Knopf Inc., 1937.

—— and F. S., *Rebel Destiny: Among the Bush Negroes of Dutch Guiana,,* New York and London, McGraw Hill Book Co., 1934.

Higham, C. S. S., *The Development of the Leeward Islands under the Restoration, 1660–1688*, Cambridge University Press, 1921.

Hobson, C. K., *The Export of Capital*, London, Constable and Co., 1914, 1963.

Hodgson, Eva M., *Second Class Citizens, First Class Men*, Hamilton, Bermuda, n.d. (1968?)

Holloway, David, *Lewis and Clark and the Crossing of North America, The Great Explorers*, Sir Vivian Fuchs (ed.), London, Weidenfeld and Nicolson, 1974.

Holly, Rev. T. J., *A Vindication of the Capacity of the Negro Race for Self-Government and Civilized Progress etc.*, New Haven, Conn., 1857.

Hopkins, A. G., *An Economic History of West Africa*, London, Longman, 1973.

Hurd, J. C., *The Law of Freedom and Bondage in the United States*, Boston, Mass., and New York, 1858, 2 vols.

Hurwitz, S. J. and Edith F., *Jamaica: a Historical Portrait*, London, Pall Mall Press, 1971.

Ikime, Obaro, *Niger Delta Rivalry: Itsekeri-Urhobo Relations and the European Presence 1884–1936*, London, Longman, 1969.

Jahn, Janheinz, *Muntu: an Outline of Neo-African Culture*, translated by Marjorie Grene, London, Faber and Faber, 1961.

James, C. L. R., *The Black Jacobins, Toussaint Louverture and the San Domingo Revolution* (original edn., London, Secker and Warburg, 1938), New York and London, Vintage Books, 1963, 2nd edn.

Jameson, Robert Francis, *Letters from the Havana during the years 1820; containing an account of present state of the island of Cuba, and observations of the slave trade*, Printed for John Miller, London, 1821.

Jay, William R., *Miscellaneous Writings on Slavery*, Boston, Mass., 1853.

Jenkins, S. W., *Pro-Slavery Thought in the Old South*, Chapel Hill, University of North Carolina Press, 1935.

Jobson, Richard, *The Golden Trade or A Discovery of the River Gambia and the Golden Trade of the Aethiopians*, 1623, reprint; Charles G. Kingsley (ed.), Teignmouth, Devonshire, 1904.

Johnson, James B., *Race Relations in Virginia and Miscegenation in the South, 1776–1860*, Amherst, Mass., 1979.

Johnson, J. C. DeGraft, *African Glory: the Story of Vanished Negro Civilization*, New York, Praeger; London, Watts and Co., 1954. Reprint, New York, Walker and Co., n.d.

Johnston, Sir Harry Hamilton, *The Negro in the New World*, London, Methuen and Co., 1910.

Jones, G. I., *The Trading States of the Oil Rivers: a Study of Political Development in Eastern Nigeria*, London, Ibadan and Accra, Oxford University Press, 1963.

―― *Efik Traders of Old Calabar: the Political Organisation of Old Calabar containing the Diary of Antera Duke an Efik Slave-trading Chief of the Eighteenth Century*, Daryll Forde (ed.), London, Oxford University Press, 1956 and 1957.

Jones, Wynne, *Black Emperor: the Story of Toussaint Louverture*, London, George G. Harrap & Co., 1949.

Jordan, Winthrop, *White Over Black: American Attitudes towards the Negro 1550–1812*, Chapel Hill, University of North Carolina Press; Institute of Early American History and Culture, Baltimore, Md., 1968; Penguin, Baltimore, Md., 1969 and 1971.

July, R. W., *The Origin of Modern African Thought*, London, Faber and Faber, 1968.

Kemble, Frances Anne, (afterwards Butler) *Journal of a Residence on a Georgian Plantation in 1838–1839*, London, Longman, Green, Longman, Roberts & Green, 1863.

Kerr, Madeline, *Personality and Conflict in Jamaica*, Liverpool, Liverpool University Press, 1952; also London, Collins; Kingston, Jamaica, Sangster Bookshop, 1963.

Kidder, Daniel P., and Fletcher, James C., *Brazil and the Brazilians Portrayed in Historical and Descriptive Sketches*, Philadelphia, 9th edn., 1857; rev., London, 1879.

Klein, H. S., *Slavery in the Americas: a Comparative Study of Virginia and Cuba*, Chicago, Ill., Quadrangle Books, 1971.

Klingberg, F. J., *The Anti-slavery Movement in England: a Study of English Humanitarianism*, New Haven, Conn., Yale Historical Publications, Miscellany 17, New Haven, Conn., 1926.

―― *Anglican Humanitarianism in Colonial New York*, Philadelphia, Pa., 1940.

―― (ed.), *Codrington Chronicle: an Experiment in Anglican Altruism on a Barbados Plantation 1710–1834*, Berkeley and Los Angeles, University of California Press, 1949.

Knorr, Klaus K., *British Colonial Theories 1570–1850*, London, Frank Cass and Co. Ltd, 1963; 1st impression, 1944.

Korngold, Ralph, *Citizen Toussaint*, London, Victor Gollancz, 1945.

Labat, Jean Baptiste, (Young C. E., and Larsen. K. H.) *The Pirates' Priest: the Life of Père Labat in the West Indies 1695–1705*, London, 1965.

―― *A Voyage to Guinea, and the adjacent islands in 1725 by the Chevalier des Marchais*, London, 1745.

―― *The Memoirs of Père Labat, 1693–1705, translated and abridged from Nouveaux Voyages aux Isles d'Amérique*, by John Eaden, with an introduction by Philip Grosse, London, Constable, 1931.

Lane, A. J. (ed.), *The Debate Over Slavery: Stanley Elkins and His Critics*, Urbana, Chicago and London, University of Illinois Press, 1971.

Latrobe, J. H. B., *Memoir of Benjamin Banneker, etc.* Maryland Historical Association, Baltimore, Md., 1845.

Lawrence, A. W., *Trade Castles and Forts of West Africa*, London, Cape, 1963.

Lenin, V. I., *Imperialism*, Petrograd, 1st edn., 1916.

Lewis, Michael Arthur, *The Hawkins Dynasty: Three Generations of a Tudor Family*, London, Allen and Unwin, 1969.

Lewis, M. G., *Journal of a Residence among the Negroes of the West Indies*, London, John Murray, 1845.

_____ *Journal of a West India Proprietor . . . 1815–17 kept during a residence in the Island of Jamaica*, London, 1834; G. Routledge & Sons, 1929.

Ligon, Richard, *A True and Exact History of the Island of Barbados, 1647–1650*, London, Humphrey Moseley, 1657; also, Peter Parker and Thomas Gray, 1673.

_____ *Memoirs of the First Settlement of the Island of Barbados*, London, 1743; reprinted Barbados, 1891.

Lloyd, Alan, *The Drums of Kumasi: the Story of the Ashanti Wars*, London, Longman, Green and Co., 1964.

Locke, Mary Stoughton, *Antislavery in America from the Introduction of African Slaves to the Prohibition of the Slave Trade (1619–1808)*, Radcliffe College Monographs, No. 11, Boston, Mass., Ginn and Co. 1901; earlier edn. 1894.

Loggins, Vernon *The Negro Author: His Development in America to 1900*, New York, Columbia University Press, 1931, 1959; reprint Port Washington, N.Y., and New York, Kennikat Press Inc., 1964.

Long, Edward, *Candid Reflections upon the Judgment lately awarded by the Court of King's Bench. The Negro Cause, in re. James Sommersett by a Planter*, London, 1772.

_____ *The History of Jamaica: General Survey of the Ancient and Modern State of that Island with Reflections etc.*, London, printed by T. Lowndes, 1774, 3 vols.

Lucas, C. P., *Introduction to a Historical Geography of British Colonies*, Oxford, 1887.

McDougall, M. G., *Fugitive Slaves 1619–1865*, Fay House Monographs No. 3, prepared under the direction of Albert Bushnell Hart, Boston, Mass., Ginn and Co., 1891.

McLeod, John, *A Voyage to Africa with some account of the Manners and Customs of the Dahomian People*, John Murray, London, 1820.

Macmillan, W. M., *Warning from the West Indies*, London, Faber and Faber, 1938.

McWilliam, H. O. A., *The Development of Education in Ghana*, London, Longman, Green and Co., 1959.

Mannix, D. P., and Cowley M., *Black Cargoes: a History of the Atlantic Slave Trade, 1518–1865*, New York and London, Longman, 1963.

Marshall, Andrew, *Brazil*, London, Thames and Hudson, 1966.

Martin, Bernard, and Spurrell, Mark (eds.), *The Journal of a Slave Trader 1750–54 with Newton's Thoughts upon the African Slave Trade*, London, Epworth Press, 1962.

Martin, E., (ed.), *Journal of a Slave Dealer: 'A View of Some Remarkable Axcedents in the Life of Nics. Owen on the Coast of Africa and America from the year 1746 to the year 1757'*, London, 1930.

Martineau, Harriet, *Society in America*, New York, Saunders and Otley, 1837, 2 vols.

Mathieson, W. L., *British Slavery and Its Abolition 1823–1849*, London, 1926.

_____ *British Slave Emancipation 1838–1849*, London, 1932.

_____ *The Sugar Colonies and Governor Eyre 1849–1866*, London, Longman, 1936.

_____ *Great Britain and the Slave Trade 1839–1865*, London, 1929; also New York, Octagon Books, 1967.

Matthews, John, *Voyage to the River Sierra Leone on the Coast of Africa . . . during the years 1785, 1786, 1787 (Lieutenant of the Royal Navy)*, London, B. White and Sons, 1788.

Maury, Ann, *Memoirs of a Huguenot Family*, translated by J. Fontaine, Williamsburg, Va. 1853.

Mellor, G. R., *British Imperial Trusteeship 1783–1850*, London, 1951.

Merivale, Herman, *Lectures on Colonisation and Colonies Delivered 1841–42*, rev. 2nd edn., 1861, for Oxford University Press, London, 1928.

Miers, S., *Britain and the Ending of the Slave Trade*, London and Harlow, Longman, 1973.

Minchinton, W. E., *The Port of Bristol in the Eighteenth Century*, Bristol, Bristol Branch Historical Association, 1962.

—— *The Growth of English Overseas Trade in the Seventeenth and Eighteenth Centuries*, London, Methuen, 1969.

Moreau, De Saint-Mery, M. L. E., *A Topographical and Political Description of the Spanish Part of Saint-Domingo*, Philadelphia, Pa., 1790, 2 vols.

Morel, E. D., *The Black Man's Burden*, London and Manchester, National Labour Press, 1919.

Moreton, J. B., *West India Customs and Manners (containing strictures on the Soil, Cultivation, Produce, Trade, Officers, and Inhabitants with the method of establishing and conducting a Sugar Plantation)*, new ed., printed for J. Parsons, London, 1793.

Mörner, Magnus, *Race Mixture in the History of Latin America*, Boston, Mass., Little Brown and Company, 1967.

—— *Race and Class in Latin America*, New York, Columbia University Press, 1971.

Newbury, C. W., *The Western Slave Coast and Its Rulers: European Trade and Administration among the Yoruba and Adja-speaking peoples of South-west Nigeria, Dahomey and Togo*, Oxford, Clarendon Press, 1961.

Newton, A. P., *The European Nations in the West Indies 1493–1699*, London, Adam and Charles Black, 1933, reprint 1966.

Newton, John, (Rector of St Mary Woolnoth), *Journal of a Slave Trader 1750–1754*, London, 1788.

Nugent, Maria (Lady), *A Journal of a Voyage and Residence in the Island of Jamaica from 1801 to 1805 and of subsequent events in England from 1805 to 1811*, London, 1839, 2 vols.

Nyakatura, J. W., *Anatomy of an African Kingdom: a History of Bunyoro-Kitara*, G. N. Uzoigwe (ed.), Anchor Books, Anchor Press and Doubleday, Garden City, N.Y., 1973.

Nye, R. B., and Murpurgo, J. E., *A History of the United States:* Vol. 1, *The Birth of the United States*, Vol. 2, *The Growth of the United States*, Harmondsworth, Penguin, 1955.

Oldmixon, J., *The British Empire in America*, London, 1708 and 1741, 2 vols.

Oliver, R., and Mathew G. *History of East Africa*, Vol. 1, Oxford, Clarendon Press, 1963.

Olivier, Sir Sydney H., 'Imperial Trusteeship', Fabian Tract no. 230, London, 1929.

—— *The Myth of Governor Eyre*, London, 1933.

—— *Jamaica: the Blessed Island*, London, Faber and Faber, 1936.

Olmsted, F. L., *Journey in the Seaboard Slave States*, New York, Dix and Edwards, 1856.

—— *A Journey in the Back Country*, London, Sampson Low, 1860.

—— *The Cotton Kingdom*, 1862.

Ortiz, Fernando, *Cuban Counterpoint — Tobacco and Sugar*, New York, 1947.

Owen, Nicholas, *Journal of A Slave Trader: a View of Some Remarkable Axcedents in the Life of Nics Owen on the Coast of Africa and America from the Year 1746 to the Year 1757*; Evangeline Martin (ed.), London, George Routledge and Sons, 1930.

Palgrave, W. G., *Dutch Guiana*, London, Macmillan and Co., 1876.

Pares, Richard, *War and Trade in the West Indies, 1739–1763*, Oxford, Clarendon Press, 1936.

_____ *Yankees and Creoles: the Trade Between North America and the West Indies Before the American Revolution*, London, Longman Green & Co., 1956.

_____ *Merchants and Planters*, Cambridge University Press, 1960.

Park, Mungo, *Journal of Travels in the Interior Districts of Africa . . . 1795, 1796, and 1797*, London, 1799, 2 vols. 1816, edn. 1817, Dublin, 1821 and 1825.

Parry, J. H., *The Age of Reconnaissance*, London, Weidenfeld and Nicolson, 1963.

_____ *The Spanish Seaborne Empire*, London, Hutchinson, 1966; 2nd edn., 1967.

_____ *The Discovery of South America*, London, Paul Elek Press, 1979.

_____ and Sherlock, P. M., *A Short History of the West Indies*, London, Macmillan; New York, St Martin's Press, 1966.

Patterson, Orlando, *The Sociology of Slavery: an Analysis of the Origins, Development and Structure of Negro Slave Society in Jamaica*, London, MacGibbon and Kee, 1967.

Payne, (Rev.) Daniel, *The History of the African Methodist Episcopal Church*, New York, reprint, 1968.

Pélissier, René, and Wheeler, Douglass L., *Angola*, London, Pall Mall Library of African Affairs.

Pennington, J. W. C., *The Reasonableness of the Abolition of Slavery etc.*, Hartford, Conn., Case Tiffany and Co., 1856.

Penson, Lilian M., *The Colonial Agent of the British West Indies*, London, 1924.

_____ *The West Indies and the Spanish American Trade 1713–1748*, Cambridge History of the British Empire, Vol. 1, 1929.

Perham, M., *The Colonial Reckoning*, London, 1963.

Philaleth, Demoticus (pseud.), *Yankee Travels Through the Island of Cuba or the Men and Government, The Laws and Customs of Cuba as Seen by American Eyes*, New York, D. Appleton & Co., 1856.

Phillips, Capt. Thomas, Commander of the Ship *Hannibal* of London, 1693, 1694, 'A Journal of a Voyage from England to Barbadoes, in the Years 1693, and 1694', in Churchill, *Collection of Voyages*, Vol. 6, London, 1732.

_____ *Journal of a Voyage Made in the Hannibal of London, Ann. 1693, 1694 from England to Cape Monseradoe in Africa thence along the Coast of Guiney to Widaw, the Island of St Thomas, And So Forward to Barbadoes, with a cursory account of the Country, the People and their Manners, Forts, Trade and co., Abstract of a Voyage Along the Coast of Guinea to Widaw*, Vol. 2, 1745.

Phillips, Ulrich Bonnell, *American Negro Slavery: a Survey of the Supply, Employment and Control of Negro Labor as Determined by the Plantation Regime*, New York and London, D. Appleton and Co., 1918.

_____ *The Slave Economy of the Old South: Selected Essays in Economic and Social History* (E. D. Genovese, ed.), Baton Rouge, Louisiana State University Press, 1966.

Phillips, Wendell, *On the murder of Lovejoy*, Faneuil Hall, Boston, Mass., 8 Dec. 1837, in Alexander Johnson (ed.), *Representative American Orations*, New York and London, G. P. Putnam's Sons, 1884, pp. 33–45.

Pierson, Donald, *Negroes in Brazil: a Study of Race Contact at Bahia*, Chicago, Ill., University of Chicago Press, 1942 and 1947.

Pinckard, Dr George, *Notes on the West Indies Written during the Expedition Under the Command of the Late General Sir Ralph Abbecromby, including observations on the Island of Barbados, and the Settlements captured by the British Troops Upon the Coast of Guiana; likewise Remarks relating to the Creoles and Slaves of the Western Colonies, and the Indians of South America; with Occasional Hints regarding the Seasoning, or Yellow Fever of Hot Climates*, London, Longman, Hurst, Rees and Orme, 1806, 3 vols.

Pitman, Emma Raymond, *The West Indies*, London, Cassell, 1881.

Pitman, F. W., *The Development of the British West Indies 1700–1763*, New Haven, Conn., Yale Historical Studies Vol. 4, 1917.

Polanyi, Karl, *Dahomey and the Slave Trade: an Analysis of an Archaic Economy*, foreword by P. Bohannan, Seattle and London, University of Washington Press, 1966; 2nd printing, 1968.

Poley, A. P., *The Imperial Commonwealth*, London, 1921.

Pope Hennessy, James, *Sins of the Father: the Atlantic Slave Traders 1441–1807*, London, Weidenfeld and Nicolson, 1967; Sphere Books, 1970.

Price, R., (ed.) *Maroon Societies: Rebel Slave Communities in the Americas*, Anchor Books, Anchor Press and Doubleday, New York, 1973.

Priestly, Margaret, *West African Trade and Coast Society: a Family Study*, London, Oxford University Press, 1969. (A Study of the Brew family.)

Quarles, Benjamin, *Frederick Douglass*, New York, 1948, 1968.

—— *The Negro in the Civil War*, 1953.

—— *The Negro in the Making of America*, New York and London, Collier-Macmillan, 1968.

—— *Black Abolitionists*, New York, Oxford University Press, 1969.

Quincy, Edmund, *An Examination of the Charges of Lewis Tappan etc. Against the America Anti-Slavery Society*, London, Whitfield, 2nd edn., 1852.

Ragatz, L. J., *The Old Plantation System in the British Caribbean*, London, Bryan Edwards Press, 1925, 1926, 1929 and 1953.

—— *Absentee Landlordism in the British Caribbean 1750–1833*, London, 1931.

—— *The Fall of the Planter Class in the British Caribbean 1763–1833*, London and New York, Century Co., 1928, 1929.

Rainsford, Marcus, *St Domingo or an Historical, Political and Military Sketch of the Black Republic etc.*, London, 1802.

—— *A Memoir of Transactions that Took Place in St Domingo in 1799 etc.*, London, 1802.

—— *An Historical Account of the Black Empire of Haiti Comprehending a view of the Principal Transactions in the Revolution of Saint Domingo with its Ancient and Modern State*, London, James Cundee, 1805.

Ramos, Arthur, *The Negro in Brazil*, Washington, D.C., Associated Publishers, 1939, 1946 (47).

Ranger, T. O. (ed.), *Emerging Themes of African History*, Nairobi, Kenya, East African Publishing House, 1968.

—— *Aspects of Central African History*, London, 1969.

Rattray, R. S., *Ashanti Law and Constitution*, Oxford, Clarendon Press, 1929.

Rawick, George. P., *The American Slave — a Composite Autobiography: From Sundown to Sun up: the Making of the Black Community*, Westport, Conn., Greenwood Publishing Co., 1972.

Raynal, (Abbé) G. T. F., *A Philosophical and Political History . . . West Indies*, trans. from the French by J. O. Justamond, London and Edinburgh, 1792 and 1798, 6 vols.

_____ *Slave Trade: a Full Account of this species of Commerce, etc.*, London, 1792.

Rees, J. F., *Mercantilism and the Colonies*, 1929.

Rees, T. M., *A History of the Quakers in Wales and their Immigration to North America* Carmarthen, W. Spurrell & Sons, 1925.

Reynolds, Edward, *Trade and Economic Change on the Gold Coast 1807–1874*, London and New York, Longman and Longman Inc., 1974.

Rhodes, J. F., preface and notes to H. S. Herbert's *The Abolition Crusade and Its Consequences*, New York, Macmillan, 1919.

Robertson, Robert *A Letter to the Rt Revd the Lord Bishop of London from an inhabitant of His Majesty's Leeward Caribbean Islands. Containing some considerations on his Lordship's two letters of May 19, 1727. The first to the masters and mistresses of families in the English plantations abroad; the second to the missionaries there. In which is inserted, a short essay concerning the conversion of the negro slaves . . . written by the same inhabitant*, London, J. Wilford, 1730.

Rodney, Walter, *West Africa and the Transatlantic Slave Trade*, Dar es Salaam, Tanzania, Historical Association of Tanzania, 1966.

_____ *A History of the Upper Guinea Coast, 1545–1880*, Oxford, Clarendon Press, 1970.

_____ *How Britain Underdeveloped Africa*, Tanzania and London, Bogle L'Ouverture Press, 1972.

Rodrigues, José Honorio, *Brazil and Africa*, translated by R. A. Mazzara and S. Hileman, Berkeley, University of California Press, 1965.

Rosher, W. G. F., *The Spanish Colonial System*, translated by E. G. Bourne, London, Longman, Hurst, Rees, Orme and Brown, 1904.

Roughley, Thomas, *The Jamaica Planter's Guide or a System of Planting etc.*, London, 1823.

Rout, Leslie, B., Jr., *The African Experience in Spanish America, 1502 to the Present Day*, Cambridge, London, New York, and Melbourne, Cambridge University Press, 1976.

Rupp, E. G., and Drewery, Benjamin, *Martin Luther, Documents of Modern History*, London, Edward Arnold, 1970, reprint 1979.

St John, Sir Spenser B., *Hayti or The Black Republic*, London, Smith, Elder and Co., 1884.

Sarbah, John Mensah, *Fanti National Constitution*, London, Clowes and Sons, 1897.

_____ *Fanti Customary Law*, London, Clowes and Sons, 1906.

[Schaw, Janet,] *Journal of a Lady of Quality, Being a Narrative of a Journey from Scotland to the West Indies, North Carolina and Portugal 1774–1776*, New Haven, Conn., Yale University Press; Oxford University Press, 1921; London, Humphrey Milford, 1921, 1939.

Schomburgk, Sir R. H. *A Description of British Guiana*, London, 1840.

—— *The Discovery of the large, rich and beautiful Empire of Guiana etc.*, London, 1848.

—— *The History of Barbados*, London, 1848.

Seeber, Edward, D., *Anti-slavery Opinion in France during the Second Half of the Eighteenth Century* Baltimore, Md., Johns Hopkins University Press; London, Oxford University Press, 1937.

Semmel, Bernard, *The Governor Eyre Controversy*, London, MacGibbon and Kee, 1962.

Sewel, William, *The History of the Rise, Increase and Progress of the Christian people called Quakers Intermixed with Several Remarkable Occurrences*, London, 1772.

Sharp, Grenville, *An Appendix to the Representation (Printed in the Year 1769) of Tolerating Injustice and Dangerous Tendency of Slavery, or of Admitting the least Claim of Private Property in the Persons of Men in England*, London, 1772.

Sheridan, R. B., *The Development of the Plantations to 1750, an Era of West Indian Prosperity 1750–1775 (Chapters in Caribbean History)*, Barbados, Caribbean Universities Press, 1970.

—— *Sugar and Slavery*, Baltimore, Md., Johns Hopkins University Press, 1974.

Shyllon, F. O., *Black Slaves in Britain*, London, New York and Ibadan, Institute of Race Relations, 1974.

Sims, P. *Trouble in Guyana*.

Simmons, (Rev.) W. J., *Men of Mark, Eminent, Progressive and Rising*, New York, 1887 and 1968.

Sinclair, William Angus, *The Aftermath of Slavery*, Boston, Mass., Small, Maynard & Co., 1905.

Smith, J., *Trade and Travels in the Gulph of Guinea*, London, 1851.

Smith, William, *A New Voyage to Guinea*, London, 1744; 2nd edn., London, F. Cass, 1967.

Snelgrave, Capt. William, *A New Account of Some Parts of Guinea and the Slave Trade*, London, 1737; reprint, London, Frank Cass, 1971.

Southey, Thomas, *Chronological History of the West Indies*, London, 1826 (2 vols.) and 1827 (3 vols.).

Sperling, J. G., *The South Sea Company*, no. 17, Boston, Mass., 1962.

Stampp, Kenneth M., *The Peculiar Institution*, New York, Vintage Books, 1956, 1964, 1967; London, Eyre and Spottiswood, 1964.

—— *The Causes of the Civil War*, Englewood Cliffs, N.J., Prentice-Hall, 1959 and 1965.

—— *The Era of Reconstruction — America after the Civil War*, London, Eyre and Spottiswood, 1964.

Stedman, J. G., *Narrative of Five Years Expedition among the Revolted Negroes of Surinam, 1772–1777*, London, 1796, 2nd edn., 1806, 2 vols.

Stein, Stanley J., *Vassouras: a Brazilian Coffee County 1850–1890: the Roles of Planter and Slave in a Changing Plantation*, Cambridge, Mass., Harvard University Press, 1957; New York, Atheneum Press, 1974.

Stroud, G. M., *Sketch of the Laws Relating to Slavery in the United States of America*, Philadelphia, Pa., 1827 and 1956.

Sturge, Joseph Harvey Thomas, *The West Indies in 1837*, London, Hamilton, Adams and Co., 1838; London, Frank Cass and Co., 1968.

Suckling, George, *An Historical Account of the Virgin Islands in the West Indies*, London, Benjamin White, 1780.

Tannenbaum, Frank, *Slave and Citizen: the Negro in the Americas*, New York, Alfred A. Knopf, 1947.

—— *Ten Keys to Latin America*, New York, Vintage Books, 1966.

Tansill, Charles C., *The United States and Santo Domingo, 1798–1873: a Chapter in Caribbean Diplomacy*, Baltimore, Md., Johns Hopkins University Press, 1938.

Tappan, Lewis, *History of the American Missionary Association*, New York, 1855.

—— *Life of Arthur Tappan*, New York, Sampson, Lowison and Marston, 1870.

Taylor, D. M., *The Black Caribs of Honduras*, New York, 1951.

Temperley, H., *British Anti-Slavery 1833–1870*, London, Longman, 1972.

Thomas, Hugh, *Cuba or The Pursuit of Freedom*, London, Eyre and Spottiswoode, Ltd., 1971.

Thompson, (Rev.) Thomas, *The African Trade for Negro Slaves Consistent with Principles of Humanity and with the Laws of Revealed Religion*, Simmons and Kirkey, in *Tracts on Slavery*, Canterbury, 1772.

Thompson, V. B., *Africa and Unity: the Evolution of Pan-Africanism*, London and Harlow, Longman, 1969.

Turnbull, David, *Travels in the West Cuba: with Notices of Porto Rico and the Slave Trade*, London, 1840.

—— *The Jamaica Movement for promoting and Enforcement of Slave trade Treaties, Prepared at the request of the Kingston Committee*, Kingston, Jamaica, 1850.

Utting, F. A. J., *The Story of Sierra Leone*, London, Longman and Co., 1931.

Uzoigwe, G. N. (ed.), *Anatomy of an African Kingdom*, New York, 1973.

Verger, Pierre (Alfred Metraux), *Haiti: Black Peasants and their Religion*, London, 1960.

—— *Bahia and the West African Trade, 1549–1851*, Ibadan, Nigeria, Ibadan University Press, 1964, 1970.

Waddell, Hope, M., *Twenty-nine Years in the West Indies and Central Africa: a Review of Missionary Work and Adventure, 1829–1858*, London, Edinburgh and New York, Nelson and Sons, 1863; reprint, London, Frank Cass, 1970, with an introduction by G. I. Jones.

Wadström, C. B., *Observations on the Slave Trade, and a Description of Some Part of Guinea During a Voyage made in 1787 and 1788 in Company with Dr A. Sparrman and Captain Arrehenius*, London, James Phillips, 1789.

Weight, Thomas, *A History of the Rise and Progress of the People called Quakers*, London, 1811.

Weinstein, Allen, and Gatell, Frank Otto (eds.), *American Negro Slavery: a Modern Reader*, New York, London, and Toronto, Oxford University Press, 2nd edn., 1973.

Weisberger, B. A., *Booker T. Washington*, New York, New American Library, 1972.

Wesley, Charles H., *Negro Labour in the United States 1850–1925: a Study in American Economic History*, New York, Vanguard Press, 1927.

—— *Richard Allen: Apostle of Freedom*, Washington, D.C., Associated Publishers, 1935.

West, Richard, *Back to Africa: a History of Sierra Leone and Liberia*, London, Jonathan Cape, 1970.

Westergaard, Waldemar, *The Danish West Indies under Company Rule (1671–1754), With a Supplementary Chapter 1755–1917*, New York, Macmillan Co., 1917.

Wheeler, Jacob, D., *A Practical Treatise on the Law of Slavery* (compilation from several courts in the U.S.A.), New York, 1837.

Wiley, Bell Irving, *Southern Negroes 1861–1865*, Yale Historical Publications, Miscellany No. 31, New Haven, Conn., 1865.

Williams, Eric E., *The Negro in the Caribbean*, Manchester, Pan-African Service, 1942.

—— *Capitalism and Slavery*, New York, Capricorn Books, 1966; Chapel Hill, University of North Carolina Press, 1944.

—— *A History of the People of Trinidad and Tobago*, Port of Spain, Trinidad, 1964.

—— *From Columbus to Castro: the History of the Caribbean 1492–1969*, London, André Deutsch, 1970.

Williams, George Washington, *History of the Negro Race in America, from 1619 to 1880, etc.* New York, G. P. Putnam's Sons, 1883, 2 vols.

—— *History of the Negro Troops in the War of Rebellion 1861–65; Preceded by a review of the military service of negroes in ancient and modern times*, London, Sampson Low and Co., 1887.

Williams, Gomer, *History of Liverpool Privateers and Letters of Marque, with an account of the Liverpool Slave Trade*, London, W. Heinemann, 1897.

Williams, J. J., *Voodoos and Obeahs: Phases in West Indian Witchcraft*, London, G. Allen and Unwin, 3rd impression, 1933.

—— *Whence the 'Black Irish' of Jamaica?* New York, Lincoln MacVeagh, 1952.

—— *Africa's God*, Anthropological Series of Boston College Graduate School, Vol. 1, no. 1, Boston, Mass., 1936.

Williams, John, *The Crisis of the Colonies Considered (the Sugar Colonies)*, 1785.

—— *A Negro Ship's Cook — Full account of a most diabolical murder etc.*, 1842.

—— *A Negro, escaped from slavery*, 1855.

Williamson, J. A., *England and the Opening of the Atlantic: the Beginning of Imperial Policy, 1649–1660 — the Colonies after the Restoration, 1660–1713*, Cambridge History of the British Empire, Cambridge, 1929.

—— *English Colonies in Guiana and the Amazon 1604–1668*, Oxford, Clarendon Press, 1923.

—— *The British Empire and Commonwealth*, 3rd edn., London, 1954.

Wilson, Charles, *Profit and Power: a Study of England and the Dutch Wars*, London, Longmans, Green & Co., 1957.

Wilson, Charles H., *Mercantilism*, No. 37, London, Routledge and Kegan Paul, 1958.

Winks, Robin, *The Blacks in Canada: a History*, Montreal, McGill Queens University Press; New Haven, Conn. and London, Yale University Press, 1st printing, 1971; 2nd printing, 1972.

Winterbottom, (Dr) Thomas, *An Account of the Native Africans in the Neighbourhood of Sierra Leone, etc.*, London, 1803, 2 vols.

Woodson, Carter G., *The Education of the Negro Prior to 1861*, New York and London, G. P. Putnam's Sons, 1915.

—— *A Century of Negro Migration*, Washington, D.C., Association for the Study of Negro Life and History, 1918.

—— *The History of the Negro Church*, Washington, D.C., Associated Publishers, 1921.

—— *The Negro in Our History*, Washington, D.C., Associated Publishers Inc., 1922, 1924.

—— *Free Negro Owners of Slaves in the United States in 1830*, Washington, D.C., 1924 and 1925.

_____ *Free Negro Heads of Families in the United States in 1830*, Washington, D.C., Association for the Study of Negro Life and History, 1925.

_____ *The Mind of the Negro as Reflected in Letters written during the Crisis 1800–1860*, Washington, D.C., 1926.

_____ *The Negro Wage Earner*, Washington, D.C., Association for the Study of Negro Life and History, Lancaster, Pa., 1930.

_____ *The Mis-education of the Negro*, Washington, D.C., 1933.

Wright, I. A., *The English Conquest of Jamaica, Miscellany*, Vol. 13 (repr. from periodicals), London, 1923.

_____ *The Early History of Cuba 1492–1586*, New York, Macmillan Co., 1916.

Wyndham, H. A., *The Atlantic and Slavery etc.* London, Oxford University Press, 1935.

_____ *The Atlantic and Emancipation*, London, Oxford University Press, 1937.

Young, E., and Larsen, K. H. (eds), *The Pirates' Priest: the Life of Père Labat in the West Indies, 1693–1705*, 1965.

Young, Sir William, *An Account of the Black Charaibs in the Island of St Vincent's with the Charaib Treaty of 1773 and other original documents*, London, 1795.

Zook, George F., *The Company of Royal Adventurers Trading to Africa*, Lancaster, Philadelphia, Pa., New Era Printing Co., 1919; reprinted from the *Journal of Negro History*, Vol. IV, No. 2 (April 1919).

b   Non-English texts

(i) French

Bastide, Roger, *Les Amériques noires: les civilisations africaines dans le Nouveau Monde* (Black America: African Civilisations in the New World), Bibliothèque scientifique, Paris, 1967.

_____ *Les Religions africaines au Brésil, Vers une sociologie des interpénétrations de civilisations*, Bibliothèque de sociologie contemporaine, Paris, 1960.

Debien, Gabriel, *La société coloniale aux XVIIᵉ et XVIIIᵉ Siècles: les engagés pour les Antilles (1634–1745)*, Société de l'Histoire des Colonies Françaises et Librairie Larose, Paris, 1952, Vol. 1.

_____ *La société coloniale aux XVIIᵉ et XVIIIᵉ Siècles: les colons de Saint-Domingue et la Révolution: Essais sur le Club Massiac (Août 1789– Août 1792)*, Librairie Armand Colin, Paris, 1953, Vol. 2.

Janvier, L. J., *La République d'Haiti et ses visiteurs 1840–1882*, Paris, 1883.

Labat, Jean Baptiste, *Voyage du Chevalier des Marchais en Guineé, Isles Voisines et à Cayenne, etc.* Paris, 1730, and Amsterdam, 1731, 4 vols.

Moreau, de Saint-Mery, *Description Topographique, Physique, Civile, Politique et Historique de la Partie Française de L'Isle Saint-Domingue (avec des Observations générales sur sa Population, sur le Caractère & les Moeurs de ses divers Habitans, sur son Climat, sa Culture, ses Productions, son Administration, & c.)*, Philadelphia, Pa., 1798, 2 vols.

Sannon, H. Pauléus, *Histoire de Toussaint-Louverture*, Haiti, Port-an-Prince, 1932.

Schoelcher, Victor, *La Vérité aux Ouvriers et Cultivateurs de la Martinique suivie des Rapports, Décrets, Arrêtes, Projects de Lois et d'Arrêtes concernant l'abolition immédiate de l'Esclavage*, Paris, 1849.

Vaissière, Pierre de, *Saint Domingue: la Société et la Vie Créoles sous l'Ancien Régime (1629–1789)*, Paris, Librairie Académique Perrin, 1909.

Verger, Pierre, *Dieux d'Afrique, Culte des Orishas et Voudons à l'ancienne Côte des Esclaves en Afrique et à Bahia la baie de Tous les saints au Brésil . . . Cent soixante photographies de l'auteur*, Paris, Paul Hartman, 1954.

(ii) Spanish

Beard, J. R., *Biografía del Libertador Toussaint L'ouverture*, . . . Introducción de Alberto Baeza Flores (traducciones de M. Morúa Delgado), La Habana, Cuba, 1957, 2 vols.

Brito, Figueroa Federico, *Historia económica y social de Venezuela, Una estructura para su estudio*, 2 vols., Universidad Central de Venezuela, Dirección de Cultura, Caracas, Venezuela, 1966; Ediciones de la Biblioteca: 1973.

—— *Las Insurrecciones de los esclavos negros en la sociedad colonial venezolana*, Caracas, Venezuela, 1961.

Carpentier, Alejo, *Historia Afro-Cubana*, Madrid, 1933.

Diaz-Soler, Luis M., *Historia de la esclavitud negra en Puerto Rico*, Rio Piedras, Palencia de Castílla, 2nd edn., 1965.

Guerra y Sanchez, R., *Azúcar y población en las Antillas*, (Sidney W. Mintz, foreword), 1964.

Guiteras, P. J., *Historia de la Isla de Cuba; con notas e ilustraciones*, New York, 1865, 2 vols.; 2nd edn., introduction by Fernando Ortiz, Habana, 1927, 3 vols.

Labra, Rafael Maria de, *Propaganda Anti-Esclavista: La Emancipación de los Esclavos de los Estados Unidos*, Madrid, 1873.

—— *Propaganda Anti-Esclavista — La Libertad de los Negros de Puerto-Rico*, Madrid, 1873.

Libra, R. M. de, *La Abolición de la Esclavitud en el orden económico*, Madrid, 1873.

Maceo, Antonio, *El Pensamiento vivo de Maceo 1876–1896*, (letters) 1917, Habana, Cuba, (José Portuondo, ed.), Habana, 1960.

Ortiz, Fernando, *Los Negros esclavos*, Habana, Cuba, Revisita bimestre Cubana, 1916.

(iii) Portuguese

Ramos, Arthur de Araujo Pereira, *O Negro Brasileiro*, Rio de Janeiro, Brazil, 1934.

—— *O Negro na civilizanção brasileira*, Rio de Janeiro, Brazil, 1956.

c *Articles in learned journals, reviews and books*

Adams, Jane Elizabeth, 'The Abolition of the Brazilian Slave Trade', *Journal of Negro History*, x, 4 (Oct. 1925), pp. 607–37.

Akinjogbin, I. A., 'Agaja and the Conquest of the Coastal Aja States', *Journal of the Nigerian Historical Society*, ii, 4 (1964), pp. 505–66.

Alexander, Herbert B., 'Brazil and United States Slavery Compared', *Journal of Negro History*, vii, 4 (Oct, 1922), pp. 349–64.

Allen, (Rt. Revd) Richard, 'An address to those who keep slaves and approve the practice', in George A, Singleton (ed.), *The Life Experience . . . of the Rt. Rev. Richard Allen*, New York, & Nashville, Tenn., 1960, pp. 69–71.

Anstey, R. T., 'Capitalism and Slavery: a Critique', *Economic History Review*, xxi, 2 (1968) pp. 307–20; first delivered at Centre for African Studies, Edinburgh University, seminar, 4–5 June 1965.

Aptheker, H., 'American Negro Slave Revolts', *Science and Society* (Summer 1937).

_____ 'Maroons within the Present Limits of the United States', *Journal of Negro History*, xxiv, 2 (April 1939), pp. 167–84.

Bastide, Roger, 'The Development of Race Relations in Brazil', in *Industrialisation and Race Relations: a Symposium*, Guy Hunter (ed.), London, 1965.

Bellegarde, Dantes, 'Alexander Petion: the Founder of Rural Democracy in Haiti', *Caribbean Quarterly*, iii, 3 (Dec. 1953), pp. 163–77.

Beltran, Auguirre, 'Tribal Origins of Slaves in Mexico', *Journal of Negro History*, xxxi, 3 (July 1946), pp. 269–352.

Bierek, Harold A. Jr., 'The Struggle for Abolition in Gran Columbia', *Hispanic American Historical Review*, xxxiii (1953), pp. 365–8.

Breathett, George, 'Catholic Missionary Activity and the Negro Slave in Haiti', *Phylon*, xxiii, 3 (1962) pp. 278–85.

Brown, George W., 'The Origins of Abolition in Santo Domingo', *Journal of Negro History*, vii, 4 (Oct. 1922), pp. 365–75.

Cade, John B., 'Out of the Mouth of Ex-Slaves', *Journal of Negro History*, xx, 3 (July 1935), pp. 294–337.

Callcott, George M., 'Omar Ibn Seid, a Slave who wrote an Autobiography in Arabic', *Journal of Negro History*, xxxix, 1 (Jan. 1954), pp. 58–62.

Chapman, Charles E., 'Palmares: the Negro Numantia', *Journal of Negro History*, iii, 1 (Jan. 1918), pp. 29–32.

Conrad, Alfred H., and Meyer, John R., 'The economics of Slavery in the Ante Bellum South', *Journal of Political Economy*, lxvii, 2 (April 1958), pp. 95–130.

Cromwell, J. W., 'The Aftermath of Nat Turner's Insurrection', *Journal of Negro History*, 2 (April 1920), pp. 208–34.

Curtin, P. D., 'The Atlantic Slave Trade 1600–1800', in *History of West Africa*, Ajayi and Crowder (eds.), London and Harlow, Longman, Vol. I, pp. 240–68.

Daaku, K. Y., 'The Slave Trade and African Society', in *Emerging Themes of African History*, Nairobi, Kenya, East African Publishing House, 1968, T. O. Ranger (ed.), pp. 134–40.

Davis, Ralph, 'English Foreign Trade 1660–1700', in *The Growth of English Overseas Trade in the Seventeenth and Eighteenth Centuries*, W. E. Minchinton (ed.), London, 1969.

Debien, Gabriel, 'Marronage in the French Caribbean', translated from the original entitled 'Le Marronage aux Antilles Françaises au XVIII siècle', *Caribbean Studies*, vi, 3 (1966), pp. 3–44.

Degler, Carl N., 'Slavery and the Genesis of American Race Prejudice', *Comparative Studies in Society and History*, Vol. 2, No. 1 (Oct. 1959), pp. 49–66.

_____ 'Slavery in Brazil and the U.S.A.,' *American Historical Review* (April 1970).

Diggs, Irene, 'The Negro in the Viceroyalty of Rio de la Plata', *Journal of Negro History*, xxxvi, 3 (July 1951), pp. 281–301.

_____ 'Color in Colonial Spanish America', *Ibid.*, xxxviii, 4 (Oct. 1953), pp. 403–27.

_____ 'Zumbi and the Republic of Os Palmares', *Phylon* (Atlanta University), xiv, 1 (1953), pp. 62–70.

Diop, Alioune, Opening Address, First International Congress of Negro Writers and Artists, 19 Sept. 1956, *Presence Africaine*, 8–9–10 (June-Nov. 1956), pp. 9–18.

Flint, John, 'Economic Change in West Africa', in *History of West Africa*, Ajayi and Crowder (eds.), Vol. 2, London, 1974, pp. 380–401.

Franklin, J. H., 'The Enslavement of the Free Negroes in North Carolina', *Journal of Negro History*, xxix, 4 (Oct. 1944), pp. 401–28.

Funke, Loretta, 'The Negro in Education', *Journal of Negro History*, 1 (Jan. 1920), pp. 1–21.

Fyfe, C., 'Reform in West Africa: the Abolition of the Slave Trade', in *History of West Africa*, Ajayi and Crowder (eds.), Vol. 2, London, 1974, 30–56.

—— 'Impact of the Slave Trade on West Africa', Proceedings of a Seminar on the Slave Trade from West Africa held at the Centre for African Studies, Edinburgh University, 4–5 June 1965.

Garnet, H. H., 'An Address to the Slaves of the United States of America', 1843, in *Negro Orators and their Orations*, C. G. Woodson (ed.), Washington, D.C., Associated Publishers, 1925, pp. 156–57.

Gobert, David L., and Handler, Jerome S. (eds.), 'Barbados in the Post-Apprenticeship period: the Observations of a French Naval Officer — 2', *Journal of the Barbados Museum and Historical Society*, xxxvi, 1 (March 1979), pp. 4–15.

—— 'Barbados in the Apprenticeship Period: the Report of a French Colonial Official', *ibid*, xxxvi, 2 (1980), pp. 108–28.

Grenville, G. S. P. Freeman, 'The Coast, 1498–1840', in *History of East Africa*, Vol. 1, R. Oliver and G. Mathew (eds.), London, 1963, pp. 129–68.

Groot, Silvia W. de, 'The Boni Maroon War, 1765–1793', *Boleti de Estudios Latino Americanos y dee Caribe*, No. 18 (June 1975) *Suriname and French Guyana in Stichting Suriname Museum*, Zorgen-Hoop, Zeelandia.

Gross, Bella, 'Freedom's Journal and the Rights of All', *Journal of Negro History*, xvii, 3 (July 1932), pp. 241–86.

Hall, D. G., 'The Apprenticeship Period in Jamaica, 1834–1838', *Caribbean Quarterly*, 2 (Dec. 1953), pp. 142–66.

Harris, J. E., 'Introduction to the African Diaspora', in *Emerging Themes of African-History*, Ranger (ed.), *op. cit.,* pp. 147–51.

Harris, Marvin, 'The Myth of the Friendly Master', in *A Reader in Comparative History*, Fonder and Genovese (eds.), *Slavery in the New World: a Reader in Comparative History*, Englewood Cliffs, N. J., Prentice-Hall Inc., 1969, pp. 38–47; reprinted from *Patterns of Race Relations*, New York, Walker and Co., 1964, pp. 65–78.

Higman, B. W., 'The West India Interests in Parliament, 1807–1833, 1', *Historical Studies: Australia and New Zealand*, University of Melbourne, xiii, 49 (Oct. 1967), pp. 1–19.

Hough, F. Harrison, 'Gregoire's Sketch of Angelo Soliman', *Journal of Negro History*, iv, 3 (July 1919), pp. 281–9.

Huston, G. D., 'John Woolman's Efforts in behalf of Freedom', *Journal of Negro History*, xi, 2 (April 1917) pp. 126–38.

Jackson, L. O., 'Religious Instruction of Negroes, 1830–1860 with special reference to South Carolina', *Journal of Negro History*, xv, 1 (Jan. 1930), pp. 72–114.

Jackson, Luther P., 'The Virginia Free Negro Farmer and Property Owners 1830–1860', *Journal of Negro History*, xxiv, 4 (Oct. 1939), pp. 390–439.

Jesse, Rev. C., 'Du Tertre and Labat on 17th-Century Slave Life in the French Antilles', *Caribbean Quarterly*, vii, 3 (Dec. 1961), pp. 137–57.

Kent, R. K., 'Palmares, an African State in Brazil', *Journal of African History*, vi, 2 (1965), pp. 161–75.

Kilson, Marion D. de B., 'Towards Freedom: an Analysis of Slave Revolts in the United States', *Phylon*, xxv, 2 (1964).

Klein, Herbert S., 'Anglicanism, Catholicism and the Negro Slave', in *Slavery in the New World: a Reader in Comparative History*, Foner and Genovese (eds.), *op. cit.*, pp. 138–66.

_____ 'The Trade in African Slaves to Rio de Janeiro, 1795–1811 — Patterns of Voyages', *Journal of African History*, x, 4 (1969), pp. 533–49.

Kunst, J., 'Notes on Negroes of Guatemala during the 17th century', *Journal of Negro History*, i, 4 (Oct. 1916) pp. 392–98.

Laudon, Fred, 'Canadian Negroes and the John Brown Raid', *Journal of Negro History*, vi, 2 (April 1921), pp. 174–82.

Lochner, H., 'Anton W. Amo', a Ghana Scholar in 18th Century Germany', *Transactions of the Historical Society of Ghana*, iii (1958), pp. 169–79.

Lofton, John M., Jr., 'Denmark Vesey's Call to Arms', *Journal of Negro History*, xxxiii, 4 (Oct. 1948), pp. 395–417.

Lumpkin, Katherine DuPre, "The General Plan Was Freedom": a Negro Secret Order on the Underground Railroad', *Phylon*, xxviii, 1 (1967).

Malecka, Alicja, 'African Studies Symposium in Cracow', *Africana Bulletin*, (Warsaw) (1967), pp. 108–13.

Malowist, Marion, 'Le Commerce d'or et d'esclaves au Soudan Occidental', *Africana Bulletin* (Warsaw) iv, (1966), pp. 49–72.

Mars, Jean Price, 'Trans-Atlantic African Survivals and the Dynamism of Negro Culture', *Presence Africaine* 8–10 (June–Nov, 1956), pp. 276–84.

Pares, Richard, 'Merchants and Planters', *Economic History Review Supplement*, No. 4, 1960.

Parkhurst, Jessie W., 'The Role of the Black Mammy in the Plantation Household', *Journal of Negro History*, xxiii, 3 (July 1938), pp. 349–69.

Penson, L. M., 'The London West India Interests in the 18th century', *English Historical Review*, xxxvi (1921), pp. 378–81.

Pi-Sunyer, Oriol, 'Historical Background of the Negro in Mexico', *Journal of Negro History*, xlii, 4 (Oct. 1957) pp. 237–46.

Pitman, Frank W., 'Slavery in the British West India Plantations in the 18th century', *Journal of Negro History*, xi, 4 (Oct. 1926), pp. 584–668.

Pitt-Rivers, Julian, 'Mestizo or Ladino', *Race*, ix, 4 (April 1969), pp. 463–77.

Porter, Dorothy B., 'Sarah Parker Redmond, Abolitionist and Physician', *Journal of Negro History*, xx, 3 (July 1935), pp. 287–94.

_____ 'The Negro in the Brazilian Abolition Movement', *ibid.*, xxxvii, 1 (Jan. 1952), pp. 54–80.

Porter, Kenneth W., 'Relations between Negroes and Indians within the present limits of the United States', *Journal of Negro History*, vii, 3 (July 1932), pp. 287–367.

_____ 'Florida Slaves and Free Negroes in the Seminole War, 1835–1842', *Journal of Negro History*, xviii (1943), pp. 390–421.

Preston, Delorus E., 'The Underground Railroad in Northwest Ohio', *Journal of Negro History*, xvii, 4 (Oct. 1932), pp. 409–36.

—— 'Genesis of the Underground Railroad', *ibid.*, xviii, 2 (April 1933), pp. 144–70.

Quarles, Benjamin, 'Ministers without Portfolio', *Journal of Negro History*, xxxix, 1 (Jan. 1954), pp. 27–42.

Rees, J. F. 'Mercantilism and the Colonies', in J. H. Rose (ed.), *Cambridge History of the British Empire*, Cambridge University Press, 1929, Vol. 1, pp. 561–602.

Riddell, W. R., 'The Slave in Upper Canada', *Journal of Negro History*, iv, 4 (Oct. 1919), pp. 372–95.

—— 'Slavery in Canada', *ibid.*, v, 3 (July 1920), pp. 261–377.

——'The Baptism of Slaves in Prince Edward Island', *ibid.*, vi, 3 (July 1921).

—— 'Le Code Noir', *ibid.*, x, 3 (July 1925), pp. 321–30.

—— 'Observations of Slavery and Privateering', *Journal of Negro History*, xv, 3 (July 1930), pp. 337–71.

Rippy, Fred J., 'The Negro and the Spanish Pioneers in the New World', *Journal of Negro History*, vi, 2 (April 1921), pp. 183–99.

Rodney, Walter, 'African Slavery and Other Forms of Social Oppression on the Upper Guinea Coast in the Context of the Atlantic Slave Trade', *Journal of African History*, vii, 3 (1966), pp. 431–43.

—— 'European activity and African reaction in Angola', in *Aspects of Central African History*, Ranger (ed.), *op. cit.*, London, 1968.

Russell, Marion, 'American Slave Discontent in Records in the High Courts', *Journal of Negro History*, xxxi, 4 (Oct. 1946), pp. 411–34.

Russell-Wood, A. J. R., 'Class, Creed and Colour in Colonial Bahia: a Study in Prejudice', *Race*, ix, 2 (Oct. 1967), pp. 133–57.

Schuler, Monica, 'Akan Slave Rebellions in the British Caribbean', *SAVACU*, i, 1 (June 1970), pp. 8–31.

Shepperson, George, 'The African Abroad or the African of the Diaspora', in *Emerging Themes of African History*, Ranger (ed.), *op. cit.*, pp. 152–76.

Sio, Arnold, 'An Interpretation of Slavery: the Slave Status in the Americas', in *A Reader etc.*, Foner and Genovese (eds.), *op. cit.*, pp. 96–112.

Southall, Eugene P., 'Negroes in Florida Prior to the Civil War', *Journal of Negro History*, xix, 1 (Jan. 1934), pp. 77–86.

Suttles, William, Jr., 'African Religious Survivals as Factors in American Slave Revolts', *Journal of Negro History*, lvi, 2 (April 1971), pp. 97–104.

Uzoigwe, G. N., 'The Slave Trade and African Societies', *Transactions of the Historical Society of Ghana*, xiv, 2 (Dec. 1973), pp. 187–212.

Walker, Dennis, 'Black Islamic Slave Revolts of South America: a Little-known Chapter in Islam's Sphere of Influence', *The Islamic Review and Arab Affairs* (Oct./Nov. 1970), pp. 9–11.

Warner, Maureen, 'Africans in 19th-century Trinidad', *Bulletin of the African Studies Association of the West Indies*, v (Dec. 1972), pp. 27–59.

Wesley, C. H., 'The Emancipation of the Free Colored Population in the British Empire', *Journal of Negro History*, xix, 2 (April 1934), pp. 137–70.

—— 'The Abolition of Negro Apprenticeship in the British Empire', *Ibid.*, xxiii, 2 (April 1938), pp. 155–99.

Westergaard, Waldemar, 'St Croix Map of 1796 with a note on its Significance in West Indian Plantation Economy', *Journal of Negro History*, xxiii, 2 (April 1938), pp. 216–28.

454

Williams, Mary Wilhelmina, 'Modern Slavery', *Encyclopedia of Social Sciences*, New York, 1934, Vol. 14, pp. 80–84.
_____ 'The Treatment of Negro Slaves in the Brazilian Empire', *Journal of Negro History*, xv, 3 (July 1930), pp. 315–36.
Wilson, Danenhower Ruth, 'Justification of Slavery, Past and Present', *Phylon* (4th quarter, 1958), xviii, pp. 407–412.
Wish, Harvey, 'American Slave Insurrections before 1861', *Journal of Negro History*, xxii, 3 (July 1937) pp. 299–320.
Woodson, C. G., 'The Beginnings of the Miscegenation of the Whites and Blacks', *Journal of Negro History*, iii, 4 (Oct. 1918), pp. 335–53.
_____ 'Attitudes of the Iberian Peninsula', *ibid.*, xx, 2 (April 1935), pp. 190–243.

4 *Unpublished theses*

Rayan, T. C. I., 'The Economics of Trading in Slaves', Ph. D. dissertation, Massachusetts Institute of Technology, 1975.
West, R. C., 'The Georgraphy of the Pacific Lowlands of Colombia', report sponsored by the US office of Naval Research, US Navy, Dept. of Geography and Anthropology, Louisiana State University, 1955.

5 *Journals*

Africana Bulletin (Warsaw)
American Historical Review
The American Museum (Washington, D.C.)
Boleti de Estudios Latino-Americanos del Caribe (Mexico)
Bulletin of the African Studies Association of the West Indies (Mona, Kingston, Jamaica)
Canadian Journal of African Studies
Caribbean Quarterly (Port of Spain, Trinidad)
Caribbean Studies
Comparative Studies in Society and History (The Hague)
Economic History Review (and Supplement) (Welwyn Garden City, Herts.)
English Historical Review
Hispanic American Historical Review (Baltimore, Md.)
Historical Studies (Australia and New Zealand), Melbourne
The Islamic Review and Arab Affairs (Woking, Surrey)
Journal of African History (Cambridge)
Journal of the Barbados Museum and Historical Society (Bridgetown, Barbados)
Journal of Negro History (Washington, D.C.)
Journal of the Nigerian Historical Society (Ibadan, Nigeria)
Journal of Political Economy (Chicago, Ill.)
Phylon (Atlanta University)
Presence Africaine (Paris)
Race (later *Race and Class*) (London)
SAVACU (Kingston, Jamaica)
Science and Society (New York)
Transactions of the Historical Society of Ghana (Legon, Ghana)

6 Newspapers and magazines

The Antigua Free Press (St John, Antigua)
The Bahama Gazetteer (Nassau, Bahamas)
Barbados Standard (Bridgetown, Barbados)
Genius of Universal Emancipation (Baltimore, Md.)
Gentleman's Magazine and Historical Chronicle (London)
Frederick Douglass Paper (Manchester, New York)
Jamaica Journal and Kingston Chronicle (Kingston, Jamaica)
The Liberator (Boston, Mass.)
The National Anti-Slavery Standard (New York)
New York Chronicle (New York)
Ohio Patriot (New Lisbon Columbiana, Ohio)

These do not in any way reflect the newspapers of the period and contain a minimum of those published by Africans of the diaspora in the Americas. Because the latter were short-lived, they seem not to have been well preserved and have not been included here. They are not always easy to come by except in libraries such as the Arthur Schomburg Collections of the New York Public Libraries. This writer spent an agonising afternoon trying to track down some Afro-American newspapers at the Rackham Library of the University of Michigan without much success, in spite of the fact that that library is reputed to have the most complete collection of anti-slavery newspapers. As his time was limited, it was not possible to revisit New York from Michigan. The author of *The Black Press, 1827–1890*, edited by Martin E. Dann, Capricorn Books, New York, 1972, provides some clues to the difficulty in locating some of these early newspapers.

INDEX